Volume Two

Xlib Reference Manual

---

for Version 11 of the
X Window System

edited by Adrian Nye

O'Reilly & Associates, Inc.

Revision and Printing History

August 1988:   First Printing
November 1988:   Second Printing. Minor revisions.
May 1989:   Third Printing. Release 3 updates added. Minor revisions.

Small Print

Volume 2: ISBN 0-937175-28-5   Set: ISBN 0-937175-26-9

Table of Contents

Page

Preface ix

About This Manual ix
Summary of Contents x
How to Use This Manual x
Assumptions xii
Font Conventions Used in This Manual xii
Related Documents xiii
Requests For Comments xiii
Licensing Information xiii
Acknowledgements xiv

Permuted Index 1

Xlib Function Reference 29

Appendix A: Function Group Summary 499

Group Listing with Brief Descriptions 499
Alphabetical Listing of Routines 514

Appendix B: Error Messages and Protocol Requests 523

Appendix C: Macros 531

Display Macros 531
Image Format Macros 535
Keysym Classification Macros 535
Resource Manager Macros 536

Appendix D: The Color Database 537

Appendix E: Event Reference 539

Meaning of Common Structure Elements 541
ButtonPress, ButtonRelease 543
CirculateNotify 545
CirculateRequest 546
ClientMessage 547
ColormapNotify 548
ConfigureNotify 549
ConfigureRequest 551
CreateNotify 553
DestroyNotify 554
EnterNotify, LeaveNotify 555
Expose 561
FocusIn, FocusOut 563
GraphicsExpose, NoExpose 569
GravityNotify 571
KeymapNotify 572
KeyPress, KeyRelease 573
MapNotify, UnmapNotify 575
MappingNotify 577
MapRequest 579
MotionNotify 580
PropertyNotify 582
ReparentNotify 583
ResizeRequest 584
SelectionClear 585
SelectionNotify 586
SelectionRequest 587
VisibilityNotify 588

Appendix F: Structure Reference 591

Description of Contents 591
Resource Types 592
Structure Definitions 592
Depth 592
Display 593
GC 594
Screen 594
ScreenFormat 595
Visual 595
XArc 596
XChar2b 596
XCharStruct 596
XClassHint 597

XColor 597
XComposeStatus 597
XExtCodes 598
XExtData 598
XFontProp 598
XFontStruct 599
XGCValues 599
XHostAddress 600
XIconSize 600
XImage 600
XKeyboardControl 601
XKeyBoardState 601
XModifierKeymap 602
XPoint 602
XRectangle 602
XSegment 602
XSetWindowAttributes 603
XSizeHints 603
XStandardColormap 604
XTextItem 604
XTextItem16 604
XTimeCoord 605
XVisualInfo 605
XWMHints 605
XWindowAttributes 606
XWindowChanges 606

Appendix G: Symbol Reference 607

Appendix H: Keysyms 623

Appendix I: The Cursor Font 641

Appendix J: Fonts 643

Appendix K: Xlib Release 3 Update 699

    New Routines 699
    Command Line Options 701
    Fonts 701
    Internal and Invisible Changes to Xlib 702
    Small Interface Changes 702
    Server Fixes 703
    The Xmu library 703
    Release 3 Protocol Clarifications 704

Window Attributes At-a-glance 707

GC At-a-glance 709

Preface

About This Manual

This manual describes the X library, the C Language programming interface to Version 11 of the X Window System. The X library, known as Xlib, is the lowest level of programming interface to X. This library enables a programmer to write applications with an advanced user interface based on windows on the screen, with complete network transparency, that will run without changes on many types of workstations and personal computers.

Xlib is powerful enough to write effective applications without additional programming tools, and is necessary for certain tasks even in applications written with higher-level "toolkits."

There are a number of these toolkits for X programming, the most notable being the DEC/MIT toolkit Xt, the Andrew toolkit developed by IBM and Carnegie-Mellon University, and the InterViews toolkit from Stanford. These toolkits are still evolving, and none of them is currently part of the X standard, although Xt is being considered for inclusion. Toolkits simplify the process of application writing considerably, providing a number of *widgets* that implement menus, command buttons, and other common features of the user interface.

This manual does not describe Xt or any other toolkit. Our intention is to provide complete documentation of the Xt toolkit in a future volume of our X Window System series. Nonetheless, all the material described in this book is essential for understanding and using the toolkits since the toolkits themselves are written using Xlib.

In Release 1 of Xlib, the resource manager (for parsing the command line and merging user preferences) was a separate library, which had been developed as part of the Xt toolkit. As of Release 2, parts of the resource manager have been incorporated into Xlib. This volume documents the Release 2 resource manager. This manual also describes the X11 routines that were provided for compatibility with X Version 10, chiefly in Volume One, Appendix B, *X10 Compatibility*.

Summary of Contents

This manual is divided into two volumes. This is the second volume, the *Xlib Reference Manual*. It includes reference pages for each of the Xlib functions (organized alphabetically), a permuted index, and numerous appendices and quick reference aids.

The first volume, the *Xlib Programming Manual*, provides a conceptual introduction to Xlib, including tutorial material and numerous programming examples. Arranged by task or topic, each chapter brings together a group of Xlib functions, describes the conceptual foundation they are based on, and illustrates how they are most often used in writing applications (or in the case of the last chapter, window managers). Volume One is structured so as to be useful as a tutorial and also as a task-oriented reference.

Volume One and Volume Two are designed to be used together. To get the most out of the examples in Volume One, you will need the exact calling sequences of each function from Volume Two. To understand fully how to use each of the functions described in Volume Two, all but the most experienced X "hacker" will need the explanation and examples in Volume One.

Both volumes include material from the original Xlib and X11 Protocol documentation provided by MIT, as well as from other documents provided on the MIT release tape. This volume is based heavily on these sources, although it has also been extensively edited and added to. We have done our best to incorporate all of the useful information from the MIT documentation, to correct code references we found to be in error, to reorganize and present it in a more useful form, and to supplement it with conceptual material, tutorials, reference aids, and examples. In other words, this manual is not only a replacement, but is a superset of the MIT documentation.

Those of you familiar with the MIT documentation will recognize that each reference page in this volume includes the detailed description of the routine found in Gettys, Newman, and Scheifler's *Xlib–C Language X Interface*, plus in many cases additional text that clarifies ambiguities and describes the context in which the routine would be used. We have also added cross-references to related reference pages and to where additional information can be found in Volume One.

How to Use This Manual

Volume Two is designed to make it as easy and fast as possible to look up virtually any fact about Xlib. It includes a permuted index, reference pages for each library function, appendices that cover macros, structures, function groups, events, fonts, colors, cursors, keysyms, and errors, and at-a-glance tables for the graphics context and window attributes.

The permuted index is the standard UNIX way of finding a particular function name given a keyword. By looking up a word in the second column that you think describes the function you are looking for, you can find the group of functions that have that word in their description lines. The description line also appears at the top of each reference page. Once you have found the routine you are looking for, you can look for its reference page.

The reference pages themselves provide all the details necessary for calling each routine, including its arguments, returned values, definitions of the structure types of arguments and returned values, and the errors it may generate. Many of the pages also give hints about how the routine is used in the context of other routines. This is the part of this volume you will use the most.

Appendix A, *Function Group Summary*, groups the routines according to function, and provides brief descriptions. You'll find it useful to have in one place a description of related routines, so their differences can be noted and the appropriate one chosen.

Appendix B, *Error Messages and Protocol Requests*, describes the errors that Xlib routines can generate. When an error is handled by the default error handler, one of these messages is printed. Also printed is the X Protocol request that caused the error. Since Protocol requests do not map directly to Xlib routines, this appendix provides a table with which you can find out which Xlib routine in your code caused the error.

Appendix C, *Macros*, describes the macros that access members of the Display structure, classify keysyms, and convert resource manager types.

Appendix D, *The Color Database*, presents the standard color database. The color names in this database should be available on all servers, though the corresponding RGB values may have been modified to account for screen variations.

Appendix E, *Event Reference*, describes each event type and structure, in a reference page format. This is an invaluable reference for event programming.

Appendix F, *Structure Reference*, describes all structures used by Xlib except the event structures described in Appendix E, including which routines use each structure.

Appendix G, *Symbol Reference*, lists in alphabetical order and describes all of the symbols defined in Xlib include files.

Appendix H, *Keysyms*, lists and describes each character in the standard keysym families, used for translating keyboard events. The characters for English and foreign language keysyms are shown where possible.

Appendix I, *The Cursor Font*, describes the standard cursor font, including a illustration of the font shapes.

Appendix J, *Fonts*, lists the standard fonts, gives a table of their metrics, and provides an illustration of each font.

Appendix K, *Xlib Release 3 Update*, describes changes to Xlib in Release 3.

Finally, Volume Two concludes with at-a-glance charts that help in setting the graphics context (GC) and the window attributes.

Assumptions

Readers should be proficient in the C programming language and should have read most of Volume One, *Xlib Programming Manual*. In addition, general familiarity with the principles of raster graphics will be helpful.

Font Conventions Used in This Manual

Italics are used for:

- UNIX pathnames, filenames, program names, user command names, and options for user commands

`Typewriter Font` is used for:

- Anything that would be typed verbatim into code, such as examples of source code and text on the screen

- The contents of include files, such as structure types, structure members, symbols (defined constants and bit flags), and macros

- Xlib functions

`Italic Typewriter Font` is used for:

- Arguments to Xlib functions, since they could be typed in code as shown but are arbitrary

Helvetica Italics are used for:

- Titles of examples, figures, and tables

Boldface is used for:

- Chapter and section headings

Related Documents

The C Programming Language by B. W. Kernighan and D. M. Ritchie

The following documents are included on the X11 source tape:

Xt Toolkit Intrinsics, by Joel McCormack, Paul Asente and Ralph Swick
Xt Toolkit Widgets, by Ralph Swick and Terry Weissman
Xlib–C Language X Interface, by Jim Gettys, Ron Newman, and Robert Scheifler

The following book on the X Window System from O'Reilly and Associates, Inc., is currently in its second printing:

Volume Three — *X Window System User's Guide*

Two more books on the X Window System are now being developed at O'Reilly & Associates, Inc., and are expected to be published in the Summer of 1989:

Volume Four — *Xt Toolkit Programming Manual*
Volume Five — *Xt Toolkit Reference Manual*

Requests For Comments

Please write to tell us about any flaws you find in this manual or how you think it could be improved, to help us provide you with the best documentation possible.

Our U.S. mail address, e-mail address, and phone number are as follows:

O'Reilly & Associates, Inc.
632 Petaluma Avenue
Sebastopol, CA 95472
(800) 338-6887

UUCP: uunet!ora!adrian   ARPA: adrian@ora.UU.NET

Licensing Information

This manual has been designed for licensing and customization by manufacturers or distributors of systems supporting X11. As of this writing, it has been licensed by Masscomp, Motorola, Apollo Computer, Silicon Graphics, and Stellar Computer. For information on licensing, call O'Reilly & Associates, Inc. at (800) 338-6887, or send e-mail to tim@ora.UU.NET.

Acknowledgements

The information contained in this manual is based in part on *Xlib–C Language X Interface*, written by Jim Gettys, Ron Newman, and Robert Scheifler, and the *X Window System Protocol, Version 11*, by Robert Scheifler (with many contributors). The X Window System software and these documents were written under the auspices of Project Athena at MIT. In addition, this manual includes material from Oliver Jones' Xlib tutorial presentation, which was given at the MIT X Conference in January 1988, and from David Rosenthal's *Inter-Client Communication Conventions Manual*.

I'd like to thank the people who helped this book come into being. It was Tim O'Reilly who originally sent me out on a contract to write a manual for X Version 10 for a workstation manufacturer, and later to another company to write a manual for X Version 11, from which this book began. I've learned most of what I know about computers and technical writing while working for Tim. For this book he acted as an editor, he helped me reorganize several chapters, he worked on the *Color* and *Managing User Preferences* chapters when time was too short for me to do it, and he kept my spirits up through this long project. While I was concentrating on the details, his eye was on the overall presentation, and his efforts improved the book enormously.

This book would not be as good (and we might still be working on it) had it not been for Daniel Gilly. Daniel was my production assistant for critical periods in the project. He dealt with formatting issues, checked for consistent usage of terms and noticed irregularities in content, and edited files from written corrections by me and by others. His job was to take as much of the work off me as possible, and with his technical skill and knowledge of UNIX he did that very well.

This manual has benefitted from the work and assistance of the entire staff of O'Reilly & Associates, Inc. Susan Willing was responsible for graphics and design, and she proofed many drafts of the book; Linda Mui tailored the troff macros to the design by Sue Willing and myself, and was invaluable in the final production process; John Strang figured out the Release 2 resource manager and wrote the section on that topic; Karen Cakebread edited a draft of the manual and established some conventions for terms and format. Peter Mui executed the "at-a-glance" tables for the inside back cover; Tom Scanlon entered written edits and performed copy fitting; Linda Walsh updated the index of the book; Valerie Quercia, Tom Van Raalte, and Donna Woonteiler all contributed in some small ways; and Cathy Brennan, Suzanne Van Hove, and Jill Berlin fielded many calls from people interested in the X manual, and saved me all the time that would have taken. A special thanks to everyone at O'Reilly & Associates for putting up with my habits of printer and terminal hogging, lugging X books around, recycling paper, and for generally being good at what they do and good-natured to boot.

I would also like to thank the people from other companies that reviewed the book or otherwise made this project possible: John Posner, Barry Kingsbury, and Jeffrey Vroom of Stellar Computer; Oliver Jones of Apollo Computer; Sam Black, Jeff Graber, and Janet Egan of Masscomp; Al Tabayoyon, Paul Shearer, and many others from Tektronix; Robert Scheifler and Jim Fulton of the X Consortium (who helped with the *Color* and *Managing User Preferences* chapters), and Peter Winston II and Aub Harden of Integrated Computer Solutions. Despite the efforts of the reviewers and everyone else, any errors that remain are my own.

— *Adrian Nye*

Permuted Index

How to Use the Permuted Index

To find the command you want, simply scan down the middle of the page, looking for a keyword of interest on the right side of the blank gutter. Once you find the keyword you want, you can read (with contortions) the brief description of the command that makes up the entry. If things still look promising, you can look all the way over to the right for the name of the relevant command page.

The Permuted Index

/get the width in pixels of an	8-bit character string.	XTextWidth
XDrawImageString: draw	8-bit image text characters.	XDrawImageString
XDrawText: draw	8-bit polytext strings.	XDrawText
only. XDrawString: draw an	8-bit text string, foreground	XDrawString
string and font metrics of a	16-bit character string. /for	XQueryTextExtents16
string and font metrics of a	16-bit character string. /get	XTextExtents16
/get the width in pixels of a	16-bit character string.	XTextWidth16
XDrawImageString16: draw	16-bit image text characters.	XDrawImageString16
XDrawText16: draw	16-bit polytext strings.	XDrawText16
deny/ XEnableAccessControl: use	access control list to allow or	XEnableAccessControl
XAddHost: add a host to the	access control list.	XAddHost
/add multiple hosts to the	access control list.	XAddHosts
/remove a host from the	access control list.	XRemoveHost
/remove multiple hosts from the	access control list.	XRemoveHosts
/disable or enable	access control.	XSetAccessControl
XDisableAccessControl: allow	access from any host.	XDisableAccessControl
/obtain a list of hosts having	access to this display.	XListHosts
XActivateScreenSaver:	activate screen blanking.	XActivateScreenSaver
/change the parameters of an	active pointer grab.	XChangeActivePointerGrab
pixel value in an/ XAddPixel:	add a constant value to every	XAddPixel
control list. XAddHost:	add a host to the access	XAddHost
XInsertModifiermapEntry:	add a new entry to an/	XInsertModifiermapEntry
XUnionRectWithRegion:	add a rectangle to a region.	XUnionRectWithRegion
string of/ XrmPutLineResource:	add a resource entry given as a	XrmPutLineResource
XrmPutStringResource:	add a resource that is/	XrmPutStringResource
a/ XrmQPutStringResource:	add a string resource value to	XrmQPutStringResource
client's/ XAddToSaveSet:	add a window's children to the	XAddToSaveSet
access control/ XAddHosts:	add multiple hosts to the	XAddHosts
the client's/ XChangeSaveSet:	add or remove a subwindow from	XChangeSaveSet

XrmUniqueQuark: allocate a new quark. .... XrmUniqueQuark
from color/ XAllocNamedColor: allocate a read-only colorcell .... XAllocNamedColor
cell with closest/ XAllocColor: allocate a read-only colormap .... XAllocColor
by English/ XStoreNamedColor: allocate a read/write colorcell .... XStoreNamedColor
structure. XCreateImage: allocate memory for an XImage .... XCreateImage
freed. Xpermalloc: allocate memory never to be .... Xpermalloc
XAllocColorPlanes: allocate read/write/ .... XAllocColorPlanes
colorcells. XAllocColorCells: allocate read/write (nonshared) .... XAllocColorCells
XFreeFontPath: free the memory allocated by XGetFontPath. .... XFreeFontPath
XFreeExtensionList: free memory allocated for a list of/ .... XFreeExtensionList
table. /free the memory allocated for an association .... XDestroyAssocTable
XDisableAccessControl: allow access from any host. .... XDisableAccessControl
/use access control list to allow or deny connection/ .... XEnableAccessControl
install default if not already installed. /a colormap; .... XUninstallColormap
XLoadFont: load a font if not already loaded; get font ID. .... XLoadFont
/move the pointer to another point on the screen. .... XWarpPointer
/insert a window between another window and its parent. .... XReparentWindow
contents of one database with another. /merge the .... XrmMergeDatabases
subtract one region from another. XSubtractRegion: .... XSubtractRegion
system from one window to another. /change the coordinate .... XTranslateCoordinates
/into a drawable with depth, applying pixel values. .... XCopyPlane
/convert a keysym to the appropriate keycode. .... XKeysymToKeycode
XDrawArc: draw an arc fitting inside a rectangle. .... XDrawArc
XSetArcMode: set the arc mode in a graphics context. .... XSetArcMode
XFillArc: fill an arc. .... XFillArc
XDrawArcs: draw multiple arcs. .... XDrawArcs
XFillArcs: fill multiple arcs. .... XFillArcs
events when these resources are grabbed. /and pointer .... XAllowEvents
XClearArea: clear a rectangular area in a window. .... XClearArea
XCopyArea: copy an area of a drawable. .... XCopyArea
fill a rectangular area. XFillRectangle: .... XFillRectangle
fill multiple rectangular areas. XFillRectangles: .... XFillRectangles
database from command line arguments. /load a resource .... XrmParseCommand
/atom (command line arguments). .... XSetCommand
/obtain RGB values for an array of pixel values. .... XQueryColors
free the font name array. XFreeFontNames: .... XFreeFontNames
properties in the properties array. /rotate .... XRotateWindowProperties
free multiple font information arrays. XFreeFontInfo: .... XFreeFontInfo
/up or translate RGB values from ASCII color name or hexadecimal/ .... XParseColor
/map a key event to ASCII string, keysym, and/ .... XLookupString
XDefineCursor: assign a cursor to a window. .... XDefineCursor
the window/ XStoreName: assign a name to a window for .... XStoreName
/deallocate storage associated with a region. .... XDestroyRegion
/change a property associated with a window. .... XChangeProperty
/deallocate memory associated with an image. .... XDestroyImage
/the GContext (resource ID) associated with the specified/ .... XGContextFromGC
XCreateAssocTable: create a new association table (X10). .... XCreateAssocTable
/delete an entry from an association table. .... XDeleteAssoc
the memory allocated for an association table. /free .... XDestroyAssocTable
/obtain data from an association table. .... XLookUpAssoc
create an entry in an association table. XMakeAssoc: .... XMakeAssoc
/set the XA_WM_COMMAND atom (command line arguments). .... XSetCommand
XInternAtom: return an atom for a given name string. .... XInternAtom
XGetWindowProperty: obtain the atom type and property format/ .... XGetWindowProperty
get a name for a given atom. XGetAtomName: .... XGetAtomName
get a font property given its atom. XGetFontProperty: .... XGetFontProperty
/change a window border tile attribute and repaint the/ .... XSetWindowBorderPixmap

/set the background pixel	attribute of a window.	XSetWindowBackground
/change the background tile	attribute of a window.	XSetWindowBackgroundPixmap
pixel/ /change a window border	attribute to the specified	XSetWindowBorder
/obtain the current	attributes of window.	XGetWindowAttributes
/set window	attributes.	XChangeWindowAttributes
create a window and set	attributes. XCreateWindow:	XCreateWindow
/turn off the keyboard	auto-repeat keys.	XAutoRepeatOff
/turn on the keyboard	auto-repeat keys.	XAutoRepeatOn
XPutBackEvent: push an event	back on the input queue.	XPutBackEvent
XSetState: set the foreground,	background, logical function,/	XSetState
XSetWindowBackground: set the	background pixel attribute of a/	XSetWindowBackground
XSetBackground: set the	background pixel value in a/	XSetBackground
window. /change the	background tile attribute of a	XSetWindowBackgroundPixmap
XAllowEvents: control the	behavior of keyboard and/	XAllowEvents
XBell: ring the	bell (Control G).	XBell
XQueryBestSize: obtain the	"best" supported cursor,/	XQueryBestSize
XQueryBestTile: obtain the	best supported fill tile shape.	XQueryBestTile
XQueryBestStipple: obtain the	best supported stipple shape.	XQueryBestStipple
parent. /insert a window	between another window and its	XReparentWindow
/calculate the difference	between the union and/	XXorRegion
XDrawLine: draw a line	between two points.	XDrawLine
XDraw: draw a polyline or curve	between vertex list (from X10).	XDraw
/convert a key string to a	binding list and a quark list.	XrmStringToBindingQuarkList
state/ XQueryKeymap: obtain a	bit vector for the current	XQueryKeymap
/create a pixmap with depth from	bitmap data.	XCreatePixmapFromBitmapData
/create a bitmap from X11	bitmap format data.	XCreateBitmapFromData
XReadBitmapFile: read a	bitmap from disk.	XReadBitmapFile
XCreateBitmapFromData: create a	bitmap from X11 bitmap format/	XCreateBitmapFromData
XWriteBitmapFile: write a	bitmap to a file.	XWriteBitmapFile
create a cursor from two	bitmaps. XCreatePixmapCursor:	XCreatePixmapCursor
graphics/ XSetFunction: set the	bitwise logical operation in a	XSetFunction
/activate screen	blanking.	XActivateScreenSaver
specified/ /change a window	border attribute to the	XSetWindowBorder
repaint the/ /change a window	border tile attribute and	XSetWindowBorderPixmap
/change the	border width of a window.	XSetWindowBorderWidth
/the window position, size,	border width, or stacking/	XConfigureWindow
pixel value and repaint the	border. /to the specified	XSetWindowBorder
tile attribute and repaint the	border. /change a window border	XSetWindowBorderPixmap
/remove the next event matching	both passed window and passed/	XCheckWindowEvent
stacking order. /circulate the	bottom child to the top of the	XCirculateSubwindowsDown
/circulate the top child to the	bottom of the stacking order.	XCirculateSubwindowsUp
function. FunctionName:	brief description of the	FunctionName
return data from cut	buffer 0. XFetchBytes:	XFetchBytes
XStoreBytes: store data in cut	buffer 0.	XStoreBytes
XPending: flush the output	buffer and return the number of/	XPending
and/ XSync: flush the output	buffer and wait for all events	XSync
XFlush: flush the output	buffer (display all queued/	XFlush
return data from a cut	buffer. XFetchBuffer:	XFetchBuffer
store data in a cut	buffer. XStoreBuffer:	XStoreBuffer
XRotateBuffers: rotate the cut	buffers.	XRotateBuffers
XUngrabButton: release a	button from grab.	XUngrabButton
/get the pointer	button mapping.	XGetPointerMapping
/set the pointer	button mapping.	XSetPointerMapping
XGrabButton: grab a pointer	button.	XGrabButton
between the union/ XXorRegion:	calculate the difference	XXorRegion
user geometry/ XGeometry:	calculate window geometry given	XGeometry
functions. /set a function	called after all Xlib	XSetAfterFunction

allocate a read-only colormap	cell with closest/ XAllocColor:	XAllocColor
with a/ XChangeProperty:	change a property associated	XChangeProperty
colormap/ XStoreColor: set or	change a read/write entry of a	XStoreColor
attribute to/ XSetWindowBorder:	change a window border	XSetWindowBorder
XSetWindowBorderPixmap:	change a window border tile/	XSetWindowBorderPixmap
XResizeWindow:	change a window's size.	XResizeWindow
context to/ XSetClipRectangles:	change clip_mask in a graphics	XSetClipRectangles
XOffsetRegion:	change offset of a region.	XOffsetRegion
the/ XStoreColors: set or	change read/write colorcells to	XStoreColors
XSetWindowBackgroundPixmap:	change the background tile/	XSetWindowBackgroundPixmap
window. XSetWindowBorderWidth:	change the border width of a	XSetWindowBorderWidth
client. XSetCloseDownMode:	change the close down mode of a	XSetCloseDownMode
XRecolorCursor:	change the color of a cursor.	XRecolorCursor
given graphics/ XChangeGC:	change the components of a	XChangeGC
from/ XTranslateCoordinates:	change the coordinate system	XTranslateCoordinates
XChangeKeyboardMapping:	change the keyboard mapping.	XChangeKeyboardMapping
such/ XChangeKeyboardControl:	change the keyboard preferences	XChangeKeyboardControl
XChangeActivePointerGrab:	change the parameters of an/	XChangeActivePointerGrab
XChangePointerControl:	change the pointer preferences.	XChangePointerControl
a window. XMoveResizeWindow:	change the size and position of	XMoveResizeWindow
siblings. XRestackWindows:	change the stacking order of	XRestackWindows
XSetStandardColormap:	change the standard colormap/	XSetStandardColormap
size, border/ XConfigureWindow:	change the window position, ...	XConfigureWindow
and font metrics of a 16-bit	character string. /for string	XQueryTextExtents16
and font metrics of a 16-bit	character string. /get string	XTextExtents16
the width in pixels of an 8-bit	character string. /get	XTextWidth
the width in pixels of a 16-bit	character string. /get	XTextWidth16
draw 8-bit image text	characters. XDrawImageString:	XDrawImageString
/draw 16-bit image text	characters.	XDrawImageString16
matching event. XCheckIfEvent:	check the event queue for a	XCheckIfEvent
the event/ XEventsQueued:	check the number of events in	XEventsQueued
stacking/ /circulate the top	child to the bottom of the	XCirculateSubwindowsUp
stacking/ /circulate the bottom	child to the top of the	XCirculateSubwindowsDown
save-set. /remove a window's	children from the client's	XRemoveFromSaveSet
XQueryTree: return a list of	children, parent, and root.	XQueryTree
XAddToSaveSet: add a window's	children to the client's/	XAddToSaveSet
/circulate the stacking order of	children up or down.	XCirculateSubwindows
the/ XCirculateSubwindowsDown:	circulate the bottom child to	XCirculateSubwindowsDown
children/ XCirculateSubwindows:	circulate the stacking order of	XCirculateSubwindows
bottom/ XCirculateSubwindowsUp:	circulate the top child to the	XCirculateSubwindowsUp
/get a resource from name and	class as quarks.	XrmQGetResource
/get a resource from name and	class as strings.	XrmGetResource
matches the desired depth and	class. /visual information that	XMatchVisualInfo
window. XClearArea:	clear a rectangular area in a	XClearArea
XClearWindow:	clear an entire window.	XClearWindow
preferences such as key	click. /change the keyboard	XChangeKeyboardControl
XKillClient: destroy a	client or its remaining/	XKillClient
XCloseDisplay: disconnect a	client program from an X server/	XCloseDisplay
XOpenDisplay: connect a	client program to an X server.	XOpenDisplay
rebind a keysym to a string for	client. XRebindKeysym:	XRebindKeysym
change the close down mode of a	client. XSetCloseDownMode:	XSetCloseDownMode
/add a window's children to the	client's save-set.	XAddToSaveSet
or remove a subwindow from the	client's save-set. /add	XChangeSaveSet
a window's children from the	client's save-set. /remove	XRemoveFromSaveSet
XSetClipOrigin: set the	clip origin in a graphics/	XSetClipOrigin
to/ XSetClipRectangles: change	clip_mask in a graphics context	XSetClipRectangles
context to the/ XSetRegion: set	clip_mask of the graphics	XSetRegion

context. XSetClipMask: set	clip_mask pixmap in a graphics	.... XSetClipMask
XSetCloseDownMode: change the	close down mode of a client.	.... XSetCloseDownMode
/entry of a colormap to the	closest available hardware/	.... XStoreColor
/read/write colorcells to the	closest available hardware/	.... XStoreColors
/a read-only colormap cell with	closest hardware-supported/	.... XAllocColor
/get database RGB values and	closest hardware-supported RGB/	.... XLookupColor
XQueryBestCursor: get the	closest supported cursor sizes.	.... XQueryBestCursor
obtain a description of error	code. XGetErrorText:	.... XGetErrorText
translate RGB values from ASCII	color name or hexadecimal/ /or	.... XParseColor
a read-only colorcell from	color name. /allocate	.... XAllocNamedColor
RGB values from	color name. /hardware-supported	.... XLookupColor
read/write colorcell by English	color name. /allocate a	.... XStoreNamedColor
XRecolorCursor: change the	color of a cursor.	.... XRecolorCursor
read/write (nonshareable)	color planes. /allocate	.... XAllocColorPlanes
with closest hardware-supported	color. /read-only colormap cell	.... XAllocColor
the closest available hardware	color. /entry of a colormap to	.... XStoreColor
name. /allocate a read/write	colorcell by English color	.... XStoreNamedColor
/allocate a read-only	colorcell from color name.	.... XAllocNamedColor
/set or change read/write	colorcells to the closest/	.... XStoreColors
allocate read/write (nonshared)	colorcells. XAllocColorCells:	.... XAllocColorCells
XFreeColormap: delete a	colormap and install the/	.... XFreeColormap
XCopyColormapAndFree: copy a	colormap and return a new/	.... XCopyColormapAndFree
/allocate a read-only	colormap cell with closest/	.... XAllocColor
XFreeColors: free	colormap cells or planes.	.... XFreeColors
XSetWindowColormap: set the	colormap for a specified/	.... XSetWindowColormap
a colormap and return a new	colormap ID. /copy	.... XCopyColormapAndFree
XUninstallColormap: uninstall a	colormap; install default if/	.... XUninstallColormap
/get the standard	colormap property.	.... XGetStandardColormap
/change the standard	colormap property.	.... XSetStandardColormap
change a read/write entry of a	colormap to the closest/ /set or	.... XStoreColor
XCreateColormap: create a	colormap.	.... XCreateColormap
and install the default	colormap. /delete a colormap	.... XFreeColormap
XInstallColormap: install a	colormap.	.... XInstallColormap
/get a list of installed	colormaps.	.... XListInstalledColormaps
the closest available hardware	colors. /colorcells to	.... XStoreColors
/load a resource database from	command line arguments.	.... XrmParseCommand
the XA_WM_COMMAND atom	(command line arguments). /set	.... XSetCommand
context. /set the line drawing	components in a graphics	.... XSetLineAttributes
context. XChangeGC: change the	components of a given graphics	.... XChangeGC
to ASCII string, keysym, and	ComposeStatus. /map a key event	.... XLookupString
regions. XIntersectRegion:	compute the intersection of two	.... XIntersectRegion
regions. XUnionRegion:	compute the union of two	.... XUnionRegion
X server. XOpenDisplay:	connect a client program to an	.... XOpenDisplay
XDrawLines: draw multiple	connected lines.	.... XDrawLines
control list to allow or deny	connection requests. /access	.... XEnableAccessControl
/report the display name when	connection to a display fails.	.... XDisplayName
XNoOp: send a NoOp to exercise	connection with the server.	.... XNoOp
value in an/ XAddPixel: add a	constant value to every pixel	.... XAddPixel
drawable into/ XGetImage: place	contents of a rectangle from	.... XGetImage
XrmMergeDatabases: merge the	contents of one database with/	.... XrmMergeDatabases
XDeleteContext: delete a	context entry for a given/	.... XDeleteContext
the/ /create a new graphics	context for a given screen with	.... XCreateGC
XUniqueContext: create a new	context ID (not graphics/	.... XUniqueContext
XFindContext: get data from the	context manager (not graphics/	.... XFindContext
/change clip_mask in a graphics	context to the list of/	.... XSetClipRectangles
/set clip_mask of the graphics	context to the specified/	.... XSetRegion
/corresponding to a window and	context type (not graphics/	.... XSaveContext

components of a given graphics context. XChangeGC: change the .... XChangeGC
XCopyGC: copy a graphics context. .... XCopyGC
context manager (not graphics context). /get data from the .... XFindContext
XFreeGC: free a graphics context. .... XFreeGC
with the specified graphics context. /ID) associated .... XGContextFromGC
and context type (not graphics context). /to a window .... XSaveContext
set the arc mode in a graphics context. XSetArcMode: .... XSetArcMode
pixel value in a graphics context. /set the background .... XSetBackground
clip_mask pixmap in a graphics context. XSetClipMask: set .... XSetClipMask
the clip origin in a graphics context. XSetClipOrigin: set .... XSetClipOrigin
(for lines) in a graphics context. /and dashes .... XSetDashes
set the fill rule in a graphics context. XSetFillRule: .... XSetFillRule
the fill style in a graphics context. XSetFillStyle: set .... XSetFillStyle
the current font in a graphics context. XSetFont: set .... XSetFont
pixel value in a graphics context. /set the foreground .... XSetForeground
logical operation in a graphics context. /set the bitwise .... XSetFunction
in a graphics context. /graphics_exposures .... XSetGraphicsExposures
components in a graphics context. /set the line drawing .... XSetLineAttributes
the plane mask in a graphics context. XSetPlaneMask: set .... XSetPlaneMask
and plane mask in a graphics context. /logical function, ... XSetState
set the stipple in a graphics context. XSetStipple: .... XSetStipple
subwindow mode in a graphics context. /set the .... XSetSubwindowMode
set the fill tile in a graphics context. XSetTile: .... XSetTile
origin in a graphics context. /set the tile/stipple .... XSetTSOrigin
a new context ID (not graphics context). /create .... XUniqueContext
of modifier keys (Shift, Control, etc.). /a mapping .... XGetModifierMapping
to be used as modifiers (Shift, Control, etc.). /set keycodes .... XSetModifierMapping
XBell: ring the bell (Control G). .... XBell
connection/ /use access control list to allow or deny .... XEnableAccessControl
add a host to the access control list. XAddHost: .... XAddHost
multiple hosts to the access control list. XAddHosts: add .... XAddHosts
remove a host from the access control list. XRemoveHost: .... XRemoveHost
multiple hosts from the access control list. /remove .... XRemoveHosts
keyboard and/ XAllowEvents: control the behavior of .... XAllowEvents
disable or enable access control. XSetAccessControl: .... XSetAccessControl
XrmStringToBindingQuarkList: convert a key string to a/ .... XrmStringToBindingQuarkList
list. XrmStringToQuarkList: convert a key string to a quark .... XrmStringToQuarkList
XKeycodeToKeysym: convert a keycode to a keysym. .... XKeycodeToKeysym
a keysym. XStringToKeysym: convert a keysym name string to .... XStringToKeysym
string. XKeysymToString: convert a keysym symbol to a .... XKeysymToString
appropriate/ XKeysymToKeycode: convert a keysym to the .... XKeysymToKeycode
XrmQuarkToString: convert a quark to a string. .... XrmQuarkToString
XrmStringToQuark: convert a string to a quark. .... XrmStringToQuark
window to another. /change the coordinate system from one .... XTranslateCoordinates
new/ XCopyColormapAndFree: copy a colormap and return a .... XCopyColormapAndFree
XCopyGC: copy a graphics context. .... XCopyGC
a location/ XGetSubImage: copy a rectangle in drawable to .... XGetSubImage
drawable into a/ XCopyPlane: copy a single plane of a .... XCopyPlane
XCopyArea: copy an area of a drawable. .... XCopyArea
XLookupKeysym: get the keysym corresponding to a keycode in/ .... XLookupKeysym
XSaveContext: save a data value corresponding to a window and/ .... XSaveContext
format/ XCreateBitmapFromData: create a bitmap from X11 bitmap .... XCreateBitmapFromData
XCreateColormap: create a colormap. .... XCreateColormap
glyphs. XCreateGlyphCursor: create a cursor from font .... XCreateGlyphCursor
standard/ XCreateFontCursor: create a cursor from the .... XCreateFontCursor
bitmaps. XCreatePixmapCursor: create a cursor from two .... XCreatePixmapCursor
string. XrmGetStringDatabase: create a database from a .... XrmGetStringDatabase

mapping/ XNewModifiermap: create a keyboard modifier .... XNewModifiermap
(X10). XCreateAssocTable: create a new association table .... XCreateAssocTable
graphics/ XUniqueContext: create a new context ID (not .... XUniqueContext
XCreateRegion: create a new empty region. .... XCreateRegion
for a given screen/ XCreateGC: create a new graphics context .... XCreateGC
XCreatePixmapFromBitmapData: create a pixmap with depth from/ .... XCreatePixmapFromBitmapData
XCreatePixmap: create a pixmap. .... XCreatePixmap
an image. XSubImage: create a subimage from part of .... XSubImage
attributes. XCreateWindow: create a window and set .... XCreateWindow
association table. XMakeAssoc: create an entry in an .... XMakeAssoc
window. XCreateSimpleWindow: create an unmapped InputOutput .... XCreateSimpleWindow
/free specified in-memory data created by an Xlib function. .... XFree
/obtain the current attributes of window. .... XGetWindowAttributes
context. XSetFont: set the current font in a graphics .... XSetFont
XGetFontPath: get the current font search path. .... XGetFontPath
XGetGeometry: obtain the current geometry of drawable. .... XGetGeometry
XGetInputFocus: return the current keyboard focus window. .... XGetInputFocus
/obtain a list of the current keyboard preferences. .... XGetKeyboardControl
XQueryPointer: get the current pointer location. .... XQueryPointer
XGetPointerControl: get the current pointer preferences. .... XGetPointerControl
XGetScreenSaver: get the current screen saver/ .... XGetScreenSaver
/obtain a bit vector for the current state of the keyboard. .... XQueryKeymap
a cursor from the standard cursor font. /create .... XCreateFontCursor
XUndefineCursor: disassociate a cursor from a window. .... XUndefineCursor
XCreateGlyphCursor: create a cursor from font glyphs. .... XCreateGlyphCursor
XCreateFontCursor: create a cursor from the standard cursor/ .... XCreateFontCursor
XCreatePixmapCursor: create a cursor from two bitmaps. .... XCreatePixmapCursor
/get the closest supported cursor sizes. .... XQueryBestCursor
/obtain the "best" supported cursor, tile, or stipple size. .... XQueryBestSize
XDefineCursor: assign a cursor to a window. .... XDefineCursor
XFreeCursor: destroy a cursor. .... XFreeCursor
change the color of a cursor. XRecolorCursor: .... XRecolorCursor
XDraw: draw a polyline or curve between vertex list (from/ .... XDraw
X10). /draw a filled polygon or curve from vertex list (from .... XDrawFilled
XFetchBytes: return data from cut buffer 0. .... XFetchBytes
XStoreBytes: store data in cut buffer 0. .... XStoreBytes
return data from a cut buffer. XFetchBuffer: .... XFetchBuffer
XStoreBuffer: store data in a cut buffer. .... XStoreBuffer
XRotateBuffers: rotate the cut buffers. .... XRotateBuffers
XSetDashes: set dash_offset and dashes (for lines) in a/ .... XSetDashes
lines) in a/ XSetDashes: set dash_offset and dashes (for .... XSetDashes
XFree: free specified in-memory data created by an Xlib/ .... XFree
XFetchBuffer: return data from a cut buffer. .... XFetchBuffer
XLookUpAssoc: obtain data from an association table. .... XLookUpAssoc
XFetchBytes: return data from cut buffer 0. .... XFetchBytes
(not/ XFindContext: get data from the context manager .... XFindContext
XStoreBuffer: store data in a cut buffer. .... XStoreBuffer
XStoreBytes: store data in cut buffer 0. .... XStoreBytes
window/ XSaveContext: save a data value corresponding to a .... XSaveContext
a bitmap from X11 bitmap format data. /create .... XCreateBitmapFromData
a pixmap with depth from bitmap data. /create .... XCreatePixmapFromBitmapData
XrmGetFileDatabase: retrieve a database from a file. .... XrmGetFileDatabase
XrmGetStringDatabase: create a database from a string. .... XrmGetStringDatabase
arguments. /load a resource database from command line .... XrmParseCommand
XrmPutFileDatabase: store a database in a file. .... XrmPutFileDatabase
resource. /search resource database levels for a given .... XrmQGetSearchResource
/return a list of database levels. .... XrmQGetSearchList

XLookupColor: get database RGB values and closest/ .... XLookupColor

/store a resource into a database using quarks. .... XrmQPutResource

a string resource value to a database using quarks. /add .... XrmQPutStringResource

/merge the contents of one database with another. .... XrmMergeDatabases

error messages from the error database. /obtain .... XGetErrorDatabaseText

store a resource into a database. XrmPutResource: .... XrmPutResource

with an image. XDestroyImage: deallocate memory associated .... XDestroyImage

with a region. XDestroyRegion: deallocate storage associated .... XDestroyRegion

or disable synchronization for debugging. /enable .... XSynchronize

a colormap and install the default colormap. /delete .... XFreeColormap

given user geometry string and default geometry. /geometry .... XGeometry

/uninstall a colormap; install default if not already/ .... XUninstallColormap

the default/ XFreeColormap: delete a colormap and install .... XFreeColormap

given window/ XDeleteContext: delete a context entry for a .... XDeleteContext

XDeleteProperty: delete a window property. .... XDeleteProperty

association/ XDeleteAssoc: delete an entry from an .... XDeleteAssoc

XDeleteModifiermapEntry: delete an entry from an/ .... XDeleteModifiermapEntry

access control list to allow or deny connection requests. /use .... XEnableAccessControl

that matches the desired depth and class. /information .... XMatchVisualInfo

/a drawable into a drawable with depth, applying pixel values. .... XCopyPlane

/create a pixmap with depth from bitmap data. .... XCreatePixmapFromBitmapData

XGetErrorText: obtain a description of error code. .... XGetErrorText

FunctionName: brief description of the function. .... FunctionName

/information that matches the desired depth and class. .... XMatchVisualInfo

remaining/ XKillClient: destroy a client or its .... XKillClient

XFreeCursor: destroy a cursor. .... XFreeCursor

XDestroyWindow: unmap and destroy a window and all/ .... XDestroyWindow

window. XDestroySubwindows: destroy all subwindows of a .... XDestroySubwindows

modifier/ XFreeModifiermap: destroy and free a keyboard .... XFreeModifiermap

a region. XPointInRegion: determine if a point is inside .... XPointInRegion

resides in a/ XRectInRegion: determine if a rectangle .... XRectInRegion

XEmptyRegion: determine if a region is empty. .... XEmptyRegion

the same size,/ XEqualRegion: determine if two regions have .... XEqualRegion

and/ XXorRegion: calculate the difference between the union .... XXorRegion

control. XSetAccessControl: disable or enable access .... XSetAccessControl

XSynchronize: enable or disable synchronization for/ .... XSynchronize

window. XUndefineCursor: disassociate a cursor from a .... XUndefineCursor

from an X/ XCloseDisplay: disconnect a client program .... XCloseDisplay

XDrawSegments: draw multiple disjoint lines. .... XDrawSegments

read a bitmap from disk. XReadBitmapFile: .... XReadBitmapFile

XFlush: flush the output buffer (display all queued requests). .... XFlush

name when connection to a display fails. /the display .... XDisplayName

a/ XDisplayName: report the display name when connection to .... XDisplayName

program from an X server and display. /disconnect a client .... XCloseDisplay

of hosts having access to this display. /obtain a list .... XListHosts

/set the name to be displayed in a window's icon. .... XSetIconName

/get the name to be displayed in an icon. .... XGetIconName

removing it from the queue; do not wait. /an event without .... XPeekIfEvent

next event that matches mask; don't wait. /remove the .... XCheckMaskEvent

queue that matches event type; don't wait. /the next event in .... XCheckTypedEvent

passed window and passed mask; don't wait. /matching both .... XCheckWindowEvent

/change the close down mode of a client. .... XSetCloseDownMode

order of children up or down. /circulate the stacking .... XCirculateSubwindows

XDrawImageString16: draw 16-bit image text/ XDrawImageString16

XDrawText16: draw 16-bit polytext strings. XDrawText16

characters. XDrawImageString: draw 8-bit image text .... XDrawImageString

XDrawText: draw 8-bit polytext strings. .... XDrawText

from vertex list/ XDrawFilled: draw a filled polygon or curve .... XDrawFilled
XDrawLine: draw a line between two points. .... XDrawLine
XDrawPoint: draw a point. .... XDrawPoint
between vertex list/ XDraw: draw a polyline or curve .... XDraw
window or pixmap. XPutImage: draw a rectangular image on a .... XPutImage
foreground only. XDrawString: draw an 8-bit text string, ... XDrawString
rectangle. XDrawArc: draw an arc fitting inside a .... XDrawArc
XDrawRectangle: draw an outline of a rectangle. .... XDrawRectangle
XDrawArcs: draw multiple arcs. .... XDrawArcs
XDrawLines: draw multiple connected lines. .... XDrawLines
XDrawSegments: draw multiple disjoint lines. .... XDrawSegments
XDrawPoints: draw multiple points. .... XDrawPoints
rectangles. XDrawRectangles: draw the outlines of multiple .... XDrawRectangles
XDrawString16: draw two-byte text strings. XDrawString16
/copy a single plane of a drawable into a drawable with/ .... XCopyPlane
contents of a rectangle from drawable into an image. /place .... XGetImage
the/ /copy a rectangle in drawable to a location within .... XGetSubImage
/plane of a drawable into a drawable with depth, applying/ .... XCopyPlane
XCopyArea: copy an area of a drawable. .... XCopyArea
given screen with the specified drawable. /context for a .... XCreateGC
obtain the current geometry of drawable. XGetGeometry: .... XGetGeometry
graphics context. /set the line drawing components in a .... XSetLineAttributes
XCreateRegion: create a new empty region. .... XCreateRegion
determine if a region is empty. XEmptyRegion: .... XEmptyRegion
XSetAccessControl: disable or enable access control. .... XSetAccessControl
synchronization/ XSynchronize: enable or disable .... XSynchronize
generate the smallest rectangle enclosing a region. XClipBox: .... XClipBox
a read/write colorcell by English color name. /allocate .... XStoreNamedColor
XClearWindow: clear an entire window. .... XClearWindow
type. /delete a context entry for a given window and .... XDeleteContext
table. XDeleteAssoc: delete an entry from an association .... XDeleteAssoc
structure. /delete an entry from an XModifierKeymap .... XDeleteModifiermapEntry
and value. /add a resource entry given as a string of name .... XrmPutLineResource
XMakeAssoc: create an entry in an association table. .... XMakeAssoc
/set or change a read/write entry of a colormap to the/ .... XStoreColor
structure. /add a new entry to an XModifierKeymap .... XInsertModifiermapEntry
obtain a description of error code. XGetErrorText: .... XGetErrorText
/obtain error messages from the error database. .... XGetErrorDatabaseText
/set a nonfatal error event handler. .... XSetErrorHandler
XGetErrorDatabaseText: obtain error messages from the error/ .... XGetErrorDatabaseText
/and wait for all events and errors to be processed by the/ .... XSync
handle fatal I/O errors. XSetIOErrorHandler: .... XSetIOErrorHandler
modifier keys (Shift, Control, etc.). /obtain a mapping of .... XGetModifierMapping
as modifiers (Shift, Control, etc.). /set keycodes to be used .... XSetModifierMapping
XPutBackEvent: push an event back on the input queue. .... XPutBackEvent
/set a nonfatal error event handler. .... XSetErrorHandler
and window. /return the next event in queue matching type .... XCheckTypedWindowEvent
event type;/ /return the next event in queue that matches .... XCheckTypedEvent
procedure. XIfEvent: wait for event matched in predicate .... XIfEvent
window and/ /remove the next event matching both passed .... XCheckWindowEvent
XWindowEvent: remove the next event matching mask and window. .... XWindowEvent
XNextEvent: get the next event of any type or window. .... XNextEvent
XCheckIfEvent: check the event queue for a matching/ .... XCheckIfEvent
the number of events in the event queue. /check .... XEventsQueued
wait. /remove the next event that matches mask; don't .... XCheckMaskEvent
XMaskEvent: remove the next event that matches mask. .... XMaskEvent
and/ XLookupString: map a key event to ASCII string, keysym, ... XLookupString

Permuted Index

event in queue that matches event type; don't wait. /next .... XCheckTypedEvent
XSelectInput: select the event types to be sent to a/ .... XSelectInput
the/ XPeekIfEvent: get an event without removing it from .... XPeekIfEvent
the queue. XPeekEvent: get an event without removing it from .... XPeekEvent
the event queue for a matching event. XCheckIfEvent: check .... XCheckIfEvent
XSendEvent: send an event. .... XSendEvent
output buffer and wait for all events and errors to be/ /the .... XSync
/check the number of events in the event queue. .... XEventsQueued
/of keyboard and pointer events when these resources are/ .... XAllowEvents
get pointer motion events. XGetMotionEvents: .... XGetMotionEvents
the number of pending input events. /buffer and return .... XPending
server. XNoOp: send a NoOp exercise connection with the .... XNoOp
XShrinkRegion: reduce or expand the size of a region. .... XShrinkRegion
XQueryExtension: get extension information. .... XQueryExtension
the/ /return a list of all extensions to X supported by .... XListExtensions
for a list of installed extensions to X. /allocated .... XFreeExtensionList
when connection to a display fails. /report the display name .... XDisplayName
XSetIOErrorHandler: handle fatal I/O errors. .... XSetIOErrorHandler
retrieve a database from a file. XrmGetFileDatabase: .... XrmGetFileDatabase
store a database in a file. XrmPutFileDatabase: .... XrmPutFileDatabase
write a bitmap to a file. XWriteBitmapFile: .... XWriteBitmapFile
XFillPolygon: fill a polygon. .... XFillPolygon
XFillRectangle: fill a rectangular area. .... XFillRectangle
XFillArc: fill an arc. .... XFillArc
XLoadQueryFont: load a font and fill information structure. .... XLoadQueryFont
XFillArcs: fill multiple arcs. .... XFillArcs
areas. XFillRectangles: fill multiple rectangular .... XFillRectangles
context. XSetFillRule: set the fill rule in a graphics .... XSetFillRule
XSetFillStyle: set the fill style in a graphics/ .... XSetFillStyle
context. XSetTile: set the fill tile in a graphics .... XSetTile
/obtain the best supported fill tile shape. .... XQueryBestTile
vertex/ XDrawFilled: draw a filled polygon or curve from .... XDrawFilled
structure that/ XGetVisualInfo: find a visual information .... XGetVisualInfo
XDrawArc: draw an arc fitting inside a rectangle. .... XDrawArc
/obtain the RGB values and flags for a specified pixel/ .... XQueryColor
return the number of/ XPending: flush the output buffer and .... XPending
wait for all events and/ XSync: flush the output buffer and .... XSync
(display all queued/ XFlush: flush the output buffer .... XFlush
return the current keyboard focus window. XGetInputFocus: .... XGetInputFocus
set the keyboard focus window. XSetInputFocus: .... XSetInputFocus
XLoadQueryFont: load a font and fill information/ .... XLoadQueryFont
font/ XFreeFont: unload a font and free storage for the .... XFreeFont
/create a cursor from font glyphs. .... XCreateGlyphCursor
font if not already loaded; get font ID. XLoadFont: load a .... XLoadFont
font ID. XLoadFont: load a font if not already loaded; get .... XLoadFont
XSetFont: set the current font in a graphics context. .... XSetFont
XFreeFontInfo: free multiple font information arrays. .... XFreeFontInfo
/query the server for string/ font metrics of a 16-bit/ XQueryTextExtents16
XTextExtents16: get string and font metrics of a 16-bit/ XTextExtents16
/query the server for string and font metrics. .... XQueryTextExtents
XTextExtents: get string and font metrics. .... XTextExtents
XFreeFontNames: free the font name array. .... XFreeFontNames
return a list of the available font names. XListFonts: .... XListFonts
XGetFontProperty: get a font property given its atom. .... XGetFontProperty
XGetFontPath: get the current font search path. .... XGetFontPath
XSetFontPath: set the font search path. .... XSetFontPath
a font and free storage for the font structure. /unload .... XFreeFont

cursor from the standard cursor font. /create a .... XCreateFontCursor
information about a loaded font. XQueryFont: return .... XQueryFont
XUnloadFont: unload a font. .... XUnloadFont
and information about loaded fonts. /obtain the names .... XListFontsWithInfo
function,/ XSetState: set the foreground, background, logical .... XSetState
draw an 8-bit text string, foreground only. XDrawString: .... XDrawString
XSetForeground: set the foreground pixel value in a/ .... XSetForeground
/create a bitmap from X11 bitmap format data. .... XCreateBitmapFromData
the atom type and property format for a window. /obtain .... XGetWindowProperty
XFreeGC: free a graphics context. .... XFreeGC
XFreeModifiermap: destroy and free a keyboard modifier/ .... XFreeModifiermap
XFreePixmap: free a pixmap ID. .... XFreePixmap
XFreeColors: free colormap cells or planes. .... XFreeColors
list of/ XFreeExtensionList: free memory allocated for a .... XFreeExtensionList
arrays. XFreeFontInfo: free multiple font information .... XFreeFontInfo
created by an Xlib/ XFree: free specified in-memory data .... XFree
XFreeFont: unload a font and free storage for the font/ .... XFreeFont
XFreeFontNames: free the font name array. .... XFreeFontNames
XGetFontPath. XFreeFontPath: free the memory allocated by .... XFreeFontPath
an/ XDestroyAssocTable: free the memory allocated for .... XDestroyAssocTable
allocate memory never to be freed. Xpermalloc: .... Xpermalloc
/foreground, background, logical function, and plane mask in a/ .... XSetState
XSetAfterFunction: set a function called after all Xlib/ .... XSetAfterFunction
brief description of the function. FunctionName: .... FunctionName
data created by an Xlib function. /specified in-memory .... XFree
of the function. FunctionName: brief description .... FunctionName
function called after all Xlib functions. /set a .... XSetAfterFunction
XBell: ring the bell (Control G). .... XBell
XGContextFromGC: obtain the GContext (resource ID)/ .... XGContextFromGC
XPolygonRegion: generate a region from points. .... XPolygonRegion
standard/ XParseGeometry: generate position and size from .... XParseGeometry
enclosing a region. XClipBox: generate the smallest rectangle .... XClipBox
XGeometry: calculate window geometry given user geometry/ .... XGeometry
/obtain the current geometry of drawable. .... XGetGeometry
/window geometry given user geometry string and default/ .... XGeometry
and size from standard window geometry string. /position .... XParseGeometry
geometry string and default geometry. /geometry given user .... XGeometry
atom. XGetFontProperty: get a font property given its .... XGetFontProperty
XListInstalledColormaps: get a list of installed/ .... XListInstalledColormaps
XGetAtomName: get a name for a given atom. .... XGetAtomName
class as/ XrmQGetResource: get a resource from name and .... XrmQGetResource
class as/ XrmGetResource: get a resource from name and .... XrmGetResource
XFetchName: get a window's name/ .... XFetchName
it from the/ XPeekIfEvent: get an event without removing .... XPeekIfEvent
it from the queue. XPeekEvent: get an event without removing .... XPeekEvent
manager (not/ XFindContext: get data from the context .... XFindContext
closest/ XLookupColor: get database RGB values and .... XLookupColor
XQueryExtension: get extension information. .... XQueryExtension
a font if not already loaded; get font ID. XLoadFont: load .... XLoadFont
XGetMotionEvents: get pointer motion events. .... XGetMotionEvents
XGetIconSizes: get preferred icon sizes. .... XGetIconSizes
a 16-bit/ XTextExtents16: get string and font metrics of XTextExtents16
XTextExtents: get string and font metrics. .... XTextExtents
cursor/ XQueryBestCursor: get the closest supported .... XQueryBestCursor
path. XGetFontPath: get the current font search .... XGetFontPath
location. XQueryPointer: get the current pointer .... XQueryPointer
XGetPointerControl: get the current pointer/ .... XGetPointerControl

parameters. XGetScreenSaver:	get the current screen saver	XGetScreenSaver
a keycode in/ XLookupKeysym:	get the keysym corresponding to	XLookupKeysym
an icon. XGetIconName:	get the name to be displayed in	XGetIconName
or window. XNextEvent:	get the next event of any type	XNextEvent
XGetPointerMapping:	get the pointer button mapping.	XGetPointerMapping
window. XListProperties:	get the property list for a	XListProperties
property of a/ XGetClassHint:	get the XA_WM_CLASS	XGetClassHint
XGetTransientForHint:	get the/	XGetTransientForHint
a window in/ XGetNormalHints:	get the size hints property of	XGetNormalHints
XGetStandardColormap:	get the standard colormap/	XGetStandardColormap
16-bit character/ XTextWidth16:	get the width in pixels of a	XTextWidth16
8-bit character/ XTextWidth:	get the width in pixels of an	XTextWidth
create a cursor from font	glyphs. XCreateGlyphCursor:	XCreateGlyphCursor
XGrabKey:	grab a key.	XGrabKey
XGrabButton:	grab a pointer button.	XGrabButton
XGrabKeyboard:	grab the keyboard.	XGrabKeyboard
XGrabPointer:	grab the pointer.	XGrabPointer
XGrabServer:	grab the server.	XGrabServer
parameters of an active pointer	grab. /change the	XChangeActivePointerGrab
release a button from	grab. XUngrabButton:	XUngrabButton
XUngrabKey: release a key from	grab.	XUngrabKey
release the keyboard from	grab. XUngrabKeyboard:	XUngrabKeyboard
release the pointer from	grab. XUngrabPointer:	XUngrabPointer
release the server from	grab. XUngrabServer:	XUngrabServer
events when these resources are	grabbed. /keyboard and pointer	XAllowEvents
screen/ XCreateGC: create a new	graphics context for a given	XCreateGC
/change clip_mask in a	graphics context to the list of/	XSetClipRectangles
specified/ /set clip_mask of the	graphics context to the	XSetRegion
the components of a given	graphics context. /change	XChangeGC
XCopyGC: copy a	graphics context.	XCopyGC
from the context manager (not	graphics context). /get data	XFindContext
XFreeGC: free a	graphics context.	XFreeGC
associated with the specified	graphics context. /ID)	XGContextFromGC
a window and context type (not	graphics context). /to	XSaveContext
set the arc mode in a	graphics context. XSetArcMode:	XSetArcMode
the background pixel value in a	graphics context. /set	XSetBackground
/set clip_mask pixmap in a	graphics context.	XSetClipMask
/set the clip origin in a	graphics context.	XSetClipOrigin
and dashes (for lines) in a	graphics context. /dash_offset	XSetDashes
/set the fill rule in a	graphics context.	XSetFillRule
/set the fill style in a	graphics context.	XSetFillStyle
set the current font in a	graphics context. XSetFont:	XSetFont
the foreground pixel value in a	graphics context. /set	XSetForeground
bitwise logical operation in a	graphics context. /set the	XSetFunction
/set graphics_exposures in a	graphics context.	XSetGraphicsExposures
line drawing components in a	graphics context. /set the	XSetLineAttributes
/set the plane mask in a	graphics context.	XSetPlaneMask
function, and plane mask in a	graphics context. /logical	XSetState
set the stipple in a	graphics context. XSetStipple:	XSetStipple
/set the subwindow mode in a	graphics context.	XSetSubwindowMode
set the fill tile in a	graphics context. XSetTile:	XSetTile
the tile/stipple origin in a	graphics context. /set	XSetTSOrigin
/create a new context ID (not	graphics context).	XUniqueContext
XSetGraphicsExposures: set	graphics_exposures in a/	XSetGraphicsExposures
XSetIOErrorHandler:	handle fatal I/O errors.	XSetIOErrorHandler
set a nonfatal error event	handler. XSetErrorHandler:	XSetErrorHandler
to the closest available	hardware color. /of a colormap	XStoreColor

to the closest available hardware colors. /colorcells .... XStoreColors
/colormap cell with closest hardware-supported color. .... XAllocColor
/database RGB values and closest hardware-supported RGB values/ .... XLookupColor
/obtain a list of hosts having access to this display. .... XListHosts
values from ASCII color name or hexadecimal value. /RGB .... XParseColor
XGetNormalHints: get the size hints property of a window in/ .... XGetNormalHints
XSetNormalHints: set the size hints property of a window in/ .... XSetNormalHints
XGetZoomHints: read the size hints property of a zoomed/ .... XGetZoomHints
XSetZoomHints: set the size hints property of a zoomed/ .... XSetZoomHints
read the window manager hints property. XGetWMHints: .... XGetWMHints
set a window manager hints property. XSetWMHints: .... XSetWMHints
list. XRemoveHost: remove a host from the access control .... XRemoveHost
list. XAddHost: add a host to the access control .... XAddHost
allow access from any host. XDisableAccessControl: .... XDisableAccessControl
XRemoveHosts: remove multiple hosts from the access control/ .... XRemoveHosts
XListHosts: obtain a list of hosts having access to this/ .... XListHosts
list. XAddHosts: add multiple hosts to the access control .... XAddHosts
XGetIconSizes: get preferred icon sizes. .... XGetIconSizes
the name to be displayed in an icon. XGetIconName: get .... XGetIconName
to be displayed in a window's icon. /set the name .... XSetIconName
in normal state (not zoomed or iconified). /of a window .... XGetNormalHints
in normal state (not zoomed or iconified). /of a window .... XSetNormalHints
/obtain the GContext (resource ID) associated with the/ .... XGContextFromGC
/create a new context ID (not graphics context). .... XUniqueContext
and return a new colormap ID. /copy a colormap .... XCopyColormapAndFree
XFreePixmap: free a pixmap ID. .... XFreePixmap
if not already loaded; get font ID. XLoadFont: load a font .... XLoadFont
XPointInRegion: determine if a point is inside a region. .... XPointInRegion
XRectInRegion: determine if a rectangle resides in a/ .... XRectInRegion
XEmptyRegion: determine if a region is empty. .... XEmptyRegion
/a colormap; install default if not already installed. .... XUninstallColormap
ID. XLoadFont: load a font if not already loaded; get font .... XLoadFont
size./ XEqualRegion: determine if two regions have the same .... XEqualRegion
XPutImage: draw a rectangular image on a window or pixmap. .... XPutImage
XDrawImageString: draw 8-bit image text characters. .... XDrawImageString
XDrawImageString16: draw 16-bit image text characters. XDrawImageString16
to every pixel value in an image. /add a constant value .... XAddPixel
memory associated with an image. /deallocate .... XDestroyImage
rectangle from drawable into an image. /place contents of a .... XGetImage
a single pixel value from an image. XGetPixel: obtain .... XGetPixel
within the pre-existing image. /drawable to a location .... XGetSubImage
set a pixel value in an image. XPutPixel: .... XPutPixel
a subimage from part of an image. XSubImage: create .... XSubImage
font. XQueryFont: return information about a loaded .... XQueryFont
/obtain the names and information about loaded fonts. .... XListFontsWithInfo
/free multiple font information arrays. .... XFreeFontInfo
XGetVisualInfo: find a visual information structure that/ .... XGetVisualInfo
/load a font and fill information structure. .... XLoadQueryFont
desired/ /obtain the visual information that matches the .... XMatchVisualInfo
XQueryExtension: get extension information. .... XQueryExtension
the stored modifier and keymap information. /update .... XRefreshKeyboardMapping
manager. XrmInitialize: initialize the resource .... XrmInitialize
Xlib/ XFree: free specified in-memory data created by an .... XFree
return the number of pending input events. /buffer and .... XPending
push an event back on the input queue. XPutBackEvent: .... XPutBackEvent
/create an unmapped InputOutput window. .... XCreateSimpleWindow
window and/ XReparentWindow: insert a window between another .... XReparentWindow

XDrawArc: draw an arc fitting	inside a rectangle.	XDrawArc
/determine if a point is	inside a region.	XPointInRegion
XInstallColormap:	install a colormap.	XInstallColormap
/uninstall a colormap;	install default if not already/	XUninstallColormap
/delete a colormap and	install the default colormap.	XFreeColormap
/get a list of	installed colormaps.	XListInstalledColormaps
/memory allocated for a list of	installed extensions to X.	XFreeExtensionList
install default if not already	installed. /a colormap;	XUninstallColormap
XIntersectRegion: compute the	intersection of two regions.	XIntersectRegion
/between the union and	intersection of two regions.	XXorRegion
/store a resource	into a database using quarks.	XrmQPutResource
/store a resource	into a database.	XrmPutResource
/a single plane of a drawable	into a drawable with depth,/	XCopyPlane
of a rectangle from drawable	into an image. /place contents	XGetImage
/handle fatal	I/O errors.	XSetIOErrorHandler
keyboard preferences such as	key click. /change the	XChangeKeyboardControl
keysym,/ XLookupString: map a	key event to ASCII string, ...	XLookupString
XUngrabKey: release a	key from grab.	XUngrabKey
and a quark list. /convert a	key string to a binding list	XrmStringToBindingQuarkList
XrmStringToQuarkList: convert a	key string to a quark list.	XrmStringToQuarkList
XGrabKey: grab a	key.	XGrabKey
when/ /control the behavior of	keyboard and pointer events	XAllowEvents
XAutoRepeatOff: turn off the	keyboard auto-repeat keys.	XAutoRepeatOff
XAutoRepeatOn: turn on the	keyboard auto-repeat keys.	XAutoRepeatOn
/return the current	keyboard focus window.	XGetInputFocus
XSetInputFocus: set the	keyboard focus window.	XSetInputFocus
XUngrabKeyboard: release the	keyboard from grab.	XUngrabKeyboard
/change the	keyboard mapping.	XChangeKeyboardMapping
structure. /destroy and free a	keyboard modifier mapping	XFreeModifiermap
XNewModifiermap: create a	keyboard modifier mapping/	XNewModifiermap
key click. /change the	keyboard preferences such as	XChangeKeyboardControl
/obtain a list of the current	keyboard preferences.	XGetKeyboardControl
XGrabKeyboard: grab the	keyboard.	XGrabKeyboard
for the current state of the	keyboard. /obtain a bit vector	XQueryKeymap
the keysym corresponding to a	keycode in structure. /get	XLookupKeysym
XKeycodeToKeysym: convert a	keycode to a keysym.	XKeycodeToKeysym
a keysym to the appropriate	keycode. /convert	XKeysymToKeycode
XSetModifierMapping: set	keycodes to be used as/	XSetModifierMapping
return symbols for	keycodes. XGetKeyboardMapping:	XGetKeyboardMapping
/update the stored modifier and	keymap information.	XRefreshKeyboardMapping
/obtain a mapping of modifier	keys (Shift, Control, etc.).	XGetModifierMapping
off the keyboard auto-repeat	keys. XAutoRepeatOff: turn	XAutoRepeatOff
on the keyboard auto-repeat	keys. XAutoRepeatOn: turn	XAutoRepeatOn
a key event to ASCII string,	keysym, and ComposeStatus. /map	XLookupString
keycode/ XLookupKeysym: get the	keysym corresponding to a	XLookupKeysym
XStringToKeysym: convert a	keysym name string to a keysym.	XStringToKeysym
XKeysymToString: convert a	keysym symbol to a string.	XKeysymToString
XRebindKeysym: rebind a	keysym to a string for client.	XRebindKeysym
XKeysymToKeycode: convert a	keysym to the appropriate/	XKeysymToKeycode
convert a keycode to a	keysym. XKeycodeToKeysym:	XKeycodeToKeysym
a keysym name string to a	keysym. /convert	XStringToKeysym
/search resource database	levels for a given resource.	XrmQGetSearchResource
return a list of database	levels. XrmQGetSearchList:	XrmQGetSearchList
resource database from command	line arguments. /load a	XrmParseCommand
/atom (command	line arguments).	XSetCommand
XDrawLine: draw a	line between two points.	XDrawLine
XSetLineAttributes: set the	line drawing components in a/	XSetLineAttributes

/set dash_offset and dashes (for lines) in a graphics context. .... XSetDashes
draw multiple connected lines. XDrawLines: .... XDrawLines
draw multiple disjoint lines. XDrawSegments: .... XDrawSegments
a key string to a binding list and a quark list. /convert .... XrmStringToBindingQuarkList
/get the property list for a window. .... XListProperties
or curve between vertex list (from X10). /a polyline .... XDraw
polygon or curve from vertex list (from X10). /draw a filled .... XDrawFilled
XListExtensions: return a list of all extensions to X/ .... XListExtensions
root. XQueryTree: return a list of children, parent, and .... XQueryTree
XrmQGetSearchList: return a list of database levels. .... XrmQGetSearchList
this/ XListHosts: obtain a list of hosts having access to .... XListHosts
XListInstalledColormaps: get a list of installed colormaps. .... XListInstalledColormaps
X. /free memory allocated for a list of installed extensions to .... XFreeExtensionList
in a graphics context to the list of rectangles. /clip_mask .... XSetClipRectangles
names. XListFonts: return a list of the available font .... XListFonts
XGetKeyboardControl: obtain a list of the current keyboard/ .... XGetKeyboardControl
connection/ /use access control list to allow or deny .... XEnableAccessControl
a host to the access control list. XAddHost: add .... XAddHost
hosts to the access control list. XAddHosts: add multiple .... XAddHosts
a host from the access control list. XRemoveHost: remove .... XRemoveHost
hosts from the access control list. /remove multiple .... XRemoveHosts
to a binding list and a quark list. /convert a key string .... XrmStringToBindingQuarkList
convert a key string to a quark list. XrmStringToQuarkList: .... XrmStringToQuarkList
information/ XLoadQueryFont: load a font and fill .... XLoadQueryFont
loaded; get font/ XLoadFont: load a font if not already .... XLoadFont
command line/ XrmParseCommand: load a resource database from .... XrmParseCommand
return information about a loaded font. XQueryFont: .... XQueryFont
the names and information about loaded fonts. /obtain .... XListFontsWithInfo
/load a font if not already loaded; get font ID. .... XLoadFont
a rectangle in drawable to a location within the/ /copy .... XGetSubImage
get the current pointer location. XQueryPointer: .... XQueryPointer
/set the foreground, background, logical function, and plane/ .... XSetState
XSetFunction: set the bitwise logical operation in a graphics/ .... XSetFunction
from ASCII color/ XParseColor: look up or translate RGB values .... XParseColor
order. XLowerWindow: lower a window in the stacking .... XLowerWindow
XGetWMHints: read the window manager hints property. .... XGetWMHints
XSetWMHints: set a window manager hints property. .... XSetWMHints
/get data from the context manager (not graphics context). .... XFindContext
initialize the resource manager. XrmInitialize: .... XrmInitialize
of properties for the window manager. /set the minimum set .... XSetStandardProperties
name to a window for the window manager. XStoreName: assign a .... XStoreName
string, keysym,/ XLookupString: map a key event to ASCII .... XLookupString
siblings. XMapRaised: map a window on top of its .... XMapRaised
XMapWindow: map a window. .... XMapWindow
XMapSubwindows: map all subwindows. .... XMapSubwindows
XGetModifierMapping: obtain a mapping of modifier keys/ .... XGetModifierMapping
and free a keyboard modifier mapping structure. /destroy .... XFreeModifiermap
/create a keyboard modifier mapping structure. .... XNewModifiermap
/change the keyboard mapping. .... XChangeKeyboardMapping
get the pointer button mapping. XGetPointerMapping: .... XGetPointerMapping
set the pointer button mapping. XSetPointerMapping: .... XSetPointerMapping
remove the next event matching mask and window. XWindowEvent: ..... XWindowEvent
the next event that matches mask; don't wait. /remove .... XCheckMaskEvent
both passed window and passed mask; don't wait. /matching .... XCheckWindowEvent
XSetPlaneMask: set the plane mask in a graphics context. .... XSetPlaneMask
/logical function, and plane mask in a graphics context. .... XSetState
the next event that matches mask. XMaskEvent: remove .... XMaskEvent

XIfEvent: wait for event matched in predicate procedure. .... XIfEvent
/the next event in queue that matches event type; don't wait. .... XCheckTypedEvent
/remove the next event that matches mask; don't wait. .... XCheckMaskEvent
remove the next event that matches mask. XMaskEvent: .... XMaskEvent
/the visual information that matches the desired depth and/ .... XMatchVisualInfo
/information structure that matches the specified template. .... XGetVisualInfo
passed/ /remove the next event matching both passed window and .... XCheckWindowEvent
check the event queue for a matching event. XCheckIfEvent: .... XCheckIfEvent
/remove the next event matching mask and window. .... XWindowEvent
/return the next event in queue matching type and window. .... XCheckTypedWindowEvent
XFreeFontPath: free the memory allocated by/ .... XFreeFontPath
XFreeExtensionList: free memory allocated for a list of/ .... XFreeExtensionList
XDestroyAssocTable: free the memory allocated for an/ .... XDestroyAssocTable
XDestroyImage: deallocate memory associated with an/ .... XDestroyImage
XCreateImage: allocate memory for an XImage structure. .... XCreateImage
Xpermalloc: allocate memory never to be freed. .... Xpermalloc
database/ XrmMergeDatabases: merge the contents of one .... XrmMergeDatabases
database. /obtain error messages from the error .... XGetErrorDatabaseText
/the server for string and font metrics of a 16-bit character/ XQueryTextExtents16
string. /get string and font metrics of a 16-bit character XTextExtents16
the server for string and font metrics. /query .... XQueryTextExtents
get string and font metrics. XTextExtents: .... XTextExtents
XSetStandardProperties: set the minimum set of properties for/ .... XSetStandardProperties
XSetArcMode: set the arc mode in a graphics context. .... XSetArcMode
/set the subwindow mode in a graphics context. .... XSetSubwindowMode
/change the close down mode of a client. .... XSetCloseDownMode
information. /update the stored modifier and keymap .... XRefreshKeyboardMapping
etc.). /obtain a mapping of modifier keys (Shift, Control, ... XGetModifierMapping
/destroy and free a keyboard modifier mapping structure. .... XFreeModifiermap
/create a keyboard modifier mapping structure. .... XNewModifiermap
/set keycodes to be used as modifiers (Shift, Control,/ .... XSetModifierMapping
XGetMotionEvents: get pointer motion events. .... XGetMotionEvents
XMoveWindow: move a window. .... XMoveWindow
point on the/ XWarpPointer: move the pointer to another .... XWarpPointer
XDrawArcs: draw multiple arcs. .... XDrawArcs
XFillArcs: fill multiple arcs. .... XFillArcs
XDrawLines: draw multiple connected lines. .... XDrawLines
XDrawSegments: draw multiple disjoint lines. .... XDrawSegments
arrays. XFreeFontInfo: free multiple font information .... XFreeFontInfo
control/ XRemoveHosts: remove multiple hosts from the access .... XRemoveHosts
control list. XAddHosts: add multiple hosts to the access .... XAddHosts
XDrawPoints: draw multiple points. .... XDrawPoints
/draw the outlines of multiple rectangles. .... XDrawRectangles
XFillRectangles: fill multiple rectangular areas. .... XFillRectangles
/get a resource from name and class as quarks. .... XrmQGetResource
/get a resource from name and class as strings. .... XrmGetResource
user preferences for program name and options. /scan the .... XGetDefault
entry given as a string of name and value. /add a resource .... XrmPutLineResource
XFreeFontNames: free the font name array. .... XFreeFontNames
XGetAtomName: get a name for a given atom. .... XGetAtomName
/RGB values from ASCII color name or hexadecimal value. .... XParseColor
XFetchName: get a window's name (XA_WM_NAME/ .... XFetchName
/convert a keysym name string to a keysym. .... XStringToKeysym
return an atom for a given name string. XInternAtom: .... XInternAtom
manager. XStoreName: assign a name to a window for the window .... XStoreName
window's/ XSetIconName: set the name to be displayed in a .... XSetIconName
icon. XGetIconName: get the name to be displayed in an .... XGetIconName

display/ /report the display name when connection to a .... XDisplayName
read-only colorcell from color name. /allocate a .... XAllocNamedColor
RGB values from color name. /hardware-supported .... XLookupColor
colorcell by English color name. /allocate a read/write .... XStoreNamedColor
XListFontsWithInfo: obtain the names and information about/ .... XListFontsWithInfo
a list of the available font names. XListFonts: return .... XListFonts
Xpermalloc: allocate memory never to be freed. .... Xpermalloc
XCreateAssocTable: create a new association table (X10). .... XCreateAssocTable
/copy a colormap and return a new colormap ID. .... XCopyColormapAndFree
XUniqueContext: create a new context ID (not graphics/ .... XUniqueContext
XCreateRegion: create a new empty region. .... XCreateRegion
XInsertModifiermapEntry: add a new entry to an XModifierKeymap/ .... XInsertModifiermapEntry
given/ XCreateGC: create a new graphics context for a .... XCreateGC
XrmUniqueQuark: allocate a new quark. .... XrmUniqueQuark
type and window. /return the next event in queue matching .... XCheckTypedWindowEvent
XCheckTypedEvent: return the next event in queue that/ .... XCheckTypedEvent
XCheckWindowEvent: remove the next event matching both passed/ .... XCheckWindowEvent
XWindowEvent: remove the next event matching mask and/ .... XWindowEvent
window. XNextEvent: get the next event of any type or .... XNextEvent
XCheckMaskEvent: remove the next event that matches mask;/ .... XCheckMaskEvent
XMaskEvent: remove the next event that matches mask. .... XMaskEvent
XSetErrorHandler: set a nonfatal error event handler. .... XSetErrorHandler
/allocate read/write (nonshareable) color planes. .... XAllocColorPlanes
/allocate read/write (nonshared) colorcells. .... XAllocColorCells
with the server. XNoOp: send a NoOp to exercise connection .... XNoOp
/hints property of a window in normal state (not zoomed or/ .... XGetNormalHints
/hints property of a window in normal state (not zoomed or/ .... XSetNormalHints
/a colormap; install default if not already installed. .... XUninstallColormap
ID. XLoadFont: load a font if not already loaded; get font .... XLoadFont
data from the context manager (not graphics context). /get .... XFindContext
/to a window and context type (not graphics context). .... XSaveContext
/create a new context ID (not graphics context). .... XUniqueContext
removing it from the queue; do not wait. /get an event without .... XPeekIfEvent
/of a window in normal state (not zoomed or iconified). .... XGetNormalHints
/of a window in normal state (not zoomed or iconified). .... XSetNormalHints
XEventsQueued: check the number of events in the event/ .... XEventsQueued
/output buffer and return the number of pending input events. .... XPending
current state of/ XQueryKeymap: obtain a bit vector for the .... XQueryKeymap
code. XGetErrorText: obtain a description of error .... XGetErrorText
access to this/ XListHosts: obtain a list of hosts having .... XListHosts
keyboard/ XGetKeyboardControl: obtain a list of the current .... XGetKeyboardControl
keys/ XGetModifierMapping: obtain a mapping of modifier .... XGetModifierMapping
from an image. XGetPixel: obtain a single pixel value .... XGetPixel
table. XLookUpAssoc: obtain data from an association .... XLookUpAssoc
error/ XGetErrorDatabaseText: obtain error messages from the .... XGetErrorDatabaseText
of pixel values. XQueryColors: obtain RGB values for an array .... XQueryColors
property/ XGetWindowProperty: obtain the atom type and .... XGetWindowProperty
cursor, tile,/ XQueryBestSize: obtain the "best" supported .... XQueryBestSize
tile shape. XQueryBestTile: obtain the best supported fill .... XQueryBestTile
stipple/ XQueryBestStipple: obtain the best supported .... XQueryBestStipple
of/ XGetWindowAttributes: obtain the current attributes .... XGetWindowAttributes
drawable. XGetGeometry: obtain the current geometry of .... XGetGeometry
ID)/ XGContextFromGC: obtain the GContext (resource .... XGContextFromGC
XListFontsWithInfo: obtain the names and/ .... XListFontsWithInfo
for a specified/ XQueryColor: obtain the RGB values and flags .... XQueryColor
that matches/ XMatchVisualInfo: obtain the visual information .... XMatchVisualInfo
keys. XAutoRepeatOff: turn off the keyboard auto-repeat .... XAutoRepeatOff

turn the screen saver on or off. XForceScreenSaver: .... XForceScreenSaver

two regions have the same size, offset, and shape. /if .... XEqualRegion

XOffsetRegion: change offset of a region. .... XOffsetRegion

8-bit text string, foreground only. XDrawString: draw an .... XDrawString

/set the bitwise logical operation in a graphics/ .... XSetFunction

for program name and options. /the user preferences .... XGetDefault

/circulate the stacking order of children up or down. .... XCirculateSubwindows

/change the stacking order of siblings. .... XRestackWindows

to the top of the stacking order. /the bottom child .... XCirculateSubwindowsDown

to the bottom of the stacking order. /circulate the top child .... XCirculateSubwindowsUp

size, border width, or stacking order. /the window position, ... XConfigureWindow

lower a window in the stacking order. XLowerWindow: .... XLowerWindow

to the top of the stacking order. /raise a window .... XRaiseWindow

XSetClipOrigin: set the clip origin in a graphics context. .... XSetClipOrigin

/set the tile/stipple origin in a graphics context. .... XSetTSOrigin

XDrawRectangle: draw an outline of a rectangle. .... XDrawRectangle

XDrawRectangles: draw the outlines of multiple/ .... XDrawRectangles

number of/ XPending: flush the output buffer and return the .... XPending

events and/ XSync: flush the output buffer and wait for all .... XSync

queued/ XFlush: flush the output buffer (display all .... XFlush

XGetSelectionOwner: return the owner of a selection. .... XGetSelectionOwner

XSetSelectionOwner: set the owner of a selection. .... XSetSelectionOwner

grab. /change the parameters of an active pointer .... XChangeActivePointerGrab

XSetScreenSaver: set the parameters of the screen saver. .... XSetScreenSaver

get the current screen saver parameters. XGetScreenSaver: .... XGetScreenSaver

return a list of children, parent, and root. XQueryTree: .... XQueryTree

between another window and its parent. /insert a window .... XReparentWindow

create a subimage from part of an image. XSubImage: .... XSubImage

matching both passed window and passed mask; don't wait. /event .... XCheckWindowEvent

/the next event matching both passed window and passed mask;/ .... XCheckWindowEvent

get the current font search path. XGetFontPath: .... XGetFontPath

set the font search path. XSetFontPath: .... XSetFontPath

buffer and return the number of pending input events. /output .... XPending

/set the background pixel attribute of a window. .... XSetWindowBackground

/attribute to the specified pixel value and repaint the/ .... XSetWindowBorder

XGetPixel: obtain a single pixel value from an image. .... XGetPixel

context. /set the background pixel value in a graphics .... XSetBackground

context. /set the foreground pixel value in a graphics .... XSetForeground

/add a constant value to every pixel value in an image. .... XAddPixel

XPutPixel: set a pixel value in an image. .... XPutPixel

and flags for a specified pixel value. /the RGB values .... XQueryColor

a drawable with depth, applying pixel values. /a drawable into .... XCopyPlane

RGB values for an array of pixel values. /obtain .... XQueryColors

XTextWidth16: get the width in pixels of a 16-bit character/ XTextWidth16

XTextWidth: get the width in pixels of an 8-bit character/ .... XTextWidth

XFreePixmap: free a pixmap ID. .... XFreePixmap

XSetClipMask: set clip_mask pixmap in a graphics context. .... XSetClipMask

data. /create a pixmap with depth from bitmap .... XCreatePixmapFromBitmapData

XCreatePixmap: create a pixmap. .... XCreatePixmap

image on a window or pixmap. /draw a rectangular .... XPutImage

from drawable into/ XGetImage: place contents of a rectangle .... XGetImage

XSetPlaneMask: set the plane mask in a graphics/ .... XSetPlaneMask

context. /logical function, and plane mask in a graphics .... XSetState

XCopyPlane: copy a single plane of a drawable into a/ .... XCopyPlane

read/write (nonshareable) color planes. /allocate .... XAllocColorPlanes

free colormap cells or planes. XFreeColors: .... XFreeColors

XPointInRegion: determine if a point is inside a region. .... XPointInRegion

/move the pointer to another point on the screen. .... XWarpPointer

XDrawPoint: draw a point. .... XDrawPoint

XGetPointerMapping: get the pointer button mapping. .... XGetPointerMapping

XSetPointerMapping: set the pointer button mapping. .... XSetPointerMapping

XGrabButton: grab a pointer button. .... XGrabButton

/the behavior of keyboard and pointer events when these/ .... XAllowEvents

XUngrabPointer: release the pointer from grab. .... XUngrabPointer

the parameters of an active pointer grab. /change .... XChangeActivePointerGrab

XQueryPointer: get the current pointer location. .... XQueryPointer

XGetMotionEvents: get pointer motion events. .... XGetMotionEvents

/change the pointer preferences. .... XChangePointerControl

/get the current pointer preferences. .... XGetPointerControl

screen. XWarpPointer: move the pointer to another point on the .... XWarpPointer

XGrabPointer: grab the pointer. .... XGrabPointer

draw a line between two points. XDrawLine: .... XDrawLine

XDrawPoints: draw multiple points. .... XDrawPoints

generate a region from points. XPolygonRegion: .... XPolygonRegion

XDrawFilled: draw a filled polygon or curve from vertex/ .... XDrawFilled

XFillPolygon: fill a polygon. .... XFillPolygon

vertex list/ XDraw: draw a polyline or curve between .... XDraw

XDrawText: draw 8-bit polytext strings. .... XDrawText

XDrawText16: draw 16-bit polytext strings. XDrawText16

XParseGeometry: generate position and size from standard/ .... XParseGeometry

/change the size and position of a window. .... XMoveResizeWindow

or stacking/ /change the window position, size, border width, ... XConfigureWindow

wait for event matched in predicate procedure. XIfEvent: .... XIfEvent

to a location within the pre-existing image. /drawable .... XGetSubImage

and/ XGetDefault: scan the user preferences for program name .... XGetDefault

/change the keyboard preferences such as key click. .... XChangeKeyboardControl

/change the pointer preferences. .... XChangePointerControl

a list of the current keyboard preferences. /obtain .... XGetKeyboardControl

/get the current pointer preferences. .... XGetPointerControl

XGetIconSizes: get preferred icon sizes. .... XGetIconSizes

for event matched in predicate procedure. XIfEvent: wait .... XIfEvent

for all events and errors to be processed by the server. /wait .... XSync

display. /disconnect a client program from an X server and .... XCloseDisplay

/scan the user preferences for program name and options. .... XGetDefault

XOpenDisplay: connect a client program to an X server. .... XOpenDisplay

/rotate properties in the properties array. .... XRotateWindowProperties

/set the minimum set of properties for the window/ .... XSetStandardProperties

XRotateWindowProperties: rotate properties in the properties/ .... XRotateWindowProperties

XChangeProperty: change a property associated with a/ .... XChangeProperty

the XA_WM_TRANSIENT_FOR property for a window. /set .... XSetTransientForHint

/obtain the atom type and property format for a window. .... XGetWindowProperty

XGetFontProperty: get a font property given its atom. .... XGetFontProperty

XListProperties: get the property list for a window. .... XListProperties

state (not/ /get the size hints property of a window in normal .... XGetNormalHints

state (not/ /set the size hints property of a window in normal .... XSetNormalHints

/get the XA_WM_CLASS property of a window. .... XGetClassHint

the XA_WM_TRANSIENT_FOR property of a window. /get .... XGetTransientForHint

/set the XA_WM_CLASS property of a window. .... XSetClassHint

/read the size hints property of a zoomed window. .... XGetZoomHints

/set the size hints property of a zoomed window. .... XSetZoomHints

XGetSizeHints: read any property of type/ .... XGetSizeHints

/set the value of any property of type/ .... XSetSizeHints

delete a window property. XDeleteProperty: .... XDeleteProperty

name (XA_WM_NAME property). /get a window's .... XFetchName

/get the standard colormap	property.	XGetStandardColormap
read the window manager hints	property. XGetWMHints:	XGetWMHints
of the XA_WM_ICON_SIZE	property. /set the value	XSetIconSizes
/change the standard colormap	property.	XSetStandardColormap
set a window manager hints	property. XSetWMHints:	XSetWMHints
queue. XPutBackEvent:	push an event back on the input	XPutBackEvent
string to a binding list and a	quark list. /convert a key	XrmStringToBindingQuarkList
/convert a key string to a	quark list.	XrmStringToQuarkList
XrmQuarkToString: convert a	quark to a string.	XrmQuarkToString
convert a string to a	quark. XrmStringToQuark:	XrmStringToQuark
XrmUniqueQuark: allocate a new	quark.	XrmUniqueQuark
resource from name and class as	quarks. XrmQGetResource: get a	XrmQGetResource
resource into a database using	quarks. /store a	XrmQPutResource
value to a database using	quarks. /add a string resource	XrmQPutStringResource
font/ XQueryTextExtents16:	query the server for string and	XQueryTextExtents16
font/ XQueryTextExtents:	query the server for string and	XQueryTextExtents
without removing it from the	queue; do not wait. /an event	XPeekIfEvent
XCheckIfEvent: check the event	queue for a matching event.	XCheckIfEvent
/return the next event in	queue matching type and window.	XCheckTypedWindowEvent
don't/ /return the next event in	queue that matches event type;	XCheckTypedEvent
number of events in the event	queue. /check the	XEventsQueued
without removing it from the	queue. /get an event	XPeekEvent
push an event back on the input	queue. XPutBackEvent:	XPutBackEvent
the output buffer (display all	queued requests). /flush	XFlush
the stacking/ XRaiseWindow:	raise a window to the top of	XRaiseWindow
XReadBitmapFile:	read a bitmap from disk.	XReadBitmapFile
XGetSizeHints:	read any property of type/	XGetSizeHints
a zoomed/ XGetZoomHints:	read the size hints property of	XGetZoomHints
property. XGetWMHints:	read the window manager hints	XGetWMHints
XAllocNamedColor: allocate a	read-only colorcell from color/	XAllocNamedColor
XAllocColor: allocate a	read-only colormap cell with/	XAllocColor
XStoreNamedColor: allocate a	read/write colorcell by English/	XStoreNamedColor
XStoreColors: set or change	read/write colorcells to the/	XStoreColors
XStoreColor: set or change a	read/write entry of a colormap/	XStoreColor
XAllocColorPlanes: allocate	read/write (nonshareable) color/	XAllocColorPlanes
XAllocColorCells: allocate	read/write (nonshared)/	XAllocColorCells
client. XRebindKeysym:	rebind a keysym to a string for	XRebindKeysym
XClipBox: generate the smallest	rectangle enclosing a region.	XClipBox
XGetImage: place contents of a	rectangle from drawable into an/	XGetImage
location/ XGetSubImage: copy a	rectangle in drawable to a	XGetSubImage
XRectInRegion: determine if a	rectangle resides in a region.	XRectInRegion
XUnionRectWithRegion: add a	rectangle to a region.	XUnionRectWithRegion
draw an arc fitting inside a	rectangle. XDrawArc:	XDrawArc
draw an outline of a	rectangle. XDrawRectangle:	XDrawRectangle
draw the outlines of multiple	rectangles. XDrawRectangles:	XDrawRectangles
graphics context to the list of	rectangles. /clip_mask in a	XSetClipRectangles
XClearArea: clear a	rectangular area in a window.	XClearArea
XFillRectangle: fill a	rectangular area.	XFillRectangle
XFillRectangles: fill multiple	rectangular areas.	XFillRectangles
or pixmap. XPutImage: draw a	rectangular image on a window	XPutImage
region. XShrinkRegion:	reduce or expand the size of a	XShrinkRegion
XSubtractRegion: subtract one	region from another.	XSubtractRegion
XPolygonRegion: generate a	region from points.	XPolygonRegion
XEmptyRegion: determine if a	region is empty.	XEmptyRegion
smallest rectangle enclosing a	region. XClipBox: generate the	XClipBox
create a new empty	region. XCreateRegion:	XCreateRegion
storage associated with a	region. /deallocate	XDestroyRegion

change offset of a region. XOffsetRegion: .... XOffsetRegion
if a point is inside a region. /determine .... XPointInRegion
if a rectangle resides in a region. /determine .... XRectInRegion
context to the specified region. /of the graphics .... XSetRegion
reduce or expand the size of a region. XShrinkRegion: .... XShrinkRegion
add a rectangle to a region. XUnionRectWithRegion: .... XUnionRectWithRegion
XEqualRegion: determine if two regions have the same size,/ .... XEqualRegion
compute the intersection of two regions. XIntersectRegion: .... XIntersectRegion
compute the union of two regions. XUnionRegion: .... XUnionRegion
union and intersection of two regions. /between the .... XXorRegion
XUngrabButton: release a button from grab. .... XUngrabButton
XUngrabKey: release a key from grab. .... XUngrabKey
XUngrabKeyboard: release the keyboard from grab. .... XUngrabKeyboard
XUngrabPointer: release the pointer from grab. .... XUngrabPointer
XUngrabServer: release the server from grab. .... XUngrabServer
/destroy a client or its remaining resources. .... XKillClient
control list. XRemoveHost: remove a host from the access .... XRemoveHost
XChangeSaveSet: add or remove a subwindow from the/ .... XChangeSaveSet
the/ XRemoveFromSaveSet: remove a window's children from .... XRemoveFromSaveSet
access control/ XRemoveHosts: remove multiple hosts from the .... XRemoveHosts
both passed/ XCheckWindowEvent: remove the next event matching .... XCheckWindowEvent
mask and window. XWindowEvent: remove the next event matching .... XWindowEvent
matches mask;/ XCheckMaskEvent: remove the next event that .... XCheckMaskEvent
matches mask. XMaskEvent: remove the next event that .... XMaskEvent
not wait. /get an event without removing it from the queue; do .... XPeekIfEvent
/get an event without removing it from the queue. .... XPeekEvent
the specified pixel value and repaint the border. /to .... XSetWindowBorder
border tile attribute and repaint the border. /a window .... XSetWindowBorderPixmap
connection to a/ XDisplayName: report the display name when .... XDisplayName
to allow or deny connection requests. /access control list .... XEnableAccessControl
buffer (display all queued requests). /flush the output .... XFlush
XResetScreenSaver: reset the screen saver. .... XResetScreenSaver
/determine if a rectangle resides in a region. .... XRectInRegion
line/ XrmParseCommand: load a resource database from command .... XrmParseCommand
XrmQGetSearchResource: search resource database levels for a/ .... XrmQGetSearchResource
XrmPutLineResource: add a resource entry given as a/ .... XrmPutLineResource
quarks. XrmQGetResource: get a resource from name and class as .... XrmQGetResource
strings. XrmGetResource: get a resource from name and class as .... XrmGetResource
the/ /obtain the GContext (resource ID) associated with .... XGContextFromGC
XrmQPutResource: store a resource into a database using/ .... XrmQPutResource
XrmPutResource: store a resource into a database. .... XrmPutResource
XrmInitialize: initialize the resource manager. .... XrmInitialize
XrmPutStringResource: add a resource that is specified as a/ .... XrmPutStringResource
using quarks. /add a string resource value to a database .... XrmQPutStringResource
database levels for a given resource. /search resource .... XrmQGetSearchResource
/and pointer events when these resources are grabbed. .... XAllowEvents
a client or its remaining resources. /destroy .... XKillClient
file. XrmGetFileDatabase: retrieve a database from a .... XrmGetFileDatabase
to X/ XListExtensions: return a list of all extensions .... XListExtensions
parent, and root. XQueryTree: return a list of children, ... XQueryTree
levels. XrmQGetSearchList: return a list of database .... XrmQGetSearchList
font names. XListFonts: return a list of the available .... XListFonts
/copy a colormap and return a new colormap ID. .... XCopyColormapAndFree
string. XInternAtom: return an atom for a given name .... XInternAtom
XFetchBuffer: return data from a cut buffer. .... XFetchBuffer
XFetchBytes: return data from cut buffer 0. .... XFetchBytes
loaded font. XQueryFont: return information about a .... XQueryFont

XGetKeyboardMapping:	return symbols for keycodes.	XGetKeyboardMapping
focus window. XGetInputFocus:	return the current keyboard	XGetInputFocus
XCheckTypedWindowEvent:	return the next event in queue/	XCheckTypedWindowEvent
that matches/ XCheckTypedEvent:	return the next event in queue	XCheckTypedEvent
/flush the output buffer and	return the number of pending/	XPending
selection. XGetSelectionOwner:	return the owner of a	XGetSelectionOwner
XLookupColor: get database	RGB values and closest/	XLookupColor
XQueryColor: obtain the	RGB values and flags for a/	XQueryColor
pixel/ XQueryColors: obtain	RGB values for an array of	XQueryColors
name or/ /look up or translate	RGB values from ASCII color	XParseColor
/and closest hardware-supported	RGB values from color name.	XLookupColor
XBell:	ring the bell (Control G).	XBell
a list of children, parent, and	root. XQueryTree: return	XQueryTree
XRotateWindowProperties:	rotate properties in the/	XRotateWindowProperties
XRotateBuffers:	rotate the cut buffers.	XRotateBuffers
XSetFillRule: set the fill	rule in a graphics context.	XSetFillRule
/read any property of type	XA_SIZE_HINTS.	XGetSizeHints
value of any property of type	XA_SIZE_HINTS. /set the	XSetSizeHints
a/ XGetClassHint: get the	XA_WM_CLASS property of	XGetClassHint
a/ XSetClassHint: set the	XA_WM_CLASS property of	XSetClassHint
(command)/ XSetCommand: set the	XA_WM_COMMAND atom	XSetCommand
property. /set the value of the	XA_WM_ICON_SIZE	XSetIconSizes
XFetchName: get a window's name	(XA_WM_NAME property).	XFetchName
XSetTransientForHint: set the	XA_WM_TRANSIENT_FOR/	XSetTransientForHint
XGetTransientForHint: get the	XA_WM_TRANSIENT_FOR/	XGetTransientForHint
/if two regions have the	same size, offset, and shape.	XEqualRegion
to a window and/ XSaveContext:	save a data value corresponding	XSaveContext
/turn the screen	saver on or off.	XForceScreenSaver
/get the current screen	saver parameters.	XGetScreenSaver
reset the screen	saver. XResetScreenSaver:	XResetScreenSaver
the parameters of the screen	saver. XSetScreenSaver: set	XSetScreenSaver
children to the client's	save-set. /add a window's	XAddToSaveSet
a subwindow from the client's	save-set. /add or remove	XChangeSaveSet
children from the client's	save-set. /remove a window's	XRemoveFromSaveSet
program name and/ XGetDefault:	scan the user preferences for	XGetDefault
XActivateScreenSaver: activate	screen blanking.	XActivateScreenSaver
XForceScreenSaver: turn the	screen saver on or off.	XForceScreenSaver
/get the current	screen saver parameters.	XGetScreenSaver
XResetScreenSaver: reset the	screen saver.	XResetScreenSaver
set the parameters of the	screen saver. XSetScreenSaver:	XSetScreenSaver
graphics context for a given	screen with the specified/ /new	XCreateGC
pointer to another point on the	screen. XWarpPointer: move the	XWarpPointer
get the current font	search path. XGetFontPath:	XGetFontPath
XSetFontPath: set the font	search path.	XSetFontPath
for a/ XrmQGetSearchResource:	search resource database levels	XrmQGetSearchResource
sent to a/ XSelectInput:	select the event types to be	XSelectInput
use the value of a	selection. XConvertSelection:	XConvertSelection
return the owner of a	selection. XGetSelectionOwner:	XGetSelectionOwner
set the owner of a	selection. XSetSelectionOwner:	XSetSelectionOwner
connection with the/ XNoOp:	send a NoOp to exercise	XNoOp
XSendEvent:	send an event.	XSendEvent
/select the event types to be	sent to a window.	XSelectInput
a client program from an X	server and display. /disconnect	XCloseDisplay
XQueryTextExtents16: query the	server for string and font/	XQueryTextExtents16
XQueryTextExtents: query the	server for string and font/	XQueryTextExtents
XUngrabServer: release the	server from grab.	XUngrabServer
XGrabServer: grab the	server.	XGrabServer

to X supported by the	server. /list of all extensions	XListExtensions
to exercise connection with the	server. XNoOp: send a NoOp	XNoOp
a client program to an X	server. XOpenDisplay: connect	XOpenDisplay
errors to be processed by the	server. /for all events and	XSync
Xlib/ XSetAfterFunction:	set a function called after all	XSetAfterFunction
handler. XSetErrorHandler:	set a nonfatal error event	XSetErrorHandler
XPutPixel:	set a pixel value in an image.	XPutPixel
property. XSetWMHints:	set a window manager hints	XSetWMHints
create a window and	set attributes. XCreateWindow:	XCreateWindow
context to the/ XSetRegion:	set clip_mask of the graphics	XSetRegion
graphics/ XSetClipMask:	set clip_mask pixmap in a	XSetClipMask
lines) in a/ XSetDashes:	set dash_offset and dashes (for	XSetDashes
XSetGraphicsExposures:	set graphics_exposures in a/	XSetGraphicsExposures
modifiers/ XSetModifierMapping:	set keycodes to be used as	XSetModifierMapping
window/ /set the minimum	set of properties for the	XSetStandardProperties
entry of a/ XStoreColor:	set or change a read/write	XStoreColor
colorcells to/ XStoreColors:	set or change read/write	XStoreColors
context. XSetArcMode:	set the arc mode in a graphics	XSetArcMode
XSetWindowBackground:	set the background pixel/	XSetWindowBackground
in a graphics/ XSetBackground:	set the background pixel value	XSetBackground
operation in a/ XSetFunction:	set the bitwise logical	XSetFunction
graphics/ XSetClipOrigin:	set the clip origin in a	XSetClipOrigin
specified/ XSetWindowColormap:	set the colormap for a	XSetWindowColormap
graphics context. XSetFont:	set the current font in a	XSetFont
context. XSetFillRule:	set the fill rule in a graphics	XSetFillRule
graphics/ XSetFillStyle:	set the fill style in a	XSetFillStyle
context. XSetTile:	set the fill tile in a graphics	XSetTile
XSetFontPath:	set the font search path.	XSetFontPath
logical function,/ XSetState:	set the foreground, background, ...	XSetState
in a graphics/ XSetForeground:	set the foreground pixel value	XSetForeground
XSetInputFocus:	set the keyboard focus window.	XSetInputFocus
in a/ XSetLineAttributes:	set the line drawing components	XSetLineAttributes
XSetStandardProperties:	set the minimum set of/	XSetStandardProperties
a window's icon. XSetIconName:	set the name to be displayed in	XSetIconName
XSetSelectionOwner:	set the owner of a selection.	XSetSelectionOwner
screen saver. XSetScreenSaver:	set the parameters of the	XSetScreenSaver
graphics/ XSetPlaneMask:	set the plane mask in a	XSetPlaneMask
XSetPointerMapping:	set the pointer button mapping.	XSetPointerMapping
property of a/ XSetClassHint:	set the XA_WM_CLASS	XSetClassHint
atom (command/ XSetCommand:	set the XA_WM_COMMAND	XSetCommand
XSetTransientForHint:	set the/	XSetTransientForHint
a window in/ XSetNormalHints:	set the size hints property of	XSetNormalHints
a zoomed/ XSetZoomHints:	set the size hints property of	XSetZoomHints
context. XSetStipple:	set the stipple in a graphics	XSetStipple
graphics/ XSetSubwindowMode:	set the subwindow mode in a	XSetSubwindowMode
a graphics/ XSetTSOrigin:	set the tile/stipple origin in	XSetTSOrigin
of type/ XSetSizeHints:	set the value of any property	XSetSizeHints
XSetIconSizes:	set the value of the/	XSetIconSizes
XChangeWindowAttributes:	set window attributes.	XChangeWindowAttributes
have the same size, offset, and	shape. /if two regions	XEqualRegion
the best supported stipple	shape. /obtain	XQueryBestStipple
the best supported fill tile	shape. XQueryBestTile: obtain	XQueryBestTile
a mapping of modifier keys	(Shift, Control, etc.). /obtain	XGetModifierMapping
/to be used as modifiers	(Shift, Control, etc.).	XSetModifierMapping
map a window on top of its	siblings. XMapRaised:	XMapRaised
change the stacking order of	siblings. XRestackWindows:	XRestackWindows
image. XGetPixel: obtain a	single pixel value from an	XGetPixel

a drawable/ XCopyPlane: copy a single plane of a drawable into .... XCopyPlane
XMoveResizeWindow: change the size and position of a window. .... XMoveResizeWindow
/change the window position, size, border width, or stacking/ .... XConfigureWindow
geometry/ /generate position and size from standard window .... XParseGeometry
in/ XGetNormalHints: get the size hints property of a window .... XGetNormalHints
in/ XSetNormalHints: set the size hints property of a window .... XSetNormalHints
XGetZoomHints: read the size hints property of a zoomed/ .... XGetZoomHints
window. XSetZoomHints: set the size hints property of a zoomed .... XSetZoomHints
/reduce or expand the size of a region. .... XShrinkRegion
/if two regions have the same size, offset, and shape. .... XEqualRegion
cursor, tile, or stipple size. /the "best" supported .... XQueryBestSize
change a window's size. XResizeWindow: .... XResizeWindow
get preferred icon sizes. XGetIconSizes: .... XGetIconSizes
the closest supported cursor sizes. XQueryBestCursor: get .... XQueryBestCursor
region. XClipBox: generate the smallest rectangle enclosing a .... XClipBox
/add a resource that is specified as a string. .... XrmPutStringResource
for a given screen with the specified drawable. /context .... XCreateGC
/ID) associated with the specified graphics context. .... XGContextFromGC
created by an Xlib/ XFree: free specified in-memory data .... XFree
window border attribute to the specified pixel value and/ /a .... XSetWindowBorder
the RGB values and flags for a specified pixel value. /obtain .... XQueryColor
of the graphics context to the specified region. /clip_mask .... XSetRegion
/structure that matches the specified template. .... XGetVisualInfo
/set the colormap for a specified window. .... XSetWindowColormap
or down. /circulate the stacking order of children up .... XCirculateSubwindows
XRestackWindows: change the stacking order of siblings. .... XRestackWindows
bottom child to the top of the stacking order. /circulate the .... XCirculateSubwindowsDown
top child to the bottom of the stacking order. /circulate the .... XCirculateSubwindowsUp
size, border width, or stacking order. /position, ... XConfigureWindow
lower a window in the stacking order. XLowerWindow: .... XLowerWindow
a window to the top of the stacking order. /raise .... XRaiseWindow
XGetStandardColormap: get the standard colormap property. .... XGetStandardColormap
/change the standard colormap property. .... XSetStandardColormap
/create a cursor from the standard cursor font. .... XCreateFontCursor
/generate position and size from standard window geometry/ .... XParseGeometry
property of a window in normal state (not zoomed or/ /hints .... XGetNormalHints
property of a window in normal state (not zoomed or/ /hints .... XSetNormalHints
a bit vector for the current state of the keyboard. /obtain .... XQueryKeymap
XSetStipple: set the stipple in a graphics context. .... XSetStipple
/obtain the best supported stipple shape. .... XQueryBestStipple
supported cursor, tile, or stipple size. /the "best" .... XQueryBestSize
XDestroyRegion: deallocate storage associated with a/ .... XDestroyRegion
/unload a font and free storage for the font structure. .... XFreeFont
XrmPutFileDatabase: store a database in a file. .... XrmPutFileDatabase
database/ XrmQPutResource: store a resource into a .... XrmQPutResource
database. XrmPutResource: store a resource into a .... XrmPutResource
XStoreBuffer: store data in a cut buffer. .... XStoreBuffer
XStoreBytes: store data in cut buffer 0. .... XStoreBytes
information. /update the stored modifier and keymap .... XRefreshKeyboardMapping
/geometry given user geometry string and default geometry. .... XGeometry
16-bit/ /query the server for string and font metrics of a XQueryTextExtents16
16-bit/ XTextExtents16: get string and font metrics of a XTextExtents16
/query the server for string and font metrics. .... XQueryTextExtents
XTextExtents: get string and font metrics. .... XTextExtents
/rebind a keysym to a string for client. .... XRebindKeysym
XDrawString: draw an 8-bit text string, foreground only. .... XDrawString
/map a key event to ASCII string, keysym, and/ .... XLookupString

/add a resource entry given as a	string of name and value.	XrmPutLineResource
XrmQPutStringResource: add a	string resource value to a/	XrmQPutStringResource
quark list. /convert a key	string to a binding list and a	XrmStringToBindingQuarkList
/convert a keysym name	string to a keysym.	XStringToKeysym
/convert a key	string to a quark list.	XrmStringToQuarkList
XrmStringToQuark: convert a	string to a quark.	XrmStringToQuark
return an atom for a given name	string. XInternAtom:	XInternAtom
convert a keysym symbol to a	string. XKeysymToString:	XKeysymToString
from standard window geometry	string. /position and size	XParseGeometry
metrics of a 16-bit character	string. /for string and font	XQueryTextExtents16
create a database from a	string. XrmGetStringDatabase:	XrmGetStringDatabase
resource that is specified as a	string. /add a	XrmPutStringResource
convert a quark to a	string. XrmQuarkToString:	XrmQuarkToString
metrics of a 16-bit character	string. /get string and font	XTextExtents16
in pixels of an 8-bit character	string. /get the width	XTextWidth
in pixels of a 16-bit character	string. /get the width	XTextWidth16
draw two-byte text	strings. XDrawString16:	XDrawString16
XDrawText: draw 8-bit polytext	strings.	XDrawText
draw 16-bit polytext	strings. XDrawText16:	XDrawText16
resource from name and class as	strings. XrmGetResource: get a	XrmGetResource
/find a visual information	structure that matches the/	XGetVisualInfo
allocate memory for an XImage	structure. XCreateImage:	XCreateImage
entry from an XModifierKeymap	structure. /delete an	XDeleteModifiermapEntry
and free storage for the font	structure. /unload a font	XFreeFont
a keyboard modifier mapping	structure. /destroy and free	XFreeModifiermap
new entry to an XModifierKeymap	structure. /add a	XInsertModifiermapEntry
a font and fill information	structure. /load	XLoadQueryFont
corresponding to a keycode in	structure. /get the keysym	XLookupKeysym
a keyboard modifier mapping	structure. /create	XNewModifiermap
XSetFillStyle: set the fill	style in a graphics context.	XSetFillStyle
XSubImage: create a	subimage from part of an image.	XSubImage
another. XSubtractRegion:	subtract one region from	XSubtractRegion
XChangeSaveSet: add or remove a	subwindow from the client's/	XChangeSaveSet
XSetSubwindowMode: set the	subwindow mode in a graphics/	XSetSubwindowMode
XUnmapSubwindows: unmap all	subwindows of a given window.	XUnmapSubwindows
XDestroySubwindows: destroy all	subwindows of a window.	XDestroySubwindows
and destroy a window and all	subwindows. /unmap	XDestroyWindow
XMapSubwindows: map all	subwindows.	XMapSubwindows
/change the keyboard preferences	such as key click.	XChangeKeyboardControl
/a list of all extensions to X	supported by the server.	XListExtensions
/get the closest	supported cursor sizes.	XQueryBestCursor
stipple/ /obtain the "best"	supported cursor, tile, or	XQueryBestSize
XQueryBestTile: obtain the best	supported fill tile shape.	XQueryBestTile
/obtain the best	supported stipple shape.	XQueryBestStipple
/convert a keysym	symbol to a string.	XKeysymToString
XGetKeyboardMapping: return	symbols for keycodes.	XGetKeyboardMapping
XSynchronize: enable or disable	synchronization for debugging.	XSynchronize
another. /change the coordinate	system from one window to	XTranslateCoordinates
/create a new association	table (X10).	XCreateAssocTable
an entry from an association	table. XDeleteAssoc: delete	XDeleteAssoc
allocated for an association	table. /free the memory	XDestroyAssocTable
obtain data from an association	table. XLookUpAssoc:	XLookUpAssoc
an entry in an association	table. XMakeAssoc: create	XMakeAssoc
that matches the specified	template. /structure	XGetVisualInfo
/draw 8-bit image	text characters.	XDrawImageString
/draw 16-bit image	text characters.	XDrawImageString16
XDrawString: draw an 8-bit	text string, foreground only.	XDrawString

XDrawString16: draw two-byte text strings. XDrawString16
border. /change a window border tile attribute and repaint the .... XSetWindowBorderPixmap
/change the background tile attribute of a window. .... XSetWindowBackgroundPixmap
XSetTile: set the fill tile in a graphics context. .... XSetTile
the "best" supported cursor, tile, or stipple size. /obtain .... XQueryBestSize
obtain the best supported fill tile shape. XQueryBestTile: .... XQueryBestTile
graphics/ XSetTSOrigin: set the tile/stipple origin in a .... XSetTSOrigin
stacking order. /circulate the top child to the bottom of the .... XCirculateSubwindowsUp
XMapRaised: map a window on top of its siblings. .... XMapRaised
/the bottom child to the top of the stacking order. .... XCirculateSubwindowsDown
/raise a window to the top of the stacking order. .... XRaiseWindow
color/ XParseColor: look up or translate RGB values from ASCII .... XParseColor
auto-repeat/ XAutoRepeatOff: turn off the keyboard .... XAutoRepeatOff
auto-repeat/ XAutoRepeatOn: turn on the keyboard .... XAutoRepeatOn
off. XForceScreenSaver: turn the screen saver on or .... XForceScreenSaver
/create a cursor from two bitmaps. .... XCreatePixmapCursor
XDrawLine: draw a line between two points. .... XDrawLine
XEqualRegion: determine if two regions have the same size./ .... XEqualRegion
compute the intersection of two regions. XIntersectRegion: .... XIntersectRegion
compute the union of two regions. XUnionRegion: .... XUnionRegion
the union and intersection of two regions. /between .... XXorRegion
XDrawString16: draw two-byte text strings. XDrawString16
window. /obtain the atom type and property format for a .... XGetWindowProperty
next event in queue matching type and window. /return the .... XCheckTypedWindowEvent
in queue that matches event type; don't wait. /next event .... XCheckTypedEvent
/to a window and context type (not graphics context). .... XSaveContext
get the next event of any type or window. XNextEvent: .... XNextEvent
/read any property of type XA_SIZE_HINTS. .... XGetSizeHints
/the value of any property of type XA_SIZE_HINTS. .... XSetSizeHints
entry for a given window and type. /delete a context .... XDeleteContext
XSelectInput: select the event types to be sent to a window. .... XSelectInput
default if/ XUninstallColormap: uninstall a colormap; install .... XUninstallColormap
/the difference between the union and intersection of two/ .... XXorRegion
XUnionRegion: compute the union of two regions. .... XUnionRegion
for the font/ XFreeFont: unload a font and free storage .... XFreeFont
XUnloadFont: unload a font. .... XUnloadFont
XUnmapWindow: unmap a window. .... XUnmapWindow
window. XUnmapSubwindows: unmap all subwindows of a given .... XUnmapSubwindows
all/ XDestroyWindow: unmap and destroy a window and .... XDestroyWindow
XCreateSimpleWindow: create an unmapped InputOutput window. .... XCreateSimpleWindow
the stacking order of children up or down. /circulate .... XCirculateSubwindows
ASCII color/ XParseColor: look up or translate RGB values from .... XParseColor
XRefreshKeyboardMapping: update the stored modifier and/ .... XRefreshKeyboardMapping
Control,/ /set keycodes to be used as modifiers (Shift, ... XSetModifierMapping
/calculate window geometry given user geometry string and/ .... XGeometry
name and/ XGetDefault: scan the user preferences for program .... XGetDefault
a resource into a database using quarks. /store .... XrmQPutResource
resource value to a database using quarks. /add a string .... XrmQPutStringResource
/to the specified pixel value and repaint the border. .... XSetWindowBorder
and/ XSaveContext: save a data value corresponding to a window .... XSaveContext
/obtain a single pixel value from an image. .... XGetPixel
/set the background pixel value in a graphics context. .... XSetBackground
/set the foreground pixel value in a graphics context. .... XSetForeground
a constant value to every pixel value in an image. /add .... XAddPixel
XPutPixel: set a pixel value in an image. .... XPutPixel
XConvertSelection: use the value of a selection. .... XConvertSelection
XSetSizeHints: set the value of any property of type/ .... XSetSizeHints

XSetIconSizes: set the value of the/ .... XSetIconSizes
quarks. /add a string resource value to a database using .... XrmQPutStringResource
an/ XAddPixel: add a constant value to every pixel value in .... XAddPixel
ASCII color name or hexadecimal value. /RGB values from .... XParseColor
and flags for a specified pixel value. /obtain the RGB values .... XQueryColor
given as a string of name and value. /add a resource entry .... XrmPutLineResource
XLookupColor: get database RGB values and closest/ .... XLookupColor
XQueryColor: obtain the RGB values and flags for a/ .... XQueryColor
XQueryColors: obtain RGB values for an array of pixel/ .... XQueryColors
/look up or translate RGB values from ASCII color name or/ .... XParseColor
closest hardware-supported RGB values from color name. /and .... XLookupColor
with depth, applying pixel values. /into a drawable .... XCopyPlane
values for an array of pixel values. /obtain RGB .... XQueryColors
the/ XQueryKeymap: obtain a bit vector for the current state of .... XQueryKeymap
a polyline or curve between vertex list (from X10). /draw .... XDraw
a filled polygon or curve from vertex list (from X10). /draw .... XDrawFilled
that/ XGetVisualInfo: find a visual information structure .... XGetVisualInfo
XMatchVisualInfo: obtain the visual information that matches/ .... XMatchVisualInfo
to/ /flush the output buffer and wait for all events and errors .... XSync
predicate procedure. XIfEvent: wait for event matched in .... XIfEvent
event that matches mask; don't wait. /remove the next .... XCheckMaskEvent
that matches event type; don't wait. /the next event in queue .... XCheckTypedEvent
window and passed mask; don't wait. /matching both passed .... XCheckWindowEvent
it from the queue; do not wait. /event without removing .... XPeekIfEvent
XTextWidth16: get the width in pixels of a 16-bit/ XTextWidth16
character/ XTextWidth: get the width in pixels of an 8-bit .... XTextWidth
/change the border width of a window. .... XSetWindowBorderWidth
window position, size, border width, or stacking order. /the .... XConfigureWindow
/unmap and destroy a window and all subwindows. .... XDestroyWindow
/a data value corresponding to a window and context type (not/ .... XSaveContext
/insert a window between another window and its parent. .... XReparentWindow
/next event matching both passed window and passed mask; don't/ .... XCheckWindowEvent
XCreateWindow: create a window and set attributes. .... XCreateWindow
a context entry for a given window and type. /delete .... XDeleteContext
XChangeWindowAttributes: set window attributes. .... XChangeWindowAttributes
and/ XReparentWindow: insert a window between another window .... XReparentWindow
XSetWindowBorder: change a window border attribute to the/ .... XSetWindowBorder
and repaint the/ /change a window border tile attribute .... XSetWindowBorderPixmap
XStoreName: assign a name to a window for the window manager. .... XStoreName
geometry/ XGeometry: calculate window geometry given user .... XGeometry
/position and size from standard window geometry string. .... XParseGeometry
/the size hints property of a window in normal state (not/ .... XGetNormalHints
/the size hints property of a window in normal state (not/ .... XSetNormalHints
XLowerWindow: lower a window in the stacking order. .... XLowerWindow
XGetWMHints: read the window manager hints property. .... XGetWMHints
XSetWMHints: set a window manager hints property. .... XSetWMHints
set of properties for the window manager. /the minimum .... XSetStandardProperties
a name to a window for the window manager. /assign .... XStoreName
XMapRaised: map a window on top of its siblings. .... XMapRaised
draw a rectangular image on a window or pixmap. XPutImage: .... XPutImage
XConfigureWindow: change the window position, size, border/ .... XConfigureWindow
XDeleteProperty: delete a window property. .... XDeleteProperty
the coordinate system from one window to another. /change .... XTranslateCoordinates
stacking/ XRaiseWindow: raise a window to the top of the .... XRaiseWindow
a property associated with a window. /change .... XChangeProperty
in queue matching type and window. /return the next event .... XCheckTypedWindowEvent
clear a rectangular area in a window. XClearArea: .... XClearArea

XClearWindow: clear an entire window. .... XClearWindow
create an unmapped InputOutput window. XCreateSimpleWindow: .... XCreateSimpleWindow
assign a cursor to a window. XDefineCursor: .... XDefineCursor
destroy all subwindows of a window. XDestroySubwindows: .... XDestroySubwindows
property of a window. /XA_WM_CLASS .... XGetClassHint
the current keyboard focus window. XGetInputFocus: return .... XGetInputFocus
/property of a window. .... XGetTransientForHint
the current attributes of window. /obtain .... XGetWindowAttributes
type and property format for a window. /obtain the atom .... XGetWindowProperty
size hints property of a zoomed window. /read the .... XGetZoomHints
get the property list for a window. XListProperties: .... XListProperties
XMapWindow: map a window. .... XMapWindow
the size and position of a window. /change .... XMoveResizeWindow
XMoveWindow: move a window. .... XMoveWindow
the next event of any type or window. XNextEvent: get .... XNextEvent
the event types to be sent to a window. XSelectInput: select .... XSelectInput
property of a window. /XA_WM_CLASS .... XSetClassHint
set the keyboard focus window. XSetInputFocus: .... XSetInputFocus
/property for a window. .... XSetTransientForHint
background pixel attribute of a window. /set the .... XSetWindowBackground
background tile attribute of a window. /change the .... XSetWindowBackgroundPixmap
change the border width of a window. XSetWindowBorderWidth: ..... XSetWindowBorderWidth
the colormap for a specified window. /set .... XSetWindowColormap
size hints property of a zoomed window. XSetZoomHints: set the .... XSetZoomHints
disassociate a cursor from a window. XUndefineCursor: .... XUndefineCursor
unmap all subwindows of a given window. XUnmapSubwindows: .... XUnmapSubwindows
XUnmapWindow: unmap a window. .... XUnmapWindow
next event matching mask and window. /remove the .... XWindowEvent
XRemoveFromSaveSet: remove a window's children from the/ .... XRemoveFromSaveSet
client's/ XAddToSaveSet: add a window's children to the .... XAddToSaveSet
the name to be displayed in a window's icon. /set .... XSetIconName
XFetchName: get a window's name/ .... XFetchName
XResizeWindow: change a window's size. .... XResizeWindow
/in drawable to a location within the pre-existing image. .... XGetSubImage
XPeekIfEvent: get an event without removing it from the/ .... XPeekIfEvent
XPeekEvent: get an event without removing it from the/ .... XPeekEvent
XWriteBitmapFile: write a bitmap to a file. .... XWriteBitmapFile
/a client program from an X server and display. .... XCloseDisplay
connect a client program to an X server. XOpenDisplay: .... XOpenDisplay
/a list of all extensions to X supported by the server. .... XListExtensions
list of installed extensions to X. /free memory allocated for a .... XFreeExtensionList
create a new association table (X10). XCreateAssocTable: .... XCreateAssocTable
curve between vertex list (from X10). /draw a polyline or .... XDraw
or curve from vertex list (from X10). /draw a filled polygon .... XDrawFilled
/create a bitmap from X11 bitmap format data. .... XCreateBitmapFromData
a window in normal state (not zoomed or iconified). /of .... XGetNormalHints
a window in normal state (not zoomed or iconified). /of .... XSetNormalHints
the size hints property of a zoomed window. /read .... XGetZoomHints
the size hints property of a zoomed window. /set .... XSetZoomHints

This page describes the format of each reference page in this volume.

Name

FunctionName — brief description of the function.

Synopsis

The Synopsis section presents the calling syntax for the routine, including the declarations of the arguments and return type. For example:

```
returntype XFunctionName(arg1, arg2, arg3);
      type1 arg1;
      type2 *arg2;              /* RETURN */
      type3 *arg3;              /* SEND and RETURN */
```

The return type `Status` is of type `int`; it returns either `True` or `False` to indicate whether the routine was successful.

Arguments

The Arguments section describes each of the arguments used by the function. There are three sorts of arguments: arguments that specify data to the function, arguments that return data from the function, and arguments that do both. An example of each type is shown below:

arg1   Specifies information for `XFunctionName`. The description of arguments that pass data to the function always begins with the word "Specifies," as shown in this example.

arg2   Returns a pointer to data to be filled in by `XFunctionName`. The description of arguments that return data from the function always begins with the word "Returns."

arg3   Specifies information for `XFunctionName`, and returns data from the function. The description of arguments that both pass data to the function and return data from the function uses both the words "Specifies" and "Returns."

Description

The Description section describes what the function does, what it returns, and what events or side-effects it causes. It also contains miscellaneous information such as examples of usage, special error cases, and pointers to related information in both volumes of this manual.

Structures

The Structures section contains the C definitions of the X-specific data types used by `FunctionName` as arguments or return values. It also contains definitions of important constants used by the function. Additional structures not shown can be found in Appendix F, *Structure Reference*.

Errors

The Errors section contains a list of the error event types that XFunctionName can generate. The general description of the error types is contained in Appendix B, *Error Messages and Protocol Requests*. Some functions generate errors due to function-specific interpretation of arguments. Where appropriate, these function-specific causes have been listed along with the error event types they generate.

Related Commands

The Related Commands section lists the Xlib functions and macros related to XFunction-Name.

XActivateScreenSaver

Name
XActivateScreenSaver — activate screen blanking.

Synopsis
```
XActivateScreenSaver(display)
    Display *display;
```

Arguments
display   Specifies a pointer to the Display structure; returned from XOpen-Display.

Description
XActivateScreenSaver turns on the screen saver using the parameters set with XSet-ScreenSaver. The screen saver blanks the screen or makes random changes to the display in order to save the phosphors from burnout if it is left unattended for an extended period of time. The interval to wait before starting screen save activity can be set with XSetScreen-Saver. Exactly how the screen saver works is server-dependent.

For more information on the screen saver, see Volume One, Chapter 13, *Other Programming Techniques.*

Related Commands
XForceScreenSaver, XResetScreenSaver, XGetScreenSaver, XSetScreen-Saver.

Name

XAddHost — add a host to the access control list.

Synopsis

```
XAddHost(display, host)
    Display *display;
    XHostAddress *host;
```

Arguments

display Specifies a pointer to the `Display` structure returned from `XOpenDisplay`.

host Specifies the network address of the host machine to be added.

Description

XAddHost adds the specified host to the access control list for the server specified by *display*. The access control list is a primitive security feature that allows access to the server only by other machines listed in a file on the machine running the server. On UNIX systems, this file is called */etc/X?.hosts*, where *?* is the number of the display.

The application that calls XAddHost and the server whose list is being updated must be running on the same host machine.

The address data must be a valid address for the type of network in which the server operates, as specified in the `family` member. Internet, DECnet and ChaosNet networks are currently supported.

For TCP/IP, the address should be in network byte order. For the DECnet family, the server performs no automatic swapping on the address bytes. A Phase IV address is two bytes long. The first byte contains the least significant eight bits of the node number. The second byte contains the most significant two bits of the node number in the least significant two bits of the byte, and the area in the most significant six bits of the byte.

For more information on access control, see Volume One, Chapter 13, *Other Programming Techniques*.

Structures

```
typedef struct {
    int family;             /* for example FamilyInternet */
    int length;             /* length of address, in bytes */
    char *address;          /* pointer to where to find the bytes */
} XHostAddress;

/* The following constants for family member */
#define FamilyInternet      0
#define FamilyDECnet        1
#define FamilyChaos         2
```

Errors

BadAccess
BadValue

Related Commands

XAddHosts, XListHosts, XRemoveHost, XRemoveHosts, XDisableAccess-
Control, XEnableAccessControl, XSetAccessControl.

Name

XAddHosts — add multiple hosts to the access control list.

Synopsis

```
XAddHosts(display, hosts, num_hosts)
    Display *display;
    XHostAddress *hosts;
    int num_hosts;
```

Arguments

display   Specifies a pointer to the Display structure; returned from XOpen-Display.

hosts   Specifies each host that is to be added.

num_hosts   Specifies the number of hosts that are to be added.

Description

XAddHosts adds each specified host to the access control list for the server specified by *display*. The access control list is a primitive security feature that allows access to the server only by other machines listed in a file on the machine running the server. On UNIX systems, this file is */etc/X?.hosts*, where *?* is the number of the display.

The application that calls XAddHosta and the server whose list is being updated must be running on the same host machine.

The address data must be a valid address for the type of network in which the server operates, as specified by the family member. Internet, DECnet and ChaosNet networks are currently supported.

For TCP/IP, the address should be in network byte order. For the DECnet family, the server performs no automatic swapping on the address bytes. A Phase IV address is two bytes long. The first byte contains the least significant eight bits of the node number. The second byte contains the most significant two bits of the node number in the least significant two bits of the byte, and the area in the most significant six bits of the byte.

For more information on access control, see Volume One, Chapter 13, *Other Programming Techniques*.

Structures

```
typedef struct {
    int family;              /* for example Family Internet */
    int length;              /* length of address, in bytes */
    char *address;           /* pointer to where to find the bytes */
} XHostAddress;

/* The following constants for family member */
#define FamilyInternet      0
#define FamilyDECnet        1
#define FamilyChaos         2
```

Errors
    BadAccess
    BadValue

Related Commands
    XAddHost, XListHosts, XRemoveHost, XRemoveHosts, XDisableAccess-
    Control, XEnableAccessControl, XSetAccessControl.

XAddPixel

Name

XAddPixel — add a constant value to every pixel value in an image.

Synopsis

```
int XAddPixel(ximage, value)
    XImage *ximage;
    unsigned long value;
```

Arguments

ximage   Specifies a pointer to the image to be modified.

value   Specifies the constant value that is to be added. Valid pixel value ranges
                depend on the visual used to create the image. If this value added to the
                existing value causes an overflow, extra bits in the result are truncated.

Description

XAddPixel adds a constant value to every pixel value in an image. This function is useful
when you have a base pixel value derived from the allocation of color resources and need to
manipulate an image so that the pixel values are in the same range.

For more information on images, see Volume One, Chapter 6, *Drawing Graphics and Text.*

Structures

```
typedef struct _XImage {
    int width, height;              /* size of image */
    int xoffset;                    /* number of pixels offset in X direction */
    int format;                     /* XYBitmap, XYPixmap, ZPixmap */
    char *data;                     /* pointer to image data */
    int byte_order;                 /* data byte order, LSBFirst, MSBFirst */
    int bitmap_unit;                /* quantity of scan line 8, 16, 32 */
    int bitmap_bit_order;           /* LSBFirst, MSBFirst */
    int bitmap_pad;                 /* 8, 16, 32 either XY or ZPixmap */
    int depth;                      /* depth of image */
    int bytes_per_line;             /* accelerator to next line */
    int bits_per_pixel;             /* bits per pixel (ZPixmap) */
    unsigned long red_mask;         /* bits in z arrangment */
    unsigned long green_mask;
    unsigned long blue_mask;
    char *obdata;                   /* hook for object routines to hang on */
    struct funcs {                  /* image manipulation routines */
    struct _XImage *(*create_image)();
    int (*destroy_image)();
    unsigned long (*get_pixel)();
    int (*put_pixel)();
    struct _XImage *(*sub_image)();
    int (*add_pixel)();
    } f;
} XImage;
```

Related Commands

XDestroyImage, XPutImage, XGetImage, XCreateImage, XSubImage, XGetSub-
Image, XPutPixel, XGetPixel, ImageByteOrder.

XAddToSaveSet

Name

XAddToSaveSet — add a window's children to the client's save-set.

Synopsis

```
XAddToSaveSet (display, w)
    Display *display;
    Window w;
```

Arguments

display   Specifies a pointer to the Display structure; returned from XOpen-Display.

w   Specifies the ID of the window whose children you want to add to the client's save-set.

Description

XAddToSaveSet adds the children of the specified window to the client's save-set.

The save-set is a safety net for windows that have been reparented by the window manager, usually to provide a shadow or other background for each window. When the window manager dies unexpectedly, the windows in the save-set are reparented to their closest living ancestor, so that they remain alive. See Volume One, Chapter 13, *Other Programming Techniques*, for more information about save-sets.

Use XRemoveFromSaveSet to remove a window's children from the client's save-set.

Errors

BadMatch   *w* not created by some other client.

BadWindow

Related Commands

XRemoveFromSaveSet, XChangeSaveSet.

XAllocColor

Name

XAllocColor — allocate a read-only colormap cell with closest hardware-supported color.

Synopsis

```
Status XAllocColor(display, cmap, colorcell_def)
    Display *display;
    Colormap cmap;
    XColor *colorcell_def; /* SENDs and RETURNs */
```

Arguments

display   Specifies a pointer to the `Display` structure; returned from `XOpenDisplay`.

cmap   Specifies the ID of the colormap in which the colorcell is to be allocated.

colorcell_def
    Specifies desired RGB values, and also returns the pixel value and the RGB values actually used in the colormap.

Description

`XAllocColor` returns in the `XColor` structure the pixel value of a read-only (shareable) colorcell with the closest RGB values available in *cmap*. `XAllocColor` also returns the red, green, and blue values actually used.

If the display hardware has an immutable hardware colormap, the entire colormap will be read-only, and the closest cell that exists will be returned. Otherwise, the colormap is read/write, and may have some read/write cells, some read-only cells, and some unallocated. If a read-only cell exists that matches the requested RGB values, that cell is returned. If no matching cell exists but there are unallocated cells, a cell is allocated to match the specified RGB values. If no matching cell exists and there are no unallocated cells, the closest available colorcell that has already been allocated (by this or any other client) is returned. Note that *colorcell_def* stores both the requested color when `XAllocColor` is called and the result when `XAllocColor` returns.

`XAllocColor` does not use or affect the `flags` member of the `XColor` structure.

`XAllocColor` returns 0 if there was some problem (typically all cells are allocated and read/write), or 1 if it succeeds.

For more information, see Volume One, Chapter 7, *Color*.

Structures

```
typedef struct {
    unsigned long pixel;
    unsigned short red, green, blue;
    char flags;                         /* DoRed, DoGreen, DoBlue */
    char pad;
} XColor;
```

Errors

BadColor

Related Commands

XAllocColorCells, XAllocColorPlanes, XAllocNamedColor, XLookupColor, XParseColor, XQueryColor, XQueryColors, XStoreColor, XStoreColors, XFreeColors, XStoreNamedColor, BlackPixel, WhitePixel.

Name

XAllocColorCells — allocate read/write (nonshared) colorcells.

Synopsis

```
Status XAllocColorCells(display, cmap, contig, plane_masks,
        nplanes, pixels, ncolors)
    Display *display;
    Colormap cmap;
    Bool contig;
    unsigned long plane_masks[nplanes]; /* RETURN */
    unsigned int nplanes;
    unsigned long pixels[ncolors];        /* RETURN pixel values */
    unsigned int ncolors;
```

Arguments

display   Specifies a pointer to the Display structure; returned from XOpen-
Display.

cmap   Specifies the ID of the colormap in which the colorcell is to be allocated.

contig   Specifies a boolean value. Pass True if the planes must be contiguous or
False if the planes need not be contiguous.

plane_mask   Returns an array of plane masks.

nplanes   Specifies the number of plane masks returned in the plane masks array.
Must be nonnegative.

pixels   Returns an array of pixel values.

ncolors   Specifies the number of pixel values returned in the pixels array. Must be
positive.

Description

XAllocColorCells allocates read/write colorcells in a read/write colormap. If ncolors
and nplanes are requested, then ncolors pixels and nplanes plane masks are returned.
No mask will have any bits in common with any other mask, or with any of the pixels. By
ORing together each of the pixels with any combination of the plane_masks, ncolors
* distinct pixels can be produced. For GrayScale or PseudoColor, each mask will have
exactly one bit, and for DirectColor each will have exactly three bits. If contig is
True, then if all plane masks are ORed together, a single contiguous set of bits will be
formed for GrayScale or PseudoColor and three contiguous sets of bits (one within each
pixel subfield) for DirectColor. The RGB values of the allocated entries are undefined
until set with XStoreColor, XStoreColors, or XStoreNamedColor.

Status is 0 on failure.

For more information, see Volume One, Chapter 7, *Color*.

Errors

BadColor

BadValue   *nplanes* is negative.
                ncolors is not positive.

Related Commands

XAllocColorPlanes, XAllocColor, XAllocNamedColor, XLookupColor,
XParseColor, XQueryColor, XQueryColors, XStoreColor, XStoreColors,
XFreeColors, XStoreNamedColor, BlackPixel, WhitePixel.

XAllocColorPlanes

Name

XAllocColorPlanes — allocate read/write (nonshareable) color planes.

Synopsis

```
Status XAllocColorPlanes (display, cmap, contig, pixels, ncolors,
        nreds, ngreens, nblues, rmask, gmask, bmask)
    Display *display;
    Colormap cmap;
    Bool contig;
    unsigned long pixels[ncolors];          /* RETURN */
    int ncolors;
    int nreds, ngreens, nblues;
    unsigned long *rmask, *gmask, *bmask;   /* RETURN */
```

Arguments

display	Specifies a pointer to the Display structure; returned from XOpenDisplay.
cmap	Specifies the ID of the colormap to be used.
contig	Specifies a boolean value. Pass True if the planes must be contiguous or False if the planes do not need to be contiguous.
pixels	Returns an array of pixel values.
ncolors	Specifies the number of pixel values returned in the pixels array. Must be positive.
nreds ngreens nblues	Specify the number of red, green, and blue planes (shades). Must be nonnegative.
rmask gmask bmask	Return bit masks for the red, green, and blue planes.

Description

If *ncolors*, *nreds*, *ngreens*, and *nblues* are requested, then *ncolors* pixels are returned, and the masks have *nreds*, *ngreens*, and *nblues* bits set to 1 respectively. Unique pixel values are generated by by ORing together subsets of masks with each item in the *pixels* list (*pixels* does not by itself contain pixel values). In doing this, *ncolors** ($2^{(nreds+ngreens+nblues)}$) distinct pixel values are allocated.

If *contig* is True, then each mask will have a contiguous set of bits. No mask will have any bits in common with any other mask, or with any of the *pixels*. For DirectColor, each mask will lie within the corresponding pixel subfield.

Note, however, that there are only *ncolors**(2^{nreds}) independent red entries, *ncolors**($2^{ngreens}$) independent green entries, and *ncolors**(2^{nblues}) independent blue entries in the colormap. This is true even for PseudoColor. This does not cause problems, though, because when the colormap entry for a pixel value is changed using XStoreColors or `XStoreNamedColor`, the pixel is decomposed according to *rmask*, *gmask*, and *bmask* and the corresponding pixel subfield entries are updated.

`Status` is 0 on failure.

For more information, see Volume One, Chapter 7, *Color*.

Errors

`BadColor`

`BadValue`   *ncolors* is not positive.
         At least one of *nreds*, *ngreens*, *nblues* is negative.

Related Commands

`XAllocColorCells`, `XAllocColor`, `XAllocNamedColor`, `XLookupColor`,
`XParseColor`, `XQueryColor`, `XQueryColors`, `XStoreColor`, `XStoreColors`,
`XFreeColors`, `XStoreNamedColor`, `BlackPixel`, `WhitePixel`.

Name

XAllocNamedColor — allocate a read-only colorcell from color name.

Synopsis

```
Status XAllocNamedColor(display, cmap, colorname,
        colorcell_def, rgb_db_def)
    Display *display;
    Colormap cmap;
    char *colorname;
    XColor *colorcell_def;      /* RETURN */
    XColor *rgb_db_def;         /* RETURN */
```

Arguments

display   Specifies a pointer to the Display structure; returned from XOpen-Display.

cmap   Specifies the ID of the colormap in which the colorcell will be allocated.

colorname   Specifies the color name string (for example, "red") you want. Upper or lower case does not matter. The string should be in ISO LATIN-1 encoding, which means that the first 128 character codes are ASCII, and the second 128 character codes are for special characters needed in western languages other than English.

colorcell_def

Returns the pixel value and RGB values actually used in the colormap. This is the closest color supported by the hardware.

rgb_db_def   Returns the exact RGB values from the database corresponding to the *colorname* supplied.

Description

XAllocNamedColor determines the RGB values for the specified *colorname* from the color database, and then allocates a read-only colorcell with the closest color available, as described under XAllocColor. Both the 'exact' database definition of the color, and the color actually allocated are returned. If the colormap is not full, the RGB values allocated are the closest supported by the hardware. If the colormap is full, XAllocNamedColor returns the closest read-only colorcell already allocated, and does not actually create or set any new colorcell.

XAllocNamedColor returns a Status of 0 when it encounters an error or 1 when it succeeds.

For more information, see Volume One, Chapter 7, *Color*.

Structures

```
typedef struct {
    unsigned long pixel;
    unsigned short red, green, blue;
    char flags;                     /* DoRed, DoGreen, DoBlue */
```

```
    char pad;
} XColor;
```

Errors
BadColor

Related Commands
XAllocColorCells, XAllocColorPlanes, XAllocColor, XLookupColor,
XParseColor, XQueryColor, XQueryColors, XStoreColor, XStoreColors,
XFreeColors, XStoreNamedColor, BlackPixel, WhitePixel.

Name

XAllowEvents — control the behavior of keyboard and pointer events when these resources
are grabbed.

Synopsis

```
XAllowEvents(display, event_mode, time)
    Display *display;
    int event_mode;
    Time time;
```

Arguments

display   Specifies a pointer to the Display structure; returned from XOpen-
Display.

event_mode   Specifies the event mode. Pass one of these constants: AsyncPointer,
SyncPointer, AsyncKeyboard, SyncKeyboard, ReplayPointer,
ReplayKeyboard, AsyncBoth, or SyncBoth.

time   Specifies the time when the grab should take place. Pass either a timestamp,
expressed in milliseconds, or the constant CurrentTime.

Description

XAllowEvents releases the events queued in the server since the last XAllowEvents call
for the same device and by the same client. Events are queued in the server (not released to
Xlib to propagate into Xlib's queues) only when the client has caused a device to "freeze"
(by grabbing the device with mode GrabModeSync). The request has no effect if *time* is
earlier than the last-grab time or later than the current server time.

The *event_mode* argument controls what device events are released for and just how and
when they are released. The *event_mode* is interpreted as follows:

AsyncPointer   If XAllowEvents is called with AsyncPointer while the
pointer is frozen by the client, pointer event processing resumes
normally, even if the pointer is frozen twice by the client on behalf
of two separate grabs. AsyncPointer has no effect if the pointer
is not frozen by the client, but the pointer need not be grabbed by
the client.

AsyncKeyboard   If XAllowEvents is called with AsyncKeyboard while the
keyboard is frozen by the client, keyboard event processing resumes
normally, even if the keyboard is frozen twice by the client on
behalf of two separate grabs. AsyncKeyboard has no effect if
the keyboard is not frozen by the client, but the keyboard need not
be grabbed by the client.

SyncPointer   If XAllowEvents is called with SyncPointer while the
pointer is frozen by the client, normal pointer event processing continues until the next ButtonPress or ButtonRelease event is
reported to the client. At this time, the pointer again appears to

freeze. However, if the reported event causes the pointer grab to be released, then the pointer does not freeze, which is the case when an automatic grab is released by a `ButtonRelease` or when `XGrab-Button` or `XGrabKey` has been called and the specified key or button is released. `SyncPointer` has no effect if the pointer is not frozen or not grabbed by the client.

SyncKeyboard
: If `XAllowEvents` is called with `SyncKeyboard` while the keyboard is frozen by the client, normal keyboard event processing continues until the next `KeyPress` or `KeyRelease` event is reported to the client. At this time, the keyboard again appears to freeze. However, if the reported event causes the keyboard grab to be released, then the keyboard does not freeze, which is the case when an automatic grab is released by a `ButtonRelease` or when `XGrabButton` or `XGrabKey` has been called and the specified key or button is released. `SyncKeyboard` has no effect if the keyboard is not frozen or not grabbed by the client.

ReplayPointer
: This symbol has an effect only if the pointer is grabbed by the client and thereby frozen as the result of an event. In other words, `XGrabButton` must have been called and the selected button/key combination pressed, or an automatic grab (initiated by a `Button-Press`) must be in effect, or a previous `XAllowEvents` must have been called with mode `SyncPointer`. If the `pointer_mode` of the `XGrabPointer` was `GrabModeSync`, then the grab is released and the releasing event is processed as if it had occurred after the release, ignoring any passive grabs at or above in the hierarchy (towards the root) on the grab-window of the grab just released.

ReplayKeyboard
: This symbol has an effect only if the keyboard is grabbed by the client and if the keyboard is frozen as the result of an event. In other words, `XGrabKey` must have been called and the selected key combination pressed, or a previous `XAllowEvents` must have been called with mode `SyncKeyboard`. If the `pointer_mode` or `keyboard_mode` of the `XGrabKey` was `GrabModeSync`, then the grab is released and the releasing event is processed as if it had occurred after the release, ignoring any passive grabs at or above in the hierarchy (towards the root).

SyncBoth
: `SyncBoth` has the effect described for both `SyncKeyboard` and `SyncPointer`. `SyncBoth` has no effect unless both pointer and keyboard are frozen by the client. If the pointer or keyboard is frozen twice by the client on behalf of two separate grabs, `Sync-Both` "thaws" for both (but a subsequent freeze for `SyncBoth` will only freeze each device once).

AsyncBoth   AsyncBoth has the effect described for both AsyncKeyboard
                  and AsyncPointer. AsyncBoth has no effect unless both
                  pointer and keyboard are frozen by the client. If the pointer and the
                  keyboard were frozen by the client, or if both are frozen twice by
                  two separate grabs, event processing (for both devices) continues
                  normally. If a device is frozen twice by the client on behalf of the
                  two separate grabs, AsyncBoth releases events for both.

AsyncPointer, SyncPointer, and ReplayPointer have no effect on the processing
of keyboard events. AsyncKeyboard, SyncKeyboard, and ReplayKeyboard have no
effect on the processing of pointer events.

It is possible for both a pointer grab and a keyboard grab (by the same or different clients) to
be active simultaneously. If a device is frozen on behalf of either grab, no event processing is
performed for the device. It is also possible for a single device to be frozen because of both
grabs. In this case, the freeze must be released on behalf of both grabs before events can
again be processed.

For more information on event handling, see Volume One, Chapter 9, *The Keyboard and
Pointer*.

Errors
BadValue   Invalid mode constant.

Related Commands
XSelectInput, XSetInputFocus, XGetInputFocus, XWindowEvent, XCheck-
WindowEvent, XCheckTypedEvent, XCheckTypedWindowEvent, XMaskEvent,
XCheckMaskEvent, XNextEvent, XEventsQueued, XGetMotionEvents,
XIfEvent, XCheckIfEvent, XPeekEvent, XPeekIfEvent, XPutBackEvent,
XPending, XSynchronize, XSendEvent, QLength.

XAutoRepeatOff

Name
XAutoRepeatOff — turn off the keyboard auto-repeat keys.

Synopsis
```
XAutoRepeatOff (display)
    Display *display;
```

Arguments
display   Specifies a pointer to the Display structure; returned from XOpen-Display.

Description
XAutoRepeatOff turns off auto-repeat for the keyboard. It sets the keyboard so that holding any non-modal key down will not result in multiple events. Keys such as Shift Lock will still not repeat.

Related Commands
XGetDefault, XAutoRepeatOn, XBell, XGetKeyboardControl, XChange-KeyboardControl, XGetPointerControl.

XAutoRepeatOn

Name

XAutoRepeatOn — turn on the keyboard auto-repeat keys.

Synopsis

```
XAutoRepeatOn (display)
    Display *display;
```

Arguments

display   Specifies a pointer to the Display structure; returned from XOpen-Display.

Description

XAutoRepeatOn sets the keyboard to auto-repeat; that is, holding any non-modal key down will result in multiple KeyPress and KeyRelease event pairs with the same keycode member. Keys such as Shift Lock will still not repeat.

Related Commands

XGetDefault, XAutoRepeatOff, XBell, XGetKeyboardControl, XChange-KeyboardControl, XGetPointerControl.

Name

XBell — ring the bell (Control G).

Synopsis

```
XBell(display, percent)
    Display *display;
    int percent;
```

Arguments

display   Specifies a pointer to the Display structure; returned from XOpenDisplay.

percent   Specifies the volume for the bell, relative to the base volume set with XChangeKeyboardControl. Possible values are –100 (off), through 0 (base volume), to 100 (loudest) inclusive.

Description

Rings the bell on the keyboard at a volume relative to the base volume for the keyboard, if possible. *percent* can range from –100 to 100 inclusive (else a BadValue error). The volume at which the bell is rung when *percent* is nonnegative is:

```
volume = base - [(base * percent) / 100] + percent
```

and when *percent* is negative:

```
volume = base + [(base * percent) / 100]
```

To change the base volume of the bell, set the bell_percent variable of XChange-KeyboardControl.

Errors

BadValue   *percent* < –100 or *percent* >100.

Related Commands

XGetDefault, XAutoRepeatOff, XAutoRepeatOn, XGetKeyboardControl, XChangeKeyboardControl, XGetPointerControl.

Name

XChangeActivePointerGrab — change the parameters of an active pointer grab.

Synopsis

```
XChangeActivePointerGrab(display, event_mask, cursor, time)
        Display *display;
        unsigned int event_mask;
        Cursor cursor;
        Time time;
```

Arguments

display   Specifies a pointer to the Display structure; returned from XOpen-Display.

event_mask   Specifies which pointer events are reported to the client. This mask is the bitwise OR of one or more of these pointer event masks: ButtonPress-Mask, ButtonReleaseMask, EnterWindowMask, LeaveWindow-Mask, PointerMotionMask, PointerMotionHintMask, Button1-MotionMask, Button2MotionMask, Button3MotionMask, Button4MotionMask, Button5MotionMask, ButtonMotionMask, KeymapStateMask.

cursor   Specifies the cursor that is displayed. A value of None will keep the current cursor.

time   Specifies the time when the grab should take place. Pass either a timestamp, expressed in milliseconds, or the constant CurrentTime.

Description

XChangeActivePointerGrab changes the specified dynamic parameters if the pointer is actively grabbed by the client and the specified time is no earlier than the last pointer grab time and no later than the current X server time. XChangeActivePointerGrab has no effect on the passive parameters of XGrabButton, or the automatic grab that occurs between ButtonPress and ButtonRelease.

event_mask is always augmented to include ButtonPress and ButtonRelease.

For more information on pointer grabbing, see Volume One, Chapter 9, *The Keyboard and Pointer*.

Errors

BadCursor

Related Commands

XQueryPointer, XWarpPointer, XGrabPointer, XUngrabPointer, XGet-PointerMapping, XSetPointerMapping, XGetPointerControl, XChange-PointerControl.

Name

XChangeGC — change the components of a given graphics context.

Synopsis

```
XChangeGC(display, gc, valuemask, values)
    Display *display;
    GC gc;
    unsigned long valuemask;
    XGCValues *values;
```

Arguments

display   Specifies a pointer to the Display structure; returned from XOpen-
             Display.

gc   Specifies the graphics context.

valuemask   Specifies the components in the graphics context that you want to change.
             This argument is the bitwise OR of one or more of the GC component
             masks.

values   Specifies a pointer to the XGCValues structure.

Description

XChangeGC changes any or all of the components of a GC. The *valuemask* specifies
which components are to be changed; it is made by combining any number of the mask sym-
bols listed in the Structures section using bitwise OR (|). The *values* structure contains the
values to be set. These two arguments operate just like they do in XCreateGC. Changing
the clip_mask overrides any previous XSetClipRectangles request for this GC.
Changing the dash_offset or dash_list overrides any previous XSetDashes request
on this GC.

Since consecutive changes to the same GC are buffered, there is no performance advantage to
using this routine over the routines that set individual members of the GC.

Even if an error occurs, a subset of the components may have already been altered.

For more information, see Volume One: Chapter 5, *The Graphics Context*; and Chapter 6,
Drawing Graphics and Text.

Structures

```
typedef struct {
    int function;              /* logical operation */
    unsigned long plane_mask;  /* plane mask */
    unsigned long foreground;  /* foreground pixel */
    unsigned long background;  /* background pixel */
    int line_width;            /* line width */
    int line_style;            /* LineSolid, LineOnOffDash, LineDoubleDash */
    int cap_style;             /* CapNotLast, CapButt, CapRound, CapProjecting */
    int join_style;            /* JoinMiter, JoinRound, JoinBevel */
    int fill_style;            /* FillSolid, FillTiled, FillStippled */
    int fill_rule;             /* EvenOddRule, WindingRule */
```

```
        int arc_mode;               /* ArcChord, ArcPieSlice */
        Pixmap tile;                /* tile pixmap for tiling operations */
        Pixmap stipple;             /* stipple 1 plane pixmap for stipping */
        int ts_x_origin;            /* offset for tile or stipple operations */
        int ts_y_origin;
        Font font;                  /* default text font for text operations */
        int subwindow_mode;         /* ClipByChildren, IncludeInferiors */
        Bool graphics_exposures;    /* generate events on XCopy, Area, XCopyPlane*/
        int clip_x_origin;          /* origin for clipping */
        int clip_y_origin;
        Pixmap clip_mask;           /* bitmap clipping; other calls for rects */
        int dash_offset;            /* patterned/dashed line information */
        char dashes;
} XGCValues;

#define GCFunction            (1L<<0)
#define GCPlaneMask           (1L<<1)
#define GCForeground          (1L<<2)
#define GCBackground          (1L<<3)
#define GCLineWidth           (1L<<4)
#define GCLineStyle           (1L<<5)
#define GCCapStyle            (1L<<6)
#define GCJoinStyle           (1L<<7)
#define GCFillStyle           (1L<<8)
#define GCFillRule            (1L<<9)
#define GCTile                (1L<<10)
#define GCStipple             (1L<<11)
#define GCTileStipXOrigin     (1L<<12)
#define GCTileStipYOrigin     (1L<<13)
#define GCFont                (1L<<14)
#define GCSubwindowMode       (1L<<15)
#define GCGraphicsExposures   (1L<<16)
#define GCClipXOrigin         (1L<<17)
#define GCClipYOrigin         (1L<<18)
#define GCClipMask            (1L<<19)
#define GCDashOffset          (1L<<20)
#define GCDashList            (1L<<21)
#define GCArcMode             (1L<<22)
```

Errors
```
BadAlloc
BadFont
BadGC
BadMatch
BadPixmap
BadValue
```

Related Commands

XCopyGC, XCreateGC, XFreeGC, XGContextFromGC, XSetStipple, XSet-
TSOrigin, XSetPlaneMask, XSetDashes, XSetLineAttributes, XSetFill-
Rule, XSetFillStyle, XSetForeground, XSetBackground, XSetFunction,
XSetGraphicsExposures, XSetArcMode, XSetClipMask, XSetClipOrigin,
XSetClipRectangles, XSetRegion, XSetState, XSetSubwindowMode,
DefaultGC.

XChangeKeyboardControl

Name

XChangeKeyboardControl — change the keyboard preferences such as key click.

Synopsis

```
XChangeKeyboardControl(display, value_mask, values)
    Display *display;
    unsigned long value_mask;
    XKeyboardControl *values;
```

Arguments

display   Specifies a pointer to the Display structure; returned from XOpen-
Display.

value_mask   Specifies a mask composed of ORed symbols from the table shown in the
Structures section below, specifying which fields to set.

values   Specifies the settings for the keyboard preferences.

Description

XChangeKeyboardControl sets user preferences such as key click, bell volume and duration, light state, and keyboard auto-repeat. Changing some or all these settings may not be
possible on all servers.

The *value_mask* argument specifies which values are to be changed; it is made by combin-
ing any number of the mask symbols listed in the Structures section using bitwise OR (|).

The *values* structure contains the values to be set, as follows:

key_click_percent sets the volume for key clicks between 0 (off) and 100 (loud)
inclusive. Setting to –1 restores the default.

The bell_percent sets the base volume for the bell between 0 (off) and 100 (loud)
inclusive. Setting to –1 restores the default.

The bell_pitch sets the pitch (specified in Hz) of the bell. Setting to –1 restores the
default.

The bell_duration sets the duration (specified in milliseconds) of the bell. Setting to -1
restores the default.

led_mode is either LedModeOn or LedModeOff. led is a number between 1 and 32
inclusive which specifies which light's state is to be changed. If both led_mode and led
are specified, then the state of the LED specified in led is changed to the state specified in
led_mode. If only led_mode is specified, then all the LEDs assume the value specified by
led_mode.

auto_repeat_mode is either AutoRepeatModeOn, AutoRepeatModeOn, or Auto-
RepeatModeDefault. key is a keycode between 7 and 255 inclusive. If both
auto_repeat_mode and key are specified, then the auto-repeat mode of the key specified
by key is set as specified by auto_repeat_mode. If only auto_repeat_mode is
specified, then the global auto_repeat mode for the entire keyboard is changed, without

affecting the settings for each key. If the `auto_repeat_mode` is `AutoRepeatMode-Default` for either case, the key or the entire keyboard is returned to its default setting for the server, which is normally to have all non-modal keys repeat.

The order in which the changes are performed is server-dependent, and some may be completed when another causes an error.

For more information on user preferences, see Volume One, Chapter 9, *The Keyboard and Pointer*.

Structures

```
/* masks for ChangeKeyboardControl */

#define KBKeyClickPercent      (1L<<0)
#define KBBellPercent          (1L<<1)
#define KBBellPitch            (1L<<2)
#define KBBellDuration         (1L<<3)
#define KBLed                  (1L<<4)
#define KBLedMode              (1L<<5)
#define KBKey                  (1L<<6)
#define KBAutoRepeatMode       (1L<<7)


/* structure for ChangeKeyboardControl */

typedef struct {
    int key_click_percent;
    int bell_percent;
    int bell_pitch;
    int bell_duration;
    int led;
    int led_mode;                /* LedModeOn or LedModeOff */
    int key;
    int auto_repeat_mode;        /* AutoRepeatModeOff, AutoRepeatModeOn,
                                    AutoRepeatModeDefault */
} XKeyboardControl;
```

Errors

BadMatch	*values.key* specified but *values.auto.repeat.mode* not specified.
	values.led specified but *values.led_mode* not specified.
BadValue	*values.key_click_percent* < –1.
	values.bell_percent < –1.
	values.bell_pitch < –1.
	values.bell_duration < –1.

Related Commands

`XGetDefault, XAutoRepeatOff, XAutoRepeatOn, XBell, XGetKeyboard-Control, XGetPointerControl.`

XChangeKeyboardMapping

Name

XChangeKeyboardMapping — change the keyboard mapping.

Synopsis

```
XChangeKeyboardMapping(display, first_code, keysyms_per_code,
        keysyms, num_codes)
    Display *display;
    int first_keycode;
    int keysyms_per_keycode;
    KeySym *keysyms;
    int num_keycodes;
```

Arguments

display   Specifies a pointer to the Display structure; returned from XOpenDisplay.

first_keycode

     Specifies the first keycode that is to be changed.

keysyms_per_keycode

     Specifies the number of keysyms that the caller is supplying for each keycode.

keysyms   Specifies a pointer to the list of keysyms.

num_keycodes

     Specifies the number of keycodes that are to be changed.

Description

Starting with *first_keycode*, XChangeKeyboardMapping defines the symbols for the specified number of keycodes. The symbols for keycodes outside this range remained unchanged. The number of elements in the keysyms list must be a multiple of *keysyms_per_keycode* (else a BadLength error). The specified *first_keycode* must be greater than or equal to min_keycode supplied at connection setup and stored in the display structure (else a BadValue error). In addition, the following expression must be less than or equal to max_keycode as returned in the connection setup (else a BadValue error):

```
max_keycode >= first_keycode + (num_keycodes / keysyms_per_keycode) - 1
```

The keysym number N (counting from 0) for keycode K has an index (counting from 0) of the following (in keysyms):

```
index = (K - first_keycode) * keysyms_per_keycode + N
```

The specified *keysyms_per_keycode* can be chosen arbitrarily by the client to be large enough to hold all desired symbols. A special keysym value of NoSymbol should be used to fill in unused elements for individual keycodes. It is legal for NoSymbol to appear in non-trailing positions of the effective list for a keycode.

XChangeKeyboardMapping generates a MappingNotify event.

Errors

BadAlloc

BadValue   *first.keycode* less than *display*->min_keycode.
display->max_keycode exceeded (see above).

Related Commands

XDeleteModifiermapEntry, XInsertModifiermapEntry, XFreeModifiermap,
XKeycodeToKeysym, XKeysymToKeycode, XKeysymToString, XNewModifier-
Map, XQueryKeymap, XStringToKeysym, XLookupKeysym, XRebindKeySym,
XGetKeyboardMapping, XRefreshKeyboardMapping, XLookupString, XSet-
ModifierMapping, XGetModifierMapping.

Name

XChangePointerControl — change the pointer preferences.

Synopsis

```
XChangePointerControl(display, do_accel, do_threshold,
        accel_numerator, accel_denominator, threshold)
    Display *display;
    Bool do_accel, do_threshold;
    int accel_numerator, accel_denominator;
    int threshold;
```

Arguments

display   Specifies a pointer to the Display structure; returned from XOpen-Display.

do_accel   Specifies a boolean value that controls whether the values for the accel_numerator or accel_denominator are set. You can pass one of these constants: True or False.

do_threshold

        Specifies a boolean value that controls whether the value for the threshold is set. You can pass one of these constants: True or False.

accel_numerator

        Specifies the numerator for the acceleration multiplier.

accel_denominator

        Specifies the denominator for the acceleration multiplier.

threshold   Specifies the acceleration threshold.

Description

XChangePointerControl defines how the pointing device moves. The acceleration is a fraction (*accel_numerator*/*accel_denominator*) which specifies how many times faster than normal the pointer moves compared to how fast it normally moves. Acceleration takes effect only when a particular pointer motion is greater than *threshold* pixels at once, and only applies to the motion beyond *threshold* pixels. The values for *do_accel* and *do_threshold* must be nonzero for the pointer values to be set; otherwise, the parameters will be unchanged. Setting any argument to −1 restores the default for that argument.

The fraction may be rounded arbitrarily by the server.

Errors

BadValue   *accel_denominator* is 0.

               Negative value for *do_accel* or *do_threshold*.

Related Commands

XQueryPointer, XWarpPointer, XGrabPointer, XChangeActivePointerGrab,
XUngrabPointer, XGetPointerMapping, XSetPointerMapping, XGetPointer-
Control.

XChangeProperty

Name

XChangeProperty — change a property associated with a window.

Synopsis

```
XChangeProperty(display, w, property, type, format, mode,
        data, nelements)
    Display *display;
    Window w;
    Atom property, type;
    int format;
    int mode;
    unsigned char *data;
    int nelements;
```

Arguments

display   Specifies a pointer to the Display structure; returned from XOpen-Display.

w   Specifies the ID of the window whose property you want to change.

property   Specifies the property atom.

type   Specifies the type of the property. X does not interpret the type, but simply passes it back to an application that later calls XGetProperty.

format   Specifies whether the data should be viewed as a list of 8-bit, 16-bit, or 32-bit quantities. This information allows the X server to correctly perform byte-swap operations as necessary. If the format is 16-bit or 32-bit, you must explicitly cast your data pointer to a (char *) in the call to XChange-Property. Possible values are 8, 16, and 32.

mode   Specifies the mode of the operation. Possible values are PropMode-Replace, PropModePrepend, PropModeAppend, or no value.

data   Specifies the property data.

nelements   Specifies the number of elements in the property.

Description

XChangeProperty changes a property and generates PropertyNotify events if they have been selected.

XChangeProperty does the following according to the *mode* argument:

- PropModeReplace
  Discards the previous property value and stores the new data.

- PropModePrepend
  Inserts the data before the beginning of the existing data. If the property is undefined, it is treated as defined with the correct type and format with zero-length data. *type* and *format* arguments must match the existing property value; otherwise a BadMatch error occurs.

- `PropModeAppend`

  Appends the data onto the end of the existing data. If the property is undefined, it is treated as defined with the correct type and format with zero-length data. `type` and `format` arguments must match the existing property value; otherwise a `BadMatch` error occurs.

The property may remain defined even after the client which defined it exits. The property becomes undefined only if the application calls `XDeleteProperty`, destroys the specified window, or closes the last connection to the X server.

The maximum size of a property is server-dependent and can vary dynamically if the server has sufficient memory.

For more information, see Volume One, Chapter 10, *Interclient Communication*.

Errors
```
BadAlloc
BadAtom
BadMatch
BadValue
BadWindow
```

Related Commands
`XSetStandardProperties`, `XGetFontProperty`, `XRotateWindowProperties`, `XDeleteProperty`, `XGetWindowProperty`, `XListProperties`, `XGetAtomName`, `XInternAtom`.

Name

XChangeSaveSet — add or remove a subwindow from the client's save-set.

Synopsis

```
XChangeSaveSet(display, w, change_mode)
    Display *display;
    Window w;
    int change_mode;
```

Arguments

display   Specifies a pointer to the Display structure; returned from XOpen-Display.

w   Specifies the ID of the window whose children you want to add or remove from the client's save-set; it must have been created by some other client.

change_mode Specifies the mode. Pass one of these constants: SetModeInsert (adds the window to this client's save-set) or SetModeDelete (deletes the window from this client's save-set).

Description

XChangeSaveSet controls the longevity of subwindows, which are normally destroyed when the parent is destroyed.

The save-set of a client is a list of other client's windows which, if they are inferiors of one of the client's windows at connection close, should not be destroyed and should be remapped if they are unmapped. For example, a window manager which wants to add decoration to a window by adding a "frame," might reparent an application's window to the "frame window." When the frame is destroyed, the application's window should not also be destroyed, but should be returned to its previous place in the window hierarchy.

Windows are removed automatically from the save-set by the server when they are destroyed. For each window in the client's save-set, if the window is an inferior of a window created by the client, the save-set window is reparented to the closest ancestor such that the save-set window is not an inferior of a window created by the client. If the save-set window is unmapped, a MapWindow request is performed on it. After save-set processing, all windows created by the client are destroyed. For each nonwindow resource created by the client, the appropriate Free request is performed. All colors and colormap entries allocated by the client are freed.

For more information on save-sets, see Volume One, Chapter 13, *Other Programming Techniques*.

Errors

BadMatch   *w* not created by some other client.

BadValue

BadWindow

Related Commands

XAddToSaveSet, XRemoveFromSaveSet.

XChangeWindowAttributes

Name

XChangeWindowAttributes — set window attributes.

Synopsis

```
XChangeWindowAttributes(display, w, valuemask, attributes)
    Display *display;
    Window w;
    unsigned long valuemask;
    XSetWindowAttributes *attributes;
```

Arguments

display   Specifies a pointer to the Display structure; returned from XOpen-Display.

w   Specifies the window ID.

valuemask   Specifies which window attributes are defined in the *attributes* argu-ment. The mask is made by combining the appropriate mask symbols listed in the Structures section using bitwise OR (|). If *valuemask* is 0, the rest is ignored, and *attributes* is not referenced. The values and restrictions are the same as for XCreateWindow.

attributes Window attributes to be changed. The *valuemask* indicates which members in this structure are referenced.

Description

XChangeWindowAttributes changes any or all of the window attributes that can be changed. For descriptions of the window attributes, see Volume One, Chapter 4, *Window Attributes*.

Changing the background does not cause the window contents to be changed. Use XClear-Window to cause the background to be repainted. Setting the border or changing the back-ground such that the border tile origin changes causes the border to be repainted. Changing the background of a root window to None or ParentRelative restores the default back-ground pixmap. Changing the border of a root window to CopyFromParent restores the default border pixmap.

Changing the win_gravity does not affect the current position of the window. Changing the backing_store of an obscured window to WhenMapped or Always may have no immediate effect. Also changing the backing_planes, backing_pixel, or save_under of a mapped window may have no immediate effect.

Multiple clients can select input on the same window; the event_mask passed are disjoint. When an event is generated it will be reported to all interested clients. Therefore, the setting of the event_mask attribute by one client will not affect the event_mask of others on the same window. However, at most, one client at a time can select each of Substructure-RedirectMask, ReSizeRedirectMask, and ButtonPressMask on any one window. If a client attempts to select on SubstructureRedirectMask, ResizeRedirectMask, or `ButtonPressMask` and some other client has already selected it on the same window, the X server generates a `BadAccess` error.

There is only one `do_not_propagate_mask` for a window, not one per client.

Changing the colormap attribute of a window generates a `ColormapNotify` event. Changing the colormap attribute of a visible window may have no immediate effect on the screen (because the map may not be installed until the window manager or client calls `XInstall-Colormap`).

Changing the cursor of a root window to `None` restores the default cursor.

For more information, see Volume One: Chapter 2, *X Concepts*; and Chapter 4, *Window Attributes*.

Structures

```
/*
 * Data structure for setting window attributes.
 */
typedef struct {
    Pixmap background_pixmap;         /* pixmap, None, or ParentRelative */
    unsigned long background_pixel;   /* background pixel */
    Pixmap border_pixmap;             /* pixmap, None, or CopyFromParent */
    unsigned long border_pixel;       /* border pixel value */
    int bit_gravity;                  /* one of bit gravity values */
    int win_gravity;                  /* one of the window gravity values */
    int backing_store;                /* NotUseful, WhenMapped, Always */
    unsigned long backing_planes;     /* planes to be preseved if possible */
    unsigned long backing_pixel;      /* value to use in restoring planes */
    Bool save_under;                  /* should bits under be saved (popups) */
    long event_mask;                  /* set of events that should be saved */
    long do_not_propagate_mask;       /* set of events that should not propagate */
    Bool override_redirect;           /* override redirected config request */
    Colormap colormap;                /* colormap to be associated with window */
    Cursor cursor;                    /* cursor to be displayed (or None) */
} XSetWindowAttributes;

/* Definitions for valuemask argument of CreateWindow and ChangeWindowAttributes */

#define CWBackPixmap         (1L<<0)
#define CWBackPixel          (1L<<1)
#define CWBorderPixmap       (1L<<2)
#define CWBorderPixel        (1L<<3)
#define CWBitGravity         (1L<<4)
#define CWWinGravity         (1L<<5)
#define CWBackingStore       (1L<<6)
#define CWBackingPlanes      (1L<<7)
#define CWBackingPixel       (1L<<8)
#define CWOverrideRedirect   (1L<<9)
#define CWSaveUnder          (1L<<10)
#define CWEventMask          (1L<<11)
#define CWDontPropagate      (1L<<12)
#define CWColormap           (1L<<13)
#define CWCursor             (1L<<14)
```

Errors
```
BadAccess
BadColor
BadCursor
BadMatch
BadPixmap
BadValue
BadWindow
```

Related Commands
XGetWindowAttributes, XSetWindowBackground, XSetWindowBackground-
Pixmap, XSetWindowBorder, XSetWindowBorderPixmap, XGetGeometry.

Name

XCheckIfEvent — check the event queue for a matching event.

Synopsis

```
Bool XCheckIfEvent (display, event, predicate, args)
    Display *display;
    XEvent *event;                 /* RETURN */
    Bool (*predicate)();
    char *args;
```

Arguments

display   Specifies a pointer to the Display structure; returned from XOpen-Display.

event   Returns the matched event.

predicate   Specifies the procedure that is called to determine if the next event matches your criteria.

arg   Specifies the user-specified argument that will be passed to the predicate procedure.

Description

XCheckIfEvent returns the next event in the queue that is matched by the specified predicate procedure. If found, that event is removed from the queue, and True is returned. If no match is found, XCheckIfEvent returns False and flushes the output buffer. No other events are removed from the queue. Later events in the queue are not searched.

The predicate procedure is called with the arguments *display*, *event*, and *arg*.

In Release 1, the output buffer was always flushed by event-getting routines. In Release 2, the output buffer is flushed only if no matching events are found on the queue. This change is compatible with applications written for Release 1.

For more information, see Volume One, Chapter 8, *Events*.

Related Commands

XSelectInput, XSetInputFocus, XGetInputFocus, XWindowEvent, XCheck-WindowEvent, XCheckTypedEvent, XCheckTypedWindowEvent, XMaskEvent, XCheckMaskEvent, XNextEvent, XEventsQueued, XAllowEvents, XGetMotion-Events, XIfEvent, XPeekEvent, XPeekIfEvent, XPutBackEvent, XPending, XSynchronize, XSendEvent, QLength.

XCheckMaskEvent

Name

XCheckMaskEvent — remove the next event that matches mask; don't wait.

Synopsis

```
Bool XCheckMaskEvent(display, mask_event, event)
    Display *display;
    unsigned long mask_event;
    XEvent *event;                  /* RETURN */
```

Arguments

display   Specifies a pointer to the Display structure; returned from XOpen-Display.

event_mask   Specifies the event types to be returned. See list under XSelectInput.

event   Returns a copy of the matched event's XEvent structure.

Description

XCheckMaskEvent removes the next event in the queue that matches the passed mask. The event is copied into an XEvent supplied by the caller and XCheckMaskEvent returns True. Other events earlier in the queue are not discarded. If no such event has been queued, XCheckMaskEvent flushes the output buffer and immediately returns False, without waiting.

In Release 1, the output buffer was always flushed by event-getting routines. In Release 2, the output buffer is flushed only if no matching events are found on the queue. This change is compatible with applications written for Release 1.

For more information, see Volume One, Chapter 8, *Events*.

Related Commands

XSelectInput, XSetInputFocus, XGetInputFocus, XWindowEvent, XCheck-WindowEvent, XCheckTypedEvent, XCheckTypedWindowEvent, XMaskEvent, XNextEvent, XEventsQueued, XAllowEvents, XGetMotionEvents, XIfEvent, XCheckIfEvent, XPeekEvent, XPeekIfEvent, XPutBackEvent, XPending, XSynchronize, XSendEvent, QLength.

XCheckTypedEvent

Name

XCheckTypedEvent — return the next event in queue that matches event type; don't wait.

Synopsis

```
Bool XCheckTypedEvent (display, event_type, report)
    Display *display;
    int event_type;
    XEvent *report;            /* RETURN */
```

Arguments

display   Specifies a pointer to the `Display` structure; returned from `XOpen-Display`.

event_type   Specifies the event type to be compared.

report   Returns a copy of the matched event structure.

Description

XCheckTypedEvent searches first the event queue, then the events available on the server connection, for the specified *event_type*. If there is a match, it returns the associated event structure. Events searched but not matched are not discarded. XCheckTypedEvent returns True if the event is found. If the event is not found, XCheckTypedEvent flushes the output buffer and returns False.

This command is similar to XCheckMaskEvent, but it searches through the queue instead of inspecting only the last item on the queue. It also matches only a single event type instead of multiple event types as specified by a mask.

In Release 1, the output buffer was always flushed by event-getting routines. In Release 2, the output buffer is flushed only if no matching events are found on the queue. This change is compatible with applications written for Release 1.

For more information, see Volume One, Chapter 8, *Events*.

Related Commands

XSelectInput, XSetInputFocus, XGetInputFocus, XWindowEvent, XCheck-WindowEvent, XCheckTypedWindowEvent, XMaskEvent, XCheckMaskEvent, XNextEvent, XEventsQueued, XAllowEvents, XGetMotionEvents, XIfEvent, XCheckIfEvent, XPeekEvent, XPeekIfEvent, XPutBackEvent, XPending, XSynchronize, XSendEvent, QLength.

XCheckTypedWindowEvent

Name

XCheckTypedWindowEvent — return the next event in queue matching type and window.

Synopsis

```
Bool XCheckTypedWindowEvent(display, w, event_type, report)
    Display *display;
    Window w;
    int event_type;
    XEvent *report;              /* RETURN */
```

Arguments

display   Specifies a pointer to the Display structure; returned from XOpen-
Display.

w   Specifies the window ID.

event_type   Specifies the event type to be compared.

report   Returns the matched event's associated structure into this client-supplied
structure.

Description

XCheckTypedWindowEvent searches first the event queue, then any events available on
the server connection, for an event that matches the specified window and the specified event
type. Events searched but not matched are not discarded.

XCheckTypedWindowEvent returns True if the event is found; it flushes the output
buffer and returns False if the event is not found.

In Release 1, the output buffer was always flushed by event-getting routines. In Release 2, the
output buffer is flushed only if no matching events are found on the queue. This change is
compatible with applications written for Release 1.

For more information, see Volume One, Chapter 8, *Events*.

Related Commands

XSelectInput, XSetInputFocus, XGetInputFocus, XWindowEvent, XCheck-
WindowEvent, XCheckTypedEvent, XMaskEvent, XCheckMaskEvent, XNext-
Event, XEventsQueued, XAllowEvents, XGetMotionEvents, XIfEvent,
XCheckIfEvent, XPeekEvent, XPeekIfEvent, XPutBackEvent, XPending,
XSynchronize, XSendEvent, QLength.

XCheckWindowEvent

Name

XCheckWindowEvent — remove the next event matching both passed window and passed mask; don't wait.

Synopsis

```
Bool XCheckWindowEvent(display, w, event_mask, event)
    Display *display;
    Window w;
    int event_mask;
    XEvent *event;                  /* RETURN */
```

Arguments

display   Specifies a pointer to the Display structure; returned from XOpen-Display.

w   Specifies the window ID. The event must match both the passed window and the passed event mask.

event_mask   Specifies the event mask. See XSelectInput for a list of mask elements.

event   Returns the XEvent structure.

Description

XCheckWindowEvent removes the next event in the queue that matches both the passed window and the passed mask. If such an event exists, it is copied into an XEvent supplied by the caller. Other events earlier in the queue are not discarded.

In Release 1, the output buffer was always flushed by event-getting routines. In Release 2, the output buffer is flushed only if no matching events are found on the queue. This change is compatible with applications written for Release 1.

If a matching event is found, XCheckWindowEvent returns True. If no such event has been queued, it flushes the output buffer and returns False, without waiting.

For more information, see Volume One, Chapter 8, *Events*.

Related Commands

XSelectInput, XSetInputFocus, XGetInputFocus, XWindowEvent, XCheck-TypedEvent, XCheckTypedWindowEvent, XMaskEvent, XCheckMaskEvent, XNextEvent, XEventsQueued, XAllowEvents, XGetMotionEvents, XIfEvent, XCheckIfEvent, XPeekEvent, XPeekIfEvent, XPutBackEvent, XPending, XSynchronize, XSendEvent, QLength.

XCirculateSubwindows

Name

XCirculateSubwindows — circulate the stacking order of children up or down.

Synopsis

```
XCirculateSubwindows(display, w, direction)
    Display *display;
    Window w;
    int direction;
```

Arguments

display   Specifies a pointer to the `Display` structure; returned from `XOpen-Display`.

w   Specifies the window ID of the parent of the subwindows to be circulated.

direction   Specifies the direction (up or down) that you want to circulate the children. Pass either `RaiseLowest` or `LowerHighest`.

Description

`XCirculateSubwindows` circulates the children of the specified window in the specified direction, either `RaiseLowest` or `LowerHighest`. If some other client has selected `SubstructureRedirectMask` on the specified window, then a `CirculateRequest` event is generated, and no further processing is performed. If you specify `RaiseLowest`, this function raises the lowest mapped child (if any) that is occluded by another child to the top of the stack. If you specify `LowerHighest`, this function lowers the highest mapped child (if any) that occludes another child to the bottom of the stack. Exposure processing is performed on formerly obscured windows.

For more information, see Volume One, Chapter 14, *Window Management*.

Errors

```
BadValue
BadWindow
```

Related Commands

XLowerWindow, XRaiseWindow, XCirculateSubwindowsDown, XCirculate-SubwindowsUp, XRestackWindows, XMoveWindow, XResizeWindow, XMove-ResizeWindow, XReparentWindow, XConfigureWindow, XQueryTree.

XCirculateSubwindowsDown

Name

XCirculateSubwindowsDown — circulate the bottom child to the top of the stacking order.

Synopsis

```
XCirculateSubwindowsDown(display, w)
    Display *display;
    Window w;
```

Arguments

display   Specifies a pointer to the Display structure; returned from XOpen-Display.

w   Specifies the window ID of the parent of the windows to be circulated.

Description

XCirculateSubwindowsDown lowers the highest mapped child of the specified window that partially or completely obscures another child. The lowered child goes to the bottom of the stack. Completely unobscured children are not affected.

This function generates exposure events on any window formerly obscured. Repeated executions lead to round-robin lowering. This is equivalent to XCirculateSubwindows (*display*, *w*, LowerHighest).

If some other client has selected SubstructureRedirectMask on the window, then a CirculateRequest event is generated, and no further processing is performed.

For more information, see Volume One, Chapter 14, *Window Management*.

Errors

BadWindow

Related Commands

XLowerWindow, XRaiseWindow, XCirculateSubwindows, XCirculate-SubwindowsUp, XRestackWindows, XMoveWindow, XResizeWindow, XMove-ResizeWindow, XReparentWindow, XConfigureWindow, XQueryTree.

Name

XCirculateSubwindowsUp — circulate the top child to the bottom of the stacking order.

Synopsis

```
XCirculateSubwindowsUp (display, w)
    Display *display;
    Window w;
```

Arguments

display   Specifies a pointer to the Display structure; returned from XOpen-Display.

w   Specifies the window ID of the parent of the windows to be circulated.

Description

XCirculateSubwindowsUp raises the lowest mapped child of the specified window that is partially or completely obscured by another child. The raised child goes to the top of the stack. Completely unobscured children are not affected. This generates exposure events on the raised child (and its descendents, if any). Repeated executions lead to round robin-raising. This is equivalent to XCirculateSubwindows (*display*, *w*, RaiseLowest).

If some other client has selected SubstructureRedirectMask on the window, then a CirculateRequest event is generated, and no further processing is performed.

For more information, see Volume One, Chapter 14, *Window Management*.

Errors

BadWindow

Related Commands

XLowerWindow, XRaiseWindow, XCirculateSubwindows, XCirculate-SubwindowsDown, XRestackWindows, XMoveWindow, XResizeWindow, XMove-ResizeWindow, XReparentWindow, XConfigureWindow, XQueryTree.

Name

XClearArea — clear a rectangular area in a window.

Synopsis

```
XClearArea(display, w, x, y, width, height, exposures)
    Display *display;
    Window w;
    int x, y;
    unsigned int width, height;
    Bool exposures;
```

Arguments

display   Specifies a pointer to the Display structure; returned from XOpenDisplay.

w   Specifies the ID of an InputOutput window.

x   Specify the x and y coordinates of the upper-left corner of the rectangle to be
y   cleared, relative to the origin of the window.

width   Specify the dimensions in pixels of the rectangle to be cleared.
height

exposures   Specifies whether exposure events are generated. Must be either True or
            False.

Description

XClearArea clears a rectangular area in a window.

If width is 0, the window is cleared from x to the right edge of the window. If height is 0, the window is cleared from y to the bottom of the window.

If the window has a defined background tile or it is ParentRelative, the rectangle is tiled with a plane_mask of all 1's and function of GXcopy. If the window has background None, the contents of the window are not changed. In either case, if exposures is True, then one or more exposure events are generated for regions of the rectangle that are either visible or are being retained in a backing store.

For more information, see Volume One, Chapter 6, *Drawing Graphics and Text*.

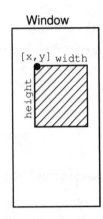

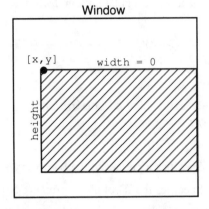

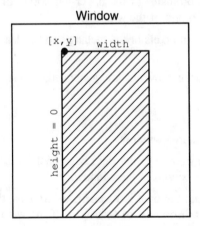

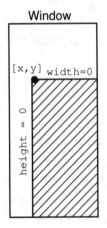

Errors

BadMatch   Window is an InputOnly class window.

BadValue

BadWindow

Related Commands

XDraw, XDrawArc, XDrawArcs, XDrawFilled, XDrawLine, XDrawLines, XDraw-
Point, XDrawPoints, XDrawRectangle, XDrawRectangles, XDrawSegments,
XCopyArea, XCopyPlane, XFillArc, XFillArcs, XFillPolygon, XFill-
Rectangle, XFillRectangles, XClearWindow.

XClearWindow

Name

XClearWindow — clear an entire window.

Synopsis

```
XClearWindow(display, w)
    Display *display;
    Window w;
```

Arguments

display   Specifies a pointer to the Display structure; returned from XOpen-
           Display.

w   Specifies the ID of the window to be cleared.

Description

XClearWindow clears a window, but does not cause exposure events. This function is
equivalent to XClearArea(display, w, 0, 0, 0, 0, False).

If the window has a defined background tile or it is ParentRelative, the rectangle is tiled
with a plane_mask of all 1's and function of GXcopy. If the window has background
None, the contents of the window are not changed.

For more information, see Volume One, Chapter 6, *Drawing Graphics and Text*.

Errors

BadMatch   If *w* is an InputOnly class window.

BadValue

BadWindow

Related Commands

XDraw, XDrawArc, XDrawArcs, XDrawFilled, XDrawLine, XDrawLines, XDraw-
Point, XDrawPoints, XDrawRectangle, XDrawRectangles, XDrawSegments,
XCopyArea, XCopyPlane, XFillArc, XFillArcs, XFillPolygon, XFill-
Rectangle, XFillRectangles, XClearArea.

Name

XClipBox — generate the smallest rectangle enclosing a region.

Synopsis

```
XClipBox(r, rect)
    Region r;
    XRectangle *rect;              /* RETURN */
```

Arguments

r   Specifies the region.

rect   Returns the smallest rectangle enclosing region r.

Description

XClipBox returns the smallest rectangle that encloses the given region.

For more information, see Volume One, Chapter 6, *Drawing Graphics and Text.*

Structures

```
typedef struct {
    short x, y;
    unsigned short width, height;
    unsigned short width, height;
} XRectangle;
/*
 * opaque reference to Region data type.
 * user won't need contents, only pointer.
 */
typedef struct _XRegion *Region;
```

Related Commands

XXorRegion, XUnionRegion, XUnionRectWithRegion, XSubtractRegion,
XShrinkRegion, XSetRegion, XRectInRegion, XPolygonRegion, XPoint-
InRegion, XOffsetRegion, XIntersectRegion, XEmptyRegion, XCreate-
Region, XDestroyRegion, XEqualRegion.

XCloseDisplay

Name

XCloseDisplay — disconnect a client program from an X server and display.

Synopsis

```
XCloseDisplay (display)
    Display *display;
```

Arguments

display   Specifies a pointer to the Display structure; returned from XOpen-Display.

Description

XCloseDisplay closes the connection between the current client and the X server specified by the Display argument.

The XCloseDisplay routine destroys all windows, resource IDs (Window, Font, Pixmap, Colormap, Cursor, and GContext), or other resources (GCs) that the client application has created on this display, unless the CloseDownMode of the client's resources has been changed by XSetCloseDownMode. Therefore, these windows, resource IDs, and other resources should not be referenced again. In addition, this routine discards any output that has been buffered but not yet sent.

Although these operations automatically (implicitly) occur when a process exits, you should call XCloseDisplay anyway.

For more information, see Volume One, Chapter 3, *Basic Window Program.*

Related Commands

XFree, XOpenDisplay, XNoOp, DefaultScreen.

Name

XConfigureWindow — change the window position, size, border width, or stacking order.

Synopsis

```
XConfigureWindow(display, w, value_mask, values)
    Display *display;
    Window w;
    unsigned int value_mask;
    XWindowChanges *values;
```

Arguments

display   Specifies a pointer to the Display structure; returned from XOpen-
               Display.

w   Specifies the ID of the window to be reconfigured.

value_mask   Specifies which values are to be set using information in the values struc-
               ture. value_mask is the bitwise OR of any number of symbols listed in
               the Structures section below.

values   Specifies a pointer to the XWindowChanges structure containing new
               configuration information. See the Structures section below.

Description

XConfigureWindow changes the window position, size, border width, and/or the stacking
order. This call should not be made without preparing for interaction with the window
manager. A ConfigureNotify event is generated to announce any changes.

If the override_redirect attribute of the window is False, and if some other client has
selected SubstructureRedirectMask on the parent, then the X server generates a
ConfigureRequest event, and no further processing is performed. If some other client
has selected ResizeRedirectMask on the window and width or height is being
changed, then a ResizeRequest event is generated and the actual size of the window is not
changed. The ResizeRequest event will be received by the other client (the window
manager) and some action taken. The client should wait for the ConfigureNotify event
to find out the size of the window. Note that the override_redirect attribute of the
window has no effect on ResizeRedirectMask and that SubstructureRedirect-
Mask on the parent has precedence over ResizeRedirectMask on the window.

When the geometry of the window is changed as specified, the window is restacked among
siblings, and a ConfigureNotify event is generated if the state of the window actually
changes. X generates GravityNotify events after generating ConfigureNotify
events.

If a window's size actually changes, the window's subwindows may move according to their
window gravity. Depending on the window's bit gravity, the contents of the window also may
be moved. See Volume One, Chapter 4, *Window Attributes* for further information.

Exposure processing is performed on formerly obscured windows, including the window itself and its inferiors, if regions of them were obscured but now are not. As a result of increasing the width or height, exposure processing is also performed on any new regions of the window and any regions where window contents are lost.

The members of XWindowChanges that you specify in *values* are:

x	Specify the x and y coordinates of the upper-left outer corner of the window
y	relative to the parent's origin.

width	Specify the inside size of the window in pixels, not including the border.
height	These arguments must be positive.

border_width
Specifies the width of the border in pixels.

sibling   Specifies the sibling window for stacking operations. If not specified, no change in the stacking order will be made. If specified, stack_mode must also be specified.

stack_mode   The stack mode can be any of these constants: Above, Below, TopIf, BottomIf, or Opposite.

The computation for the BottomIf, TopIf, and Opposite stacking modes is performed with respect to window *w*'s final size and position (as controlled by the other arguments to XConfigureWindow, not its initial position.) It is an error if *sibling* is specified without *stack_mode*. If *sibling* and *stack_mode* are specified, the window is restacked as follows:

Stacking Flag	Position
Above	*w* is placed just above *sibling*
Below	*w* is placed just below *sibling*
TopIf	if *sibling* obscures *w*, then *w* is placed at the top of the stack
BottomIf	if *w* obscures *sibling*, then *w* is placed at the bottom of the stack
Opposite	if *sibling* occludes *w*, then *w* is placed at the top of the stack, else if *w* occludes *sibling*, then *w* is placed at the bottom of the stack

If a `stack_mode` is specified but no sibling is specified, the window is restacked as follows:

Stacking Flag	Position
Above	*w* is placed at the top of the stack
Below	*w* is placed at the bottom of the stack
TopIf	if any sibling obscures *w*, then *w* is placed at the top of the stack
BottomIf	if *w* obscures any sibling, then window is placed at the bottom of the stack
Opposite	if any sibling occludes *w*, then *w* is placed at the top of the stack, else if *w* occludes any sibling, then *w* is placed at the bottom of the stack

Structures

```
typedef struct {
    int x, y;
    int width, height;
    int border_width;
    Window sibling;
    int stack_mode;
} XWindowChanges;

/* ConfigureWindow structure */
/* ChangeWindow value bits definitions for valuemask */
#define CWX                 (1<<0)
#define CWY                 (1<<1)
#define CWWidth             (1<<2)
#define CWHeight            (1<<3)
#define CWBorderWidth       (1<<4)
#define CWSibling           (1<<5)
#define CWStackMode         (1<<6)
```

Errors

BadMatch   Nonzero *border_width* of InputOnly window.
            sibling specified without a *stack_mode*.
            The *sibling* window is not actually a sibling.

BadValue   *width* or *height* is 0.

BadWindow

Related Commands

XLowerWindow, XRaiseWindow, XCirculateSubwindows, XCirculate-SubwindowsDown, XCirculateSubwindowsUp, XRestackWindows, XMove-Window, XResizeWindow, XMoveResizeWindow, XReparentWindow, XQuery-Tree.

Name

XConvertSelection — use the value of a selection.

Synopsis

```
XConvertSelection(display, selection, target, property,
        requestor, time)
    Display *display;
    Atom selection, target;
    Atom property;                  /* may be None */
    Window requestor;
    Time time;
```

Arguments

display   Specifies a pointer to the Display structure; returned from XOpen-
             Display.

selection   Specifies the selection atom. XA_PRIMARY and XA_SECONDARY are the
             standard selection atoms.

target   Specifies the atom of the type property that specifies the desired format for
             the data.

property   Specifies the property in which the requested data is to be placed. None is
             also valid, but current conventions specify that the requestor is in a better
             position to select a property than the selection owner.

requestor   Specifies the requesting window.

time   Specifies the time when the conversion should take place. Pass either a
             timestamp, expressed in milliseconds, or the constant CurrentTime.

Description

XConvertSelection causes a SelectionRequest event to be sent to the current
selection owner if there is one, specifying the property to store the data in (selection), the
format to convert that data into before storing it (target), the property to place the information in (property), the window that wants the information (requestor), and the time to
make the conversion (time).

The selection owner responds by sending a SelectionNotify event, which confirms the
selected atom and type. If no owner for the specified selection exists, or if the owner could
not convert to the type specified by requestor, the X server generates a SelectionNotify
event to the *requestor* with property None. Whether or not the owner exists, the arguments
are passed unchanged. See Volume One, Chapter 10, *Interclient Communication*, for a
description of selection events and selection conventions.

Errors

BadAtom
BadWindow

Related Commands

XSetSelectionOwner, XGetSelectionOwner.

Name

XCopyArea — copy an area of a drawable.

Synopsis

```
XCopyArea(display, src, dest, gc, src_x, src_y, width,
        height, dest_x, dest_y)
    Display *display;
    Drawable src, dest;
    GC gc;
    int src_x, src_y;
    unsigned int width, height;
    int dest_x, dest_y;
```

Arguments

display	Specifies a pointer to the Display structure; returned from XOpen-Display.
src *dest*	Specify the source and destination rectangles to be combined. *src* and *dest* must have the same root and depth.
gc	Specifies the graphics context.
src_x *src_y*	Specify the x and y coordinates of the upper-left corner of the source rectangle relative to the origin of the source drawable.
width *height*	Specify the dimensions in pixels of both the source and destination rectangles.
dest_x *dest_y*	Specify the x and y coordinates within the destination window.

Description

XCopyArea combines the specified rectangle of *src* with the specified rectangle of *dest*. *src* and *dest* must have the same root and depth.

If regions of the source rectangle are obscured and have not been retained in backing_store, or if regions outside the boundaries of the source drawable are specified, then those regions are not copied. Instead, the following occurs on all corresponding destination regions that are either visible or are retained in backing_store. If *dest* is a window with a background other than None, the corresponding regions of the destination are tiled (with plane_mask of all 1's and function GXcopy) with that background. Regardless of tiling, if the destination is a window and graphics_exposure in *gc* is True, then GraphicsExpose events for all corresponding destination regions are generated. If graphics_exposure is True but no regions are exposed, then a NoExpose event is generated.

If regions of the source rectangle are not obscured and graphics_exposure is False, one NoExpose event is generated on the destination.

XCopyArea uses these graphics context components: `function`, `plane_mask`, `subwindow_mode`, `graphics_exposures`, `clip_x_origin`, `clip_y_origin`, and `clip_mask`.

Errors

BadDrawable

BadGC

BadMatch   The *src* and *dest* rectangles do not have the same root and depth.

Related Commands

XDraw, XDrawArc, XDrawArcs, XDrawFilled, XDrawLine, XDrawLines, XDraw-Point, XDrawPoints, XDrawRectangle, XDrawRectangles, XDrawSegments, XCopyPlane, XFillArc, XFillArcs, XFillPolygon, XFillRectangle, XFill-Rectangles, XClearArea, XClearWindow.

XCopyColormapAndFree

Name

XCopyColormapAndFree — copy a colormap and return a new colormap ID.

Synopsis

```
Colormap XCopyColormapAndFree (display, cmap)
    Display *display;
    Colormap cmap;
```

Arguments

display   Specifies a pointer to the Display structure; returned from XOpen-Display.

cmap   Specifies the colormap you are moving out of.

Description

XCopyColormapAndFree is used to obtain a new virtual colormap when allocating color-cells out of a previous colormap has failed due to resource exhaustion (that is, too many cells or planes were in use in the original colormap).

XCopyColormapAndFree moves all of the client's existing allocations from cmap to the returned Colormap and frees those entries in cmap. Values in other entries of the new colormap are undefined. The visual type and screen for the new colormap is the same as for the old.

If cmap was created by the client with the alloc argument set to AllocAll, the new colormap is also created with AllocAll, all color values for all entries are copied from cmap, and then all entries in cmap are freed.

If cmap was created by the client with AllocNone, the allocations to be moved are all those pixels and planes that have been allocated by the client using XAllocColor, XAlloc-NamedColor, XAllocColorCells, or XAllocColorPlanes and that have not been freed since they were allocated.

For more information, see Volume One, Chapter 7, *Color*.

Errors

```
BadAlloc
BadColor
```

Related Commands

XCreateColormap, XFreeColormap, XGetStandardColormap, XInstall-Colormap, XUninstallColormap, XSetStandardColormap, XListInstalled-Colormaps, XSetWindowColormap, DefaultColormap, DisplayCells.

Name

XCopyGC — copy a graphics context.

Synopsis

```
XCopyGC(display, src, valuemask, dest)
    Display *display;
    GC src, dest;
    unsigned long valuemask;
```

Arguments

display   Specifies a pointer to the Display structure; returned from XOpen-Display.

src   Specifies the components of the source graphics context.

valuemask   Specifies the components in the source GC structure to be copied into the destination GC. valuemask is made by combining any number of the mask symbols listed in the Structures section using bitwise OR (|).

dest   Specifies the destination graphics context.

Description

XCopyGC copies the selected elements of one graphics context to another. See Volume One, Chapter 5, *The Graphics Context*, for a description of the graphics context.

Structures

The GC structure contains the following elements:

```
/*
 * Data structure for setting graphics context.
 */
typedef struct {
    int function;              /* logical operation */
    unsigned long plane_mask;  /* plane mask */
    unsigned long foreground;  /* foreground pixel */
    unsigned long background;  /* background pixel */
    int line_width;            /* line width */
    int line_style;            /* Solid, OnOffDash, DoubleDash */
    int cap_style;             /* NotLast, Butt, Round, Projecting */
    int join_style;            /* Miter, Round, Bevel */
    int fill_style;            /* Solid, Tiled, Stippled */
    int fill_rule;             /* EvenOdd, Winding */
    int arc_mode;              /* PieSlice */
    Pixmap tile;               /* tile pixmap for tiling operations */
    Pixmap stipple;            /* stipple 1 plane pixmap for stipping */
    int ts_x_origin;           /* offset for tile or stipple operations */
    int ts_y_origin;
    Font font;                 /* default text font for text operations */
    int subwindow_mode;        /* ClipByChildren, IncludeInferiors */
```

```
    Bool graphics_exposures;   /* boolean, should exposures be generated */
    int clip_x_origin;         /* origin for clipping */
    int clip_y_origin;
    Pixmap clip_mask;          /* bitmap clipping; other calls for rects */
    int dash_offset;           /* patterned/dashed line information */
    char dashes;
} XGCValues;

/* GC components: masks used in XCreateGC, XCopyGC, XChangeGC, OR'ed into
   GC.stateChanges */

#define GCFunction          (1L<<0)
#define GCPlaneMask         (1L<<1)
#define GCForeground        (1L<<2)
#define GCBackground        (1L<<3)
#define GCLineWidth         (1L<<4)
#define GCLineStyle         (1L<<5)
#define GCCapStyle          (1L<<6)
#define GCJoinStyle         (1L<<7)
#define GCFillStyle         (1L<<8)
#define GCFillRule          (1L<<9)
#define GCTile              (1L<<10)
#define GCStipple           (1L<<11)
#define GCTileStipXOrigin   (1L<<12)
#define GCTileStipYOrigin   (1L<<13)
#define GCFont              (1L<<14)
#define GCSubwindowMode     (1L<<15)
#define GCGraphicsExposures (1L<<16)
#define GCClipXOrigin       (1L<<17)
#define GCClipYOrigin       (1L<<18)
#define GCClipMask          (1L<<19)
#define GCDashOffset        (1L<<20)
#define GCDashList          (1L<<21)
#define GCArcMode           (1L<<22)
```

Errors

```
BadAlloc
BadGC
BadMatch        src and dest do not have the same root and depth.
```

Related Commands

XChangeGC, XCreateGC, XFreeGC, XGContextFromGC, XSetStipple, XSet-
TSOrigin, XSetPlaneMask, XSetDashes, XSetLineAttributes, XSetFill-
Rule, XSetFillStyle, XSetForeground, XSetBackground, XSetFunction,
XSetGraphicsExposures, XSetArcMode, XSetClipMask, XSetClipOrigin,
XSetClipRectangles, XSetState, XSetSubwindowMode, DefaultGC.

XCopyPlane

Name

XCopyPlane — copy a single plane of a drawable into a drawable with depth, applying pixel values.

Synopsis

```
XCopyPlane (display, src, dest, gc, src_x, src_y, width,
       height, dest_x, dest_y, plane)
    Display *display;
    Drawable src, dest;
    GC gc;
    int src_x, src_y;
    unsigned int width, height;
    int dest_x, dest_y;
    unsigned long plane;
```

Arguments

display	Specifies a pointer to the Display structure; returned from XOpen-Display.
src *dest*	Specify the source and destination drawables.
gc	Specifies the graphics context.
src_x *src_y*	Specify the x and y coordinates of the upper-left corner of the source rectangle relative to the origin of the drawable.
width *height*	Specify the width and height in pixels. These are the dimensions of both the source and destination rectangles.
dest_x *dest_y*	Specify the x and y coordinates at which the copied area will be placed relative to the origin of the destination drawable.
plane	Specifies the source bit-plane. You must set exactly one bit.

Description

XCopyPlane copies a single plane of a rectangle in the source into the entire depth of a corresponding rectangle in the destination. The plane of the source drawable and the foreground/background pixel values in *gc* are combined to form a pixmap of the same depth as the destination drawable, and the equivalent of an XCopyArea is performed, with all the same exposure semantics.

XCopyPlane uses these graphics context components: function, plane_mask, foreground, background, subwindow_mode, graphics_exposures, clip_x_origin, clip_y_origin, and clip_mask.

src and *dest* must have the same root, but need not have the same depth.

For more information, see Volume One, Chapter 5, *The Graphics Context*.

Errors

`BadDrawable`

`BadGC`

`BadMatch`   *src* and *dest* do not have the same root.

`BadValue`   *plane* does not have exactly one bit set.

Related Commands

XDraw, XDrawArc, XDrawArcs, XDrawFilled, XDrawLine, XDrawLines, XDraw-
Point, XDrawPoints, XDrawRectangle, XDrawRectangles, XDrawSegments,
XCopyArea, XFillArc, XFillArcs, XFillPolygon, XFillRectangle, XFill-
Rectangles, XClearArea, XClearWindow.

Name
XCreateAssocTable — create a new association table (X10).

Synopsis
```
XAssocTable *XCreateAssocTable(size)
    int size;
```

Arguments
size   Specifies the number of buckets in the hashed association table.

Description
XCreateAssocTable creates an association table, which allows you to associate your own structures with X resources in a fast lookup table. This function is provided for compatibility with X Version 10. To use it you must include the file *<X11/X10.h>* and link with the library *-loldX*.

The size argument specifies the number of buckets in the hash system of XAssocTable. For reasons of efficiency the number of buckets should be a power of two. Some size suggestions might be: use 32 buckets per 100 objects; a reasonable maximum number of object per buckets is 8.

If there is an error allocating memory for the XAssocTable, a NULL pointer is returned.

For more information on association tables, see Volume One, Chapter 13, *Other Programming Techniques*.

Structures
```
typedef struct {
    XAssoc *buckets;        /* pointer to first bucket in array */
    int size;               /* table size (number of buckets) */
}XAssocTable;
```

Related Commands
XDeleteAssoc, XDestroyAssocTable, XLookUpAssoc, XMakeAssoc.

XCreateBitmapFromData

Name
XCreateBitmapFromData — create a bitmap from X11 bitmap format data.

Synopsis
```
Pixmap XCreateBitmapFromData(display, drawable, data,
        width, height)
    Display *display;
    Drawable drawable;
    char *data;
    unsigned int width, height;
```

Arguments

display   Specifies a pointer to the Display structure; returned from XOpen-Display.

drawable   Specifies the drawable. This determines which screen to create the bitmap on.

data   Specifies the location of the bitmap data.

width   Specify the dimensions in pixels of the created bitmap. If smaller than the
height   original bitmap, the upper-left corner is used.

Description

XCreateBitmapFromData creates a single-plane pixmap from an array of hexadecimal data. This data may be defined in the program or included. The bitmap data must be in X version 11 format as shown below (it cannot be in X10 format). The following format is assumed for the data, where the variables are members of the XImage structure described in Volume One, Chapter 6, *Drawing Graphics and Text*:

```
format=XYPixmap
bit_order=LSBFirst
byte_order=LSBFirst
bitmap_unit=8
bitmap_pad=8
xoffset=0
no extra bytes per line
```

XCreateBitmapFromData creates an image with the specified data and copies it into the created pixmap. The following is an example of creating a bitmap:

```
#define gray_width 16
#define gray_height 16
#define gray_x_hot 8
#define gray_y_hot 8
static char gray_bits[] =
        {
        0xf81f, 0xe3c7, 0xcff3, 0x9ff9,
        0xbffd, 0x33cc, 0x7ffe, 0x7ffe,
        0x7e7e, 0x7ffe, 0x37ec, 0xbbdd,
        0x9c39, 0xcff3, 0xe3c7, 0xf81f
        };
```

```
Pixmap XCreateBitmapFromData(display, window, gray_bits,
    gray_width, gray_height);
```

If insufficient working storage was allocated, XCreateBitmapFromData returns NULL.
The user should free the bitmap using XFreePixmap when it is no longer needed.

For more information, see Volume One, Chapter 6, *Drawing Graphics and Text.*

Errors

BadAlloc

Related Commands

XSetTile, XQueryBestTile, XSetWindowBorderPixmap, XSetWindow-
BackgroundPixmap, XCreatePixmap, XCreatePixmapFromBitmapData, XFree-
Pixmap, XQueryBestSize, XQueryBestStipple, XWriteBitmapFile, XRead-
BitmapFile, XCreatePixmapFromBitmapData.

XCreateColormap

Name

XCreateColormap — create a colormap.

Synopsis

```
Colormap XCreateColormap(display, w, visual, alloc)
    Display *display;
    Window w;
    Visual *visual;
    int alloc;
```

Arguments

display   Specifies a pointer to the Display structure; returned from XOpen-Display.

w   Specifies a window ID. The colormap created will be associated with the same screen as the window.

visual   Specifies a pointer to the Visual structure for the colormap. The visual class and depth must be supported by the screen.

alloc   Specifies how many colormap entries to allocate. Pass either AllocNone or AllocAll.

Description

XCreateColormap creates a colormap of the specified visual type and allocates either none or all of its entries, and returns the colormap ID.

It is legal to specify any visual class in the structure pointed to by the *visual* argument. If the class is StaticColor, StaticGray, or TrueColor, the colorcells will have pre-allocated read-only values defined by the individual server but unspecified by the X11 protocol. In these cases, *alloc* must be specified as AllocNone (else a BadMatch error).

For the other visual classes, PseudoColor, DirectColor, and GrayScale, you can pass either AllocAll or AllocNone to the *alloc* argument. If you pass AllocNone, the colormap has no allocated entries. This allows your client programs to allocate read-only colorcells with XAllocColor or read/write cells with XAllocColorCells, Alloc-ColorPlanes and XStoreColors. If you pass the constant AllocAll, the entire color-map is allocated writable (all the entries are read/write, nonshareable and have undefined initial values), and the colors can be set with XStoreColors. However, you cannot free these entries with XFreeColors, and no relationships between the entries are defined.

If the visual class is PseudoColor or GrayScale and *alloc* is AllocAll, this function simulates many calls to the function XAllocColor returning all pixel values from 1 to (map_entries - 1). For a visual class of DirectColor, the processing for Alloc-All simulates a call to the function XAllocColorPlanes, returning a pixel value of 0 and mask values the same as the red_mask, green_mask, and blue_mask members in *visual*.

The *visual* structure should be as returned from the DefaultVisual macro, XMatch-
VisualInfo, or XGetVisualInfo. The red_mask, green_mask, and blue_mask
members specify which bits of the pixel value are allocated to each primary color. The
map_entries member specifies the number of colormap entries.

For more information on creating colormaps, see Volume One, Chapter 7, *Color*.

Errors

BadAlloc

BadMatch   Didn't use AllocNone for StaticColor, StaticGray, or
                     TrueColor.
                     visual type not supported on screen.

BadValue

BadWindow

Related Commands

XCopyColormapAndFree, XFreeColormap, XGetStandardColormap, XInstall-
Colormap, XUninstallColormap, XSetStandardColormap, XListInstalled-
Colormaps, XSetWindowColormap, DefaultColormap, DisplayCells.

XCreateFontCursor

Name

XCreateFontCursor — create a cursor from the standard cursor font.

Synopsis

```
#include <X11/cursorfont.h>
Cursor XCreateFontCursor(display, shape)
    Display *display;
    unsigned int shape;
```

Arguments

display   Specifies a pointer to the `Display` structure; returned from `XOpenDisplay`.

shape   Specifies which character in the standard cursor font should be used for the cursor.

Description

X provides a set of standard cursor shapes in a special font named "cursor." Programs are encouraged to use this interface for their cursors, since the font can be customized for the individual display type and swapped between clients.

The hotspot comes from the information stored in the font. The initial colors of the cursor are black for the `foreground` and white for the `background`. `XRecolorCursor` can be used to change the colors of the cursor to those desired.

For more information about cursors and their shapes in fonts, see Appendix I, *The Cursor Font*.

Errors
```
BadAlloc
BadMatch
BadValue
```

Related Commands
XDefineCursor, XUndefineCursor, XCreateGlyphCursor, XCreatePixmap-
Cursor, XFreeCursor, XRecolorCursor, XQueryBestCursor, XQueryBest-
Size.

Name

XCreateGC — create a new graphics context for a given screen with the depth of the specified drawable.

Synopsis

```
GC XCreateGC (display, drawable, valuemask, values)
    Display *display;
    Drawable drawable;
    unsigned long valuemask;
    XGCValues *values;
```

Arguments

display   Specifies a pointer to the Display structure; returned from XOpen-Display.

drawable   Specifies the drawable.

valuemask   Specifies which members of the GC are to be set using information in the *values* structure. *valuemask* is made by combining any number of the mask symbols listed in the Structures section.

values   Specifies a pointer to an XGCValues structure which will provide components for the new GC.

Description

This function creates a new GC, replacing the old one if there was one. The specified components of the new graphics context in *valuemask* are set to the values passed in the *values* argument. Unset components default as follows:

Component	Value
function	GXcopy
plane_mask	all 1's
foreground	0
background	1
line_width	0
line_style	LineSolid
cap_style	CapButt
join_style	JoinMiter
fill_style	FillSolid
fill_rule	EvenOddRule
arc_mode	ArcPieSlice
tile	Pixmap filled with foreground pixel
stipple	Pixmap filled with 1's
ts_x_origin	0
ts_y_origin	0

Component	Value
font	(implementation dependent)
subwindow_mode	ClipByChildren
graphics_exposures	True
clip_x_origin	0
clip_y_origin	0
clip_mask	None
dash_offset	0
dash_list	4 (i.e., the list [4, 4])

For more information, see Volume One, Chapter 5, *The Graphics Context.*

Structures

```
typedef struct {
     int function;                  /* logical operation */
     unsigned long plane_mask;      /* plane mask */
     unsigned long foreground;      /* foreground pixel */
     unsigned long background;      /* background pixel */
     int line_width;                /* line width */
     int line_style;                /* LineSolid, LineOnOffDash, LineDoubleDash */
     int cap_style;                 /* CapNotLast, CapButt, CapRound, CapProjecting */
     int join_style;                /* JoinMiter, JoinRound, JoinBevel */
     int fill_style;                /* FillSolid, FillTiled, FillStippled */
     int fill_rule;                 /* EvenOddRule, WindingRule */
     int arc_mode;                  /* ArcPieSlice, ArcChord */
     Pixmap tile;                   /* tile pixmap for tiling operations */
     Pixmap stipple;                /* stipple 1 plane pixmap for stipping */
     int ts_x_origin;               /* offset for tile or stipple operations */
     int ts_y_origin;
     Font font;                     /* default text font for text operations */
     int subwindow_mode;            /* ClipByChildren, IncludeInferiors */
     Bool graphics_exposures;       /* generate events on XCopyArea, XCopyPlane */
     int clip_x_origin;             /* origin for clipping */
     int clip_y_origin;
     Pixmap clip_mask;              /* bitmap clipping; other calls for rects */
     int dash_offset;               /* patterned/dashed line information */
     char dashes;
} XGCValues;

#define GCFunction           (1L<<0)
#define GCPlaneMask          (1L<<1)
#define GCForeground         (1L<<2)
#define GCBackground         (1L<<3)
#define GCLineWidth          (1L<<4)
#define GCLineStyle          (1L<<5)
#define GCCapStyle           (1L<<6)
#define GCJoinStyle          (1L<<7)
#define GCFillStyle          (1L<<8)
#define GCFillRule           (1L<<9)
#define GCTile               (1L<<10)
```

```
#define GCStipple            (1L<<11)
#define GCTileStipXOrigin    (1L<<12)
#define GCTileStipYOrigin    (1L<<13)
#define GCFont               (1L<<14)
#define GCSubwindowMode      (1L<<15)
#define GCGraphicsExposures  (1L<<16)
#define GCClipXOrigin        (1L<<17)
#define GCClipYOrigin        (1L<<18)
#define GCClipMask           (1L<<19)
#define GCDashOffset         (1L<<20)
#define GCDashList           (1L<<21)
#define GCArcMode            (1L<<22)
```

Errors

```
BadAlloc
BadDrawable
BadFont
BadMatch
BadPixmap
BadValue
```

Related Commands

XChangeGC, XCopyGC, XFreeGC, XGContextFromGC, XSetStipple, XSet-
TSOrigin, XSetPlaneMask, XSetDashes, XSetLineAttributes, XSetFill-
Rule, XSetFillStyle, XSetForeground, XSetBackground, XSetFunction,
XSetGraphicsExposures, XSetArcMode, XSetClipMask, XSetClipOrigin,
XSetClipRectangles, XSetState, XSetSubwindowMode, DefaultGC.

XCreateGlyphCursor

Name

XCreateGlyphCursor — create a cursor from font glyphs.

Synopsis

```
Cursor XCreateGlyphCursor(display, source_font, mask_font,
        source_char, mask_char, foreground_color,
        background_color)
    Display *display;
    Font source_font, mask_font;
    unsigned int source_char, mask_char;
    XColor *foreground_color;
    XColor *background_color;
```

Arguments

display　　　　Specifies a pointer to the `Display` structure; returned from `XOpen-Display`.

source_font　Specifies the font from which a character is to be used for the cursor.

mask_font　　Specifies the mask font. Optional; specify 0 if not needed.

source_char　Specifies the index into the cursor shape font.

mask_char　　Specifies the index into the mask shape font. Optional; specify 0 if not needed.

foreground_color
　　　　　　Specifies the red, green, and blue (RGB) values for the foreground.

background_color
　　　　　　Specifies the red, green, and blue (RGB) values for the background.

Description

XCreateGlyphCursor is similar to XCreatePixmapCursor, but the source and mask bitmaps are obtained from separate font characters, perhaps in separate fonts. The mask font and character are optional. If *mask_char* is not specified, all pixels of the source are displayed.

The x offset for the hotspot of the created cursor is the left-bearing for the source character, and the y offset is the ascent, each measured from the upper-left corner of the bounding rectangle of the character.

The origins of the source and mask (if it is defined) characters are positioned coincidently and define the hotspot. The source and mask need not have the same bounding box metrics, and there is no restriction on the placement of the hotspot relative to the bounding boxes.

Note that *source_char* and *mask_char* are of type unsigned int, not of type XChar2b. For two-byte matrix fonts, the 16-bit value should be formed with the byte1 member in the most significant byte and the byte2 member in the least significant byte.

You can free the fonts with XFreeFont if they are no longer needed after creating the glyph cursor.

For more information on fonts and cursors, see Volume One, Chapter 6, *Drawing Graphics and Text*.

Structures

```
typedef struct {
    unsigned long pixel;
    unsigned short red, green, blue;
    char flags;                     /* DoRed, DoGreen, DoBlue */
    char pad;
} XColor;
```

Errors

BadAlloc

BadFont

BadValue   *source_char* not defined in *source_font*.
                mask_char not defined in *mask_font* (if *mask_font* defined).

Related Commands

XDefineCursor, XUndefineCursor, XCreateFontCursor, XCreatePixmap-Cursor, XFreeCursor, XRecolorCursor, XQueryBestCursor, XQueryBest-Size.

XCreateImage

Name

XCreateImage — allocate memory for an `XImage` structure.

Synopsis

```
#include <X11/Xutil.h>
XImage *XCreateImage(display, visual, depth, format, offset,
        data, width, height, bitmap_pad, bytes_per_line)
    Display *display;
    Visual *visual;
    unsigned int depth;
    int format;
    int offset;
    char *data;
    unsigned int width;
    unsigned int height;
    int bitmap_pad;
    int bytes_per_line;
```

Arguments

display　　　Specifies a pointer to the `Display` structure; returned from `XOpen-Display`.

visual　　　Specifies a pointer to a visual that should match the visual of the window the image is to be displayed in.

depth　　　Specifies the depth of the image.

format　　　Specifies the format for the image. Pass one of these constants: `XYPixmap`, or `ZPixmap`.

offset　　　Specifies the number of pixels beyond the beginning of the data (pointed to by *data*) where the image actually begins. This is useful if the image is not aligned on an even addressable boundary.

data　　　Specifies a pointer to the image data.

width
height　　　Specify the width and height in pixels of the image.

bitmap_pad　　　Specifies the quantum of a scan line. In other words, the start of one scan line is separated in client memory from the start of the next scan line by an integer multiple of this many bits. You must pass one of these values: 8, 16, or 32.

bytes_per_line

Specifies the number of bytes in the client image between the start of one scan line and the start of the next. If you pass a value of 0 here, Xlib assumes that the scan lines are contiguous in memory and thus calculates the value of `bytes_per_line` itself.

Description

XCreateImage allocates the memory needed for an XImage structure for the specified display and visual.

This function does not allocate space for the image itself. It initializes the structure with byte order, bit order, and bitmap unit values, and returns a pointer to the XImage structure. The red, green, and blue mask values are defined for ZPixmap format images only and are derived from the Visual structure passed in.

For a description of images, see Volume One, Chapter 6, *Drawing Graphics and Text*.

Related Commands

XDestroyImage, XPutImage, XGetImage, XSubImage, XGetSubImage, XAddPixel, XPutPixel, XGetPixel, ImageByteOrder.

Name

XCreatePixmap — create a pixmap.

Synopsis

```
Pixmap XCreatePixmap(display, drawable, width, height, depth)
    Display *display;
    Drawable drawable;
    unsigned int width, height;
    unsigned int depth;
```

Arguments

display   Specifies a pointer to the Display structure; returned from XOpen-Display.

drawable   Specifies the drawable. May be an InputOnly window.

width   Specify the width and height in pixels of the pixmap. The values must be
height   nonzero.

depth   Specifies the depth of the pixmap. The depth must be supported by the screen of the specified drawable.

Description

XCreatePixmap creates a *pixmap* resource and returns its pixmap ID. The initial contents of the pixmap are undefined.

The server uses the *drawable* argument to determine which screen the pixmap is stored on. The pixmap can only be used on this screen. The pixmap can only be used with other drawables of the same depth, except in XCopyPlane.

A bitmap is a single-plane pixmap. There is no separate bitmap type in X Version 11.

Pixmaps should be considered a precious resource, since many systems have limits on the amount of off-screen memory available.

For more information, see Volume One, Chapter 6, *Drawing Graphics and Text*.

Errors

BadAlloc

BadDrawable

BadValue   *width* or *height* is 0.
               depth is not supported by root window.

Related Commands

XSetTile, XQueryBestTile, XSetWindowBorderPixmap, XSetWindow-BackgroundPixmap, XCreatePixmapFromBitmapData, XFreePixmap, XQuery-BestSize, XQueryBestStipple, XWriteBitmapFile, XReadBitmapFile, XCreateBitmapFromData.

Name

XCreatePixmapCursor — create a cursor from two bitmaps.

Synopsis

```
Cursor XCreatePixmapCursor(display, source, mask,
        foreground_color, background_color, x_hot, y_hot)
    Display *display;
    Pixmap source;
    Pixmap mask;
    XColor *foreground_color;
    XColor *background_color;
    unsigned int x_hot, y_hot;
```

Arguments

display   Specifies a pointer to the Display structure; returned from XOpen-Display.

source   Specifies the shape of the source cursor. A pixmap of depth 1.

mask   Specifies the bits of the cursor that are to be displayed (the mask or stipple). A pixmap of depth 1.

foreground_color
        Specifies the red, green, and blue (RGB) values for the foreground.

background_color
        Specifies the red, green, and blue (RGB) values for the background.

x_hot   Specify the coordinates of the cursor's hotspot relative to the source's origin.
y_hot   Must be a point within the source.

Description

XCreatePixmapCursor creates a cursor and returns a cursor ID. Foreground and background RGB values must be specified using *foreground_color* and *background_color*, even if the server only has a monochrome screen. The *foreground_color* is used for the 1 bits in the source, and the background is used for the 0 bits. Both source and mask (if specified) must have depth 1, but can have any root. The mask pixmap defines the shape of the cursor; that is, the 1 bits in the mask define which source pixels will be displayed. If no mask is given, all pixels of the source are displayed. The mask, if present, must be the same size as the source.

The pixmaps can be freed immediately if no further explicit references to them are to be made.

For more information on the cursor font, see Appendix I, *The Cursor Font*. See also the description of cursors in Volume One, Chapter 6, *Drawing Graphics and Text*.

Structures

```
typedef struct {
    unsigned long pixel;
    unsigned short red, green, blue;
    char flags;                         /* DoRed, DoGreen, DoBlue */
    char pad;
} XColor;
```

Related Commands

XSetTile, XQueryBestTile, XSetWindowBorderPixmap, XSetWindow-
BackgroundPixmap, XCreatePixmap, XFreePixmap, XQueryBestSize, XQuery-
BestStipple, XWriteBitmapFile, XReadBitmapFile, XCreateBitmapFrom-
Data.

XCreatePixmapFromBitmapData

Name

XCreatePixmapFromBitmapData — create a pixmap with depth from bitmap data.

Synopsis

```
Pixmap XCreatePixmapFromBitmapData(display, drawable, data,
        width, height, fg, bg, depth)
    Display *display;
    Drawable drawable;
    char *data;
    unsigned int width, height;
    unsigned long fg, bg;
    unsigned int depth;
```

Arguments

display	Specifies a pointer to the Display structure, returned from XOpen-Display.
drawable	Specifies a drawable ID which indicates which screen the pixmap is to be used on.
data	Specifies the data in bitmap format.
width *height*	Specify the width and height in pixels of the pixmap to create.
fg *bg*	Specify the foreground and background pixel values to use.
depth	Specifies the depth of the pixmap. Must be valid on the screen specified by *drawable*.

Description

XCreatePixmapFromBitmapData creates a pixmap of the given depth using bitmap data and foreground and background pixel values.

The following format for the data is assigned by default, where the variables are members of the XImage structure described in Volume One, Chapter 6, *Drawing Graphics and Text*:

```
format=XYPixmap
bit_order=LSBFirst
byte_order=LSBFirst
bitmap_unit=8
bitmap_pad=8
xoffset=0
no extra bytes per line
```

XCreatePixmapFromBitmapData creates an image from the data and uses XPutImage to place the data into the pixmap. For example:

```
#define gray_width 16
#define gray_height 16
#define gray_x_hot 8
#define gray_y_hot 8
static char gray_bits[] =
        {
        0xf81f, 0xe3c7, 0xcff3, 0x9ff9,
        0xbffd, 0x33cc, 0x7ffe, 0x7ffe,
        0x7e7e, 0x7ffe, 0x37ec, 0xbbdd,
        0x9c39, 0xcff3, 0xe3c7, 0xf81f/* example data */
        };
unsigned long foreground, background;
unsigned int depth;

/* open display, determine colors and depth */

Pixmap XCreatePixmapFromBitmapData(display, window, gray_bits,
        gray_width, gray_height, foreground, background, depth);
```

If you want to use data of a different format, it is straightforward to write a routine that does this yourself, using images.

Pixmaps should be considered a precious resource, since many systems have limits on the amount of off-screen memory available.

Errors
```
BadAlloc
BadMatch
```

Related Commands
```
XSetTile, XQueryBestTile, XSetWindowBorderPixmap, XSetWindow-
BackgroundPixmap, XCreatePixmap, XFreePixmap, XQueryBestSize, XQuery-
BestStipple, XWriteBitmapFile, XReadBitmapFile, XCreateBitmapFrom-
Data.
```

XCreateRegion

Name

XCreateRegion — create a new empty region.

Synopsis

```
Region XCreateRegion()
```

Description

XCreateRegion creates a new region of undefined size. XPolygonRegion can be used to create a region with a defined shape and size. Many of the functions that perform operations on regions can also create regions.

For a description of regions, see Volume One, Chapter 6, *Drawing Graphics and Text*.

Structures

```
typedef struct _XREGION *Region;/* opaque reference to region type */
```

Related Commands

XXorRegion, XUnionRegion, XUnionRectWithRegion, XSubtractRegion, XShrinkRegion, XSetRegion, XRectInRegion, XPolygonRegion, XPoint-InRegion, XOffsetRegion, XIntersectRegion, XEmptyRegion, XDestroy-Region, XEqualRegion, XClipBox.

Name

XCreateSimpleWindow — create an unmapped `InputOutput` window.

Synopsis

```
Window XCreateSimpleWindow(display, parent, x, y, width,
        height, border_width, border, background)
    Display *display;
    Window parent;
    int x, y;
    unsigned int width, height, border_width;
    unsigned long border;
    unsigned long background;
```

Arguments

display	Specifies a pointer to the `Display` structure; returned from `XOpenDisplay`.
parent	Specifies the parent window ID. Must be an `InputOutput` window.
x *y*	Specify the x and y coordinates of the upper-left pixel of the new window's border relative to the origin of the parent (inside the parent window's border).
width *height*	Specify the width and height, in pixels, of the new window. These are the inside dimensions, not including the new window's borders, which are entirely outside of the window. Must be nonzero. Any part of the window that extends outside its parent window is clipped.
border_width	Specifies the width, in pixels, of the new window's border.
border	Specifies the pixel value for the border of the window.
background	Specifies the pixel value for the background of the window.

Description

XCreateSimpleWindow creates an unmapped `InputOutput` subwindow of the specified parent window. Use XCreateWindow to set the attributes to create an `InputOnly` window while creating a window.

XCreateSimpleWindow returns the ID of the created window. The new window is placed on top of the stacking order relative to its siblings. Note that the window is unmapped when it is created—use XMapWindow to display it. This function generates a CreateNotify event.

The initial conditions of the window are as follows:

The window inherits its depth, class, and visual from its parent. All other window attributes have their default values.

All properties have undefined values.

The new window will not have a cursor defined; the cursor will be that of the window's parent until the cursor attribute is set with XDefineCursor.

If no background or border is specified, CopyFromParent is implied.

For more information, see Volume One, Chapter 2, *X Concepts* and Volume One, Chapter 3, *Basic Window Program.*

Errors

BadAlloc

BadMatch

BadValue   *width* or *height* is 0.

BadWindow   Specified parent is an InputOnly window.

Related Commands

XCreateWindow, XDestroySubwindows, XDestroyWindow.

XCreateWindow

Name

XCreateWindow — create a window and set attributes.

Synopsis

```
Window XCreateWindow(display, parent, x, y, width, height,
        border_width, depth, class, visual, valuemask,
        attributes)
    Display *display;
    Window parent;
    int x, y;
    unsigned int width, height;
    unsigned int border_width;
    int depth;
    unsigned int class;
    Visual *visual
    unsigned long valuemask;
    XSetWindowAttributes *attributes;
```

Arguments

display   Specifies a pointer to the Display structure; returned from XOpenDisplay.

parent   Specifies the parent window. Parent must be InputOutput if class of window created is to be InputOutput.

x   Specify the x and y coordinates of the upper-left pixel of the new window's
y   border relative to the origin of the parent (upper left inside the parent's border).

width   Specify the width and height, in pixels, of the window. These are the new
height   window's inside dimensions. These dimensions do not include the new window's borders, which are entirely outside of the window. Must be nonzero, otherwise XCreateWindow generates a BadValue error.

border_width
              Specifies the width, in pixels, of the new window's border. Must be 0 for InputOnly windows, otherwise a BadMatch error is returned.

depth   Specifies the depth of the window, which is not necessarily the same as the parent's depth. A depth of 0 for class InputOutput or CopyFromParent means the depth is taken from the parent.

class   Specifies the new window's class. Pass one of these constants: InputOutput, InputOnly, or CopyFromParent.

visual   Specifies a pointer to the visual structure describing the colormaps to be used with this window. CopyFromParent is valid.

valuemask   Specifies which window attributes are defined in the attributes argument. If valuemask is 0, the rest is ignored, and attributes is not referenced. This mask is the inclusive OR of the valid attribute mask bits.

attributes   Attributes of the window to be set at creation time should be set in this structure. The *valuemask* should have the appropriate bits set to indicate which attributes have been set in the structure.

Description

To create an unmapped subwindow for a specified parent window from an application, you can use XCreateWindow or XCreateSimpleWindow. XCreateWindow is a more general function that allows you to set specific window attributes when you create it. If you do not want to set specific attributes when you create a window, use XCreateSimpleWindow, which creates a window that inherits its attributes from its parent. XCreateSimpleWindow creates InputOutput windows only.

XCreateWindow returns the ID of the created window. XCreateWindow causes the X server to generate a CreateNotify event. The newly created window is placed on top of its siblings in the stacking order.

Extension packages may define other classes of windows.

The visual should be DefaultVisual or one returned by XGetVisualInfo or XMatch-VisualInfo.

For more information, see Volume One, Chapter 4, *Window Attributes*.

Structures

```
/*
 * Data structure for setting window attributes.
 */
typedef struct {
    Pixmap background_pixmap;         /* background or None or ParentRelative */
    unsigned long background_pixel;   /* background pixel */
    Pixmap border_pixmap;             /* border of the window */
    unsigned long border_pixel;       /* border pixel value */
    int bit_gravity;                  /* one of bit gravity values */
    int win_gravity;                  /* one of the window gravity values */
    int backing_store;                /* NotUseful, WhenMapped, Always */
    unsigned long backing_planes;     /* planes to be preseved if possible */
    unsigned long backing_pixel;      /* value to use in restoring planes */
    Bool save_under;                  /* should bits under be saved (popups) */
    long event_mask;                  /* set of events that should be saved */
    long do_not_propagate_mask;       /* set of events that should not propagate */
    Bool override_redirect;           /* boolean value for override-redirect */
    Colormap colormap;                /* colormap to be associated with window */
    Cursor cursor;                    /* cursor to be displayed (or None) */
} XSetWindowAttributes;

/* Window attributes for CreateWindow and ChangeWindowAttributes */

/* Definitions for valuemask argument */

#define CWBackPixmap              (1L<<0)
#define CWBackPixel               (1L<<1)
#define CWBorderPixmap            (1L<<2)
#define CWBorderPixel             (1L<<3)
```

```
#define CWBitGravity        (1L<<4)
#define CWWinGravity        (1L<<5)
#define CWBackingStore      (1L<<6)
#define CWBackingPlanes     (1L<<7)
#define CWBackingPixel      (1L<<8)
#define CWOverrideRedirect  (1L<<9)
#define CWSaveUnder         (1L<<10)
#define CWEventMask         (1L<<11)
#define CWDontPropagate     (1L<<12)
#define CWColormap          (1L<<13)
#define CWCursor            (1L<<14)
```

Errors

BadAlloc   Attribute besides win_gravity, event_mask, do_not_propagate_mask, override_redirect or cursor specified for InputOnly.

BadColor   *depth* nonzero for InputOnly.

BadCursor   Parent of InputOutput is InputOnly.

BadMatch   *border_width* is nonzero for InputOnly.

BadPixmap   *depth* not supported on screen for InputOutput.

BadValue   *width* or *height* is 0.

BadWindow   *visual* type not supported on screen (either InputOnly or InputOutput).

Related Commands

XCreateSimpleWindow, XDestroySubwindows, XDestroyWindow.

Name

XDefineCursor — assign a cursor to a window.

Synopsis

```
XDefineCursor(display, w, cursor)
    Display *display;
    Window w;
    Cursor cursor;
```

Arguments

display   Specifies a pointer to the Display structure; returned from XOpen-
            Display.

w   Specifies the ID of the window for which the cursor is to be assigned.

cursor   Specifies the cursor to be displayed when the pointer is in the specified win-
            dow. Pass None to have the parent's cursor displayed in the window, or for
            the root window, to have the default cursor displayed.

Description

Sets the cursor attribute of a window, so that the specified cursor is shown whenever this window is visible and the pointer is inside. If XDefineCursor is not called, the parent's cursor
is used by default.

For more information on available cursors, see Appendix I, *The Cursor Font*.

Errors

```
BadCursor
BadWindow
```

Related Commands

XUndefineCursor, XCreateFontCursor, XCreateGlyphCursor, XCreate-
PixmapCursor, XFreeCursor, XRecolorCursor, XQueryBestCursor, XQuery-
BestSize.

Name

XDeleteAssoc — delete an entry from an association table.

Synopsis

```
XDeleteAssoc(display, table, x_id)
    Display *display;
    XAssocTable *table;
    XID x_id;
```

Arguments

display   Specifies a pointer to the Display structure; returned from XOpen-Display.

table   Specifies one of the association tables created by XCreateAssocTable.

x_id   Specifies the X resource ID of the association to be deleted.

Description

This function is provided for compatibility with X Version 10. To use it you must include the file *<X11/X10.h>* and link with the library *-loldX*.

XDeleteAssoc deletes an association in an XAssocTable keyed on its XID. Redundant deletes (and deletes of nonexistent XID's) are meaningless and cause no problems. Deleting associations in no way impairs the performance of an XAssocTable.

For more information on association tables, see Volume One, Chapter 13, *Other Programming Techniques*.

Structures

```
typedef struct {
    XAssoc *buckets;        /* pointer to first bucket in array */
    int size;               /* table size (number of buckets) */
}XAssocTable;
```

Related Commands

XCreateAssocTable, XDestroyAssocTable, XLookUpAssoc, XMakeAssoc.

XDeleteContext

Name

XDeleteContext — delete a context entry for a given window and type.

Synopsis

```
int XDeleteContext(display, w, context)
    Display *display;
    Window w;
    XContext context;
```

Arguments

display   Specifies a pointer to the Display structure; returned from XOpen-Display.

w   Specifies the window with which the data is associated.

context   Specifies the context type to which the data belongs.

Description

XDeleteContext deletes the entry for the given window and type from the context data structure defined in *<X11/Xutil.h>*. This function returns XCNOENT if the context could not be found, or 0 if it succeeds. XDeleteContext does not free the data whose address was saved.

See Volume One, Chapter 13, *Other Programming Techniques*, for a description of context management.

Structures

```
typedef int XContext;
```

Related Commands

XFindContext, XSaveContext, XUniqueContext.

Name

XDeleteModifiermapEntry — delete an entry from an XModifierKeymap structure.

Synopsis

```
XModifierKeymap *XDeleteModifiermapEntry(modmap,
        keysym_entry, modifier)
    XModifierKeymap *modmap;
    KeyCode keysym_entry;
    int modifier;
```

Arguments

modmap   Specifies a pointer to an XModifierKeymap structure.

keysym_entry
                Specifies the KeyCode of the key to be deleted from modmap.

modifier   Specifies the modifier you no longer want mapped to the keycode specified
                in keysym_entry. This should be one of the constants: ShiftMap-
                Index, LockMapIndex, ControlMapIndex, Mod1MapIndex, Mod2-
                MapIndex, Mod3MapIndex, Mod4MapIndex, or Mod5MapIndex.

Description

XDeleteModifiermapEntry returns an XModifierKeymap structure suitable for calling XSetModifierMapping, in which the specified keycode is deleted from the set of
keycodes that is mapped to the specified modifier (like Shift or Control). XDelete-
ModifiermapEntry does not change the mapping itself.

This function is normally used by calling XGetModifierMapping to get a pointer to the
current XModifierKeymap structure for use as the modmap argument to XDelete-
ModifiermapEntry.

Note that the structure pointed to by modmap is freed by XDeleteModifiermapEntry.
It should not be freed or otherwise used by applications.

For a description of the modifier map, see XSetModifierMapping.

Structures

```
typedef struct {
    int max_keypermod;      /* server's max number of keys per modifier */
    KeyCode *modifiermap;   /* an 8 by max_keypermod array of
                             * keycodes to be used as modifiers */
} XModifierKeymap;

#define ShiftMapIndex       0
#define LockMapIndex        1
#define ControlMapIndex     2
#define Mod1MapIndex        3
#define Mod2MapIndex        4
#define Mod3MapIndex        5
```

```
#define Mod4MapIndex        6
#define Mod5MapIndex        7
```

Related Commands

InsertModifiermapEntry, XGetModifierMapping, XSetModifierMapping,
XNewModifiermap, XFreeModifiermap, XKeycodeToKeysym, XKeysym-
ToKeycode, XKeysymToString, XQueryKeymap, XStringToKeysym, XLookup-
Keysym, XRebindKeySym, XGetKeyboardMapping, XRefreshKeyboardMapping,
XLookupString.

XDeleteProperty

Name

XDeleteProperty — delete a window property.

Synopsis

```
XDeleteProperty(display, w, property)
    Display *display;
    Window w;
    Atom property;
```

Arguments

display   Specifies a pointer to the Display structure; returned from XOpen-Display.

w   Specifies the ID of the window whose property you want to delete.

property   Specifies the atom of the property to be deleted.

Description

XDeleteProperty deletes a window property, so that it no longer contains any data. Its atom, specified by *property*, still exists after the call so that it can be used again later by any application that knows the ID of the window the property is defined on. If the property was defined on the specified window, XDeleteProperty generates a PropertyNotify event.

See the introduction to properties in Volume One, Chapter 2, *X Concepts*, or more detailed information in Volume One, Chapter 10, *Interclient Communication*.

Errors

```
BadAtom
BadWindow
```

Related Commands

XSetStandardProperties, XGetFontProperty, XRotateWindowProperties, XChangeProperty, XGetWindowProperty, XListProperties, XGetAtomName, XInternAtom.

XDestroyAssocTable

Name

XDestroyAssocTable — free the memory allocated for an association table.

Synopsis

```
XDestroyAssocTable(table)
    XAssocTable *table;
```

Arguments

table   Specifies the association table whose memory is to be freed.

Description

This function is provided for compatibility with X Version 10. To use it you must include the file *<X11/X10.h>* and link with the library *-loldX*.

Using an XAssocTable after it has been destroyed will have unpredictable and probably disastrous consequences.

For more information on association tables, see Volume One, Chapter 13, *Other Programming Techniques*.

Structures

```
typedef struct {
    XAssoc *buckets;        /* pointer to first bucket in array */
    int size;               /* table size (number of buckets) */
}XAssocTable;
```

Related Commands

XCreateAssocTable, XDeleteAssoc, XLookUpAssoc, XMakeAssoc.

XDestroyImage

Name

XDestroyImage — deallocate memory associated with an image.

Synopsis

```
int XDestroyImage(ximage)
    XImage *ximage;
```

Arguments

ximage   Specifies a pointer to the image.

Description

XDestroyImage deallocates the memory associated with an XImage structure. This memory includes both the memory holding the XImage structure, and the memory holding the actual image data.

For more information on images, see Volume One, Chapter 6, *Drawing Graphics and Text*.

Related Commands

XPutImage, XGetImage, XCreateImage, XSubImage, XGetSubImage, XAddPixel, XPutPixel, XGetPixel, ImageByteOrder.

Name

XDestroyRegion — deallocate storage associated with a region.

Synopsis

```
XDestroyRegion(r)
    Region r;
```

Arguments

r   Specifies the region to be destroyed.

Description

XDestroyRegion frees the memory associated with a region.

See Volume One, Chapter 6, *Drawing Graphics and Text*, for a description of regions.

Related Commands

XXorRegion, XUnionRegion, XUnionRectWithRegion, XSubtractRegion, XShrinkRegion, XSetRegion, XRectInRegion, XPolygonRegion, XPoint-InRegion, XOffsetRegion, XIntersectRegion, XEmptyRegion, XCreate-Region, XEqualRegion, XClipBox.

XDestroySubwindows

Name

XDestroySubwindows — destroy all subwindows of a window.

Synopsis

```
XDestroySubwindows (display, w)
    Display *display;
    Window w;
```

Arguments

display   Specifies a pointer to the `Display` structure; returned from `XOpen-Display`.

w   Specifies the ID of the window whose subwindows are to be destroyed.

Description

This function destroys all descendants of the specified window, in bottom to top stacking order.

`XDestroySubwindows` generates exposure events on window *w*, if any mapped subwindows were actually destroyed. This is much more efficient than deleting many subwindows one at a time, since much of the work need only be performed once for all of the windows rather than for each window. It also saves multiple exposure events on the windows about to be destroyed. The subwindows should never again be referenced.

`XCloseDisplay` automatically destroys all windows that have been created by that client on the specified display (unless called after a fork system call).

Errors

`BadWindow`

Related Commands

`XCreateSimpleWindow, XCreateWindow, XDestroyWindow.`

Name

XDestroyWindow — unmap and destroy a window and all subwindows.

Synopsis

```
XDestroyWindow(display, window)
    Display *display;
    Window window;
```

Arguments

display   Specifies a pointer to the `Display` structure; returned from XOpen-Display.

window   Specifies the ID of the window to be destroyed.

Description

If *window* is mapped, an `UnmapWindow` request is performed automatically. The window and all inferiors are then destroyed, and a `DestroyNotify` event is generated for each window. The ordering of the `DestroyNotify` events is such that for any given window, `DestroyNotify` is generated on all inferiors of the window before being generated on the window itself. The ordering among siblings and across subhierarchies is not otherwise constrained.

The windows should never again be referenced.

Destroying a mapped window will generate exposure events on other windows that were obscured by the windows being destroyed. `XDestroyWindow` may also generate `Enter-Window` events if *window* was mapped and contained the pointer.

No windows are destroyed if you try to destroy the root window.

Errors

BadWindow

Related Commands

XCreateSimpleWindow, XCreateWindow, XDestroySubwindows.

Name

XDisableAccessControl — allow access from any host.

Synopsis

```
XDisableAccessControl(display)
    Display *display;
```

Arguments

display   Specifies a pointer to the Display structure; returned from XOpen-Display.

Description

XDisableAccessControl instructs the server to allow access from clients on any host. This overrides the host access list.

This routine can only be called from a client running on the same host as the server.

For more information on access control, see Volume One, Chapter 13, *Other Programming Techniques.*

Errors

BadAccess

Related Commands

XAddHost, XAddHosts, XListHosts, XRemoveHost, XRemoveHosts, XEnable-AccessControl, XSetAccessControl.

Name

XDisplayName — report the display name when connection to a display fails.

Synopsis

```
char *XDisplayName (string)
    char *string;
```

Arguments

string   Specifies the character string.

Description

XDisplayName is normally used to report the name of the display the program attempted to open with OpenDisplay. This is necessary because X error handling begins only after the connection to the server succeeds. If a NULL string is specified, XDisplayName looks in the environment for the display and returns the display name that the user was requesting. Otherwise, XDisplayName returns its own argument. This makes it easier to report to the user precisely which display the program attempted to open.

For more information, see Volume One, Chapter 3, *Basic Window Program.*

Related Commands

XGetErrorDatabaseText, XGetErrorText, XSetErrorHandler, XSetIOError-Handler, XSynchronize, XSetAfterFunction.

Name

XDraw — draw a polyline or curve between vertex list (from X10).

Synopsis

```
Status XDraw(display, drawable, gc, vlist, vcount)
    Display *display;
    Drawable drawable;
    GC gc;
    Vertex *vlist;
    int vcount;
```

Arguments

display   Specifies a pointer to the `Display` structure; returned from `XOpen-Display`.

drawable   Specifies the drawable.

gc   Specifies the graphics context.

vlist   Specifies a pointer to the list of vertices that indicates what to draw.

vcount   Specifies how many vertices are in *vlist*.

Description

This function is provided for compatibility with X Version 10. To use it you must include the file *<X11/X10.h>* and link with the library *-loldX*.

`XDraw` achieves the effects of the X10 `XDraw`, `XDrawDashed`, and `XDrawPatterned` functions.

`XDraw` draws an arbitrary polygon or curve. The figure drawn is defined by the specified list of vertices (*vlist*). The points are connected by lines as specified in the flags each the `Vertex` structure.

The `Vertex` structure contains an x,y coordinate and a bitmask called `flags` that specifies the drawing parameters.

The x and y elements of `Vertex` are the coordinates of the vertex that are relative to either the previous vertex (if `VertexRelative` is 1) or the upper-left inside corner of the drawable (if `VertexRelative` is 0). If `VertexRelative` is 0 the coordinates are said to be absolute. The first vertex must be an absolute vertex.

If the `VertexDontDraw` bit is 1, no line or curve is drawn from the previous vertex to this one. This is analogous to picking up the pen and moving to another place before drawing another line.

If the `VertexCurved` bit is 1, a spline algorithm is used to draw a smooth curve from the previous vertex, through this one, to the next vertex. Otherwise, a straight line is drawn from the previous vertex to this one. It makes sense to set `VertexCurved` to 1 only if a previous and next vertex are both defined (either explicitly in the array, or through the definition of a closed curve—see below.)

It is permissible for `VertexDontDraw` bits and `VertexCurved` bits to both be 1. This is useful if you want to define the previous point for the smooth curve, but you do not want an actual curve drawing to start until this point.

If `VertexStartClosed` bit is 1, then this point marks the beginning of a closed curve. This vertex must be followed later in the array by another vertex whose absolute coordinates are identical and which has `VertexEndClosed` bit of 1. The points in between form a cycle for the purpose of determining predecessor and successor vertices for the spline algorithm.

`XDraw` uses the following graphics context components: `function`, `plane_mask`, `line_width`, `line_style`, `cap_style`, `join_style`, `fill_style`, `subwindow_mode`, `clip_x_origin`, `clip_y_origin`, and `clip_mask`. This function also uses these graphics context mode-dependent components: `foreground`, `background`, `tile`, `stipple`, `ts_x_origin`, `ts_y_origin`, `dash_offset`, and `dash_list`.

A `Status` of 0 is returned on failure.

For more information, see Volume One, Appendix B, *X10 Compatibility*.

Structures

```
typedef struct _Vertex {
    short x,y;
    unsigned short flags;
} Vertex;

/* defined constants for use as flags */
#define VertexRelative       0x0001    /* else absolute */
#define VertexDontDraw       0x0002    /* else draw */
#define VertexCurved         0x0004    /* else straight */
#define VertexStartClosed    0x0008    /* else not */
#define VertexEndClosed      0x0010    /* else not */
```

Related Commands

`XDrawArc`, `XDrawArcs`, `XDrawFilled`, `XDrawLine`, `XDrawLines`, `XDrawPoint`, `XDrawPoints`, `XDrawRectangle`, `XDrawRectangles`, `XDrawSegments`, `XCopyArea`, `XCopyPlane`, `XFillArc`, `XFillArcs`, `XFillPolygon`, `XFillRectangle`, `XFillRectangles`, `XClearArea`, `XClearWindow`.

Name

XDrawArc — draw an arc fitting inside a rectangle.

Synopsis

```
XDrawArc(display, drawable, gc, x, y, width, height,
        angle1, angle2)
    Display *display;
    Drawable drawable;
    GC gc;
    int x, y;
    unsigned int width, height;
    int angle1, angle2;
```

Arguments

display	Specifies a pointer to the Display structure; returned from XOpen-Display.
drawable	Specifies the drawable.
gc	Specifies the graphics context.
x *y*	Specify the x and y coordinates of the upper-left corner of the rectangle that contains the arc, relative to the origin of the specified drawable.
width *height*	Specify the width and height in pixels of the major and minor axes of the arc.
angle1	Specifies the start of the arc relative to the three-o'clock position from the center. Angles are specified in 64ths of a degree, (360 * 64 is a complete circle).
angle2	Specifies the path and extent of the arc relative to the start of the arc. Angles are specified in 64ths of a degree, (360 * 64 is a complete circle).

Description

XDrawArc draws a circular or elliptical arc. An arc is specified by a rectangle and two angles. The *x* and *y* coordinates are relative to the origin of the drawable, and define the upper-left corner of the rectangle. The center of the circle or ellipse is the center of the rectangle, and the major and minor axes are specified by the width and height, respectively. The angles are signed integers in 64ths of a degree, with positive values indicating counterclockwise motion and negative values indicating clockwise motion, truncated to a maximum of 360 degrees. The start of the arc is specified by *angle1* relative to the three-o'clock position from the center, and the path and extent of the arc is specified by *angle2* relative to the start of the arc.

By specifying one axis to be 0, a horizontal or vertical line can be drawn.

Angles are computed based solely on the coordinate system and ignore the aspect ratio. In other words, if the bounding rectangle of the arc is not square and *angle1* is 0 and *angle2* is (45x64), a point drawn from the center of the bounding box through the endpoint of the arc will not pass through the corner of the rectangle.

XDrawArc uses these graphics context components: function, plane_mask, line_width, line_style, cap_style, join_style, fill_style, subwindow_ mode, clip_x_origin, clip_y_origin, and clip_mask. This function also uses these graphics context mode-dependent components: foreground, background, tile, stipple, ts_x_origin, ts_y_origin, dash_offset, and dash_list. XDraw-Arc is not affected by the tile or stipple in the GC.

For more information, see Volume One, Chapter 6, *Drawing Graphics and Text.*

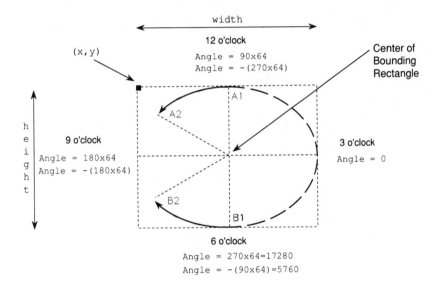

Example 1:
Arc from A1 to A2, Counterclockwise
A1 = 90 x 64
A2 = 45 x 64

Example 2:
Arc from B1 to B2, Clockwise
A1 = 270 x 64
A2 = -(45 x 64)

Errors

BadDrawable
BadGC
BadMatch

Related Commands

XDraw, XDrawArcs, XDrawFilled, XDrawLine, XDrawLines, XDrawPoint, XDrawPoints, XDrawRectangle, XDrawRectangles, XDrawSegments, XCopyArea, XCopyPlane, XFillArc, XFillArcs, XFillPolygon, XFillRectangle, XFillRectangles, XClearArea, XClearWindow.

XDrawArcs

Name

XDrawArcs — draw multiple arcs.

Synopsis

```
XDrawArcs(display, drawable, gc, arcs, narcs)
    Display *display;
    Drawable drawable;
    GC gc;
    XArc *arcs;
    int narcs;
```

Arguments

display   Specifies a pointer to the Display structure; returned from XOpen-Display.

drawable   Specifies the drawable.

gc   Specifies the graphics context.

arcs   Specifies a pointer to an array of arcs.

narcs   Specifies the number of arcs in the array.

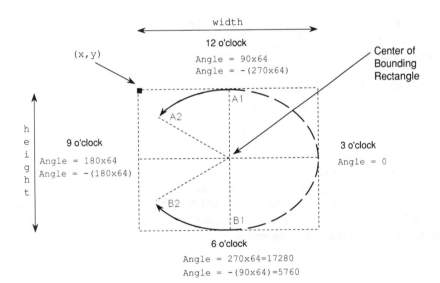

Example 1:
Arc from A1 to A2, Counterclockwise
A1 = 90 x 64
A2 = 45 x 64

Example 2:
Arc from B1 to B2, Clockwise
A1 = 270 x 64
A2 = -(45 x 64)

Description

This is the plural version of XDrawArc. See XDrawArc for details of drawing a single arc.

The arcs are drawn in the order listed in the *arcs* array. For any given arc, no pixel is drawn more than once. If arcs intersect, pixels will be drawn multiple times. If the last point in one arc coincides with the first point in the following arc, the two arcs will join correctly according to the GC. If the first point in the first arc coincides with the last point in the last arc, the two arcs will join correctly according to the join_style specified in the GC. By specifying one axis to be 0, a horizontal or vertical line can be drawn. Angles are computed based solely on the coordinate system, ignoring the aspect ratio.

By specifying one axis to be 0, a horizontal or vertical line can be drawn. Angles are computed based solely on the coordinate system and ignore the aspect ratio.

For any given arc, no pixel is drawn more than once. If two arcs join correctly and if line_width is greater than 0 and the arcs intersect, no pixel is drawn more than once. Otherwise, the intersecting pixels of intersecting arcs are drawn multiple times. Specifying an arc with one endpoint and a clockwise extent draws the same pixels as specifying the other endpoint and an equivalent counterclockwise extent, except as it affects joins.

If the last point in one arc coincides with the first point in the following arc, the two arcs will join correctly. If the first point in the first arc coincides with the last point in the last arc, the two arcs will join correctly.

XDrawArcs uses these graphics context components: function, plane_mask, line_width, line_style, cap_style, join_style, fill_style, subwindow_mode, clip_x_origin, clip_y_origin, and clip_mask. This function also uses these graphics context mode-dependent components: foreground, background, tile, stipple, ts_x_origin, ts_y_origin, dash_offset, and dash_list. XDrawArcs is not affected by the tile or stipple in the GC.

The following is a technical explanation of the points drawn by XDrawArcs. For an arc specified as [x, y, width, height, angle1, angle2], the origin of the major and minor axes is at [x+(width/2), y+(height/2)], and the infinitely thin path describing the entire circle or ellipse intersects the horizontal axis at [x, y+(height/2)] and [x+width, y+(height/2)] and intersects the vertical axis at [x+(width/2),y] and [x+(width/2), y+height]. These coordinates can be fractional. That is, they are not truncated to discrete coordinates. The path should be defined by the ideal mathematical path. For a wide line with line width line_width, the bounding outlines for filling are given by the infinitely thin paths describing the arcs:

```
[x+dx/2, y+dy/2, width-dx, height-dy, angle1, angle2]
```

and

```
[x-line_width/2, y-line_width/2, width+line_width, height+line_width,
angle1, angle2]
```

where

```
dx=min(line_width,width)
dy=min(line_width,height)
```

If (`height != width`) the angles must be specified in the effectively skewed coordinate system of the ellipse (for a circle, the angles and coordinate systems are identical). The relationship between these angles and angles expressed in the normal coordinate system of the screen (as measured with a protractor) is as follows:

```
skewed-angle = atan(tan(normal-angle) * width/height) + adjust
```

The skewed-angle and normal-angle are expressed in radians (rather than in 64ths of a degree) in the range `[0,2*PI]`, and where `atan` returns a value in the range `[-PI/2,PI/2]`, and where `adjust` is:

```
0          for normal-angle in the range [0,PI/2]
PI         for normal-angle in the range [PI/2,(3*PI)/2]
2*PI       for normal-angle in the range [(3*PI)/2,2*PI]
```

For more information, see Volume One, Chapter 6, *Drawing Graphics and Text*.

Structures
```
typedef struct {
    short x, y;
    unsigned short width, height;
    short angle1, angle2;              /*  Degrees * 64  */
} XArc;
```

Errors
```
BadDrawable
BadGC
BadMatch
```

Related Commands
XDraw, XDrawArc, XDrawFilled, XDrawLine, XDrawLines, XDrawPoint, XDraw-
Points, XDrawRectangle, XDrawRectangles, XDrawSegments, XCopyArea,
XCopyPlane, XFillArc, XFillArcs, XFillPolygon, XFillRectangle, XFill-
Rectangles, XClearArea, XClearWindow.

Name

XDrawFilled — draw a filled polygon or curve from vertex list (from X10).

Synopsis

```
Status XDrawFilled(display, drawable, gc, vlist, vcount)
    Display *display;
    Drawable drawable;
    GC gc;
    Vertex *vlist;
    int vcount;
```

Arguments

display   Specifies a pointer to the Display structure; returned from XOpen-Display.

drawable   Specifies the drawable.

gc   Specifies the graphics context.

vlist   Specifies a pointer to the list of vertices.

vcount   Specifies how many vertices are in vlist.

Description

This function is provided for compatibility with X Version 10. To use it you must include the file <X11/X10.h> and link with the library -loldX. XDrawFilled achieves the effects of the X Version 10 XDrawTiled and XDrawFilled functions.

XDrawFilled draws arbitrary polygons or curves, according to the same rules as XDraw, and then fills them.

XDrawFilled uses the following graphics context components: function, plane_mask, line_width, line_style, cap_style, join_style, fill_style, subwindow_mode, clip_x_origin, clip_y_origin, and clip_mask. This function also uses these graphics context mode-dependent components: foreground, background, tile, stipple, ts_x_origin, ts_y_origin, dash_offset, dash_list, fill_style and fill_rule.

XDrawFilled returns a Status of 0 on failure.

For more information, see Volume One, Appendix B, *X10 Compatibility*.

Related Commands

XDraw, XDrawArc, XDrawArcs, XDrawLine, XDrawLines, XDrawPoint, XDraw-Points, XDrawRectangle, XDrawRectangles, XDrawSegments, XCopyArea, XCopyPlane, XFillArc, XFillArcs, XFillPolygon, XFillRectangle, XFill-Rectangles, XClearArea, XClearWindow.

XDrawImageString

Name

XDrawImageString — draw 8-bit image text characters.

Synopsis

```
XDrawImageString(display, drawable, gc, x, y, string, length)
    Display *display;
    Drawable drawable;
    GC gc;
    int x, y;
    char *string;
    int length;
```

Arguments

display   Specifies a pointer to the Display structure; returned from XOpen-
            Display.

drawable   Specifies the drawable.

gc   Specifies the graphics context.

x   Specify the x and y coordinates of the baseline starting position for the
y   image text character, relative to the origin of the specified drawable.

string   Specifies the character string.

length   Specifies the number of characters in the string argument.

Description

XDrawImageString draws a string, but unlike XDrawString it can draw both the foreground and the background of the characters, if the GC is set accordingly.

XDrawImageString uses these graphics context components: plane_mask, foreground, background, font, subwindow_mode, clip_x_origin, clip_y_
origin, and clip_mask. The function and fill_style defined in gc are ignored;
the effective function is GXcopy and the effective fill_style is FillSolid.

XDrawImageString first fills a destination rectangle with the background pixel defined
in gc, and then paints the text with the foreground pixel. The upper-left corner of the
filled rectangle is at [x, y - font_ascent], the width is overall->width and the
height is Xascent + descent.

The overall->width, ascent, and descent are as would be returned by XQuery-
TextExtents using gc and string.

For more information, see Volume One: Chapter 6, *Drawing Graphics and Text*; and Chapter
5, *The Graphics Context*.

Errors

    BadDrawable
    BadGC
    BadMatch

Related Commands

    XQueryTextExtents, XQueryTextExtents16, XDrawImageString16, XDraw-
    String, XDrawString16, XDrawText, XDrawText16, XTextExtents, XText-
    Extents16, XTextWidth, XTextWidth16.

XDrawImageString16

Name

XDrawImageString16 — draw 16-bit image text characters.

Synopsis

```
XDrawImageString16(display, drawable, gc, x, y, string, length)
    Display *display;
    Drawable drawable;
    GC gc;
    int x, y;
    XChar2b *string;
    int length;
```

Arguments

display	Specifies a pointer to the `Display` structure; returned from `XOpen-Display`.
drawable	Specifies the drawable.
gc	Specifies the graphics context.
x	Specify the x and y coordinates of the baseline starting position for the
y	image text character, relative to the origin of the specified drawable.
string	Specifies the character string.
length	Specifies the number of characters in the *string* argument.

Description

XDrawImageString16 draws a string, but unlike XDrawString16 it can draw both the foreground and the background of the characters, if the GC is set accordingly.

XDrawImageString16 uses these graphics context components: plane_mask, foreground, background, font, subwindow_mode, clip_x_origin, clip_y_origin, and clip_mask. The function and fill_style defined in *gc* are ignored; the effective function is GXcopy and the effective fill_style is FillSolid.

XDrawImageString16 first fills a destination rectangle with the background pixel defined in *gc*, and then paints the text with the foreground pixel. The upper-left corner of the filled rectangle is at [x, y - font_ascent], the width is overall->width and the height is ascent + descent.

The overall->width, ascent, and descent are as would be returned by XQuery-TextExtents16 using *gc* and *string*.

For more information, see Volume One: Chapter 6, *Drawing Graphics and Text*; and Chapter 5, *The Graphics Context*.

Structures

```
typedef struct {
    unsigned char byte1;
    unsigned char byte2;
} XChar2b;
```

Errors

```
BadDrawable
BadGC
BadMatch
```

Related Commands

XQueryTextExtents, XQueryTextExtents16, XDrawImageString, XDraw-
String, XDrawString16, XDrawText, XDrawText16, XTextExtents, XText-
Extents16, XTextWidth, XTextWidth16.

Name

XDrawLine — draw a line between two points.

Synopsis

```
XDrawLine(display, drawable, gc, x1, y1, x2, y2)
    Display *display;
    Drawable drawable;
    GC gc;
    int x1, y1, x2, y2;
```

Arguments

display   Specifies a pointer to the Display structure; returned from XOpen-
                Display.

drawable   Specifies the drawable.

gc   Specifies the graphics context.

x1   Specify the coordinates of the endpoints of the line relative to the drawable
y1   origin. XLine connects point (x1, y1) to point (x2, y2).
x2
y2

Description

XDrawLine uses the components of the specified graphics context to draw a line between
two points in the specified drawable. No pixel is drawn more than once.

XDrawLine uses these graphics context components: function, plane_mask,
line_width, line_style, cap_style, fill_style, subwindow_mode, clip_
x_origin, clip_y_origin, and clip_mask. XDrawLine also uses these graphics
context mode-dependent components: foreground, background, tile, stipple,
ts_x_origin, ts_y_origin, dash_offset, and dash_list.

XDrawLine is not affected by tile or stipple in the GC.

For more information, see Volume One: Chapter 6, *Drawing Graphics and Text*; and Chapter
5, *The Graphics Context*.

Errors

```
BadDrawable
BadGC
BadMatch
```

Related Commands

XDraw, XDrawArc, XDrawArcs, XDrawFilled, XDrawLines, XDrawPoint, XDraw-
Points, XDrawRectangle, XDrawRectangles, XDrawSegments, XCopyArea,
XCopyPlane, XFillArc, XFillArcs, XFillPolygon, XFillRectangle, XFill-
Rectangles, XClearArea, XClearWindow.

Name

XDrawLines — draw multiple connected lines.

Synopsis

```
XDrawLines(display, drawable, gc, points, npoints, mode)
    Display *display;
    Drawable drawable;
    GC gc;
    XPoint *points;
    int npoints;
    int mode;
```

Arguments

display   Specifies a pointer to the Display structure; returned from XOpen-Display.

drawable   Specifies the drawable.

gc   Specifies the graphics context.

points   Specifies a pointer to an array of points.

npoints   Specifies the number of points in the array.

mode   Specifies the coordinate mode. Pass either CoordModeOrigin or Coord-ModePrevious.

Description

XDrawLines does the following:

- Draws lines connecting each point in the list (*points* array) to the next point in the list. The lines are drawn in the order listed in the *points* array. For any given line, no pixel is drawn more than once. If thin (zero line width) lines intersect, pixels will be drawn multiple times. If the first and last points coincide, the first and last lines will join correctly. If wide lines intersect, the intersecting pixels are drawn only once, as though the entire multiline request were a single filled shape.

- Uses the components of the specified graphics context to draw multiple connected lines in the specified drawable. Specifically, XDrawLines uses these graphics context components: function, plane_mask, line_width, line_style, cap_style, join_style, fill_style, subwindow_mode, clip_x_origin, clip_y_origin, and clip_mask. This function also uses these graphics context mode-dependent components: foreground, background, tile, stipple, ts_x_origin, ts_y_origin, dash_offset, and dash_list.

The *mode* argument may have two values:

- CoordModeOrigin indicates that all points are relative to the drawable's origin.

- CoordModePrevious indicates that all points after the first are relative to the previous point. (The first point is always relative to the drawable's origin.)

XDrawLines is not affected by the tile or stipple in the GC.

For more information, see Volume One: Chapter 6, *Drawing Graphics and Text*; and Chapter 5, *The Graphics Context*.

Structures

```
typedef struct {
    short x, y;
} XPoint;
```

Errors

```
BadDrawable
BadGC
BadMatch
BadValue
```

Related Commands

XDraw, XDrawArc, XDrawArcs, XDrawFilled, XDrawLine, XDrawPoint, XDraw-Points, XDrawRectangle, XDrawRectangles, XDrawSegments, XCopyArea, XCopyPlane, XFillArc, XFillArcs, XFillPolygon, XFillRectangle, XFill-Rectangles, XClearArea, XClearWindow.

Name

XDrawPoint — draw a point.

Synopsis

```
XDrawPoint(display, drawable, gc, x, y)
    Display *display;
    Drawable drawable;
    GC gc;
    int x, y;
```

Arguments

display   Specifies a pointer to the Display structure; returned from XOpen-Display.

drawable Specifies the drawable.

gc   Specifies the graphics context.

x   Specify the x and y coordinates of the point, relative to the corner of the
y   drawable.

Description

XDrawPoint uses the foreground pixel and function components of the graphics context to draw a single point into the specified drawable. XDrawPoint uses these graphics context components: function, plane_mask, foreground, subwindow_mode, clip_x_origin, clip_y_origin, and clip_mask. Use XDrawPoints to draw multiple points.

For more information, see Volume One: Chapter 6, *Drawing Graphics and Text*; and Chapter 5, *The Graphics Context*.

Errors

BadDrawable
BadGC
BadMatch

Related Commands

XDraw, XDrawArc, XDrawArcs, XDrawFilled, XDrawLine, XDrawLines, XDraw-Points, XDrawRectangle, XDrawRectangles, XDrawSegments, XCopyArea, XCopyPlane, XFillArc, XFillArcs, XFillPolygon, XFillRectangle, XFill-Rectangles, XClearArea, XClearWindow.

XDrawPoints

Name

XDrawPoints — draw multiple points.

Synopsis

```
XDrawPoints(display, drawable, gc, points, npoints, mode)
    Display *display;
    Drawable drawable;
    GC gc;
    XPoint *points;
    int npoints;
    int mode;
```

Arguments

display   Specifies a pointer to the Display structure; returned from XOpen-Display.

drawable   Specifies the drawable.

gc   Specifies the graphics context.

points   Specifies a pointer to an array of XPoint structures containing the positions of the points.

npoints   Specifies the number of points to be drawn.

mode   Specifies the coordinate mode. CoordModeOrigin treats all coordinates as relative to the origin, while CoordModePrevious treats all coordinates after the first as relative to the previous point, while the first is still relative to the origin.

Description

XDrawPoints uses the foreground pixel and function components of the graphics context to draw one or more points into the specified drawable.

XDrawPoints uses these graphics context components: function, plane_mask, foreground, subwindow_mode, clip_x_origin, clip_y_origin, and clip_mask.

For more information, see Volume One: Chapter 6, *Drawing Graphics and Text*; and Chapter 5, *The Graphics Context*.

Structures

```
typedef struct {
    short x, y;
} XPoint;
```

Errors

```
BadDrawable
BadGC
BadMatch
BadValue
```

Related Commands

XDraw, XDrawArc, XDrawArcs, XDrawFilled, XDrawLine, XDrawLines, XDraw-
Points, XDrawRectangle, XDrawRectangles, XDrawSegments, XCopyArea,
XCopyPlane, XFillArc, XFillArcs, XFillPolygon, XFillRectangle, XFill-
Rectangles, XClearArea, XClearWindow.

XDrawRectangle

Name

XDrawRectangle — draw an outline of a rectangle.

Synopsis

```
XDrawRectangle(display, drawable, gc, x, y, width, height)
    Display *display;
    Drawable drawable;
    GC gc;
    int x, y;
    unsigned int width, height;
```

Arguments

display	Specifies a pointer to the Display structure; returned from XOpenDisplay.
drawable	Specifies the drawable.
gc	Specifies the graphics context.
x y	Specify the x and y coordinates of the upper-left corner of the rectangle, relative to the drawable's origin.
width height	Specify the width and height in pixels. These dimensions define the outline of the rectangle.

XDrawRectangle(display, drawable, gc, 0, 0, 19, 11);

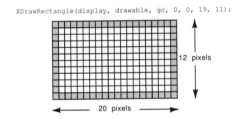

XFillRectangle(display, drawable, gc, 0, 0, 19, 11);

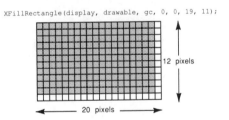

Description

XDrawRectangle draws the outline of the rectangle by using the *x* and *y* coordinates, *width* and *height*, and graphics context you specify. Specifically, XDrawRectangle uses these graphics context components: function, plane_mask, line_width, line_style, cap_style, join_style, fill_style, subwindow_mode, clip_x_origin, clip_y_origin, and clip_mask. This function also uses these graphics context mode-dependent components: foreground, background, tile, stipple, ts_x_origin, ts_y_origin, dash_offset, and dash_list.

XDrawRectangle is not affected by the tile or stipple in the GC. For the specified rectangle, no pixel is drawn more than once.

For more information, see Volume One: Chapter 6, *Drawing Graphics and Text*; and Chapter 5, *The Graphics Context*.

Structure
```
typedef struct {
    short x, y;
    unsigned short width, height;
} XRectangle;
```

Errors
```
BadDrawable
BadGC
BadMatch
```

Related Commands

XDraw, XDrawArc, XDrawArcs, XDrawFilled, XDrawLine, XDrawLines, XDraw-Point, XDrawPoints, XDrawRectangles, XDrawSegments, XCopyArea, XCopy-Plane, XFillArc, XFillArcs, XFillPolygon, XFillRectangle, XFill-Rectangles, XClearArea, XClearWindow.

XDrawRectangles

Name

XDrawRectangles — draw the outlines of multiple rectangles.

Synopsis

```
XDrawRectangles(display, drawable, gc, rectangles, nrectangles)
    Display *display;
    Drawable drawable;
    GC gc;
    XRectangle rectangles[];
    int nrectangles;
```

Arguments

display   Specifies a pointer to the Display structure; returned from XOpen-Display.

drawable   Specifies the drawable.

gc   Specifies the graphics context.

rectangles   Specifies a pointer to an array of rectangles containing position and size information.

nrectangles   Specifies the number of rectangles in the array.

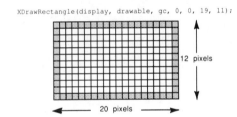

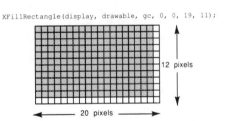

Description

XDrawRectangles draws the outlines of the specified rectangles by using the position and size values in the array of rectangles. The x and y coordinates of each rectangle are relative to the drawable's origin, and define the upper-left corner of the rectangle. This function uses these graphics context components: function, plane_mask, line_width, line_style, cap_style, join_style, fill_style, subwindow_mode, clip_x_origin, clip_y_origin, and clip_mask. XDrawRectangles also uses these graphics context mode-dependent components: foreground, background, tile, stipple, ts_x_origin, ts_y_origin, dash_offset, and dash_list.

The rectangles are drawn in the order listed. For any given rectangle, no pixel is drawn more than once. If rectangles intersect, pixels are drawn multiple times.

XDrawRectangles is not affected by tile or stipple in the GC.

For more information, see Volume One: Chapter 6, *Drawing Graphics and Text*; and Chapter 5, *The Graphics Context*.

Structures

```
typedef struct {
    short x, y;
    unsigned short width, height;
    unsigned short width, height;
} XRectangle;
```

Errors

```
BadDrawable
BadGC
BadMatch
```

Related Commands

XDraw, XDrawArc, XDrawArcs, XDrawFilled, XDrawLine, XDrawLines, XDraw-Point, XDrawPoints, XDrawRectangle, XDrawSegments, XCopyArea, XCopy-Plane, XFillArc, XFillArcs, XFillPolygon, XFillRectangle, XFill-Rectangles, XClearArea, XClearWindow.

XDrawSegments

Name

XDrawSegments — draw multiple disjoint lines.

Synopsis

```
XDrawSegments(display, drawable, gc, segments, nsegments)
    Display *display;
    Drawable drawable;
    GC gc;
    XSegment *segments;
    int nsegments;
```

Arguments

display   Specifies a pointer to the Display structure; returned from XOpen-Display.

drawable   Specifies the drawable.

gc   Specifies the graphics context.

segments   Specifies a pointer to an array of line segments.

nsegments   Specifies the number of segments in the array.

Description

XDrawSegments draws multiple line segments into the specified drawable. Each line is specified by a pair of points, so the line may be connected or disjoint.

For each segment, XDrawSegments draws a line between ($x1$, $y1$) and ($x2$, $y2$). The lines are drawn in the order listed in segments. For any given line, no pixel is drawn more than once. If lines intersect, pixels will be drawn multiple times. The lines will be drawn separately, without regard to the join_style.

XDrawSegments uses these graphics context components: function, plane_mask, line_width, line_style, cap_style, fill_style, subwindow_mode, clip_x_origin, clip_y_origin, and clip_mask. XDrawSegments also uses these graphics context mode-dependent components: foreground, background, tile, stipple, ts_x_origin, ts_y_origin, dash_offset, and dash_list.

XDrawSegments is not affected by the tile or stipple in the GC.

For more information, see Volume One: Chapter 6, *Drawing Graphics and Text*; and Chapter 5, *The Graphics Context*.

Structures

```
typedef struct {
    short x1, y1, x2, y2;
} XSegment;
```

Errors
```
BadDrawable
BadGC
BadMatch
```

Related Commands

XDraw, XDrawArc, XDrawArcs, XDrawFilled, XDrawLine, XDrawLines, XDraw-
Point, XDrawPoints, XDrawRectangle, XDrawRectangles, XCopyArea, XCopy-
Plane, XFillArc, XFillArcs, XFillPolygon, XFillRectangle, XFill-
Rectangles, XClearArea, XClearWindow.

XDrawString

Name
XDrawString — draw an 8-bit text string, foreground only.

Synopsis
```
XDrawString (display, drawable, gc, x, y, string, length)
    Display *display;
    Drawable drawable;
    GC gc;
    int x, y;
    char *string;
    int length;
```

Arguments

display   Specifies a pointer to the Display structure; returned from XOpen-Display.

drawable   Specifies the drawable.

gc   Specifies the graphics context.

x   Specify the x and y coordinates of the baseline starting position for the char-
y   acter, relative to the origin of the specified drawable.

string   Specifies the character string.

length   Specifies the number of characters in the string argument.

Description
XDrawString draws the given string into a drawable using the foreground only to draw set bits in the font. It does not affect any other pixels in the bounding box for each character.

The y coordinate defines the baseline row of pixels while the x coordinate is the point for measuring the lbearing, rbearing, and width from.

XDrawString uses these graphics context components: function, plane_mask, fill_style, font, subwindow_mode, clip_x_origin, clip_y_origin, and clip_mask. This function also uses these graphics context mode-dependent components: foreground, tile, stipple, ts_x_origin, and ts_y_origin. Each character image, as defined by the font in gc, is treated as an additional mask for a fill operation on the drawable.

For more information, see Volume One: Chapter 6, *Drawing Graphics and Text*; and Chapter 5, *The Graphics Context*.

Errors
```
BadDrawable
BadFont
BadGC
BadMatch
```

Related Commands

XQueryTextExtents, XQueryTextExtents16, XDrawImageString, XDraw-
ImageString16, XDrawString16, XDrawText, XDrawText16, XTextExtents,
XTextExtents16, XTextWidth, XTextWidth16.

Name

XDrawString16 — draw two-byte text strings.

Synopsis

```
XDrawString16 (display, drawable, gc, x, y, string, length)
    Display *display;
    Drawable drawable;
    GC gc;
    int x, y;
    XChar2b *string;
    int length;
```

Arguments

display	Specifies a pointer to the Display structure; returned from XOpen-Display.
drawable	Specifies the drawable.
gc	Specifies the graphics context.
x y	Specify the x and y coordinates of the baseline starting position for the character, relative to the origin of the specified drawable.
string	Specifies the character string. Characters are two bytes wide.
length	Specifies the number of characters in the string argument.

Description

XDrawString16 draws a string in the foreground pixel value without drawing the surrounding pixels.

The y coordinate defines the baseline row of pixels while the x coordinate is the point for measuring the lbearing, rbearing, and width from. For more information on text placement, see Volume One, Chapter 6, *Drawing Graphics and Text*.

XDrawString16 uses these graphics context components: function, plane_mask, fill_style, font, subwindow_mode, clip_x_origin, clip_y_origin, and clip_mask. This function also uses these graphics context mode-dependent components: foreground, tile, stipple, ts_x_origin, and ts_y_origin. Each character image, as defined by the font in gc, is treated as an additional mask for a fill operation on the drawable.

For more information, see Volume One: Chapter 6, *Drawing Graphics and Text*; and Chapter 5, *The Graphics Context*.

Structures

```
typedef struct {
    unsigned char byte1;
    unsigned char byte2;
} XChar2b;
```

Errors

BadDrawable
BadFont
BadGC
BadMatch

Related Commands

XQueryTextExtents, XQueryTextExtents16, XDrawImageString, XDraw-
ImageString16, XDrawString, XDrawText, XDrawText16, XTextExtents,
XTextExtents16, XTextWidth, XTextWidth16.

Name

XDrawText — draw 8-bit polytext strings.

Synopsis

```
XDrawText(display, drawable, gc, x, y, items, nitems)
    Display *display;
    Drawable drawable;
    GC gc;
    int x, y;
    XTextItem *items;
    int nitems;
```

Arguments

display   Specifies a pointer to the Display structure; returned from XOpen-Display.

drawable   Specifies the drawable.

gc   Specifies the graphics context.

x
y   Specify the x and y coordinates of the baseline starting position for the initial string, relative to the origin of the specified drawable.

items   Specifies a pointer to an array of text items.

nitems   Specifies the number of text items in the *items* array.

Description

XDrawText is capable of drawing multiple strings and changing fonts between strings. Each XTextItem structure contains a string, the number of characters in the string, the delta offset from the starting position for the string, and the font. Each text item is processed in turn. The font in each XTextItem is stored in the specified GC and used for subsequent text. If the XTextItem.font is *None*, the font in the GC is used for drawing and is not changed. Switching between fonts with different drawing directions is permitted.

The delta in each XTextItem specifies the change in horizontal position before the string is drawn. The delta is always added to the character origin and is not dependent on the draw direction of the font. For example, if x = 40, y = 20, and items[0].delta = 8, the string specified by items[0].chars would be drawn starting at x = 48, y = 20. The delta for the second string begins at the rbearing of the last character in the first string. A negative delta would tend to overlay subsequent strings on the end of the previous string.

Only the pixels selected in the font are drawn (the background member of the GC is not used).

XDrawText uses the following elements in the specified GC: function, plane_mask, fill_style, font, subwindow_mode, clip_x_origin, clip_y_origin, and clip_mask. This function also uses these graphics context mode-dependent components: foreground, tile, stipple, ts_x_origin, and ts_y_origin.

For more information, see Volume One: Chapter 6, *Drawing Graphics and Text*; and Chapter 5, *The Graphics Context*.

Structures

```
typedef struct {
    char *chars;            /* pointer to string */
    int nchars;             /* number of characters */
    int delta;              /* delta between strings */
    Font font;              /* font to print it in, None don't change */
} XTextItem;
```

Errors

```
BadDrawable
BadFont
BadGC
BadMatch
```

Related Commands

XQueryTextExtents, XQueryTextExtents16, XDrawImageString, XDraw-
ImageString16, XDrawString, XDrawString16, XDrawText16, XTextExtents,
XTextExtents16, XTextWidth, XTextWidth16.

Name

XDrawText16 — draw 16-bit polytext strings.

Synopsis

```
XDrawText16(display, drawable, gc, x, y, items, nitems)
    Display *display;
    Drawable drawable;
    GC gc;
    int x, y;
    XTextItem16 *items;
    int nitems;
```

Arguments

display	Specifies a pointer to the Display structure; returned from XOpen-Display.
drawable	Specifies the drawable.
gc	Specifies the graphics context.
x	Specify the x and y coordinates of the baseline starting position for the initial
y	string, relative to the origin of the specified drawable.
items	Specifies a pointer to an array of text items using two-byte characters.
nitems	Specifies the number of text items in the array.

Description

XDrawText16 is capable of drawing multiple strings and changing fonts between strings. Each XTextItem structure contains a string, the number of characters in the string, the delta offset from the starting position for the string, and the font. Each text item is processed in turn. The font in each XTextItem is stored in the specified GC and used for subsequent text. If the XTextItem16.font is None, the font in the GC is used for drawing and is not changed. Switching between fonts with different drawing directions is permitted.

The delta in each XTextItem specifies the change in horizontal position before the string is drawn. The delta is always added to the character origin and is not dependent on the drawing direction of the font. For example, if x = 40, y = 20, and items[0].delta = 8, the string specified by items[0].chars would be drawn starting at x = 48, y = 20. The delta for the second string begins at the rbearing of the last character in the first string. A negative delta would tend to overlay subsequent strings on the end of the previous string.

Only the pixels selected in the font are drawn (the background member of the GC is not used).

XDrawText16 uses the following elements in the specified GC: function, plane_mask, fill_style, font, subwindow_mode, clip_x_origin, clip_y_origin, and clip_mask. This function also uses these graphics context mode-dependent components: foreground, tile, stipple, ts_x_origin, and ts_y_origin.

Note that the chars member of the XTextItem16 structure is of type XChar2b, rather than of type char as it is in the XTextItem structure. For fonts defined with linear indexing rather than two-byte matrix indexing, the X server will interpret each member of the XChar2b structure as a 16-bit number that has been transmitted most significant byte first. In other words, the byte1 member of the XChar2b structure is taken as the most significant byte.

For more information, see Volume One: Chapter 6, *Drawing Graphics and Text*; and Chapter 5, *The Graphics Context*.

Structures

```
typedef struct {
    XChar2b *chars;        /* 2 byte characters */
    int nchars;            /* number of characters */
    int delta;             /* delta between strings */
    Font font;             /* font to print it in, None don't change */
} XTextItem16;

typedef struct {           /* normal 16 bit characters are two bytes */
    unsigned char byte1;
    unsigned char byte2;
} XChar2b;
```

Errors

```
BadDrawable
BadFont
BadGC
BadMatch
```

Related Commands

XQueryTextExtents, XQueryTextExtents16, XDrawImageString, XDraw-ImageString16, XDrawString, XDrawString16, XDrawText, XTextExtents, XTextExtents16, XTextWidth, XTextWidth16.

Name

XEmptyRegion — determine if a region is empty.

Synopsis

```
int XEmptyRegion(r)
    Region r;
```

Arguments

r   Specifies the region to be checked.

Description

XEmptyRegion will return True if the specified region is empty.

Structures

```
/*
 * opaque reference to Region data type.
 * user won't need contents, only pointer.
 */
typedef struct _XRegion *Region;
```

Related Commands

XXorRegion, XUnionRegion, XUnionRectWithRegion, XSubtractRegion, XShrinkRegion, XSetRegion, XRectInRegion, XPolygonRegion, XPoint-InRegion, XOffsetRegion, XIntersectRegion, XCreateRegion, XDestroy-Region, XEqualRegion, XClipBox.

Name

XEnableAccessControl — use access control list to allow or deny connection requests.

Synopsis

```
XEnableAccessControl(display)
    Display *display;
```

Arguments

display   Specifies a pointer to the Display structure; returned from XOpen-
                 Display.

Description

XEnableAccessControl instructs the server to use the host access list to determine whether access should be granted to clients seeking a connection with the server.

By default, the host access list is used. If access has not been disabled with XDisable-AccessControl or XSetAccessControl, this routine does nothing.

This routine can only be called by clients running on the same host as the server.

For more information, see Volume One, Chapter 13, *Other Programming Techniques*.

Related Commands

XAddHost, XAddHosts, XListHosts, XRemoveHost, XRemoveHosts, XDisable-AccessControl, XSetAccessControl.

Name

XEqualRegion — determine if two regions have the same size, offset, and shape.

Synopsis

```
int XEqualRegion(r1, r2)
    Region r1, r2;
```

Arguments

r1
r2   Specify the two regions you want to compare.

Description

XEqualRegion returns True if the two regions are identical; i.e., they have the same offset, size and shape.

Regions are located using an offset from a point (the *region origin*) which is common to all regions. It is up to the application to interpret the location of the region relative to a drawable.

For more information, see Volume One, Chapter 6, *Drawing Graphics and Text*.

Structures

```
/*
 * opaque reference to Regiondata type.
 * user won't need contents, only pointer.
 */
typedef struct _XRegion *Region;
```

Related Commands

XXorRegion, XUnionRegion, XUnionRectWithRegion, XSubtractRegion, XShrinkRegion, XSetRegion, XRectInRegion, XPolygonRegion, XPoint-InRegion, XOffsetRegion, XIntersectRegion, XEmptyRegion, XCreate-Region, XDestroyRegion, XClipBox.

XEventsQueued

Name

XEventsQueued — check the number of events in the event queue.

Synopsis

```
int XEventsQueued(display, mode)
    Display *display;
    int mode;
```

Arguments

display   Specifies a pointer to the Display structure, returned from XOpen-Display.

mode   Specifies whether the output buffer is flushed if there are no events in Xlib's queue. You can specify one of these constants: QueuedAlready, QueuedAfterFlush, QueuedAfterReading.

Description

XEventsQueued checks whether events are queued. If there are events in Xlib's queue, the routine returns immediately to the calling routine. Its return value is the number of events regardless of *mode*.

mode specifies what happens if no events are found on Xlib's queue.

- If *mode* is QueuedAlready, and there are no events in the queue, XEvents-Queued returns 0 (it does not flush the output buffer or attempt to read more events from the connection).

- If *mode* is QueuedAfterFlush, and there are no events in the queue, XEvents-Queued flushes the output buffer, attempts to read more events out of the application's connection, and returns the number read.

- If *mode* is QueuedAfterReading, and there are no events in the queue, XEventsQueued attempts to read more events out of the application's connection without flushing the output buffer and returns the number read.

Note that XEventsQueued always returns immediately without I/O if there are events already in the queue.

XEventsQueued with mode QueuedAfterFlush is identical in behavior to XPending. XEventsQueued with mode QueuedAlready is identical to the QLength macro (see Appendix C, *Macros*).

For more information, see Volume One, Chapter 8, *Events*.

Related Commands

XSelectInput, XSetInputFocus, XGetInputFocus, XWindowEvent, XCheck-WindowEvent, XCheckTypedEvent, XCheckTypedWindowEvent, XMaskEvent, XCheckMaskEvent, XNextEvent, XAllowEvents, XGetMotionEvents, XIfEvent, XCheckIfEvent, XPeekEvent, XPeekIfEvent, XPutBackEvent, XSynchronize, XSendEvent, QLength, XPending.

XFetchBuffer

Name
XFetchBuffer — return data from a cut buffer.

Synopsis
```
char *XFetchBuffer(display, nbytes, buffer)
    Display *display;
    int *nbytes;                /* RETURN */
    int buffer;
```

Arguments

display   Specifies a pointer to the Display structure; returned from XOpen-Display.

nbytes   Returns the number of bytes in *buffer* returned by XFetchBuffer. If there is no data in the buffer, *nbytes* is set to 0.

buffer   Specifies which buffer you want data from. Specify an integer from 0 to 7.

Description

XFetchBuffer returns data from one of the 8 buffers provided for interclient communication. If the buffer contains data, XFetchBuffer returns the number of bytes in *nbytes*, otherwise it returns NULL and sets *nbytes* to 0. The appropriate amount of storage is allocated and the pointer returned; the client must free this storage when finished with it. Note that the cut buffer does not necessarily contain text, so it may contain embedded null bytes and may not terminate with a null byte.

Selections are the preferred communication scheme.

For more information on cut buffers, see Volume One, Chapter 13, *Other Programming Techniques*.

Errors
BadValue

Related Commands
XStoreBuffer, XStoreBytes, XFetchBytes, XRotateBuffers.

XFetchBytes

Name

XFetchBytes — return data from cut buffer 0.

Synopsis

```
char *XFetchBytes(display, nbytes)
    Display *display;
    int *nbytes;                    /* RETURN */
```

Arguments

display Specifies a pointer to the Display structure; returned from XOpen-Display.

nbytes Returns the number of bytes in the string returned by XFetchBytes. If there is no data in the buffer, *nbytes* is set to 0.

Description

XFetchBytes returns data from cut buffer 0 of the 8 buffers provided for interclient communication. If the buffer contains data, XFetchBytes returns the number of bytes in *nbytes*, otherwise it returns NULL and sets *nbytes* to 0. The appropriate amount of storage is allocated and the pointer returned; the client must free this storage when finished with it by calling XFree. Note that the cut buffer does not necessarily contain text, so it may contain embedded null bytes and may not terminate with a null byte.

Use XFetchBuffer to fetch data from any specified cut buffer.

Selections are the preferred communication method.

For more information on cut buffers, see Volume One, Chapter 13, *Other Programming Techniques*.

Related Commands

XStoreBuffer, XStoreBytes, XFetchBuffer, XRotateBuffers.

XFetchName

Name

XFetchName — get a window's name (XA_WM_NAME property).

Synopsis

```
Status XFetchName(display, w, window_name)
    Display *display;
    Window w;
    char **window_name;          /* RETURN */
```

Arguments

display   Specifies a pointer to the Display structure; returned from XOpen-Display.

w   Specifies the ID of the window whose name you want a pointer set to.

window_name Returns a pointer to the window name, which will be a null-terminated string. If the XA_WM_NAME property has not been set for this window, XFetchName sets *windowname* to NULL. When finished with it, a client must free the name string using XFree.

Description

XFetchName returns the current value of the XA_WM_NAME property for the specified window. XFetchName return value is nonzero if it succeeds, and 0 if the property has not been set for the argument window.

For more information, see Volume One: Chapter 10, *Interclient Communication*; and Chapter 14, *Window Management*.

Errors

BadWindow

Related Commands

XGetClassHint, XSetClassHint, XGetSizeHints, XSetSizeHints, XGet-WMHints, XSetWMHints, XGetZoomHints, XSetZoomHints, XGetNormalHints, XSetNormalHints, XGetTransientForHint, XSetTransientForHint, XGet-IconName, XSetIconName, XStoreName, XGetIconSizes, XSetIconSizes, XSetCommand.

Name

XFillArc — fill an arc.

Synopsis

```
XFillArc(display, drawable, gc,  x, y, width, height,
        angle1, angle2)
    Display *display;
    Drawable drawable;
    GC gc;
    int x, y;
    unsigned int width, height;
    int angle1, angle2;
```

Arguments

display   Specifies a pointer to the Display structure; returned from XOpen-Display.

drawable   Specifies the drawable.

gc   Specifies the graphics context.

x   Specify the x and y coordinates of the upper-left corner of the bounding box
y   containing the arc, relative to the origin of the drawable.

width   Specify the width and height in pixels. These are the major and minor axes
height   of the arc.

angle1   Specifies the start of the arc relative to the three-o'clock position from the
                center. Angles are specified in degrees, multiplied by 64.

angle2   Specifies the path and extent of the arc relative to the start of the arc. Angles
                are specified in degrees, multiplied by 64.

Description

XFillArc fills an arc according to the arc_mode in the GC. The *x*, *y*, *width*, and *height* arguments specify the bounding box for the arc. See XDrawArc for the description of how this bounding box is used to compute the arc. Some, but not all, of the pixels drawn with XDrawArc will be drawn by XFillArc with the same arguments.

The arc forms one boundary of the area to be filled. The other boundary is determined by the arc_mode in the GC. If the arc_mode in the GC is ArcChord, the single line segment joining the endpoints of the arc is used. If ArcPieSlice, the two line segments joining the endpoints of the arc with the center point are used.

XFillArc uses these graphics context components: function, plane_mask, fill_style, arc_mode, subwindow_mode, clip_x_origin, clip_y_origin, and clip_mask. This function also uses these graphics context mode-dependent components: foreground, background, tile, stipple, ts_x_origin, and ts_y_origin.

For more information, see Volume One: Chapter 6, *Drawing Graphics and Text*; and Chapter 5, *The Graphics Context*.

Errors
```
BadDrawable
BadGC
BadMatch
```

Related Commands
XDraw, XDrawArc, XDrawArcs, XDrawFilled, XDrawLine, XDrawLines, XDraw-Point, XDrawPoints, XDrawRectangle, XDrawRectangles, XDrawSegments, XCopyArea, XCopyPlane, XFillArcs, XFillPolygon, XFillRectangle, XFill-Rectangles, XClearArea, XClearWindow.

XFillArcs

Name

XFillArcs — fill multiple arcs.

Synopsis

```
XFillArcs(display, drawable, gc, arcs, narcs)
    Display *display;
    Drawable drawable;
    GC gc;
    XArc *arcs;
    int narcs;
```

Arguments

display   Specifies a pointer to the Display structure; returned from XOpenDisplay.

drawable   Specifies the drawable.

gc   Specifies the graphics context.

arcs   Specifies a pointer to an array of arc definitions.

narcs   Specifies the number of arcs in the array.

Description

For each arc, XFillArcs fills the region closed by the specified arc and one or two line segments, depending on the arc_mode specified in the GC. It does not draw the complete outlines of the arcs, but some pixels may overlap.

The arc forms one boundary of the area to be filled. The other boundary is determined by the arc_mode in the GC. If the arc_mode in the GC is ArcChord, the single line segment joining the endpoints of the arc is used. If ArcPieSlice, the two line segments joining the endpoints of the arc with the center point are used. The arcs are filled in the order listed in the array. For any given arc, no pixel is drawn more than once. If regions intersect, pixels will be drawn multiple times.

XFillArcs use these graphics context components: function, plane_mask, fill_style, arc_mode, subwindow_mode, clip_x_origin, clip_y_origin, and clip_mask. This function also uses these graphics context mode-dependent components: foreground, background, tile, stipple, ts_x_origin, and ts_y_origin.

For more information, see Volume One: Chapter 6, *Drawing Graphics and Text*; and Chapter 5, *The Graphics Context*.

Structures

```
typedef struct {
    short x, y;
    unsigned short width, height;
    unsigned short width, height;
    short angle1, angle2;               /*  Degrees * 64  */
} XArc;
```

Errors
```
BadDrawable
BadGC
BadMatch
```

Related Commands

XDraw, XDrawArc, XDrawArcs, XDrawFilled, XDrawLine, XDrawLines, XDraw-
Point, XDrawPoints, XDrawRectangle, XDrawRectangles, XDrawSegments,
XCopyArea, XCopyPlane, XFillArc, XFillPolygon, XFillRectangle, XFill-
Rectangles, XClearArea, XClearWindow.

Name

XFillPolygon — fill a polygon.

Synopsis

```
XFillPolygon(display, drawable, gc, points, npoints, shape, mode)
    Display *display;
    Drawable drawable;
    GC gc;
    XPoint *points;
    int npoints;
    int shape;
    int mode;
```

Arguments

display	Specifies a pointer to the Display structure; returned from XOpen-Display.
drawable	Specifies the drawable.
gc	Specifies the graphics context.
points	Specifies a pointer to an array of points.
npoints	Specifies the number of points in the array.
shape	Specifies an argument that helps the server to improve performance. Pass the last constant in this list that is valid for the polygon to be filled: Complex, Nonconvex, or Convex.
mode	Specifies the coordinate mode. Pass either CoordModeOrigin or CoordModePrevious.

Description

XFillPolygon fills the region closed by the specified path. Some but not all of the path itself will be drawn. The path is closed automatically if the last point in the list does not coincide with the first point. No pixel of the region is drawn more than once.

The *mode* argument affects the interpretation of the points that define the polygon:

- CoordModeOrigin indicates that all points are relative to the drawable's origin.

- CoordModePrevious indicates that all points after the first are relative to the previous point. (The first point is always relative to the drawable's origin.)

The *shape* argument allows the fill routine to optimize its performance given tips on the configuration of the area.

- Complex indicates the path may self-intersect. The fill_rule of the GC must be consulted to determine which areas are filled. See Volume One, Chapter 5, *The Graphics Context*, for a discussion of the fill rules EvenOddRule and WindingRule.

- Nonconvex indicates the path does not self-intersect, but the shape is not wholly convex. If known by the client, specifying Nonconvex instead of Complex may improve performance. If you specify Nonconvex for a self-intersecting path, the graphics results are undefined.

- Convex indicates the path is wholly convex. This can improve performance even more, but if the path is not convex, the graphics results are undefined.

XFillPolygon uses these graphics context components when filling the polygon area: function, plane_mask, fill_style, fill_rule, subwindow_mode, clip_ x_origin, clip_y_origin, and clip_mask. This function also uses these mode-dependent components of the GC: foreground, background, tile, stipple, ts_x_origin, and ts_y_origin.

For more information, see Volume One: Chapter 6, *Drawing Graphics and Text*; and Chapter 5, *The Graphics Context*.

Structures
```
typedef struct {
    short x, y;
} XPoint;
```

Errors
```
BadDrawable
BadGC
BadMatch
BadValue
```

Related Commands

XDraw, XDrawArc, XDrawArcs, XDrawFilled, XDrawLine, XDrawLines, XDraw-Point, XDrawPoints, XDrawRectangle, XDrawRectangles, XDrawSegments, XCopyArea, XCopyPlane, XFillArc, XFillArcs, XFillRectangle, XFill-Rectangles, XClearArea, XClearWindow.

XFillRectangle

Name

XFillRectangle — fill a rectangular area.

Synopsis

```
XFillRectangle(display, drawable, gc, x, y, width, height)
    Display *display;
    Drawable drawable;
    GC gc;
    int x, y;
    unsigned int width, height;
```

Arguments

display   Specifies a pointer to the Display structure; returned from XOpenDisplay.

drawable   Specifies the drawable.

gc   /   Specifies the graphics context.

x   Specify the x and y coordinates of the upper-left corner of the rectangle, rela-
y   tive to the origin of the drawable.

width   Specify the dimensions in pixels of the rectangle to be filled.
height

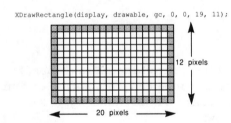

XDrawRectangle(display, drawable, gc, 0, 0, 19, 11);

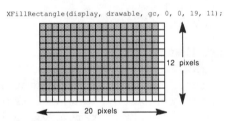

XFillRectangle(display, drawable, gc, 0, 0, 19, 11);

Description

XFillRectangle fills the rectangular area in the specified drawable using the x and y coordinates, width and height dimensions, and graphics context you specify. XFill-Rectangle draws some but not all of the path drawn by XDrawRectangle with the same arguments.

XFillRectangle uses these graphics context components: function, plane_mask, fill_style, subwindow_mode, clip_x_origin, clip_y_origin, and clip_mask. This function also uses these graphics context components depending on the fill_style: foreground, background tile, stipple, ts_x_origin, and ts_y_origin.

For more information, see Volume One: Chapter 6, *Drawing Graphics and Text*; and Chapter 5, *The Graphics Context*.

Errors
BadDrawable
BadGC
BadMatch

Related Commands
XDraw, XDrawArc, XDrawArcs, XDrawFilled, XDrawLine, XDrawLines, XDraw-
Point, XDrawPoints, XDrawRectangle, XDrawRectangles, XDrawSegments,
XCopyArea, XCopyPlane, XFillArc, XFillArcs, XFillPolygon, XFill-
Rectangles, XClearArea, XClearWindow.

XFillRectangles

Name

XFillRectangles — fill multiple rectangular areas.

Synopsis

```
XFillRectangles(display, drawable, gc, rectangles, nrectangles)
    Display *display;
    Drawable drawable;
    GC gc;
    XRectangle *rectangles;
    int nrectangles;
```

Arguments

display   Specifies a pointer to the Display structure; returned from XOpen-
                Display.

drawable   Specifies the drawable.

gc   Specifies the graphics context.

rectangles   Specifies a pointer to an array of rectangles.

nrectangles   Specifies the number of rectangles in the array.

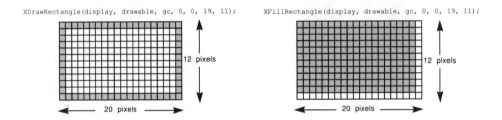

Description

XFillRectangles fills multiple rectangular areas in the specified drawable using the
graphics context.

The x and y coordinates of each rectangle are relative to the drawable's origin, and define the
upper left corner of the rectangle. The rectangles are drawn in the order listed. For any given
rectangle, no pixel is drawn more than once. If rectangles intersect, the intersecting pixels will
be drawn multiple times.

XFillRectangles uses these graphics context components: function, plane_mask,
fill_style, subwindow_mode, clip_x_origin, clip_y_origin, and clip_
mask. This function also uses these graphics context components depending on the fill_
style: foreground, background, tile, stipple, ts_x_origin, and ts_y_
origin.

For more information, see Volume One: Chapter 6, *Drawing Graphics and Text*; and Chapter 5, *The Graphics Context*.

Structures

```
typedef struct {
    short x, y;
    unsigned short width, height;
    unsigned short width, height;
} XRectangle;
```

Errors

```
BadDrawable
BadGC
BadMatch
```

Related Commands

XDraw, XDrawArc, XDrawArcs, XDrawFilled, XDrawLine, XDrawLines, XDraw-
Point, XDrawPoints, XDrawRectangle, XDrawRectangles, XDrawSegments,
XCopyArea, XCopyPlane, XFillArc, XFillArcs, XFillPolygon, XFill-
Rectangle, XFillRectangles, XClearArea, XClearWindow.

Name

XFindContext — get data from the context manager (not graphics context).

Synopsis

```
int XFindContext(display, w, context, data)
    Display *display;
    Window w;
    XContext context;
    caddr_t *data;                /* RETURN */
```

Arguments

display   Specifies a pointer to the Display structure; returned from XOpen-Display.

w   Specifies the window with which the data is associated.

context   Specifies the context type to which the data corresponds.

data   Returns the data.

Description

XFindContext gets data that has been assigned to the specified window and context ID. The context manager is used to associate data with windows for use within an application.

This application should have called XUniqueContext to get a unique ID, and then XSave-Context to save the data into the array. The meaning of the data is indicated by the context ID, but is completely up to the client.

XFindContext returns XCNOENT (a nonzero error code) if the context could not be found and zero (0) otherwise.

For more information on the context manager, see Volume One, Chapter 13, *Other Programming Techniques*.

Structures

```
typedef int XContext
```

Related Commands

XDeleteContext, XSaveContext, XUniqueContext.

Name

XFlush — flush the output buffer (display all queued requests).

Synopsis

```
XFlush (display)
    Display *display;
```

Arguments

display Specifies a pointer to the `Display` structure; returned from `XOpen-Display`.

Description

`XFlush` sends to the display (''flushes'') all output requests that have been buffered but not yet sent.

Flushing is done automatically when input is read if no matching events are in Xlib's queue (with `XPending`, `XNextEvent`, or `XWindowEvent`), or when a call is made that gets information from the server (such as `XQueryPointer`, `XGetFontInfo`) so `XFlush` is seldom needed. It is used when the buffer must be flushed before any of these calls are reached.

For more information, see Volume One: Chapter 2, *X Concepts*; and Chapter 3, *Basic Window Program*.

Related Commands

XSync

XForceScreenSaver

Name
XForceScreenSaver — turn the screen saver on or off.

Synopsis
```
XForceScreenSaver(display, mode)
    Display *display;
    int mode;
```

Arguments
display   Specifies a pointer to the Display structure; returned from XOpen-
               Display.

mode   Specifies whether the screen saver is active or reset. The possible modes
               are: ScreenSaverActive or ScreenSaverReset.

Description
XForceScreenSaver resets or activates the screen saver.

If the specified mode is ScreenSaverActive and the screen saver currently is disabled,
the screen saver is activated, even if the screen saver had been disabled by calling XSet-
ScreenSaver with a timeout of zero (0). This means that the screen may go blank or have
some random change take place to save the phosphors.

If the specified mode is ScreenSaverReset and the screen saver currently is enabled, the
screen is returned to normal, the screen saver is deactivated and the activation timer is reset to
its initial state (as if device input had been received). Expose events may be generated on all
visible windows if the server cannot save the entire screen contents.

For more information on the screen saver, see Volume One, Chapter 13, *Other Programming
Techniques*.

Errors
BadValue

Related Commands
XActivateScreenSaver, XResetScreenSaver, XGetScreenSaver, XSet-
ScreenSaver.

XFree

Name

XFree — free specified in-memory data created by an Xlib function.

Synopsis

```
XFree(data)
    caddr_t data;
```

Arguments

data   Specifies a pointer to the data that is to be freed.

Description

XFree is a general purpose routine for freeing data allocated by Xlib calls.

Related Commands

XOpenDisplay, XCloseDisplay, XNoOp, DefaultScreen.

XFreeColormap

Name

XFreeColormap — delete a colormap and install the default colormap.

Synopsis

```
XFreeColormap(display, cmap)
    Display *display;
    Colormap cmap;
```

Arguments

display   Specifies a pointer to the Display structure; returned from XOpen-Display.

cmap   Specifies the colormap to delete.

Description

XFreeColormap destroys the specified colormap, unless it is the default colormap for a screen. That is, it not only uninstalls *cmap* from the hardware colormap if it is installed, but also frees the associated memory including the colormap ID.

XFreeColormap performs the following processing:

- If *cmap* is an installed map for a screen, it uninstalls the colormap and installs the default if not already installed.

- If *cmap* is defined as the colormap attribute for a window (by XCreateWindow or XChangeWindowAttributes), it changes the colormap associated with the window to the constant None, generates a ColormapNotify event, and frees the colormap. The colors displayed with a colormap of None are server-dependent, since the default colormap is normally used.

For more information, see Volume One, Chapter 7, *Color*.

Errors

BadColor

Related Commands

XCopyColormapAndFree, XCreateColormap, XGetStandardColormap, XInstallColormap, XUninstallColormap, XSetStandardColormap, XList-InstalledColormaps, XSetWindowColormap, DefaultColormap, Display-Cells.

XFreeColors

Name

XFreeColors — free colormap cells or planes.

Synopsis

```
XFreeColors(display, cmap, pixels, npixels, planes)
    Display *display;
    Colormap cmap;
    unsigned long pixels[];
    int npixels;
    unsigned long planes;
```

Arguments

display Specifies a pointer to the Display structure; returned from XOpen-Display.

cmap Specifies the colormap.

pixels Specifies an array of pixel values. These pixel values map to the cells in the specified colormap.

npixels Specifies the number of pixels.

planes Specifies the planes you want to free.

Description

XFreeColors frees the cells whose values are computed by ORing together subsets of the *planes* argument with each pixel value in the *pixels* array.

If the cells are read/write, they become available for reuse, unless they were allocated with XAllocColorPlanes, in which case all the related pixels may need to be freed before any become available.

If the cells were read-only, they become available only if this is the last client to have allocated those shared cells.

For more information, see Volume One, Chapter 7, *Color*.

Errors

BadAccess A colorcell allocated by client (either unallocated or allocated by another client).

BadColor

BadValue A pixel value is not a valid index into *cmap*.

Note: if more than one pixel value is in error, the one reported is arbitrary.

Related Commands

XAllocColorCells, XAllocColorPlanes, XAllocColor, XAllocNamedColor, XLookupColor, XParseColor, XQueryColor, XQueryColors, XStoreColor, XStoreColors, XStoreNamedColor, BlackPixel, WhitePixel.

Name

XFreeCursor — destroy a cursor.

Synopsis

```
XFreeCursor(display, cursor)
    Display *display;
    Cursor cursor;
```

Arguments

display   Specifies a pointer to the Display structure; returned from XOpen-Display.

cursor   Specifies the ID of the cursor to be affected.

Description

XFreeCursor deletes the association between the cursor ID and the specified cursor. The cursor storage is freed when all other clients have freed it. Windows with their cursor attribute set to this cursor will be changed to None (which implies CopyFromParent). The specified cursor ID should not be referred to again.

Errors

BadCursor

Related Commands

XDefineCursor, XUndefineCursor, XCreateFontCursor, XCreateGlyph-Cursor, XCreatePixmapCursor, XRecolorCursor, XQueryBestCursor, XQueryBestSize.

Name

XFreeExtensionList — free memory allocated for a list of installed extensions to X.

Synopsis

```
XFreeExtensionList(list)
    char **list;
```

Arguments

list   Specifies a pointer to the list of extensions returned from XList-
                Extensions.

Description

XFreeExtensionList frees the memory allocated by XListExtensions.

For more information, see Volume One, Chapter 13, *Other Programming Techniques.*

Related Commands

XListExtensions, XQueryExtension.

XFreeFont

Name

XFreeFont — unload a font and free storage for the font structure.

Synopsis

```
XFreeFont(display, font_struct)
    Display *display;
    XFontStruct *font_struct;
```

Arguments

display   Specifies a pointer to the Display structure; returned from XOpen-Display.

font_struct Specifies the storage associated with the font.

Description

XFreeFont frees the memory allocated for the *font_struct* font information structure (XFontStruct) filled by XQueryFont or XLoadQueryFont. XFreeFont frees all storage associated with the *font_struct* argument. Neither the data nor the font should be referenced again.

The font itself is unloaded if no other client has loaded it.

For more information, see Volume One, Chapter 6, *Drawing Graphics and Text*.

Structures

```
typedef struct {
    XExtData *ext_data;               /* hook for extension to hang data */
    Font fid;                         /* Font ID for this font */
    unsigned direction;               /* hint about direction the font is painted */
    unsigned min_char_or_byte2;       /* first character */
    unsigned max_char_or_byte2;       /* last character */
    unsigned min_byte1;               /* first row that exists */
    unsigned max_byte1;               /* last row that exists */
    Bool all_chars_exist;             /* flag if all characters have nonzero size*/
    unsigned default_char;            /* char to print for undefined character */
    int n_properties;                 /* how many properties there are */
    XFontProp *properties;            /* pointer to array of additional properties*/
    XCharStruct min_bounds;           /* minimum bounds over all existing char*/
    XCharStruct max_bounds;           /* minimum bounds over all existing char*/
    XCharStruct *per_char;            /* first_char to last_char information */
    int ascent;                       /* logical extent above baseline for spacing */
    int descent;                      /* logical descent below baseline for spacing */
} XFontStruct;
```

Errors

BadFont

Related Commands

XLoadFont, XLoadQueryFont, XFreeFontInfo, XListFonts, XListFontsWith-Info, XFreeFontNames, XFreeFontPath, XGetFontPath, XQueryFont, XSet-Font, XSetFontPath, XUnloadFont, XGetFontProperty, XCreateFontCursor.

XFreeFontInfo

Name

XFreeFontInfo — free multiple font information arrays.

Synopsis

```
XFreeFontInfo(names, info, actual_count)
    char **names;
    XFontStruct *info;
    int actual_count;
```

Arguments

names   Specifies a pointer to the list of font names that were returned by XList-FontsWithInfo.

info   Specifies a pointer to the list of font information that was returned by XListFontWithInfo.

actual_count
                Specifies the number of matched font names returned by XListFontWith-Info.

Description

XFreeFontInfo frees the list of font information structures allocated by XListFonts-WithInfo. It does not unload the specified fonts themselves.

Structures

```
typedef struct {
    XExtData *ext_data;          /* hook for extension to hang data */
    Font fid;                    /* Font ID for this font */
    unsigned direction;          /* hint about direction the font is painted */
    unsigned min_char_or_byte2;  /* first character */
    unsigned max_char_or_byte2;  /* last character */
    unsigned min_byte1;          /* first row that exists */
    unsigned max_byte1;          /* last row that exists */
    Bool all_chars_exist;        /* flag if all characters have nonzero size*/
    unsigned default_char;       /* char to print for undefined character */
    int n_properties;            /* how many properties there are */
    XFontProp *properties;       /* pointer to array of additional properties*/
    XCharStruct min_bounds;      /* minimum bounds over all existing char*/
    XCharStruct max_bounds;      /* minimum bounds over all existing char*/
    XCharStruct *per_char;       /* first_char to last_char information */
    int ascent;                  /* logical extent above baseline for spacing */
    int descent;                 /* logical descent below baseline for spacing */
} XFontStruct;
```

Related Commands

XLoadFont, XLoadQueryFont, XFreeFont, XListFonts, XListFontsWithInfo, XFreeFontNames, XGetFontPath, XQueryFont, XSetFont, XSetFontPath, XUnloadFont, XGetFontProperty, XCreateFontCursor.

Name

XFreeFontNames — free the font name array.

Synopsis

```
XFreeFontNames (list)
    char *list[];
```

Arguments

list   Specifies the array of font name strings to be freed.

Description

XFreeFontNames frees the array of strings returned by XListFonts.

Related Commands

XLoadFont, XLoadQueryFont, XFreeFont, XFreeFontInfo, XListFonts, XListFontsWithInfo, XFreeFontPath, XGetFontPath, XQueryFont, XSetFont, XSetFontPath, XUnloadFont, XGetFontProperty, XCreateFontCursor.

XFreeFontPath

Name

XFreeFontPath — free the memory allocated by XGetFontPath.

Synopsis

```
XFreeFontPath(list)
    char **list;
```

Arguments

list   Specifies an array of strings allocated by XGetFontPath.

Description

XFreeFontPath frees the data used by the array of pathnames returned by XGetFont-Path.

For more information, see Volume One, Chapter 6, *Drawing Graphics and Text.*

Related Commands

XLoadFont, XLoadQueryFont, XFreeFont, XFreeFontInfo, XListFonts, XListFontsWithInfo, XFreeFontNames, XGetFontPath, XQueryFont, XSet-Font, XSetFontPath, XUnloadFont, XGetFontProperty, XCreateFontCursor.

Name

XFreeGC — free a graphics context.

Synopsis

```
XFreeGC(display, gc)
    Display *display;
    GC gc;
```

Arguments

display   Specifies a pointer to the Display structure; returned from XOpen-
               Display.

gc   Specifies the graphics context to be freed.

Description

XFreeGC frees all memory associated with a graphics context, and removes the GC from the server and display hardware.

For more information, see Volume One, Chapter 5, *The Graphics Context.*

Errors

BadGC

Related Commands

XChangeGC, XCopyGC, XCreateGC, XGContextFromGC, XSetStipple, XSet-
TSOrigin, XSetPlaneMask, XSetDashes, XSetLineAttributes, XSetFill-
Rule, XSetFillStyle, XSetForeground, XSetBackground, XSetFunction,
XSetGraphicsExposures, XSetArcMode, XSetClipMask, XSetClipOrigin,
XSetClipRectangles, XSetState, XSetSubwindowMode, DefaultGC.

XFreeModifiermap

Name

XFreeModifiermap — destroy and free a keyboard modifier mapping structure.

Synopsis

```
XFreeModifiermap(modmap)
     XModifierKeymap *modmap;
```

Arguments

modmap   Specifies a pointer to the XModifierKeymap structure to be freed.

Description

XFreeModifiermap frees the specified XModifierKeymap structure.

For more information, see Volume One, Chapter 9, *The Keyboard and Pointer*.

Structures

```
typedef struct {
    int max_keypermod;    /* server's max number of keys per modifier */
    KeyCode *modifiermap; /* an 8 by max_keypermod array of
                           * keycodes to be used as modifiers */

} XModifierKeymap;
```

Related Commands

XDeleteModifiermapEntry, XInsertModifiermapEntry, XKeycodeToKeysym,
XKeysymToKeycode, XKeysymToString, XNewModifierMap, XQueryKeymap,
XStringToKeysym, XLookupKeysym, XRebindKeySym, XGetKeyboardMapping,
XChangeKeyboardMapping, XRefreshKeyboardMapping, XLookupString,
XSetModifierMapping, XGetModifierMapping.

XFreePixmap

Name

XFreePixmap — free a pixmap ID.

Synopsis

```
XFreePixmap(display, pixmap)
    Display *display;
    Pixmap pixmap;
```

Arguments

display   Specifies a pointer to the Display structure; returned from XOpen-
            Display.

pixmap   Specifies the pixmap whose ID should be freed.

Description

XFreePixmap disassociates a pixmap ID from its resource. If no other client has an ID for
that resource, it is freed. The Pixmap should never be referenced again by this client. If it
is, the ID will be unknown and a BadPixmap error will result.

Errors

BadPixmap

Related Commands

XSetTile, XQueryBestTile, XSetWindowBorderPixmap, XSetWindow-
BackgroundPixmap, XCreatePixmap, XCreatePixmapFromBitmapData,
XQueryBestSize, XQueryBestStipple, XWriteBitmapFile, XReadBitmap-
File, XCreateBitmapFromData.

Name

XGContextFromGC — obtain the GContext (resource ID) associated with the specified graphics context.

Synopsis

```
GContext XGContextFromGC(gc)
    GC gc;
```

Arguments

gc   Specifies the graphics context of the desired resource ID.

Description

XGContextFromGC extracts the resource ID from the GC structure. Using the *gc* argument, *gc->gid* does the same thing, except that applications shouldn't reference members of the *gc* structure directly.

Related Commands

XChangeGC, XCopyGC, XCreateGC, XFreeGC, XSetStipple, XSetTSOrigin, XSetPlaneMask, XSetDashes, XSetLineAttributes, XSetFillRule, XSetFillStyle, XSetForeground, XSetBackground, XSetFunction, XSetGraphicsExposures, XSetArcMode, XSetClipMask, XSetClipOrigin, XSetClipRectangles, XSetState, XSetSubwindowMode, DefaultGC.

XGeometry

Name

XGeometry — calculate window geometry given user geometry string and default geometry.

Synopsis

```
int XGeometry(display, screen, user_geom, default_geom, bwidth,
fwidth, fheight, xadder, yadder, x, y, width, height)
    Display *display;
    int screen;
    char *user_geom, *default_geom;
    unsigned int bwidth;
    unsigned int fwidth, fheight;
    int xadder, yadder;
    int *x, *y, *width, *height;/* RETURN */
```

Arguments

display	Specifies a pointer to the `Display` structure; returned from `XOpen-Display`.
screen	Specifies which screen the window is on.
user_geom	Specifies the user or program supplied geometry string, perhaps incomplete.
default_geom	Specifies the default geometry string and must be complete.
bwidth	Specifies the border width.
fheight *fwidth*	Specify the font height and width in pixels (increment size).
xadder *yadder*	Specify additional interior padding in pixels needed in the window.
width *height*	Return the window dimensions in pixels.
x *y*	Return the user-specified or default coordinates of the window.

Description

XGeometry returns the position and size of a window given a user-supplied geometry (allowed to be partial) and a default geometry. Each user-supplied specification is copied into the appropriate returned argument, unless it is not present, in which case the default specification is used. The default geometry should be complete while the user-supplied one may not be.

XGeometry is useful for processing command line options and user preferences. These geometry strings are of the form:

```
=<width>x<height>{+-}<xoffset>{+-}<yoffset>
```

The "=" at the beginning of the string is now optional. (Items enclosed in <> are integers, and items enclosed in { } are a set from which one item is to be chosen. Note that the brackets should not appear in the actual string.)

The XGeometry return value is a bitmask that indicates which values were present in *user_geom*. This bitmask is composed of the exclusive OR of the symbols XValue, YValue, WidthValue, HeightValue, XNegative, or YNegative.

If the function returns either XValue or YValue, you should place the window at the requested position. The border width (*bwidth*), size of the width and height increments (typically *fwidth* and *fheight*), and any additional interior space (*xadder* and *yadder*) are passed in to make it easy to compute the resulting size.

Related Commands

XParseGeometry, XTranslateCoordinates.

XGetAtomName

Name

XGetAtomName — get a name for a given atom.

Synopsis

```
char *XGetAtomName(display, atom)
    Display *display;
    Atom atom;
```

Arguments

display   Specifies a pointer to the Display structure; returned from XOpen-Display.

atom   Specifies the atom whose string name you want returned.

Description

An atom is a symbol (actually a number) identifying a property. XGetAtomName returns a string version of the atom name. If the specified atom is not defined, XGetAtomName returns NULL. XA_WM_CLASS (a symbol) is returned as "XA_WM_CLASS" (a string).

XInternAtom performs the inverse function. To free the resulting string, call XFree.

Errors

BadAtom

Related Commands

XSetStandardProperties, XGetFontProperty, XRotateWindowProperties, XDeleteProperty, XChangeProperty, XGetWindowProperty, XList-Properties, XInternAtom.

Name

XGetClassHint — get the XA_WM_CLASS property of a window.

Synopsis

```
Status XGetClassHint(display, w, class_hints)
    Display *display;
    Window w;
    XClassHint *class_hints;   /* RETURN */
```

Arguments

display Specifies a pointer to the Display structure; returned from XOpen-Display.

w   Specifies the ID of the window for which the property is desired.

class_hints Returns the XClassHints structure.

Description

XGetClassHint obtains the XA_WM_CLASS property for the specified window.

XGetClassHint returns a Status of 0 on failure, nonzero on success.

The XClassHint structure returned contains res_class, which is the name of the client such as "emacs", and res_name, which is the first of the following that applies:

- command line option (*–rn name*)

- a specific environment variable (e.g., RESOURCE_NAME)

- the trailing component of argv[0] (after the last /)

To free res_name and res_class when finished with the strings, use XFree.

For more information on using hints, see Volume One, Chapter 10, *Interclient Communication*.

Structures

```
typedef struct {
    char *res_name;
    char *res_class;
} XClassHint;
```

Errors

BadWindow

Related Commands

XSetClassHint, XGetSizeHints, XSetSizeHints, XGetWMHints, XSet-WMHints, XGetZoomHints, XSetZoomHints, XGetNormalHints, XSetNormal-Hints, XGetTransientForHint, XSetTransientForHint, XFetchName, XGet-IconName, XSetIconName, XStoreName, XGetIconSizes, XSetIconSizes, XSetCommand.

Name

XGetDefault — scan the user preferences for program name and options.

Synopsis

```
char *XGetDefault (display, program, option)
    Display *display;
    char *program;
    char *option;
```

Arguments

display   Specifies a pointer to the Display structure; returned from XOpenDisplay.

program   Specifies the program name to be looked for in the user's resource database. The program name is usually argv [0], the first argument on the UNIX command line.

option   Specifies the option name or keyword. Lines containing both the *program* name and the *option* name will be matched.

Description

XGetDefault returns a character string containing the user's default value for the specified *program* name and *option* name. XGetDefault returns NULL if no key can be found that matches *option* and *program*. For a description of the matching rules, see XrmGet-Resource.

The strings returned by XGetDefault are owned by Xlib and should not be modified or freed by the client.

Lines in the user's resource database look like this:

```
xterm.foreground:       #c0c0ff
xterm.geometry:         =81x28
xterm.saveLines:        256
xterm.font:             8x13
xterm.keyMapFile:       /usr/black/.keymap
xterm.activeIcon:       on
xmh.header.font         9x15
```

The portion on the left is known as a key; the portion on the right is the value. Upper or lower case is important in keys. In some programs the standard is to capitalize only the second and successive words in each option, if any. In others, the first word is also capitalized.

Defaults are usually loaded into the XA_RESOURCE_MANAGER property on the root window at login. If no such property exists, a resource file in the user's home directory is loaded. On a UNIX system, this file is *$HOME/.Xdefaults*. After loading these defaults, XGetDefault merges additional defaults specified by the XENVIRONMENT environment variable. If XENVIRONMENT is defined, it contains a full path name for the additional resource file. If XENVIRONMENT is not defined, XGetDefault looks for *$HOME/.Xdefaults*-name, where *name* specifies the name of the machine on which the application is running.

The first invocation of XGetDefault reads the defaults into memory so that subsequent requests are fast. Therefore, changes to the defaults files from the program will not be felt until the next invocation.

For more information, see Volume One, Chapter 11, *Managing User Preferences.*

Related Commands

XAutoRepeatOff, XAutoRepeatOn, XBell, XGetKeyboardControl, XChange-
KeyboardControl, XGetPointerControl.

Name

XGetErrorDatabaseText — obtain error messages from the error database.

Synopsis

```
XGetErrorDatabaseText (display, name, message,
        default_string, buffer, length)
    Display display;
    char *name, *message;
    char *default_string;
    char *buffer;                    /* RETURN */
    int length;
```

Arguments

display   Specifies a pointer to the `Display` structure; returned from `XOpenDisplay`.

name   Specifies the name of the application.

message   Specifies the type of the error message. One of `XProtoError`, `Xlib-Message`, or `XRequestMajor` (see Description below).

default_string
    Specifies the default error message.

buffer   Returns the error description.

length   Specifies the size of the return buffer.

Description

`XGetErrorDatabaseText` returns a message from the error message database. Given *name* and *message* as keys, `XGetErrorDatabaseText` uses the resource manager to look up a string and returns it in the buffer argument. Xlib uses this function internally to look up its error messages. On a UNIX system, the error message database is */usr/lib/Xerror-DB*.

The *name* argument should generally be the name of your application. The *message* argument should indicate which type of error message you want. Three predefined *message* types are used by Xlib to report errors:

- `XProtoError`
  The protocol error number is used as a string for the message argument.

- `XlibMessage`
  These are the message strings that are used internally by the library.

- `XRequestMajor`
  The major request protocol number is used for the message argument.

If no string is found in the error database, `XGetErrorDatabaseText` returns the default_string that you specify to the buffer.

The string in *buffer* will be of length *length*.

For more information, see Volume One, Chapter 3, *Basic Window Program.*

Related Commands

`XDisplayName, XGetErrorText, XSetErrorHandler, XSetIOErrorHandler, XSynchronize, XSetAfterFunction.`

Name

XGetErrorText — obtain a description of error code.

Synopsis

```
XGetErrorText(display, code, buffer, length)
    Display *display;
    int code;
    char *buffer;                    /* RETURN */
    int length;
```

Arguments

display   Specifies a pointer to the Display structure; returned from XOpen-
            Display.

code   Specifies the error code for which you want to obtain a description.

buffer   Returns a pointer to the error description text.

length   Specifies the size of the buffer.

Description

XGetErrorText obtains textual descriptions of errors. XGetErrorText returns a pointer
to a null-terminated string describing the specified error code with length *length*. This
string is copied from static data and therefore may be freed. This routine allows extensions to
the Xlib library to define their own error codes and error strings, which can be accessed easily.

For more information, see Volume One, Chapter 3, *Basic Window Program.*

Related Commands

XDisplayName, XGetErrorDatabaseText, XSetErrorHandler, XSetIOError-
Handler, XSynchronize, XSetAfterFunction.

Name

XGetFontPath — get the current font search path.

Synopsis

```
char **XGetFontPath(display, npaths)
    Display *display;
    int *npaths;                    /* RETURN number of elements */
```

Arguments

display   Specifies a pointer to the `Display` structure; returned from `XOpen-Display`.

npaths   Returns the number of strings in the font path array.

Description

`XGetFontPath` allocates and returns an array of strings containing the search path for fonts. The data in the font path should be freed when no longer needed.

Related Commands

`XLoadFont`, `XLoadQueryFont`, `XFreeFont`, `XFreeFontInfo`, `XListFonts`, `XListFontsWithInfo`, `XFreeFontNames`, `XFreeFontPath`, `XQueryFont`, `XSet-Font`, `XSetFontPath`, `XUnloadFont`, `XGetFontProperty`, `XCreateFontCursor`.

XGetFontProperty

Name

XGetFontProperty — get a font property given its atom.

Synopsis

```
Bool XGetFontProperty(font_struct, atom, value)
    XFontStruct *font_struct;
    Atom atom;
    unsigned long *value;        /* RETURN */
```

Arguments

font_struct Specifies the storage associated with the font.

atom   Specifies the atom associated with the property name you want returned.

value   Returns the value of the font property.

Description

XGetFontProperty returns the value of the specified font property, given the atom for that property. The function returns 0 if the atom was not defined, or 1 if was defined.

There are a set of predefined atoms for font properties which can be found in *<X11/Xatom.h>*. These atoms are listed and described in Volume One, Chapter 6, *Drawing Graphics and Text*. This set contains the standard properties associated with a font. The predefined font properties are likely but not guaranteed to be present on any given server.

Structures

```
typedef struct {
    XExtData *ext_data;              /* hook for extension to hang data */
    Font fid;                        /* Font ID for this font */
    unsigned direction;              /* hint about direction the font is painted */
    unsigned min_char_or_byte2;      /* first character */
    unsigned max_char_or_byte2;      /* last character */
    unsigned min_byte1;              /* first row that exists */
    unsigned max_byte1;              /* last row that exists */
    Bool all_chars_exist;            /* flag if all characters have nonzero size*/
    unsigned default_char;           /* char to print for undefined character */
    int n_properties;                /* how many properties there are */
    XFontProp *properties;           /* pointer to array of additional properties*/
    XCharStruct min_bounds;          /* minimum bounds over all existing char*/
    XCharStruct max_bounds;          /* minimum bounds over all existing char*/
    XCharStruct *per_char;           /* first_char to last_char information */
    int ascent;                      /* logical extent above baseline for spacing */
    int descent;                     /* logical descent below baseline for spacing */
} XFontStruct;
```

Related Commands

XSetStandardProperties, XRotateWindowProperties, XDeleteProperty, XChangeProperty, XGetWindowProperty, XListProperties, XGetAtomName, XInternAtom.

XGetGeometry

Name
XGetGeometry — obtain the current geometry of drawable.

Synopsis
```
Status XGetGeometry(display, drawable, root, x, y,
        width, height, border_width, depth)
    Display *display;
    Drawable drawable;
    Window *root;                       /* RETURN */
    int *x, *y;                         /* RETURN */
    unsigned int *width, *height;       /* RETURN */
    unsigned int *border_width;         /* RETURN */
    unsigned int *depth;                /* RETURN */
```

Arguments

display	Specifies a pointer to the Display structure; returned from XOpenDisplay.
drawable	Specifies the drawable, either a window or a pixmap.
root	Returns the root window ID of the specified window.
x y	Return the coordinates of the upper-left pixel of the window's border, relative to its parent's origin. For pixmaps, these coordinates are always 0.
width height	Return the dimensions of the drawable. For a window, these return the inside size (not including the border). For a pixmap, they just return the size.
border_width	Returns the borderwidth, in pixels, of the window's border, if the drawable is a window. Returns 0 if the drawable is a pixmap.
depth	Returns the depth of the pixmap (bits per pixel for the object). The depth must be supported by the root of the specified drawable.

Description
This function gets complete information about the root window and the current geometry of a drawable.

XGetGeometry returns a Status of 0 on failure, or 1 on success.

Errors
BadDrawable

Related Commands
XGetWindowAttributes, XMoveWindow, XMoveResizeWindow, XResizeWindow, XConfigureWindow.

XGetIconName

Name

XGetIconName — get the name to be displayed in an icon.

Synopsis

```
Status XGetIconName(display, w, icon_name)
    Display *display;
    Window w;
    char **icon_name;              /* RETURN */
```

Arguments

display   Specifies a pointer to the Display structure; returned from XOpen-
           Display.

w   Specifies the ID of the window whose icon name you want to learn.

icon_name Returns a pointer to the name to be displayed in the window's icon. The
           name should be a null-terminated string. If a name hasn't been assigned to
           the window, XGetIconName sets this argument to NULL. When finished
           with it, a client must free the icon name string using XFree.

Description

XGetIconName reads the icon name property of a window. This function is primarily used
by window managers to get the name to be written in that window's icon when they need to
display that icon.

XGetIconName returns a nonzero Status if it succeeds, and 0 if no icon name has been
set for the argument window.

For more information, see Volume One, Chapter 10, *Interclient Communication*.

Errors

BadWindow

Related Commands

XGetClassHint, XSetClassHint, XGetSizeHints, XSetSizeHints, XGet-
WMHints, XSetWMHints, XGetZoomHints, XSetZoomHints, XGetNormalHints,
XSetNormalHints, XGetTransientForHint, XSetTransientForHint, XFetch-
Name, XSetIconName, XStoreName, XGetIconSizes, XSetIconSizes, XSet-
Command.

XGetIconSizes

Name

XGetIconSizes — get preferred icon sizes.

Synopsis

```
Status XGetIconSizes(display, w, size_list, count)
    Display *display;
    Window w;
    XIconSize **size_list;      /* RETURN */
    int *count;                 /* RETURN */
```

Arguments

display   Specifies a pointer to the Display structure; returned from XOpenDisplay.

w   Specifies the window ID (usually of the root window).

size_list   Returns a pointer to the size list.

count   Returns the number of items in the size list.

Description

XGetIconSizes reads the XA_WM_ICON_SIZE property that should be set by the window manager to specify its desired icon sizes. XGetIconSizes returns a Status of 0 if a window manager has not set icon sizes, and a nonzero Status otherwise. This function should be called by all programs to find out what icon sizes are preferred by the window manager. The application should then use XSetWMHints to supply the window manager with an icon pixmap or window in one of the supported sizes. To free the data allocated in size_list, use XFree.

For more information, see Volume One, Chapter 10, *Interclient Communication*.

Structures

```
typedef struct {
    int min_width, min_height;
    int max_width, max_height;
    int width_inc, height_inc;
} XIconSize;

/* width_inc and height_inc provide the preferred
 * increment of sizes in the range from min_width
 * to max_width and min_height to max_height. */
```

Errors

BadWindow

Related Commands

XGetClassHint, XSetClassHint, XGetSizeHints, XSetSizeHints, XGet-WMHints, XSetWMHints, XGetZoomHints, XSetZoomHints, XGetNormalHints, XSetNormalHints, XGetTransientForHint, XSetTransientForHint, XFetch-Name, XGetIconName, XStoreName, XSetIconSizes, XSetCommand.

Name

XGetImage — place contents of a rectangle from drawable into an image.

Synopsis

```
XImage *XGetImage(display, drawable, x, y, width, height,
        plane_mask, format)
    Display *display;
    Drawable drawable;
    int x, y;
    unsigned int width, height;
    unsigned long plane_mask;
    int format;
```

Arguments

display   Specifies a pointer to the Display structure; returned from XOpen-
              Display.

drawable   Specifies the drawable to get the data from.

x   Specify the x and y coordinates of the upper-left corner of the rectangle, rela-
y   tive to the origin of the drawable.

width   Specify the width and height in pixels of the image.
height

plane_mask   Specifies a plane mask that indicates which planes are represented in the
              image.

format   Specifies the format for the image. Pass either XYPixmap or ZPixmap.

Description

XGetImage provides a mechanism to perform a rudimentary screen dump.

XGetImage returns an XImage structure. This structure provides you with the contents of
the specified rectangle of the drawable in the format you specify. Depending on which format
you pass to the format argument, the function does the following:

- If the format is XYPixmap

  Gets only the bit planes you passed to the *plane_mask* argument.

- If the format is ZPixmap

  Sets to 0 the bits in all planes not specified in the *plane_mask* argument. The function performs no range checking on the values in *plane_mask*, and ignores extraneous
  bits.

XGetImage returns the depth of the image to the depth member of the XImage structure.
The depth of the image is as specified when the drawable was created.

If the drawable is a pixmap, the specified rectangle must be completely inside the pixmap, or a
BadMatch error will occur. If XGetImage fails, it returns NULL.

If the drawable is a window, the window must be mapped, and it must be the case that, if there were no inferiors or overlapping windows, the specified rectangle of the window would be fully visible on the screen. Otherwise, a `BadMatch` error will occur. The returned image will include any visible portions of inferiors or overlapping windows contained in the rectangle. The specified area can include the borders. The returned contents of visible regions of inferiors of different depth than the specified window are undefined.

If the window has a backing-store, the backing-store contents are returned for regions of the window that are obscured by noninferior windows. Otherwise, the return contents of such obscured regions are undefined. Also undefined are the returned contents of visible regions of inferiors of different depth than the specified window.

For `XYFormat` *format* data, the `bit_order` member of `XImage` specifies the bit order in which your server expects the data.

For more information, see Volume One, Chapter 6, *Drawing Graphics and Text*.

Errors

`BadDrawable`

`BadMatch`   See Description above.

`BadValue`

Related Commands

`XDestroyImage`, `XPutImage`, `XCreateImage`, `XSubImage`, `XGetSubImage`, `XAdd-Pixel`, `XPutPixel`, `XGetPixel`, `ImageByteOrder`.

Name

XGetInputFocus — return the current keyboard focus window.

Synopsis

```
XGetInputFocus(display, focus, revert_to)
    Display *display;
    Window *focus;              /* RETURN */
    int *revert_to;             /* RETURN */
```

Arguments

display   Specifies a pointer to the Display structure; returned from XOpen-Display.

focus   Returns the ID of the focus window, or one of the constants PointerRoot or None.

revert_to   Returns the window to which the focus would revert if the focus window became invisible. This is one of these constants: RevertToParent, RevertToPointerRoot, or RevertToNone. Must not be a window ID.

Description

XGetInputFocus returns the current focus window and the window to which the focus would revert if the focus window became invisible.

XGetInputFocus does not report the last focus change time. This is available only from events.

Related Commands

XSelectInput, XSetInputFocus, XWindowEvent, XCheckWindowEvent, XCheckTypedEvent, XCheckTypedWindowEvent, XMaskEvent, XCheckMask-Event, XNextEvent, XEventsQueued, XAllowEvents, XGetMotionEvents, XIfEvent, XCheckIfEvent, XPeekEvent, XPeekIfEvent, XPutBackEvent, XPending, XSynchronize, XSendEvent, QLength.

XGetKeyboardControl

Name
XGetKeyboardControl — obtain a list of the current keyboard preferences.

Synopsis
```
XGetKeyboardControl(display, values)
    Display *display;
    XKeyboardState *values;  /* RETURN */
```

Arguments
display Specifies a pointer to the Display structure; returned from XOpen-Display.

values Returns filled XKeyboardState structure.

Description
XGetKeyboardControl returns the current control values for the keyboard. For the LEDs, the least significant bit of *led_mask* corresponds to LED 1, and each bit that is set to 1 in *led_mask* indicates an LED that is lit. auto_repeats is a bit vector; each bit that is set to 1 indicates that auto-repeat is enabled for the corresponding key. The vector is represented as 32 bytes. Byte N (from 0) contains the bits for keys 8N to 8N+7, with the least significant bit in the byte representing key 8N. *global_auto_repeat* is either Auto-RepeatModeOn or AutoRepeatModeOff.

For the ranges of each member of XKeyboardState, see the description of the routine that sets that value.

For more information, see Volume One, Chapter 9, *The Keyboard and Pointer*.

Structures
```
typedef struct {
    int key_click_percent;
    int bell_percent;
    unsigned int bell_pitch, bell_duration;
    unsigned long led_mask;
    int global_auto_repeat;
    char auto_repeats[32];
} XKeyboardState;
```

Related Commands
XGetDefault, XAutoRepeatOff, XAutoRepeatOn, XBell, XChangeKeyboard-Control, XGetPointerControl.

Name

XGetKeyboardMapping — return symbols for keycodes.

Synopsis

```
KeySym *XGetKeyboardMapping(display, first_keycode,
        keycode_count, keysyms_per_keycode)
    Display *display;
    KeyCode first_keycode;
    int keycode_count;
    int *keysyms_per_keycode;  /* RETURN */
```

Arguments

display   Specifies a pointer to the Display structure; returned from XOpenDisplay.

first_keycode

      Specifies the first keycode that is to be returned.

keycode_count

      Specifies the number of keycodes that are to be returned.

keysyms_per_keycode

      Returns the number of keysyms per keycode.

Description

Starting with *first_keycode*, XGetKeyboardMapping returns the symbols for the specified number of keycodes. The specified *first_keycode* must be greater than or equal to min_keycode as returned in the Display structure, otherwise a BadValue error occurs. In addition, the following expression must be less than or equal to max_keycode as returned in the Display structure, otherwise a BadValue error occurs:

    first_keycode + *keycode_count* − 1

The number of elements in the keysyms list is:

    keycode_count * *keysyms_per_keycode*

Then, keysym number N (counting from 0) for keycode K has an index (counting from 0) of the following (in keysyms):

    (K − *first_keycode*) * *keysyms_per_keycode* + N

The keysyms_per_keycode value is chosen arbitrarily by the server to be large enough to report all requested symbols. A special KeySym value of NoSymbol is used to fill in unused elements for individual keycodes.

Use XFree to free the returned keysym list when you no longer need it.

For more information, see Volume One, Chapter 9, *The Keyboard and Pointer*.

Errors

BadValue   *first_keycode* less than *display*->min_keycode.

                display->max_keycode exceeded.

Related Commands

XDeleteModifiermapEntry, XInsertModifiermapEntry, XFreeModifiermap,
XKeycodeToKeysym, XKeysymToKeycode, XKeysymToString, XNewModifier-
Map, XQueryKeymap, XStringToKeysym, XLookupKeysym, XRebindKeySym,
XChangeKeyboardMapping, XRefreshKeyboardMapping, XLookupString,
XSetModifierMapping, XGetModifierMapping.

XGetModifierMapping

Name

XGetModifierMapping — obtain a mapping of modifier keys (Shift, Control, etc.).

Synopsis

```
XModifierKeymap *XGetModifierMapping(display)
    Display *display;
```

Arguments

display   Specifies a pointer to the Display structure; returned from XOpen-
Display.

Description

XGetModifierMapping returns the keycodes of the keys being used as modifiers.

There are eight modifiers, represented by the symbols ShiftMapIndex, LockMapIndex, ControlMapIndex, Mod1MapIndex, Mod2MapIndex, Mod3MapIndex, Mod4Map-Index, and Mod5MapIndex. The modifiermap member of the XModifierKeymap structure contains eight sets of keycodes, each set containing max_keypermod keycodes. Zero keycodes are not meaningful. If an entire modifiermap is filled with 0's, the corresponding modifier is disabled. No keycode will appear twice anywhere in the map.

Structures

```
typedef struct {
    int max_keypermod;     /* server's max number of keys per modifier */
    KeyCode *modifiermap;  /* an 8 by max_keypermod array of
                            * keycodes to be used as modifiers */

} XModifierKeymap;

/* modifier names.  Used to build a SetModifierMapping request or
   to read a GetModifierMapping request.  These correspond to the
   masks defined above. */
#define ShiftMapIndex     0
#define LockMapIndex      1
#define ControlMapIndex   2
#define Mod1MapIndex      3
#define Mod2MapIndex      4
#define Mod3MapIndex      5
#define Mod4MapIndex      6
#define Mod5MapIndex      7
```

Related Commands

XDeleteModifiermapEntry, XInsertModifiermapEntry, XFreeModifiermap, XKeycodeToKeysym, XKeysymToKeycode, XKeysymToString, XNewModifier-Map, XQueryKeymap, XStringToKeysym, XLookupKeysym, XRebindKeySym, XGetKeyboardMapping, XChangeKeyboardMapping, XRefreshKeyboard-Mapping, XLookupString, XSetModifierMapping.

        July 26, 1988

Name
XGetMotionEvents — get pointer motion events.

Synopsis
```
XTimeCoord *XGetMotionEvents(display, w, start, stop, nevents)
    Display *display;
    Window w;
    Time start, stop;
    int *nevents;                    /* RETURN */
```

Arguments

display   Specifies a pointer to the Display structure; returned from XOpenDisplay.

w   Specifies the ID of the window whose associated pointer motion events will be returned.

start   Specify the time interval in which the events are returned from the motion his-
stop   tory buffer. Pass a time stamp (in milliseconds) or CurrentTime.

nevents   Returns the number of events returned from the motion history buffer.

Description
XGetMotionEvents returns all events in the motion history buffer that fall between the specified start and stop times (inclusive) and that have coordinates that lie within (including borders) the specified window at its present placement. The x and y coordinates of the XTimeCoord return structure are reported relative to the origin of *w*. If XGetMotion-Event fails, it returns NULL.

If the start time is later than the stop time, or if the start time is in the future, no events are returned. If the stop time is in the future, it is equivalent to specifying the constant CurrentTime.

The motion history buffer may not be available on all servers. If display.motion_buffer > 0, it exists. The pointer position at each pointer hardware interrupt may then be stored for later retrieval.

Use XFree to free the returned XTimeCoord structures when they are no longer needed.

For more information, see Volume One, Chapter 9, *The Keyboard and Pointer*.

Structures
```
typedef struct _XTimeCoord {
    Time time;
    unsigned short x, y;
} XTimeCoord;
```

Errors
BadWindow

Related Commands

XSelectInput, XSetInputFocus, XGetInputFocus, XWindowEvent, XCheck-
WindowEvent, XCheckTypedEvent, XCheckTypedWindowEvent, XMaskEvent,
XCheckMaskEvent, XNextEvent, XEventsQueued, XAllowEvents, XIfEvent,
XCheckIfEvent, XPeekEvent, XPeekIfEvent, XPutBackEvent, XPending,
XSynchronize, XSendEvent, QLength.

XGetNormalHints

Name

XGetNormalHints — get the size hints property of a window in normal state (not zoomed or iconified).

Synopsis

```
Status XGetNormalHints(display, w, hints)
    Display *display;
    Window w;
    XSizeHints *hints;              /* RETURN */
```

Arguments

display   Specifies a pointer to the Display structure; returned from XOpen-Display.

w   Specifies the ID of the window to be queried.

hints   Returns the sizing hints for the window in its normal state.

Description

XGetNormalHints returns the size hints for a window in its normal state by reading the XA_WM_NORMAL_HINTS property. This function is normally used only by a window manager. It returns a nonzero Status if it succeeds, and 0 if it fails (e.g., the application specified no normal size hints for this window.)

For more information on using hints, see Volume One, Chapter 10, *Interclient Communication.*

Structures

```
typedef struct {
    long flags;    /* which fields in structure are defined */
    int x, y;
    int width, height;
    int min_width, min_height;
    int max_width, max_height;
    int width_inc, height_inc;
    struct {
                int x;   /* numerator */
                int y;   /* denominator */
    } min_aspect, max_aspect;
} XSizeHints;

/* flags argument in size hints */
#define USPosition (1L << 0)/* user specified x, y */
#define USSize     (1L << 1)/* user specified width, height */

#define PPosition  (1L << 2)/* program specified position */
#define PSize      (1L << 3)/* program specified size */
#define PMinSize   (1L << 4)/* program specified minimum size */
#define PMaxSize   (1L << 5)/* program specified maximum size */
```

```
#define PResizeInc (1L << 6)/* program specified resize increments */
#define PAspect    (1L << 7)/* program specified min/max aspect ratios */
#define PAllHints (PPosition|PSize|PMinSize|PMaxSize|PResizeInc|PAspect)
```

Errors

BadWindow

Related Commands

XGetClassHint, XSetClassHint, XGetSizeHints, XSetSizeHints, XGet-
WMHints, XSetWMHints, XGetZoomHints, XSetZoomHints, XSetNormalHints,
XGetTransientForHint, XSetTransientForHint, XFetchName, XGetIcon-
Name, XSetIconName, XStoreName, XGetIconSizes, XSetIconSizes, XSet-
Command.

XGetPixel

Name

XGetPixel — obtain a single pixel value from an image.

Synopsis

```
unsigned long XGetPixel(ximage, x, y)
    XImage *ximage;
    int x;
    int y;
```

Arguments

ximage   Specifies a pointer to the image.

x

y   Specify the x and y coordinates of the pixel whose value is to be returned.

Description

XGetPixel returns the specified pixel from the named image. The *x* and *y* coordinates are relative to the origin (upper left [0,0]) of the image. The pixel value is returned in normalized format; that is, the least significant byte (LSB) of the long is the least significant byte of the pixel. The x and y coordinates must be contained in the image.

For more information, see Volume One, Chapter 6, *Drawing Graphics and Text*.

Structures

```
typedef struct _XImage {
    int width, height;              /* size of image */
    int xoffset;                    /* number of pixels offset in X direction */
    int format;                     /* XYBitmap, XYPixmap, ZPixmap */
    char *data;                     /* pointer to image data */
    int byte_order;                 /* data byte order, LSBFirst, MSBFirst */
    int bitmap_unit;                /* quant. of scan line 8, 16, 32 */
    int bitmap_bit_order;           /* LSBFirst, MSBFirst */
    int bitmap_pad;                 /* 8, 16, 32 either XY or ZPixmap */
    int depth;                      /* depth of image */
    int bytes_per_line;             /* accelerator to next line */
    int bits_per_pixel;             /* bits per pixel (ZPixmap) */
    unsigned long red_mask;         /* bits in z arrangment */
    unsigned long green_mask;
    unsigned long blue_mask;
    char *obdata;                   /* hook for the object routines to hang on */
    struct funcs {                  /* image manipulation routines */
    struct _XImage *(*create_image)();
    int (*destroy_image)();
    unsigned long (*get_pixel)();
    int (*put_pixel)();
    struct _XImage *(*sub_image)();
    int (*add_pixel)();
    } f;
} XImage;
```

Related Commands

XDestroyImage, XPutImage, XGetImage, XCreateImage, XSubImage, XGetSub-
Image, XAddPixel, XPutPixel, ImageByteOrder.

Name

XGetPointerControl — get the current pointer preferences.

Synopsis

```
XGetPointerControl(display, accel_numerator, accel_denominator,
        threshold)
    Display *display;
    int *accel_numerator, *accel_denominator;  /* RETURN */
    int *threshold;                            /* RETURN */
```

Arguments

display   Specifies a pointer to the Display structure; returned from XOpen-
Display.

accel_numerator
Returns the numerator for the acceleration multiplier.

accel_denominator
Returns the denominator for the acceleration multiplier.

threshold   Returns the acceleration threshold in pixels. The pointer must move more
than this amount before acceleration takes effect.

Description

XGetPointerControl gets the pointer acceleration parameters.

accel_numerator/accel_denominator is the number of pixels the cursor moves per
unit of motion of the pointer, applied only to the amount of movement over *threshold*.

Related Commands

XQueryPointer, XWarpPointer, XGrabPointer, XChangeActivePointerGrab,
XUngrabPointer, XGetPointerMapping, XSetPointerMapping, XChange-
PointerControl.

XGetPointerMapping

Name

XGetPointerMapping — get the pointer button mapping.

Synopsis

```
int XGetPointerMapping(display, map, nmap)
    Display *display;
    unsigned char map[];        /* RETURN */
    int nmap;
```

Arguments

display   Specifies a pointer to the Display structure; returned from XOpenDisplay.

map   Returns the mapping list. Array begins with map[].

nmap   Specifies the number of items in mapping list.

Description

XGetPointerMapping returns the current mapping of the pointer buttons. Information is returned in both the arguments and the function's return value. map is an array of the numbers of the buttons as they are currently mapped. Elements of the list are indexed starting from 1. The nominal mapping for a pointer is the identity mapping: map[i]=i. If map[3]=2, it means that the third physical button triggers the second logical button.

nmap indicates the desired number of button mappings.

The return value of the function is the actual number of elements in the pointer list, which may be greater or less than nmap.

Related Commands

XQueryPointer, XWarpPointer, XGrabPointer, XChangeActivePointerGrab, XUngrabPointer, XSetPointerMapping, XGetPointerControl, XChange-PointerControl.

Name

XGetScreenSaver — get the current screen saver parameters.

Synopsis

```
XGetScreenSaver(display, timeout, interval, prefer_blanking,
        allow_exposures)
    Display *display;
    int *timeout, *interval;    /* RETURN */
    int *prefer_blanking;       /* RETURN */
    int *allow_exposures;       /* RETURN */
```

Arguments

display   Specifies a pointer to the Display structure; returned from XOpen-Display.

timeout   Returns the timeout, in seconds, until the screen saver turns on.

interval   Returns the interval between screen saver invocations, in seconds.

prefer_blanking
            Returns the current screen blanking preference, one of these constants:
            DontPreferBlanking, PreferBlanking, or DefaultBlanking.

allow_exposures
            Returns the current screen save control value, either DontAllow-Exposures, AllowExposures, or DefaultExposures.

Description

XGetScreenSaver returns the current settings of the screen saver, which may be set with XSetScreenSaver.

A positive *timeout* indicates that the screen saver is enabled. A *timeout* of 0 indicates that the screen saver is disabled. If no input from devices (keyboard, mouse, etc.) is generated for the specified number of *timeout* seconds, the screen saver is activated.

If the server-dependent screen saver method supports periodic change, *interval* serves as a hint about the length of the change period, and 0 serves as a hint that no periodic change should be made. Examples of ways to change the screen include scrambling the colormap periodically, moving an icon image about the screen periodically, or tiling the screen with the root window background tile, randomly reoriginated periodically. An *interval* of 0 indicates that random pattern motion is disabled.

For more information on the screen saver, see Volume One, Chapter 13, *Other Programming Techniques*.

Related Commands

XForceScreenSaver, XActivateScreenSaver, XResetScreenSaver, XSet-ScreenSaver.

Name

XGetSelectionOwner — return the owner of a selection.

Synopsis

```
Window XGetSelectionOwner(display, selection)
    Display *display;
    Atom selection;
```

Arguments

display   Specifies a pointer to the Display structure; returned from XOpen-Display.

selection   Specifies the selection atom whose owner you want returned.

Description

XGetSelectionOwner returns the window ID of the current owner of the specified selection. If no selection was specified, or there is no owner, the function returns the constant None.

For more information on selections, see Volume One, Chapter 10, *Interclient Communication*.

Errors

BadAtom

Related Commands

XSetSelectionOwner, XConvertSelection.

Name

XGetSizeHints — read any property of type XA_SIZE_HINTS.

Synopsis

```
Status XGetSizeHints(display, w, hints, property)
    Display *display;
    Window w;
    XSizeHints *hints;          /* RETURN */
    Atom property;
```

Arguments

display   Specifies a pointer to the Display structure; returned from XOpen-Display.

w   Specifies the ID of the window for which size hints will be returned.

hints   Returns the size hints structure.

property   Specifies a property atom of type XA_WM_SIZE_HINTS. May be XA_WM_NORMAL_HINTS, XA_WM_ZOOM_HINTS, or a property defined by an application.

Description

XGetSizeHints returns the XSizeHints structure for the named property and the specified window. This is used by XGetNormalHints and XGetZoomHints, and can be used to retrieve the value of any property of type XA_WM_SIZE_HINTS; thus, it is useful if other properties of that type get defined. This function is used almost exclusively by window managers.

XGetSizeHints returns a nonzero Status if a size hint was defined, and 0 otherwise.

For more information on using hints, see Volume One, Chapter 10, *Interclient Communication*.

Structures

```
typedef struct {
    long flags;     /* which fields in structure are defined */
    int x, y;
    int width, height;
    int min_width, min_height;
    int max_width, max_height;
    int width_inc, height_inc;
    struct {
                int x;    /* numerator */
                int y;    /* denominator */
    } min_aspect, max_aspect;
} XSizeHints;

/* flags argument in size hints */
#define USPosition (1L << 0) /* user specified x, y */
```

```
#define USSize      (1L << 1) /* user specified width, height */

#define PPosition  (1L << 2) /* program specified position */
#define PSize      (1L << 3) /* program specified size */
#define PMinSize   (1L << 4) /* program specified minimum size */
#define PMaxSize   (1L << 5) /* program specified maximum size */
#define PResizeInc (1L << 6) /* program specified resize increments */
#define PAspect    (1L << 7) /* program specified min/max aspect ratios */
#define PAllHints  (PPosition|PSize|PMinSize|PMaxSize|PResizeInc|PAspect)
```

Errors

BadAtom
BadWindow

Related Commands

XGetClassHint, XSetClassHint, XSetSizeHints, XGetWMHints, XSet-
WMHints, XGetZoomHints, XSetZoomHints, XGetNormalHints, XSetNormal-
Hints, XGetTransientForHint, XSetTransientForHint, XFetchName, XGet-
IconName, XSetIconName, XStoreName, XGetIconSizes, XSetIconSizes,
XSetCommand.

XGetStandardColormap

Name

XGetStandardColormap — get the standard colormap property.

Synopsis

```
Status XGetStandardColormap(display, w, cmap_info, property)
    Display *display;
    Window w;
    XStandardColormap *cmap_info;/* RETURN */
    Atom property;
```

Arguments

display   Specifies a pointer to the Display structure; returned from XOpen-
                 Display.

w   Specifies the ID of the window on which the property is set. This is nor-
                 mally the root window.

cmap_info   Returns the filled colormap information structure.

property   Specifies the atom indicating the type of standard colormap desired. The
                 predefined standard colormap atoms are XA_RGB_BEST_MAP,
                 XA_RGB_RED_MAP, XA_RGB_GREEN_MAP, XA_RGB_BLUE_MAP,
                 XA_RGB_DEFAULT_MAP, and XA_RGB_GRAY_MAP.

Description

XGetStandardColormap gets a property on a window (normally the root window) that
describes a standard colormap.

This call does not load the colormap into the hardware colormap, it does not allocate entries,
and it does not even create a virtual colormap. It just provides information about one design
of colormap. The application can then attempt to create a virtual colormap of the appropriate
type, and allocate its entries according to the information in the XStandardColormap
structure. Installing the colormap must then be done with XInstallColormap, in coopera-
tion with the window manager. Any of these steps could fail, and the application should be
prepared.

If the server has already created a standard colormap of this type, then its ID will be returned
in the colormap member of the XStandardColormap structure. Some servers, particular
on high-performance workstations, will create some or all of the standard colormaps so they
can be quickly installed when needed by applications.

An application should go through the standard colormap creation process only if it needs the
special qualities of the standard colormaps. For one, they allow the application to convert
RGB values into pixel values quickly because the mapping is predictable. Given an
XStandardColormap structure for an XA_RGB_BEST_MAP colormap, and floating point
RGB coefficients in the range 0.0 to 1.0, you can compose pixel values with the following C
expression:

```
pixel = base_pixel
    + ((unsigned long) (0.5 + r * red_max)) * red_mult
    + ((unsigned long) (0.5 + g * green_max)) * green_mult
    + ((unsigned long) (0.5 + b * blue_max)) * blue_mult;
```

The use of addition rather than logical-OR for composing pixel values permits allocations where the RGB value is not aligned to bit boundaries.

See Volume One, Chapter 7, *Color*, for a complete description of standard colormaps.

Structures

```
typedef struct {
    Colormap colormap;    /* ID of colormap created by XCreateColormap */
    unsigned long red_max;
    unsigned long red_mult;
    unsigned long green_max;
    unsigned long green_mult;
    unsigned long blue_max;
    unsigned long blue_mult;
    unsigned long base_pixel;
} XStandardColormap;
```

Errors

```
BadAtom
BadWindow
```

Related Commands

XCopyColormapAndFree, XCreateColormap, XFreeColormap, XInstall-
Colormap, XUninstallColormap, XSetStandardColormap, XListInstalled-
Colormaps, XSetWindowColormap, DefaultColormap, DisplayCells.

Name

XGetSubImage — copy a rectangle in drawable to a location within the pre-existing image.

Synopsis

```
XImage *XGetSubImage (display, drawable, x, y, width, height,
        plane_mask, format, dest_image, dest_x, dest_y)
    Display *display;
    Drawable drawable;
    int x, y;
    unsigned int width, height;
    unsigned long plane_mask;
    int format;
    XImage *dest_image;
    int dest_x, dest_y;
```

Arguments

display   Specifies a pointer to the Display structure; returned from XOpen-Display.

drawable   Specifies the drawable from which the rectangle is to be copied.

x   Specify the x and y coordinates of the upper-left corner of the rectangle, rela-
y   tive to the origin of the drawable.

width   Specify the width and height in pixels of the subimage taken.
height

plane_mask   Specifies which planes of the drawable are transferred to image.

format   Specifies the format for the image. Either XYPixmap or ZPixmap.

dest_image   Specifies the the destination image.

dest_x   Specify the x and y coordinates of the destination rectangle's upper left
dest_y   corner, relative to the image's origin.

Description

XGetSubImage updates the *dest_image* with the specified subimage in the same manner
as XGetImage, except that it does not create the image or necessarily fill the entire image. If
format is XYPixmap, the function transmits only the bit planes you specify in
plane_mask. If *format* is ZPixmap, the function transmits as 0 the bits in all planes not
specified in *plane_mask*. The function performs no range checking on the values in
plane_mask and ignores extraneous bits.

The depth of the destination XImage structure must be the same as that of the drawable. Otherwise, a BadMatch error is generated. If the specified subimage does not fit at the specified
location on the destination image, the right and bottom edges are clipped. If the drawable is a
window, the window must be mapped or held in backing store, and it must be the case that, if
there were no inferiors or overlapping windows, the specified rectangle of the window would
be fully visible on the screen. Otherwise, a BadMatch error is generated.

If the window has a backing store, the backing store contents are returned for regions of the window that are obscured by noninferior windows. Otherwise, the return contents of such obscured regions are undefined. Also undefined are the returned contents of visible regions of inferiors of different depth than the specified window.

XSubImage extracts a subimage from an image, instead of from a drawable like XGetSub-Image.

For more information on images, see Volume One, Chapter 6, *Drawing Graphics and Text*.

Errors

BadDrawable

BadGC

BadMatch   Depth of *dest_image* is not the same as depth of *drawable*. See also Description.

BadValue

Related Commands

XDestroyImage, XPutImage, XGetImage, XCreateImage, XSubImage, XAdd-Pixel, XPutPixel, XGetPixel, ImageByteOrder.

Name

XGetTransientForHint — get the XA_WM_TRANSIENT_FOR property of a window.

Synopsis

```
Status XGetTransientForHint(display, w, prop_window)
    Display *display;
    Window w;
    Window *prop_window;         /* RETURN */
```

Arguments

display   Specifies a pointer to the Display structure; returned from XOpen-Display.

w   Specifies the ID of the window to be queried.

prop_window Returns the XA_WM_TRANSIENT_FOR property of the specified window.

Description

XGetTransientForHint obtains the XA_WM_TRANSIENT_FOR property for the specified window. This function is normally used by a window manager. This property should be set for windows that are to appear only temporarily on the screen, such as pop-up menus and dialog boxes.

XGetTransientForHint returns a Status of 0 on failure, and nonzero on success.

For more information on using hints, see Volume One, Chapter 10, *Interclient Communication*.

Errors

BadWindow

Related Commands

XGetClassHint, XSetClassHint, XGetSizeHints, XSetSizeHints, XGet-WMHints, XSetWMHints, XGetZoomHints, XSetZoomHints, XGetNormalHints, XSetNormalHints, XSetTransientForHint, XFetchName, XGetIconName, XSetIconName, XStoreName, XGetIconSizes, XSetIconSizes, XSetCommand.

XGetVisualInfo

Name

XGetVisualInfo — find a visual information structure that matches the specified template.

Synopsis

```
XVisualInfo *XGetVisualInfo(display, vinfo_mask,
        vinfo_template, nitems)
   Display *display;
   long vinfo_mask;
   XVisualInfo *vinfo_template;
   int *nitems;                  /* RETURN */
```

Arguments

display   Specifies a pointer to the Display structure; returned from XOpen-Display.

vinfo_mask   Specifies the visual mask value. Indicates which elements in template are to be matched.

vinfo_template
                 Specifies the visual attributes that are to be used in matching the visual structures.

nitems   Returns the number of matching visual structures.

Description

XGetVisualInfo returns a list of visual structures that match the attributes specified by the *vinfo_template* argument. If no visual structures match the template, XGetVisual-Info returns a NULL. To free the data returned by this function, use XFree.

For more information, see Volume One, Chapter 7, *Color*.

Structures

```
typedef struct {
    Visual *visual;
    VisualID visualid;
    int screen;
    unsigned int depth;
    int class;
    unsigned long red_mask;
    unsigned long green_mask;
    unsigned long blue_mask;
    int colormap_size;
    int bits_per_rgb;
} XVisualInfo;
```

```
/* The symbols for the vinfo_mask argument are: */

#define VisualNoMask            0x0
#define VisualIDMask            0x1
#define VisualScreenMask        0x2
```

```
#define VisualDepthMask            0x4
#define VisualClassMask            0x8
#define VisualRedMaskMask          0x10
#define VisualGreenMaskMask        0x20
#define VisualBlueMaskMask         0x40
#define VisualColormapSizeMask     0x80
#define VisualBitsPerRGBMask       0x100
#define VisualAllMask              0x1FF
```

Related Commands

XMatchVisualInfo, DefaultVisual.

Name

XGetWindowAttributes — obtain the current attributes of window.

Synopsis

```
Status XGetWindowAttributes(display, w, window_attributes)
    Display *display;
    Window w;
    XWindowAttributes *window_attributes; /* RETURN */
```

Arguments

display   Specifies a pointer to the Display structure; returned from XOpenDisplay.

w   Specifies the window whose current attributes you want.

window_attributes

      Returns a filled XWindowAttributes structure, containing the current attributes for the specified window.

Description

XGetWindowAttributes returns the XWindowAttributes structure containing the current window attributes.

While *w* is defined as type Window, a Pixmap can also be used, in which case all the returned members will be 0 except width, height, depth, and screen.

The following list briefly describes each member of the XWindowAttributes structure. For more information, see Volume One, Chapter 4, *Window Attributes*.

x, y   The current position of the upper-left pixel of the window's border, relative to the origin of its parent.

width, height The current dimensions in pixels of this window.

border_width   The current border width of the window.

depth   The number of bits per pixel in this window.

visual   The visual structure.

root   The root window ID of the screen containing the window.

class   The window class. One of these constants: InputOutput or InputOnly.

bit_gravity   The new position for existing contexts on resize. One of the constants ForgetGravity, StaticGravity, or CenterGravity, or one of the compass constants (NorthWestGravity, NorthGravity, etc.).

win_gravity   The new position for subwindow on parent resize. One of the constants CenterGravity, UnmapGravity, StaticGravity, or one of the compass constants.

backing_store When to maintain contents of the window. One of these constants: NotUseful, WhenMapped, or Always.

backing_planes
:   The bit planes to be preserved in a backing store.

backing_pixel The pixel value used when restoring planes from a partial backing store.

save_under
:   A boolean value, indicating whether saving bits under this window would be useful.

colormap
:   The colormap ID to be used in this window, or None.

map_installed A boolean value, indicating whether the colormap is currently installed. If True, the window is being displayed in its chosen colors.

map_state
:   The window's map state. One of these constants: IsUnmapped, IsUnviewable, or IsViewable. IsUnviewable indicates that the specified window is mapped but some ancestor is unmapped.

all_event_masks
:   The set of events any client have selected. This member is the bitwise inclusive OR of all event masks selected on the window by all clients.

your_event_mask
:   The bitwise inclusive OR of all event mask symbols selected by the querying client.

do_not_propagate_mask
:   The bitwise inclusive OR of the event mask symbols that specify the set of events that should not propagate. This is global across all clients.

override_redirect
:   A boolean value, indicating whether this window will override structure control facilities. This is usually only used for temporary pop-up windows. Either True or False.

screen
:   A pointer to the Screen structure for the screen containing this window.

XGetWindowAttributes returns a Status of 0 on failure, or 1 on success.

Structures

The XWindowAttributes structure contains:

```
typedef struct {
    int x, y;                     /* location of window */
    int width, height;            /* width and height of window */
    int border_width;             /* border width of window */
    int depth;                    /* depth of window */
    Visual *visual;               /* the associated visual structure */
    Window root;                  /* root of screen containing window */
    int class;                    /* InputOutput, InputOnly*/
    int bit_gravity;              /* one of bit gravity values */
    int win_gravity;              /* one of the window gravity values */
    int backing_store;            /* NotUseful, WhenMapped, Always */
    unsigned long backing_planes;/* planes to be preserved if possible */
    unsigned long backing_pixel; /* value to be used when restoring planes */
```

```
        Bool save_under;                /* boolean, should bits under be saved */
        Colormap colormap;              /* colormap to be associated with window */
        Bool map_installed;             /* boolean, is colormap currently installed*/
        int map_state;                  /* IsUnmapped, IsUnviewable, IsViewable */
        long all_event_masks;           /* set of events all people have interest in*/
        long your_event_mask;           /* my event mask */
        long do_not_propagate_mask;     /* set of events that should not propagate */
        Bool override_redirect;         /* boolean value for override-redirect */
        Screen *screen;                 /* pointer to correct screen */
} XWindowAttributes;
```

Related Commands

XChangeWindowAttributes, XSetWindowBackground, XSetWindow-
BackgroundPixmap, XSetWindowBorder, XSetWindowBorderPixmap, XGet-
Geometry.

XGetWindowProperty

Name

XGetWindowProperty — obtain the atom type and property format for a window.

Synopsis

```
int XGetWindowProperty(display, w, property, long_offset,
        long_length, delete, req_type, actual_type,
        actual_format, nitems, bytes_after, prop)
    Display *display;
    Window w;
    Atom property;
    long long_offset, long_length;
    Bool delete;
    Atom req_type;
    Atom *actual_type;          /* RETURN */
    int *actual_format;         /* RETURN */
    unsigned long *nitems;      /* RETURN */
    unsigned long *bytes_after; /* RETURN */
    unsigned char **prop;       /* RETURN */
```

Arguments

display   Specifies a pointer to the Display structure; returned from XOpen-Display.

w   Specifies the ID of the window whose atom type and property format you want to obtain.

property   Specifies the property atom.

long_offset   Specifies the offset in 32-bit quantities where data will be retrieved.

long_length   Specifies the length in 32-bit multiples of the data to be retrieved.

delete   Specifies a boolean value of True or False. If you pass True and a property is returned, the property is deleted from the window and a Property-Notify event is generated on the window.

req_type   If AnyPropertyType is specified, returns the property from the specified window regardless of its type. If a type is specified, the function returns the property only if its type equals the specified type.

actual_type   Returns the actual type of the property.

actual_format

Returns the actual data type of the returned data.

nitems   Returns the actual number of 8-, 16-, or 32-bit items returned in *prop*.

bytes_after   Returns the number of bytes remaining to be read in the property if a partial read was performed.

prop   Returns a pointer to the data actually returned, in the specified format. XGetWindowProperty always allocates one extra byte after the data and sets it to ASCII Null. This byte is not counted in *nitems*.

Description

XGetWindowProperty gets the value of a property if it is the desired type. XGet-WindowProperty sets the return arguments acccording to the following rules:

- If the specified property does not exist for the specified window, then: *actual_type* is None; *actual_format* = *0*; and *bytes_after* = *0*. *delete* is ignored in this case, and *nitems* is empty.

- If the specified property exists, but its type does not match *req_type*, then: *actual_type* is the actual property type; *actual_format* is the actual property format (never 0); and *bytes_after* is the property length in bytes (even if *actual_format* is 16 or 32). *delete* is ignored in this case, and *nitems* is empty.

- If the specified property exists, and either *req_type* is AnyPropertyType or the specified type matches the actual property type, then: *actual_type* is the actual property type; and *actual_format* is the actual property format (never 0). *bytes_after* and *nitems* are defined by combining the following values:

  N = actual length of stored property in bytes (even if *actual_format* is 16 or 32)
  I = 4 * *long_offset* (convert offset from *longs* into bytes)
  L = MINIMUM((N - I), 4 * *long_length*) (BadValue if L < 0)
  bytes_after = N - (I + L) (number of trailing unread bytes in stored property)

  The returned data (in *prop*) starts at byte index I in the property (indexing from 0). The actual length of the returned data in bytes is *L*. *L* is converted into the number of 8-, 16-, or 32-bit items returned by dividing by 1, 2, or 4 respectively and this value is returned in *nitems*. The number of trailing unread bytes is returned in *bytes_after*.

  If *delete* == True and *bytes_after* == 0 the function deletes the property from the window and generates a PropertyNotify event on the window.

When XGetWindowProperty executes successfully, it returns Success. If it fails, it returns 1. Note that these return values are the opposite values of routines that return int or Status. To free the resulting data, use XFree. If the specified window did not exist, it generates a BadWindow error. If the type you passed in *req_type* did not exist or did not match the property type returned in *actual_type*, the function generates a BadMatch error.

For more information, see Volume One, Chapter 10, *Interclient Communication*.

Errors

BadAtom

BadMatch

BadValue   Value of *long_offset* caused *L* to be negative above.

BadWindow

Related Commands

XSetStandardProperties, XGetFontProperty, XRotateWindowProperties,
XDeleteProperty, XChangeProperty, XListProperties, XGetAtomName,
XInternAtom.

Name

XGetWMHints — read the window manager hints property.

Synopsis

```
XWMHints *XGetWMHints(display, w)
    Display *display;
    Window w;
```

Arguments

display   Specifies a pointer to the Display structure; returned from XOpenDisplay.

w   Specifies the ID of the window to be queried.

Description

This function is primarily for window managers. XGetWMHints returns NULL if no XA_WM_HINTS property was set on window *w*, and returns a pointer to an XWMHints structure if it succeeds. Programs must free the space used for that structure by calling XFree.

For more information on using hints, see Volume One, Chapter 10, *Interclient Communication.*

Structures

```
typedef struct {
        long flags;             /* marks which fields in this structure are defined */
        Bool input;             /* does application need window manager for input */
        int initial_state;      /* see below */
        Pixmap icon_pixmap;     /* pixmap to be used as icon */
        Window icon_window;     /* window to be used as icon */
        int icon_x, icon_y;     /* initial position of icon */
        Pixmap icon_mask;       /* icon mask bitmap */
        XID window_group;       /* ID of related window group */
        /* this structure may be extended in the future */
} XWMHints;

/* initial state flag: */
#define DontCareState    0
#define NormalState      1
#define ZoomState        2
#define IconicState      3
#define InactiveState    4
```

Errors

BadWindow

Related Commands

XGetClassHint, XSetClassHint, XGetSizeHints, XSetSizeHints, XSet-
WMHints, XGetZoomHints, XSetZoomHints, XGetNormalHints, XSetNormal-
Hints, XGetTransientForHint, XSetTransientForHint, XFetchName, XGet-
IconName, XSetIconName, XStoreName, XGetIconSizes, XSetIconSizes,
XSetCommand.

Name

XGetZoomHints — read the size hints property of a zoomed window.

Synopsis

```
Status XGetZoomHints(display, w, zhints)
    Display *display;
    Window w;
    XSizeHints *zhints;          /* RETURN */
```

Arguments

display   Specifies a pointer to the Display structure; returned from XOpenDisplay.

w   Specifies the ID of the window to be queried.

zhints   Returns a pointer to the zoom hints.

Description

XGetZoomHints is primarily for window managers. XGetZoomHints returns the size hints for a window in its zoomed state (not normal or iconified) read from the XA_WM_ZOOM_HINTS property. It returns a nonzero Status if it succeeds, and 0 if the application did not specify zoom size hints for this window.

For more information on using hints, see Volume One, Chapter 10, *Interclient Communication*.

Structures

```
typedef struct {
    long flags;      /* which fields in structure are defined */
    int x, y;
    int width, height;
    int min_width, min_height;
    int max_width, max_height;
    int width_inc, height_inc;
    struct {
                int x;    /* numerator */
                int y;    /* denominator */
    } min_aspect, max_aspect;
} XSizeHints;

/* flags argument in size hints */
#define USPosition (1L << 0) /* user specified x, y */
#define USSize     (1L << 1) /* user specified width, height */

#define PPosition  (1L << 2) /* program specified position */
#define PSize      (1L << 3) /* program specified size */
#define PMinSize   (1L << 4) /* program specified minimum size */
#define PMaxSize   (1L << 5) /* program specified maximum size */
#define PResizeInc (1L << 6) /* program specified resize increments */
#define PAspect    (1L << 7) /* program specified min/max aspect ratios */
#define PAllHints  (PPosition|PSize|PMinSize|PMaxSize|PResizeInc|PAspect)
```

Errors

`BadWindow`

Related Commands

`XGetClassHint`, `XSetClassHint`, `XGetSizeHints`, `XSetSizeHints`, `XGet-WMHints`, `XSetWMHints`, `XSetZoomHints`, `XGetNormalHints`, `XSetNormal-Hints`, `XGetTransientForHint`, `XSetTransientForHint`, `XFetchName`, `XGet-IconName`, `XSetIconName`, `XStoreName`, `XGetIconSizes`, `XSetIconSizes`, `XSetCommand`.

XGrabButton

Name

XGrabButton — grab a pointer button.

Synopsis

```
XGrabButton(display, button, modifiers, grab_window,
       owner_events, event_mask, pointer_mode, keyboard_mode,
       confine_to, cursor)
  Display *display;
  unsigned int button;
  unsigned int modifiers;
  Window grab_window;
  Bool owner_events;
  unsigned int event_mask;
  int pointer_mode, keyboard_mode;
  Window confine_to;
  Cursor cursor;
```

Arguments

display   Specifies a pointer to the `Display` structure; returned from `XOpen-Display`.

button   Specifies the mouse button. May be `Button1`, `Button2`, `Button3`, `Button4`, `Button5`, or `AnyButton`. The constant `AnyButton` is equivalent to issuing the grab request for all possible buttons. The button symbols cannot be ORed.

modifiers   Specifies a set of keymasks. This is a bitwise OR of one or more of the following symbols: `ShiftMask`, `LockMask`, `ControlMask`, `Mod1Mask`, `Mod2Mask`, `Mod3Mask`, `Mod4Mask`, `Mod5Mask`, or `AnyModifier`. `AnyModifier` is equivalent to issuing the grab key request for all possible modifier combinations (including no modifiers).

grab_window Specifies the ID of the window you want to grab.

owner_events

               Specifies a boolean value of either `True` or `False`. See Description below.

event_mask Specifies the event mask. This mask is the bitwise OR of one or more of the event masks listed on the reference page for `XSelectInput`.

pointer_mode

               Controls further processing of pointer events. Pass one of these constants: `GrabModeSync` or `GrabModeAsync`.

keyboard_mode

               Controls further processing of keyboard events. Pass one of these constants: `GrabModeSync` or `GrabModeAsync`.

confine_to   Specifies the ID of the window to confine the pointer. One possible value is the constant `None`, in which case the pointer is not confined to any window.

cursor   Specifies the cursor to be displayed during the grab. One possible value you can pass is the constant None.

Description

XGrabButton establishes a passive grab, such that an active grab may take place when the specified key/button combination is pressed. After this call, if

1)   the specified button is pressed when the specified modifier keys are down (and no other buttons or modifier keys are down),

2)   *grab_window* contains the pointer,

3)   the *confine_to* window (if any) is viewable, and

4)   these constraints are not satisfied for any ancestor,

then the pointer is actively grabbed as described in GrabPointer, the last_pointer_grab time is set to the time at which the button was pressed, and the ButtonPress event is reported.

The interpretation of the remaining arguments is as for XGrabPointer. The active grab is terminated automatically when all buttons are released (independent of the state of modifier keys).

A modifier of AnyModifier is equivalent to issuing the grab request for all possible modifier combinations (including no modifiers). A button of AnyButton is equivalent to issuing the request for all possible buttons (but at least one).

The request fails if some other client has already issued a GrabButton with the same button/key combination on the same window. When using AnyModifier or AnyButton, the request fails completely (no grabs are established) if there is a conflicting grab for any combination. The request has no effect on an active grab.

The *owner_events* argument specifies whether the grab window should receive all events (True) or whether the grabbing application should receive all events normally (False).

The *pointer_mode* and *keyboard_mode* control the processing of events during the grab. If either is GrabModeSync, events for that device are not queued for applications until XAllowEvents is called to release the events. If either is GrabModeAsync, events for that device are processed normally.

An automatic grab takes place between a ButtonPress and a ButtonRelease, so this call is not necessary in some of the most common situations.

For more information on grabbing, see Volume One, Chapter 9, *The Keyboard and Pointer*.

Errors

BadAccess   When using `AnyModifier` or `AnyButton` and there is a conflicting grab
                by another client. No grabs are established.

                Another client has already issued an *XGrabButton* request with the same
                key/button combination on the same window.

BadAlloc

BadCursor

BadValue

BadWindow

Related Commands

XGrabKey, XUngrabKey, XGrabKeyboard, XUngrabKeyboard, XUngrabButton,
XGrabPointer, XUngrabPointer, XChangeActivePointerGrab, XGrabServer,
XUngrabServer.

Name

XGrabKey — grab a key.

Synopsis

```
XGrabKey(display, keycode, modifiers, grab_window,
        owner_events, pointer_mode, keyboard_mode)
    Display *display;
    int keycode;
    unsigned int modifiers;
    Window grab_window;
    Bool owner_events;
    int pointer_mode, keyboard_mode;
```

Arguments

display   Specifies a pointer to the Display structure; returned from XOpen-
Display.

keycode   Specifies the keycode to be grabbed. It may be a modifier key. Specifying
AnyKey is equivalent to issuing the request for all key codes.

modifiers   Specifies a set of keymasks. This is a bitwise OR of one or more of the following symbols: ShiftMask, LockMask, ControlMask, Mod1Mask,
Mod2Mask, Mod3Mask, Mod4Mask, Mod5Mask, or AnyModifier.
AnyModifier is equivalent to issuing the grab key request for all possible
modifier combinations (including no modifiers). All specified modifiers do
not need to have currently assigned keycodes.

grab_window Specifies the window from which you want to receive input from the
grabbed key combination.

owner_events

Specifies whether the grab window should receive all events (True) or
whether the grabbing application should receive all events normally
(False).

pointer_mode

Controls further processing of pointer events. Pass one of these constants:
GrabModeSync or GrabModeAsync.

keyboard_mode

Controls further processing of keyboard events. Pass one of these constants:
GrabModeSync or GrabModeAsync.

Description

XGrabKey establishes a passive grab on the specified keys, such that when the specified
key/modifier combination is pressed, the keyboard is grabbed, and all keyboard events are sent
to this application. More formally:

- IF the keyboard is not grabbed and the specified key, which itself can be a modifier key, is logically pressed when the specified modifier keys logically are down (and no other keys are down),

- AND no other modifier keys logically are down,

- AND EITHER the grab window is an ancestor of (or is) the focus window OR the grab window is a descendent of the focus window and contains the pointer,

- AND a passive grab on the same key combination does not exist on any ancestor of the grab window,

- THEN the keyboard is actively grabbed, as for XGrabKeyboard, the last keyboard grab time is set to the time at which the key was pressed (as transmitted in the Key-Press event), and the KeyPress event is reported.

The active grab is terminated automatically when the specified key is released (independent of the state of the modifier keys).

The *pointer_mode* and *keyboard_mode* control the processing of events during the grab. If either is GrabModeSync, events for that device are not queued for applications until XAllowEvents is called to release the events. If either is GrabModeAsync, events for that device are processed normally.

For more information on grabbing, see Volume One, Chapter 9, *The Keyboard and Pointer*.

Errors

BadAccess   When using AnyModifier or AnyKey and another client has grabbed any overlapping combinations. In this case, no grabs are established.

Another client has issued XGrabKey for the same key combination in *grab_window*.

BadValue   *keycode* is not in the range between min_keycode and max_keycode in the display structure.

BadWindow

Related Commands

XUngrabKey, XGrabKeyboard, XUngrabKeyboard, XGrabButton, XUngrab-Button, XGrabPointer, XUngrabPointer, XChangeActivePointerGrab, XGrabServer, XUngrabServer.

XGrabKeyboard

Name

XGrabKeyboard — grab the keyboard.

Synopsis

```
int XGrabKeyboard(display, grab_window, owner_events,
        pointer_mode, keyboard_mode, time)
    Display *display;
    Window grab_window;
    Bool owner_events;
    int pointer_mode, keyboard_mode;
    Time time;
```

Arguments

display Specifies a pointer to the Display structure; returned from XOpen-Display.

grab_window Specifies the ID of the window that requires continuous keyboard input.

owner_events

Specifies a boolean value of either True or False. See Description below.

pointer_mode

Controls further processing of pointer events. Pass either GrabModeSync or GrabModeAsync.

keyboard_mode

Controls further processing of keyboard events. Pass either GrabMode-Sync or GrabModeAsync.

time Specifies the time when the grab should take place. Pass either a timestamp, expressed in milliseconds, or the constant CurrentTime.

Description

XGrabKeyboard actively grabs control of the main keyboard. Further key events are reported only to the grabbing client. This request generates FocusIn and FocusOut events.

XGrabKeyboard processing is controlled by the value in the *owner_events* argument:

- If *owner_events* is False, all generated key events are reported to *grab_window*.

- If *owner_events* is True, then if a generated key event would normally be reported to this client, it is reported normally. Otherwise the event is reported to *grab_window*.

  Both KeyPress and KeyRelease events are always reported, independent of any event selection made by the client.

XGrabKeyboard processing of pointer events and keyboard events are controlled by *pointer_mode* and *keyboard_mode*:

- If the *pointer_mode* or *keyboard_mode* is GrabModeAsync, event processing for the respective device continues normally.

- For *keyboard_mode* GrabModeAsync only: if the keyboard was currently frozen by this client, then processing of keyboard events is resumed.

- If the *pointer_mode* or *keyboard_mode* is GrabModeSync, events for the respective device are queued until a releasing XAllowEvents request occurs or until the keyboard grab is released as described above.

If the grab is successful, it returns the constant GrabSuccess. XGrabKeyboard processing fails under the following conditions and returns the following:

- If the keyboard is actively grabbed by some other client, it returns AlreadyGrabbed.

- If *grab_window* is not viewable, it returns GrabNotViewable.

- If *time* is earlier than the last keyboard grab time or later than the current server time, it returns GrabInvalidTime.

- If the pointer is frozen by an active grab of another client, the request fails with a status GrabFrozen.

If the grab succeeds, the last keyboard grab time is set to the specified time, with Current-Time replaced by the current X server time.

For more information on grabbing, see Volume One, Chapter 9, *The Keyboard and Pointer*.

Errors
```
BadValue
BadWindow
```

Related Commands
XGrabKey, XUngrabKey, XUngrabKeyboard, XGrabButton, XUngrabButton, XGrabPointer, XUngrabPointer, XChangeActivePointerGrab, XGrabServer, XUngrabServer.

Name

XGrabPointer — grab the pointer.

Synopsis

```
int XGrabPointer(display, grab_window, owner_events,
        event_mask, pointer_mode, keyboard_mode, confine_to,
        cursor, time)
    Display *display;
    Window grab_window;
    Bool owner_events;
    unsigned int event_mask;
    int pointer_mode, keyboard_mode;
    Window confine_to;
    Cursor cursor;
    Time time;
```

Arguments

display   Specifies a pointer to the Display structure; returned from XOpen-Display.

grab_window   Specifies the ID of the window that should grab the pointer input independent of pointer location.

owner_events

Specifies if the pointer events are to be reported normally within this application (pass True) or only to the grab window if selected by the event mask (pass False).

event_mask   Specifies the event mask. See XSelectInput for a complete list of event masks.

pointer_mode

Controls further processing of pointer events. Pass either GrabModeSync or GrabModeAsync.

keyboard_mode

Controls further processing of keyboard events. Pass either GrabMode-Sync or GrabModeAsync.

confine_to   Specifies the ID of the window to confine the pointer. One option is None, in which case the pointer is not confined to any window.

cursor   Specifies the ID of the cursor that is displayed with the pointer during the grab. One option is None, which causes the cursor to keep its current pattern.

time   Specifies the time when the grab request took place. Pass either a timestamp, expressed in milliseconds (from an event), or the constant Current-Time.

Description

XGrabPointer actively grabs control of the pointer. Further pointer events are only reported to the grabbing client.

event_mask is always augmented to include ButtonPressMask and ButtonRelease-Mask. If *owner_events* is False, all generated pointer events are reported with respect to *grab_window*, and are only reported if selected by *event_mask*. If *owner_events* is True, then if a generated pointer event would normally be reported to this client, it is reported normally; otherwise the event is reported with respect to the *grab_window*, and is only reported if selected by *event_mask*. For either value of *owner_events*, unreported events are discarded.

pointer_mode controls further processing of pointer events, and *keyboard_mode* controls further processing of main keyboard events. If the mode is GrabModeAsync, event processing continues normally. If the mode is GrabModeSync, events for the device are queued but not sent to clients until the grabbing client issues a releasing XAllowEvents request or an XUngrabPointer request.

If a cursor is specified, then it is displayed regardless of what window the pointer is in. If no cursor is specified, then when the pointer is in *grab_window* or one of its subwindows, the normal cursor for that window is displayed. Otherwise, the cursor for *grab_window* is displayed.

If a *confine_to* window is specified, then the pointer will be restricted to that window. The *confine_to* window need have no relationship to the *grab_window*. If the pointer is not initially in the *confine_to* window, then it is warped automatically to the closest edge (and enter/leave events generated normally) just before the grab activates. If the *confine_to* window is subsequently reconfigured, the pointer will be warped automatically as necessary to keep it contained in the window.

The *time* argument lets you avoid certain circumstances that come up if applications take a long while to respond or if there are long network delays. Consider a situation where you have two applications, both of which normally grab the pointer when clicked on. If both applications specify the timestamp from the ButtonPress event, the second application will successfully grab the pointer, while the first will get a return value of AlreadyGrabbed, indicating that the other application grabbed the pointer before its request was processed. This is the desired response because the latest user action is most important in this case.

XGrabPointer generates EnterNotify and LeaveNotify events.

If the grab is successful, it returns the constant GrabSuccess. The XGrabPointer function fails under the following conditions, with the following return values:

- If *grab_window* or *confine_to* window is not viewable, GrabNotViewable is returned.

- If the pointer is actively grabbed by some other client, the constant AlreadyGrabbed is returned.

- If the pointer is frozen by an active grab of another client, GrabFrozen is returned.

- If the specified time is earlier than the last-pointer-grab time or later than the current X server time, GrabInvalidTime is returned. (If the call succeeds, the last pointer grab time is set to the specified time, with the constant CurrentTime replaced by the current X server time.)

For more information on grabbing, see Volume One, Chapter 9, *The Keyboard and Pointer*.

Errors
    BadCursor
    BadValue
    BadWindow

Related Commands
    XGrabKey, XUngrabKey, XGrabKeyboard, XUngrabKeyboard, XGrabButton,
    XUngrabButton, XUngrabPointer, XChangeActivePointerGrab, XGrab-
    Server, XUngrabServer.

Name

XGrabServer — grab the server.

Synopsis

```
XGrabServer (display)
    Display *display;
```

Arguments

display   Specifies a pointer to the Display structure; returned from XOpen-
Display.

Description

Grabbing the server means that only requests by the calling client will be acted on. All others
will be queued in the server until the next XUngrabServer call. The X server should not
be grabbed any more than is absolutely necessary.

Related Commands

XGrabKey, XUngrabKey, XGrabKeyboard, XUngrabKeyboard, XGrabButton,
XUngrabButton, XGrabPointer, XUngrabPointer, XChangeActivePointer-
Grab, XUngrabServer.

Name

XIfEvent — wait for event matched in predicate procedure.

Synopsis

```
XIfEvent (display, event, predicate, args)
    Display *display;
    XEvent *event;                /* RETURN */
    Bool (*predicate)();
    char *args;
```

Arguments

display   Specifies a pointer to the `Display` structure; returned from `XOpen-Display`.

event   Returns the matched event.

predicate   Specifies the procedure to be called to determine if the next event satisfies your criteria.

args   Specifies the user-specified arguments to be passed to the predicate procedure.

Description

`XIfEvent` checks the event queue for events, uses the user-supplied routine to check if they meet certain criteria, and removes the matching event from the input queue. `XIfEvent` returns only when the specified predicate procedure returns `True` for an event. The specified predicate is called each time an event is added to the queue, with the arguments *display*, *event*, and *arg*.

If no matching events exist on the queue, `XIfEvent` flushes the output buffer and waits for an appropriate event to arrive. Use `XCheckIfEvent` if you don't want to wait for an event.

In Release 1, the output buffer was always flushed by event-getting routines. In Release 2, the output buffer is flushed only if no matching events are found on the queue. This change is compatible with applications written for Release 1.

For more information, see Volume One, Chapter 8, *Events*.

Related Commands

`XSelectInput`, `XSetInputFocus`, `XGetInputFocus`, `XWindowEvent`, `XCheck-WindowEvent`, `XCheckTypedEvent`, `XCheckTypedWindowEvent`, `XMaskEvent`, `XCheckMaskEvent`, `XNextEvent`, `XEventsQueued`, `XAllowEvents`, `XGetMotion-Events`, `XCheckIfEvent`, `XPeekEvent`, `XPeekIfEvent`, `XPutBackEvent`, `XPending`, `XSynchronize`, `XSendEvent`, `QLength`.

XInsertModifiermapEntry

Name

XInsertModifiermapEntry — add a new entry to an XModifierKeymap structure.

Synopsis

```
XModifierKeymap *XInsertModifiermapEntry(modmap,
        keysym_entry, modifier)
    XModifierKeymap *modmap;
    KeyCode keysym_entry;
    int modifier;
```

Arguments

modmap   Specifies a pointer to an XModifierKeymap structure.

keysym_entry

        Specifies the keycode of the key to be added to *modmap*.

modifier   Specifies the modifier you want mapped to the keycode specified in *keysym_entry*. This should be one of the constants: ShiftMapIndex, LockMapIndex, ControlMapIndex, Mod1MapIndex, Mod2Map-Index, Mod3MapIndex, Mod4MapIndex, or Mod5MapIndex.

Description

XInsertModifiermapEntry returns an XModifierKeymap structure suitable for calling XSetModifierMapping, in which the specified keycode is deleted from the set of keycodes that is mapped to the specified modifier (like Shift or Control). XInsert-ModifiermapEntry does not change the mapping itself.

This function is normally used by calling XGetModifierMapping to get a pointer to the current XModifierKeymap structure for use as the *modmap* argument to XInsert-ModifiermapEntry.

Note that the structure pointed to by *modmap* is freed by XInsertModifiermapEntry. It should not be freed or otherwise used by applications.

For a description of the modifier map, see XSetModifierMapping.

Structures

```
typedef struct {
    int max_keypermod;     /* server's max number of keys per modifier */
    KeyCode *modifiermap;  /* an 8 by max_keypermod array of
                            * keycodes to be used as modifiers */
} XModifierKeymap;

#define ShiftMapIndex     0
#define LockMapIndex      1
#define ControlMapIndex   2
#define Mod1MapIndex      3
#define Mod2MapIndex      4
#define Mod3MapIndex      5
```

```
#define Mod4MapIndex    6
#define Mod5MapIndex    7
```

Related Commands

XDeleteModifiermapEntry, XGetModifierMapping, XSetModifierMapping,
XNewModifierMap, XFreeModifiermap, XKeycodeToKeysym, XKeysym-
ToKeycode, XKeysymToString, XQueryKeymap, XStringToKeysym, XLookup-
Keysym, XRebindKeySym, XGetKeyboardMapping, XRefreshKeyboardMapping,
XLookupString.

XInstallColormap

Name

XInstallColormap — install a colormap.

Synopsis

```
XInstallColormap(display, cmap)
    Display *display;
    Colormap cmap;
```

Arguments

display   Specifies a pointer to the `Display` structure; returned from `XOpen-Display`.

cmap   Specifies the colormap to install.

Description

If there is only one hardware colormap, `XInstallColormap` loads a virtual colormap into the hardware colormap. All windows associated with this colormap immediately display with their chosen colors. Other windows associated with the old colormap will display with false colors.

If additional hardware colormaps are possible, `XInstallColormap` loads the new hardware map and keeps the existing ones. Other windows will then remain in their true colors unless the limit for colormaps has been reached. If the maximum number of allowed hardware colormaps is already installed, an old colormap is swapped out. The `MinCmaps-OfScreen(screen)` and `MaxCmapsOfScreen(screen)` macros can be used to determine how many hardware colormaps are supported.

If *cmap* is not already an installed map, a `ColormapNotify` event is generated on every window having *cmap* as an attribute. If a colormap is uninstalled as a result of the install, a `ColormapNotify` event is generated on every window having that colormap as an attribute.

Colormaps are usually installed and uninstalled by the window manager, not by clients.

At any time, there is a subset of the installed colormaps, viewed as an ordered list, called the "required list." The length of the required list is at most the min_maps specified for each screen in the `Display` structure. When a colormap is installed with `XInstallColormap` it is added to the head of the required list and the last colormap in the list is removed if necessary to keep the length of the list at mim_maps. When a colormap is uninstalled with `XUninstallColormap` and it is in the required list, it is removed from the list. No other actions by the server or the client change the required list. It is important to realize that on all but high-performance workstations, min_maps is likely to be 1.

For more information, see Volume One, Chapter 7, *Color*.

Errors

`BadColor`

Related Commands

XCopyColormapAndFree, XCreateColormap, XFreeColormap, XGetStandard-
Colormap, XUninstallColormap, XSetStandardColormap, XListInstalled-
Colormaps, XSetWindowColormap, DefaultColormap, DisplayCells.

XInternAtom

Name

XInternAtom — return an atom for a given name string.

Synopsis

```
Atom XInternAtom(display, property_name, only_if_exists)
    Display *display;
    char *property_name;
    Bool only_if_exists;
```

Arguments

display   Specifies a pointer to the Display structure; returned from XOpen-Display.

property_name

      Specifies the name associated with the property you want the atom for. Upper or lower case is important. The string should be in ISO LATIN-1 encoding, which means that the first 128 character codes are ASCII, and the second 128 character codes are for special characters needed in western languages other than English.

only_if_exists

      Specifies a boolean value that indicates whether XInternAtom should return None or should create the atom if no such *property_name* exists.

Description

XInternAtom returns the atom identifier corresponding to *property_name*.

If the atom does not exist, then XInternAtom either returns None (if *only_if_exists* is True) or creates the atom and returns its ID (if *only_if_exists* is False). The string name should be a null-terminated ASCII string. Case matters: the strings ''thing,'' ''Thing,'' and ''thinG'' all designate different atoms. The atom will remain defined even after the client that defined it has exited. It will become undefined only when the last connection to the X server closes.

This function is the opposite of XGetAtomName, which returns the atom name when given an atom ID.

Predefined atoms are defined in *<X11/Xatom.h>* and begin with the prefix ''XA_''.

Errors

```
BadAlloc
BadValue
```

Related Commands

XSetStandardProperties, XGetFontProperty, XRotateWindowProperties, XDeleteProperty, XChangeProperty, XGetWindowProperty, XList-Properties, XGetAtomName.

Name

XIntersectRegion — compute the intersection of two regions.

Synopsis

```
XIntersectRegion(sra, srb, dr)
    Region sra, srb;
    Region dr;                    /* RETURN */
```

Arguments

sra   Specify the two regions with which to perform the computation.
srb

dr   Returns the result of the computation.

Description

XIntersectRegion generates a region that is the intersection of two regions.

Structures

```
/*
 * opaque reference to Regiondata type.
 * user won't need contents, only pointer.
 */
typedef struct _XRegion *Region;
```

Related Commands

XXorRegion, XUnionRegion, XUnionRectWithRegion, XSubtractRegion,
XShrinkRegion, XSetRegion, XRectInRegion, XPolygonRegion, XPoint-
InRegion, XOffsetRegion, XEmptyRegion, XCreateRegion, XDestroyRegion,
XEqualRegion, XClipBox.

XKeycodeToKeysym

Name

XKeycodeToKeysym — convert a keycode to a keysym.

Synopsis

```
KeySym XKeycodeToKeysym(display, keycode, index)
    Display *display;
    KeyCode keycode;
    int index;
```

Arguments

display   Specifies a pointer to the Display structure; returned from XOpen-Display.

keycode   Specifies the keycode.

index   Specifies which keysym to return.

Description

XKeycodeToKeysym returns the keysym defined for the specified *keycode*. XKeycode-ToKeysym uses internal Xlib tables. *index* specifies which keysym in the array of keysyms corresponding to a keycode should be returned. If no symbol is defined, XKeycode-ToKeysym returns NoSymbol.

Related Commands

XDeleteModifiermapEntry, XInsertModifiermapEntry, XFreeModifiermap, XKeysymToKeycode, XKeysymToString, XNewModifierMap, XQueryKeymap, XStringToKeysym, XLookupKeysym, XRebindKeySym, XGetKeyboardMapping, XChangeKeyboardMapping, XRefreshKeyboardMapping, XLookupString, XSetModifierMapping, XGetModifierMapping, IsKeypadKey, IsCursorKey, IsPFKey, IsFunctionKey, IsMiscFunctionKey, IsModifierKey.

Name

XKeysymToKeycode — convert a keysym to the appropriate keycode.

Synopsis

```
KeyCode XKeysymToKeycode(display, keysym_kcode)
    Display *display;
    Keysym keysym_kcode;
```

Arguments

display   Specifies a pointer to the Display structure; returned from XOpen-Display.

keysym_kcode
                Specifies the keysym that is to be searched for.

Description

XKeysymToKeycode returns the keycode corresponding to the specified keysym symbol in the current mapping. If the specified keysym is not defined for any keycode, XKeysym-ToKeycode returns 0.

Related Commands

XDeleteModifiermapEntry, XInsertModifiermapEntry, XFreeModifiermap, XKeycodeToKeysym, XKeysymToString, XNewModifierMap, XQueryKeymap, XStringToKeysym, XLookupKeysym, XRebindKeySym, XGetKeyboardMapping, XChangeKeyboardMapping, XRefreshKeyboardMapping, XLookupString, XSetModifierMapping, XGetModifierMapping, IsKeypadKey, IsCursorKey, IsPFKey, IsFunctionKey, IsMiscFunctionKey, IsModifierKey.

XKeysymToString

Name

XKeysymToString — convert a keysym symbol to a string.

Synopsis

```
char *XKeysymToString(keysym_str)
    KeySym keysym_str;
```

Arguments

keysym_str   Specifies the keysym that is to be converted.

Description

XKeysymToString converts a keysym symbol (a number) into a character string. The returned string is in a static area and must not be modified. If the specified keysym is not defined, XKeysymToString returns NULL. For example, XKeysymToString converts XK_Shift to "Shift".

Note that XKeysymString does not return the string that is mapped to the keysym, but only a string version of the keysym itself. In other words, even if the F1 key is mapped to the string "STOP" using XRebindKeysym, XKeysymToString still returns "F1". XLookupString, however, would return "STOP".

Related Commands

XDeleteModifiermapEntry, XInsertModifiermapEntry, XFreeModifiermap, XKeycodeToKeysym, XKeysymToKeycode, XNewModifierMap, XQueryKeymap, XStringToKeysym, XLookupKeysym, XRebindKeysym, XGetKeyboardMapping, XChangeKeyboardMapping, XRefreshKeyboardMapping, XLookupString, XSetModifierMapping, XGetModifierMapping, IsKeypadKey, IsCursorKey, IsPFKey, IsFunctionKey, IsMiscFunctionKey, IsModifierKey.

Name

XKillClient — destroy a client or its remaining resources.

Synopsis

```
XKillClient(display, resource)
    Display *display;
    XID resource;
```

Arguments

display   Specifies a pointer to the Display structure; returned from XOpen-
               Display.

resource   Specifies any resource created by the client you want to destroy, or the con-
               stant AllTemporary.

Description

If a valid resource is specified, XKillClient forces a close-down of the client that created
the resource. If the client has already terminated in either RetainPermanent or Retain-
Temporary mode, all of the client's resources are destroyed. If AllTemporary is
specified in the *resource* argument, then the resources of all clients that have terminated in
RetainTemporary are destroyed.

For more information, see Volume One, Chapter 13, *Other Programming Techniques*.

Errors

BadValue

Related Commands

XSetCloseDownMode

Name

XListExtensions — return a list of all extensions to X supported by the server.

Synopsis

```
char **XListExtensions(display, nextensions)
    Display *display;
    int *nextensions;               /* RETURN */
```

Arguments

display   Specifies a pointer to the Display structure; returned from XOpen-
Display.

nextensions Returns the number of extensions in the returned list.

Description

XListExtensions lists all the X extensions supported by the current server. Upper or lower case is important. The returned strings will be in ISO LATIN-1 encoding, which means that the first 128 character codes are ASCII, and the second 128 character codes are for special characters needed in western languages other than English.

For more information on extensions, see Volume One, Chapter 13, *Other Programming Techniques*.

Related Commands

XQueryExtension, XFreeExtensionList.

Name

XListFonts — return a list of the available font names.

Synopsis

```
char **XListFonts(display, pattern, maxnames, actual_count)
    Display *display;
    char *pattern;
    int maxnames;
    int *actual_count;              /* RETURN */
```

Arguments

display   Specifies a pointer to the Display structure; returned from XOpen-
            Display.

pattern   Specifies the string associated with the font names you want returned. You
            can specify any string, an asterisk (*), or a question mark. The asterisk indi-
            cates a wildcard for any number of characters and the question mark indi-
            cates a wildcard for a single character. Upper or lower case is not important.
            The string should be in ISO LATIN-1 encoding, which means that the first
            128 character codes are ASCII, and the second 128 character codes are for
            special characters needed in western languages other than English.

maxnames   Specifies the maximum number of names that are to be in the returned list.

actual_count
            Returns the actual number of font names in the list.

Description

XListFonts returns a list of font names that match the string *pattern*. Each string is terminated by NULL. The maximum number of names returned in the list depends on the value
you passed to *maxnames*. The function returns the actual number of font names in
actual_count. The client should call XFreeFontNames when done with this list to free
the memory.

The font search path (the order in which font names are compared to *pattern*) is set by
XSetFontPath.

For more information on fonts, see Volume One, Chapter 6, *Drawing Graphics and Text*.

Related Commands

XLoadFont, XLoadQueryFont, XFreeFont, XFreeFontInfo, XListFontsWith-
Info, XFreeFontNames, XFreeFontPath, XGetFontPath, XQueryFont, XSet-
Font, XSetFontPath, XUnloadFont, XGetFontProperty, XCreateFontCursor.

Name

XListFontsWithInfo — obtain the names and information about loaded fonts.

Synopsis

```
char **XListFontsWithInfo(display, pattern, maxnames,
        count, info)
    Display *display;
    char *pattern;              /* null-terminated */
    int maxnames;
    int *count;                 /* RETURN */
    XFontStruct **info;         /* RETURN */
```

Arguments

display   Specifies a pointer to the Display structure; returned from XOpen-Display.

pattern   Specifies the string associated with the font names you want returned. You can specify any string, an asterisk (*), or a question mark. The asterisk indicates a wildcard on any number of characters and the question mark indicates a wildcard on a single character.

maxnames   Specifies the maximum number of names that are to be in the returned list.

count   Returns the actual number of matched font names.

info   Returns the font information. XListFontsWithInfo provides enough space for *maxnames* pointers.

Description

XListFontsWithInfo returns a list of font names that match the specified pattern and a list of their associated font information. The list of names is limited to a size specified by the *maxnames* argument. To free the allocated name array, the client should call XFreeFont-Names. To free the font information array, the client should call XFreeFontInfo.

The information returned for each font is identical to what XQueryFont would return, except that the per-character metrics (lbearing, rbearing, width, ascent, descent for single characters) are not returned.

XListFontsWithInfo returns NULL on failure.

For more information on fonts, see Volume One, Chapter 6, *Drawing Graphics and Text*.

Structures

```
typedef struct {
    XExtData *ext_data;        /* hook for extension to hang data */
    Font fid;                  /* Font ID for this font */
    unsigned direction;        /* hint about direction the font is painted */
    unsigned min_char_or_byte2; /* first character */
    unsigned max_char_or_byte2; /* last character */
    unsigned min_byte1;        /* first row that exists */
    unsigned max_byte1;        /* last row that exists */
```

```
        Bool all_chars_exist;       /* flag if all characters have nonzero size*/
        unsigned default_char;      /* char to print for undefined character */
        int n_properties;           /* how many properties there are */
        XFontProp *properties;      /* pointer to array of additional properties*/
        XCharStruct min_bounds;     /* minimum bounds over all existing char*/
        XCharStruct max_bounds;     /* minimum bounds over all existing char*/
        XCharStruct *per_char;      /* first_char to last_char information */
        int ascent;                 /* logical extent above baseline for spacing */
        int descent;                /* logical descent below baseline for spacing */
} XFontStruct;
```

Related Commands

XLoadFont, XLoadQueryFont, XFreeFont, XFreeFontInfo, XListFonts,
XFreeFontNames, XFreeFontPath, XGetFontPath, XQueryFont, XSetFont,
XSetFontPath, XUnloadFont, XGetFontProperty, XCreateFontCursor.

Name

XListHosts — obtain a list of hosts having access to this display.

Synopsis

```
XHostAddress *XListHosts(display, nhosts, state)
    Display *display;
    int *nhosts;                    /* RETURN */
    Bool *state;                    /* RETURN */
```

Arguments

display   Specifies a pointer to the Display structure; returned from XOpen-Display.

nhosts   Returns the number of hosts currently in the access control list.

state   Returns the state of access to the control list at connection setup. True if enabled, False if disabled.

Description

XListHosts returns the current access control list as well as whether the use of the list was enabled or disabled when this client connected to the display. XListHosts allows a program to find out what machines can make connections, by looking at the list of host structures. This XHostAddress list should be freed with XFree when it is no longer needed. XList-Hosts returns NULL on failure.

For more information on access control lists, see Volume One, Chapter 13, *Other Programming Techniques*.

Structures

```
typedef struct {
    int family;
    int length;
    char *address;
} XHostAddress;
```

Related Commands

XAddHost, XAddHosts, XRemoveHost, XRemoveHosts, XDisableAccess-Control, XEnableAccessControl, XSetAccessControl.

Name

XListInstalledColormaps — get a list of installed colormaps.

Synopsis

```
Colormap *XListInstalledColormaps(display, w, num)
    display *display;
    Window w;
    int *num;                       /* RETURN */
```

Arguments

display   Specifies a pointer to the Display structure; returned from XOpen-Display.

w   Specifies the ID of the window for whose screen you want the list of currently installed colormaps.

num   Returns the number of currently installed colormaps in the returned list.

Description

XListInstalledColormaps returns a list of the currently installed colormaps for the screen of the specified window. The order in the list is not significant. There is no distinction in the list between colormaps actually being used by windows and colormaps no longer in use which have not yet been freed or destroyed. The allocated list should be freed using XFree when it is no longer needed. XListInstalledColormaps returns None on failure and sets *num* to 0.

For more information on installing colormaps, see Volume One, Chapter 7, *Color*.

Errors

BadWindow

Related Commands

XCopyColormapAndFree, XCreateColormap, XFreeColormap, XGetStandard-Colormap, XInstallColormap, XUninstallColormap, XSetStandard-Colormap, XSetWindowColormap, DefaultColormap, DisplayCells.

XListProperties

Name

XListProperties — get the property list for a window.

Synopsis

```
Atom *XListProperties(display, w, num_prop)
    Display *display;
    Window w;
    int *num_prop;                 /* RETURN */
```

Arguments

display   Specifies a pointer to the Display structure; returned from XOpen-Display.

w   Specifies the window whose property list you want.

num_prop   Returns the length of the properties array.

Description

XListProperties returns a pointer to an array of atom properties that are defined for the specified window. To free the memory allocated by this function, use XFree. XList-Properties returns NULL on failure and sets *num_prop* to 0.

For more information, see Volume One, Chapter 10, *Interclient Communication*.

Errors

BadWindow

Related Commands

XSetStandardProperties, XGetFontProperty, XRotateWindowProperties, XDeleteProperty, XChangeProperty, XGetWindowProperty, XGetAtomName, XInternAtom.

XLoadFont

Name

XLoadFont — load a font if not already loaded; get font ID.

Synopsis

```
Font XLoadFont(display, name)
    Display *display;
    char *name;
```

Arguments

display   Specifies a pointer to the `Display` structure; returned from `XOpen-Display`.

name   Specifies the name of the font in a null terminated string. Upper or lower case is not important. The string should be in ISO LATIN-1 encoding, which means that the first 128 character codes are ASCII, and the second 128 character codes are for special characters needed in western languages other than English.

Description

`XLoadFont` loads a font into the server if it has not already been loaded by another client. `XLoadFont` returns the font ID or, if it was unsuccessful, returns a 0 and generates a `Bad-Name` error. When the font is no longer needed, the client should call `XUnloadFont`. Fonts are not associated with a particular screen. Once the font ID is available, it can be set in the `font` member of any GC, and thereby used in subsequent drawing requests.

Font information is usually necessary for locating the text. Call `XLoadFontWithInfo` to get the info at the time you load the font, or call `XQueryFont` if you used `XLoadFont` to load the font.

For more information on fonts, see Volume One, Chapter 6, *Drawing Graphics and Text*.

Errors

`BadAlloc`

`BadName`   name specifies an unavailable font.

Related Commands

`XLoadQueryFont, XFreeFont, XFreeFontInfo, XListFonts, XListFontsWith-Info, XFreeFontNames, XFreeFontPath, XGetFontPath, XQueryFont, XSet-Font, XSetFontPath, XUnloadFont, XGetFontProperty, XCreateFontCursor`.

Name

XLoadQueryFont — load a font and fill information structure.

Synopsis

```
XFontStruct *XLoadQueryFont(display, name)
    Display *display;
    char *name;
```

Arguments

display   Specifies a pointer to the Display structure; returned from XOpen-
Display.

name   Specifies the name of the font. This name is a null terminated string.

Description

XLoadQueryFont performs a XLoadFont and XQueryFont in a single operation. XLoadQueryFont provides the easiest way to get character-size tables for placing a proportional font. That is, XLoadQueryFont both opens (loads) the specified font and returns a pointer to the appropriate XFontStruct structure. If the font does not exist, XLoadQuery-Font returns NULL.

The XFontStruct structure consists of the font-specific information and a pointer to an array of XCharStruct structures for each character in the font.

For more information on fonts, see Volume One, Chapter 6, *Drawing Graphics and Text*.

Errors

BadAlloc

BadName   name specifies an unavailable font.

Structures

```
typedef struct {
    XExtData *ext_data;          /* hook for extension to hang data */
    Font fid;                    /* Font ID for this font */
    unsigned direction;          /* hint about direction the font is painted */
    unsigned min_char_or_byte2;  /* first character */
    unsigned max_char_or_byte2;  /* last character */
    unsigned min_byte1;          /* first row that exists */
    unsigned max_byte1;          /* last row that exists */
    Bool all_chars_exist;        /* flag if all characters have nonzero size*/
    unsigned default_char;       /* char to print for undefined character */
    int n_properties;            /* how many properties there are */
    XFontProp *properties;       /* pointer to array of additional properties*/
    XCharStruct min_bounds;      /* minimum bounds over all existing char*/
    XCharStruct max_bounds;      /* minimum bounds over all existing char*/
    XCharStruct *per_char;       /* first_char to last_char information */
    int ascent;                  /* logical extent above baseline for spacing */
    int descent;                 /* logical descent below baseline for spacing */
} XFontStruct;
```

```
typedef struct {
    short lbearing;              /* origin to left edge of character */
    short rbearing;              /* origin to right edge of character */
    short width;                 /* advance to next char's origin */
    short ascent;                /* baseline to top edge of character */
    short descent;               /* baseline to bottom edge of character */
    unsigned short attributes;   /* per char flags (not predefined) */
} XCharStruct;
```

Errors
BadAlloc

Related Commands
XLoadFont, XFreeFont, XFreeFontInfo, XListFonts, XListFontsWithInfo,
XFreeFontNames, XFreeFontPath, XGetFontPath, XQueryFont, XSetFont,
XSetFontPath, XUnloadFont, XGetFontProperty, XCreateFontCursor.

XLookUpAssoc

Name
XLookUpAssoc — obtain data from an association table.

Synopsis
```
caddr_t XLookUpAssoc(display, table, x_id)
    Display *display;
    XAssocTable *table;
    XID x_id;
```

Arguments

display Specifies a pointer to the Display structure; returned from XOpen-Display.

table Specifies the association table.

x_id Specifies the X resource ID.

Description
This function is provided for compatibility with X Version 10. To use it you must include the file *<X11/X10.h>* and link with the library *-loldX*.

Association tables provide a way of storing data and accessing by ID. This information is available to all clients. XLookUpAssoc retrieves the data stored in an XAssocTable by its XID. If the matching XID can be found in the table, the routine returns the data associated with it. If the *x_id* cannot be found in the table the routine returns NULL.

For more information on association tables, see Volume One, Chapter 13, *Other Programming Techniques*.

Structures
```
typedef struct {
    XAssoc *buckets;        /* pointer to first bucket in bucket array */
    int size;               /* table size (number of buckets) */
} XAssocTable;

typedef struct _XAssoc {
    struct _XAssoc *next;   /* next object in this bucket */
    struct _XAssoc *prev;   /* previous object in this bucket */
    Display *display;       /* display which owns the ID */
    XID x_id;               /* X Window System ID */
    char *data;             /* pointer to untyped memory */
} XAssoc;
```

Related Commands
XCreateAssocTable, XDeleteAssoc, XDestroyAssocTable, XMakeAssoc.

XLookupColor

Name

XLookupColor — get database RGB values and closest hardware-supported RGB values from color name.

Synopsis

```
Status XLookupColor(display, cmap, colorname, rgb_db_def,
        hardware_def)
    Display *display;
    Colormap cmap;
    char *colorname;
    XColor *rgb_db_def, *hardware_def; /* RETURN */
```

Arguments

display   Specifies a pointer to the Display structure; returned from XOpen-Display.

cmap   Specifies the colormap.

colorname   Specifies the color name string (for example "red"). Upper or lower case does not matter. The string should be in ISO LATIN1 encoding, which means that the first 128 character codes are ASCII, and the second 128 character codes are for special characters needed in western languages other than English.

rgb_db_def   Returns the exact RGB values for the specified color name from the /usr/lib/rgb database.

hardware_def   Returns the closest RGB values possible on the hardware.

Description

XLookupColor looks up the string name of a color with respect to the screen associated with the specified cmap and returns both the exact color values and the closest values possible on that screen.

XLookupColor returns 1 if colorname exists in the RGB database or 0 if it does not exist.

To determine the exact RGB values, XLookupColor uses a database on the X server. On UNIX, this database is /usr/lib/rgb. To read the colors provided by the database on a UNIX system, see /usr/lib/rgb.txt. The location, name, and contents of this file are server-dependent.

For more information see Volume One, Chapter 7, Color, and Appendix D, The Color Database, in this volume.

Structures

```
typedef struct {
    unsigned long pixel;
    unsigned short red, green, blue;
    char flags;                         /* DoRed, DoGreen, DoBlue */
    char pad;
} XColor;
```

Related Commands

XAllocColorCells, XAllocColorPlanes, XAllocColor, XAllocNamedColor,
XParseColor, XQueryColor, XQueryColors, XStoreColor, XStoreColors,
XFreeColors, XStoreNamedColor, BlackPixel, WhitePixel.

Name

XLookupKeysym — get the keysym corresponding to a keycode in structure.

Synopsis

```
KeySym XLookupKeysym(event, index)
    XKeyEvent *event;
    int index;
```

Arguments

event   Specifies the KeyPress or KeyRelease event that is to be used.

index   Specifies which keysym from the list associated with the keycode in the event to return. These correspond to the modifier keys, and the symbols ShiftMap-Index, LockMapIndex, ControlMapIndex, Mod1MapIndex, Mod2-MapIndex, Mod3MapIndex, Mod4MapIndex, and Mod5MapIndex can be used.

Description

Given a keyboard event and the index into the list of keysyms for that keycode, XLookup-Keysym returns the keysym from the list that corresponds to the keycode in the event. If no keysym is defined for the keycode of the event, XLookupKeysym returns NoSymbol.

Each keycode may have a list of associated keysyms, which are portable symbols representing the meanings of the key. The index specifies which keysym in the list is desired, indicating the combination of modifier keys that are currently pressed. Therefore, the program must interpret the state member of the XKeyEvent structure to determine the index before calling this function. The exact mapping of modifier keys into the list of keysyms for each keycode is server-dependent beyond the fact that the first keysym corresponds to the keycode without modifier keys, and the second corresponds to the keycode with Shift pressed.

XLookupKeysym simply calls XKeycodeToKeysym, using arguments taken from the specified event structure.

Note that some hardware can't support KeyRelease events for every key. You may wish to avoid using them in your code.

Structures

```
typedef struct {
    int type;                /* of event */
    Display *display;        /* display the event was read from */
    Window window;           /* "event" window it is reported relative to */
    Window root;             /* root window that the event occured on */
    Window subwindow;        /* child window */
    Time time;               /* milliseconds */
    int x, y;                /* pointer x, y coordinates in event window */
    int x_root, y_root;      /* coordinates relative to root */
    unsigned int state;      /* key or button mask */
    unsigned int keycode;    /* detail */
    Bool same_screen;        /* same screen flag */
} XKeyEvent;
```

Related Commands

XDeleteModifiermapEntry, XInsertModifiermapEntry, XFreeModifiermap,
XKeycodeToKeysym, XKeysymToKeycode, XKeysymToString, XNewModifier-
Map, XQueryKeymap, XStringToKeysym, XRebindKeysym, XGetKeyboard-
Mapping, XChangeKeyboardMapping, XRefreshKeyboardMapping, XLookup-
String, XSetModifierMapping, XGetModifierMapping.

Name

XLookupString — map a key event to ASCII string, keysym, and `ComposeStatus`.

Synopsis

```
int XLookupString(event, buffer, num_bytes, keysym, status)
    XKeyEvent *event;
    char *buffer;                 /* RETURN */
    int num_bytes;
    KeySym *keysym;               /* RETURN */
    XComposeStatus *status;       /* not implemented */
```

Arguments

event   Specifies the key event to be used.

buffer   Returns the resulting string.

num_bytes   Specifies the length of the buffer. No more than *num_bytes* of translation are returned.

keysym   If this argument is not NULL, it specifies the keysym ID computed from the event.

status   Specifies the XCompose structure that contains compose key state information and that allows the compose key processing to take place. This can be NULL if the caller is not interested in seeing compose key sequences. Not implemented in Release 1 or 2.

Description

XLookupString gets an ASCII string and a keysym that are currently mapped to the key-code in a KeyPress or KeyRelease event, using the modifier bits in the key event to deal with shift, lock and control. The XLookupString return value is the length of the translated string and the string's bytes are copied into the user's buffer. The length may be greater than 1 if the event's keycode translates into a keysym that was rebound with XRebindKeysym.

The compose *status* is not implemented in Release 1 or 2.

Structures

```
/*
 * Compose sequence status structure, used in calling XLookupString.
 */
typedef struct _XComposeStatus {
    char *compose_ptr;     /* state table pointer */
    int chars_matched;     /* match state */
} XComposeStatus;

typedef struct {
    int type;              /* of event */
    Display *display;      /* Display the event was read from */
    Window window;         /* "event" window it is reported relative to */
```

```
        Window root;            /* root window that the event occured on */
        Window subwindow;       /* child window */
        Time time;              /* milliseconds */
        int x, y;               /* pointer x, y coordinates in event window */
        int x_root, y_root;     /* coordinates relative to root */
        unsigned int state;     /* key or button mask */
        unsigned int keycode;   /* detail */
        Bool same_screen;       /* same screen flag */
    } XKeyEvent;
```

Related Commands

XDeleteModifiermapEntry, XInsertModifiermapEntry, XFreeModifiermap,
XKeycodeToKeysym, XKeysymToKeycode, XKeysymToString, XNewModifier-
Map, XQueryKeymap, XStringToKeysym, XLookupKeysym, XRebindKeySym,
XGetKeyboardMapping, XChangeKeyboardMapping, XRefreshKeyboard-
Mapping, XSetModifierMapping, XGetModifierMapping.

XLowerWindow

Name

XLowerWindow — lower a window in the stacking order.

Synopsis

```
XLowerWindow(display, w)
    Display *display;
    Window w;
```

Arguments

display   Specifies a pointer to the Display structure; returned from XOpen-
             Display.

w   Specifies the ID of the window to be lowered.

Description

XLowerWindow lowers a window in the stacking order of its siblings so that it does not
obscure any sibling windows. If the windows are regarded as overlapping sheets of paper
stacked on a desk, then lowering a window is analogous to moving the sheet to the bottom of
the stack, while leaving its x and y location on the desk constant. Lowering a mapped window will generate exposure events on any windows it formerly obscured.

If the override_redirect attribute of the window (see Chapter 4, *Window Attributes*) is
False and some other client has selected SubstructureRedirectMask on the parent,
then a ConfigureRequest event is generated, and no further processing is performed.
Otherwise, the window is lowered to the bottom of the stack.

LeaveNotify events are sent to the lowered window if the pointer was inside it, and
EnterNotify events are sent to the window which was immediately below the lowered
window at the pointer position.

For more information, see Volume One, Chapter 14, *Window Management*.

Errors

BadWindow

Related Commands

XRaiseWindow, XCirculateSubwindows, XCirculateSubwindowsDown,
XCirculateSubwindowsUp, XRestackWindows, XMoveWindow, XResizeWindow,
XMoveResizeWindow, XReparentWindow, XConfigureWindow, XQueryTree.

XMakeAssoc

Name

XMakeAssoc — create an entry in an association table.

Synopsis

```
XMakeAssoc(display, table, x_id, data)
    Display *display;
    XAssocTable *table;
    XID x_id;
    caddr_t data;
```

Arguments

display   Specifies a pointer to the Display structure; returned from XOpenDisplay.

table   Specifies the association table in which an entry is to be made.

x_id   Specifies the X resource ID.

data   Specifies the data to be associated with the X resource ID.

Description

XMakeAssoc inserts data into an XAssocTable keyed on an XID. Association tables allow you to easily associate data with resource ID's for later retrieval by any application.

This function is provided for compatibility with X Version 10. To use it you must include the file *<X11/X10.h>* and link with the library *-loldX*.

Data is inserted into the table only once. Redundant inserts are meaningless and cause no problems. The queue in each association bucket is sorted from the lowest XID to the highest XID.

For more information, see Volume One, Chapter 13, *Other Programming Techniques*.

Structure

```
typedef struct {
    XAssoc *buckets;        /* pointer to first bucket in bucket array */
    int size;               /* table size (number of buckets) */
} XAssocTable;

typedef struct _XAssoc {
    struct _XAssoc *next;   /* next object in this bucket */
    struct _XAssoc *prev;   /* previous object in this bucket */
    Display *display;       /* display which owns the ID */
    XID x_id;               /* X Window System ID */
    char *data;             /* pointer to untyped memory */
} XAssoc;
```

Related Commands

XCreateAssocTable, XDeleteAssoc, XDestroyAssocTable, XLookUpAssoc.

Name

XMapRaised — map a window on top of its siblings.

Synopsis

```
XMapRaised(display, w)
    Display *display;
    Window w;
```

Arguments

display   Specifies a pointer to the Display structure; returned from XOpenDisplay.

w   Specifies the window ID.

Description

XMapRaised marks a window as eligible to be displayed. It will actually be displayed if its ancestors are mapped, it is on top of sibling windows, and it is not obscured by unrelated windows. XMapRaised is similar to XMapWindow, except it additionally raises the specified window to the top of the stack among its siblings. Mapping an already mapped window with XMapRaised raises the window. See XMapWindow for further details.

For more information, see Volume One, Chapter 14, *Window Management*.

Errors

BadWindow

Related Commands

XMapSubwindows, XMapWindow, XUnmapSubwindows, XUnmapWindow.

XMapSubwindows

Name

XMapSubwindows — map all subwindows.

Synopsis

```
XMapSubwindows (display, w)
    Display *display;
    Window w;
```

Arguments

display   Specifies a pointer to the `Display` structure; returned from `XOpenDisplay`.

w   Specifies the ID of the window whose subwindows are to be mapped.

Description

XMapSubwindows maps all subwindows of a window in top-to-bottom stacking order. XMapSubwindows also generates an `Expose` event on each newly displayed window. This is much more efficient than mapping many windows one at a time, as much of the work need only be performed once for all of the windows rather than for each window.

For more information, see Volume One, Chapter 14, *Window Management*.

Errors

BadWindow

Related Commands

XMapRaised, XMapWindow, XUnmapSubwindows, XUnmapWindow.

Name

XMapWindow — map a window.

Synopsis

```
XMapWindow(display, w)
    Display *display;
    Window w;
```

Arguments

display   Specifies a pointer to the Display structure; returned from XOpenDisplay.

w   Specifies the ID of the window to be mapped.

Description

XMapWindow maps a window, making it eligible for display depending on its stacking order among its siblings, the mapping status of its ancestors, and the placement of other visible windows. If all the ancestors are mapped, and it is not obscured by siblings higher in the stacking order, the window and all of its mapped subwindows are displayed.

Mapping a window that has an unmapped ancestor does not display the window but marks it as eligible for display when its ancestors become mapped. Mapping an already mapped window has no effect (it does not raise the window).

If the window is opaque, XMapWindow generates Expose events on each opaque window that it causes to become displayed. If the client first maps the window, then paints the window, then begins processing input events, the window is painted twice. To avoid this, the client should use either of two strategies:

1. Map the window, call XSelectInput for exposure events, wait for the first Expose event, and repaint each window explicitly.

2. Call XSelectInput for exposure events, map, and process input events normally. Exposure events are generated for each window that has appeared on the screen, and the client's normal response to an Expose event should be to repaint the window.

The latter method is preferred as it usually leads to simpler programs. If you fail to wait for the Expose event in the first method, it can cause incorrect behavior with certain window managers that intercept the request.

Errors

BadWindow

Related Commands

XMapRaised, XMapSubwindows, XUnmapSubwindows, XUnmapWindow.

XMaskEvent

Name

XMaskEvent — remove the next event that matches mask.

Synopsis

```
XMaskEvent(display, event_mask, rep)
    Display *display;
    unsigned long event_mask;
    XEvent *rep;                    /* RETURN */
```

Arguments

display   Specifies a pointer to the Display structure; returned from XOpen-
            Display.

event_mask Specifies the event mask. See XSelectInput for a complete list of event
            masks.

rep   Returns the event removed from the input queue.

Description

XMaskEvent removes the next event in the queue which matches the passed mask. The event is copied into an XEvent supplied by the caller. Other events in the queue are not discarded. If no such event has been queued, XMaskEvent flushes the output buffer and waits until one is received. Use XCheckMaskEvent if you do not wish to wait.

In Release 1, the output buffer was always flushed by event-getting routines. In Release 2, the output buffer is flushed only if no matching events are found on the queue. This change is compatible with applications written for Release 1.

Related Commands

XSelectInput, XSetInputFocus, XGetInputFocus, XWindowEvent, XCheck-WindowEvent, XCheckTypedEvent, XCheckTypedWindowEvent, XCheckMask-Event, XNextEvent, XEventsQueued, XAllowEvents, XGetMotionEvents, XIfEvent, XCheckIfEvent, XPeekEvent, XPeekIfEvent, XPutBackEvent, XPending, XSynchronize, XSendEvent, QLength.

XMatchVisualInfo

Name

XMatchVisualInfo — obtain the visual information that matches the desired depth and class.

Synopsis

```
Status XMatchVisualInfo(display, screen, depth, class, vinfo)
    Display *display;
    int screen;
    int depth;
    int class;
    XVisualInfo *vinfo;        /* RETURN */
```

Arguments

display   Specifies a pointer to the Display structure; returned from XOpenDisplay.

screen   Specifies the screen.

depth   Specifies the desired depth of the visual.

class   Specifies the desired class of the visual, such as PseudoColor or True-Color.

vinfo   Returns the matched visual information.

Description

XMatchVisualInfo returns the visual information for a visual that matches the specified depth and class for a screen. Because multiple visuals that match the specified depth and class can exist, the exact visual chosen is undefined.

If a visual is found, this function returns a nonzero value and the information on the visual is returned to vinfo. If a visual is not found, it returns 0.

For more information on visuals, see Volume One, Chapter 7, Color.

Structures

```
typedef struct {
    Visual *visual;
    VisualID visualid;
    int screen;
    unsigned int depth;
    int class;
    unsigned long red_mask;
    unsigned long green_mask;
    unsigned long blue_mask;
    int colormap_size;
    int bits_per_rgb;
} XVisualInfo;
```

Related Commands

XGetVisualInfo, DefaultVisual.

XMoveResizeWindow

Name

XMoveResizeWindow — change the size and position of a window.

Synopsis

```
XMoveResizeWindow(display, w, x, y, width, height)
    Display *display;
    Window w;
    int x, y;
    unsigned int width, height;
```

Arguments

display   Specifies a pointer to the Display structure; returned from XOpenDisplay.

w   Specifies the ID of the window to be reconfigured.

x
y   Specify the new x and y coordinates of the upper-left pixel of the window's border, relative to the window's parent.

width
height   Specify the width and height in pixels. These arguments define the interior size of the window.

Description

XMoveResizeWindow moves or resizes a window or both. XMoveResizeWindow does not raise the window. Configuring a mapped window may lose its contents and generate an Expose event on that window depending on the bit_gravity and backing store attributes. Configuring a window may generate exposure events on windows that the window formerly obscured, depending on the new size and location parameters.

If the override_redirect attribute of the window is False (see Volume One, Chapter 4, *Window Attributes*) and some other client has selected SubstructureRedirectMask on the parent, then a ConfigureRequest event is generated, and no further processing is performed.

If some other client has selected StructureNotifyMask on the window, then a ConfigureNotify event is generated after the move and resize takes place, and the event will contain the final position and size of the window.

Errors

```
BadMatch
BadValue
BadWindow
```

Related Commands

XLowerWindow, XRaiseWindow, XCirculateSubwindows, XCirculate-SubwindowsDown, XCirculateSubwindowsUp, XRestackWindows, XMove-Window, XResizeWindow, XReparentWindow, XConfigureWindow, XQueryTree.

Name

XMoveWindow — move a window.

Synopsis

```
XMoveWindow(display, w, x, y)
    Display *display;
    Window w;
    int x, y;
```

Arguments

display   Specifies a pointer to the Display structure; returned from XOpenDisplay.

w   Specifies the ID of the window to be moved.

x   Specify the new x and y coordinates of the upper-left pixel of the window's
y   border (or of the window itself, if it has no border), relative to the window's
            parent.

Description

XMoveWindow changes the position of the origin of the specified window relative to its
parent. XMoveWindow does not change the mapping state, size, or stacking order of the window, nor does it raise the window. Moving a mapped window will lose its contents if:

- Its background_pixmap attribute is ParentRelative.

- The window is obscured by nonchildren and no backing store exists.

If the contents are lost, exposure events will be generated for the window and any mapped
subwindows. Moving a mapped window will generate exposure events on any formerly
obscured windows.

If the override_redirect attribute of the window is False (see Volume One, Chapter
4, *Window Attributes*) and some other client has selected SubstructureRedirectMask
on the parent, then a ConfigureRequest event is generated, and no further processing is
performed.

If some other client has selected StructureNotifyMask on the window, then a
ConfigureNotify event is generated after the move takes place, and the event will contain
the final position of the window.

Errors

BadWindow

Related Commands

XLowerWindow, XRaiseWindow, XCirculateSubwindows, XCirculate-
SubwindowsDown, XCirculateSubwindowsUp, XRestackWindows, XResize-
Window, XMoveResizeWindow, XReparentWindow, XConfigureWindow, XQuery-
Tree.

XNewModifiermap

Name
XNewModifiermap — create a keyboard modifier mapping structure.

Synopsis
```
XModifierKeymap *XNewModifiermap(max_keys_per_mod)
     int max_keys_per_mod;
```

Arguments
max_keys_per_mod
>Specifies the maximum number of keycodes assigned to any of the modifiers in the map.

Description
XNewModifiermap returns a XModifierKeymap structure and allocates the needed space. This function is used when more than one XModifierKeymap structure is needed. *max_keys_per_mod* depends on the server and should be gotten from the XModifier-Keymap returned by XGetModifierMapping.

For more information on keyboard preferences, see Volume One, Chapter 9, *The Keyboard and Pointer*.

Structures
```
typedef struct {
    int max_keypermod;      /* server's max number of keys per modifier */
    KeyCode *modifiermap;   /* An 8 by max_keypermod array
                             * of the modifiers */
} XModifierKeymap;
```

Related Commands
XDeleteModifiermapEntry, XInsertModifiermapEntry, XFreeModifiermap, XKeycodeToKeysym, XKeysymToKeycode, XKeysymToString, XQueryKeymap, XStringToKeysym, XLookupKeysym, XRebindKeysym, XGetKeyboardMapping, XChangeKeyboardMapping, XRefreshKeyboardMapping, XLookupString, XSetModifierMapping, XGetModifierMapping.

Name

XNextEvent — get the next event of any type or window.

Synopsis

```
XNextEvent(display, report)
    Display *display;
    XEvent *report;                    /* RETURN */
```

Arguments

display   Specifies a pointer to the Display structure; returned from XOpen-Display.

report   Returns the event removed from the input queue.

Description

XNextEvent removes an input event from the head of the event queue and copies it into an XEvent supplied by the caller. If the event queue is empty, XNextEvent flushes the output buffer and waits (blocks) until an event is received. Use XCheckNextEvent if you do not want to wait.

In Release 1, the output buffer was always flushed by event-getting routines. In Release 2, the output buffer is flushed only if no matching events are found on the queue. This change is compatible with applications written for Release 1.

For more information, see Volume One, Chapter 8, *Events*.

Related Commands

XSelectInput, XSetInputFocus, XGetInputFocus, XWindowEvent, XCheck-WindowEvent, XCheckTypedEvent, XCheckTypedWindowEvent, XMaskEvent, XCheckMaskEvent, XEventsQueued, XAllowEvents, XGetMotionEvents, XIfEvent, XCheckIfEvent, XPeekEvent, XPeekIfEvent, XPutBackEvent, XPending, XSynchronize, XSendEvent, QLength.

Name

XNoOp — send a NoOp to exercise connection with the server.

Synopsis

```
XNoOp (display)
    Display *display;
```

Arguments

display   Specifies a pointer to the Display structure; returned from XOpen-
               Display.

Description

XNoOp sends a NoOperation request to the X server, thereby exercising the connection.
This request can be used to measure the response time of the network connection. XNoOp
does not flush the output buffer.

Related Commands

XFree, XOpenDisplay, XCloseDisplay, DefaultScreen.

Name

XOffsetRegion — change offset of a region.

Synopsis

```
XOffsetRegion(r, dx, dy)
    Region r;
    int dx, dy;
```

Arguments

r   Specifies the region.

dx   Specify the amount to move the specified region relative to the origin of all
dy   regions.

Description

XOffsetRegion changes the offset of the region the specified amounts in the x and y directions.

Regions are located using an offset from a point (the *region origin*) which is common to all regions. It is up to the application to interpret the location of the region relative to a drawable. If the region is to be used as a clip_mask by calling XSetRegion, the upper-left corner of the region relative to the drawable used in the graphics request will be at (xoffset + clip_x_origin, yoffset + clip_y_origin), where xoffset and yoffset are the offset of the region and clip_x_origin and clip_y_origin are elements of the GC used in the graphics request.

Structures

```
/*
 * opaque reference to Regiondata type.
 * user won't need contents, only pointer.
 */
typedef struct _XRegion *Region;
```

Related Commands

XXorRegion, XUnionRegion, XUnionRectWithRegion, XSubtractRegion, XShrinkRegion, XSetRegion, XRectInRegion, XPolygonRegion, XPoint-InRegion, XIntersectRegion, XEmptyRegion, XCreateRegion, XDestroy-Region, XEqualRegion, XClipBox.

XOpenDisplay

Name

XOpenDisplay — connect a client program to an X server.

Synopsis

```
Display *XOpenDisplay(display_name)
    char *display_name;
```

Arguments

display_name

> Specifies the display name, which determines the hardware display and communications domain to be used. See Description below.

Description

The XOpenDisplay routine connects the client to the server controlling the hardware display through TCP, UNIX, or DECnet streams.

If display_name is NULL, the value defaults to the contents of the DISPLAY environment variable on UNIX systems. On non-UNIX systems, see that operating system's Xlib manual for the default display_name. The display_name or DISPLAY environment variable is a string that has the format hostname:server or hostname:server.screen. For example, frog:0.2 would specify screen 2 of server 0 on the machine frog.

hostname Specifies the name of the host machine on which the display is physically connected. You follow the hostname with either a single colon (:) or a double colon (::), which determines the communications domain to use. Any or all of the communication protocols can be used simultaneously on a server built to support them.

- If hostname is a host machine name and a single colon (:) separates the hostname and display number, XOpenDisplay connects the hardware display to TCP streams.

- If hostname is "unix" and a single colon (:) separates it from the display number, XOpenDisplay connects the hardware display to UNIX domain IPC streams.

- If hostname is a host machine name and a double colon (::) separates the hostname and display number, XOpenDisplay connects the hardware display to DECnet streams. To use DECnet, however, you must build all software for DECnet. A single X server will accept both TCP and DECnet connections if it has been built for DECnet.

server Specifies the number of the server on its host machine. This display number may be followed by a period (.). A single CPU can have more than one display; the displays are usually numbered starting from 0.

    screen   Specifies the number of the default screen on *server*. Multiple screens can be connected to (controlled by) a single X server, but they are used as a single display by a single user. *screen* merely sets an internal variable that is returned by the DefaultScreen macro. If *screen* is omitted, it defaults to 0.

If successful, XOpenDisplay returns a pointer to a Display. This structure provides many of the specifications of the server and its screens. If XOpenDisplay does not succeed, it returns a NULL.

After a successful call to XOpenDisplay, all of the screens on the server may be used by the application. The screen number specified in the *display_name* argument serves only to specify the value that will be returned by the DefaultScreen macro. After opening the display, you can use the ScreenCount macro to determine how many screens are available. Then you can reference each screen with integer values between 0 and the value returned by ScreenCount.

For more information, see Volume One: Chapter 2, *X Concepts*; and Chapter 3, *Basic Window Program*.

Structures

```
/*
 * Display datatype maintaining display specific data.
 */
typedef struct _XDisplay {
    XExtData *ext_data;            /* hook for extension to hang data */
    struct _XDisplay *next;        /* next open Display on list */
    int fd;                        /* network socket */
    int lock;                      /* is someone in critical section */
    int proto_major_version;       /* major version of server's X protocol */
    int proto_minor_version;       /* minor version of server's X protocol */
    char *vendor;                  /* vendor of the server hardware */
    long resource_base;            /* resource ID base */
    long resource_mask;            /* resource ID mask bits */
    long resource_id;              /* allocator current ID */
    int resource_shift;            /* allocator shift to correct bits */
    XID (*resource_alloc)();       /* allocator function */
    int byte_order;                /* screen byte order, LSBFirst, MSBFirst */
    int bitmap_unit;               /* padding and data requirements */
    int bitmap_pad;                /* padding requirements on bitmaps */
    int bitmap_bit_order;          /* LeastSignificant or MostSignificant */
    int nformats;                  /* number of pixmap formats in list */
    ScreenFormat *pixmap_format;   /* pixmap format list */
    int vnumber;                   /* Xlib's X protocol version number */
    int release;                   /* release of the server */
    struct _XSQEvent *head, *tail; /* input event queue */
    int qlen;                      /* length of input event queue */
    int last_request_read;         /* sequence number of last event read */
    int request;                   /* sequence number of last request */
    char *last_req;                /* beginning of last request, or dummy */
    char *buffer;                  /* output buffer starting address */
    char *bufptr;                  /* output buffer index pointer */
```

```
    char *bufmax;                    /* output buffer maximum+1 address */
    unsigned max_request_size;      /* maximum number 32 bit words in request*/
    struct _XrmHashBucketRec *db;
    int (*synchandler)();           /* synchronization handler */
    char *display_name;             /* "host:display" string used on this connect*/
    int default_screen;             /* default screen for operations */
    int nscreens;                   /* number of screens on this server*/
    Screen *screens;                /* pointer to list of screens */
    int motion_buffer;              /* size of motion buffer */
    Window current;                 /* for use internally for KeymapNotify */
    int min_keycode;                /* minimum defined keycode */
    int max_keycode;                /* maximum defined keycode */
    KeySym *keysyms;                /* this server's keysyms */
    XModifierKeymap *modifiermap;   /* this server's modifier keymap */
    int keysyms_per_keycode;        /* number of rows */
    char *xdefaults;                /* contents of defaults from server */
    char *scratch_buffer;           /* place to hang scratch buffer */
    unsigned long scratch_length;   /* length of scratch buffer */
    int ext_number;                 /* extension number on this display */
    _XExtension *ext_procs;         /* extensions initialized on this display */
    /*
     * The following can be fixed size, as the protocol defines how much
     * address space is available.  While this could be done using the
     * extension vector, there may be MANY events processed, so a search
     * through the extension list to find the right procedure for each
     * event might be expensive if many extensions are being used.
     */
    Bool (*event_vec[128])();       /* vector for wire to event */
    Status (*wire_vec[128])();      /* vector for event to wire */
} Display;


/*
 * Information about the screen
 */
typedef struct {
    XExtData *ext_data;             /* hook for extension to hang data */
    struct _XDisplay *display;      /* back pointer to display structure */
    Window root;                    /* root window ID */
    int width, height;              /* width and height of screen */
    int mwidth, mheight;            /* width and height of in millimeters */
    int ndepths;                    /* number of depths possible */
    Depth *depths;                  /* list of allowable depths on the screen */
    int root_depth;                 /* bits per pixel */
    Visual *root_visual;            /* root visual */
    GC default_gc;                  /* GC for the root root visual */
    Colormap cmap;                  /* default colormap */
    unsigned long white_pixel;
    unsigned long black_pixel;      /* white and black pixel values */
    int max_maps, min_maps;         /* max and min colormaps */
    int backing_store;              /* Never, WhenMapped, Always */
    Bool save_unders;
    long root_input_mask;           /* initial root input mask */
} Screen;
```

```
/*
 * Format structure; describes ZFormat data the screen will understand.
 */
typedef struct {
    XExtData *ext_data;          /* hook for extension to hang data */
    int depth;                   /* depth of this image format */
    int bits_per_pixel;          /* bits/pixel at this depth */
    int scanline_pad;            /* scan line must padded to this multiple */
} ScreenFormat;
```

Related Commands

XFree, XCloseDisplay, XNoOp, DefaultScreen.

XParseColor

Name

XParseColor — look up or translate RGB values from ASCII color name or hexadecimal value.

Synopsis

```
Status XParseColor(display, colormap, spec, rgb_db_def)
    Display *display;
    Colormap colormap;
    char *spec;
    XColor *rgb_db_def;        /* RETURN */
```

Arguments

display   Specifies a pointer to the `Display` structure; returned from `XOpen-Display`.

cmap   Specifies a colormap. This argument is required but is not used. The same code is used to process `XParseColor` and `XLookupColor`, but only `XLookupColor` returns actual values from the colormap.

spec   Specifies the color specification, either as a color name or as hexadecimal coded in ASCII (see below). Upper or lower case does not matter. The string must be null-terminated, and should be in ISO LATIN-1 encoding, which means that the first 128 character codes are ASCII, and the second 128 character codes are for special characters needed in western languages other than English.

rgb_db_def   Returns the RGB values corresponding to the specified color name or hexadecimal specification, and sets its `DoRed`, `DoGreen` and `DoBlue` flags.

Description

`XParseColor` returns the RGB values corresponding to the English color name or hexadecimal values specified, by looking up the color name in the color database, or translating the hexadecimal code into separate RGB values. It takes a string specification of a color, typically from a command line or `XGetDefault` option, and returns the corresponding red, green, and blue values, suitable for a subsequent call to `XAllocColor` or `XStoreColor`. *spec* can be given either as an English color name (as in `XAllocNamedColor`) or as an initial sharp sign character followed by a hexadecimal specification in one of the following formats:

#RGB	(one character per color)
#RRGGBB	(two characters per color)
#RRRGGGBBB	(three characters per color)
#RRRRGGGGBBBB	(four characters per color)

where R, G, and B represent single hexadecimal digits (upper or lower case).

The hexadecimal strings must be null-terminated so that `XParseColor` knows when it has reached the end. When fewer than 16 bits each are specified, they represent the most significant bits of the value. For example, #3a7 is the same as #3000a0007000. The colormap is used to determine which screen to look up the color on. The screen's default colormap is a reliable choice.

This routine will fail and return a Status of 0 if the initial character is a sharp sign but the string otherwise fails to fit one of the above formats, or if the initial character is not a sharp sign and the named color does not exist in the server's database.

Status is 0 on failure, 1 on success.

For more information, see Volume One, Chapter 7, *Color*.

Structures

```
typedef struct {
    unsigned long pixel;
    unsigned short red, green, blue;
    char flags;                      /* DoRed, DoGreen, DoBlue */
    char pad;
} XColor;
```

Errors

```
BadColor
```

Related Commands

```
XAllocColorCells, XAllocColorPlanes, XAllocColor, XAllocNamedColor,
XLookupColor, XQueryColor, XQueryColors, XStoreColor, XStoreColors,
XFreeColors, XStoreNamedColor, BlackPixel, WhitePixel.
```

Name

XParseGeometry — generate position and size from standard window geometry string.

Synopsis

```
int XParseGeometry(parsestring, x, y, width, height)
    char *parsestring;
    int *x, *y;                           /* RETURN */
    unsigned int *width, *height;         /* RETURN */
```

Arguments

parsestring   Specifies the string you want to parse.

x
y   Return the x and y coordinates (offsets) from the string.

width
height   Return the width and height in pixels from the string.

Description

By convention, X applications use a standard string to indicate window size and placement. XParseGeometry makes it easy to conform to this standard because it allows you to parse the standard window geometry string. Specifically, this function lets you parse strings of the form:

   =<width>x<height>{+-}<xoffset>{+-}<yoffset>

The items in this string map into the arguments associated with this function. (Items enclosed in <> are integers and items enclosed in {} are a set from which one item is allowed. Note that the brackets should not appear in the actual string.)

XParseGeometry returns a bitmask that indicates which of the four values (width, height, xoffset, and yoffset) were actually found in the string, and whether the x and y values are negative. The bits are represented by these constants: XValue, YValue, WidthValue, HeightValue, XNegative, and YNegative, and are defined in <X11/Xutil.h>. For each value found, the corresponding argument is updated and the corresponding bitmask element set; for each value not found, the argument is left unchanged, and the bitmask element is not set.

For more information, see Volume One, Chapter 11, *Managing User Preferences*.

Related Commands

XGeometry, XTranslateCoordinates.

Name

XPeekEvent — get an event without removing it from the queue.

Synopsis

```
XPeekEvent (display, report)
    Display *display;
    XEvent *report;                    /* RETURN */
```

Arguments

display   Specifies a pointer to the Display structure; returned from XOpen-Display.

report   Returns the event peeked from the input queue.

Description

XPeekEvent peeks at an input event from the head of the event queue and copies it into an XEvent supplied by the caller, without removing it from the input queue. If the queue is empty, XPeekEvent flushes the output buffer and waits (blocks) until an event is received. If you do not want to wait, use the QLength macro to determine if there are any events to peek at, or use XPeekIfEvent. In Release 2, XEventsQueued can perform the function of either QLength or XPending and more.

In Release 1, the output buffer was always flushed by event-getting routines. In Release 2, the output buffer is flushed only if no matching events are found on the queue. This change is compatible with applications written for Release 1.

For more information, see Volume One, Chapter 8, *Events*.

Related Commands

XSelectInput, XSetInputFocus, XGetInputFocus, XWindowEvent, XCheck-WindowEvent, XCheckTypedEvent, XCheckTypedWindowEvent, XMaskEvent, XCheckMaskEvent, XNextEvent, XEventsQueued, XAllowEvents, XGetMotion-Events, XIfEvent, XCheckIfEvent, XPeekIfEvent, XPutBackEvent, XPending, XSynchronize, XSendEvent, QLength.

Name

XPeekIfEvent — get an event without removing it from the queue; do not wait.

Synopsis

```
XPeekIfEvent (display, event, predicate, args)
    Display *display;
    XEvent *event;                /* RETURN */
    Bool (*predicate)();
    char *args;
```

Arguments

display   Specifies a pointer to the Display structure; returned from XOpen-Display.

event   Returns the matched event.

predicate   Specifies the procedure to be called to determine if each event that arrives in the queue is the desired one.

args   Specifies the user-specified arguments that will be passed to the predicate procedure.

Description

XPeekIfEvent returns an event only when the specified predicate procedure returns True for the event. The event is copied into *event* but not removed from the queue. The specified predicate is called each time an event is added to the queue, with the arguments *display*, *event*, and *arg*.

XPeekIfEvent flushes the output buffer if no matching events could be found on the queue, and then waits for the next matching event.

In Release 1, the output buffer was always flushed by event-getting routines. In Release 2, the output buffer is flushed only if no matching events are found on the queue. This change is compatible with applications written for Release 1.

For more information, see Volume One, Chapter 8, *Events*.

Related Commands

XSelectInput, XSetInputFocus, XGetInputFocus, XWindowEvent, XCheck-WindowEvent, XCheckTypedEvent, XCheckTypedWindowEvent, XMaskEvent, XCheckMaskEvent, XNextEvent, XEventsQueued, XAllowEvents, XGetMotion-Events, XIfEvent, XCheckIfEvent, XPeekEvent, XPutBackEvent, XPending, XSynchronize, XSendEvent, QLength.

Name

XPending — flush the output buffer and return the number of pending input events.

Synopsis

```
int XPending(display)
    Display *display;
```

Arguments

display   Specifies a pointer to the Display structure; returned from XOpen-
Display.

Description

XPending returns the number of input events that have been received from the server, but not yet removed from the queue. If there are no events on the queue, XPending flushes the output buffer, and returns the number of events transferred to the input queue as a result of the flush.

The QLength macro returns the number of events on the queue, but without flushing the output buffer first.

For more information, see Volume One, Chapter 8, *Events*.

Related Commands

XSelectInput, XSetInputFocus, XGetInputFocus, XWindowEvent, XCheck-
WindowEvent, XCheckTypedEvent, XCheckTypedWindowEvent, XMaskEvent,
XCheckMaskEvent, XNextEvent, XEventsQueued, XAllowEvents, XGetMotion-
Events, XIfEvent, XCheckIfEvent, XPeekEvent, XPeekIfEvent, XPutBack-
Event, XSynchronize, XSendEvent, QLength.

Xpermalloc

Name
Xpermalloc — allocate memory never to be freed.

Synopsis
```
char *Xpermalloc(size)
    unsigned int size;
```

Arguments
size   Specifies the size in bytes of the space to be allocated. This specification is rounded to the nearest 4-byte boundary.

Description
Xpermalloc allocates some memory that will not be freed until the process exits. Xpermalloc is used by some toolkits for permanently allocated storage and allows some performance and space savings over the completely general memory allocator.

Name

XPointInRegion — determine if a point is inside a region.

Synopsis

```
int XPointInRegion(r, x, y)
    Region r;
    int x, y;
```

Arguments

r   Specifies the region.

x   Specify the x and y coordinates of the point relative to the region's origin.

y

Description

XPointInRegion returns True if the point x, y is contained in the region r. A point exactly on the boundary of the region is considered inside the region.

Regions are located using an offset from a point (the *region origin*) which is common to all regions. It is up to the application to interpret the location of the region relative to a drawable.

For more information on regions, see Volume One, Chapter 6, *Drawing Graphics and Text*.

Structures

```
/*
 * opaque reference to Regiondata type.
 * user won't need contents, only pointer.
 */
typedef struct _XRegion *Region;
```

Related Commands

XXorRegion, XUnionRegion, XUnionRectWithRegion, XSubtractRegion, XShrinkRegion, XSetRegion, XRectInRegion, XPolygonRegion, XOffset-Region, XIntersectRegion, XEmptyRegion, XCreateRegion, XDestroy-Region, XEqualRegion, XClipBox.

Name

XPolygonRegion — generate a region from points.

Synopsis

```
Region XPolygonRegion(points, n, fill_rule)
    XPoint points[];
    int n;
    int fill_rule;
```

Arguments

points   Specifies a pointer to an array of points.

n   Specifies the number of points in the polygon.

fill_rule   Specifies whether areas overlapping an odd number of times should be part of the region (WindingRule) or not part of the region (EvenOddRule). See Volume One, Chapter 5, *The Graphics Context*, for a description of the fill rule.

Description

XPolygonRegion creates a region defined by connecting the specified points, and returns a pointer to be used to refer to the region.

Regions are located relative to a point (the *region origin*) which is common to all regions. In XPolygonRegion, the coordinates specified in *points* are relative to the region origin. By specifying all points relative to the drawable in which they will be used, the region origin can be coincident with the drawable origin. It is up to the application whether to interpret the location of the region relative to a drawable or not.

If the region is to be used as a clip_mask by calling XSetRegion, the upper-left corner of the region relative to the drawable used in the graphics request will be at (xoffset + clip_x_origin, yoffset + clip_y_origin), where xoffset and yoffset are the offset of the region (if any) and clip_x_origin and clip_y_origin are elements of the GC used in the graphics request. The *fill_rule* can be either of these values:

- EvenOddRule   Areas overlapping an odd number of times are *not* part of the region.

- WindingRule   Overlapping areas are always filled.

For more information on structures, see Volume One, Chapter 6, *Drawing Graphics and Text*.

Structures

```
typedef struct {
    short x,y;
} XPoint;

/*
 * opaque reference to Regiondata type.
 * user won't need contents, only pointer.
 */
typedef struct _XRegion *Region;
```

Related Commands

XXorRegion, XUnionRegion, XUnionRectWithRegion, XSubtractRegion, XShrinkRegion, XSetRegion, XRectInRegion, XPointInRegion, XOffset-Region, XIntersectRegion, XEmptyRegion, XCreateRegion, XDestroy-Region, XEqualRegion, XClipBox.

XPutBackEvent

Name

XPutBackEvent — push an event back on the input queue.

Synopsis

```
XPutBackEvent(display, event)
    Display *display;
    XEvent *event;
```

Arguments

display   Specifies a pointer to the Display structure; returned from XOpen-
            Display.

event   Specifies a pointer to the event to be requeued.

Description

XPutBackEvent pushes an event back onto the head of the current display's input queue (so that it would become the next one returned by the next XNextEvent call). This can be useful if you have read an event and then decide that you'd rather deal with it later. There is no limit to how many times you can call XPutBackEvent in succession.

For more information, see Volume One, Chapter 8, *Events*.

Related Commands

XSelectInput, XSetInputFocus, XGetInputFocus, XWindowEvent, XCheck-
WindowEvent, XCheckTypedEvent, XCheckTypedWindowEvent, XMaskEvent,
XCheckMaskEvent, XNextEvent, XEventsQueued, XAllowEvents, XGetMotion-
Events, XIfEvent, XCheckIfEvent, XPeekEvent, XPeekIfEvent, XPending,
XSynchronize, XSendEvent, QLength.

Name

XPutImage — draw a rectangular image on a window or pixmap.

Synopsis

```
XPutImage(display, drawable, gc, image, src_x, src_y,
        dst_x, dst_y, width, height)
    Display *display;
    Drawable drawable;
    GC gc;
    XImage *image;
    int src_x, src_y;
    int dst_x, dst_y;
    unsigned int width, height;
```

Arguments

display	Specifies a pointer to the Display structure; returned from XOpen-Display.
drawable	Specifies the drawable.
gc	Specifies the graphics context.
image	Specifies the image you want combined with the rectangle.
src_x *src_y*	Specify the coordinates of the upper-left corner of the rectangle to be copied, relative to the origin of the image.
dst_x *dst_y*	Specify the x and y coordinates, relative to the origin of the drawable, where the upper-left corner of the copied rectangle will be placed.
width *height*	Specify the width and height in pixels of the rectangular area to be copied.

Description

XPutImage draws a section of an image on a rectangle in a window or pixmap. The section of the image is defined by *src_x*, *src_y*, *width* and *height*.

XPutImage uses these graphics context components: function, plane_mask, subwindow_mode, clip_x_origin, clip_y_origin, and clip_mask. This function also uses these graphics context mode-dependent components: foreground and background.

If an XYBitmap format image is used, then the depth of *drawable* must be 1 and the image must be XYFormat, otherwise a BadMatch error is generated. The foreground pixel in *gc* defines the source for set bits in the image, and the background pixel defines the source for the bits set to 0.

For XYPixmap and ZPixmap format images, the depth of the image must match the depth of *drawable*. For XYPixmap, the image must be sent in XYFormat. For ZPixmap, the image must be sent in the ZFormat defined for the given depth.

Structures

```
typedef struct _XImage {
    int width, height;      /* size of image */
    int xoffset;            /* number of pixels offset in x direction */
    int format;             /* XYBitmap, XYPixmap, ZPixmap */
    char *data;             /* pointer to image data */
    int byte_order;         /* data byte order, LSBFirst, MSBFirst */
    int bitmap_unit;        /* quant. of scan line 8, 16, 32 */
    int bitmap_bit_order;   /* LSBFirst, MSBFirst */
    int bitmap_pad;         /* 8, 16, 32 either XY or ZPixmap */
    int depth;              /* depth of image */
    int bytes_per_line;     /* accelerator to next line */
    int bits_per_pixel;     /* bits per pixel (ZPixmap) */
    char *obdata;           /* hook for the object routines to hang on */
    struct funcs {          /* image manipulation routines */
    struct _XImage *(*create_image)();
    int (*destroy_image)();
    unsigned long (*get_pixel)();
    int (*put_pixel)();
    struct _XImage *(*sub_image)();
    int (*add_pixel)();
    } f;
} XImage;
```

Errors

BadDrawable

BadGC

BadMatch   See Description above.

BadValue

Related Commands

XDestroyImage, XGetImage, XCreateImage, XSubImage, XGetSubImage, XAdd-
Pixel, XPutPixel, XGetPixel, ImageByteOrder.

Name

XPutPixel — set a pixel value in an image.

Synopsis

```
int XPutPixel(ximage, x, y, pixel)
    XImage *ximage;
    int x;
    int y;
    unsigned long pixel;
```

Arguments

ximage   Specifies a pointer to the image to be modified.

x   Specify the x and y coordinates of the pixel to be set, relative to the origin of
y   the image.

pixel   Specifies the new pixel value.

Description

XPutPixel overwrites the pixel in the named image with the specified pixel value. The x
and y coordinates are relative to the origin (upper left [0,0]) of the image. The input pixel
value must be in normalized format (that is, the Least Significant Byte (LSB) of the long is the
LSB of the pixel). The x and y coordinates must be contained in the image.

Structures

```
typedef struct _XImage {
    int width, height;              /* size of image */
    int xoffset;                    /* number of pixels offset in x direction */
    int format;                     /* XYBitmap, XYPixmap, ZPixmap */
    char *data;                     /* pointer to image data */
    int byte_order;                 /* data byte order, LSBFirst, MSBFirst */
    int bitmap_unit;                /* quant. of scan line 8, 16, 32 */
    int bitmap_bit_order;           /* LSBFirst, MSBFirst */
    int bitmap_pad;                 /* 8, 16, 32 either XY or ZPixmap */
    int depth;                      /* depth of image */
    int bytes_per_line;             /* accelerator to next line */
    int bits_per_pixel;             /* bits per pixel (ZPixmap) */
    unsigned long red_mask;         /* bits in z arrangment */
    unsigned long green_mask;
    unsigned long blue_mask;
    char *obdata;                   /* hook for the object routines to hang on */
    struct funcs {                  /* image manipulation routines */
    struct _XImage *(*create_image)();
    int (*destroy_image)();
    unsigned long (*get_pixel)();
    int (*put_pixel)();
    struct _XImage *(*sub_image)();
    int (*add_pixel)();
    } f;
} XImage;
```

Related Commands

XDestroyImage, XPutImage, XGetImage, XCreateImage, XSubImage, XGetSub-
Image, XAddPixel, XGetPixel, ImageByteOrder.

XQueryBestCursor

Name

XQueryBestCursor — get the closest supported cursor sizes.

Synopsis

```
Status XQueryBestCursor(display, drawable, width, height,
        rwidth, rheight)
    Display *display;
    Drawable drawable;
    unsigned int width, height;
    unsigned int *rwidth, *rheight; /* RETURN */
```

Arguments

display	Specifies a pointer to the Display structure; returned from XOpen-Display.
drawable	Specifies a drawable that indicates which screen the cursor is to be used on. The best cursor may be different on different screens.
width *height*	Specify the preferred width and height, in pixels.
rwidth *rheight*	Return pointers to the closest supported cursor dimensions, in pixels, on the display hardware.

Description

XQueryBestCursor returns the closest cursor dimensions actually supported by the display hardware to the dimensions you specify.

Call this function if you wish to use a cursor size other than 16 by 16. XQueryBest-Cursor provides a way to find out what size cursors are actually possible on the display. Applications should be prepared to use smaller cursors on displays which cannot support large ones.

XQueryBestCursor returns 1 if the call succeeded in getting a supported size (may be the same or different from the specified size), or 0 if the call failed.

Errors

BadDrawable

Related Commands

XDefineCursor, XUndefineCursor, XCreateFontCursor, XCreateGlyph-Cursor, XCreatePixmapCursor, XFreeCursor, XRecolorCursor, XQueryBest-Size.

XQueryBestSize

Name

XQueryBestSize — obtain the ''best'' supported cursor, tile, or stipple size.

Synopsis

```
Status XQueryBestSize(display, class, drawable, width,
        height, rwidth, rheight)
    Display *display;
    int class;
    Drawable drawable;
    unsigned int width, height;
    unsigned int *rwidth, *rheight; /* RETURN */
```

Arguments

display   Specifies a pointer to the Display structure; returned from XOpen-Display.

class   Specifies the class that you are interested in. Pass one of these constants: TileShape, CursorShape, or StippleShape.

drawable   Specifies a drawable ID that tells the server which screen you want the best size for.

width
height   Specify the preferred width and height in pixels.

rwidth
rheight   Return the closest supported width and height, in pixels, available for the object on the display hardware.

Description

XQueryBestSize returns the ''fastest'' or ''closest'' size to the specified size. For *class* of CursorShape, this is the closest size that can be fully displayed on the screen. For TileShape and StippleShape, this is the closest size that can be tiled or stippled ''fastest.''

For CursorShape, the drawable indicates the desired screen. For TileShape and StippleShape, the drawable indicates the screen and possibly the visual class and depth (server-dependent). An InputOnly window cannot be used as the drawable for Tile-Shape or StippleShape (else a BadMatch error occurs).

XQueryBestSize returns 1 if the call succeeded in getting a supported size (may be the same or different from the specified size), or 0 if the call failed.

Errors

BadDrawable

BadMatch   InputOnly drawable for *class* TileShape or StippleShape.

BadValue

Related Commands

XSetTile, XQueryBestTile, XSetWindowBorderPixmap, XSetWindow-
BackgroundPixmap, XCreatePixmap, XCreatePixmapFromBitmapData, XFree-
Pixmap, XQueryBestStipple, XWriteBitmapFile, XReadBitmapFile,
XCreateBitmapFromData.

Name

XQueryBestStipple — obtain the best supported stipple shape.

Synopsis

```
Status XQueryBestStipple(display, drawable, width, height,
        rwidth, rheight)
    Display *display;
    Drawable drawable;
    unsigned int width, height;
    unsigned int *rwidth, *rheight; /* RETURN */
```

Arguments

display	Specifies a pointer to the Display structure; returned from XOpen-Display.
drawable	Specifies a drawable that tells the server which screen you want the best size for.
width height	Specify the preferred width and height in pixels.
rwidth rheight	Return the width and height, in pixels, of the stipple best supported by the display hardware.

Description

XQueryBestStipple returns the closest stipple size that can be stippled fastest. The drawable indicates the screen and possibly the visual class and depth. An InputOnly window cannot be used as the drawable (else a BadMatch error occurs).

XQueryBestStipple returns 1 if the call succeeded in getting a supported size (may be the same or different from the specified size), or 0 if the call failed.

For more information on stipples, see Volume One, Chapter 5, *The Graphics Context.*

Errors

BadDrawable

BadMatch   InputOnly window.

Related Commands

XSetTile, XQueryBestTile, XSetWindowBorderPixmap, XSetWindow-BackgroundPixmap, XCreatePixmap, XCreatePixmapFromBitmapData, XFree-Pixmap, XQueryBestSize, XWriteBitmapFile, XReadBitmapFile, XCreate-BitmapFromData.

Name

XQueryBestTile — obtain the best supported fill tile shape.

Synopsis

```
Status XQueryBestTile(display, drawable, width, height,
        rwidth, rheight)
    Display *display;
    Drawable drawable;
    unsigned int width, height;
    unsigned int *rwidth, *rheight;  /* RETURN */
```

Arguments

display   Specifies a pointer to the Display structure; returned from XOpen-
              Display.

drawable   Specifies a drawable that tells the server which screen you want the best size
              for.

width   Specify the preferred width and height in pixels.
height

rwidth   Return the width and height, in pixels, of the tile best supported by the
rheight   display hardware.

Description

XQueryBestTile returns the "closest" size that can be tiled "fastest." The drawable indicates the screen and possibly the visual class and depth. An InputOnly window cannot be
used as the drawable.

XQueryBestTile returns 1 if the call succeeded in getting a supported size (may be the
same or different from the specified size), or 0 if the call failed.

For more information on tiles, see Volume One, Chapter 5, *The Graphics Context*.

Errors

BadDrawable

BadMatch   InputOnly drawable specified.

Related Commands

XSetTile, XSetWindowBorderPixmap, XSetWindowBackgroundPixmap,
XCreatePixmap, XCreatePixmapFromBitmapData, XFreePixmap, XQueryBest-
Size, XQueryBestStipple, XWriteBitmapFile, XReadBitmapFile, XCreate-
BitmapFromData.

Name

XQueryColor — obtain the RGB values and flags for a specified pixel value.

Synopsis

```
XQueryColor(display, cmap, colorcell_def)
    Display *display;
    Colormap cmap;
    XColor *colorcell_def;        /* SEND and RETURN */
```

Arguments

display   Specifies a pointer to the Display structure; returned from XOpen-Display.

cmap   Specifies the ID of the colormap from which RGB values will be retrieved.

colorcell_def
              Specifies the pixel value and returns the RGB contents of that colorcell.

Description

XQueryColor returns the RGB values in colormap cmap for the colorcell corresponding to the pixel value specified in the pixel member of the XColor structure colorcell_def. The RGB values are returned in the red, green, and blue members of that same structure, and the flags member of that structure is set to (DoRed | DoGreen | DoBlue). The values returned for an unallocated entry are undefined.

For more information, see Volume One, Chapter 7, *Color*.

Structures

```
typedef struct {
    unsigned long pixel;
    unsigned short red, green, blue;
    char flags;                    /* DoRed, DoGreen, DoBlue */
    char pad;
} XColor;
```

Errors

BadColor

BadValue   Pixel not valid index into cmap.

Related Commands

XAllocColorCells, XAllocColorPlanes, XAllocColor, XAllocNamedColor, XLookupColor, XParseColor, XQueryColors, XStoreColor, XStoreColors, XFreeColors, XStoreNamedColor, BlackPixel, WhitePixel.

XQueryColors

Name

XQueryColors — obtain RGB values for an array of pixel values.

Synopsis

```
XQueryColors(display, cmap, colorcell_defs, ncolors)
    Display *display;
    Colormap cmap;
    XColor colorcell_defs[ncolors];    /* SEND and RETURN */
    int ncolors;
```

Arguments

display Specifies a pointer to the Display structure; returned from XOpen-Display.

cmap Specifies the ID of the colormap from which RGB values will be retrieved.

colorcell_defs
 Specifies an array of XColor structures. In each one, pixel is set to indicate which colorcell in the colormap to return, and the RGB values in that colorcell are returned in red, green, and blue.

ncolors Specifies the number of XColor structures in the color definition array.

Description

XQueryColors is similar to XQueryColor, but it returns an array of RGB values. It returns the RGB values in colormap *cmap* for the colorcell corresponding to the pixel value specified in the pixel member of the XColor structure colorcell_def. The RGB values are returned in the red, green, and blue members of that same structure, and sets the flags member in each XColor structure to (DoRed | DoGreen | DoBlue).

For more information, see Volume One, Chapter 7, *Color*.

Structures

```
typedef struct {
    unsigned long pixel;
    unsigned short red, green, blue;
    char flags;                    /* DoRed, DoGreen, DoBlue */
    char pad;
} XColor;
```

Errors

BadColor

BadValue Pixel not valid index into *cmap*.

Note: if more than one pixel value is in error, the one reported is arbitrary.

Related Commands

XAllocColorCells, XAllocColorPlanes, XAllocColor, XAllocNamedColor, XLookupColor, XParseColor, XQueryColor, XStoreColor, XStoreColors, XFreeColors, XStoreNamedColor, BlackPixel, WhitePixel.

XQueryExtension

Name

XQueryExtension — get extension information.

Synopsis

```
Bool XQueryExtension(display, name, major_opcode,
        first_event, first_error)
    Display *display;
    char *name;
    int *major_opcode;        /* RETURN */
    int *first_event;         /* RETURN */
    int *first_error;         /* RETURN */
```

Arguments

display   Specifies a pointer to the Display structure; returned from XOpen-
                 Display.

name   Specifies the name of the desired extension. Upper or lower case is impor-
                 tant. The string should be in ISO LATIN-1 encoding, which means that the
                 first 128 character codes are ASCII, and the second 128 character codes are
                 for special characters needed in western languages other than English.

major_opcode
                 Returns the major opcode of the extension, for use in error handling routines.

first_event   Returns the code of the first custom event type created by the extension.

first_error   Returns the code of the first custom error defined by the extension.

Description

XQueryExtension determines if the named extension is present, and returns True if it is.
If so, the routines in the extension can be used just as if they were core Xlib requests, except
that they may return new types of events or new error codes. The available extensions can be
listed with XListExtensions.

The major_opcode for the extension is returned, if it has one. Otherwise, 0 is returned.
This opcode will appear in errors generated in the extension.

If the extension involves additional event types, the base event type code is returned in
first_event. Otherwise, 0 is returned in first_event. The format of the events is
specific to the extension.

If the extension involves additional error codes, the base error code is returned in
first_error. Otherwise, 0 is returned. The format of additional data in the errors is
specific to the extension.

See Volume One, Chapter 13, *Other Programming Techniques*, for more information on using
extensions, and Volume One, Appendix C, *Writing Extensions to X*, for information on writing
them.

Related Commands

    XListExtensions, XFreeExtensionList.

Name

XQueryFont — return information about a loaded font.

Synopsis

```
XFontStruct *XQueryFont (display, font_ID)
    Display *display;
    XID font_ID;
```

Arguments

display   Specifies a pointer to the Display structure; returned from XOpen-Display.

font_ID   Specifies either the font ID or the graphics context ID. You can declare the data type for this argument as either Font or GContext (both X IDs).

Description

XQueryFont returns a pointer to the XFontStruct structure information associated with the font. This call is needed if you loaded the font with XLoadFont, but need the font information to place text. If the font hasn't been loaded, XQueryFont returns NULL.

If *font_ID* is declared as data type GContext (also a resource ID), this function queries the font stored in the GC specified by this ID. However, in this case the GContext ID will be the ID stored in the returned XFontStruct, and you can't use that ID in XSetFont or XUnloadFont, since it is not itself the ID of the font.

Use XFreeFontInfo to free this data. Use XLoadQueryFont to both load and get information about a font.

For more information on fonts, see Volume One, Chapter 6, *Drawing Graphics and Text*.

Errors

BadAlloc

BadfFont

Structures

```
typedef struct {
    XExtData *ext_data;          /* hook for extension to hang data */
    Font fid;                    /* font ID for this font */
    unsigned direction;          /* hint about direction font is painted */
    unsigned min_char_or_byte2;  /* first character */
    unsigned max_char_or_byte2;  /* last character */
    unsigned min_byte1;          /* first row that exists */
    unsigned max_byte1;          /* last row that exists */
    Bool all_chars_exist;        /* flag if all characters have nonzero size*/
    unsigned default_char;       /* char to print for undefined character */
    int n_properties;            /* how many properties there are */
    XFontProp *properties;       /* pointer to array of additional properties*/
    XCharStruct min_bounds;      /* minimum bounds over all existing char*/
    XCharStruct max_bounds;      /* minimum bounds over all existing char*/
    XCharStruct *per_char;       /* first_char to last_char information */
```

```
    int ascent;                 /* logical extent above baseline for spacing */
    int descent;                /* logical descent below baseline for spacing */
} XFontStruct;
```

Related Commands

XLoadFont, XLoadQueryFont, XFreeFont, XFreeFontInfo, XListFonts, XListFontsWithInfo, XFreeFontNames, XFreeFontPath, XGetFontPath, XSetFont, XSetFontPath, XUnloadFont, XGetFontProperty, XCreateFont-Cursor.

Name

XQueryKeymap — obtain a bit vector for the current state of the keyboard.

Synopsis

```
XQueryKeymap(display, keys)
    Display *display;
    char keys[32];                /* RETURN */
```

Arguments

display   Specifies a pointer to the Display structure; returned from XOpen-Display.

keys   Returns an array of bytes that identifies which keys are pressed down. Each bit represents one key of the keyboard.

Description

XQueryKeymap returns a bit vector for the logical state of the keyboard, where each bit set to 1 indicates that the corresponding key is currently pressed down. The vector is represented as 32 bytes. Byte N (from 0) contains the bits for keys $8N$ to $8N+7$ with the least significant bit in the byte representing key $8N$. Note that the logical state may lag the physical state if device event processing is frozen due to a grab.

Related Commands

XDeleteModifiermapEntry, XInsertModifiermapEntry, XFreeModifiermap, XKeycodeToKeysym, XKeysymToKeycode, XKeysymToString, XNewModifier-Map, XStringToKeysym, XLookupKeysym, XRebindKeysym, XGetKeyboard-Mapping, XChangeKeyboardMapping, XRefreshKeyboardMapping, XLookup-String, XSetModifierMapping, XGetModifierMapping.

Name

XQueryPointer — get the current pointer location.

Synopsis

```
Bool XQueryPointer(display, w, root, child, root_x, root_y,
        win_x, win_y, keys_buttons)
    Display *display;
    Window w;
    Window *root, *child;           /* RETURN */
    int *root_x, *root_y;           /* RETURN */
    int *win_x, *win_y;             /* RETURN */
    unsigned int *keys_buttons;     /* RETURN */
```

Arguments

display   Specifies a pointer to the Display structure; returned from XOpenDisplay.

w   Specifies a window which indicates which screen the pointer position is returned for, and child will be a child of this window if pointer is inside a child.

root   Returns the root window ID the pointer is currently on.

child   Returns the ID of the child of w the pointer is located in, or 0 if it not in a child.

root_x
root_y   Return the x and y coordinates of the pointer relative to the root's origin.

win_x
win_y   Return the x and y coordinates of the pointer relative to the origin of window w.

keys_buttons
     Returns the current state of the modifier keys and pointer buttons. This is a mask composed of the OR of any number of the following symbols: Shift-Mask, LockMask, ControlMask, Mod1Mask, Mod2Mask, Mod3Mask, Mod4Mask, Mod5Mask, Button1Mask, Button2Mask, Button3Mask, Button4Mask, Button5Mask.

Description

XQueryPointer gets the pointer coordinates relative to a window and relative to the root window, the root window ID and the child window ID (if any) the pointer is currently in, and the current state of modifier keys and buttons.

If XQueryPointer returns False, then the pointer is not on the same screen as w, child is None, and win_x and win_y are zero. However, root, root_x, and root_y are still valid. If XQueryPointer returns True, then the pointer is on the same screen as the window w, and all return values are valid.

The logical state of the pointer buttons and modifier keys can lag behind their physical state if device event processing is frozen due to a grab.

Errors
BadWindow

Related Commands
XWarpPointer, XGrabPointer, XChangeActivePointerGrab, XUngrab-
Pointer, XGetPointerMapping, XSetPointerMapping, XGetPointerControl,
XChangePointerControl.

Name

XQueryTextExtents — query the server for string and font metrics.

Synopsis

```
int XQueryTextExtents(display, font_ID, string, nchars,
        direction, ascent, descent, overall)
    Display *display;
    XID font_ID;
    char *string;
    int nchars;
    int *direction;            /* RETURN */
    int *ascent, *descent;     /* RETURN */
    XCharStruct *overall;      /* RETURN */
```

Arguments

display	Specifies a pointer to the Display structure; returned from XOpen-Display.
font_ID	Specifies the appropriate font ID previously returned by XLoadFont, or the GContext that specifies the font.
string	Specifies the character string for which metrics are to be returned.
nchars	Specifies the number of characters in the character string.
direction	Returns the direction the string would be drawn using the specified font. Either FontLeftToRight or FontRightToLeft.
ascent	Returns the maximum ascent for the specified font.
descent	Returns the maximum descent for the specified font.
overall	Returns the overall characteristics of the string. These are the sum of the width measurements for each character, the maximum ascent and descent, the minimum lbearing added to the width of all characters up to the character with the smallest lbearing, and the maximum rbearing added to the width of all characters up to the character with the largest rbearing.

Description

XQueryTextExtents returns the dimensions in pixels that specify the bounding box of the specified string of characters in the named font, and the maximum ascent and descent for the entire font. This function queries the server and, therefore, suffers the round trip overhead that is avoided by XTextExtents, but it does not require a filled XFontInfo structure.

The returned *ascent* and *descent* should usually be used to calculate the line spacing, while the width, rbearing, and lbearing members of *overall* should be used for horizontal measures. The total height of the bounding rectangle, good for any string in this font, is *ascent* + *descent*.

overall.ascent is the maximum of the ascent metrics of all characters in the string. The *overall.descent* is the maximum of the descent metrics. The *overall.width* is the sum of the character-width metrics of all characters in the string. The *overall.lbearing* is the lbearing of the character in the string with the smallest lbearing plus the width of all the characters up to but not including that character. The *overall.rbearing* is the rbearing of the character in the string with the largest lbearing plus the width of all the characters up to but not including that character.

For more information on drawing text, see Volume One, Chapter 6, *Drawing Graphics and Text*.

XQueryTextExtents returns 1 on success, 0 on failure.

Structures
```
typedef struct {
    short lbearing;         /* origin to left edge of character */
    short rbearing;         /* origin to right edge of character */
    short width;            /* advance to next char's origin */
    short ascent;           /* baseline to top edge of character */
    short descent;          /* baseline to bottom edge of character */
    unsigned short attributes;/* per char flags (not predefined) */
} XCharStruct;
```

Errors
```
BadFont
BadGC
```

Related Commands
XQueryTextExtents16, XDrawImageString, XDrawImageString16, XDraw-String, XDrawString16, XDrawText, XDrawText16, XTextExtents, XText-Extents16, XTextWidth, XTextWidth16.

XQueryTextExtents16

Name

XQueryTextExtents16 — query the server for string and font metrics of a 16-bit character string.

Synopsis

```
int XQueryTextExtents16(display, font_ID, string, nchars,
        direction, ascent, descent, overall)
    Display *display;
    XID font_ID;
    XChar2b *string;
    int nchars;
    int *direction;              /* RETURN */
    int *ascent, *descent;       /* RETURN */
    XCharStruct *overall;        /* RETURN */
```

Arguments

display   Specifies a pointer to the Display structure; returned from XOpen-Display.

font_ID   Specifies the appropriate font ID previously returned by XLoadFont, or the GContext that specifies the font.

string   Specifies the character string for which metrics are to be returned.

nchars   Specifies the number of characters in the character string.

direction   Returns the direction of painting in the specified font. Either FontLeftto-Right or FontRighttoLeft.

ascent   Returns the maximum ascent in pixels for the specified font.

descent   Returns the maximum descent in pixels for the specified font.

overall   Returns the overall characteristics of the string. These are the sum of the width measurements for each character, the maximum ascent and descent, the minimum lbearing added to the width of all characters up to the character with the smallest lbearing, and the maximum rbearing added to the width of all characters up to the character with the largest rbearing.

Description

XQueryTextExtents16 returns the dimensions in pixels that specify the bounding box of the specified string of characters in the named font, and the maximum ascent and descent for the entire font. This function queries the server and, therefore, suffers the round trip overhead that is avoided by XTextExtents16, but it does not require a filled XFontInfo structure.

The returned *ascent* and *descent* should usually be used to calculate the line spacing, while the width, rbearing, and lbearing members of *overall* should be used for horizontal measures. The total height of the bounding rectangle, good for any string in this font, is *ascent + descent*.

overall.ascent is the maximum of the ascent metrics of all characters in the string. The *overall.descent* is the maximum of the descent metrics. The *overall.width* is the sum of the character-width metrics of all characters in the string. The *overall.lbearing* is the lbearing of the character in the string with the smallest lbearing plus the width of all the characters up to but not including that character. The *overall.rbearing* is the rbearing of the character in the string with the largest lbearing plus the width of all the characters up to but not including that character.

For fonts defined with linear indexing rather than two-byte matrix indexing, the server interprets each XChar2b as a 16-bit number that has been transmitted with the most significant byte first. That is, byte 1 of the XChar2b is taken as the most significant byte.

If the font has no defined default character, then undefined characters in the string are taken to have all 0 metrics. XQueryTextExtents16 returns 1 on success, 0 on failure.

Structures

```
typedef struct {              /* normal 16-bit characters are two bytes */
    unsigned char byte1;
    unsigned char byte2;
} XChar2b;

typedef struct {
    short lbearing;           /* origin to left edge of character */
    short rbearing;           /* origin to right edge of character */
    short width;              /* advance to next char's origin */
    short ascent;             /* baseline to top edge of character */
    short descent;            /* baseline to bottom edge of character */
    unsigned short attributes;/* per char flags (not predefined) */
} XCharStruct;
```

Errors

```
BadFont
BadGC
```

Related Commands

XQueryTextExtents, XDrawImageString, XDrawImageString16, XDraw-String, XDrawString16, XDrawText, XDrawText16, XTextExtents, XText-Extents16, XTextWidth, XTextWidth16.

Name

XQueryTree — return a list of children, parent, and root.

Synopsis

```
Status XQueryTree(display, w, root, parent, children,
        nchildren)
    Display *display;
    Window w;
    Window *root;              /* RETURN */
    Window *parent;            /* RETURN */
    Window **children;         /* RETURN */
    unsigned int *nchildren;   /* RETURN */
```

Arguments

display   Specifies a pointer to the Display structure; returned from XOpen-Display.

w   Specifies the ID of the window to be queried. For this window, XQuery-Tree will list its children, its root, its parent, and the number of children.

root   Returns the root ID for the specified window.

parent   Returns the parent window of the specified window.

children   Returns the list of children associated with the specified window.

nchildren   Returns the number of children associated with the specified window.

Description

XQueryTree uses its last four arguments to return the root ID, the parent ID, a pointer to a list of children and the number of children in that list, all for the specified window w. The children are listed in current stacking order, from bottommost (first) to topmost (last). XQueryTree returns 0 if it fails, 1 if it succeeds.

You should deallocate the list of children with XFree when it is no longer needed.

Related Commands

XLowerWindow, XRaiseWindow, XCirculateSubwindows, XCirculate-SubwindowsDown, XCirculateSubwindowsUp, XRestackWindows, XMove-Window, XResizeWindow, XMoveResizeWindow, XReparentWindow, XConfigureWindow.

XRaiseWindow

Name

XRaiseWindow — raise a window to the top of the stacking order.

Synopsis

```
XRaiseWindow(display, w)
    Display *display;
    Window w;
```

Arguments

display   Specifies a pointer to the Display structure; returned from XOpen-
Display.

w   Specifies the ID of the window to be raised to the top of the stack.

Description

XRaiseWindow moves a window to the top of the stacking order among its siblings. If the windows are regarded as overlapping sheets of paper stacked on a desk, then raising a window is analogous to moving the sheet to the top of the stack, while leaving its x and y location on the desk constant.

Raising a mapped window may generate exposure events for that window and any mapped subwindows of that window that were formerly obscured.

If the override_redirect attribute of the window (see Volume One, Chapter 4, *Window Attributes*) is False and some other client has selected SubstructureRedirectMask on the parent, then a ConfigureRequest event is generated, and no further processing is performed.

Errors

BadWindow

Related Commands

XLowerWindow, XCirculateSubwindows, XCirculateSubwindowsDown, XCirculateSubwindowsUp, XRestackWindows, XMoveWindow, XResizeWindow, XMoveResizeWindow, XReparentWindow, XConfigureWindow, XQueryTree.

Name

XReadBitmapFile — read a bitmap from disk.

Synopsis

```
int XReadBitmapFile(display, drawable, filename, width,
        height, bitmap, x_hot, y_hot)
    Display *display;
    Drawable drawable;
    char *filename;
    unsigned int *width, *height;        /* RETURN */
    Pixmap *bitmap;                      /* RETURN */
    int *x_hot, *y_hot;                  /* RETURN */
```

Arguments

display   Specifies a pointer to the Display structure; returned from XOpen-Display.

drawable   Specifies the drawable.

filename   Specifies the filename to use. The format of the filename is operating system specific.

width
height   Return the dimensions in pixels of the bitmap that is read.

bitmap   Returns the pixmap resource ID that is created.

x_hot
y_hot   Return the hotspot coordinates in the file (or –1,–1 if none present).

Description

XReadBitmapFile reads in a file containing a pixmap of depth 1 (a bitmap). The file can be either in the standard X Version 10 format or in the newer X Version 11 bitmap format (which is only slightly different).

XReadBitmapFile creates a pixmap of the appropriate size, reads the bitmap data from the file into the pixmap. The caller must free the bitmap using XFreePixmap when done.

If the file cannot be opened, XReadBitmapFile returns BitmapOpenFailed. If the file can be opened but does not contain valid bitmap data, XReadBitmapFile returns Bitmap-FileInvalid. If insufficient working storage is allocated, XReadBitmapFile returns BitmapNoMemory. If the file is readable and valid, XReadBitmapFile returns Bitmap-Success.

Here is an X Version 11 example bitmap file:

```
#define name_width 16
#define name_height 16
#define name_x_hot 8
#define name_y_hot 8
static char name_bits[] = {
   0xf8, 0x1f, 0xe3, 0xc7, 0xcf, 0xf3, 0x9f, 0xf9, 0xbf, 0xfd, 0x33, 0xcc,
   0x7f, 0xfe, 0x7f, 0xfe, 0x7e, 0x7e, 0x7f, 0xfe, 0x37, 0xec, 0xbb, 0xdd,
   0x9c, 0x39, 0xcf, 0xf3, 0xe3, 0xc7, 0xf8, 0x1f};
```

For more information, see Volume One, Chapter 6, *Drawing Graphics and Text.*

Related Commands

XSetTile, XQueryBestTile, XSetWindowBorderPixmap, XSetWindow-
BackgroundPixmap, XCreatePixmap, XCreatePixmapFromBitmapData, XFree-
Pixmap, XQueryBestSize, XQueryBestStipple, XWriteBitmapFile, XCreate-
BitmapFromData.

XRebindKeysym

Name

XRebindKeysym — rebind a keysym to a string for client.

Synopsis

```
XRebindKeysym(display, keysym, mod_list, mod_count, string,
        num_bytes)
    Display *display;
    KeySym keysym;
    KeySym *mod_list;
    int mod_count;
    unsigned char *string;
    int num_bytes;
```

Arguments

display   Specifies a pointer to the Display structure; returned from XOpen-
               Display.

keysym   Specifies the keysym to be rebound.

mod_list   Specifies a pointer to an array of keysyms that are being used as modifiers.

mod_count   Specifies the number of modifiers in the modifier list.

string   Specifies a pointer to the string that is to be copied and returned by
               XLookupString.

num_bytes   Specifies the length of the string.

Description

XRebindKeysym binds the ASCII *string* to the specified *keysym*, so that *string* and
keysym are returned when that key is pressed and the modifiers specified in *mod_list* are
also being held down. This function rebinds the meaning of a keysym for a client. It does not
redefine the keycode in the server but merely provides an easy way for long strings to be
attached to keys. Note that you are allowed to rebind a keysym that may not exist.

See Volume One, Chapter 9, *The Keyboard and Pointer*, for a description of keysyms and
keyboard mapping.

Related Commands

XDeleteModifiermapEntry, XInsertModifiermapEntry, XFreeModifiermap,
XKeycodeToKeysym, XKeysymToKeycode, XKeysymToString, XNewModifier-
Map, XQueryKeymap, XStringToKeysym, XLookupKeysym, XGetKeyboard-
Mapping, XChangeKeyboardMapping, XRefreshKeyboardMapping, XLookup-
String, XSetModifierMapping, XGetModifierMapping.

Name

XRecolorCursor — change the color of a cursor.

Synopsis

```
XRecolorCursor(display, cursor, foreground_color,
        background_color)
    Display *display;
    Cursor cursor;
    XColor *foreground_color, *background_color;
```

Arguments

display   Specifies a pointer to the Display structure; returned from XOpen-Display.

cursor   Specifies the cursor ID.

foreground_color

        Specifies the red, green, and blue (RGB) values for the foreground.

background_color

        Specifies the red, green, and blue (RGB) values for the background.

Description

XRecolorCursor applies a foreground and background color to a cursor. Cursors are normally created using a single plane pixmap, composed of 0's and 1's, with one pixel value assigned to 1's and another assigned to 0's. XRecolorCursor changes these pixel values. If the cursor is being displayed on a screen, the change is visible immediately. On some servers, these color selections are read/write cells from the colormap, and can't be shared by applications.

Structures

```
typedef struct {
    unsigned long pixel;
    unsigned short red, green, blue;
    char flags;                     /* DoRed, DoGreen, DoBlue */
    char pad;
} XColor;
```

Errors

BadCursor

Related Commands

XDefineCursor, XUndefineCursor, XCreateFontCursor, XCreateGlyph-Cursor, XCreatePixmapCursor, XFreeCursor, XQueryBestCursor, XQuery-BestSize.

XRectInRegion

Name

XRectInRegion — determine if a rectangle resides in a region.

Synopsis

```
int XRectInRegion(r, x, y, width, height)
    Region r;
    int x, y;
    unsigned int width, height;
```

Arguments

r   Specifies the region.

x   Specify the x and y coordinates of the upper-left corner of the rectangle, rela-
y   tive to the region's origin.

width   Specify the width and height in pixels of the rectangle.
height

Description

XRectInRegion returns RectangleIn if the rectangle is completely contained in the
region r, RectangleOut if it is completely outside, and RectanglePart if it is partially
inside.

Regions are located using an offset from a point (the *region origin*) which is common to all
regions. It is up to the application to interpret the location of the region relative to a drawable.
If the region is to be used as a clip_mask by calling XSetRegion, the upper-left corner of
region relative to the drawable used in the graphics request will be at (xoffset +
clip_x_origin, yoffset + clip_y_origin), where xoffset and yoffset are
the offset of the region and clip_x_origin and clip_y_origin are the clip origin in
the GC used.

For this function, the x and y arguments are interpreted relative to the region origin, not the
drawable origin.

Structures

```
/*
 * opaque reference to Regiondata type.
 * user won't need contents, only pointer.
 */
typedef struct _XRegion *Region;
```

Related Commands

XXorRegion, XUnionRegion, XUnionRectWithRegion, XSubtractRegion,
XShrinkRegion, XSetRegion, XPolygonRegion, XPointInRegion, XOffset-
Region, XIntersectRegion, XEmptyRegion, XCreateRegion, XDestroy-
Region, XEqualRegion, XClipBox.

XRefreshKeyboardMapping

Name

XRefreshKeyboardMapping — update the stored modifier and keymap information.

Synopsis

```
XRefreshKeyboardMapping(event)
    XMappingEvent *event;
```

Arguments

event   Specifies the mapping event that is to be used.

Description

XRefreshKeyboardMapping causes the library to update the mapping between keycodes and keysyms. This updates the client application's knowledge of the keyboard.

You usually want to call XRefreshKeyboardMapping when a MappingNotify event occurs. MappingNotify events occur when some client has called XChangeKeyboard-Mapping.

For more information, see Volume One, Chapter 9, *The Keyboard and Pointer*.

Structures

```
typedef struct {
    int type;
    Display *display;      /* display the event was read from */
    Window window;         /* unused */
    int request;           /* one of MappingModifier, MappingKeyboard,
                                 MappingPointer */
    int first_keycode;     /* first keycode */
    int count;             /* defines range of change with first_keycode*/
} XMappingEvent;
```

Related Commands

XDeleteModifiermapEntry, XInsertModifiermapEntry, XFreeModifiermap, XKeycodeToKeysym, XKeysymToKeycode, XKeysymToString, XNewModifier-Map, XQueryKeymap, XStringToKeysym, XLookupKeysym, XRebindKeysym, XGetKeyboardMapping, XChangeKeyboardMapping, XLookupString, XSet-ModifierMapping, XGetModifierMapping.

Name

XRemoveFromSaveSet — remove a window's children from the client's save-set.

Synopsis

```
XRemoveFromSaveSet(display, w)
    Display *display;
    Window w;
```

Arguments

display   Specifies a pointer to the Display structure; returned from XOpen-Display.

w   Specifies the window whose children you want to remove from this client's save-set. This window must have been created by a client other than the client making this call.

Description

XRemoveFromSaveSet removes a window's children from the save-set of the calling application. Usually, this call is invoked by a window manager, using the RootWindow macro for *w*, to remove all top-level windows on a screen from the save-set.

The save-set is a safety net for windows that have been reparented by the window manager, usually to provide a shadow or other background for each window. When the window manager dies unexpectedly, the windows in the save-set are reparented to their closest living ancestor, so that they remain alive.

This call is not necessary when a window is destroyed since destroyed windows are automatically removed from the save-set. See Volume One, Chapter 14, *Window Management*, for more information about save-sets.

Errors

BadMatch   *w* not created by some other client.

BadWindow

Related Commands

XAddToSaveSet, XChangeSaveSet.

Name

XRemoveHost — remove a host from the access control list.

Synopsis

```
XRemoveHost(display, host)
    Display *display;
    XHostAddress *host;
```

Arguments

display   Specifies a pointer to the Display structure; returned from XOpen-Display.

host   Specifies the network address of the machine to be removed.

Description

XRemoveHost removes the specified host from the access control list on the host running the server controlling the current display. The display hardware must be on the same host as the calling process in order to change the access control list.

If you remove your own machine from the access control list, you can no longer connect to that server, and there is no way back from this call other than to log out and reset the server.

The address data must be a valid address for the type of network in which the server operates, as specified in the family member.

For TCP/IP, the address should be in network byte order. For the DECnet family, the server performs no automatic swapping on the address bytes. A Phase IV address is two bytes long. The first byte contains the least significant eight bits of the node number. The second byte contains the most significant two bits of the node number in the least significant two bits of the byte, and the area in the most significant six bits of the byte.

For more information on access control lists, see Volume One, Chapter 13, *Other Programming Techniques*.

Structures

```
typedef struct {
    int family;             /* for example Family Internet */
    int length;             /* length of address, in bytes */
    char *address;          /* pointer to where to find the bytes */
} XHostAddress;

/* constants used for family member of XHostAddress */
#define FamilyInternet        0
#define FamilyDECnet          1
#define FamilyChaos           2
```

Errors

BadAccess
BadValue

Related Commands

XAddHost, XAddHosts, XListHosts, XRemoveHosts, XDisableAccessControl,
XEnableAccessControl, XSetAccessControl.

XRemoveHosts

Name

XRemoveHosts — remove multiple hosts from the access control list.

Synopsis

```
XRemoveHosts(display, hosts, num_hosts)
    Display *display;
    XHostAddress *hosts;
    int num_hosts;
```

Arguments

display Specifies a pointer to the Display structure; returned from XOpen-Display.

hosts Specifies the list of hosts that are to be removed.

num_hosts Specifies the number of hosts that are to be removed.

Description

XRemoveHosts removes each specified host from the access control list on the local machine running the server. The display hardware must be on the same host as the client process, in order to change the access control list.

If you remove your machine from the access control list, you can no longer connect to that server, and there is no way back from this call except to log out and reset the server.

The address data must be a valid address for the type of network in which the server operates, as specified in the family member.

For TCP/IP, the address should be in network byte order. For the DECnet family, the server performs no automatic swapping on the address bytes. A Phase IV address is two bytes long. The first byte contains the least significant eight bits of the node number. The second byte contains the most significant two bits of the node number in the least significant two bits of the byte, and the area in the most significant six bits of the byte.

For more information on access control lists, see Volume One, Chapter 13, *Other Programming Techniques*.

Structures

```
typedef struct {
    int family;          /* for example Family Internet */
    int length;          /* length of address, in bytes */
    char *address;       /* pointer to where to find the bytes */
} XHostAddress;

/* constants used for family member of XHostAddress */
#define FamilyInternet      0
#define FamilyDECnet        1
#define FamilyChaos         2
```

Errors
    BadAccess
    BadValue

Related Commands
    XAddHost, XAddHosts, XListHosts, XRemoveHost, XDisableAccessControl,
    XEnableAccessControl, XSetAccessControl.

XReparentWindow

Name

XReparentWindow — insert a window between another window and its parent.

Synopsis

```
XReparentWindow(display, win, parent, x, y)
    Display *display;
    Window win;
    Window parent;
    int x, y;
```

Arguments

display   Specifies a pointer to the `Display` structure; returned from `XOpen-Display`.

win   Specifies the ID of the window to be reparented.

parent   Specifies the window ID of the new parent window.

x
y   Specify the coordinates of the window relative to the new parent.

Description

`XReparentWindow` modifies the window hierarchy by placing window *win* as a child of window *parent*. This function is usually used by a window manager to put a decoration window behind application windows. In the case of the window manager, the new parent window must first be created as a child of the root window.

If *win* is mapped, an `XUnmapWindow` request is performed on it automatically. *win* is then removed from its current position in the hierarchy, and is inserted as a child of the specified parent. *win* is placed on top in the stacking order with respect to siblings.

A `ReparentNotify` event is then generated. The `override_redirect` member of the structure returned by this event is set to either `True` or `False`. Window manager clients normally should ignore this event if this member is set to `True`.

Finally, if the window was originally mapped, an `XMapWindow` request is performed automatically.

Descendants of *win* remain descendants of *win*; they are not reparented to the old parent of *win*.

Normal exposure processing on formerly obscured windows is performed. The server might not generate exposure events for regions from the initial unmap that are immediately obscured by the final map. The request fails if the new parent is not on the same screen as the old parent, or if the new parent is the window itself or an inferior of the window.

Errors

BadMatch

> *parent* not on same screen as old parent of *win*.
>
> *win* has a ParentRelative background and *parent* is not the same depth as *win*.
>
> *parent* is *win* or an inferior of *win*.

BadWindow

Related Commands

XLowerWindow, XRaiseWindow, XCirculateSubwindows, XCirculate-SubwindowsDown, XCirculateSubwindowsUp, XRestackWindows, XMove-Window, XResizeWindow, XMoveResizeWindow, XConfigureWindow, XQuery-Tree.

XResetScreenSaver

Name
XResetScreenSaver — reset the screen saver.

Synopsis
```
XResetScreenSaver (display)
    Display *display;
```

Arguments
display   Specifies a pointer to the Display structure; returned from XOpen-Display.

Description
XResetScreenSaver redisplays the screen if the screen saver was activated. This may result in exposure events to all visible windows if the server cannot save the screen contents. If the screen is already active, nothing happens.

For more information on the screen saver, see Volume One, Chapter 13, *Other Programming Techniques*.

Related Commands
XForceScreenSaver, XActivateScreenSaver, XGetScreenSaver, XSet-ScreenSaver.

Name

XResizeWindow — change a window's size.

Synopsis

```
XResizeWindow(display, w, width, height)
    Display *display;
    Window w;
    unsigned int width, height;
```

Arguments

display   Specifies a pointer to the Display structure; returned from XOpen-Display.

w   Specifies the ID of the window to be resized.

width
height   Specify the new dimensions of the window in pixels.

Description

XResizeWindow changes the inside dimensions of the window. The border is resized to match but its width is not changed. XResizeWindow does not raise the window, or change its origin. Changing the size of a mapped window may lose its contents and generate an Expose event, depending on the bit_gravity attribute (see Volume One, Chapter 4, *Window Attributes*). If a mapped window is made smaller, exposure events will be generated on windows that it formerly obscured.

If the override_redirect attribute of the window is False and some other client has selected SubstructureRedirectMask on the parent, then a ConfigureRequest event is generated, and no further processing is performed.

If some other client has selected StructureNotifyMask on the window, then a ConfigureNotify event is generated after the move takes place, and the event will contain the final size of the window.

Errors

BadValue
BadWindow

Related Commands

XLowerWindow, XRaiseWindow, XCirculateSubwindows, XCirculate-SubwindowsDown, XCirculateSubwindowsUp, XRestackWindows, XMove-Window, XMoveResizeWindow, XReparentWindow, XConfigureWindow, XQuery-Tree.

XRestackWindows

Name

XRestackWindows — change the stacking order of siblings.

Synopsis

```
XRestackWindows(display, windows, nwindows);
    Display *display;
    Window windows[];
    int nwindows;
```

Arguments

display   Specifies a pointer to the Display structure; returned from XOpen-Display.

windows   Specifies an array containing the windows to be restacked. All the windows must have a common parent.

nwindows   Specifies the number of windows to be restacked.

Description

XRestackWindows restacks the windows in the order specified, from top to bottom. The stacking order of the first window in the windows array will be on top, and the other windows will be stacked underneath it in the order of the array. Note that other siblings may not be included in the windows array and so the top window in that array will not move relative to these other siblings.

For each window in the window array that is not a child of the specified window, a Bad-Match error will be generated. If the override_redirect attribute of the window is False and some other client has selected SubstructureRedirectMask on the parent, then ConfigureRequest events are generated for each window whose override_redirect is not set, and no further processing is performed. Otherwise, the windows will be restacked in top to bottom order.

Errors

BadMatch
BadWindow

Related Commands

XLowerWindow, XRaiseWindow, XCirculateSubwindows, XCirculate-SubwindowsDown, XCirculateSubwindowsUp, XMoveWindow, XResizeWindow, XMoveResizeWindow, XReparentWindow, XConfigureWindow, XQueryTree.

XrmGetFileDatabase

Name

XrmGetFileDatabase — retrieve a database from a file.

Synopsis

```
XrmDatabase XrmGetFileDatabase(filename)
    char *filename;
```

Arguments

filename   Specifies the resource database filename.

Description

XrmGetFileDatabase opens the specified file, creates a new resource database, and loads it with the data read in from the file. The return value of the function is subsequently used as a pointer to the created database.

The specified file must contain lines in the format accepted by XrmPutLineResource. If it cannot open the specified file, XrmGetFileDatabase returns NULL.

For more information, see Volume One, Chapter 11, *Managing User Preferences*.

Structures

XrmDatabase is a pointer to an opaque data type.

Related Commands

XrmGetResource, XrmGetStringDatabase, XrmInitialize, XrmMerge-
Databases, XrmParseCommand, XrmPutFileDatabase, XrmPutLineResource,
XrmPutResource, XrmPutStringResource, XrmQGetResource, XrmQGet-
SearchList, XrmQGetSearchResource, XrmQPutResource, XrmQPutString-
Resource, XrmQuarkToString, XrmStringToBindingQuarkList, XrmString-
ToQuarkList, XrmStringToQuark, XrmUniqueQuark.

XrmGetResource

Name

XrmGetResource — get a resource from name and class as strings.

Synopsis

```
Bool XrmGetResource(database, str_name, str_class,
        str_type, value)
    XrmDatabase database;
    char *str_name;
    char *str_class;
    char **str_type;           /* RETURN */
    XrmValue *value;           /* RETURN */
```

Arguments

database	Specifies the database that is to be used.
str_name	Specifies the fully qualified name of the value being retrieved (as a string). str_name is an instance of a name retrieval key as described below.
str_class	Specifies the fully qualified class of the value being retrieved (as a string). str_class is an instance of a class retrieval key as described below.
str_type	Returns a pointer to the representation type of the destination. In this function, the representation type is itself represented as a string, not as an Xrm-Representation.
value	Returns the value in the database. Do not modify or free this data.

Description

The resource manager manages databases of resources consisting of lines containing resource name/class strings followed by a colon and the value of the resource. XrmGetResource retrieves a resource from the specified database. It takes fully qualified name and class strings, and returns the representation and value of the matching resource. The value returned points into database memory; therefore, you must not modify that data. If a resource was found, XrmGetResource returns True. Otherwise, it returns False.

Currently, the database only frees or overwrites entries when new data is stored with Xrm-MergeDatabases, or XrmPutResource and related routines. A client that avoids these functions should be safe using the address passed back at any time until it exits.

XrmGetResource is very similar to XrmQGetResource, except that in XrmQGet-Resource, the equivalent arguments to str_name, str_class, and str_type are quarks instead of strings.

To understand how data is stored and retrieved from the database, you must understand:

1) The basic components that make up the storage key and retrieval keys.

2) How keys are made up from components.

3) The two ways that components can be bound together.

4)   What sort of keys are used to store and retrieve data.

5)   How the storage key and retrieval keys are compared to determine whether they match.

6)   If there are multiple matches, how the best match is chosen so only that corresponding value is returned.

Each will be covered in turn.

1)   The storage key and retrieval keys are composed of a variable number of components, bound together. There are two types of components: names and classes. By convention, names begin with a lower case character and classes begin with an upper case character. Therefore, xmh, background, and toc are examples of names, while Xmh, Box, and Command are examples of classes. A name key (like *str_name*) consists purely of name components. A class key (like *str_class*) consists purely of class components. The retrieval keys are a pair of keys, one composed of purely name components, the other of purely class components. A storage key (like *specifier* in XrmPutResource) consists of a mixture of name and class components.

2)   A key is composed of multiple components bound together in sequence. This allows you to build logical keys for your application. For example, at the top level, the application might consist of a paned window (that is, a window divided into several sections) named toc. One pane of the paned window is a button box window named buttons filled with command buttons. One of these command buttons is used to retrieve (include) new mail and has the name include. This window has a fully qualified name xmh.toc.buttons.include and a fully qualified class Xmh.VPaned.Box.Command. Its fully qualified name is the name of its parent, xmh.toc.buttons, followed by its name include. Its class is the class of its parent, Xmh.VPaned.Box, followed by its particular class, Command.

3)   The components in a key can be bound together in two ways: by a tight binding (a dot ".") or by a loose binding (an asterisk "*"). Thus xmhtoc.background has three name components tightly bound together, while Xmh*Command.foreground uses both a loose and a tight binding. Bindings can also precede the first component (but may not follow the last component). By convention, if no binding is specified before the first component, a tight binding is assumed. For example, xmh.background and .xmh.background both begin with tight bindings before the xmh, while *xmh.background begins with a loose binding.

The difference between tight and loose bindings comes when comparing two keys. A tight binding means that the components on either side of the binding must be sequential. A loose binding is a sort of wildcard, meaning that there may be unspecified components between the two components that are loosely bound togehter. For example, xmh.toc.background would match xmh*background and *background but not xmh.background or background.

4)   A key used to store data into the database can use both loose and tight bindings. This allows you to specify a data value which can match to many different retrieval keys. In contrast, keys used to retrieve data from the database can use only tight bindings. You

can only look up one item in the database at a time. Remember also that a storage key can mix name and class components, while the retrieval keys are a pair of keys, one consisting purely of name (first character lower case) components and one consisting purely of class (capitalized) components.

5)   The resource manager must solve the problem of how to compare the pair of retrieval keys to a single storage key. (Actually, to many single storage keys, since the resource manager will compare the retrieval keys against every key in the database, but one at a time.) The solution of comparing a pair of keys to a single key is simple. The resource manager compares component by component, comparing a component from the storage key against both the corresponding component from the name retrieval key, and the corresponding component from the class retrieval key. If the storage key component matches either retrieval key component, then that component is considered to match. For example, the storage key `xmh.toc.Foreground` matches the name key `xmh.toc.foreground` with the class key `Xmh.Box.Foreground`. This is why storage keys can mix name and class components, while retrieval keys cannot.

6)   Because the resource manager allows loose bindings (wildcards) and mixing names and classes in the storage key, it is possible for many storage keys to match a single name/class retrieval key pair. To solve this problem, the resource manager uses the following precedence rules to determine which is the best match (and only the value from that match will be returned). The precedence rules are, in order of preference:

1.   The attribute of the name and class must match. For example, queries for

```
xterm.scrollbar.background    (name)
XTerm.Scrollbar.Background    (class)
```

will not match the following database entry:

```
xterm.scrollbar:        on
```

because background does not appear in the database entry.

2.   Database entries with name or class prefixed by a dot (.) are more specific than those prefixed by an asterisk (*). For example, the entry `xterm.geometry` is more specific than the entry `xterm*geometry`.

3.   Names are more specific than classes. For example, the entry `*scrollbar.-background` is more specific than the entry `*Scrollbar.Background`.

4.   A name or class is more specific than omission. For example, the entry `Scrollbar*Background` is more specific than the entry `*Background`.

5.   Left components are more specific than right components. For example, to query for `.xterm.scrollbar.background`, the entry `xterm*background` is more specific than the entry `scrollbar*background`.

Names and classes can be mixed. As an example of these rules, assume the following user preference specification:

```
xmh*background:                      red
*command.font:                       8x13
*command.background:                 blue
*Command.Foreground:                 green
xmh.toc*Command.activeForeground:    black
```

A query for the name `xmh.toc.messagefunctions.include.activeForeground` and class `Xmh.VPaned.Box.Command.Foreground` would match `xmh.toc*-Command.activeForeground` and return `black`. However, it also matches `*Command.Foreground` but with lower preference, so it would not return `green`.

For more information, see Volume One, Chapter 11, *Managing User Preferences.*

Structures

`XrmDatabase` is a pointer to an opaque data type.

```
typedef struct {
    unsigned int    size;
    caddr_t         addr;
} XrmValue;
```

Related Commands

`XrmGetFileDatabase, XrmGetStringDatabase, XrmInitialize, XrmMerge-Databases, XrmParseCommand, XrmPutFileDatabase, XrmPutLineResource, XrmPutResource, XrmPutStringResource, XrmQGetResource, XrmQGet-SearchList, XrmQGetSearchResource, XrmQPutResource, XrmQPutString-Resource, XrmQuarkToString, XrmStringToBindingQuarkList, XrmString-ToQuarkList, XrmStringToQuark, XrmUniqueQuark.`

XrmGetStringDatabase

Name
XrmGetStringDatabase — create a database from a string.

Synopsis
```
XrmDatabase XrmGetStringDatabase(data)
    char *data;
```

Arguments
data   Specifies the database contents using a string.

Description
XrmGetStringDatabase creates a new database and stores in it the resources specified in *data*. The return value is subsequently used to refer to the created database. XrmGet-StringDatabase is similar to XrmGetFileDatabase, except that it reads the information out of a string instead of a file. Each line is separated by a new line character in the format accepted by XrmPutLineResource.

For more information, see Volume One, Chapter 11, *Managing User Preferences.*

Structures
XrmDatabase is a pointer to an opaque data type.

Related Commands
XrmGetFileDatabase, XrmGetResource, XrmInitialize, XrmMerge-Databases, XrmParseCommand, XrmPutFileDatabase, XrmPutLineResource, XrmPutResource, XrmPutStringResource, XrmQGetResource, XrmQGet-SearchList, XrmQGetSearchResource, XrmQPutResource, XrmQPutString-Resource, XrmQuarkToString, XrmStringToBindingQuarkList, XrmString-ToQuarkList, XrmStringToQuark, XrmUniqueQuark.

Name

XrmInitialize — initialize the resource manager.

Synopsis

```
void XrmInitialize();
```

Description

XrmInitialize initializes the resource manager, and should be called once before using any other resource manager functions. All it does is to create a representation type of ''String'' for values defined as strings. This representation type is used by XrmPutString-Resource and XrmQPutStringResource, which require a value as a string. See Xrm-QPutResource for a description of representation types.

For more information, see Volume One, Chapter 11, *Managing User Preferences*.

Related Commands

XrmGetFileDatabase, XrmGetResource, XrmGetStringDatabase, XrmMerge-Databases, XrmParseCommand, XrmPutFileDatabase, XrmPutLineResource, XrmPutResource, XrmPutStringResource, XrmQGetResource, XrmQGet-SearchList, XrmQGetSearchResource, XrmQPutResource, XrmQPutString-Resource, XrmQuarkToString, XrmStringToBindingQuarkList, XrmString-ToQuarkList, XrmStringToQuark, XrmUniqueQuark.

XrmMergeDatabases

Name

XrmMergeDatabases — merge the contents of one database with another.

Synopsis

```
void XrmMergeDatabases(source_db, target_db)
    XrmDatabase source_db, *target_db;
```

Arguments

source_db   Specifies the descriptor of the resource database to be merged into the existing database.

target_db   Specifies a pointer to the descriptor of the resource database into which the *source_db* database will be merged.

Description

XrmMergeDatabases overwrites entries in the destination database. This procedure is used to combine databases, for example, an application specific database of defaults and a database of user preferences. The merge is destructive; it destroys the original *source_db* database and modifies the original *target_db*.

For more information, see Volume One, Chapter 11, *Managing User Preferences*.

Structures

XrmDatabase is a pointer to an opaque data type.

Related Commands

XrmGetFileDatabase, XrmGetResource, XrmGetStringDatabase, Xrm-
Initialize, XrmParseCommand, XrmPutFileDatabase, XrmPutLineResource,
XrmPutResource, XrmPutStringResource, XrmQGetResource, XrmQGet-
SearchList, XrmQGetSearchResource, XrmQPutResource, XrmQPutString-
Resource, XrmQuarkToString, XrmStringToBindingQuarkList, XrmString-
ToQuarkList, XrmStringToQuark, XrmUniqueQuark.

Name

XrmParseCommand — load a resource database from command line arguments.

Synopsis

```
void XrmParseCommand(db, table, table_count, name, argc,
        argv)
    XrmDatabase *db;
    XrmOptionDescList table;
    int table_count;
    char *name;
    int *argc;                    /* SEND and RETURN */
    char **argv;                  /* SEND and RETURN */
```

Arguments

database	Specifies a pointer to the resource database. If *database* contains NULL, a new resource database is created and a pointer to it is returned in *database*.
table	Specifies table of command line arguments to be parsed.
table_count	Specifies the number of entries in the table.
name	Specifies the application name.
argc	Before the call, specifies the number of arguments. After the call, returns the number of arguments not parsed.
argv	Before the call, specifies a pointer to the command line arguments. After the call, returns a pointer to a string containing the command line arguments that could not be parsed.

Description

XrmParseCommand parses an (*argc*, *argv*) pair according to the specified option table, loads recognized options into the specified database, and modifies the (*argc*, *argv*) pair to remove all recognized options.

The specified table is used to parse the command line. Recognized entries in the table are removed from *argv*, and entries are made in the specified resource database. The table entries contain information on the option string, the option name, which style of option and a value to provide if the option kind is XrmoptionNoArg. See the example table below.

argc specifies the number of arguments in *argv* and is set to the remaining number of arguments that were not parsed. *name* should be the name of your application for use in building the database entry. *name* is prepended to the resourceName in the option table before storing the specification. No separating (binding) character is inserted. The table must contain either a dot (".") or an asterisk ("*") as the first character in each resourceName entry. The resourceName entry can contain multiple components.

The following is a typical options table:

```
static XrmOptionDescRec opTable[ ] = {
{"-background",  "*background",                    XrmoptionSepArg, (caddr_t) NULL},
{"-bd",          "*borderColor",                   XrmoptionSepArg, (caddr_t) NULL},
{"-bg",          "*background",                    XrmoptionSepArg, (caddr_t) NULL},
{"-borderwidth", "*TopLevelShell.borderWidth",     XrmoptionSepArg, (caddr_t) NULL},
{"-bordercolor", "*borderColor",                   XrmoptionSepArg, (caddr_t) NULL},
{"-bw",          "*TopLevelShell.borderWidth",     XrmoptionSepArg, (caddr_t) NULL},
{"-display",     ".display",                       XrmoptionSepArg, (caddr_t) NULL},
{"-fg",          "*foreground",                    XrmoptionSepArg, (caddr_t) NULL},
{"-fn",          "*font",                          XrmoptionSepArg, (caddr_t) NULL},
{"-font",        "*font",                          XrmoptionSepArg, (caddr_t) NULL},
{"-foreground",  "*foreground",                    XrmoptionSepArg, (caddr_t) NULL},
{"-geometry",    ".TopLevelShell.geometry",        XrmoptionSepArg, (caddr_t) NULL},
{"-iconic",      ".TopLevelShell.iconic",          XrmoptionNoArg,  (caddr_t) "on"},
{"-name",        ".name",                          XrmoptionSepArg, (caddr_t) NULL},
{"-reverse",     "*reverseVideo",                  XrmoptionNoArg,  (caddr_t) "on"},
{"-rv",          "*reverseVideo",                  XrmoptionNoArg,  (caddr_t) "on"},
{"-synchronous", ".synchronous",                   XrmoptionNoArg,  (caddr_t) "on"},
{"-title",       ".TopLevelShell.title",           XrmoptionSepArg, (caddr_t) NULL},
{"-xrm",         NULL,                             XrmoptionResArg, (caddr_t) NULL},
};
```

In this table, if the *-background* (or *-bg*) option is used to set background colors, the stored resource specifier will match all resources of attribute background. If the *-borderwidth* option is used, the stored resource specifier applies only to border width attributes of class `Top-LevelShell` (that is, outermost windows, including pop-up windows). If the *-title* option is used to set a window name, only the topmost application windows receive the resource.

When parsing the command line, any unique unambiguous abbreviation for an option name in the table is considered a match for the option. Note that upper case and lower case matter.

For more information, see Volume One, Chapter 11, *Managing User Preferences.*

Structures

`XrmDatabase` is a pointer to an opaque data type.

```
typedef enum {
    XrmoptionNoArg,       /* value is specified in OptionDescRec.value */
    XrmoptionIsArg,       /* value is the option string itself */
    XrmoptionStickyArg,   /* value is chars immediately following option */
    XrmoptionSepArg,      /* value is next argument in argv */
    XrmoptionResArg,      /* resource and value in next argument in argv */
    XrmoptionSkipArg,     /* ignore this option and next argument in argv */
    XrmoptionSkipLine     /* ignore this option and the rest of argv */
} XrmOptionKind;

typedef struct {
    char *option;          /* option specification string in argv */
    char *resourceName;    /* binding & resource name (w/out application name) */
    XrmOptionKind argKind; /* which style of option it is */
    caddr_t value;         /* value to provide if XrmoptionNoArg */
} XrmOptionDescRec, *XrmOptionDescList;
```

Related Commands

XrmGetFileDatabase, XrmGetResource, XrmGetStringDatabase, Xrm-
Initialize, XrmMergeDatabases, XrmPutFileDatabase, XrmPutLine-
Resource, XrmPutResource, XrmPutStringResource, XrmQGetResource, Xrm-
QGetSearchList, XrmQGetSearchResource, XrmQPutResource, XrmQPut-
StringResource, XrmQuarkToString, XrmStringToBindingQuarkList, Xrm-
StringToQuarkList, XrmStringToQuark, XrmUniqueQuark.

Name

XrmPutFileDatabase — store a database in a file.

Synopsis

```
void XrmPutFileDatabase(database, stored_db)
    XrmDatabase database;
    char *stored_db;
```

Arguments

database   Specifies the database that is to be saved.

stored_db   Specifies the filename for the stored database.

Description

XrmPutFileDatabase stores a copy of the application's current database in the specified file. The file is an ASCII text file that contains lines in the format that is accepted by Xrm-PutLineResource.

For more information, see Volume One, Chapter 11, *Managing User Preferences*.

Structures

XrmDatabase is a pointer to an opaque data type.

Related Commands

XrmGetFileDatabase, XrmGetResource, XrmGetStringDatabase, Xrm-Initialize, XrmMergeDatabases, XrmParseCommand, XrmPutLineResource, XrmPutResource, XrmPutStringResource, XrmQGetResource, XrmQGet-SearchList, XrmQGetSearchResource, XrmQPutResource, XrmQPutString-Resource, XrmQuarkToString, XrmStringToBindingQuarkList, XrmString-ToQuarkList, XrmStringToQuark, XrmUniqueQuark.

XrmPutLineResource

Name

XrmPutLineResource — add a resource entry given as a string of name and value.

Synopsis

```
void XrmPutLineResource (database, line)
    XrmDatabase *database; /* SEND, and if NULL, RETURN */
    char *line;
```

Arguments

database   Specifies a pointer to the resource database. If `database` contains NULL, a new resource database is created and a pointer to it is returned in `database`.

line   Specifies the resource name and value pair as a single string, in the format `resource:value`. A single colon (":") separates the resource name from the value, for example, `xterm*background:green\n`.

Description

`XrmPutLineResource` adds a single resource entry to the specified database.

`XrmPutLineResource` is similar to `XrmPutStringResource`, except that instead of having separate string arguments for the resource and its value, `XrmPutLineResource` takes a single string argument (`line`) which consists of the resource name, a colon, then the value. Since the value is a string, it is stored into the database with representation type `String`.

Any whitespace before or after the name or colon in the `line` argument is ignored. The value is terminated by a new-line or a NULL character. The value may contain embedded new-line characters represented by the "\" and "n" two character pair (not the single "\n" character), which are converted into a single linefeed character. In addition, the value may run over onto the next line, this is indicated by a "\" character at the end of the line immediately preceding the "\n" character.

Null-terminated strings without a new line are also permitted. `XrmPutResource`, `XrmQPutResource`, `XrmPutStringResource`, `XrmQPutStringResource` and `XrmPutLineResource` all store data into a database. See `XrmQPutResource` for the most complete description of this process.

For more information, see Volume One, Chapter 11, *Managing User Preferences*.

Structures

`XrmDatabase` is a pointer to an opaque data type.

Related Commands

XrmGetFileDatabase, XrmGetResource, XrmGetStringDatabase, Xrm-
Initialize, XrmMergeDatabases, XrmParseCommand, XrmPutFileDatabase,
XrmPutResource, XrmPutStringResource, XrmQGetResource, XrmQGet-
SearchList, XrmQGetSearchResource, XrmQPutResource, XrmQPutString-
Resource, XrmQuarkToString, XrmStringToBindingQuarkList, XrmString-
ToQuarkList, XrmStringToQuark, XrmUniqueQuark.

Name

XrmPutResource — store a resource into a database.

Synopsis

```
void XrmPutResource(database, specifier, type, value)
    XrmDatabase *database; /* SEND, and if NULL, RETURN */
    char *specifier;
    char *type;
    XrmValue *value;
```

Arguments

database   Specifies a pointer to the resource database. If database contains NULL, a new resource database is created and a pointer to it is returned in *database*.

specifier   Specifies a complete or partial specification of the resource.

type   Specifies the type of the resource.

value   Specifies the value of the resource.

Description

XrmPutResource is one of several functions which store data into a database.

XrmQPutResource first converts *specifier* into a binding list and a quark list by calling XrmStringToBindingQuarkList, and converts *type* into an XrmRepresentation by calling XrmStringToRepresentation. Finally, it puts the data into the database.

XrmPutResource, XrmQPutResource, XrmPutStringResource, XrmQPut-StringResource and XrmPutLineResource all store data into a database. See the description of XrmQPutResource for the most complete description of this process.

For more information, see Volume One, Chapter 11, *Managing User Preferences*.

Structures

XrmDatabase is a pointer to an opaque data type.

```
typedef struct {
    unsigned int    size;
    caddr_t         addr;
} XrmValue, *XrmValuePtr;
```

Related Commands

XrmGetFileDatabase, XrmGetResource, XrmGetStringDatabase, Xrm-
Initialize, XrmMergeDatabases, XrmParseCommand, XrmPutFileDatabase,
XrmPutLineResource, XrmPutStringResource, XrmQGetResource, XrmQGet-
SearchList, XrmQGetSearchResource, XrmQPutResource, XrmQPutString-
Resource, XrmQuarkToString, XrmStringToBindingQuarkList, XrmString-
ToQuarkList, XrmStringToQuark, XrmUniqueQuark.

Name

XrmPutStringResource — add a resource that is specified as a string.

Synopsis

```
void XrmPutStringResource (database, resource, value)
    XrmDatabase *database; /* SEND, and if NULL, RETURN */
    char *resource;
    char *value;
```

Arguments

database   Specifies a pointer to the resource database. If *database* contains NULL, a new resource database is created and a pointer to it is returned in *database*.

resource   Specifies the resource as a string.

value   Specifies the value of the resource. The value is specified as a string.

Description

XrmPutStringResource adds a resource with the specified value to the specified database. The *resource* string may contain both names and classes, bound with either loose (*) or tight (.) bindings. See the description of XrmGetResource for more information about bindings.

The representation type used in the database is String.

XrmPutResource, XrmQPutResource, XrmPutStringResource, XrmQPut-StringResource and XrmPutLineResource all store data into a database. See Xrm-QPutResource for the most complete description of this process.

For more information, see Volume One, Chapter 11, *Managing User Preferences*.

Structures

XrmDatabase is a pointer to an opaque data type.

Related Commands

XrmGetFileDatabase, XrmGetResource, XrmGetStringDatabase, Xrm-Initialize, XrmMergeDatabases, XrmParseCommand, XrmPutFileDatabase, XrmPutLineResource, XrmPutResource, XrmQGetResource, XrmQGetSearch-List, XrmQGetSearchResource, XrmQPutResource, XrmQPutStringResource, XrmQuarkToString, XrmStringToBindingQuarkList, XrmStringToQuark-List, XrmStringToQuark, XrmUniqueQuark.

Name

XrmQGetResource — get a resource from name and class as quarks.

Synopsis

```
Bool XrmQGetResource(database, quark_name, quark_class,
        quark_type, value)
    XrmDatabase database;
    XrmNameList quark_name;
    XrmClassList quark_class;
    XrmRepresentation *quark_type;  /* RETURN */
    XrmValue *value;                /* RETURN */
```

Arguments

database   Specifies the database that is to be used.

quark_name   Specifies the fully qualified name of the value being retrieved (as a list of quarks).

quark_class   Specifies the fully qualified class of the value being retrieved (as a list of quarks).

quark_type   Returns a pointer to the representation type of the destination. In this function, the representation type is itself represented as a quark.

value   Returns a pointer to the value in the database. Do not modify or free this data.

Description

XrmQGetResource retrieves a resource from the specified database. It takes fully qualified name and class strings, and returns the representation and value of the matching resource. The value returned points into database memory; therefore, you must not modify that data. If a resource was found, XrmQGetResource returns True. Otherwise, it returns False.

Currently, the database only frees or overwrites entries when new data is stored with Xrm-MergeDatabases, or XrmPutResource and related routines. A client that avoids these functions should be safe using the address passed back at any time until it exits.

XrmQGetResource is very similar to XrmGetResource, except that in XrmGet-Resource, the equivalent arguments to *quark_name*, *quark_class*, and *quark_type* arguments are strings instead of quarks.

See XrmGetResource for a full description of how data is looked up in the database.

For more information, see Volume One, Chapter 11, *Managing User Preferences*.

Structures

`XrmDatabase` is a pointer to an opaque data type.

```
typedef XrmQuarkList XrmNameList;
typedef XrmQuarkList XrmClassList;
typedef XrmQuark     XrmRepresentation;

typedef struct {
    unsigned int    size;
    caddr_t         addr;
} XrmValue, *XrmValuePtr;
```

Related Commands

`XrmGetFileDatabase`, `XrmGetResource`, `XrmGetStringDatabase`, `Xrm-Initialize`, `XrmMergeDatabases`, `XrmParseCommand`, `XrmPutFileDatabase`, `XrmPutLineResource`, `XrmPutResource`, `XrmPutStringResource`, `XrmQGet-SearchList`, `XrmQGetSearchResource`, `XrmQPutResource`, `XrmQPutString-Resource`, `XrmQuarkToString`, `XrmStringToBindingQuarkList`, `XrmString-ToQuarkList`, `XrmStringToQuark`, `XrmUniqueQuark`.

Name

XrmQGetSearchList — return a list of database levels.

Synopsis

```
Bool XrmQGetSearchList(database, names, classes,
        search_list, list_length)
    XrmDatabase database;
    XrmNameList names;
    XrmClassList classes;
    XrmSearchList search_list; /* RETURN */
    int list_length;
```

Arguments

database   Specifies the database that is to be used.

names   Specifies a list of resource names.

classes   Specifies a list of resource classes.

search_list   Returns a search list for further use. The caller must allocate sufficient space for the list before calling XrmQGetSearchList.

list_length Specifies the number of entries (not the byte size) allocated for list.

Description

XrmQGetSearchList is a tool for searching the database more efficiently. It is used in combination with XrmGetSearchResource. Often, one searches the database for many similar resources which differ only in their final component (e.g. xmh.toc.foreground, xmh.toc.background, etc). Rather than looking for each resource in its entirety, Xrm-GetSearchList searches the database for the common part of the resource name, returning a whole list of items in the database that match it. This list is called the *search list*. This search list is then used by XrmQGetSearchList, which searches for the last components one at a time. In this way, the common work of searching for similar resources is done only once, and the specific part of the search is done on the much shorter search list.

XrmQGetSearchList takes a list of names and classes and returns a list of database levels where a match might occur. The returned list is in best-to-worst order and uses the same algorithm as XrmGetResource for determining precedence. If *search_list* was large enough for the search list, XrmQGetSearchList returns True. Otherwise, it returns False.

The size of the search list that must be allocated by the caller is dependent upon the number of levels and wildcards in the resource specifiers that are stored in the database. The worst case length is 3^n, where n is the number of name or class components in *names* or *classes*.

Only the common prefix of a resource name should be specified in the name and class list to XrmQGetSearchList. In the example above, the common prefix would be xmh.toc. However, note that XrmQGetSearchResource requires that *name* represent a single component only. Therefore, the common prefix must be all but the last component of the name and class.

For more information, see Volume One, Chapter 11, *Managing User Preferences.*

Structures

XrmDatabase is a pointer to an opaque data type.

```
typedef XrmQuarkList XrmNameList;
typedef XrmQuarkList XrmClassList;
typedef XrmQuark     XrmRepresentation;
```

XrmSearchList is a pointer to an opaque data type.

Related Commands

XrmGetFileDatabase, XrmGetResource, XrmGetStringDatabase, Xrm-
Initialize, XrmMergeDatabases, XrmParseCommand, XrmPutFileDatabase,
XrmPutLineResource, XrmPutResource, XrmPutStringResource, XrmQGet-
Resource, XrmQGetSearchResource, XrmQPutResource, XrmQPutString-
Resource, XrmQuarkToString, XrmStringToBindingQuarkList, XrmString-
ToQuarkList, XrmStringToQuark, XrmUniqueQuark.

XrmQGetSearchResource

Name

XrmQGetSearchResource — search resource database levels for a given resource.

Synopsis

```
Bool XrmQGetSearchResource(search_list, name, class,
        type, value)
    XrmSearchList search_list;
    XrmName name;
    XrmClass class;
    XrmRepresentation *type;   /* RETURN */
    XrmValue *value;           /* RETURN */
```

Arguments

search_list Specifies the search list returned by XrmQGetSearchList.

name   Specifies the resource name.

class   Specifies the resource class.

type   Returns the data representation type.

value   Returns the value in the database.

Description

XrmQGetSearchResource is a tool for searching the database more efficiently. It is used in combination with XrmGetSearchList. Often, one searches the database for many similar resources which differ only in their final component (e.g., xmh.toc.foreground, xmh.toc.background, etc). Rather than looking for each resource in its entirety, Xrm-GetSearchList searches the database for the common part of the resource name, returning a whole list of items in the database that match it. This list is called the *search list*. Xrm-QGetSearchResource searches the search list for the resource that is fully identified by *name* and *class*. The search stops with the first match. XrmQGetSearchResource returns True if the resource was found; otherwise, it returns False.

A call to XrmQGetSearchList with a name and class list containing all but the last component of a resource name followed by a call to XrmQGetSearchResource with the last component name and class returns the same database entry as XrmGetResource or Xrm-QGetResource would with the fully qualified name and class.

For more information, see Volume One, Chapter 11, *Managing User Preferences*.

Structures

XrmDatabase is a pointer to an opaque data type.

```
typedef XrmQuark XrmName;
typedef XrmQuark XrmClass;
typedef XrmQuark XrmRepresentation;

typedef struct {
    unsigned int    size;
    caddr_t         addr;
} XrmValue, *XrmValuePtr;
```

XrmSearchList is a pointer to an opaque data type.

Related Commands

XrmGetFileDatabase, XrmGetResource, XrmGetStringDatabase, Xrm-
Initialize, XrmMergeDatabases, XrmParseCommand, XrmPutFileDatabase,
XrmPutLineResource, XrmPutResource, XrmPutStringResource, XrmQGet-
Resource, XrmQGetSearchList, XrmQPutResource, XrmQPutStringResource,
XrmQuarkToString, XrmStringToBindingQuarkList, XrmStringToQuark-
List, XrmStringToQuark, XrmUniqueQuark.

XrmQPutResource

Name

XrmQPutResource — store a resource into a database using quarks.

Synopsis

```
void XrmQPutResource(database, bindings, quarks, type, value)
    XrmDatabase *database;  /* SEND, and if NULL, RETURN */
    XrmBindingList bindings;
    XrmQuarkList quarks;
    XrmRepresentation type;
    XrmValue *value;
```

Arguments

database   Specifies a pointer to the resource database. If database contains NULL, a new resource database is created and a pointer to it is returned in *database*.

bindings   Specifies a list of bindings for binding together the *quarks* argument.

quarks   Specifies the complete or partial name or class list of the resource to be stored.

type   Specifies the type of the resource.

value   Specifies the value of the resource.

Description

XrmQPutResource stores a resource into the database.

database can be a previously defined database, as returned by XrmGetString-Database, XrmGetFileDatabase, or from XrmMergeDatabases. If *database* is NULL, a new database is created and a pointer to it returned in *database*.

bindings and *quarks* together specify where the value should be stored in the database. See XrmStringToBindingQuarkList for a brief description of binding and quark lists. See XrmGetResource for a description of the resource manager naming conventions and lookup rules.

type is the representation type of *value*. This provides a way to distinguish between different representations of the same information. Representation types are user defined character strings describing the way the data is represented. For example, a color may be specified by a color name ("red"), or be coded in a hexadecimal string ("#4f6c84") (if it is to be used as an argument to XParseColor.) The representation type would distinguish between these two. Representation types are created from simple character strings by using the macro Xrm-StringToRepresentation. The type XrmRepresentation is actually the same type as XrmQuark, since it is an ID for a string. The representation is stored along with the value in the database, and is returned when the database is accessed.

value is the value of the resource, specified as an XrmValue.

XrmGetResource contains the complete description of how data is accessed from the database, and so provides a good perspective on how it is stored.

For more information, see Volume One, Chapter 11, *Managing User Preferences.*

Structures

XrmDatabase is a pointer to an opaque data type.

```
typedef enum {XrmBindTightly, XrmBindLoosely} XrmBinding, *XrmBindingList

typedef int XrmQuark, *XrmQuarkList;
typedef XrmQuarkList XrmNameList;
typedef XrmQuark XrmRepresentation;

typedef struct {
    unsigned int size;
    caddr_t addr;
} XrmValue, *XrmValuePtr;
```

Related Commands

XrmGetFileDatabase, XrmGetResource, XrmGetStringDatabase, Xrm-
Initialize, XrmMergeDatabases, XrmParseCommand, XrmPutFileDatabase,
XrmPutLineResource, XrmPutResource, XrmPutStringResource, XrmQGet-
Resource, XrmQGetSearchList, XrmQGetSearchResource, XrmQPutString-
Resource, XrmQuarkToString, XrmStringToBindingQuarkList, XrmString-
ToQuarkList, XrmStringToQuark, XrmUniqueQuark.

XrmQPutStringResource

Name
XrmQPutStringResource — add a string resource value to a database using quarks.

Synopsis
```
void XrmQPutStringResource(database, bindings, quarks, value)
    XrmDatabase *database; /* SEND, and if NULL, RETURN */
    XrmBindingList bindings;
    XrmQuarkList quarks;
    char *value;
```

Arguments
database   Specifies a pointer to the resource database. If database contains NULL, a new
            resource database is created and a pointer to it is returned in database.

bindings   Specifies a list of bindings for binding together the quarks argument.

quarks   Specifies the complete or partial name or class list of the resource to be stored.

value   Specifies the value of the resource as a string.

Description
XrmQPutStringResource stores a resource into the specified database.

XrmQPutStringResource is a cross between XrmQPutResource and XrmPut-
StringResource. Like XrmQPutResource, it specifies the resource by quarks and
bindings, two lists that together make a name/class list with loose and tight bindings. Like
XrmPutStringResource, it specifies the value to be stored as a string, that value is converted into an XrmValue, and the default representation type String is used.

XrmPutResource, XrmQPutResource, XrmPutStringResource, XrmQPut-
StringResource and XrmPutLineResource all store data into a database. See Xrm-
QPutResource for the most complete description of this process.

For more information, see Volume One, Chapter 11, *Managing User Preferences.*

Structures
XrmDatabase is a pointer to an opaque data type.

```
typedef enum {XrmBindTightly, XrmBindLoosely} XrmBinding, *XrmBindingList;

typedef int XrmQuark, *XrmQuarkList;
```

Related Commands
XrmGetFileDatabase, XrmGetResource, XrmGetStringDatabase, Xrm-
Initialize, XrmMergeDatabases, XrmParseCommand, XrmPutFileDatabase,
XrmPutLineResource, XrmPutResource, XrmPutStringResource, XrmQGet-
Resource, XrmQGetSearchList, XrmQGetSearchResource, XrmQPutResource,
XrmQuarkToString, XrmStringToBindingQuarkList, XrmStringToQuark-
List, XrmStringToQuark, XrmUniqueQuark.

Name

XrmQuarkToString — convert a quark to a string.

Synopsis

```
char *XrmQuarkToString(quark)
    XrmQuark quark;
```

Arguments

quark   Specifies the quark for which the equivalent string is desired.

Description

XrmQuarkToString returns the string for which the quark is serving as a shorthand symbol. The quark was earlier set to represent the string by XrmStringToQuark. The string pointed to by the return value must not be modified or freed, because that string is in the data structure used by the resource manager for assigning quarks. If no string exists for that quark, these routines return NULL.

Quarks are used by the resource manager to represent strings. Since the resource manager needs to make many comparisons of strings when it gets data from the database, it is more efficient to convert these strings into quarks, and to compare quarks instead. Since quarks are presently represented by integers, comparing quarks is trivial.

The three #define statements in the Structures section provide an extra level of abstraction. They define macros so that names, classes and representations can also be represented as quarks.

For more information, see Volume One, Chapter 11, *Managing User Preferences*.

Structures

```
typedef int XrmQuark;

/* macro definitions from <X11/resource.h> */

#define XrmNameToString(name) XrmQuarkToString(name)
#define XrmClassToString(class) XrmQuarkToString(class)
#define XrmRepresentationToString(type) XrmQuarkToString(type)
```

Related Commands

XrmGetFileDatabase, XrmGetResource, XrmGetStringDatabase, XrmInitialize, XrmMergeDatabases, XrmParseCommand, XrmPutFileDatabase, XrmPutLineResource, XrmPutResource, XrmPutStringResource, XrmQGetResource, XrmQGetSearchList, XrmQGetSearchResource, XrmQPutResource, XrmQPutStringResource, XrmStringToBindingQuarkList, XrmStringToQuarkList, XrmStringToQuark, XrmUniqueQuark.

Name

XrmStringToBindingQuarkList — convert a key string to a binding list and a quark list.

Synopsis

```
XrmStringToBindingQuarkList (string, bindings, quarks)
    char *string;
    XrmBindingList bindings; /* RETURN */
    XrmQuarkList quarks;     /* RETURN */
```

Arguments

string   Specifies the string for which the list of quarks and list of bindings are to be generated. Must be NULL terminated.

bindings   Returns the binding list. The caller must allocate sufficient space for the binding list before the call.

quark   Returns the list of quarks. The caller must allocate sufficient space for the quarks list before the call.

Description

XrmStringToBindingQuarkList converts the string into two lists—one of quarks and one of bindings. Component names in the list are separated by a dot (".") indicating a tight binding or an asterisk ("*") indicating a loose binding. If the string does not start with dot or asterisk, a dot (".") is assumed.

A tight binding means that the quarks on either side of the binding are consecutive in the key. A loose binding, on the other hand, is a wildcard that can match any number of unspecified components in between the two quarks separated by the binding. Tight and loose bindings are used in the match rules, which compare multicomponent strings to find matches and determine the best match. See XrmGetResource for a full description of lookup rules.

For example, *a.b*c becomes:

quarks	bindings
"a"	XrmBindLoosely
"b"	XrmBindTightly
"c"	XrmBindLoosely

For more information, see Volume One, Chapter 11, *Managing User Preferences*.

Structures

```
typedef int XrmQuark, *XrmQuarkList;
typedef enum (XrmBindLoosely, XrmBindTightly) XrmBinding, *XrmBindingList;
```

Related Commands

XrmGetFileDatabase, XrmGetResource, XrmGetStringDatabase, Xrm-
Initialize, XrmMergeDatabases, XrmParseCommand, XrmPutFileDatabase,
XrmPutLineResource, XrmPutResource, XrmPutStringResource, XrmQGet-
Resource, XrmQGetSearchList, XrmQGetSearchResource, XrmQPutResource,
XrmQPutStringResource, XrmQuarkToString, XrmStringToQuarkList, Xrm-
StringToQuark, XrmUniqueQuark.

XrmStringToQuark

Name

XrmStringToQuark — convert a string to a quark.

Synopsis

```
XrmQuark XrmStringToQuark (string)
    char *string;
```

Arguments

string   Specifies the string for which a quark is to be allocated.

Description

XrmStringToQuark returns a quark that is equivalent to the specified string. If a quark already exists for the string, that previously existing quark is returned. If no quark exists for the string, then a new quark is created, assigned to the string, and string is copied into the quark table. (Since string is copied, it may be freed. However, the copy of the string in the quark table must not be modified or freed.) XrmQuarkToString performs the inverse function.

Quarks are used by the resource manager to represent strings. Since the resource manager needs to make many comparisons of strings when it gets data from the database, it is more efficient to convert these strings into quarks, and to compare quarks instead. Since quarks are presently represented by integers, comparing quarks is trivial.

The three #define statements in the Structures section provide an extra level of abstraction. They define macros so that names, classes, and representations can also be represented as quarks.

For more information, see Volume 1, Chapter 11, *Managing User Preferences.*

Structures

```
typedef int XrmQuark;

/* macro definitions from <X11/resource.h> */

#define XrmStringToName(string) XrmStringToQuark(string)
#define XrmStringToClass(string) XrmStringToQuark(string)
#define XrmStringToRepresentation(string) XrmStringToQuark(string)
```

Related Commands

XrmGetFileDatabase, XrmGetResource, XrmGetStringDatabase, XrmInitialize, XrmMergeDatabases, XrmParseCommand, XrmPutFileDatabase, XrmPutLineResource, XrmPutResource, XrmPutStringResource, XrmQGetResource, XrmQGetSearchList, XrmQGetSearchResource, XrmQPutResource, XrmQPutStringResource, XrmQuarkToString, XrmStringToBindingQuarkList, XrmStringToQuarkList, XrmUniqueQuark.

Name

XrmStringToQuarkList — convert a key string to a quark list.

Synopsis

```
void XrmStringToQuarkList(string, quarks)
    char *string;
    XrmQuarkList quarks;        /* RETURN */
```

Arguments

string   Specifies the string for which a list of quarks is to be generated. Must be null-terminated. The components may be separated by the "." character (tight binding) or the "*" character (loose binding).

quarks   Returns the list of quarks.

Description

XrmStringToQuarkList converts *string* (generally a fully qualified name/class string) to a list of quarks. Components of the string may be separated by a tight binding (the "." character) or a loose binding ("*"). Use XrmStringToBindingQuarkList for lists which contain both tight and loose bindings. See XrmGetResource for a description of tight and loose binding.

Each component of the string is individually converted into a quark. See XrmString-ToQuark for information about quarks and converting strings to quarks. *quarks* is a null-terminated list of quarks.

For example, xmh.toc.command.background is converted into a list of four quarks: the quarks for xmh, toc, command, and background, in that order. A NULLQUARK is appended to the end of the list.

Note that XrmStringToNameList and XrmStringToClassList are macros that perform exactly the same function as XrmStringToQuarkList. These may be used in cases where they clarify the code.

For more information, see Volume One, Chapter 11, *Managing User Preferences*.

Structures

```
typedef int XrmQuark *XrmQuarkList;

#define XrmStringToNameList(str, name)   XrmStringToQuarkList((str), (name))
#define XrmStringToClassList(str,class)  XrmStringToQuarkList((str), (class))
```

Related Commands

XrmGetFileDatabase, XrmGetResource, XrmGetStringDatabase, Xrm-
Initialize, XrmMergeDatabases, XrmParseCommand, XrmPutFileDatabase,
XrmPutLineResource, XrmPutResource, XrmPutStringResource, XrmQGet-
Resource, XrmQGetSearchList, XrmQGetSearchResource, XrmQPutResource,
XrmQPutStringResource, XrmQuarkToString, XrmStringToBindingQuark-
List, XrmStringToQuark, XrmUniqueQuark.

Name

XrmUniqueQuark — allocate a new quark.

Synopsis

```
XrmQuark XrmUniqueQuark()
```

Description

XrmUniqueQuark allocates a quark that is guaranteed not to represent any existing string. For most applications, XrmStringToQuark is more useful, as it binds a quark to a string. However, on some occasions, you may want to allocate a quark that has no string equivalent.

The shorthand name for a string is called a *quark* and is the type XrmQuark. Quarks are used to improve performance of the resource manager, which must make many string comparisons. Quarks are presently represented as ints. Simple comparisons of quarks can be performed rather than lengthy string comparisons.

A quark is to a string what an atom is to a property name in the server, but its use is entirely local to your application.

For more information, see Volume One, Chapter 11, *Managing User Preferences*.

Structures

```
typedef int XrmQuark;
```

Related Commands

XrmGetFileDatabase, XrmGetResource, XrmGetStringDatabase, XrmInitialize, XrmMergeDatabases, XrmParseCommand, XrmPutFileDatabase, XrmPutLineResource, XrmPutResource, XrmPutStringResource, XrmQGetResource, XrmQGetSearchList, XrmQGetSearchResource, XrmQPutResource, XrmQPutStringResource, XrmQuarkToString, XrmStringToBindingQuarkList, XrmStringToQuarkList, XrmStringToQuark.

XRotateBuffers

Name
XRotateBuffers — rotate the cut buffers.

Synopsis
```
XRotateBuffers(display, rotate)
    Display *display;
    int rotate;
```

Arguments

display   Specifies a pointer to the Display structure; returned from XOpen-Display.

rotate   Specifies how many positions to rotate the cut buffers.

Description

XRotateBuffers rotates the 8 cut buffers the amount specified by *rotate*. Buffer 0 becomes buffer *rotate*, buffer 1 becomes buffer *rotate*+1 mod 8, buffer 2 becomes buffer *rotate*+2 mod 8, and so on. This cut buffer numbering is global to the display. This routine will not work if any of the buffers have not been stored into with XStoreBuffer.

See the description of cut buffers in Volume One, Chapter 13, *Other Programming Techniques*.

Errors
```
BadAtom
BadMatch
BadWindow
```

Related Commands
XStoreBuffer, XStoreBytes, XFetchBuffer, XFetchBytes.

Name

XRotateWindowProperties — rotate properties in the properties array.

Synopsis

```
XRotateWindowProperties(display, w, properties, num_prop,
        npositions)
    Display *display;
    Window w;
    Atom properties[];
    int num_prop;
    int npositions;
```

Arguments

display   Specifies a pointer to the Display structure; returned from XOpen-
               Display.

w   Specifies the ID of the window whose properties are to be rearranged.

properties   Specifies the property list.

num_prop   Specifies the length of the properties array.

npositions   Specifies the number of positions to rotate the property list. The sign con-
               trols the direction of rotation.

Description

XRotateWindowProperties rotates the contents of an array of properties on a window.
If the property names in the *properties* array are viewed as if they were numbered starting
from 0 and if there are *num_prop* property names in the list, then the value associated with
property name *I* becomes the value associated with property name (*I* + *npositions*) mod
num_prop, for all *I* from 0 to *num_prop* – 1. Therefore, the sign of *npositions* controls the direction of rotation. The effect is to rotate the states by *npositions* places
around the virtual ring of property names (right for positive *npositions*, left for negative
nposition).

If *npositions* mod *num_prop* is nonzero, a PropertyNotify event is generated for
each property, in the order listed.

If a BadAtom or BadMatch error is generated, no properties are changed.

Error

BadAtom   Atom occurs more than once in list for the window.
               No property with that name for the window.

BadMatch

BadWindow

Related Commands

XSetStandardProperties, XGetFontProperty, XDeleteProperty, XChange-
Property, XGetWindowProperty, XListProperties, XGetAtomName, XIntern-
Atom.

Name

XSaveContext — save a data value corresponding to a window and context type (not graphics context).

Synopsis

```
int XSaveContext(display, w, context, data)
    Display *display;
    Window w;
    XContext context;
    caddr_t data;
```

Arguments

display   Specifies a pointer to the Display structure; returned from XOpen-Display.

w   Specifies the ID of the window with which the data is associated.

context   Specifies the context type to which the data corresponds.

data   Specifies the data to be associated with the window and type.

Description

XSaveContext saves *data* to the context manager database, according to the specified window and *context* ID. The context manager is used for associating data with windows within an application. The client must have called XUniqueContext to get the *context* ID before calling this function. The meaning of the *data* is indicated by the *context* ID, but is completely up to the client.

If an entry with the specified window and *context* ID already exists, XSaveContext writes over it with the specified data.

The XSaveContext function returns XCNOMEM (a nonzero error code) if an error has occurred and zero (0) otherwise. For more information, see the description of the context manager in Volume One, Chapter 13, *Other Programming Techniques*.

Structures

```
typedef int XContext;
```

Related Commands

XDeleteContext, XFindContext, XUniqueContext.

Name

XSelectInput — select the event types to be sent to a window.

Synopsis

```
XSelectInput(display, w, event_mask)
    Display *display;
    Window w;
    unsigned long event_mask;
```

Arguments

display   Specifies a pointer to the Display structure; returned from XOpen-Display.

w   Specifies the ID of the window interested in the input events.

event_mask Specifies the event mask. This mask is the bitwise OR of one or more of the valid event mask bits (see below).

Description

XSelectInput defines which input events the window is interested in. If a window is not interested in an event, it propagates up to the closest ancestor unless otherwise specified in the do_not_propagate_mask attribute.

The bits of the mask are defined in *<X11/X.h>* :

ButtonPressMask	NoEventMask
ButtonReleaseMask	KeyPressMask
EnterWindowMask	KeyReleaseMask
LeaveWindowMask	ExposureMask
PointerMotionMask	VisibilityChangeMask
PointerMotionHintMask	StructureNotifyMask
Button1MotionMask	ResizeRedirectMask
Button2MotionMask	SubstructureNotifyMask
Button3MotionMask	SubstructureRedirectMask
Button4MotionMask	FocusChangeMask
Button5MotionMask	PropertyChangeMask
ButtonMotionMask	ColormapChangeMask
KeymapStateMask	OwnerGrabButtonMask

A call on XSelectInput overrides any previous call on XSelectInput for the same window from the same client but not for other clients. Multiple clients can select input on the same window; their event_masks are disjoint. When an event is generated it will be reported to all interested clients. However, only one client at a time can select for each of SubstructureRedirectMask, ResizeRedirectMask, and ButtonPress.

If a window has both ButtonPressMask and ButtonReleaseMask selected, then a ButtonPress event in that window will automatically grab the mouse until all buttons are released, with events sent to windows as described for XGrabPointer. This ensures that a window will see the `ButtonRelease` event corresponding to the `ButtonPress` event, even though the mouse may have exited the window in the meantime.

If `PointerMotionMask` is selected, events will be sent independent of the state of the mouse buttons. If instead, one or more of `Button1MotionMask`, `Button2MotionMask`, `Button3MotionMask`, `Button4MotionMask`, `Button5MotionMask` is selected, `MotionNotify` events will be generated only when one or more of the specified buttons is depressed.

`XOpenDisplay` sets the *event_mask* attribute; this attribute can also be set directly with `XChangeWindowAttributes`.

For more information, see Volume One, Chapter 8, *Events*.

Errors
`BadValue`
`BadWindow`

Related Commands
`XSetInputFocus`, `XGetInputFocus`, `XWindowEvent`, `XCheckWindowEvent`, `XCheckTypedEvent`, `XCheckTypedWindowEvent`, `XMaskEvent`, `XCheckMaskEvent`, `XNextEvent`, `XEventsQueued`, `XAllowEvents`, `XGetMotionEvents`, `XIfEvent`, `XCheckIfEvent`, `XPeekEvent`, `XPeekIfEvent`, `XPutBackEvent`, `XPending`, `XSynchronize`, `XSendEvent`, `QLength`.

XSendEvent

Name

XSendEvent — send an event.

Synopsis

```
Status XSendEvent(display, w, propagate, event_mask, event)
    Display *display;
    Window w;
    Bool propagate;
    unsigned long event_mask;
    XEvent *event;
```

Arguments

display   Specifies a pointer to the Display structure; returned from XOpen-Display.

w   Specifies the ID of the window where you want to send the event. Pass the window resource ID, PointerWindow, or InputFocus.

propagate Specifies how the sent event should propagate depending on event_mask. See description below. May be True or False.

event_mask Specifies the event mask. See XSelectInput for a detailed list of the event masks.

event   Specifies a pointer to the event to be sent.

Description

XSendEvent sends an event from one client to another (or conceivably to itself). This function is used for communication between clients using selections, for simulating user actions in demos, and for other purposes.

The specified event is sent to the window indicated by w regardless of active grabs.

If w is set to PointerWindow, the destination of the event will be the window that the pointer is in. If w is InputFocus is specified, then the destination is the focus window, regardless of pointer position.

If propagate is False, then the event is sent to every client selecting on the window specified by w any of the event types in event_mask. If propagate is True and no clients have been selected on w any of the event types in event_mask, then the event propagates like any other event.

The event code must be one of the core events, or one of the events defined by a loaded extension, so that the server can correctly byte swap the contents as necessary. The contents of the event are otherwise unaltered and unchecked by the server except that in Release 1 the most significant bit of XEvent.type is set to 1. In Release 2, the high bit is no longer set. Instead, a new flag send_event has been added to each event, which if True indicates that the event was sent with XSendEvent.

Under Release 1, if a client wants to read events sent by XSendEvent as normal events, it must ignore the high bit by ORing the event type with the following expression:

```
XEvent report;
XNextEvent(display, &report);
report.type &= 0x7f;
/* now sent event looks like any other */
```

This function is often used in selection processing. For example, the owner of a selection should use XSendEvent to send a SelectionNotify event to a requestor when a selection has been converted and stored as a property. See Volume One, Chapter 10, *Interclient Communication* for more information.

The status returned by XSendEvent indicates whether or not the given XEvent structure was successfully converted into a wire event. Along with changes in the extensions mechanism, this makes merging of two wire events into a single user-visible event possible.

Structures

See Appendix F, *Structure Reference*, for the contents of specific event structures.

Related Commands

XSelectInput, XSetInputFocus, XGetInputFocus, XWindowEvent, XCheck-
WindowEvent, XCheckTypedEvent, XCheckTypedWindowEvent, XMaskEvent,
XCheckMaskEvent, XNextEvent, XEventsQueued, XAllowEvents, XGetMotion-
Events, XIfEvent, XCheckIfEvent, XPeekEvent, XPeekIfEvent, XPutBack-
Event, XPending, XSynchronize, QLength.

XSetAccessControl

Name

XSetAccessControl — disable or enable access control.

Synopsis

```
XSetAccessControl(display, mode)
    Display *display;
    int mode;
```

Arguments

display   Specifies a pointer to the `Display` structure; returned from `XOpen-Display`.

mode   Specifies whether you want to enable or disable the access control. Pass one of these constants: `EnableAccess` or `DisableAccess`.

Description

`XSetAccessControl` specifies whether to check the host access list before allowing access to clients running on remote hosts. If the constant used is `DisableAccess`, clients from any host have access unchallenged.

This routine can only be called from a client running on the same host as the server.

For more information on access control lists, see Volume One, Chapter 13, *Other Programming Techniques*.

Errors

```
BadAccess
BadValue
```

Related Commands

XAddHost, XAddHosts, XListHosts, XRemoveHost, XRemoveHosts, XDisable-AccessControl, XEnableAccessControl.

Name

XSetAfterFunction — set a function called after all Xlib functions.

Synopsis

```
int (*XSetAfterFunction(display, func))()
    Display *display;
    int (*func)();
```

Arguments

display   Specifies a pointer to the Display structure; returned from XOpen-
               Display.

func   Specifies the user-defined function to be called after each Xlib function.
               This function is called with one argument, the display pointer.

Description

All Xlib functions that generate protocol requests can call what is known as an *after function* after completing their work (normally, they don't). XSetAfterFunction allows you to write a function to be called.

XSynchronize sets an after function to make sure that the input and output buffers are flushed after every Xlib routine.

For more information, see Volume One, Chapter 13, *Other Programming Techniques*.

Related Commands

XDisplayName, XGetErrorDatabaseText, XGetErrorText, XSetError-
Handler, XSetIOErrorHandler, XSynchronize.

Name

XSetArcMode — set the arc mode in a graphics context.

Synopsis

```
XSetArcMode(display, gc, arc_mode)
    Display *display;
    GC gc;
    int arc_mode;
```

Arguments

display   Specifies a pointer to the Display structure; returned from XOpen-Display.

gc   Specifies the graphics context.

arc_mode Specifies the arc mode for the specified graphics context. Possible values are ArcChord or ArcPieSlice.

Description

XSetArcMode sets the *arc_mode* member of the GC, which controls filling in the XFill-Arcs function. ArcChord specifies that the area between the arc and a line segment joining the endpoints of the arc is filled. ArcPieSlice specifies that the area filled is delimited by the arc and two line segments connecting the ends of the arc to the center point of the rectangle defining the arc.

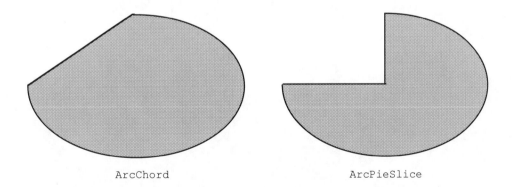

ArcChord   ArcPieSlice

Errors
    BadAlloc
    BadGC
    BadValue

Related Commands
    XChangeGC, XCopyGC, XCreateGC, XFreeGC, XGContextFromGC, XSetStipple,
    XSetTSOrigin, XSetPlaneMask, XSetDashes, XSetLineAttributes, XSet-
    FillRule, XSetFillStyle, XSetForeground, XSetBackground, XSet-
    Function, XSetGraphicsExposures, XSetClipMask, XSetClipOrigin, XSet-
    ClipRectangles, XSetState, XSetSubwindowMode, DefaultGC.

XSetBackground

Name

XSetBackground — set the background pixel value in a graphics context.

Synopsis

```
XSetBackground(display, gc, background)
    Display *display;
    GC gc;
    unsigned long background;
```

Arguments

display   Specifies a pointer to the `Display` structure; returned from `XOpen-Display`.

gc   Specifies the graphics context.

background Specifies the background you want to set for the specified graphics context.

Description

`XSetBackground` sets the *background* pixel value for graphics requests. Note that this is different from the `background` of a window, which can be set with either `XSetWindow-Background` or `XSetWindowBackgroundPixmap`.

Errors

```
BadAlloc
BadGC
```

Related Commands

`XChangeGC`, `XCopyGC`, `XCreateGC`, `XFreeGC`, `XGContextFromGC`, `XSetStipple`, `XSetTSOrigin`, `XSetPlaneMask`, `XSetDashes`, `XSetLineAttributes`, `XSet-FillRule`, `XSetFillStyle`, `XSetForeground`, `XSetFunction`, `XSetGraphics-Exposures`, `XSetArcMode`, `XSetClipMask`, `XSetClipOrigin`, `XSetClip-Rectangles`, `XSetState`, `XSetSubwindowMode`, `DefaultGC`.

Name

XSetClassHint — set the XA_WM_CLASS property of a window.

Synopsis

```
XSetClassHint(display, w, class_hints)
    Display *display;
    Window w;
    XClassHint *class_hints;
```

Arguments

display   Specifies a pointer to the Display structure; returned from XOpen-Display.

w   Specifies the ID of the window for which the class hint is to be set.

class_hints Specifies the XClassHint structure that is to be used.

Description

XSetClassHint sets the XA_WM_CLASS property for the specified window.

XSetClassHint returns a Status of 0 on failure, and nonzero on success.

The XClassHint structure set contains res_class, which is the name of the client such as "emacs", and res_name, which is the first of the following that applies:

- command line option (*–rn name*)

- a specific environment variable (e.g., RESOURCE_NAME)

- the trailing component of argv[0] (after the last /)

For more information, see Volume One, Chapter 10, *Interclient Communication*.

Errors

```
BadAlloc
BadWindow
```

Structures

```
typedef struct {
    char *res_name;
    char *res_class;
} XClassHint;
```

Related Commands

XGetClassHint, XGetSizeHints, XSetSizeHints, XGetWMHints, XSet-WMHints, XGetZoomHints, XSetZoomHints, XGetNormalHints, XSetNormal-Hints, XGetTransientForHint, XSetTransientForHint, XFetchName, XGet-IconName, XSetIconName, XStoreName, XGetIconSizes, XSetIconSizes, XSetCommand.

Name

XSetClipMask — set `clip_mask` pixmap in a graphics context.

Synopsis

```
XSetClipMask(display, gc, clip_mask)
    Display *display;
    GC gc;
    Pixmap clip_mask;
```

Arguments

display   Specifies a pointer to the `Display` structure; returned from `XOpen-Display`.

gc   Specifies the graphics context.

clip_mask   Specifies a pixmap of depth 1 to be used as the clip mask. Pass the constant `None` if no clipping is desired.

Description

`XSetClipMask` sets the `clip_mask` member of a GC to a pixmap. The `clip_mask` filters which pixels in the destination are drawn. If `clip_mask` is set to `None`, the pixels are always drawn, regardless of the clip origin. Use `XSetClipRectangles` to set `clip_mask` to a set of rectangles, or `XSetRegion` to set `clip_mask` to a region.

For more information, see Volume One, Chapter 5, *The Graphics Context*.

Errors

```
BadAlloc
BadGC
BadMatch
BadValue
```

Related Commands

XChangeGC, XCopyGC, XCreateGC, XFreeGC, XGContextFromGC, XSetStipple, XSetTSOrigin, XSetPlaneMask, XSetDashes, XSetLineAttributes, XSet-FillRule, XSetFillStyle, XSetForeground, XSetBackground, XSet-Function, XSetGraphicsExposures, XSetArcMode, XSetClipOrigin, XSet-ClipRectangles, XSetState, XSetSubwindowMode, DefaultGC.

Name

XSetClipOrigin — set the clip origin in a graphics context.

Synopsis

```
XSetClipOrigin(display, gc, clip_x_origin, clip_y_origin)
    Display *display;
    GC gc;
    int clip_x_origin, clip_y_origin;
```

Arguments

display   Specifies a pointer to the Display structure; returned from XOpen-
                 Display.

gc   Specifies the graphics context.

clip_x_origin   Specify the coordinates of the clip origin relative to the window
clip_y_origin   specified in the GC.

Description

XSetClipOrigin sets the clip_x_origin and clip_y_origin members of the GC.
The clip origin controls the position of the clip_mask in the GC, which filters which pixels
in the destination are drawn.

For more information, see Volume One, Chapter 5, *The Graphics Context*.

Errors

BadAlloc
BadGC

Related Commands

XChangeGC, XCopyGC, XCreateGC, XFreeGC, XGContextFromGC, XSetStipple,
XSetTSOrigin, XSetPlaneMask, XSetDashes, XSetLineAttributes, XSet-
FillRule, XSetFillStyle, XSetForeground, XSetBackground, XSet-
Function, XSetGraphicsExposures, XSetArcMode, XSetClipMask, XSetClip-
Rectangles, XSetState, XSetSubwindowMode, DefaultGC.

Name

XSetClipRectangles — change clip_mask in a graphics context to the list of rectangles.

Synopsis

```
XSetClipRectangles(display, gc, clip_x_origin,
        clip_y_origin, rectangles, nrects, ordering)
    Display *display;
    GC gc;
    int clip_x_origin, clip_y_origin;
    XRectangle rectangles[];
    int nrects;
    int ordering;
```

Arguments

display	Specifies a pointer to the Display structure; returned from XOpen-Display.
gc	Specifies the graphics context.
clip_x_origin clip_y_origin	Specify the x and y coordinates of the clip origin, relative to the window specified in the drawing request.
rectangles	Specifies an array of rectangles. These are the rectangles you want output clipped to.
nrects	Specifies the number of rectangles.
ordering	Specifies the ordering relations on the rectangles. Possible values are Unsorted, YSorted, YXSorted, or YXBanded.

Description

XSetClipRectangles changes the clip_mask in the specified GC to the specified list of rectangles and sets the clip origin to clip_x_origin and clip_y_origin. The rectangle coordinates are interpreted relative to the clip origin. The output from drawing requests using that GC are henceforth clipped to remain contained within the rectangles. The rectangles should be nonintersecting, or the graphics results will be undefined. If the list of rectangles is empty, output is effectively disabled as all space is clipped in that GC. This is the opposite of a clip_mask of None in XCreateGC, XChangeGC, or XSetClipMask.

If known by the client, ordering relations on the rectangles can be specified with the *ordering* argument. This may provide faster operation by the server. If an incorrect ordering is specified, the X server may generate a BadMatch error, but it is not required to do so. If no error is generated, the graphics results are undefined. Unsorted means the rectangles are in arbitrary order. YSorted means that the rectangles are nondecreasing in their y origin. YXSorted additionally constrains YSorted order in that all rectangles with an equal y origin are nondecreasing in their x origin. YXBanded additionally constrains YXSorted by requiring that, for every possible horizontal y scan line, all rectangles that include that scan line have identical y origins and y extents.

To cancel the effect of this command, so that there is no clipping, pass `None` as the `clip_mask` in `XChangeGC` or `XSetClipMask`.

For more information, see Volume One, Chapter 5, *The Graphics Context.*

Structures

```
typedef struct {
    short x,y;
    unsigned short width, height;
} XRectangle;
```

Errors

`BadAlloc`

`BadGC`

`BadMatch`   Incorrect ordering (error message server-dependent).

`BadValue`

Related Commands

`XChangeGC`, `XCopyGC`, `XCreateGC`, `XFreeGC`, `XGContextFromGC`, `XSetStipple`, `XSetTSOrigin`, `XSetPlaneMask`, `XSetDashes`, `XSetLineAttributes`, `XSetFillRule`, `XSetFillStyle`, `XSetForeground`, `XSetBackground`, `XSetFunction`, `XSetGraphicsExposures`, `XSetArcMode`, `XSetClipMask`, `XSetClipOrigin`, `XSetState`, `XSetSubwindowMode`, `DefaultGC`.

XSetCloseDownMode

Name

XSetCloseDownMode — change the close down mode of a client.

Synopsis

```
XSetCloseDownMode(display, close_mode)
    Display *display;
    int close_mode;
```

Arguments

display   Specifies a pointer to the `Display` structure; returned from `XOpen-Display`.

close_mode   Specifies the client close down mode you want. Pass one of these constants: `DestroyAll`, `RetainPermanent`, or `RetainTemporary`.

Description

`XSetCloseDownMode` defines what will happen to the client's resources at connection close. A connection between a client and the server starts in `DestroyAll` mode, and all resources associated with that connection will be freed when the client process dies. If the close down mode is `RetainTemporary` or `RetainPermanent` when the client dies, its resources live on until a call to `XKillClient`. The *resource* argument of `XKill-Client` can be used to specify which client to kill, or it may be the constant `All-Temporary`, in which case `XKillClient` kills all resources of all clients that have terminated in `RetainTemporary` mode.

One use of `RetainTemporary` or `RetainPermanent` might be to allow an application to recover from a failure of the network connection to the display server. After restarting, the application would need to be able to identify its own resources and reclaim control of them.

Errors

`BadValue`

Related Commands

`XKillClient`

XSetCommand

Name

XSetCommand — set the XA_WM_COMMAND atom (command line arguments).

Synopsis

```
XSetCommand(display, w, argv, argc)
    Display *display;
    Window w;
    char **argv;
    int argc;
```

Arguments

display   Specifies a pointer to the Display structure; returned from XOpenDisplay.

w   Specifies the ID of the window whose atom is to be set.

argv   Specifies a pointer to the command and arguments used to start the application.
            The application is an array of pointers to null-terminated strings.

argc   Specifies the number of arguments.

Description

XSetCommand is used by the application to set the XA_WM_COMMAND property for the window manager with the UNIX shell command and its arguments used to invoke the application.

Use this command only if not calling XSetStandardProperties.

Errors

BadAlloc
BadWindow

Related Commands

XGetClassHint, XSetClassHint, XGetSizeHints, XSetSizeHints, XGet-
WMHints, XSetWMHints, XGetZoomHints, XSetZoomHints, XGetNormalHints,
XSetNormalHints, XGetTransientForHint, XSetTransientForHint, XFetch-
Name, XGetIconName, XSetIconName, XStoreName, XGetIconSizes, XSetIcon-
Sizes.

Name

XSetDashes — set `dash_offset` and `dashes` (for lines) in a graphics context.

Synopsis

```
XSetDashes(display, gc, dash_offset, dash_list, n)
    Display *display;
    GC gc;
    int dash_offset;
    char dash_list[];
    int n;
```

Arguments

display   Specifies a pointer to the Display structure; returned from XOpen-Display.

gc   Specifies the graphics context.

dash_offset   Specifies the phase of the pattern for the dashed line style.

dash_list   Specifies the dash list for the dashed line style. An odd-length list is equivalent to the same list concatenated with itself to produce an even-length list.

n   Specifies the length of the dash list argument.

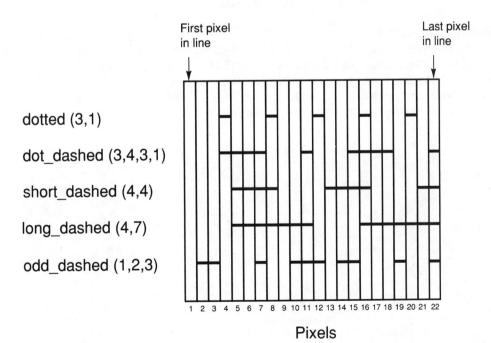

Description

XSetDashes sets the dashes member of the GC. The initial and alternating elements of the *dash_list* are the dashes, the others are the gaps. All of the elements must be nonzero. The *dash_offset* defines the phase of the pattern, specifying how many pixels into the *dash_list* the pattern should actually begin in the line drawn by the request.

n specifies the length of *dash_list*. An odd value for *n* is interpreted as specifying the *dash_list* concatenated with itself to produce twice as long a list.

The unit of measure for dashes is the same as in the ordinary coordinate system. Ideally, a dash length is measured along the slope of the line, but server implementors are only required to match this ideal for horizontal and vertical lines. Failing the ideal semantics, it is suggested that the length be measured along the major axis of the line. The major axis is defined as the x axis for lines drawn at an angle of between –45 and +45 degrees or between 315 and 225 degrees from the x axis. For all other lines, the major axis is the y axis.

See Volume One, Chapter 5, *The Graphics Context*, for further information.

Errors

BadAlloc

BadGC

BadValue   No values in *dash_list*.

                       Element in *dash_list* is 0.

Related Commands

XChangeGC, XCopyGC, XCreateGC, XFreeGC, XGContextFromGC, XSetStipple, XSetTSOrigin, XSetPlaneMask, XSetLineAttributes, XSetFillRule, XSetFillStyle, XSetForeground, XSetBackground, XSetFunction, XSetGraphicsExposures, XSetArcMode, XSetClipMask, XSetClipOrigin, XSetClipRectangles, XSetState, XSetSubwindowMode, DefaultGC.

XSetErrorHandler

Name

XSetErrorHandler — set a nonfatal error event handler.

Synopsis

```
XSetErrorHandler(handler)
    int (* handler)(Display *, XErrorEvent *)
```

Arguments

handler   The user-defined function to be called to handle error events. If a NULL
pointer, reinvoke the default handler, which prints a message and exits.

Description

The error handler function specified in `handler` will be called by Xlib whenever an XError
event is received. These are nonfatal conditions, such as unexpected values for arguments. It
is acceptable for this procedure to return, though the default handler simply prints a message
and exits. However, the error handler should NOT perform any operations (directly or
indirectly) on the `Display`.

The function is called with two arguments, the display variable and a pointer to the XError-
Event structure. Here is a trivial example of a user-defined error handler:

```
int myhandler (display, myerr)
Display *display;
XErrorEvent *myerr;
{
char msg[80];
XGetErrorText(display, myerr->error_code, msg, 80);
fprintf(stderr, "Error code %s\n", msg);
}
```

This is how the example routine would be used in XSetErrorHandler.

```
XSetErrorHandler(myhandler);
```

Note that `XSetErrorHandler` is one of the few routines that does not require a display
argument. The routine that calls the error handler gets the display variable from the XError-
Event structure.

The error handler is not called on BadName errors from OpenFont, LookupColor,
AllocNamedColor, protocol requests, on BadFont errors from a QueryFont protocol
request, or on BadAlloc or BadAccess errors. These errors are all indicated by a 0 return
value in the corresponding Xlib routines, and can be caught and handled by the application.

Use XIOErrorHandler to to provide a handler for fatal errors.

In the XErrorEvent structure shown below, the `serial` member is the number of requests
(starting from 1) sent over the network connection since it was opened. It is the number that
was the value of the request sequence number immediately after the failing call was made.
The `request_code` member is a protocol representation of the name of the procedure that
failed and is defined in *<X11/X.h>*.

For more information, see Volume One, Chapter 3, *Basic Window Program.*

Structures

```
typedef struct {
    int type
    Display *display;          /* display the event was read from */
    unsigned long serial;      /* serial number of failed request */
    char error_code;           /* error code of failed request */
    char request_code;         /* major opcode of failed request */
    char minor_code;           /* minor opcode of failed request */
    XID resourceid;            /* resource ID */
} XErrorEvent;
```

Related Commands

XDisplayName, XGetErrorDatabaseText, XGetErrorText, XSetIOError-
Handler, XSynchronize, XSetAfterFunction.

XSetFillRule

Name

XSetFillRule — set the fill rule in a graphics context.

Synopsis

```
XSetFillRule(display, gc, fill_rule)
    Display *display;
    GC gc;
    int fill_rule;
```

Arguments

display   Specifies a pointer to the Display structure; returned from XOpen-Display.

gc   Specifies the graphics context.

fill_rule   Specifies the fill rule you want to set for the specified graphics context. Possible values are EvenOddRule or WindingRule.

Description

XSetFillRule sets the *fill_rule* member of a GC. The *fill_rule* member of the GC determines what pixels are drawn in XFillPolygon requests. Simply put, Winding-Rule fills overlapping areas of the polygon, while EvenOddRule does not fill areas that overlap an odd number of times. Technically, EvenOddRule means that the point is drawn if an arbitrary ray drawn from the point would cross the path determined by the request an odd number of times. WindingRule indicates that a point is drawn if a point crosses an unequal number of clockwise and counterclockwise path segments, as seen from the point.

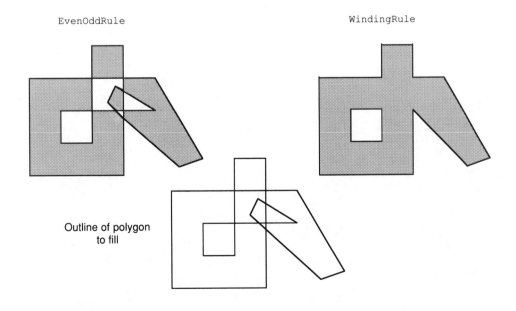

A clockwise-directed path segment is one which crosses the ray from left to right as observed from the point. A counterclockwise segment is one which crosses the ray from right to left as observed from the point. The case where a directed line segment is coincident with the ray is uninteresting because you can simply choose a different ray that is not coincident with a segment.

All calculations are performed on infinitely small points, so that if any point within a pixel is considered inside, the entire pixel is drawn. Pixels with centers exactly on boundaries are considered inside only if the filled area is to the right, except that on horizontal boundaries, the pixel is considered inside only if the filled area is below the pixel.

See Volume One, Chapter 5, *The Graphics Context*, for more information.

Errors
```
BadAlloc
BadGC
BadValue
```

Related Commands

XChangeGC, XCopyGC, XCreateGC, XFreeGC, XGContextFromGC, XSetStipple, XSetTSOrigin, XSetPlaneMask, XSetDashes, XSetLineAttributes, XSet-FillStyle, XSetForeground, XSetBackground, XSetFunction, XSet-GraphicsExposures, XSetArcMode, XSetClipMask, XSetClipOrigin, XSet-ClipRectangles, XSetState, XSetSubwindowMode, DefaultGC.

XSetFillStyle

Name

XSetFillStyle — set the fill style in a graphics context.

Synopsis

```
XSetFillStyle(display, gc, fill_style)
    Display *display;
    GC gc;
    int fill_style;
```

Arguments

display   Specifies a pointer to the Display structure; returned from XOpen-Display.

gc   Specifies the graphics context.

fill_style   Specifies the fill style for the specified graphics context. Possible values are FillSolid, FillTiled, FillStippled, or FillOpaque-Stippled.

Description

XSetFillStyle sets the *fill_style* member of the GC. The *fill_style* defines the contents of the source for line, text, and fill requests. FillSolid indicates that the pixels represented by set bits in the source are drawn in the foreground pixel value, and unset bits in the source are not drawn. FillTiled uses the tile specified in the GC to determine the pixel values for set bits in the source. FillOpaqueStippled specifies that bits set in the stipple are drawn in the foreground pixel value and unset bits are drawn in the background. FillStippled draws bits set in the source and set in the stipple in the foreground color, and leaves unset bits alone.

For more information, see Volume One, Chapter 5, *The Graphics Context*.

Errors

```
BadAlloc
BadGC
BadValue
```

Related Commands

XChangeGC, XCopyGC, XCreateGC, XFreeGC, XGContextFromGC, XSetStipple, XSetTSOrigin, XSetPlaneMask, XSetDashes, XSetLineAttributes, XSet-FillRule, XSetForeground, XSetBackground, XSetFunction, XSetGraphics-Exposures, XSetArcMode, XSetClipMask, XSetClipOrigin, XSetClip-Rectangles, XSetState, XSetSubwindowMode, DefaultGC.

Name

XSetFont — set the current font in a graphics context.

Synopsis

```
XSetFont(display, gc, font)
    Display *display;
    GC gc;
    Font font;
```

Arguments

display   Specifies a pointer to the Display structure; returned from XOpen-
                Display.

gc   Specifies the graphics context.

font   Specifies the ID of the font to be used.

Description

XSetFont sets the *font* in the GC. Text drawing requests using this GC will use this font
only if it is loaded. Otherwise, the text will not be drawn.

For more information, see Volume One, Chapter 5, *The Graphics Context.*

Errors

BadAlloc
BadFont
BadGC

Related Commands

XLoadFont, XLoadQueryFont, XFreeFont, XFreeFontInfo, XListFonts,
XListFontsWithInfo, XFreeFontNames, XFreeFontPath, XGetFontPath,
XQueryFont, XSetFontPath, XUnloadFont, XGetFontProperty, XCreateFont-
Cursor.

Name

XSetFontPath — set the font search path.

Synopsis

```
XSetFontPath(display, directories, ndirs)
    Display *display;
    char **directories;
    int ndirs;
```

Arguments

display   Specifies a pointer to the `Display` structure; returned from `XOpen-Display`.

directories Specifies the directory path used to look for the font. Setting the path to the empty list restores the default path defined for the X server.

ndirs   Specifies the number of directories in the path.

Description

`XSetFontPath` defines the directory search path for font lookup for all clients. Therefore the user should construct a new directory search path carefully by adding to the old directory search path obtained by `XGetFontPath`. Passing an invalid path can result in preventing the server from accessing any fonts. Also avoid restoring the default path, since some other client may have changed the path on purpose.

The interpretation of the strings is operating system dependent, but they are intended to specify directories to be searched in the order listed. Also, the contents of these strings are operating system specific and are not intended to be used by client applications.

As a side-effect of executing this request, the server is guaranteed to flush all cached information about fonts for which there are currently no explicit resource IDs allocated. The meaning of errors from this request is system specific.

Errors

BadValue

Related Commands

XLoadFont, XLoadQueryFont, XFreeFont, XFreeFontInfo, XListFonts, XListFontsWithInfo, XFreeFontNames, XFreeFontPath, XGetFontPath, XQueryFont, XSetFont, XUnloadFont, XGetFontProperty, XCreateFont-Cursor.

XSetForeground

Name

XSetForeground — set the foreground pixel value in a graphics context.

Synopsis

```
XSetForeground(display, gc, foreground)
    Display *display;
    GC gc;
    unsigned long foreground;
```

Arguments

display   Specifies a pointer to the `Display` structure; returned from `XOpen-Display`.

gc   Specifies the graphics context.

foreground   Specifies the foreground pixel value you want for the specified graphics context.

Description

XSetForeground sets the *foreground* member in a GC. This pixel value is used for set bits in the source according to the `fill_style`.

See Volume One, Chapter 5, *The Graphics Context*, for more information on the GC.

Errors

BadAlloc
BadGC

Related Commands

XChangeGC, XCopyGC, XCreateGC, XFreeGC, XGContextFromGC, XSetStipple, XSetTSOrigin, XSetPlaneMask, XSetDashes, XSetLineAttributes, XSet-FillRule, XSetFillStyle, XSetBackground, XSetFunction, XSetGraphics-Exposures, XSetArcMode, XSetClipMask, XSetClipOrigin, XSetClip-Rectangles, XSetState, XSetSubwindowMode, DefaultGC.

XSetFunction

Name

XSetFunction — set the bitwise logical operation in a graphics context.

Synopsis

```
XSetFunction(display, gc, function)
    Display *display;
    GC gc;
    int function;
```

Arguments

display   Specifies a pointer to the `Display` structure; returned from `XOpenDisplay`.

gc   Specifies the graphics context.

function   Specifies the logical operation you want for the specified graphics context. See Description for the choices and their meanings.

Description

XSetFunction sets the logical operation applied between the source pixel values (generated by the drawing request) and existing destination pixel values (already in the window or pixmap) to generate the final destination pixel values in a drawing request (what is actually drawn to the window or pixmap). Of course, the `plane_mask` and `clip_mask` in the GC also affect this operation by preventing drawing to planes and pixels respectively.

See Volume One, Chapter 5, *The Graphics Context*, for more information about the logical function.

The *function* symbols and their logical definitions are:

Symbol	Bit	Meaning
GXclear	0x0	0
GXand	0x1	src AND dst
GXandReverse	0x2	src AND (NOT dst)
GXcopy	0x3	src
GXandInverted	0x4	(NOT src) AND dst
GXnoop	0x5	dst
GXxor	0x6	src XOR dst
GXor	0x7	src OR dst
GXnor	0x8	(NOT src) AND (NOT dst)
GXequiv	0x9	(NOT src) XOR dst
GXinvert	0xa	(NOT dst)
GXorReverse	0xb	src OR (NOT dst)
GXcopyInverted	0xc	(NOT src)
GXorInverted	0xd	(NOT src) OR dst
GXnand	0xe	(NOT src) OR (NOT dst)
GXset	0xf	1

Errors

```
BadAlloc
BadGC
BadValue
```

Related Commands

XChangeGC, XCopyGC, XCreateGC, XFreeGC, XGContextFromGC, XSetStipple, XSetTSOrigin, XSetPlaneMask, XSetDashes, XSetLineAttributes, XSet-FillRule, XSetFillStyle, XSetForeground, XSetBackground, XSet-GraphicsExposures, XSetArcMode, XSetClipMask, XSetClipOrigin, XSet-ClipRectangles, XSetState, XSetSubwindowMode, DefaultGC.

XSetGraphicsExposures

Name

XSetGraphicsExposures — set `graphics_exposures` in a graphics context.

Synopsis

```
XSetGraphicsExposures(display, gc, graphics_exposures)
    Display *display;
    GC gc;
    Bool graphics_exposures;
```

Arguments

display   Specifies a pointer to the `Display` structure; returned from `XOpenDisplay`.

gc   Specifies the graphics context.

graphics_exposures

Specifies whether you want `GraphicsExpose` and `NoExpose` events when calling `XCopyArea` and `XCopyPlane` with this graphics context.

Description

`XSetGraphicsExposure` sets the *graphics_exposures* member of the GC. If *graphics_exposures* is `True`, `GraphicsExpose` events will be generated when `XCopyArea` and `XCopyPlane` requests cannot be completely satisfied because a source region is obscured, and `NoExpose` events are generated when they can be completely satisfied. If *graphics_exposures* is `False`, these events are not generated.

These events are not selected in the normal way with `XSelectInput`. Setting the *graphics_exposures* member of the GC used in the `CopyArea` or `CopyPlane` request is the only way to select these events.

For more information, see Volume One, Chapter 5, *The Graphics Context*.

Errors

```
BadAlloc
BadGC
BadValue
```

Related Commands

`XChangeGC`, `XCopyGC`, `XCreateGC`, `XFreeGC`, `XGContextFromGC`, `XSetStipple`, `XSetTSOrigin`, `XSetPlaneMask`, `XSetDashes`, `XSetLineAttributes`, `XSet-FillRule`, `XSetFillStyle`, `XSetForeground`, `XSetBackground`, `XSet-Function`, `XSetArcMode`, `XSetClipMask`, `XSetClipOrigin`, `XSetClip-Rectangles`, `XSetState`, `XSetSubwindowMode`, `DefaultGC`.

Name

XSetIconName — set the name to be displayed in a window's icon.

Synopsis

```
XSetIconName(display, w, icon_name)
    Display *display;
    Window w;
    char *icon_name;
```

Arguments

display   Specifies a pointer to the Display structure; returned from XOpen-Display.

w   Specifies the ID of the window whose icon name is being set.

icon_name   Specifies the name to be displayed in the window's icon. The name should be a null-terminated string. This name is returned by any subsequent call to XGetIconName.

Description

XSetIconName sets the XA_WM_ICON_NAME property for a window. This is usually set by an application for the window manager. The name should be short, since it is to be displayed in association with an icon.

XSetStandardProperties also sets this property.

For more information, see Volume One, Chapter 10, *Interclient Communication*.

Errors

BadAlloc
BadWindow

Related Commands

XGetClassHint, XSetClassHint, XGetSizeHints, XSetSizeHints, XGet-WMHints, XSetWMHints, XGetZoomHints, XSetZoomHints, XGetNormalHints, XSetNormalHints, XGetTransientForHint, XSetTransientForHint, XFetch-Name, XGetIconName, XStoreName, XGetIconSizes, XSetIconSizes, XSet-Command.

XSetIconSizes

Name

XSetIconSizes — set the value of the XA_WM_ICON_SIZE property.

Synopsis

```
XSetIconSizes(display, w, size_list, count)
    Display *display;
    Window w;
    XIconSize *size_list;
    int count;
```

Arguments

display   Specifies a pointer to the Display structure; returned from XOpen-
             Display.

w   Specifies the ID of the window whose icon size property is to be set. Nor-
             mally the root window.

size_list   Specifies a pointer to the size list.

count   Specifies the number of items in the size list.

Description

XSetIconSizes is normally used by a window manager to set the range of preferred icon
sizes in the XA_WM_ICON_SIZE property of the root window.

Applications can then read the property with XGetIconSizes.

Structures

```
typedef struct {
    int min_width, min_height;
    int max_width, max_height;
    int width_inc, height_inc;
} XIconSize;
```

Errors

```
BadAlloc
BadWindow
```

Related Commands

XGetClassHint, XSetClassHint, XGetSizeHints, XSetSizeHints, XGet-
WMHints, XSetWMHints, XGetZoomHints, XSetZoomHints, XGetNormalHints,
XSetNormalHints, XGetTransientForHint, XSetTransientForHint, XFetch-
Name, XGetIconName, XSetIconName, XStoreName, XGetIconSizes, XSet-
Command.

Name

XSetInputFocus — set the keyboard focus window.

Synopsis

```
XSetInputFocus(display, focus, revert_to, time)
    Display *display;
    Window focus;
    int revert_to;
    Time time;
```

Arguments

display   Specifies a pointer to the Display structure; returned from XOpenDisplay.

focus   Specifies the ID of the window you want to be the keyboard focus. Pass the window ID, PointerRoot, or None.

revert_to   Specifies which window the keyboard focus reverts to if the focus window becomes not viewable. Pass one of these constants: RevertToParent, RevertToPointerRoot, or RevertToNone. Must not be a window ID.

time   Specifies the time when the focus change should take place. Pass either a timestamp, expressed in milliseconds, or the constant CurrentTime. Also returns the time of the focus change when CurrentTime is specified.

Description

XSetInputFocus changes the keyboard focus and the last-focus-change time. The function has no effect if *time* is earlier than the current last-focus-change time or later than the current X server time. Otherwise, the last-focus-change time is set to the specified time, with CurrentTime replaced by the current X server time.

XSetInputFocus generates FocusIn and FocusOut events if *focus* is different from the current focus.

XSetInputFocus executes as follows, depending on what value you assign to the *focus* argument:

- If you assign None, all keyboard events are discarded until you set a new focus window. In this case, *revert_to* is ignored.

- If you assign a window ID, it becomes the main keyboard's focus window. If a generated keyboard event would normally be reported to this window or one of its inferiors, the event is reported normally; otherwise, the event is reported with respect to the focus window.

- If you assign PointerRoot, the focus window is dynamically taken to be the root window of whatever screen the pointer is on at each keyboard event. In this case, *revert_to* is ignored.

The specified focus window must be viewable at the time of the request (else a BadMatch error). If the focus window later becomes not viewable, the focus window will change to the *revert_to* argument.

If the focus window later becomes not viewable, XSetInputFocus evaluates the *revert_to* argument to determine the new focus window:

- If you assign RevertToParent, the focus reverts to the parent (or the closest viewable ancestor) automatically with a new *revert_to* argument of RevertToName.

- If you assign RevertToPointerRoot or RevertToNone, the focus reverts to that value automatically. FocusIn and FocusOut events are generated when the focus reverts, but the last_focus_change_time is not affected.

Errors

BadMatch   *focus* window not viewable when XSetInputFocus called.

BadValue

BadWindow

Related Commands

XSelectInput, XGetInputFocus, XWindowEvent, XCheckWindowEvent, XCheckTypedEvent, XCheckTypedWindowEvent, XMaskEvent, XCheckMask-Event, XNextEvent, XEventsQueued, XAllowEvents, XGetMotionEvents, XIfEvent, XCheckIfEvent, XPeekEvent, XPeekIfEvent, XPutBackEvent, XPending, XSynchronize, XSendEvent, QLength.

Name

XSetIOErrorHandler — handle fatal I/O errors.

Synopsis

```
XSetIOErrorHandler(handler)
    int (*handler)(Display *);
```

Arguments

handler   Specifies a pointer to a user-defined fatal error handling routine. If NULL, reinvoke the default fatal error handler.

Description

XSetIOErrorHandler specifies a user-defined error handling routine for fatal errors. This error handler will be called by Xlib if any sort of system call error occurs, such as the connection to the server being lost. The called routine should not return. If the I/O error handler does return, the client process will exit.

If handler is a NULL pointer, the default error handler is reinvoked. The default I/O error handler prints an error message and exits.

For more information, see Volume One, Chapter 3, *Basic Window Program*.

Related Commands

XDisplayName, XGetErrorDatabaseText, XGetErrorText, XSetError-Handler, XSynchronize, XSetAfterFunction.

Name

XSetLineAttributes — set the line drawing components in a graphics context.

Synopsis

```
XSetLineAttributes(display, gc, line_width, line_style,
        cap_style, join_style)
    Display *display;
    GC gc;
    unsigned int line_width;
    int line_style;
    int cap_style;
    int join_style;
```

Arguments

display   Specifies a pointer to the Display structure; returned from XOpen-
Display.

gc   Specifies the graphics context.

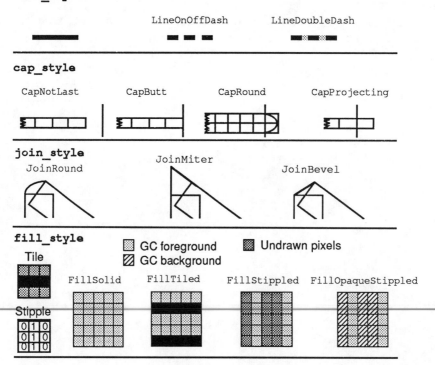

line_width   Specifies the line width you want to set for the specified graphics context.

line_style   Specifies the line style you want to set for the specified graphics context. Possible values are LineSolid, LineOnOffDash, or LineDouble-Dash.

cap_style   Specifies the line and cap style you want to set for the specified graphics context. Possible values are CapNotLast, CapButt, CapRound, or CapProjecting.

join_style   Specifies the line-join style you want to set for the specified graphics context. Possible values are JoinMiter, JoinRound, or JoinBevel.

Description

XSetLineAttributes sets four types of line characteristics in the GC: *line_width*, *line_style*, *cap_style*, and *join_style*.

See the description of line and join styles in Volume One, Chapter 5, *The Graphics Context*. See also XSetDashes.

A *line_width* of zero (0) means to use the fastest algorithm for drawing a line of one pixel width. These lines may not meet properly with lines specified as width 1 or more.

Errors

BadGC
BadValue

Related Commands

XChangeGC, XCopyGC, XCreateGC, XFreeGC, XGContextFromGC, XSetStipple, XSetTSOrigin, XSetPlaneMask, XSetDashes, XSetFillRule, XSetFillStyle, XSetForeground, XSetBackground, XSetFunction, XSetGraphicsExposures, XSetArcMode, XSetClipMask, XSetClipOrigin, XSetClipRectangles, XSet-State, XSetSubwindowMode, DefaultGC.

Name

XSetModifierMapping — set keycodes to be used as modifiers (Shift, Control, etc.).

Synopsis

```
int XSetModifierMapping(display, mod_map)
    Display *display;
    XModifierKeymap *mod_map;
```

Arguments

display   Specifies a pointer to the `Display` structure; returned from `XOpenDisplay`.

mod_map   Specifies a pointer to the `XModifierKeymap` structure.

Description

`XSetModifierMapping` is one of two ways to specify the keycodes of the keys that are to be used as modifiers (like Shift, Control, etc.). `XSetModifierMapping` specifies all the keycodes for all the modifiers at once. The other, easier, way is to use `XInsertModifiermapEntry` and `XDeleteModifiermapEntry`, which add or delete a single keycode for a single modifier key. `XSetModifierMapping` does the work in a single call, but the price of this call is that you need to manually set up the `XModifierKeymap` structure pointed to by *mod_map*. This requires you to know how the `XModifierKeymap` structure is defined and organized, as described in the next three paragraphs.

The `XModifierKeymap` structure for the *mod_map* argument should be created using `XNewModifierMap` or `XGetModifierMapping`. The `max_keypermod` element of the structure specifies the maximum number of keycodes that can be mapped to each modifier. You define this number but there may be an upper limit on a particular server.

The `modifiermap` element of the structure is an array of keycodes. There are eight by `max_keypermod` keycodes in this array: eight because there are eight modifiers, and `max_keypermod` because that is the number of keycodes that must be reserved for each modifier.

The eight modifiers are represented by the constants `ShiftMapIndex`, `LockMapIndex`, `ControlMapIndex`, `Mod1MapIndex`, `Mod2MapIndex`, `Mod3MapIndex`, `Mod4MapIndex`, and `Mod5MapIndex`. These are not actually used as arguments, but they are convenient for referring to each row in the `modifiermap` structure while filling it. The definitions of these constants are shown in the Structures section below.

Now you can interpret the `modifiermap` array. For each modifier in a given `modifiermap`, the keycodes which correspond are from `modifiermap[index * max_keypermod]` to `modifiermap[[(index + 1) * max_keyspermod] -1]` where `index` is the appropriate modifier index definition (`ShiftMapIndex`, `LockMapIndex`, etc.). You must set the *mod_map* array up properly before calling `XSetModifierMapping`. Now you know why `XInsertModifierMapEntry` and `XDeleteModifierMapEntry` were created!

Zero keycodes are ignored. No keycode may appear twice anywhere in the map (otherwise, a `BadValue` error is generated). In addition, all of the nonzero keycodes must be in the range specified by `min_keycode` and `max_keycode` in the `Display` structure (otherwise a `BadValue` error occurs).

A server can impose restrictions on how modifiers can be changed. For example, certain keys may not generate up transitions in hardware, or multiple modifier keys may not be supported. If a restriction is violated, then the status reply is `MappingFailed`, and none of the modifiers are changed.

If the new keycodes specified for a modifier differ from those currently defined and any (current or new) keys for that modifier are in the down state, then the status reply is `MappingBusy`, and none of the modifiers are changed.

`XSetModifierMapping` generates a `MappingNotify` event on a `MappingSuccess` status.

A value of 0 for `modifiermap` indicates that no keys are valid as any modifier.

Structures
```
typedef struct {
    int max_keypermod;      /* server's max # of keys per modifier */
    KeyCode *modifiermap;   /* an 8 by max_keypermod array */
} XModifierKeymap;

/* modifier names.  Used to build a SetModifierMapping request or
   to read a GetModifierMapping request.  These correspond to the
   masks defined above. */
#define ShiftMapIndex       0
#define LockMapIndex        1
#define ControlMapIndex     2
#define Mod1MapIndex        3
#define Mod2MapIndex        4
#define Mod3MapIndex        5
#define Mod4MapIndex        6
#define Mod5MapIndex        7
```

Errors
`BadAlloc`

`BadValue`   Keycode appears twice in the map.

Keycode < *display*->min_keycode or
keycode > *display*->max_keycode.

Related Commands
`XDeleteModifiermapEntry`, `XInsertModifiermapEntry`, `XFreeModifiermap`, `XKeycodeToKeysym`, `XKeysymToKeycode`, `XKeysymToString`, `XNewModifier-Map`, `XQueryKeymap`, `XStringToKeysym`, `XLookupKeysym`, `XRebindKeysym`, `XGetKeyboardMapping`, `XChangeKeyboardMapping`, `XRefreshKeyboard-Mapping`, `XLookupString`, `XGetModifierMapping`, `XInsertModifiermap-Entry`, `XDeleteModifiermapEntry`.

Name

XSetNormalHints — set the size hints property of a window in normal state (not zoomed or iconified).

Synopsis

```
void XSetNormalHints(display, w, hints)
    Display *display;
    Window w;
    XSizeHints *hints;
```

Arguments

display   Specifies a pointer to the Display structure; returned from XOpen-Display.

w   Specifies the window ID.

hints   Specifies a pointer to the sizing hints for the window in its normal state.

Description

XSetNormalHints sets the XA_WM_NORMAL_HINTS property for the specified window. Applications use XSetNormalHints to inform the window manager of the size or position desirable for that window. In addition, an application wanting to move or resize itself should call XSetNormalHints specifying its new desired location and size, in addition to making direct X calls to move or resize. This is because some window managers may redirect window configuration requests, but ignore the resulting events and pay attention to property changes instead.

To set size hints, an application must not only assign values to the appropriate elements in the hints structure, but also must set the flags field of the structure to indicate which members have assigned values and the source of the assignment. These flags are listed in the Structures section below.

For more information on using hints, see Volume One, Chapter 10, *Interclient Communication*.

Structures

```
typedef struct {
    long flags;     /* which fields in structure are defined */
    int x, y;
    int width, height;
    int min_width, min_height;
    int max_width, max_height;
    int width_inc, height_inc;
    struct {
        int x;     /* numerator */
        int y;     /* denominator */
    } min_aspect, max_aspect;
} XSizeHints;
```

```
/* flags argument in size hints */
#define USPosition (1L << 0) /* user specified x, y */
#define USSize     (1L << 1) /* user specified width, height */

#define PPosition  (1L << 2) /* program specified position */
#define PSize      (1L << 3) /* program specified size */
#define PMinSize   (1L << 4) /* program specified minimum size */
#define PMaxSize   (1L << 5) /* program specified maximum size */
#define PResizeInc (1L << 6) /* program specified resize increments */
#define PAspect    (1L << 7) /* program specified min/max aspect ratios */
#define PAllHints  (PPosition|PSize|PMinSize|PMaxSize|PResizeInc|PAspect)
```

Errors

BadAlloc
BadWindow

Related Commands

XGetClassHint, XSetClassHint, XGetSizeHints, XSetSizeHints, XGet-
WMHints, XSetWMHints, XGetZoomHints, XSetZoomHints, XGetNormalHints,
XGetTransientForHint, XSetTransientForHint, XFetchName, XGetIcon-
Name, XSetIconName, XStoreName, XGetIconSizes, XSetIconSizes, XSet-
Command.

XSetPlaneMask

Name

XSetPlaneMask — set the plane mask in a graphics context.

Synopsis

```
XSetPlaneMask(display, gc, plane_mask)
    Display *display;
    GC gc;
    unsigned long plane_mask;
```

Arguments

display   Specifies a pointer to the Display structure; returned from XOpen-Display.

gc   Specifies the graphics context.

plane_mask   Specifies the plane mask. You can use the macro AllPlanes if desired.

Description

XSetPlaneMask sets the plane_mask member of the specified GC. The plane_mask determines which planes of the destination drawable are affected by a graphics request.

For more information, see Volume One, Chapter 5, *The Graphics Context*.

Errors

BadAlloc
BadGC

Related Commands

XChangeGC, XCopyGC, XCreateGC, XFreeGC, XGContextFromGC, XSetStipple, XSetTSOrigin, XSetDashes, XSetLineAttributes, XSetFillRule, XSetFill-Style, XSetForeground, XSetBackground, XSetFunction, XSetGraphics-Exposures, XSetArcMode, XSetClipMask, XSetClipOrigin, XSetClip-Rectangles, XSetState, XSetSubwindowMode, DefaultGC.

Name

XSetPointerMapping — set the pointer button mapping.

Synopsis

```
int XSetPointerMapping(display, map, nmap)
    Display *display;
    unsigned char map[];
    int nmap;
```

Arguments

display   Specifies a pointer to the Display structure; returned from XOpen-
Display.

map   Specifies the mapping list.

nmap   Specifies the number of items in the mapping list.

Description

XSetPointerMapping sets the mapping of the pointer. Elements of the *map* list are indexed starting from 1. The length of the list *nmap* must be the same as XGetPointer-Mapping returns (you must call that first). The index is a physical button number, and the element of the list defines the effective button number. In other words, if map[2] is set to 1, when the second physical button is pressed, a ButtonPress event will be generated if Button1Mask was selected but not if Button2Mask was selected. The button member in the event will read Button1.

No two elements can have the same nonzero value. A value of 0 for an element of *map* disables a button, and values for elements are not restricted in value by the number of physical buttons. If any of the buttons to be altered are currently in the down state, the status reply is MappingBusy and the mapping is not changed.

This function returns either MappingSuccess or MappingBusy. XSetPointer-Mapping generates a MappingNotify event on a status of MappingSuccess.

Errors

BadValue   Two elements of *map*[] have same nonzero value.

nmap not equal to XGetPointerMapping return value.

Related Commands

XQueryPointer, XWarpPointer, XGrabPointer, XChangeActivePointerGrab, XUngrabPointer, XGetPointerMapping, XGetPointerControl, XChange-PointerControl.

Name

XSetRegion — set `clip_mask` of the graphics context to the specified region.

Synopsis

```
XSetRegion(display, gc, r)
    Display *display;
    GC gc;
    Region r;
```

Arguments

display   Specifies a pointer to the `Display` structure; returned from `XOpen-Display`.

gc   Specifies the graphics context.

r   Specifies the region.

Description

`XSetRegion` sets the `clip_mask` of the GC to the specified region. Thereafter, all output requests made with `gc` will be confined to the region.

Regions are located using an offset from a point (the *region origin*) which is common to all regions. It is up to the application to interpret the location of the region relative to a drawable. When the region is to be used as a `clip_mask` by calling `XSetRegion`, the upper-left corner of region relative to the drawable used in the graphics request will be at (`xoffset` + `clip_x_origin`, `yoffset` + `clip_y_origin`), where `xoffset` and `yoffset` are the offset of the region and `clip_x_origin` and `clip_y_origin` are elements of the GC used in the graphics request.

For more information on regions, see Volume One: Chapter 5, *The Graphics Context*; and Chapter 6, *Drawing Graphics and Text*.

Structures

```
/*
 * opaque reference to Regiondata type.
 * user won't need contents, only pointer.
 */
typedef struct _XRegion *Region;
```

Related Commands

XXorRegion, XUnionRegion, XUnionRectWithRegion, XSubtractRegion, XShrinkRegion, XRectInRegion, XPolygonRegion, XPointInRegion, XOffsetRegion, XIntersectRegion, XEmptyRegion, XCreateRegion, XDestroyRegion, XEqualRegion, XClipBox.

XSetScreenSaver

Name

XSetScreenSaver — set the parameters of the screen saver.

Synopsis

```
XSetScreenSaver(display, timeout, interval,
        prefer_blanking, allow_exposures)
    Display *display;
    int timeout, interval;
    int prefer_blanking;
    int allow_exposures;
```

Arguments

display   Specifies a pointer to the Display structure; returned from XOpen-Display.

timeout   Specifies the time of inactivity, in seconds, before the screen saver turns on.

interval   Specifies the interval, in seconds, between screen saver invocations. This is for intermittent changes to the display, not blanking.

prefer_blanking
                Specifies whether to enable screen blanking. Possible values are DontPreferBlanking, PreferBlanking, or DefaultBlanking.

allow_exposures
                Specifies the current screen saver control values. Possible values are DontAllowExposures, AllowExposures, or DefaultExposures.

Description

XSetScreenSaver sets the parameters that control the screen saver. *timeout* and *interval* are specified in seconds. A positive *timeout* enables the screen saver. A *timeout* of 0 disables the screen saver, while a timeout of −1 restores the default. An *interval* of 0 disables the random pattern motion. If no input from devices (keyboard, mouse, etc.) is generated for the specified number of timeout seconds, the screen saver is activated.

For each screen, if blanking is preferred and the hardware supports video blanking, the screen will simply go blank. Otherwise, if either exposures are allowed or the screen can be regenerated without sending exposure events to clients, the screen is tiled with the root window background tile, with a random origin, each *interval* seconds. Otherwise, the state of the screen does not change. All screen states are restored at the next input from a device.

If the server-dependent screen saver method supports periodic change, *interval* serves as a hint about how long the change period should be, and a value of 0 hints that no periodic change should be made. Examples of ways to change the screen include scrambling the color map periodically, moving an icon image about the screen periodically, or tiling the screen with the root window background tile, randomly reoriginated periodically.

For more information on the screen saver, see Volume One, Chapter 13, *Other Programming Techniques*.

Errors

    BadValue   *timeout* < –1.

Related Commands

XForceScreenSaver, XActivateScreenSaver, XResetScreenSaver, XGet-
ScreenSaver.

XSetSelectionOwner

Name

XSetSelectionOwner — set the owner of a selection.

Synopsis

```
XSetSelectionOwner(display, selection, owner, time)
    Display *display;
    Atom selection;
    Window owner;
    Time time;
```

Arguments

display   Specifies a pointer to the Display structure; returned from XOpen-
             Display.

selection   Specifies the selection atom. Predefined atoms are XA_PRIMARY and
             XA_SECONDARY.

owner   Specifies the present owner of the specified selection atom. This value is
             either a window ID or None.

time   Specifies the time when the grab should take place. Pass either a timestamp,
             expressed in milliseconds, or the constant CurrentTime.

Description

XSetSelectionOwner sets the owner and last-change time of a selection property. This
should be called by an application that supports cutting and pasting between windows (or at
least cutting), when the user has made a selection of any kind of text, graphics, or data. This
makes the information available so that other applications can request the data from the new
selection owner using XConvertSelection, which generates a SelectionRequest
event specifying the desired type and format of the data. Then the selection owner sends a
SelectionNotify using XSendEvent, which notes that the information is stored in the
selection property in the desired format or indicates that it couldn't do the conversion to the
desired type.

If owner is specified as None, then the new owner of the selection is None. Otherwise, the
new owner is the client executing the request.

If the new owner is not the same as the current owner of the selection, and the current owner
is a window, then the current owner is sent a SelectionClear event. This indicates to
that window that the selection should be unhighlighted.

If the selection owner window is later destroyed, the owner of the selection automatically
reverts to None.

The value you pass to the time argument must be no earlier than the last-change time of the
specified selection, and no later than the current time, or the selection is not affected. The new
last-change time recorded is the specified time, with CurrentTime replaced by the current
server time. If the X server reverts a selection owner to None, the last-change time is not
affected.

For more information on selections, see Volume One, Chapter 10, *Interclient Communication*.

Errors
```
BadAtom
BadWindow
```

Related Commands
`XGetSelectionOwner`, `XConvertSelection`.

Name

XSetSizeHints — set the value of any property of type XA_SIZE_HINTS.

Synopsis

```
XSetSizeHints(display, w, hints, property)
    Display *display;
    Window w;
    XSizeHints *hints;
    Atom property;
```

Arguments

display   Specifies a pointer to the Display structure; returned from XOpen-
              Display.

w   Specifies the window ID.

hints   Specifies a pointer to the size hints.

property   Specifies the property atom.

Description

XSetSizeHints sets the named property on the specified window to the specified XSize-
Hints structure. This routine is useful if new properties of type XA_WM_SIZE_HINTS are
defined. The predefined properties of that type have their own set and get functions, XSet-
NormalHints and XSetZoomHints.

The flags member of XSizeHints must be set to the OR of the symbols representing each
member to be set.

For more information on using hints, see Volume One, Chapter 10, *Interclient Communication*.

Structures

```
typedef struct {
    long flags;    /* which fields in structure are defined */
    int x, y;
    int width, height;
    int min_width, min_height;
    int max_width, max_height;
    int width_inc, height_inc;
    struct {
        int x;     /* numerator */
        int y;     /* denominator */
    } min_aspect, max_aspect;
} XSizeHints;

/* flags argument in size hints */
#define USPosition (1L << 0)/* user specified x, y */
#define USSize     (1L << 1)/* user specified width, height */

#define PPosition  (1L << 2)/* program specified position */
```

```
#define PSize      (1L << 3) /* program specified size */
#define PMinSize   (1L << 4) /* program specified minimum size */
#define PMaxSize   (1L << 5) /* program specified maximum size */
#define PResizeInc (1L << 6) /* program specified resize increments */
#define PAspect    (1L << 7) /* program specified min/max aspect ratios */
#define PAllHints (PPosition|PSize|PMinSize|PMaxSize|PResizeInc|PAspect)
```

Errors
```
BadAlloc
BadAtom
BadWindow
```

Related Commands

XGetClassHint, XSetClassHint, XGetSizeHints, XGetWMHints, XSet-
WMHints, XGetZoomHints, XSetZoomHints, XGetNormalHints, XSetNormal-
Hints, XGetTransientForHint, XSetTransientForHint, XFetchName, XGet-
IconName, XSetIconName, XStoreName, XGetIconSizes, XSetIconSizes,
XSetCommand.

XSetStandardColormap

Name

XSetStandardColormap — change the standard colormap property.

Synopsis

```
void XSetStandardColormap(display, w, cmap, property)
    Display *display;
    Window w;
    XStandardColormap *cmap;
    Atom property;
```

Arguments

display   Specifies a pointer to the `Display` structure; returned from `XOpenDisplay`.

w   Specifies the ID of the window with which this colormap will be associated.

cmap   Specifies the filled colormap information structure.

property   Specifies the standard colormap property to set. The predefined standard colormaps are: `XA_RGB_BEST_MAP`, `XA_RGB_RED_MAP`, `XA_RGB_GREEN_MAP`, `XA_RGB_BLUE_MAP`, `XA_RGB_DEFAULT_MAP`, and `XA_RGB_GRAY_MAP`.

Description

`XSetStandardColormap` defines or changes a colormap property. It is usually used only by window managers. To create a standard colormap, follow this procedure:

1. Open a new connection to the same server.

2. Grab the server.

3. See if *property* is on the property list of the root window for the display, using `XGetStandardColormap`. If it is, the colormap already exists.

4. If the desired property is not present, do the following:

    - Create a colormap (not required for `XA_RGB_DEFAULT_MAP`).

    - Determine the color capabilities of the display.

    - Call `XAllocColorPlanes` or `XAllocColorCells` to allocate cells in the colormap.

    - Call `XStoreColors` to store appropriate color values in the colormap.

    - Fill in the descriptive fields in the structure.

    - Call `XSetStandardColormap` to set the property on the root window.

    - Use `XSetCloseDownMode` to make the resource permanent.

5. Ungrab the server.

See description of predefined standard colormap atoms in Volume One, Chapter 7, *Color*.

Errors

```
BadAlloc
BadAtom
BadWindow
```

Structures

```
typedef struct {
    Colormap colormap;          /* ID of colormap made by XCreateColormap */
    unsigned long red_max;
    unsigned long red_mult;
    unsigned long green_max;
    unsigned long green_mult;
    unsigned long blue_max;
    unsigned long blue_mult;
    unsigned long base_pixel;
} XStandardColormap;
```

Related Commands

XCopyColormapAndFree, XCreateColormap, XFreeColormap, XGetStandard-
Colormap, XInstallColormap, XUninstallColormap, XListInstalled-
Colormaps, XSetWindowColormap, DefaultColormap, DisplayCells.

Name

XSetStandardProperties — set the minimum set of properties for the window manager.

Synopsis

```
XSetStandardProperties(display, w, window_name, icon_name,
        icon_pixmap, argv, argc, hints)
    Display *display;
    Window w;
    char *window_name;
    char *icon_name;
    Pixmap icon_pixmap;
    char **argv;
    int argc;
    XSizeHints *hints
```

Arguments

display	Specifies a pointer to the Display structure; returned from XOpen-Display.
w	Specifies the window ID.
window_name	Specifies the name of the window.
icon_name	Specifies the name to be displayed in the window's icon.
icon_pixmap	Specifies the pixmap that is to be used for the icon, or None. This pixmap should normally be of depth 1.
argv	Specifies a pointer to the command and arguments used to start the application. The application is an array of pointers to null-terminated strings.
argc	Specifies the number of arguments.
hints	Specifies a pointer to the size hints for the window in its normal state.

Description

XSetStandardProperties sets in a single call the most essential properties for a quickie application. XSetStandardProperties gives a window manager some information about your program's preferences; it probably will not be sufficient for complex programs. See Volume One, Chapter 10, *Interclient Communication* for a description of standard properties.

Structures

```
typedef struct {
    long flags;                  /* which fields in structure are defined */
    int x, y;
    int width, height;
    int min_width, min_height;
    int max_width, max_height;
    int width_inc, height_inc;
    struct {
```

```
        int x;      /* numerator */
        int y;      /* denominator */
    } min_aspect, max_aspect;
} XSizeHints;

/* flags argument in size hints */
#define USPosition  (1L << 0)/* user specified x, y */
#define USSize      (1L << 1)/* user specified width, height */

#define PPosition   (1L << 2)/* program specified position */
#define PSize       (1L << 3)/* program specified size */
#define PMinSize    (1L << 4)/* program specified minimum size */
#define PMaxSize    (1L << 5)/* program specified maximum size */
#define PResizeInc  (1L << 6)/* program specified resize increments */
#define PAspect     (1L << 7)/* program specified min and max aspect ratios */
#define PAllHints (PPosition|PSize|PMinSize|PMaxSize|PResizeInc|PAspect)
```

Errors
```
BadAlloc
BadWindow
```

Related Commands

XGetFontProperty, XRotateWindowProperties, XDeleteProperty, XChange-
Property, XGetWindowProperty, XListProperties, XGetAtomName, XIntern-
Atom.

Name

XSetState — set the foreground, background, logical function, and plane mask in a graphics context.

Synopsis

```
XSetState(display, gc, foreground, background, function,
        plane_mask)
    Display *display;
    GC gc;
    unsigned long foreground, background;
    int function;
    unsigned long plane_mask;
```

Arguments

display   Specifies a pointer to the Display structure; returned from XOpen-Display.

gc   Specifies the graphics context.

foreground   Specifies the foreground you want for the specified graphics context.

background   Specifies the background you want for the specified graphics context.

function   Specifies the function you want for the specified graphics context.

plane_mask   Specifies the plane mask you want for the specified graphics context.

Description

XSetState sets the foreground and background pixel values, the logical function, and the plane_mask in a GC. See XSetForeground, XSetBackground, XSet-Function, and XSetPlaneMask for what these members do and appropriate values.

See Volume One, Chapter 5, *The Graphics Context*, for more information.

Errors

BadAlloc
BadGC
BadValue

Related Commands

XChangeGC, XCopyGC, XCreateGC, XFreeGC, XGContextFromGC, XSetStipple, XSetTSOrigin, XSetPlaneMask, XSetDashes, XSetLineAttributes, XSet-FillRule, XSetFillStyle, XSetForeground, XSetBackground, XSet-Function, XSetGraphicsExposures, XSetArcMode, XSetClipMask, XSetClip-Origin, XSetClipRectangles, XSetSubwindowMode, DefaultGC.

Name
XSetStipple — set the stipple in a graphics context.

Synopsis
```
XSetStipple(display, gc, stipple)
    Display *display;
    GC gc;
    Pixmap stipple;
```

Arguments

display   Specifies a pointer to the Display structure; returned from XOpenDisplay.

gc   Specifies the graphics context.

stipple   Specifies the stipple you want to set for the specified graphics context.

Description

XSetStipple sets the stipple member of the GC. The *stipple* is a pixmap of depth 1. It is laid out like a tile. Set bits in the stipple determine which pixels in an area are drawn in the foreground pixel value. Unset bits in the stipple determine which pixels are drawn in the background pixel value if the fill_style is FillOpaqueStippled. If fill_style is FillStippled, pixels overlayed with unset bits in the stipple are not drawn. If fill_style is FillTiled or FillSolid, the stipple is not used.

For more information, see Volume One, Chapter 5, *The Graphics Context*.

Errors

```
BadAlloc
BadGC
BadMatch
BadPixmap
```

Related Commands

XChangeGC, XCopyGC, XCreateGC, XFreeGC, XGContextFromGC, XSetTSOrigin, XSetPlaneMask, XSetDashes, XSetLineAttributes, XSetFillRule, XSet-FillStyle, XSetForeground, XSetBackground, XSetFunction, XSet-GraphicsExposures, XSetArcMode, XSetClipMask, XSetClipOrigin, XSet-ClipRectangles, XSetState, XSetSubwindowMode, DefaultGC.

Name

XSetSubwindowMode — set the subwindow mode in a graphics context.

Synopsis

```
XSetSubwindowMode(display, gc, subwindow_mode)
    Display *display;
    GC gc;
    int subwindow_mode;
```

Arguments

display   Specifies a pointer to the Display structure; returned from XOpenDisplay.

gc   Specifies the graphics context.

subwindow_mode
                 Specifies the subwindow mode you want to set for the specified graphics context. Possible values are ClipByChildren or IncludeInferiors.

Description

XSetSubwindowMode sets the subwindow_mode member of the GC. Clip-ByChildren means that graphics requests will be clipped by all viewable children. IncludeInferiors means draw through all subwindows.

For more information, see Volume One, Chapter 5, *The Graphics Context*.

Errors

BadAlloc
BadGC
BadValue

Related Commands

XChangeGC, XCopyGC, XCreateGC, XFreeGC, XGContextFromGC, XSetStipple, XSetTSOrigin, XSetPlaneMask, XSetDashes, XSetLineAttributes, XSet-FillRule, XSetFillStyle, XSetForeground, XSetBackground, XSet-Function, XSetGraphicsExposures, XSetArcMode, XSetClipMask, XSetClip-Origin, XSetClipRectangles, XSetState, DefaultGC.

XSetTile

Name

XSetTile — set the fill tile in a graphics context.

Synopsis

```
XSetTile(display, gc, tile)
    Display *display;
    GC gc;
    Pixmap tile;
```

Arguments

display   Specifies a pointer to the Display structure; returned from XOpenDisplay.

gc   Specifies the graphics context.

tile   Specifies the desired tile for the specified graphics context.

Description

XSetTile sets the tile member of the GC. This member of the GC determines the pixmap used to tile areas. The tile must have the same depth as the destination drawable.

For more information, see Volume One, Chapter 5, *The Graphics Context*.

Errors

```
BadAlloc
BadGC
BadMatch
BadPixmap
```

Related Commands

XQueryBestTile, XSetWindowBorderPixmap, XSetWindowBackgroundPixmap, XCreatePixmap, XCreatePixmapFromBitmapData, XFreePixmap, XQueryBest-Size, XQueryBestStipple, XWriteBitmapFile, XReadBitmapFile, XCreate-BitmapFromData.

XSetTransientForHint

Name

XSetTransientForHint — set the XA_WM_TRANSIENT_FOR property for a window.

Synopsis

```
XSetTransientForHint(display, w, prop_window)
    Display *display;
    Window w;
    Window prop_window;
```

Arguments

display   Specifies a pointer to the Display structure; returned from XOpen-Display.

w   Specifies the window ID.

prop_window   Specifies the window ID that the XA_WM_TRANSIENT_FOR property is to be set to.

Description

XSetTransientForHint sets the XA_WM_TRANSIENT_FOR property of the specified window. This should be done when the window *w* is a temporary child (for example, a dialog box) and the main top-level window of its application is *prop_window*. Some window managers may use this information to unmap an application's dialog boxes (for example, when the main application window gets iconified).

For more information, see Volume One, Chapter 10, *Interclient Communication*.

Errors

BadAlloc
BadWindow

Related Commands

XGetClassHint, XSetClassHint, XGetSizeHints, XSetSizeHints, XGet-WMHints, XSetWMHints, XGetZoomHints, XSetZoomHints, XGetNormalHints, XSetNormalHints, XGetTransientForHint, XFetchName, XGetIconName, XSetIconName, XStoreName, XGetIconSizes, XSetIconSizes, XSetCommand.

Name

XSetTSOrigin — set the tile/stipple origin in a graphics context.

Synopsis

```
XSetTSOrigin(display, gc, ts_x_origin, ts_y_origin)
    Display *display;
    GC gc;
    int ts_x_origin, ts_y_origin;
```

Arguments

display   Specifies a pointer to the Display structure; returned from XOpen-
                 Display.

gc   Specifies the graphics context.

ts_x_origin   Specify the x and y coordinates of the tile/stipple origin.
ts_y_origin

Description

XSetTSOrigin sets the ts_x_origin and ts_y_origin in the GC, which are measured relative to the origin of the drawable specified in the drawing request that uses the GC.
This controls the placement of the tile or the stipple pattern that patterns an area. To tile or
stipple a child so that the pattern matches the parent, you need to subtract the current position
of the child window from ts_x_origin and ts_y_origin.

For more information, see Volume One, Chapter 5, *The Graphics Context*.

Errors

BadAlloc
BadGC

Related Commands

XChangeGC, XCopyGC, XCreateGC, XFreeGC, XGContextFromGC, XSetStipple,
XSetPlaneMask, XSetDashes, XSetLineAttributes, XSetFillRule, XSet-
FillStyle, XSetForeground, XSetBackground, XSetFunction, XSet-
GraphicsExposures, XSetArcMode, XSetClipMask, XSetClipOrigin, XSet-
ClipRectangles, XSetState, XSetSubwindowMode, DefaultGC.

XSetWindowBackground

Name

XSetWindowBackground — set the background pixel attribute of a window.

Synopsis

```
XSetWindowBackground(display, w, background_pixel)
    Display *display;
    Window w;
    unsigned long background_pixel;
```

Arguments

display   Specifies a pointer to the Display structure; returned from XOpenDisplay.

w   Specifies the window ID. Must be an InputOutput window.

background_pixel
     Specifies which entry in the colormap is used as the background.

Description

XSetWindowBackground sets the background attribute of a window, setting the pixel value to be used to fill the background. The current window contents are not changed. The background is automatically repainted after Expose events, in the area affected by the exposure.

When XSetWindowBackground and XSetWindowBackgroundPixmap are both used on a window, whichever is called last will control the current background. Trying to change the background of an InputOnly window will generate a BadMatch error.

For more information, see Volume One, Chapter 4, *Window Attributes*.

Errors

BadMatch
BadWindow

Related Commands

XGetWindowAttributes, XChangeWindowAttributes, XSetWindow-BackgroundPixmap, XSetWindowBorder, XSetWindowBorderPixmap, XGet-Geometry.

Name

XSetWindowBackgroundPixmap — change the background tile attribute of a window.

Synopsis

```
XSetWindowBackgroundPixmap(display, w, background_tile)
    Display *display;
    Window w;
    Pixmap background_tile;
```

Arguments

display Specifies a pointer to the Display structure; returned from XOpenDisplay.

w   Specifies the window ID. Must be an InputOutput class window.

background_tile

    Specifies a pixmap ID, None, or ParentRelative to be used as a background.

Description

XSetWindowBackgroundPixmap sets the background_pixmap attribute of a window. If no background pixmap is specified, the background pixmap of the window's parent is used. On the root window, the default background will be restored. The old, unused background pixmap can immediately be freed if no further explicit references to it are to be made.

XSetWindowBackgroundPixmap can only be performed on an InputOutput window. An error will result otherwise.

This does not change the current contents of the window, so you may wish to call XClear-Window to repaint the window after this function.

XSetWindowBackground may be used if a solid color instead of a tile is desired. If *background_tile* is specified as ParentRelative, the windows will get an Expose event when it is moved and its background will be repainted. When XSetWindow-Background and XSetWindowBackgroundPixmap are both used on a window, whichever is called last will control the current background.

For more information, see Volume One, Chapter 4, *Window Attributes*.

Errors

```
BadMatch
BadPixmap
BadWindow
```

Related Commands

XSetTile, XQueryBestTile, XSetWindowBorderPixmap, XCreatePixmap, XCreatePixmapFromBitmapData, XFreePixmap, XQueryBestSize, XQuery-BestStipple, XWriteBitmapFile, XReadBitmapFile, XCreateBitmapFrom-Data.

XSetWindowBorder

Name

XSetWindowBorder — change a window border attribute to the specified pixel value and repaint the border.

Synopsis

```
XSetWindowBorder(display, w, border_pixel)
    Display *display;
    Window w;
    unsigned long border_pixel;
```

Arguments

display   Specifies a pointer to the Display structure; returned from XOpenDisplay.

w   Specifies the window ID. Must be an InputOutput window.

border_pixel
    Specifies the entry in the colormap. XSetWindowBorder uses this entry to paint the border.

Description

XSetWindowBorder sets the border_pixel attribute of window *w* to a pixel value, and repaints the border. The border is also automatically repainted after Expose events.

Use XSetWindowBorderPixmap to create a tiled border.

For more information, see Volume One, Chapter 4, *Window Attributes*.

Errors

BadMatch
BadWindow

Related Commands

XGetWindowAttributes, XChangeWindowAttributes, XSetWindow-Background, XSetWindowBackgroundPixmap, XSetWindowBorderPixmap, XGetGeometry.

Name

XSetWindowBorderPixmap — change a window border tile attribute and repaint the border.

Synopsis

```
XSetWindowBorderPixmap(display, w, border_tile)
    Display *display;
    Window w;
    Pixmap border_tile;
```

Arguments

display   Specifies a pointer to the `Display` structure; returned from `XOpen-Display`.

w   Specifies the ID of an `InputOutput` window whose border is to be changed.

border_tile Specifies any pixmap or `None`.

Description

`XSetWindowBorderPixmap` sets the `border_pixmap` attribute of a window and repaints the border. The `border_tile` can be freed immediately after the call if no further explicit references to it are to be made.

This function can only be performed on an `InputOutput` window.

Errors

```
BadMatch
BadPixmap
BadWindow
```

Related Commands

XSetTile, XQueryBestTile, XSetWindowBackgroundPixmap, XCreatePixmap, XCreatePixmapFromBitmapData, XFreePixmap, XQueryBestSize, XQuery-BestStipple, XWriteBitmapFile, XReadBitmapFile, XCreateBitmapFrom-Data.

Name

XSetWindowBorderWidth — change the border width of a window.

Synopsis

```
XSetWindowBorderWidth(display, w, width)
    Display *display;
    Window w;
    unsigned int width;
```

Arguments

display   Specifies a pointer to the `Display` structure; returned from `XOpenDisplay`.

w   Specifies the ID of the window whose border is to be changed.

width   Specifies the width of the window border.

Description

`XSetWindowBorderWidth` changes the border width of a window. This request is often used by the window manager as an indication of the current input focus window, so other clients should not change it.

Errors

BadWindow

Related Commands

XLowerWindow, XRaiseWindow, XCirculateSubwindows, XCirculate-
SubwindowsDown, XCirculateSubwindowsUp, XRestackWindows, XMove-
Window, XResizeWindow, XMoveResizeWindow, XReparentWindow,
XConfigureWindow, XQueryTree.

XSetWindowColormap

Name

XSetWindowColormap — set the colormap for a specified window.

Synopsis

```
XSetWindowColormap(display, w, cmap)
    Display *display;
    Window w;
    Colormap cmap;
```

Arguments

display Specifies a pointer to the Display structure; returned from XOpenDisplay.

w   Specifies the ID of the window for which you want to set the colormap.

cmap   Specifies the colormap.

Description

XSetWindowColormap sets the colormap attribute of the specified window. The color-map need not be installed to be set as an attribute. *cmap* will be used to translate pixel values drawn into this window when *cmap* is installed in the hardware.

Eventually, window managers will install and uninstall the proper colormaps according to this attribute and the pointer position or some other convention. For now, applications must install their own colormaps if they cannot use the default colormap.

The colormap must have the same visual as the window.

Errors

```
BadColor
BadMatch
BadWindow
```

Related Commands

XGetWindowAttributes, XChangeWindowAttributes, XSetWindow-Background, XSetWindowBackgroundPixmap, XSetWindowBorder, XSet-WindowBorderPixmap, XGetGeometry.

XSetWMHints

Name

XSetWMHints — set a window manager hints property.

Synopsis

```
XSetWMHints(display, w, wmhints)
    Display *display;
    Window w;
    XWMHints *wmhints;
```

Arguments

display   Specifies a pointer to the Display structure; returned from XOpenDisplay.

w   Specifies the ID for which window manager hints are to be set.

wmhints   Specifies a pointer to the window manager hints.

Description

XSetWMHints sets the window manager hints that include icon information and location, the initial state of the window, and whether the application relies on the window manager to get keyboard input. See Volume One, Chapter 10, *Interclient Communication*, for a description of each XWMHints structure member.

Structures

```
typedef struct {
    long flags;              /* marks defined fields in structure */
    Bool input;              /* does application need window manager for
                              * keyboard input */
    int initial_state;       /* see below */
    Pixmap icon_pixmap;      /* pixmap to be used as icon */
    Window icon_window;      /* window to be used as icon */
    int icon_x, icon_y;      /* initial position of icon */
    Pixmap icon_mask;        /* icon mask bitmap */
    XID window_group;        /* ID of related window group */
    /* this structure may be extended in the future */
} XWMHints;

/* definitions for the flags field: */
#define InputHint        (1L << 0)
#define StateHint        (1L << 1)
#define IconPixmapHint   (1L << 2)
#define IconWindowHint   (1L << 3)
#define IconPositionHint (1L << 4)
#define IconMaskHint     (1L << 5)
#define WindowGroupHint  (1L << 6)
#define AllHints (InputHint|StateHint|IconPixmapHint|IconWindowHint| \
    IconPositionHint|IconMaskHint|WindowGroupHint)
```

```
/* definitions for the initial state flag: */
#define DontCareState   0     /* don't know or care */
#define NormalState     1     /* most applications want to start this way */
#define ZoomState       2     /* application wants to start zoomed */
#define IconicState     3     /* application wants to start as an icon */
#define InactiveState   4     /* application believes it is seldom used;
                                 some wm's may put it on inactive menu */
```

Errors
BadAlloc
BadWindow

Related Commands
XGetClassHint, XSetClassHint, XGetSizeHints, XSetSizeHints, XGet-
WMHints, XGetZoomHints, XSetZoomHints, XGetNormalHints, XSetNormal-
Hints, XGetTransientForHint, XSetTransientForHint, XFetchName, XGet-
IconName, XSetIconName, XStoreName, XGetIconSizes, XSetIconSizes,
XSetCommand.

XSetZoomHints

Name

XSetZoomHints — set the size hints property of a zoomed window.

Synopsis

```
XSetZoomHints(display, w, zhints)
    Display *display;
    Window w;
    XSizeHints *zhints;
```

Arguments

display   Specifies a pointer to the `Display` structure; returned from `XOpenDisplay`.

w   Specifies the ID of the window for which zoom hints are to be set.

zhints   Specifies a pointer to the zoom hints.

Description

`XSetZoomHints` sets the `XA_WM_ZOOM_HINTS` property for an application's top-level window in its zoomed state. Many window managers think of windows in three states: iconified, normal, or zoomed, corresponding to small, medium, and large. Applications use `XSetZoomHints` to inform the window manager of the size or position desirable for the zoomed window.

In addition, an application wanting to move or resize its zoomed window should call `XSetZoomHints` specifying its new desired location and size, in addition to making direct X calls to move or resize. This is because some window managers may redirect window configuration requests, but ignore the resulting events and pay attention to property changes instead.

To set size hints, an application must not only assign values to the appropriate elements in the hints structure, but also must set the `flags` field of the structure to indicate which members have assigned values and the source of the assignment. These flags are listed in the Structures section below.

For more information on using hints, see Volume One, Chapter 10, *Interclient Communication*.

Structures

```
typedef struct {
    long flags;                /* marks defined fields in structure */
    int x, y;
    int width, height;
    int min_width, min_height;
    int max_width, max_height;
    int width_inc, height_inc;
    struct {
        int x;                 /* numerator */
        int y;                 /* denominator */
    } min_aspect, max_aspect;
```

```
/* flags argument in size hints */
#define USPosition (1L << 0)  /* user specified x, y */
#define USSize     (1L << 1)  /* user specified width, height */

#define PPosition  (1L << 2)  /* program specified position */
#define PSize      (1L << 3)  /* program specified size */
#define PMinSize   (1L << 4)  /* program specified minimum size */
#define PMaxSize   (1L << 5)  /* program specified maximum size */
#define PResizeInc (1L << 6)  /* program specified resize increments */
#define PAspect    (1L << 7)  /* program specified min/max aspect ratios */
#define PAllHints (PPosition|PSize|PMinSize|PMaxSize|PResizeInc|PAspect)
} XSizeHints;
```

Errors

BadAlloc
BadWindow

Related Commands

XGetClassHint, XSetClassHint, XGetSizeHints, XSetSizeHints, XGet-
WMHints, XSetWMHints, XGetZoomHints, XGetNormalHints, XSetNormal-
Hints, XGetTransientForHint, XSetTransientForHint, XFetchName, XGet-
IconName, XSetIconName, XStoreName, XGetIconSizes, XSetIconSizes,
XSetCommand.

Name

XShrinkRegion — reduce or expand the size of a region.

Synopsis

```
XShrinkRegion(r, dx, dy)
    Region r;
    int dx, dy;
```

Arguments

r   Specifies the region.

dx   Specify the amounts by which you want to shrink or expand the specified

dy   region. Positive values expand the region while negative values shrink the
region.

Description

XShrinkRegion changes the width of the specified region by the ratio:

```
(currentwidth + dx)/currentwidth
```

and the height by the ratio:

```
(currentheight + dy)/currentheight .
```

Counter to the name of the routine and the MIT documentation, the code seems to show that
positive values expand the region; negative values shrink the region. The offset of the region
is changed to keep the center of the resized region near its original position.

Structures

```
/*
 * opaque reference to Regiondata type.
 * user won't need contents, only pointer.
 */
typedef struct _XRegion *Region;
```

Related Commands

XXorRegion, XUnionRegion, XUnionRectWithRegion, XSubtractRegion,
XSetRegion, XRectInRegion, XPolygonRegion, XPointInRegion, XOffset-
Region, XIntersectRegion, XEmptyRegion, XCreateRegion, XDestroy-
Region, XEqualRegion, XClipBox.

Name

XStoreBuffer — store data in a cut buffer.

Synopsis

```
XStoreBuffer(display, bytes, nbytes, buffer)
    Display *display;
    char bytes[];
    int nbytes;
    int buffer;
```

Arguments

display Specifies a pointer to the Display structure; returned from XOpenDisplay.

bytes Specifies the string of bytes you want stored. The byte string is not necessarily ASCII or null-terminated.

nbytes Specifies the number of bytes in the string.

buffer Specifies the cut buffer in which to store the byte string. Must be in the range 0-7.

Description

XStoreBuffer stores the specified data into one of the eight cut buffers. All eight buffers must be stored into before they can be circulated with XRotateBuffers. The cut buffers are numbered 0 through 7. Use XFetchBuffer to recover data from any cut buffer.

Note that selections are the preferred method of transferring data between applications.

For more information on cut buffers, see Volume One, Chapter 13, *Other Programming Techniques*. For more information on selections, see Volume One, Chapter 10, *Interclient Communication*.

Errors

```
BadAlloc
BadAtom
```

Related Commands

XStoreBytes, XFetchBuffer, XFetchBytes, XRotateBuffers.

XStoreBytes

Name

XStoreBytes — store data in cut buffer 0.

Synopsis

```
XStoreBytes(display, bytes, nbytes)
    Display *display;
    char bytes[];
    int nbytes;
```

Arguments

display   Specifies a pointer to the `Display` structure; returned from `XOpenDisplay`.

bytes   Specifies the string of bytes you want stored. The byte string is not necessarily ASCII or null-terminated.

nbytes   Specifies the number of bytes that you want stored.

Description

`XStoreBytes` stores data in cut buffer 0, usually for reading by another client that already knows the meaning of the contents. Note that the cut buffer's contents need not be text, so null bytes are not special.

The cut buffer's contents may be retrieved later by any client calling `XFetchBytes`.

Use `XStoreBuffer` to store data in buffers 1-7. Note that selections are the preferred method of transferring data between applications.

For more information on cut buffers, see Volume One, Chapter 13, *Other Programming Techniques*. For more information on selections, see Volume One, Chapter 10, *Interclient Communication*.

Errors

BadAlloc

Related Commands

XStoreBuffer, XFetchBuffer, XFetchBytes, XRotateBuffers.

XStoreColor

Name

XStoreColor — set or change a read/write entry of a colormap to the closest available hardware color.

Synopsis

```
XStoreColor(display, cmap, colorcell_def)
    Display *display;
    Colormap cmap;
    XColor *colorcell_def;
```

Arguments

display   Specifies a pointer to the `Display` structure; returned from `XOpen-Display`.

cmap   Specifies the colormap.

colorcell_def   Specifies a pixel value and the desired RGB values.

Description

XStoreColor changes the RGB values of a colormap entry specified by *colorcell_def.pixel* to the closest values available on the hardware. This pixel value must be a read/write cell and a valid index into *cmap*. XStoreColor changes the red, green, and/or blue color components in the cell according to the `colorcell_def.flags` member, which you set by ORing the constants `DoRed`, `DoGreen`, and/or `DoBlue`.

If the colormap is an installed map for its screen, the changes are visible immediately.

For more information, see Volume One, Chapter 7, *Color*.

Structures

```
typedef struct {
    unsigned long pixel;
    unsigned short red, green, blue;
    char flags;                        /* DoRed, DoGreen, DoBlue */
    char pad;
} XColor;
```

Errors

BadColor

BadValue   *pixel* not valid index into *cmap*.

Related Commands

XAllocColorCells, XAllocColorPlanes, XAllocColor, XAllocNamedColor, XLookupColor, XParseColor, XQueryColor, XQueryColors, XStoreColors, XFreeColors, XStoreNamedColor, BlackPixel, WhitePixel.

XStoreColors

Name

XStoreColors — set or change read/write colorcells to the closest available hardware colors.

Synopsis

```
XStoreColors(display, cmap, colorcell_defs, ncolors)
    Display *display;
    Colormap cmap;
    XColor colorcell_defs[ncolors];
    int ncolors;
```

Arguments

display   Specifies a pointer to the `Display` structure; returned from `XOpenDisplay`.

cmap   Specifies the colormap.

colorcell_defs
        Specifies an array of color definition structures.

ncolors   Specifies the number of `XColor` structures in *colorcell_defs*.

Description

XStoreColors changes the RGB values of each colormap entry specified by *colorcell_defs[].pixel* to the closest available hardware colors. Each pixel value must be a read/write cell and a valid index into *cmap*. XStoreColors changes the red, green, and/or blue color components in each cell according to the *colorcell_defs[].flags* member, which you set by ORing the constants DoRed, Do-Green, and/or DoBlue. The specified pixels are changed if they are writable by any client, even if one or more pixels generates an error.

If the colormap is an installed map for its screen, the changes are visible immediately. For more information, see Volume One, Chapter 7, *Color*.

Structures

```
typedef struct {
    unsigned long pixel;
    unsigned short red, green, blue;
    char flags;                         /* DoRed, DoGreen, DoBlue */
    char pad;
} XColor;
```

Errors

BadAccess   A specified pixel is unallocated or read-only.

BadColor

BadValue   A specified pixel is not a valid entry into *cmap*.

Related Commands

XAllocColorCells, XAllocColorPlanes, XAllocColor, XAllocNamedColor, XLookupColor, XParseColor, XQueryColor, XQueryColors, XStoreColor, XFreeColors, XStoreNamedColor, BlackPixel, WhitePixel.

Name

XStoreName — assign a name to a window for the window manager.

Synopsis

```
XStoreName (display, w, window_name)
    Display *display;
    Window w;
    char *window_name;
```

Arguments

display   Specifies a pointer to the Display structure; returned from XOpen-
                Display.

w   Specifies the ID of the window to which you want to assign a name.

window_name   Specifies the name of the window. The name should be a null-terminated
                string. This name is returned by any subsequent call to XFetchName.

Description

XStoreName sets the XA_WM_NAME property, which should be used by the application to communicate the following information to the window manager, according to current conventions:

- To permit the user to identify one of a number of instances of the same client.

- To provide the user with noncritical state information.

Clients can assume that at least the beginning of this string is visible to the user.

The XA_WM_CLASS property, on the other hand, has two members which should be used to identify the client in general and each instance in particular. It is used for obtaining resources. See XSetClassHint for details.

For more information, see Volume One, Chapter 10, *Interclient Communication*.

Errors

BadAlloc
BadWindow

Related Commands

XGetClassHint, XSetClassHint, XGetSizeHints, XSetSizeHints, XGet-
WMHints, XSetWMHints, XGetZoomHints, XSetZoomHints, XGetNormalHints,
XSetNormalHints, XGetTransientForHint, XSetTransientForHint, XFetch-
Name, XGetIconName, XSetIconName, XGetIconSizes, XSetIconSizes, XSet-
Command.

XStoreNamedColor

Name

XStoreNamedColor — allocate a read/write colorcell by English color name.

Synopsis

```
XStoreNamedColor(display, cmap, colorname, pixel, flags)
    Display *display;
    Colormap cmap;
    char *colorname;
    unsigned long pixel;
    int flags;
```

Arguments

display   Specifies a pointer to the Display structure; returned from XOpenDisplay.

cmap   Specifies the colormap.

colorname Specifies the color name string (for example, "red"). This cannot be in hex format (as used in XParseColor). Upper or lower case is not important. The string should be in ISO LATIN-1 encoding, which means that the first 128 character codes are ASCII, and the second 128 character codes are for special characters needed in western languages other than English.

pixel   Specifies the entry in the colormap to store color in.

flags   Specifies which red, green, and blue indexes are set.

Description

XStoreNamedColor looks up the named *color* in the database, with respect to the screen associated with *cmap*, then stores the result in the cell of *cmap* specified by *pixel*. Upper or lower case in name does not matter. The *flags* argument, a bitwise OR of the constants DoRed, DoGreen, and DoBlue, determines which subfields within the pixel value in the cell are written.

For more information, see Volume One, Chapter 7, *Color*.

Errors

BadAccess   *pixel* is unallocated or read-only.

BadColor

BadName

BadValue   *pixel* is not a valid index into *cmap*.

Related Commands

XCopyColormapAndFree, XCreateColormap, XFreeColormap, XGetStandard-Colormap, XInstallColormap, XUninstallColormap, XSetStandard-Colormap, XListInstalledColormaps, XSetWindowColormap, Default-Colormap, DisplayCells.

Name

XStringToKeysym — convert a keysym name string to a keysym.

Synopsis

```
KeySym XStringToKeysym(string)
    char *string;
```

Arguments

string   Specifies the name of the keysym that is to be converted.

Description

XStringToKeysym translates the character string version of a keysym name ("Shift") to the matching keysym which is a constant (XK_Shift). Valid keysym names are listed in *<X11/keysymdef.h>*. If the specified string does not match a valid keysym, XString-ToKeysym returns NoSymbol.

This string is not the string returned in the *buffer* argument of XLookupString, which can be set with XRebindKeysym. If that string is used, XStringToKeysym will return NoSymbol except by coincidence.

For more information, see Volume One, Chapter 9, *The Keyboard and Pointer*.

Related Commands

XDeleteModifiermapEntry, XInsertModifiermapEntry, XFreeModifiermap, XKeycodeToKeysym, XKeysymToKeycode, XKeysymToString, XNewModifier-Map, XQueryKeymap, XLookupKeysym, XRebindKeysym, XGetKeyboardMapping, XChangeKeyboardMapping, XRefreshKeyboardMapping, XLookupString, XSetModifierMapping, XGetModifierMapping.

XSubImage

Name

XSubImage — create a subimage from part of an image.

Synopsis

```
XImage *XSubImage(ximage, x, y, subimage_width,
        subimage_height)
    XImage *ximage;
    int x;
    int y;
    unsigned int subimage_width;
    unsigned int subimage_height;
```

Arguments

ximage   Specifies a pointer to the image.

x   Specify the x and y coordinates of the origin of the subimage.
y

subimage_width
subimage_height
            Specify the width and height (in pixels) of the new subimage.

Description

XSubImage creates a new image that is a subsection of an existing one. It allocates the memory necessary for the new XImage structure and returns a pointer to the new image. The data is copied from the source image, and the rectangle defined by x, y, subimage_width, and subimage_height must by contained in the image.

XSubImage extracts a subimage from an image, while XGetSubImage extracts an image from a drawable.

For more information on images, see Volume One, Chapter 6, *Drawing Graphics and Text*.

Related Commands

XDestroyImage, XPutImage, XGetImage, XCreateImage, XGetSubImage, XAddPixel, XPutPixel, XGetPixel, ImageByteOrder.

Name

XSubtractRegion — subtract one region from another.

Synopsis

```
XSubtractRegion(sra, srb, dr)
    Region sra, srb;
    Region dr;                     /* RETURN */
```

Arguments

sra
srb   Specify the two regions in which you want to perform the computation.

dr   Returns the result of the computation.

Description

XSubtractRegion calculates the difference between the two regions specified (sra – srb) and puts the result in dr.

This function returns a region which contains all parts of sra that are not also in srb.

For more information on regions, see Volume One, Chapter 6, *Drawing Graphics and Text*.

Structures

```
/*
 * opaque reference to Regiondata type.
 * user won't need contents, only pointer.
 */
typedef struct _XRegion *Region;
```

Related Commands

XXorRegion, XUnionRegion, XUnionRectWithRegion, XShrinkRegion, XSet-Region, XRectInRegion, XPolygonRegion, XPointInRegion, XOffsetRegion, XIntersectRegion, XEmptyRegion, XCreateRegion, XDestroyRegion, XEqualRegion, XClipBox.

Name

XSync — flush the output buffer and wait for all events and errors to be processed by the server.

Synopsis

```
XSync(display, discard)
    Display *display;
    int discard;
```

Arguments

display   Specifies a pointer to the Display structure; returned from XOpen-Display.

discard   Specifies whether XSync discards all events on the input queue. This argument is either True or False.

Description

XSync flushes the output buffer, then waits until all events and errors resulting from previous calls have been received and processed by the X server. Events (and errors) are placed on the input queue. The client's XError routine is called once for each error received.

If discard is True, XSync discards all events on the input queue (including those events that were on the queue before XSync was called).

XSync is sometimes used with window manipulation functions (by the window manager) to wait for all resulting exposure events. Very few clients need to use this function.

Related Commands

XFlush

Name

XSynchronize — enable or disable synchronization for debugging.

Synopsis

```
int (*XSynchronize(display, onoff))()
    Display *display;
    int onoff;
```

Arguments

display   Specifies a pointer to the Display structure; returned from XOpen-
                 Display.

onoff   Specifies whether to enable or disable synchronization. You can pass 0 (dis-
                 able synchronization) or nonzero (enable synchronization).

Description

XSynchronize turns on or off synchronous mode for debugging. If *onoff* is nonzero, it
turns on synchronous behavior; *0* resets the state to off.

When events are synchronized, they are reported as they occur instead of at some later time,
but server performance is many times slower. This can be useful for debugging complex
event handling routines. Under UNIX, the same result can be achieved without hardcoding by
setting the global variable _Xdebug to True.

If synchronous mode was off before the call, XSynchronize returns NULL.

For more information, see Volume One, Chapter 3, *Basic Window Program.*

Related Commands

XSelectInput, XSetInputFocus, XGetInputFocus, XWindowEvent, XCheck-
WindowEvent, XCheckTypedEvent, XCheckTypedWindowEvent, XMaskEvent,
XCheckMaskEvent, XNextEvent, XEventsQueued, XAllowEvents, XGetMotion-
Events, XIfEvent, XCheckIfEvent, XPeekEvent, XPeekIfEvent, XPutBack-
Event, XPending, XSendEvent, QLength.

Name

XTextExtents — get string and font metrics.

Synopsis

```
XTextExtents(font_struct, string, nchars, direction,
        ascent, descent, overall)
    XFontStruct *font_struct;
    char *string;
    int nchars;
    int *direction;              /* RETURN */
    int *ascent, *descent;       /* RETURN */
    XCharStruct *overall;        /* RETURN */
```

Arguments

font_struct   Specifies a pointer to the XFontStruct structure.

string   Specifies the character string for which metrics are to be returned.

nchars   Specifies the number of characters in the character string.

direction   Returns the value of the direction element of the XFontStruct. Either FontRightToLeft or FontLeftToRight.

ascent   Returns the font ascent element of the XFontStruct. This is the overall maximum ascent for the font.

descent   Returns the font descent element of the XFontStruct. This is the overall maximum descent for the font.

overall   Returns the overall characteristics of the string. These are the sum of the width measurements for each character, the maximum ascent and descent, the minimum lbearing added to the width of all characters up to the character with the smallest lbearing, and the maximum rbearing added to the width of all characters up to the character with the largest rbearing.

Description

XTextExtents returns the dimensions in pixels that specify the bounding box of the specified string of characters in the named font, and the maximum ascent and descent for the entire font. This function performs the size computation locally and, thereby, avoids the roundtrip overhead of XQueryTextExtents, but it requires a filled XFontStruct.

ascent and *descent* return information about the font, while *overall* returns information about the given string. The returned *ascent* and *descent* should usually be used to calculate the line spacing, while the width, rbearing, and lbearing members of *overall* should be used for horizontal measures. The total height of the bounding rectangle, good for any string in this font, is *ascent* + *descent*.

overall.ascent is the maximum of the ascent metrics of all characters in the string. The *overall.descent* is the maximum of the descent metrics. The *overall.width* is the sum of the character-width metrics of all characters in the string. The *overall.lbearing* is the lbearing of the character in the string with the smallest lbearing plus the width of all the characters up to but not including that character. The *overall.rbearing* is the rbearing of the character in the string with the largest rbearing plus the width of all the characters up to but not including that character.

For more information on drawing text, see Volume One, Chapter 6, *Drawing Graphics and Text*.

Structures

```
typedef struct {
    XExtData *ext_data;        /* hook for extension to hang data */
    Font fid;                  /* font ID for this font */
    unsigned direction;        /* hint about direction the font is painted */
    unsigned min_char_or_byte2;/* first character */
    unsigned max_char_or_byte2;/* last character */
    unsigned min_byte1;        /* first row that exists */
    unsigned max_byte1;        /* last row that exists */
    Bool all_chars_exist;      /* flag if all characters have nonzero size*/
    unsigned default_char;     /* char to print for undefined character */
    int n_properties;          /* how many properties there are */
    XFontProp *properties;     /* pointer to array of additional properties*/
    XCharStruct min_bounds;    /* minimum bounds over all existing char*/
    XCharStruct max_bounds;    /* minimum bounds over all existing char*/
    XCharStruct *per_char;     /* first_char to last_char information */
    int ascent;                /* logical extent above baseline for spacing */
    int descent;               /* logical descent below baseline for spacing */
} XFontStruct;

typedef struct {
    short lbearing;            /* origin to left edge of character */
    short rbearing;            /* origin to right edge of character */
    short width;               /* advance to next char's origin */
    short ascent;              /* baseline to top edge of character */
    short descent;             /* baseline to bottom edge of character */
    unsigned short attributes; /* per char flags (not predefined) */
} XCharStruct;
```

Related Commands

XQueryTextExtents, XQueryTextExtents16, XDrawImageString, XDraw-ImageString16, XDrawString, XDrawString16, XDrawText, XDrawText16, XTextExtents16, XTextWidth, XTextWidth16.

XTextExtents16

Name

XTextExtents16 — get string and font metrics of a 16-bit character string.

Synopsis

```
XTextExtents16(font_struct, string, nchars, direction,
        ascent, descent, overall)
    XFontStruct *font_struct;
    XChar2b *string;
    int nchars;
    int *direction;            /* RETURN */
    int *ascent, *descent;     /* RETURN */
    XCharStruct *overall;      /* RETURN */
```

Arguments

font_struct   Specifies a pointer to the XFontStruct structure.

string   Specifies the character string made up of XChar26 structures.

nchars   Specifies the number of characters in the character string.

direction   Returns the value of the direction element of the XFontStruct. Font-RightToLeft of FontLeftToRight.

ascent   Returns the font ascent element of the XFontStruct. This is the overall maximum ascent for the font.

descent   Returns the font descent element of the XFontStruct. This is the overall maximum descent for the font.

overall   Returns the overall characteristics of the string. These are the sum of the width measurements for each character, the maximum ascent and descent, the minimum lbearing added to the width of all characters up to the character with the smallest lbearing, and the maximum rbearing added to the width of all characters up to the character with the largest rbearing.

Description

XTextExtents16 returns the dimensions in pixels that specify the bounding box of the specified string of characters in the named font, and the maximum ascent and descent for the entire font. This function performs the size computation locally and, thereby, avoids the roundtrip overhead of XQueryTextExtents16, but it requires a filled XFontStruct.

ascent and descent return information about the font, while overall returns information about the given string. The returned ascent and descent should usually be used to calculate the line spacing, while the width, rbearing, and lbearing members of overall should be used for horizontal measures. The total height of the bounding rectangle, good for any string in this font, is ascent + descent.

overall.ascent is the maximum of the ascent metrics of all characters in the string. The overall.descent is the maximum of the descent metrics. The overall.width is the sum of the character-width metrics of all characters in the string. The overall.lbearing is the lbearing of the character in the string with the smallest lbearing plus the width of all the characters up to but not including that character. The *overall.rbearing* is the rbearing of the character in the string with the largest rbearing plus the width of all the characters up to but not including that character.

For more information on drawing text, see Volume One, Chapter 6, *Drawing Graphics and Text*.

Structures

```
typedef struct {
    short lbearing;                /* origin to left edge of character */
    short rbearing;                /* origin to right edge of character */
    short width;                   /* advance to next char's origin */
    short ascent;                  /* baseline to top edge of character */
    short descent;                 /* baseline to bottom edge of character */
    unsigned short attributes;     /* per char flags (not predefined) */
} XCharStruct;

typedef struct {
    XExtData *ext_data;            /* hook for extension to hang data */
    Font fid;                      /* font ID for this font */
    unsigned direction;            /* hint about direction the font is painted */
    unsigned min_char_or_byte2;    /* first character */
    unsigned max_char_or_byte2;    /* last character */
    unsigned min_byte1;            /* first row that exists */
    unsigned max_byte1;            /* last row that exists */
    Bool all_chars_exist;          /* flag if all characters have nonzero size*/
    unsigned default_char;         /* char to print for undefined character */
    int n_properties;              /* how many properties there are */
    XFontProp *properties;         /* pointer to array of additional properties*/
    XCharStruct min_bounds;        /* minimum bounds over all existing char*/
    XCharStruct max_bounds;        /* minimum bounds over all existing char*/
    XCharStruct *per_char;         /* first_char to last_char information */
    int ascent;                    /* logical extent above baseline for spacing */
    int descent;                   /* logical descent below baseline for spacing */
} XFontStruct;

typedef struct {                   /* normal 16 bit characters are two bytes */
    unsigned char byte1;
    unsigned char byte2;
} XChar2b;
```

Related Commands

XQueryTextExtents, XQueryTextExtents16, XDrawImageString, XDraw-
ImageString16, XDrawString, XDrawString16, XDrawText, XDrawText16,
XTextExtents, XTextWidth, XTextWidth16.

XTextWidth

Name

XTextWidth — get the width in pixels of an 8-bit character string.

Synopsis

```
int XTextWidth(font_struct, string, count)
    XFontStruct *font_struct;
    char *string;
    int count;
```

Arguments

font_struct   Specifies the font description structure of the font in which you want to draw the string.

string   Specifies the character string whose width is to be returned.

count   Specifies the character count in string.

Description

XTextWidth returns the width in pixels of the specified string using the specified font. This is the sum of the XCharStruct.width for each character in the string. This is also equivalent to the value of overall.width returned by XQueryTextExtents or XText-Extents. The characters in string are 8-bit characters.

For more information on drawing text, see Volume One, Chapter 6, *Drawing Graphics and Text*.

Structures

```
typedef struct {
    XExtData *ext_data;          /* hook for extension to hang data */
    Font fid;                    /* font ID for this font */
    unsigned direction;          /* hint about direction the font is painted */
    unsigned min_char_or_byte2;  /* first character */
    unsigned max_char_or_byte2;  /* last character */
    unsigned min_byte1;          /* first row that exists */
    unsigned max_byte1;          /* last row that exists */
    Bool all_chars_exist;        /* flag if all characters have nonzero size*/
    unsigned default_char;       /* char to print for undefined character */
    int n_properties;            /* how many properties there are */
    XFontProp *properties;       /* pointer to array of additional properties*/
    XCharStruct min_bounds;      /* minimum bounds over all existing char*/
    XCharStruct max_bounds;      /* minimum bounds over all existing char*/
    XCharStruct *per_char;       /* first_char to last_char information */
    int ascent;                  /* logical extent above baseline for spacing */
    int descent;                 /* logical descent below baseline for spacing */
} XFontStruct;
```

Related Commands

XQueryTextExtents, XQueryTextExtents16, XDrawImageString, XDraw-ImageString16, XDrawString, XDrawString16, XDrawText, XDrawText16, XTextExtents, XTextExtents16, XTextWidth16.

XTextWidth16

Name

XTextWidth16 — get the width in pixels of a 16-bit character string.

Synopsis

```
int XTextWidth16(font_struct, string, count)
    XFontStruct *font_struct;
    XChar2b *string;
    int count;
```

Arguments

font_struct   Specifies the font description structure of the font in which you want to draw
               the string.

string   Specifies a character string made up of XChar2b structures.

count   Specifies the character count in string.

Description

XTextWidth16 returns the width in pixels of the specified string using the specified font.
This is the sum of the XCharStruct.width for each character in the string. This is also
equivalent to the value of overall.width returned by XQueryTextExtents16 or
XTextExtents16.

The characters in string are 16-bit characters.

For more information on drawing text, see Volume One, Chapter 6, *Drawing Graphics and
Text*.

Structures

```
typedef struct {
    XExtData *ext_data;          /* hook for extension to hang data */
    Font fid;                    /* font ID for this font */
    unsigned direction;          /* hint about direction the font is painted */
    unsigned min_char_or_byte2;  /* first character */
    unsigned max_char_or_byte2;  /* last character */
    unsigned min_byte1;          /* first row that exists */
    unsigned max_byte1;          /* last row that exists */
    Bool all_chars_exist;        /* flag if all characters have nonzero size*/
    unsigned default_char;       /* char to print for undefined character */
    int n_properties;            /* how many properties there are */
    XFontProp *properties;       /* pointer to array of additional properties*/
    XCharStruct min_bounds;      /* minimum bounds over all existing char*/
    XCharStruct max_bounds;      /* minimum bounds over all existing char*/
    XCharStruct *per_char;       /* first_char to last_char information */
    int ascent;                  /* logical extent above baseline for spacing */
    int descent;                 /* logical descent below baseline for spacing */
} XFontStruct;
```

Related Commands

XQueryTextExtents, XQueryTextExtents16, XDrawImageString, XDraw-
ImageString16, XDrawString, XDrawString16, XDrawText, XDrawText16,
XTextExtents, XTextExtents16, XTextWidth.

XTranslateCoordinates

Name

XTranslateCoordinates — change the coordinate system from one window to another.

Synopsis

```
Bool XTranslateCoordinates (display, src_w, dest_w, src_x,
        src_y, dest_x, dest_y, child)
    Display *display;
    Window src_w, dest_w;
    int src_x, src_y;
    int *dest_x, *dest_y;        /* RETURN */
    Window *child;               /* RETURN */
```

Arguments

display   Specifies a pointer to the Display structure; returned from XOpenDisplay.

src_w   Specifies the ID of the source window.

dest_w   Specifies the ID of the destination window.

src_x
src_y   Specify the x and y coordinates within the source window.

dest_x
dest_y   Return the translated x and y coordinates within the destination window.

child   If the point is contained in a mapped child of the destination window, then that child ID is returned in *child*.

Description

XTranslateCoordinates translates coordinates from the frame of reference of one window to another. This should be avoided in most applications since it requires a roundtrip request to the server. Most applications benefit from the window-based coordinate system anyway and don't need global coordinates.

XTranslateCoordinates returns False and *dest_x* and *dest_y* are set to 0 if *src_w* and *dest_w* are on different screens. In addition, if the coordinates are contained in a mapped child of *dest_w*, then that child is returned in the *child* argument. Otherwise, XTranslateCoordinates returns True, sets *dest_x* and *dest_y* to the location of the point relative to *dest_w*, and sets *child* to None.

Window managers often need to perform a coordinate transformation from the coordinate space of one window to another, or unambiguously determine which subwindow a coordinate lies in. XTranslateCoordinates fulfills this need, while avoiding any race conditions by asking the server to perform this operation.

Errors

BadWindow

Related Commands

XGeometry, XParseGeometry.

XUndefineCursor

Name

XUndefineCursor — disassociate a cursor from a window.

Synopsis

```
XUndefineCursor(display, w)
    Display *display;
    Window w;
```

Arguments

display Specifies a pointer to the Display structure; returned from XOpen-Display.

w Specifies the ID of the window whose cursor is to be undefined.

Description

XUndefineCursor sets the cursor for a window to its parent's cursor, undoing the effect of a previous XDefineCursor for this window. On the root window, with no cursor specified, the default cursor is restored.

Errors

BadWindow

Related Commands

XDefineCursor, XCreateFontCursor, XCreateGlyphCursor, XCreatePixmap-Cursor, XFreeCursor, XRecolorCursor, XQueryBestCursor, XQueryBest-Size.

Name

XUngrabButton — release a button from grab.

Synopsis

```
XUngrabButton(display, button, modifiers, w)
    Display *display;
    unsigned int button;
    unsigned int modifiers;
    Window w;
```

Arguments

display   Specifies a pointer to the Display structure; returned from XOpen-Display.

button   Specifies the mouse button to be released from grab. Specify Button1, Button2, Button3, Button4, Button5, or the constant AnyButton, which is equivalent to issuing the ungrab request for all possible buttons.

modifiers   Specifies a set of keymasks. This is a bitwise OR of one or more of the following symbols: ShiftMask, LockMask, ControlMask, Mod1Mask, Mod2Mask, Mod3Mask, Mod4Mask, Mod5Mask, or AnyModifier. AnyModifier is equivalent to issuing the ungrab button request for all possible modifier combinations (including no modifiers).

w   Specifies the ID of the window you want to release the button grab.

Description

XUngrabButton cancels the passive grab on a button/key combination on the specified window if it was grabbed by this client. A *modifiers* of AnyModifier is equivalent to issuing the ungrab request for all possible modifier combinations (including the combination of no modifiers). A *button* of AnyButton is equivalent to issuing the request for all possible buttons. This call has no effect on an active grab.

For more information, see Volume One, Chapter 9, *The Keyboard and Pointer*.

Errors

BadWindow

Related Commands

XGrabKey, XUngrabKey, XGrabKeyboard, XUngrabKeyboard, XGrabButton, XGrabPointer, XUngrabPointer, XChangeActivePointerGrab, XGrabServer, XUngrabServer.

Name

XUngrabKey — release a key from grab.

Synopsis

```
XUngrabKey(display, keycode, modifiers, w)
    Display *display;
    int keycode;
    unsigned int modifiers;
    Window w;
```

Arguments

display   Specifies a pointer to the Display structure; returned from XOpen-
             Display.

keycode   Specifies the keycode. This keycode maps to the specific key you want to
             ungrab. Pass either a keycode or AnyKey.

modifiers   Specifies a set of keymasks. This is a bitwise OR of one or more of the fol-
             lowing symbols: ShiftMask, LockMask, ControlMask, Mod1Mask,
             Mod2Mask, Mod3Mask, Mod4Mask, Mod5Mask, or AnyModifier.
             AnyModifier is equivalent to issuing the ungrab key request for all possi-
             ble modifier combinations (including no modifiers).

w   Specifies the ID of the window for which you want to ungrab the specified
             keys.

Description

XUngrabKey cancels the passive grab on the key combination on the specified window if it
was grabbed by this client. A *modifiers* of AnyModifier is equivalent to issuing the
request for all possible modifier combinations (including the combination of no modifiers). A
keycode of AnyKey is equivalent to issuing the request for all possible nonmodifier key
codes. This call has no effect on an active grab.

For more information, see Volume One, Chapter 9, *The Keyboard and Pointer*.

Errors

BadWindow

Related Commands

XGrabKey, XGrabKeyboard, XUngrabKeyboard, XGrabButton, XUngrabButton,
XGrabPointer, XUngrabPointer, XChangeActivePointerGrab, XGrabServer,
XUngrabServer.

XUngrabKeyboard

Name

XUngrabKeyboard — release the keyboard from grab.

Synopsis

```
XUngrabKeyboard(display, time)
    Display *display;
    Time time;
```

Arguments

display Specifies a pointer to the Display structure; returned from XOpen-Display.

time Specifies the time. Pass either a timestamp, expressed in milliseconds, or the constant CurrentTime. If this time is earlier than the last-keyboard-grab time or later than the current server time, the keyboard will not be ungrabbed.

Description

XUngrabKeyboard releases any active grab on the keyboard by this client. It executes as follows:

- Releases the keyboard and any queued events if this client has it actively grabbed from either XGrabKeyboard or XGrabKey.

- Does not release the keyboard and any queued events if *time* is earlier than the last-keyboard-grab time or is later than the current X server time.

- Generates FocusIn and FocusOut events.

The X server automatically performs an UngrabKeyboard if the event_window that initiated an active keyboard grab becomes unviewable.

For more information, see Volume One, Chapter 9, *The Keyboard and Pointer*.

Related Commands

XGrabKey, XUngrabKey, XGrabKeyboard, XGrabButton, XUngrabButton, XGrabPointer, XUngrabPointer, XChangeActivePointerGrab, XGrabServer, XUngrabServer.

Name

XUngrabPointer — release the pointer from grab.

Synopsis

```
XUngrabPointer(display, time)
    Display *display;
    Time time;
```

Arguments

display   Specifies a pointer to the Display structure; returned from XOpen-Display.

time   Specifies the time when the grab should take place. Pass either a timestamp, expressed in milliseconds, or the constant CurrentTime. If this time is earlier than the last-pointer-grab time or later than current server time, the pointer will not be grabbed.

Description

XUngrabPointer releases an active grab on the pointer by the calling client. It executes as follows:

- Releases the pointer and any queued events, if this client has actively grabbed the pointer from XGrabPointer, XGrabButton, or from a normal button press.

- Does not release the pointer if the specified time is earlier than the last-pointer-grab time or is later than the current X server time.

- Generates EnterNotify and LeaveNotify events.

The X server performs an XUngrabPointer automatically if the event_window or confine_to window for an active pointer grab becomes not viewable.

For more information, see Volume One, Chapter 9, *The Keyboard and Pointer.*

Related Commands

XQueryPointer, XWarpPointer, XGrabPointer, XChangeActivePointerGrab, XGetPointerMapping, XSetPointerMapping, XGetPointerControl, XChange-PointerControl.

XUngrabServer

Name

XUngrabServer — release the server from grab.

Synopsis

```
XUngrabServer (display)
    Display *display;
```

Arguments

display   Specifies a pointer to the Display structure; returned from XOpen-
               Display.

Description

XUngrabServer releases the grabbed server, and begins execution of all the graphics
requests queued during the grab. XUngrabServer is called automatically when a client
closes its connection.

For more information, see Volume One, Chapter 9, *The Keyboard and Pointer*.

Related Commands

XGrabKey, XUngrabKey, XGrabKeyboard, XUngrabKeyboard, XGrabButton,
XUngrabButton, XGrabPointer, XUngrabPointer, XChangeActivePointer-
Grab, XGrabServer.

Name

XUninstallColormap — uninstall a colormap; install default if not already installed.

Synopsis

```
XUninstallColormap(display, cmap)
    Display *display;
    Colormap cmap;
```

Arguments

display   Specifies a pointer to the Display structure; returned from XOpen-
            Display.

cmap   Specifies the colormap to be uninstalled.

Description

If cmap is an installed map for its screen, it is uninstalled. If the screen's default colormap is not installed, it is installed.

If cmap is an installed map, a ColormapNotify event is generated on every window having this colormap as an attribute. If a colormap is installed as a result of the uninstall, a ColormapNotify event is generated on every window having that colormap as an attribute.

At any time, there is a subset of the installed colormaps, viewed as an ordered list, called the *required list*. The length of the required list is at most the min_maps specified for each screen in the Display structure. When a colormap is installed with XInstallColormap it is added to the head of the required list and the last colormap in the list is removed if necessary to keep the length of the list at min_maps. When a colormap is uninstalled with XUninstallColormap and it is in the required list, it is removed from the list. No other actions by the server or the client change the required list. It is important to realize that on all but high-performance workstations, min_maps is likely to be 1.

For more information on installing and uninstalling colormaps, see Volume One, Chapter 7, *Color*.

Related Commands

XCopyColormapAndFree, XCreateColormap, XFreeColormap, XGetStandard-Colormap, XInstallColormap, XSetStandardColormap, XListInstalled-Colormaps, XSetWindowColormap, DefaultColormap, DisplayCells.

Name

XUnionRectWithRegion — add a rectangle to a region.

Synopsis

```
XUnionRectWithRegion(rectangle, src_region, dest_region)
    XRectangle *rectangle;
    Region src_region;
    Region dest_region;
```

Arguments

rectangle   Specifies the rectangle to add to the region.

src_region   Specifies the source region to be used.

dest_region Specifies the resulting region. May be the same as *src_region*.

Description

XUnionRectWithRegion computes the destination region from a union of the specified rectangle and the specified source region. The source and destination regions may be the same.

One common application of this function is to simplify the combining of the rectangles specified in Expose events into a clip_mask in the GC, thus restricting the redrawn areas to the exposed rectangles. Use XUnionRectWithRegion to combine the rectangle in each Expose event into a region, then call XSetRegion. XSetRegion sets the clip_mask in a GC to the region. In this case, *src_region* and *dest_region* would be the same region.

If *src_region* and *dest_region* are not the same region, *src_region* is copied to *dest_region* before the rectangle is added to *dest_region*.

For more information on regions, see Volume One, Chapter 6, *Drawing Graphics and Text.*

Structures

```
typedef struct {
    short x, y;
    unsigned short width, height;
} XRectangle;
```

The Region type is a pointer to an opaque data type. Its definition is not needed by programs.

Related Commands

XClipBox, XDestroyRegion, XEmptyRegion, XEqualRegion, XIntersect-
Region, XOffsetRegion, XPointInRegion, XPolygonRegion, XRectInRegion,
XSetRegion, XShrinkRegion, XSubtractRegion, XUnionRegion, XXorRegion.

XUnionRegion

Name

XUnionRegion — compute the union of two regions.

Synopsis

```
XUnionRegion(sra, srb, dr)
    Region sra, srb;
    Region dr;
```

Arguments

sra   Specify the two regions in which you want to perform the computation.
srb

dr   Returns the result of the computation.

Description

XUnionRegion computes the union of two regions and places the result in dr. The resulting region will contain all the area of both the source regions.

For more information on regions, see Volume One, Chapter 6, *Drawing Graphics and Text*.

Structures

```
/*
 * opaque reference to Regiondata type.
 * user won't need contents, only pointer.
 */
typedef struct _XRegion *Region;
```

Related Commands

XXorRegion, XUnionRectWithRegion, XSubtractRegion, XShrinkRegion, XSetRegion, XRectInRegion, XPolygonRegion, XPointInRegion, XOffset-Region, XIntersectRegion, XEmptyRegion, XCreateRegion, XDestroy-Region, XEqualRegion, XClipBox.

Name

XUniqueContext — create a new context ID (not graphics context).

Synopsis

```
XContext XUniqueContext()
```

Description

The context manager allows association of arbitrary data with a resource ID. This call creates an instance of the XContext structure with a unique resource ID that will be used in subsequent calls to XFindContext, XDeleteContext, and XSaveContext.

For more information on the context manager, see Volume One, Chapter 13, *Other Programming Techniques*.

Structures

```
typedef int XContext;
```

Related Commands

XDeleteContext, XFindContext, XSaveContext.

Name

XUnloadFont — unload a font.

Synopsis

```
XUnloadFont(display, font)
    Display *display;
    Font font;
```

Arguments

display　　　　Specifies a pointer to the Display structure; returned from XOpen-
　　　　　　　Display.

font　　　　　Specifies the ID of the font to be unloaded.

Description

XUnloadFont indicates to the server that this client no longer needs the specified font. The font may be unloaded on the X server if this is the last client that needs the font. In any case, the font should never again be referenced by this client because X destroys the resource ID.

For more information on loading and unloading fonts, see Volume One, Chapter 6, *Drawing Graphics and Text*.

Errors

BadFont

Related Commands

XLoadFont, XLoadQueryFont, XFreeFont, XFreeFontInfo, XListFonts, XListFontsWithInfo, XFreeFontNames, XFreeFontPath, XGetFontPath, XQueryFont, XSetFont, XSetFontPath, XGetFontProperty, XCreateFont-Cursor.

Name

XUnmapSubwindows — unmap all subwindows of a given window.

Synopsis

```
XUnmapSubwindows(display, w)
    Display *display;
    Window w;
```

Arguments

display   Specifies a pointer to the Display structure; returned from XOpen-
              Display.

w   Specifies the ID of the window whose subwindows are to be unmapped.

Description

XUnmapSubwindows performs an XUnmapWindow on all mapped children of w, in bottom
to top stacking order.

XUnmapSubwindows also generates an UnmapNotify event on each subwindow and generates exposure events on formerly obscured windows. This is much more efficient than
unmapping many subwindows one at a time, since much of the work need only be performed
once for all of the subwindows rather than for each subwindow.

For more information on window mapping, see Volume One, Chapter 2, *X Concepts*.

Errors

BadWindow

Related Commands

XMapRaised, XMapSubwindows, XMapWindow, XUnmapWindow.

XUnmapWindow

Name

XUnmapWindow — unmap a window.

Synopsis

```
XUnmapWindow(display, w)
    Display *display;
    Window w;
```

Arguments

display   Specifies a pointer to the Display structure; returned from XOpen-
              Display.

w   Specifies the window ID.

Description

XUnmapWindow removes *w* and all its descendants from the screen. If *w* is already
unmapped, XUnmapWindow has no effect. Otherwise, *w* is unmapped and an Unmap-
Notify event is generated. Normal exposure processing on formerly obscured windows is
performed.

Descendants of *w* will not be visible until *w* is mapped again. In other words, the subwindows
are still mapped, but are not visible because *w* is unmapped. Unmapping a *w* will generate
exposure events on windows that were formerly obscured by *w* and its children.

For more information on window mapping, see Volume One, Chapter 2, *X Concepts*.

Errors

BadWindow

Related Commands

XMapRaised, XMapSubwindows, XMapWindow, XUnmapSubwindows.

Name

XWarpPointer — move the pointer to another point on the screen.

Synopsis

```
XWarpPointer(display, src_w, dest_w, src_x, src_y,
        src_width, src_height, dest_x, dest_y)
    Display *display;
    Window src_w, dest_w;
    int src_x, src_y;
    unsigned int src_width, src_height;
    int dest_x, dest_y;
```

Arguments

display   Specifies a pointer to the Display structure; returned from XOpen-Display.

src_w   Specifies the ID of the source window. You can also pass None.

dest_w   Specifies the ID of the destination window. You can also pass None.

src_x
src_y   Specify the x and y coordinates within the source window. These are used with *src_width* and *src_height* to determine the rectangle the pointer must be in. They are not the present pointer position. If *src_y* is None, these coordinates are relative to the root window of *src_w*.

src_width
src_height   Specify the width and height in pixels of the source window. Used with *src_x* and *src_y*.

dest_x
dest_y   Specify the destination x and y coordinates within the destination window. If *dest_y* is None, these coordinates are relative to the root window of *dest_w*.

Description

XWarpPointer moves the pointer suddenly from one point on the screen to another.

If *dest_w* is a window, XWarpPointer moves the pointer to [*dest_x*, *dest_y*] relative to the destination window's origin. If *dest_w* is None, XWarpPointer moves the pointer according to the offsets [*dest_x*, *dest_y*] relative to the current position of the pointer.

If *src_window* is None, the move is independent of the current cursor position (*dest_x* and *dest_y* use global coordinates). If the source window is not None, the move only takes place if the pointer is currently contained in a visible portion of the rectangle of the source window (including its inferiors) specified by *src_x*, *src_y*, *src_width* and *src_height*. If *src_width* is zero (0), the pointer must be between *src_x* and the right edge of the window to be moved. If *src_height* is zero (0), the pointer must be between *src_y* and the bottom edge of the window to be moved.

XWarpPointer cannot be used to move the pointer outside the confine_to window of an active pointer grab. If this is attempted the pointer will be moved to the point on the border of the confine_to window nearest the requested destination.

XWarpPointer generates events as if the user had (instantaneously) moved the pointer.

This function should not be used unless absolutely necessary, and then only in tightly controlled, predictable situations. It has the potential to confuse the user.

Errors
BadWindow

Related Commands
XQueryPointer, XGrabPointer, XChangeActivePointerGrab, XUngrab-
Pointer, XGetPointerMapping, XSetPointerMapping, XGetPointerControl,
XChangePointerControl.

XWindowEvent

Name

XWindowEvent — remove the next event matching mask and window.

Synopsis

```
XWindowEvent (display, w, event_mask, rep)
    Display *display;
    Window w;
    long event_mask;
    XEvent *rep;                    /* RETURN */
```

Arguments

display   Specifies a pointer to the Display structure; returned from XOpen-Display.

w   Specifies the ID of the window whose next matched event you want to remove.

event_mask   Specifies the event mask. See XSelectInput for a complete list of event masks.

rep   Specifies the event removed from the input queue. XWindowEvent returns this event to this argument.

Description

XWindowEvent searches the event queue for specific event types from the specified window. XWindowEvent removes the next event in the queue which matches both the passed window and the passed mask. The event is copied into an XEvent supplied by the caller. Other events in the queue are not discarded. If no such event has been queued, XWindowEvent flushes the output buffer and waits until one is received.

In Release 1, the output buffer was always flushed by event-getting routines. In Release 2, the output buffer is flushed only if no matching events are found on the queue. This change is compatible with applications written for Release 1.

Structures

See individual event structures described in Volume One, Chapter 8, *Events*, and Appendix F, *Structure Reference* in this volume.

Related Commands

XSelectInput, XSetInputFocus, XGetInputFocus, XCheckWindowEvent, XCheckTypedEvent, XCheckTypedWindowEvent, XMaskEvent, XCheckMask-Event, XNextEvent, XEventsQueued, XAllowEvents, XGetMotionEvents, XIfEvent, XCheckIfEvent, XPeekEvent, XPeekIfEvent, XPutBackEvent, XPending, XSynchronize, XSendEvent, QLength.

Name

XWriteBitmapFile — write a bitmap to a file.

Synopsis

```
int XWriteBitmapFile(display, filename, bitmap, width,
        height, x_hot, y_hot)
    Display *display;
    char *filename;
    Pixmap bitmap;
    unsigned int width, height;
    int x_hot, y_hot;
```

Arguments

display   Specifies a pointer to the Display structure; returned from XOpen-
              Display.

filename   Specifies the filename to use. The format of the filename is operating system
              specific.

bitmap   Specifies the bitmap to be written.

width   Specify the width and height in pixels of the bitmap to be written.
height

x_hot   Specify where to place the hotspot coordinates (or –1,–1 if none present) in
y_hot   the file.

Description

XWriteBitmapFile writes a bitmap to a file. The file is written out in X version 11 bitmap format, which is the format created by the X version 11 *bitmap* program. Refer to that
program's reference pages for details. While XReadBitmapFile can read in either X Version 10 format or X Version 11 format, XWriteBitmapFile always writes out X Version
11 format only. The difference between these formats is slight.

If the file cannot be opened for writing, XWriteBitmapFile returns BitmapOpen-
Failed. If insufficient memory is allocated XWriteBitmapFile returns Bitmap-
NoMemory. Otherwise, on no error, XWriteBitmapFile returns BitmapSuccess.

If x_hot and y_hot are not –1, –1, then XWriteBitmapFile writes them out as the
hotspot coordinates for the bitmap.

The following is an example of the contents of a bitmap file created. The name used ("gray"
in this example) is the portion of filename after the last "/".

```
#define gray_width 16
#define gray_height 16
#define gray_x_hot 8
#define gray_y_hot 8
static char gray_bits[] = {
    0xf8, 0x1f, 0xe3, 0xc7, 0xcf, 0xf3, 0x9f, 0xf9, 0xbf, 0xfd, 0x33, 0xcc,
    0x7f, 0xfe, 0x7f, 0xfe, 0x7e, 0x7e, 0x7f, 0xfe, 0x37, 0xec, 0xbb, 0xdd,
    0x9c, 0x39, 0xcf, 0xf3, 0xe3, 0xc7, 0xf8, 0x1f};
```

For more information on bitmaps, see Volume One, Chapter 6, *Drawing Graphics and Text*.

Errors

```
BadDrawable
BadMatch
```

Related Commands

XSetTile, XQueryBestTile, XSetWindowBorderPixmap, XSetWindow-
BackgroundPixmap, XCreatePixmap, XCreatePixmapFromBitmapData, XFree-
Pixmap, XQueryBestSize, XQueryBestStipple, XReadBitmapFile, XCreate-
BitmapFromData.

Name

XXorRegion — calculate the difference between the union and intersection of two
regions.

Synopsis

```
XXorRegion(sra, srb, dr)
    Region sra, srb;
    Region dr;                       /* RETURN */
```

Arguments

sra   Specify the two regions on which you want to perform the computation.
srb

dr   Returns the result of the computation.

Description

XXorRegion calculates the union minus the intersection of two regions, and places it in *dr*.
Xor is short for "Exclusive OR", meaning that a pixel is included in *dr* if it is set in either
sra or *srb* but not in both.

For more information on regions, see Volume One, Chapter 6, *Drawing Graphics and Text*.

Structures

```
/*
 * opaque reference to Regiondata type.
 * user won't need contents, only pointer.
 */
typedef struct _XRegion *Region;
```

Related Commands

XUnionRegion, XUnionRectWithRegion, XSubtractRegion, XShrinkRegion,
XSetRegion, XRectInRegion, XPolygonRegion, XPointInRegion, XOffset-
Region, XIntersectRegion, XEmptyRegion, XCreateRegion, XDestroy-
Region, XEqualRegion, XClipBox.

A
Function Group Summary

This quick reference is intended to help you find and use the right function for a particular task. It supplies two lists:

- Listing of Functions by Groups

- Alphabetical Listing of Functions

Both functions and macros are listed in all the groups in which they belong. Therefore, several of them are listed more than once.

Remember that Xlib functions begin with the letter "X"; macros do not.

Group Listing with Brief Descriptions

Association Tables

XCreateAssocTable	Create a new association table (X10).
XDeleteAssoc	Delete an entry from an association table.
XDestroyAssocTable	Free the memory allocated for an association table.
XLookUpAssoc	Obtain data from an association table.
XMakeAssoc	Create an entry in an association table.

Buffers

XStoreBuffer	Store data in a cut buffer.
XStoreBytes	Store data in cut buffer 0.
XFetchBuffer	Return data from a cut buffer.
XFetchBytes	Return data from cut buffer 0.
XRotateBuffers	Rotate the cut buffers.

Client Connections

XKillClient	Destroy a client or its remaining resources.
XSetCloseDownMode	Change the close down mode of a client.

Colorcells

XAllocColor	Allocate a read-only colormap cell with closest hardware-supported color.
XAllocColorCells	Allocate read/write (nonshared) colorcells.
XAllocColorPlanes	Allocate read/write (nonshareable) color planes.
XAllocNamedColor	Allocate a read-only colorcell from color name.
XLookupColor	Get database RGB values and closest hardware-supported RGB values from color name.
XParseColor	Look up or translate RGB values from color name or hexadecimal value.
XQueryColor	Obtain the RGB values for a specified pixel value.
XQueryColors	Obtain RGB values and flags for each specified pixel value.
XStoreColor	Set or change a read/write entry of a colormap to the closest available hardware color.
XStoreColors	Set or change read/write colorcells to the closest available hardware colors.
XStoreNamedColor	Allocate a read/write colorcell by English color name.
XFreeColors	Free colormap cells or planes.
BlackPixel	Return a black pixel value on the default colormap of screen.
WhitePixel	Return a pixel value representing white in default colormap.

Colormaps

XCopyColormapAndFree	Copy a colormap and return a new colormap ID.
XCreateColormap	Create a colormap.
XFreeColormap	Delete a colormap and install the default colormap.
XGetStandardColormap	Get the standard colormap property.
XSetStandardColormap	Change the standard colormap property.
XSetWindowColormap	Set the colormap for a specified window.
XInstallColormap	Install a colormap.
XUninstallColormap	Uninstall a colormap; install default if not already installed.
XListInstalledColormaps	Get a list of installed colormaps.
DefaultColormap	Return the default colormap on the default screen.
DefaultColormapOfScreen	Return the default colormap on the specified screen.
DisplayCells	Return the maximum number of colormap cells on the connected display.

Context Manager

XDeleteContext	Delete a context entry for a given window and type.
XFindContext	Get data from the context manager (not graphics context).

Context Manager (continued)

| XSaveContext | Save a data value corresponding to a window and context type (not graphics context). |
| XUniqueContext | Create a new context ID (not graphics context). |

Cursors

XDefineCursor	Assign a cursor to a window.
XUndefineCursor	Disassociate a cursor from a window.
XCreateFontCursor	Create a cursor from the standard cursor font.
XCreateGlyphCursor	Create a cursor from font glyphs.
XCreatePixmapCursor	Create a cursor from two bitmaps.
XFreeCursor	Destroy a cursor.
XRecolorCursor	Change the color of a cursor.
XQueryBestCursor	Get the closest supported cursor sizes.
XQueryBestSize	Obtain the "best" supported cursor, tile, or stipple size.

Display Specifications

DefaultColormap	Return the default colormap on the specified screen.
DefaultDepth	Return the depth of the default root window for a screen.
DefaultGC	Return the default graphics context for the root window of a screen.
DefaultScreen	Return the screen integer; the last segment of a string passed to XOpenDisplay, or the DISPLAY environment variable if NULL was used.
DefaultVisual	Return the default visual structure for a screen.
DisplayCells	Return the maximum number of colormap cells on the connected display.
DisplayHeight	Return an integer that describes the height of the screen in pixels.
DisplayHeightMM	Return the height of the specified screen in millimeters.
DisplayPlanes	Return the number of planes on the connected display.
DisplayString	Return the string that was passed to XOpenDisplay or if that was NULL, the DISPLAY variable.
DisplayWidth	Return the width of the screen in pixels.
DisplayWidthMM	Return the width of the specified screen in millimeters.
RootWindow	Return the ID of the root window.
ScreenCount	Return the number of available screens.

Drawing Primitives

XDraw	Draw a polyline or curve between vertex list (from X10).
XDrawArc	Draw an arc fitting inside a rectangle.
XDrawArcs	Draw multiple arcs.
XDrawFilled	Draw a filled polygon or curve from vertex list (from X10).
XDrawLine	Draw a line between two points.

Drawing Primitives (continued)

XDrawLines	Draw multiple connected lines.
XDrawPoint	Draw a point.
XDrawPoints	Draw multiple points.
XDrawRectangle	Draw an outline of a rectangle.
XDrawRectangles	Draw the outlines of multiple rectangles.
XDrawSegments	Draw multiple disjoint lines.
XCopyArea	Copy an area of a drawable.
XCopyPlane	Copy a single plane of a drawable into a drawable with depth, applying pixel values.
XFillArc	Fill an arc.
XFillArcs	Fill multiple arcs.
XFillPolygon	Fill a polygon.
XFillRectangle	Fill a rectangular area.
XFillRectangles	Fill multiple rectangular areas.
XClearArea	Clear a rectangular area in a window.
XClearWindow	Clear an entire window.

Errors

XGetErrorDatabaseText	Obtain error messages from the error database.
XGetErrorText	Obtain a description of error code.
XSetErrorHandler	Set a nonfatal error event handler.
XSetIOErrorHandler	Handle fatal I/O errors.
XDisplayName	Report the display name when connection to a display fails.
XSetAfterFunction	Set a function called after all Xlib functions.
XSynchronize	Enable or disable synchronization for debugging.

Events

XSelectInput	Select the event types to be sent to a window.
XSendEvent	Send an event.
XSetInputFocus	Set the keyboard focus window.
XGetInputFocus	Return the current keyboard focus window.
XWindowEvent	Remove the next event matching mask and window.
XCheckWindowEvent	Remove the next event matching both passed window and passed mask; don't wait.
XCheckTypedEvent	Return the next event in queue that matches event type; don't wait.
XCheckTypedWindowEvent	Return the next event in queue matching type and window.
XMaskEvent	Remove the next event that matches mask.
XCheckMaskEvent	Remove the next event that matches mask; don't wait.
XIfEvent	Wait for matching event.
XCheckIfEvent	Check the event queue for a matching event.

Events (continued)

XPeekEvent	Get an event without removing it from the queue.
XPeekIfEvent	Get an event without recovering it from the queue; don't wait.
XAllowEvents	Control the behavior of keyboard and pointer events when these resources are grabbed.
XGetMotionEvents	Get pointer motion events.
XNextEvent	Get the next event of any type or window.
XPutBackEvent	Push an event back on the input queue.
XEventsQueued	Check the number of events in the event queue.
XPending	Flush the output buffer and return the number of pending input events.
XSynchronize	Enable or disable synchronization for debugging.
QLength	Return the current length of the input queue on the connected display.

Extensions

XFreeExtensionList	Free memory allocated for a list of installed extensions to X.
XListExtensions	Return a list of all extensions to X supported by the server.
XQueryExtension	Get extension information.

Fonts

XLoadFont	Load a font if not already loaded; get font ID.
XUnloadFont	Unload a font.
XFreeFont	Unload a font and free storage for the font structure.
XFreeFontInfo	Free multiple font information arrays.
XFreeFontNames	Free the font name array.
XFreeFontPath	Free the memory allocated by XGetFontPath.
XListFonts	Return a list of the available font names.
XListFontsWithInfo	Obtain the names and information about loaded fonts.
XQueryFont	Return information about a loaded font.
XSetFont	Set the current font in a graphics context.
XSetFontPath	Set the font search path.
XGetFontPath	Get the current font search path.
XGetFontProperty	Get a font property given its atom.
XCreateFontCursor	Create a cursor from the standard cursor font.

Grabbing

XGrabKey	Grab a key.
XUngrabKey	Release a key from grab.
XGrabKeyboard	Grab the keyboard.
XUngrabKeyboard	Release the keyboard from grab.

Grabbing (continued)

XGrabButton	Grab a pointer button.
XUngrabButton	Release a button from grab.
XGrabPointer	Grab the pointer.
XUngrabPointer	Release the pointer from grab.
XGrabServer	Grab the server grab.
XUngrabServer	Release the server from grab.
XChangeActivePointerGrab	Change the parameters of an active pointer grab.

Graphics Context

XGContextFromGC	Obtain the GContext (resource ID) associated with the specified graphics context.
XCreateGC	Create a new graphics context for a given screen with the depth of the specified drawable.
XChangeGC	Change the components of a given graphics context.
XCopyGC	Copy a graphics context.
XFreeGC	Free a graphics context.
XSetArcMode	Set the arc mode in a graphics context.
XSetClipMask	Set clip_mask pixmap in a graphics context.
XSetClipOrigin	Set the clip origin in a graphics context.
XSetClipRectangles	Set clip_mask in a graphics context to the list of rectangles.
XSetRegion	Set clip_mask of the graphics context to the specified region.
XSetDashes	Set dash_offset and dashes (for lines) in a graphics context.
XSetLineAttributes	Set the line drawing components in a graphics context.
XSetFillRule	Set the fill rule in a graphics context.
XSetFillStyle	Set the fill style in a graphics context.
XSetTile	Set the fill tile in a graphics context.
XSetStipple	Set the stipple in a graphics context.
XSetTSOrigin	Set the tile/stipple origin in a graphics context.
XSetGraphicsExposures	Set graphics_exposures in a graphics context.
XSetForeground	Set the foreground pixel value in a graphics context.
XSetBackground	Set the background pixel value in a graphics context.
XSetFunction	Set the bitwise logical operation in a graphics context.
XSetPlaneMask	Set the plane mask in a graphics context.
XSetState	Set the foreground, background, logical function and plane mask in a graphics context.
XSetSubwindowMode	Set the subwindow mode in a graphics context.
DefaultGC	Return the default graphics context for the root window of a screen.

Host Access

XAddHost	Add a host to the access control list.
XAddHosts	Add multiple hosts to the access control list.
XListHosts	Obtain a list of hosts having access to this display.
XRemoveHost	Remove a host from the access control list.
XRemoveHosts	Remove multiple hosts from the access control list.
XDisableAccessControl	Allow access from any host.
XEnableAccessControl	Use access control list to allow or deny connection requests.
XSetAccessControl	Disable or enable access control.

HouseKeeping

XFree	Free specified in-memory data created by an Xlib function.
XOpenDisplay	Connect a client program to an X server.
XCloseDisplay	Disconnect a client program from an X server and display.
XNoOp	Send a NoOp to exercise connection with the server.
DefaultScreen	Return the screen integer; the last segment of a string passed to XOpenDisplay, or the DISPLAY environment variable if NULL was used.

Images

XCreateImage	Allocate memory for an XImage structure.
XDestroyImage	Deallocate memory associated with an image.
XPutImage	Draw a rectangular image on a window or pixmap.
XSubImage	Create a subimage from part of an image.
XGetImage	Place contents of a rectangle from drawable into an image.
XGetSubImage	Copy a rectangle in drawable to a location within the pre-existing image.
XAddPixel	Add a constant value to every pixel value in an image.
XPutPixel	Set a pixel value in an image.
XGetPixel	Obtain a single pixel value from an image.
ImageByteOrder	Specify the required byte order for images for each scan line unit in XYFormat (bitmap) or for each pixel value in ZFormat. Returns either LSBFirst or MSBFirst.

Keyboard

XKeycodeToKeysym	Convert a keycode to a keysym.
XKeysymToKeycode	Convert a keysym to the appropriate keycode.
XKeysymToString	Convert a keysym symbol to a string.
XStringToKeysym	Convert a keysym name string to a keysym.
XLookupKeysym	Get the keysym corresponding to a keycode in a structure.
XRebindKeysym	Rebind a keysym to a string for client.

Keyboard (continued)

XLookupString	Map a key event to ASCII string, keysym, and Compose-Status.
XQueryKeymap	Obtain a bit vector for the current state of the keyboard.
XGetKeyboardMapping	Return symbols for keycodes.
XChangeKeyboardMapping	Change the keyboard mapping.
XRefreshKeyboardMapping	Update the stored modifier and keymap information.
XSetModifierMapping	Set keycodes to be used as modifiers (Shift, Control, etc.).
XGetModifierMapping	Obtain modifier key mapping (Shift, Control, etc.).
XDeleteModifiermapEntry	Delete an entry from an XModifierKeymap structure.
XInsertModifiermapEntry	Add a new entry to an XModifierKeymap structure.
XNewModifiermap	Create a keyboard modifier mapping structure.
XFreeModifiermap	Destroy and free a keyboard modifier mapping structure.

Macros, Display

AllPlanes	Return an unsigned long value with all bits set.
BlackPixel	Return a black pixel value on the default colormap of screen.
BlackPixelOfScreen	Return the black pixel value in the default colormap of the specified screen.
CellsOfScreen	Return the number of colormap cells of the specified screen.
ConnectionNumber	Return the connection number (file descriptor on UNIX system).
DefaultColormap	Return the default colormap on the specified screen.
DefaultColormapOfScreen	Return the default colormap of the specified screen.
DefaultDepth	Return the depth of the default root window for a screen.
DefaultDepthOfScreen	Return the default depth of the specified screen.
DefaultGC	Return the default graphics context for the root window of a screen.
DefaultGCOfScreen	Return the default graphics context (GC) of the specified screen.
DefaultRootWindow	Return the root window for the default screen.
DefaultScreen	Return the screen integer; the last segment of a string passed to XOpenDisplay, or the DISPLAY environment variable if NULL was used.
DefaultScreenOfDisplay	Return the default screen of the specified display.
DefaultVisual	Return the default visual structure for a screen.
DefaultVisualOfScreen	Return the default visual of the specified screen.
DisplayCells	Return the maximum number of colormap cells on the connected display.
DisplayHeight	Return an integer that describes the height of the screen in pixels.
DisplayHeightMM	Return the height of the specified screen in millimeters.
DisplayOfScreen	Return the display of the specified screen.
DisplayPlanes	Return the number of planes on the connected display.

Macros, Display (continued)

DisplayString	Return the string that was passed to XOpenDisplay or if that was NULL, the DISPLAY variable.
DisplayType	Return the connected display manufacturer, as defined in <X11/Xvendors.h>.
DisplayWidth	Return the width of the screen in pixels.
DisplayWidthMM	Return the width of the specified screen in millimeters.
DoesBackingStore	Return a value indicating whether the screen supports backing stores. Return one of WhenMapped, NotUseful, or Always.
DoesSaveUnders	Return whether the screen supports save unders. True or False.
dpyno	Return the file descriptor of the connected display.
EventMaskOfScreen	Return the initial root event mask for the specified screen.
HeightOfScreen	Return the height of the specified screen.
HeightMMOfScreen	Return the height of the specified screen in millimeters.
Keyboard	Return the device ID for the main keyboard connected to the display.
LastKnownRequest-Processed	Return the serial ID of the last known protocol request to have been issued.
MaxCmapsOfScreen	Return the maximum number of colormaps supported by a screen.
MinCmapsOfScreen	Return the minimum number of colormaps supported by a screen.
NextRequest	Return the serial ID of the next protocol request to be issued.
PlanesOfScreen	Return the number of planes in a screen.
ProtocolRevision	Return the minor protocol revision number of the X server.
ProtocolVersion	Return the version number of the X protocol on the connected display.
QLength	Return the current length of the input queue on the connected display.
RootWindow	Return the ID of the root window.
RootWindowOfScreen	Return the root window of the specified screen.
ScreenCount	Return the number of available screens.
ScreenOfDisplay	Return the specified screen of the specified display.
ServerVendor	Return a pointer to a null-terminated string giving some identification of the maker of the X server implementation.
VendorRelease	Return a number related to the release of the X server by the vendor.
WhitePixel	Return a pixel value representing white in default colormap.
WhitePixelOfScreen	Return the white pixel value in the default colormap of the specified screen.
WidthOfScreen	Return the width of the specified screen.
WidthMMOfScreen	Return the width of the specified screen in millimeters.

Function Groups

Macros, Image Format

BitmapBitOrder	Return LeastSignificant or MostSignificant. Indicates the bit order in BitmapUnit.
BitmapPad	Each scan line is padded to a multiple of bits specified by the value returned by this macro.
BitmapUnit	The scan line is quantized (calculated) in multiples of this value.
ByteOrder	Specifies the required byte order for images for each scan line unit in XYFormat (bitmap) or for each pixel value in ZFormat. Possible values are LSBFirst or MSBFirst.
ImageByteOrder	Specifies the required byte order for images for each scan line unit in XYFormat (bitmap) or for each pixel value in ZFormat. Return either LSBFirst or MSBFirst.

Macros, Keysym Classification

IsCursorKey	Return True if the keysym is on the cursor key.
IsFunctionKey	Return True if the keysym is on the function keys.
IsKeypadKey	Return True if the keysym is on the key pad.
IsMiscFunctionKey	Return True if the keysym is on the miscellaneous function keys.
IsModifierKey	Return True if the keysym is on the modifier keys.
IsPFKey	Return True if the keysym is on the PF keys.

Mapping

(see Window Mapping, Keyboard, or Pointer)

Output Buffer

XFlush	Flush the output buffer.
XSync	Flush the output buffer and wait for all events to be processed by the server.

Pointers

XQueryPointer	Get the current pointer location.
XWarpPointer	Move the pointer to another point on the screen.
XGrabPointer	Grab the pointer.
XUngrabPointer	Release the pointer from grab.
XGetPointerMapping	Get the pointer button mapping.
XSetPointerMapping	Set the pointer button mapping.
XGetPointerControl	Get the current pointer preferences.
XChangePointerControl	Change the pointer preferences.
XChangeActivePointerGrab	Change the parameters of an active pointer grab.

Properties

XListProperties	Get the property list for a window.
XDeleteProperty	Delete a window property.
XChangeProperty	Change a property associated with a window.
XSetStandardProperties	Set the minimum set of properties for the window manager.
XRotateWindowProperties	Rotate properties in the properties array.
XGetAtomName	Get a name for a given atom.
XGetFontProperty	Get a font property given its atom.
XGetWindowProperty	Obtain the atom type and property format for a window.
XInternAtom	Return an atom for a given name string.

Regions

XCreateRegion	Create a new empty region.
XDestroyRegion	Deallocate storage associated with a region.
XEmptyRegion	Determine if a region is empty.
XPolygonRegion	Generate a region from points.
XPointInRegion	Determine if a point resides in a region.
XRectInRegion	Determine if a rectangle resides in a region.
XUnionRectWithRegion	Add a rectangle to a region.
XClipBox	Generate the smallest rectangle enclosing a region.
XOffsetRegion	Change offset of a region.
XShrinkRegion	Reduce the size of a region.
XEqualRegion	Determine if two regions have the same size, offset, and space.
XSetRegion	Set clip_mask of the graphics context to the specified region.
XSubtractRegion	Subtract one region from another.
XIntersectRegion	Compute the intersection of two regions.
XUnionRegion	Compute the union of two regions.
XXorRegion	Calculate the difference between the union and intersection of 2 regions.

Resource Manager and DataBase (Release 2 only)

XrmGetFileDatabase	Retrieve a database from a file.
XrmGetResource	Get a resource from name and class as strings.
XrmGetStringDatabase	Create a database from a string.
XrmInitialize	Initialize the resource manager.
XrmMergeDatabases	Merge the contents of one database with another.
XrmParseCommand	Load a resource database from command line arguments.
XrmPutFileDatabase	Store a database in a file.
XrmPutLineResource	Add a resource entry given as a string of name and value.
XrmPutResource	Store a resource into a database.
XrmPutStringResource	Add a resource that is specified as a string.

Resource Manager and DataBase (Release 2 only) (continued)

XrmQGetResource	Get a resource from name and class as quarks.
XrmQGetSearchList	Return a list of database levels.
XrmQGetSearchResource	Search resource database levels for a given resource.
XrmQPutResource	Store a resource into a database using quarks.
XrmQPutStringResource	Add a string resource value to a database using quarks.
XrmQuarkToString	Convert a quark to a string.
XrmStringToBinding- QuarkList	Convert a key string to a binding list and a quark list.
XrmStringToQuarkList	Convert a key string to a quark list.
XrmStringToQuark	Convert a string to a quark.
XrmUniqueQuark	Allocate a new quark.
Xpermalloc	Allocate memory never to be freed.

Save Set

XAddToSaveSet	Add a window's children to the client's save-set.
XRemoveFromSaveSet	Remove a window's children from the client's save-set.
XChangeSaveSet	Add or remove a subwindow from the client's save-set.

Screen Saver

XActivateScreenSaver	Activate screen blanking.
XForceScreenSaver	Turn the screen saver on or off.
XResetScreenSaver	Reset the screen saver.
XGetScreenSaver	Get the current screen saver parameters.
XSetScreenSaver	Set the parameters of the screen saver.

Selections

XGetSelectionOwner	Return the owner of a selection.
XSetSelectionOwner	Set the owner of a selection.
XConvertSelection	Use the value of a selection.

Standard Geometry

XGeometry	Calculate window geometry given user geometry string and default geometry.
XParseGeometry	Generate position and size from standard window geometry string.
XTranslateCoordinates	Change the coordinate system from one window to another.

Text

XDrawImageString	Draw 8-bit image text characters.
XDrawImageString16	Draw 16-bit image text characters.
XDrawString	Draw an 8-bit text string, foreground only.

Text (continued)

XDrawString16	Draw two-byte text strings.
XDrawText	Draw 8-bit polytext strings.
XDrawText16	Draw 16-bit polytext strings.
XQueryTextExtents	Query the server for string and font metrics.
XQueryTextExtents16	Query the server for string and font metrics of a 16-bit character string.
XTextExtents	Get string and font metrics.
XTextExtents16	Get string and font metrics of a 16-bit character string.
XTextWidth	Get the width in pixels of an 8-bit character string.
XTextWidth16	Get the width in pixels of a 16-bit character string.

Tile, Pixmap, Stipple and Bitmap

XCreatePixmap	Create a pixmap.
XFreePixmap	Free a pixmap ID.
XQueryBestSize	Obtain the "best" supported cursor, tile, or stipple size.
XQueryBestStipple	Obtain the best supported stipple shape.
XQueryBestTile	Obtain the best supported fill tile shape.
XSetTile	Set the fill tile in a graphics context.
XSetWindowBorderPixmap	Change a window border tile attribute and repaint the border.
XSetWindowBackgroundPixmap	Change the background tile attribute of a window.
XReadBitmapFile	Read a bitmap from disk.
XWriteBitmapFile	Write a bitmap to a file.
XCreateBitmapFromData	Create a bitmap from X11 bitmap format data.
XCreatePixmapFromBitmapData	Create a pixmap with depth from bitmap data.

User Preferences

XAutoRepeatOff	Turn off the keyboard auto-repeat keys.
XAutoRepeatOn	Turn on the keyboard auto-repeat keys.
XBell	Ring the bell (Control G).
XGetDefault	Scan the user preferences for program name and options.
XGetPointerControl	Get the current pointer preferences.
XGetKeyboardControl	Obtain a list of the current keyboard preferences.
XChangeKeyboardControl	Change the keyboard preferences.

Visuals

XGetVisualInfo	Find a visual information structure that matches the specified template.
XMatchVisualInfo	Obtain the visual information that matches the desired depth and class.
DefaultVisual	Return the default visual structure for a screen.

Window Attributes

XGetWindowAttributes	Obtain the current attributes of window.
XChangeWindowAttributes	Set window attributes.
XSetWindowBackground	Set the background pixel attribute of a window.
XSetWindowBackgroundPixmap	Change the background tile attribute of a window.
XSetWindowBorder	Change a window border attribute to the specified pixel value and repaint the border.
XSetWindowBorderPixmap	Change a window border tile attribute and repaint the border.
XSetWindowColormap	Set the colormap for a specified window.
XDefineCursor	Assign a cursor to a window.
XGetGeometry	Obtain the current geometry of drawable.
XSelectInput	Select the event types to be sent to a window.

Window Configuration

XMoveWindow	Move a window.
XResizeWindow	Change a window's size.
XMoveResizeWindow	Change the size and position of a window.
XSetWindowBorderWidth	Change the border width of a window.
XRestackWindows	Change the stacking order of siblings.
XConfigureWindow	Change the window position, size, border width, or stacking order.
XGetGeometry	Obtain the current geometry of drawable.

Window Existence

XCreateSimpleWindow	Create an unmapped InputOutput subwindow.
XCreateWindow	Create a window and set attributes.
XDestroySubwindows	Destroy all subwindows of a window.
XDestroyWindow	Unmap and destroy a window and all subwindows.

Window Manager Hints

XGetClassHint	Get the XA_WM_CLASS property of a window.
XSetClassHint	Set the XA_WM_CLASS property of a window.
XGetNormalHints	Get the size hints property of a window in normal state (not zoomed or iconified).
XSetNormalHints	Set the size hints property of a window in normal state (not zoomed or iconified).
XGetSizeHints	Read any property of type XA_WM_SIZE_HINTS.
XSetSizeHints	Set the value of any property of type XA_WM_SIZE_HINTS.
XGetTransientForHint	Get the XA_WM_TRANSIENT_FOR property of a window.

Window Manager Hints (continued)

XSetTransientForHint	Set the XA_WM_TRANSIENT_FOR property of a window.
XGetWMHints	Read a window manager hints property.
XSetWMHints	Set a window manager hints property.
XGetZoomHints	Read the size hints property of a zoomed window.
XSetZoomHints	Set the size hints property of a zoomed window.
XFetchName	Get a window's name (XA_WM_NAME property).
XStoreName	Assign a name to a window for the window manager.
XGetIconName	Get the name to be displayed in an icon.
XSetIconName	Set the name to be displayed in a window's icon.
XGetIconSizes	Get preferred icon sizes.
XSetIconSizes	Set the value of the XA_WM_ICON_SIZE property.
XSetCommand	Set the XA_WM_COMMAND atom (command line arguments).

Window Manipulation

XLowerWindow	Lower a window in the stacking order.
XRaiseWindow	Raise a window to the top of the stacking order.
XCirculateSubwindows	Circulate the stacking order of children up or down.
XCirculateSubwindowsDown	Circulate the bottom child to the top of the stacking order.
XCirculateSubwindowsUp	Circulate the top child to the bottom of the stacking order.
XQueryTree	Return a list of children, parent, and root.
XReparentWindow	Change a window's parent.
XMoveWindow	Move a window.
XResizeWindow	Change a window's size.
XMoveResizeWindow	Change the size and position of a window.
XSetWindowBorderWidth	Change the border width of a window.
XRestackWindows	Change the stacking order of siblings.
XConfigureWindow	Change the window position, size, border width, or stacking order.

Window Mapping

XMapRaised	Map a window on top of its siblings.
XMapSubwindows	Map all subwindows.
XMapWindow	Map a window.
XUnmapSubwindows	Unmap all subwindows of a given window.
XUnmapWindow	Unmap a window.

Alphabetical Listing of Routines

Table A-1. Alphabetical Listing of Routines

Routine	Description
XActivateScreenSaver	Activate screen blanking.
XAddHost	Add a host to the access control list.
XAddHosts	Add multiple hosts to the access control list.
XAddPixel	Add a constant value to every pixel value in an image.
XAddToSaveSet	Add a window's children to the client's save-set.
XAllocColor	Allocate a read-only colormap cell with closest hardware-supported color.
XAllocColorCells	Allocate read/write (nonshared) colorcells.
XAllocColorPlanes	Allocate read/write (nonshareable) color planes.
XAllocNamedColor	Allocate a read-only colorcell from color name.
XAllowEvents	Control the behavior of keyboard and pointer events when these resources are grabbed.
XAutoRepeatOff	Turn off the keyboard auto-repeat keys.
XAutoRepeatOn	Turn on the keyboard auto-repeat keys.
XBell	Ring the bell (Control G).
XChangeActivePointerGrab	Change the parameters of an active pointer grab.
XChangeGC	Change the components of a given graphics context.
XChangeKeyboardControl	Change the keyboard preferences such as key click.
XChangeKeyboardMapping	Change the keyboard mapping.
XChangePointerControl	Change the pointer preferences.
XChangeProperty	Change a property associated with a window.
XChangeSaveSet	Add or remove a subwindow from the client's save-set.
XChangeWindowAttributes	Set window attributes.
XCheckIfEvent	Check the event queue for a matching event.
XCheckMaskEvent	Remove the next event that matches mask; don't wait.
XCheckTypedEvent	Return the next event in queue that matches event type; don't wait.
XCheckTypedWindowEvent	Return the next event in queue matching type and window.
XCheckWindowEvent	Remove the next event matching both passed window and passed mask; don't wait.
XCirculateSubwindows	Circulate the stacking order of children up or down.
XCirculateSubwindowsDown	Circulate the bottom child to the top of the stacking order.
XCirculateSubwindowsUp	Circulate the top child to the bottom of the stacking order.
XClearArea	Clear a rectangular area in a window.
XClearWindow	Clear an entire window.
XClipBox	Generate the smallest rectangle enclosing a region.

Routine	Description
XCloseDisplay	Disconnect a client program from an X server and display.
XConfigureWindow	Change the window position, size, border width, or stacking order.
XConvertSelection	Use the value of a selection.
XCopyArea	Copy an area of a drawable.
XCopyColormapAndFree	Copy a colormap and return a new colormap ID.
XCopyGC	Copy a graphics context.
XCopyPlane	Copy a single plane of a drawable into a drawable with depth, applying pixel values.
XCreateAssocTable	Create a new association table (X10).
XCreateBitmapFromData	Create a bitmap from X11 bitmap format data.
XCreateColormap	Create a colormap.
XCreateFontCursor	Create a cursor from the standard cursor font.
XCreateGC	Create a new graphics context for a given screen with the depth of the specified drawable.
XCreateGlyphCursor	Create a cursor from font glyphs.
XCreateImage	Allocate memory for an XImage structure.
XCreatePixmap	Create a pixmap.
XCreatePixmapCursor	Create a cursor from two bitmaps.
XCreatePixmapFrom-BitmapData	Create a pixmap with depth from bitmap data.
XCreateRegion	Create a new empty region.
XCreateSimpleWindow	Create an unmapped InputOutput window.
XCreateWindow	Create a window and set attributes.
XDefineCursor	Assign a cursor to a window.
XDeleteAssoc	Delete an entry from an association table.
XDeleteContext	Delete a context entry for a given window and type.
XDeleteModifiermapEntry	Delete an entry from an XModifierKeymap structure.
XDeleteProperty	Delete a window property.
XDestroyAssocTable	Free the memory allocated for an association table.
XDestroyImage	Deallocate memory associated with an image.
XDestroyRegion	Deallocate storage associated with a region.
XDestroySubwindows	Destroy all subwindows of a window.
XDestroyWindow	Unmap and destroy a window and all subwindows.
XDisableAccessControl	Allow access from any host.
XDisplayName	Report the display name when connection to a display fails.
XDraw	Draw a polyline or curve between vertex list (from X10).
XDrawArc	Draw an arc fitting inside a rectangle.
XDrawArcs	Draw multiple arcs.
XDrawFilled	Draw a filled polygon or curve from vertex list (from X10).
XDrawImageString	Draw 8-bit image text characters.

Function Groups

Routine	Description
XDrawImageString16	Draw 16-bit image text characters.
XDrawLine	Draw a line between two points.
XDrawLines	Draw multiple connected lines.
XDrawPoint	Draw a point.
XDrawPoints	Draw multiple points.
XDrawRectangle	Draw an outline of a rectangle.
XDrawRectangles	Draw the outlines of multiple rectangles.
XDrawSegments	Draw multiple disjoint lines.
XDrawString	Draw an 8-bit text string, foreground only.
XDrawString16	Draw two-byte text strings.
XDrawText	Draw 8-bit polytext strings.
XDrawText16	Draw 16-bit polytext strings.
XEmptyRegion	Determine if a region is empty.
XEnableAccessControl	Use access control list to allow or deny connection requests.
XEqualRegion	Determine if two regions have the same size, offset, and shape.
XEventsQueued	Check the number of events in the event queue.
XFetchBuffer	Return data from a cut buffer.
XFetchBytes	Return data from cut buffer 0.
XFetchName	Get a window's name (XA_WM_NAME property).
XFillArc	Fill an arc.
XFillArcs	Fill multiple arcs.
XFillPolygon	Fill a polygon.
XFillRectangle	Fill a rectangular area.
XFillRectangles	Fill multiple rectangular areas.
XFindContext	Get data from the context manager (not graphics context).
XFlush	Flush the output buffer (display all queued requests).
XForceScreenSaver	Turn the screen saver on or off.
XFree	Free specified in-memory data created by an Xlib function.
XFreeColormap	Delete a colormap and install the default colormap.
XFreeColors	Free colormap cells or planes.
XFreeCursor	Destroy a cursor.
XFreeExtensionList	Free memory allocated for a list of installed extensions to X.
XFreeFont	Unload a font and free storage for the font structure.
XFreeFontInfo	Free multiple font information arrays.
XFreeFontNames	Free the font name array.
XFreeFontPath	Free the memory allocated by XGetFontPath.
XFreeGC	Free a graphics context.
XFreeModifiermap	Destroy and free a keyboard modifier mapping structure.
XFreePixmap	Free a pixmap ID.
XGContextFromGC	Obtain the GContext (resource ID) associated with the specified graphics context.

Routine	Description
XGeometry	Calculate window geometry given user geometry string and default geometry.
XGetAtomName	Get a name for a given atom.
XGetClassHint	Get the XA_WM_CLASS property of a window.
XGetDefault	Scan the user preferences for program name and options.
XGetErrorDatabaseText	Obtain error messages from the error database.
XGetErrorText	Obtain a description of error code.
XGetFontPath	Get the current font search path.
XGetFontProperty	Get a font property given its atom.
XGetGeometry	Obtain the current geometry of drawable.
XGetIconName	Get the name to be displayed in an icon.
XGetIconSizes	Get preferred icon sizes.
XGetImage	Place contents of a rectangle from drawable into an image.
XGetInputFocus	Return the current keyboard focus window.
XGetKeyboardControl	Obtain a list of the current keyboard preferences.
XGetKeyboardMapping	Return symbols for keycodes.
XGetModifierMapping	Obtain a mapping of modifier keys (Shift, Control, etc.)
XGetMotionEvents	Get pointer motion events.
XGetNormalHints	Get the size hints property of a window in normal state (not zoomed or iconified).
XGetPixel	Obtain a single pixel value from an image.
XGetPointerControl	Get the current pointer preferences.
XGetPointerMapping	Get the pointer button mapping.
XGetScreenSaver	Get the current screen saver parameters.
XGetSelectionOwner	Return the owner of a selection.
XGetSizeHints	Read any property of type XA_WM_SIZE_HINTS.
XGetStandardColormap	Get the standard colormap property.
XGetSubImage	Copy a rectangle in drawable to a location within the pre-existing image.
XGetTransientForHint	Get the XA_WM_TRANSIENT_FOR property of a window.
XGetVisualInfo	Find a visual information structure that matches the specified template.
XGetWindowAttributes	Obtain the current attributes of window.
XGetWindowProperty	Obtain the atom type and property format for a window.
XGetWMHints	Read a window manager hints property.
XGetZoomHints	Read the size hints property of a zoomed window.
XGrabButton	Grab a pointer button.
XGrabKey	Grab a key.
XGrabKeyboard	Grab the keyboard.
XGrabPointer	Grab the pointer.
XGrabServer	Grab the server.
XIfEvent	Wait for matching event.

Routine	Description
XInsertModifiermapEntry	Add a new entry to an XModifierKeymap structure.
XInstallColormap	Install a colormap.
XInternAtom	Return an atom for a given name string.
XIntersectRegion	Compute the intersection of two regions.
XKeycodeToKeysym	Convert a keycode to a keysym.
XKeysymToKeycode	Convert a keysym to the appropriate keycode.
XKeysymToString	Convert a keysym symbol to a string.
XKillClient	Destroy a client or its remaining resources.
XListExtensions	Return a list of all extensions to X supported by the server.
XListFonts	Return a list of the available font names.
XListFontsWithInfo	Obtain the names and information about loaded fonts.
XListHosts	Obtain a list of hosts having access to this display.
XListInstalledColormaps	Get a list of installed colormaps.
XListProperties	Get the property list for a window.
XLoadFont	Load a font if not already loaded; get font ID.
XLoadQueryFont	Load a font and fill information structure.
XLookUpAssoc	Obtain data from an association table.
XLookupColor	Get database RGB values and closest hardware-supported RGB values from color name.
XLookupKeysym	Get the keysym corresponding to a keycode in structure.
XLookupString	Map a key event to ASCII string, keysym, and ComposeStatus.
XLowerWindow	Lower a window in the stacking order.
XMakeAssoc	Create an entry in an association table.
XMapRaised	Map a window on top of its siblings.
XMapSubwindows	Map all subwindows.
XMapWindow	Map a window.
XMaskEvent	Remove the next event that matches mask.
XMatchVisualInfo	Obtain the visual information that matches the desired depth and class.
XMoveResizeWindow	Change the size and position of a window.
XMoveWindow	Move a window.
XNewModifiermap	Create a keyboard modifier mapping structure.
XNextEvent	Get the next event of any type or window.
XNoOp	Send a NoOp to exercise connection with the server.
XOffsetRegion	Change offset of a region.
XOpenDisplay	Connect a client program to an X server.
XParseColor	Look up or translate RGB values from ASCII color name or hexadecimal value.
XParseGeometry	Generate position and size from standard window geometry string.
XPeekEvent	Get an event without removing it from the queue.

Routine	Description
XPeekIfEvent	Get an event without removing it from the queue; do not wait.
XPending	Flush the output buffer and return the number of pending input events.
Xpermalloc	Allocate memory never to be freed.
XPointInRegion	Determine if a point is inside a region.
XPolygonRegion	Generate a region from points.
XPutBackEvent	Push an event back on the input queue.
XPutImage	Draw a rectangular image on a window or pixmap.
XPutPixel	Set a pixel value in an image.
XQueryBestCursor	Get the closest supported cursor sizes.
XQueryBestSize	Obtain the "best" supported cursor, tile, or stipple size.
XQueryBestStipple	Obtain the best supported stipple shape.
XQueryBestTile	Obtain the best supported fill tile shape.
XQueryColor	Obtain the RGB values and flags for a specified pixel value.
XQueryColors	Obtain RGB values for an array of pixel values.
XQueryExtension	Get extension information.
XQueryFont	Return information about a loaded font.
XQueryKeymap	Obtain a bit vector for the current state of the keyboard.
XQueryPointer	Get the current pointer location.
XQueryTextExtents	Query the server for string and font metrics.
XQueryTextExtents16	Query the server for string and font metrics of a 16-bit character string.
XQueryTree	Return a list of children, parent, and root.
XRaiseWindow	Raise a window to the top of the stacking order.
XReadBitmapFile	Read a bitmap from disk.
XRebindKeysym	Rebind a keysym to a string for client.
XRecolorCursor	Change the color of a cursor.
XRectInRegion	Determine if a rectangle resides in a region.
XRefreshKeyboardMapping	Update the stored modifier and keymap information.
XRemoveFromSaveSet	Remove a window's children from the client's save-set.
XRemoveHost	Remove a host from the access control list.
XRemoveHosts	Remove multiple hosts from the access control list.
XReparentWindow	Change a window's parent.
XResetScreenSaver	Reset the screen saver.
XResizeWindow	Change a window's size.
XRestackWindows	Change the stacking order of siblings.
XrmGetFileDatabase	Retrieve a database from a file.
XrmGetResource	Get a resource from name and class as strings.
XrmGetStringDatabase	Create a database from a string.
XrmInitialize	Initialize the resource manager.
XrmMergeDatabases	Merge the contents of one database with another.

Routine	Description
XrmParseCommand	Load a resource database from command line arguments.
XrmPutFileDatabase	Store a database in a file.
XrmPutLineResource	Add a resource entry given as a string of name and value.
XrmPutResource	Store a resource into a database.
XrmPutStringResource	Add a resource that is specified as a string.
XrmQGetResource	Get a resource from name and class as quarks.
XrmQGetSearchList	Return a list of database levels.
XrmQGetSearchResource	Search resource database levels for a given resource.
XrmQPutResource	Store a resource into a database using quarks.
XrmQPutStringResource	Add a string resource value to a database using quarks.
XrmQuarkToString	Convert a quark to a string.
XrmStringToBindingQuarkList	Convert a key string to a binding list and a quark list.
XrmStringToQuark	Convert a string to a quark.
XrmStringToQuarkList	Convert a key string to a quark list.
XrmUniqueQuark	Allocate a new quark.
XRotateBuffers	Rotate the cut buffers.
XRotateWindowProperties	Rotate properties in the properties array.
XSaveContext	Save a data value corresponding to a window and context type (not graphics context).
XSelectInput	Select the event types to be sent to a window.
XSendEvent	Send an event.
XSetAccessControl	Disable or enable access control.
XSetAfterFunction	Set a function called after all Xlib functions.
XSetArcMode	Set the arc mode in a graphics context.
XSetBackground	Set the background pixel value in a graphics context.
XSetClassHint	Set the XA_WM_CLASS property of a window.
XSetClipMask	Set clip_mask pixmap in a graphics context.
XSetClipOrigin	Set the clip origin in a graphics context.
XSetClipRectangles	Change clip_mask in a graphics context to the list of rectangles.
XSetCloseDownMode	Change the close down mode of a client.
XSetCommand	Set the XA_WM_COMMAND atom (command line arguments).
XSetDashes	Set dash_offset and dashes (for lines) in a graphics context.
XSetErrorHandler	Set a nonfatal error event handler.
XSetFillRule	Set the fill rule in a graphics context.
XSetFillStyle	Set the fill style in a graphics context.
XSetFont	Set the current font in a graphics context.

Routine	Description
XSetFontPath	Set the font search path.
XSetForeground	Set the foreground pixel value in a graphics context.
XSetFunction	Set the bitwise logical operation in a graphics context.
XSetGraphicsExposures	Set graphics_exposures in a graphics context.
XSetIconName	Set the name to be displayed in a window's icon.
XSetIconSizes	Set the value of the XA_WM_ICON_SIZE property.
XSetInputFocus	Set the keyboard focus window.
XSetIOErrorHandler	Handle fatal I/O errors.
XSetLineAttributes	Set the line drawing components in a graphics context.
XSetModifierMapping	Set keycodes to be used as modifiers (Shift, Control, etc.).
XSetNormalHints	Set the size hints property of a window in normal state (not zoomed or iconified).
XSetPlaneMask	Set the plane mask in a graphics context.
XSetPointerMapping	Set the pointer button mapping.
XSetRegion	Set clip_mask of the graphics context to the specified region.
XSetScreenSaver	Set the parameters of the screen saver.
XSetSelectionOwner	Set the owner of a selection.
XSetSizeHints	Set the value of any property of type XA_WM_SIZE_HINTS.
XSetStandardColormap	Change the standard colormap property.
XSetStandardProperties	Set the minimum set of properties for the window manager.
XSetState	Set the foreground, background, logical function, and plane mask in a graphics context.
XSetStipple	Set the stipple in a graphics context.
XSetSubwindowMode	Set the subwindow mode in a graphics context.
XSetTile	Set the fill tile in a graphics context.
XSetTransientForHint	Set the XA_WM_TRANSIENT_FOR property of a window.
XSetTSOrigin	Set the tile/stipple origin in a graphics context.
XSetWindowBackground	Set the background pixel attribute of a window.
XSetWindowBackgroundPixmap	Change the background tile attribute of a window.
XSetWindowBorder	Change a window border attribute to the specified pixel value and repaint the border.
XSetWindowBorderPixmap	Change a window border tile attribute and repaint the border.
XSetWindowBorderWidth	Change the border width of a window.
XSetWindowColormap	Set the colormap for a specified window.
XSetWMHints	Set a window manager hints property.
XSetZoomHints	Set the size hints property of a zoomed window.

Routine	Description
XShrinkRegion	Reduce or expand the size of a region.
XStoreBuffer	Store data in a cut buffer.
XStoreBytes	Store data in cut buffer 0.
XStoreColor	Set or change a read/write entry of a colormap to the closest available hardware color.
XStoreColors	Set or change read/write colorcells to the closest available hardware colors.
XStoreName	Assign a name to a window for the window manager.
XStoreNamedColor	Allocate a read/write colorcell by English color name.
XStringToKeysym	Convert a keysym name string to a keysym.
XSubImage	Create a subimage from part of an image.
XSubtractRegion	Subtract one region from another.
XSync	Flush the output buffer and wait for all events and errors to be processed by the server.
XSynchronize	Enable or disable synchronization for debugging.
XTextExtents	Get string and font metrics.
XTextExtents16	Get string and font metrics of a 16-bit character string.
XTextWidth	Get the width in pixels of an 8-bit character string.
XTextWidth16	Get the width in pixels of a 16-bit character string.
XTranslateCoordinates	Change the coordinate system from one window to another.
XUndefineCursor	Disassociate a cursor from a window.
XUngrabButton	Release a button from grab.
XUngrabKey	Release a key from grab.
XUngrabKeyboard	Release the keyboard from grab.
XUngrabPointer	Release the pointer from grab.
XUngrabServer	Release the server from grab.
XUninstallColormap	Uninstall a colormap; install default if not already installed.
XUnionRectWithRegion	Add a rectangle to a region.
XUnionRegion	Compute the union of two regions.
XUniqueContext	Create a new context ID (not graphics context).
XUnloadFont	Unload a font.
XUnmapSubwindows	Unmap all subwindows of a given window.
XUnmapWindow	Unmap a window.
XWarpPointer	Move the pointer to another point on the screen.
XWindowEvent	Remove the next event matching mask and window.
XWriteBitmapFile	Write a bitmap to a file.
XXorRegion	Calculate the difference between the union and intersection of two regions.

B
Error Messages and Protocol Requests

This appendix contains two tables: Table B-1 describes the standard error codes (the error_code member of XErrorEvent) and what causes them, and Table B-2 describes the mapping between protocol requests and Xlib functions. Each reference page in this volume describes in more detail the errors that may occur because of that Xlib routine. Volume One, Chapter 3, *Basic Window Program*, describes the handling of errors in general.

A protocol request is the actual network message that is sent from Xlib to the server. Many convenience functions are provided in Xlib to make programs easier to write and more readable. When any one of several convenience routines is called it will be translated into one type of protocol request. For example, XMoveWindow and XResizeWindow are convenience routines for the more general XConfigureWindow. Both of these Xlib routines use the protocol request X_ConfigureWindow. The protocol request that causes an error, along with other information about the error is printed to the standard error output by the default error handlers. In order to find out where in your code the error ocurred, you will need to know what Xlib function to look for. Use Table B-2 to find this function.

Xlib functions that do not appear in Table B-2 do not generate protocol requests. They perform their function without affecting the display and without requiring information from the server. If errors can occur in them, the errors are reported in the returned value.

Table B-1. Error Messages

Error Codes	Possible Cause
BadAccess	Client attempted to grab a key/button combination that is already grabbed by another client.
	Client attempted to free a colormap entry that is not allocated by the client.
	Client attempted to store into a read-only colormap entry.
	Client attempted to modify the access control list from other than the local (or otherwise authorized) host.
	Client attempted to select an event type that only one client can select at a time, when another client has already selected it.
BadAlloc	The server failed to allocate the requested resource.

Table B-1. Error Messages (continued)

Error Codes:	Possible Cause
BadAtom	A value for an Atom argument does not name a defined Atom.
BadColor	A value for a Colormap argument does not name a defined Colormap.
BadCursor	A value for a Cursor argument does not name a defined Cursor.
BadDrawable	A value for a Drawable argument does not name a defined Window or Pixmap.
BadFont	A value for a Font or GContext argument does not name a defined Font.
BadGC	A value for a GContext argument does not name a defined GContext.
BadIDChoice	The value chosen for a resource identifier is either not included in the range assigned to the client, or is already in use.
BadImplemen -tation	The server does not implement some aspect of the request. A server that generates this error for a core request is deficient. Clients should be prepared to receive such errors and either handle or discard them.
BadLength	The length of a request is shorter or longer than that required to minimally contain the arguments. This usually indicates an internal Xlib error.
BadMatch	An InputOnly window is used as a Drawable.
	Some argument (or pair of arguments) has the correct type and range, but fails to "match" in some other way required by the request.
BadName	A font or color of the specified name does not exist.
BadPixmap	A value for a Pixmap argument does not name a defined Pixmap.
BadRequest	The major or minor opcode does not specify a valid request.
BadValue	Some numeric value falls outside the range of values accepted by the request. Unless a specific range is specified for an argument, the full range defined by the argument's type is accepted. Any argument defined as a set of alternatives can generate this error.
BadWindow	A value for a Window argument does not name a defined Window.

The BadAtom, BadColor, BadCursor, BadDrawable, BadFont, BadGC, Bad-Pixmap, and BadWindow errors are also used when the argument type should be among a set of fixed alternatives (for example, a window ID, PointerRoot, or None) and some other constant or variable is used.

Protocol Request	Xlib Function
X_AllocColor	`XAllocColor`
X_AllocColorCells	`XAllocColorCells`
X_AllocColorPlanes	`XAllocColorPlanes`
X_AllocNamedColor	`XAllocNamedColor`
X_AllowEvents	`XAllowEvents`
X_Bell	`XBell`
X_ChangeActivePointerGrab	`XChangeActivePointerGrab`

X_ChangeGC	`XChangeGC`
	`XSetArcMode`
	`XSetBackground`
	`XSetClipMask`
	`XSetClipOrigin`
	`XSetFillRule`
	`XSetFillStyle`
	`XSetFont`
	`XSetForeground`
	`XSetFunction`
	`XSetGraphicsExposures`
	`XSetLineAttributes`
	`XSetPlaneMask`
	`XSetState`
	`XSetStipple`
	`XSetSubwindowMode`
	`XSetTile`
	`XSetTSOrigin`

X_ChangeHosts	`XAddHost`
	`XAddHosts`
	`XRemoveHost`
	`XRemoveHosts`

X_ChangeKeyboardControl	`XAutoRepeatOff`
	`XAutoRepeatOn`
	`XChangeKeyboardControl`

X_ChangeKeyboardMapping	`XChangeKeyboardMapping`
X_ChangePointerControl	`XChangePointerControl`

X_ChangeProperty	`XChangeProperty`
	`XSetCommand`
	`XSetIconSizes`
	`XSetIconWindow`
	`XSetNormalHints`
	`XSetResizeHint`
	`XSetSizeHints`

Protocol Request	Xlib Function
	XSetStandardProperties
	XSetWMHints
	XSetZoomHints
	XStoreBuffer
	XStoreBytes
	XStoreName
X_ChangeSaveSet	XAddToSaveSet
	XChangeSaveSet
	XRemoveFromSaveSet
X_ChangeWindowAttributes	XChangeWindowAttributes
	XDefineCursor
	XSelectInput
	XSetWindowBackground
	XSetWindowBackgroundPixmap
	XSetWindowBorder
	XSetWindowBorderPixmap
	XSetWindowColormap
	XUndefineCursor
X_CirculateWindow	XCirculateSubwindows
	XCirculateSubwindowsDown
	XCirculateSubwindowsUp
X_ClearArea	XClearArea
	XClearWindow
X_CloseFont	XFreeFont
	XUnloadFont
X_ConfigureWindow	XConfigureWindow
	XLowerWindow
	XMapRaised
	XMoveResizeWindow
	XMoveWindow
	XRaiseWindow
	XResizeWindow
	XRestackWindows
	XSetWindowBorderWidth
X_ConvertSelection	XConvertSelection
X_CopyArea	XCopyArea
X_CopyColormapAndFree	XCopyColormapAndFree
X_CopyGC	XCopyGC
X_CopyPlane	XCopyPlane
X_CreateColormap	XCreateColormap
X_CreateCursor	XCreatePixmapCursor

Protocol Request	Xlib Function
X_CreateGC	XCreateGC XOpenDisplay
X_CreateGlyphCursor	XCreateFontCursor XCreateGlyphCursor
X_CreatePixmap	XCreatePixmap
X_CreateWindow	XCreateSimpleWindow XCreateWindow
X_DeleteProperty	XDeleteProperty
X_DestroySubwindows	XDestroySubwindows
X_DestroyWindow	XDestroyWindow
X_FillPoly	XFillPolygon
X_ForceScreenSaver	XActivateScreenSaver XForceScreenSaver XResetScreenSaver
X_FreeColormap	XFreeColormap
X_FreeColors	XFreeColors
X_FreeCursor	XFreeCursor
X_FreeGC	XFreeGC
X_FreePixmap	XFreePixmap
X_GetAtomName	XGetAtomName
X_GetFontPath	XGetFontPath
X_GetGeometry	XGetGeometry XGetWindowAttributes
X_GetImage	XGetImage
X_GetInputFocus	XGetInputFocus XSync
X_GetKeyboardControl	XGetKeyboardControl
X_GetKeyboardMapping	XGetKeyboardMapping
X_GetModifierMapping	XGetModifierMapping
X_GetMotionEvents	XGetMotionEvents
X_GetPointerControl	XGetPointerControl
X_GetPointerMapping	XGetPonterMapping
X_GetProperty	XClearIconWindow XFetchBytes

Errors

Protocol Request	Xlib Function
	`XFetchName`
	`XGetIconSizes`
	`XGetIconWindow`
	`XGetNormalHints`
	`XGetSizeHints`
	`XGetWindowProperty`
	`XGetWMHints`
	`XGetZoomHints`
X_GetScreenSaver	`XGetScreenSaver`
X_GetSelectionOwner	`XGetSelectionOwner`
X_GetWindowAttributes	`XGetWindowAttributes`
X_GrabButton	`XGrabButton`
X_GrabKey	`XGrabKey`
X_GrabKeyboard	`XGrabKeyboard`
X_GrabPointer	`XGrabPointer`
X_GrabServer	`XGrabServer`
X_ImageText8	`XDrawImageString`
X_ImageText16	`XDrawImageString16`
X_InstallColormap	`XInstallColormap`
X_InternAtom	`XInternAtom`
X_KillClient	`XKillClient`
X_ListExtensions	`XListExtensions`
X_ListFonts	`XListFonts`
X_ListFontsWithInfo	`XListFontsWithInfo`
X_ListHosts	`XListHosts`
X_ListInstalledColormaps	`XListInstalledColormaps`
X_ListProperties	`XListProperties`
X_LookupColor	`XLookupColor`
	`XParseColor`
X_MapSubwindows	`XMapSubwindows`
X_MapWindow	`XMapRaised`
	`XMapWindow`
X_NoOperation	`XNoOp`
X_OpenFont	`XLoadFont`
	`XLoadQueryFont`

Protocol Request	Xlib Function
X_PolyArc	`XDrawArc` `XDrawArcs`
X_PolyFillArc	`XFillArc` `XFillArcs`
X_PolyFillRectangle	`XFillRectangle` `XFillRectangles`
X_PolyLine	`XDrawLines`
X_PolyPoint	`XDrawPoint` `XDrawPoints`
X_PolyRectangle	`XDrawRectangle` `XDrawRectangles`
X_PolySegment	`XDrawLine` `XDrawSegments`
X_PolyText8	`XDrawString` `XDrawText`
X_PolyText16	`XDrawString16` `XDrawText16`
X_PutImage	`XPutImage`

X_QueryBestSize	`XQueryBestCursor`
	`XQueryBestSize`
	`XQueryBestStipple`
	`XQueryBestTile`

X_QueryColors	`XQueryColor` `XQueryColors`
X_QueryExtension	`XInitExtension` `XQueryExtension`
X_QueryFont	`XLoadQueryFont`
X_QueryKeymap	`XQueryKeymap`
X_QueryPointer	`XQueryPointer`
X_QueryTextExtents	`XQueryTextExtents` `XQueryTextExtents16`
X_QueryTree	`XQueryTree`
X_RecolorCursor	`XRecolorCursor`
X_ReparentWindow	`XReparentWindow`
X_RotateProperties	`XRotateBuffers` `XRotateWindowProperties`

Errors

Protocol Request	Xlib Function
X_SendEvent	XSendEvent
X_SetAccessControl	XDisableAccessControl
	XEnableAccessControl
	XSetAccessControl
X_SetClipRectangles	XSetClipRectangles
X_SetCloseDownMode	XSetCloseDownMode
X_SetDashes	XSetDashes
X_SetFontPath	XSetFontPath
X_SetInputFocus	XSetInputFocus
X_SetModifierMapping	XSetModifierMapping
X_SetPointerMapping	XSetPointerMapping
X_SetScreenSaver	XSetScreenSaver
X_SetSelectionOwner	XSetSelectionOwner
X_StoreColors	XStoreColor
	XStoreColors
X_StoreNamedColor	XStoreNamedColor
X_TranslateCoords	XTranslateCoordinates
X_UngrabButton	XUngrabButton
X_UngrabKey	XUngrabKey
X_UngrabKeyboard	XUngrabKeyboard
X_UngrabPointer	XUngrabPointer
X_UngrabServer	XUngrabServer
X_UninstallColormap	XUninstallColormap
X_UnmapSubwindows	XUnmapSubWindows
X_UnmapWindow	XUnmapWindow
X_WarpPointer	XWarpPointer

C
Macros

Once you have successfully connected your application to an X server, you can obtain data from the `Display` structure associated with that display. The Xlib interface provides a number of useful C language macros and corresponding functions for other language bindings which return data from the `Display` structure.

The function versions of these macros have the same names as the macros except that the function forms begin with the letter "X." They use the same arguments. Using the macro versions is slightly more efficient in C because it eliminates function call overhead.

For the purposes of this appendix, the macros are divided into four categories: Display macros, Image Format macros, Keysym Classification macros, and Resource Manager macros. The macros are listed alphabetically within each category.

Note that some macros take as arguments an integer screen (*scr_num*) or pointer to a screen structure (*scr_pnt*). *scr_num* is returned by the `DefaultScreen` macro and *scr_pnt* is returned by the `DefaultScreenOfDisplay` macro.

Display Macros

`AllPlanes()`	Return a value with all bits set suitable for use as a plane mask argument.
`BlackPixel(`*display*`,`*scr_num*`)`	Return the black pixel value in the default colormap that is created by `XOpenDisplay`.
`BlackPixelOfScreen(`*scr_pnt*`)`	Return the black pixel value in the default colormap of the specified screen.
`CellsOfScreen(`*scr_pnt*`)`	Return the number of colormap cells in the default colormap of the specified screen.
`ConnectionNumber(`*display*`)`	Return a connection number for the specified display. On a UNIX system, this is the file descriptor of the connection.

`DefaultColormap(`*`display,scr_num`*`)`	Return the default colormap for the specified screen. Most routine allocations of color should be made out of this colormap.
`DefaultColormapOfScreen(`*`scr_pnt`*`)`	Return the default colormap of the specified screen.
`DefaultDepth(`*`display,scr_num`*`)`	Return the depth (number of planes) of the root window for the specified screen. Other depths may also be supported on this screen. See Volume One, Chapter 7, *Color*, or the reference pages for `XMatchVisualInfo` and `XGetVisualInfo` to find out how to determine what depths are available.
`DefaultDepthOfScreen(`*`scr_pnt`*`)`	Return the default depth of the specified screen.
`DefaultGC(`*`display,scr_num`*`)`	Return the default graphics context for the specified screen.
`DefaultGCOfScreen(`*`scr_pnt`*`)`	Return the default graphics context (GC) of the specified screen.
`DefaultRootWindow(`*`display`*`)`	Return the ID of the root window on the default screen. Most applications should use `RootWindow` instead so that screen selection is supported.
`DefaultScreen(`*`display`*`)`	Return the integer that was specified in the last segment of the string passed to `XOpenDisplay`, or from the DISPLAY environment variable if `NULL` was used. For example, if the DISPLAY environment were `Ogre:0.1` then `DefaultScreen` would return 1.
`DefaultScreenOfDisplay(`*`display`*`)`	Return the default screen of the specified display.
`DefaultVisual(`*`display,scr_num`*`)`	Return a pointer to the default visual structure for the specified screen.
`DefaultVisualOfScreen(`*`scr_pnt`*`)`	Return the default visual of the specified screen.
`DisplayCells(`*`display,scr_num`*`)`	Return the maximum possible number of colormap cells on the specified screen. This macro is misnamed: it should have been `ScreenCells`.
`DisplayHeight(`*`display,scr_num`*`)`	Return the height in pixels of the screen. This macro is misnamed: it should have been `ScreenHeight`.
`DisplayHeightMM(`*`display,scr_num`*`)`	Return the height in millimeters of the specified screen. This macro is misnamed: it should have been `ScreenHeightMM`.

`DisplayOfScreen(scr_pnt)`	Return the display associated with the specified screen.
`DisplayPlanes(display,scr_num)`	Return the number of planes on the specified screen. This macro is misnamed: it should have been `ScreenPlanes`.
`DisplayString(display)`	Return the string that was passed to `XOpen-Display` when the current display was opened (or, if that was `NULL`, the value of the DISPLAY environment variable). This macro is useful in applications which invoke the fork system call and want to open a new connection to the same display from the child process.
`DisplayWidth(display,scr_num)`	Return the width in pixels of the screen. This macro is misnamed: it should have been `ScreenWidth`.
`DisplayWidthMM(display,scr_num)`	Return the width in millimeters of the specified screen. This macro is misnamed: it should have been `ScreenWidthMM`.
`DoesBackingStore(scr_pnt)`	Return a value indicating whether the screen supports backing stores. Values are `When-Mapped`, `NotUseful`, or `Always`. See Volume One, Section 4.3.5 for a discussion of the backing store.
`DoesSaveUnders(scr_pnt)`	Return a Boolean value indicating whether the screen supports save unders. If `True`, the screen supports save unders. If `False`, the screen does not support save unders. See Volume One, Section 4.3.6 for a discussion of the save under.
`dpyno(display)`	Return the file descriptor of the connected display. On a UNIX system, you can then pass this returned file descriptor to the *select*(3) system call when your application program is driving more than one display at a time.
`EventMaskOfScreen(scr_pnt)`	Return the initial event mask for the root window of the specified screen.
`HeightOfScreen(scr_pnt)`	Return the height in pixels of the specified screen.
`HeightMMOfScreen(scr_pnt)`	Return the height in millimeters of the specified screen.
`Keyboard(display)`	Return the device ID for the main keyboard connected to the display.

Macros

`LastKnownRequestProcessed` (*display*)	Return the serial ID of the last known protocol request to have been issued. This can be useful in processing errors, since the serial number of failing requests are provided in the `XError-Event` structure.
`MaxCmapsOfScreen(`*scr_pnt*`)`	Return the maximum number of installed (hardware) colormaps supported by the specified screen.
`MinCmapsOfScreen(`*scr_pnt*`)`	Return the minimum number of installed (hardware) colormaps supported by the specified screen.
`NextRequest(`*display*`)`	Return the serial ID of the next protocol request to be issued. This can be useful in processing errors, since the serial number of failing requests are provided in the `XErrorEvent` structure.
`PlanesOfScreen(`*scr_pnt*`)`	Return the number of planes in the specified screen.
`ProtocolRevision(`*display*`)`	Return the minor protocol revision number of the X server.
`ProtocolVersion(`*display*`)`	Return the version number of the X protocol associated with the connected display. This is currently 11.
`QLength(`*display*`)`	Return the number of events that can be queued by the specified display.
`RootWindow(`*display,scr_num*`)`	Return the ID of the root window. This macro is necessary for routines that reference the root window or create a top-level window for an application.
`RootWindowOfScreen(`*scr_pnt*`)`	Return the ID of the root window of the specified screen.
`ScreenCount(`*display*`)`	Return the number of available screens on a specified display.
`ScreenOfDisplay(`*display,scr_num*`)`	Return the specified screen of the specified display.
`ServerVendor(`*display*`)`	Return a pointer to a null terminated string giving some identification of the owner of the X server implementation.
`VendorRelease(`*display*`)`	Return a number related to the release of the X server by the vendor.

WhitePixel(*display,scr_num*)	Return the white pixel value in the default colormap that is created by XOpenDisplay.
WhitePixelOfScreen(*scr_pnt*)	Return the white pixel value in the default colormap of the specified screen.
WidthOfScreen(*scr_pnt*)	Return the width of the specified screen.
WidthMMOfScreen(*scr_pnt*)	Return the width of the specified screen in millimeters.

Image Format Macros

BitmapBitOrder(*display*)	Within each BitmapUnit, the leftmost bit in the bitmap as displayed on the screen is either the least or most significant bit in the unit. Values are Least-Significant or MostSignificant.
BitmapPad(*display*)	Each scan line must be padded to a multiple of bits specified by the value returned by this macro.
BitmapUnit(*display*)	Return the size of a bitmap's unit. The scan line is quantized (calculated) in multiples of this value.
ByteOrder(*display*)	Specifies the required byte order for images for each scan line unit in XYFormat (bitmap) or for each pixel value in ZFormat. Values are LSBFirst or MSBFirst.
ImageByteOrder(*display*)	Specifies the required byte order for images for each scan line unit in XYFormat (bitmap) or for each pixel value in ZFormat. Values are LSBFirst or MSBFirst.

Keysym Classification Macros

You may want to test if a keysym of the defined set (XK_MISCELLANY) is, for example, on the key pad or the function keys. You can use the keysym macros to perform the following tests:

IsCursorKey(*keysym*)	Return True if the keysym represents a cursor key.
IsFunctionKey(*keysym*)	Return True if the keysym represents a function key.
IsKeypadKey(*keysym*)	Return True if the keysym represents a key pad.
IsMiscFunctionKey(*keysym*)	Return True if the keysym represents a miscellaneous function key.

`IsModifierKey(keysym)`	Return `True` if the keysym represents a modifier key.
`IsPFKey(keysym)`	Return `True` if the keysym represents a PF key.

Resource Manager Macros

These macros convert from strings to quarks and quarks to strings. They are used by the resource manager. Note that they do not follow the normal naming conventions for macros, since they begin with an X.

`XrmStringToName(string)`	Convert string to `XrmName`. Same as `XStringToQuark`.
`XrmStringToClass(string)`	Convert string to `XrmClass`. Same as `XStringToQuark`.
`XrmStringToRepresentation` `(string)`	Convert string to `XrmRepresentation`. Same as `XStringToQuark`.
`XrmNameToString(name)`	Convert `XrmName` to string. Same as `XrmQuarkToString`.
`XrmClassToString(class)`	Convert `XrmClass` to string. Same as `XrmQuarkToString`.
`XrmRepresentationToString` `(type)`	Convert `XrmRepresentation` to string. Same as `XrmQuarkToString`.

D
The Color Database

The color database is used by `XParseColor`, `XLookupColor`, and `XStoreNamed-Color`. These routines make it easier to allow the user to specify color names. Use of these names for routine color allocation of read-only colorcells is encouraged since this increases the chance of sharing colorcells and thereby makes the colormap go further before running out of colorcells. The location in the file system of the text version of the color database is an implementation detail, but by default on a UNIX system it is *lusr/lib/X11/rgb.txt*.

It should be noted that while these color names are present in the standard X11 distribution, they are not specified by the X11 Protocol or Xlib. Therefore, it is permissible for server vendors to change the color names, though most will probably only add colors rather than take them away. Furthermore, hardware vendors must change the RGB values for each display hardware to achieve the proper "gamma correction" so that the colors described by the name really generate that color. The RGB values in the standard file are for the DEC VR290 display. The color that appears on a Sun system given these RGB values for "pink," for example, looks more like light burgundy.

Each color in Table D-1 (see next page) may be used in the form shown or in mixed case, with initial capitals and all spaces eliminated.

Colors

Table D-1. The Text Version of the Color Database

English Words	Red	Green	Blue	English Words	Red	Green	Blue
aquamarine	112	219	147	medium aquamarine	50	204	153
black	0	0	0	medium blue	50	50	204
blue	0	0	255	medium forest green	107	142	35
blue violet	159	95	159	medium goldenrod	234	234	173
brown	165	42	42	medium orchid	147	112	219
cadet blue	95	159	159	medium sea green	66	111	66
coral	255	127	0	medium slate blue	127	0	255
cornflower blue	66	66	111	medium spring green	127	255	0
cyan	0	255	255	medium turquoise	112	219	219
dark green	47	79	47	medium violet red	219	112	147
dark olive green	79	79	47	midnight blue	47	47	79
dark orchid	153	50	204	navy	35	35	142
dark slate blue	107	35	142	navy blue	35	35	142
dark slate gray	47	79	79	orange	204	50	50
dark slate grey	47	79	79	orange red	255	0	127
dark turquoise	112	147	219	orchid	219	112	219
dim gray	84	84	84	pale green	143	188	143
dim grey	84	84	84	pink	188	143	143
firebrick	142	35	35	plum	234	173	234
forest green	35	142	35	red	255	0	0
gold	204	127	50	salmon	111	66	66
goldenrod	219	219	112	sea green	35	142	107
gray	192	192	192	sienna	142	107	35
green	0	255	0	sky blue	50	153	204
green yellow	147	219	112	slate blue	0	127	255
grey	192	192	192	spring green	0	255	127
indian red	79	47	47	steel blue	35	107	142
khaki	159	159	95	tan	219	147	112
light blue	191	216	216	thistle	216	191	216
light gray	168	168	168	turquoise	173	234	234
light grey	168	168	168	violet	79	47	79
light steel blue	143	143	188	violet red	204	50	153
lime green	50	204	50	wheat	216	216	191
magenta	255	0	255	white	252	252	252
maroon	142	35	107	yellow	255	255	0
				yellow green	153	204	50

E
Event Reference

This appendix describes each event structure in detail and briefly shows how each event type is used. It covers the most common uses of each event type, the information contained in each event structure, how the event is selected, and the side effects of the event, if any. Each event is described on a separate reference page.

Table E-1 lists each event mask, its associated event types, and the associated structure definition. See Volume One, Chapter 8, *Events* for more information on events.

Table E-1. Event Masks, Event Types, and Event Structures

Event Mask	Event Type	Structure
KeyPressMask	KeyPress	XKeyPressedEvent
KeyReleaseMask	KeyRelease	XKeyReleasedEvent
ButtonPressMask	ButtonPress	XButtonPressedEvent
ButtonReleaseMask	ButtonRelease	XButtonReleasedEvent
OwnerGrabButtonMask	n/a	n/a
KeymapStateMask	KeymapNotify	XKeymapEvent
PointerMotionMask PointerMotionHintMask ButtonMotionMask Button1MotionMask Button2MotionMask Button3MotionMask Button4MotionMask Button5MotionMask	MotionNotify	XPointerMovedEvent
EnterWindowMask	EnterNotify	XEnterWindowEvent
LeaveWindowMask	LeaveNotify	XLeaveWindowEvent
FocusChangeMask	FocusIn FocusOut	XFocusInEvent XFocusOutEvent
ExposureMask	Expose	XExposeEvent

Table E-1. Event Masks, Event Types, and Event Structures (continued)

Event Mask	Event Type	Structure
selected in GC by graphics_expose member)	GraphicsExpose NoExpose	XGraphicsExposeEvent XNoExposeEvent
ColormapChangeMask	ColormapNotify	XColormapEvent
PropertyChangeMask	PropertyNotify	XPropertyEvent
VisibilityChangeMask	VisibilityNotify	XVisibilityEvent
ResizeRedirectMask	ResizeRequest	XResizeRequestEvent
StructureNotifyMask	CirculateNotify ConfigureNotify DestroyNotify GravityNotify MapNotify ReparentNotify UnmapNotify	XCirculateEvent XConfigureEvent XDestroyWindowEvent XGravityEvent XMapEvent XReparentEvent XUnmapEvent
SubstructureNotifyMask	CirculateNotify ConfigureNotify CreateNotify DestroyNotify GravityNotify MapNotify ReparentNotify UnmapNotify	XCirculateEvent XConfigureEvent XCreateWindowEvent XDestroyWindowEvent XGravityEvent XMapEvent XReparentEvent XUnmapEvent
SubstructureRedirectMask	CirculateRequest ConfigureRequest MapRequest	XCirculateRequestEvent XConfigureRequestEvent XMapRequestEvent
(always selected)	MappingNotify	XMappingEvent
(always selected)	ClientMessage	XClientMessageEvent
(always selected)	SelectionClear	XSetSelectClearEvent
(always selected)	SelectionNotify	XSelectionEvent
(always selected)	SelectionRequest	XSelectionRequestEvent

Meaning of Common Structure Elements

Example E-1 shows the XEvent union and a simple event structure that is one member of the union. Several of the members of this structure are present in nearly every event structure. They are described here before we go into the event-specific members (see also Volume One, Section 8.2.2).

Example E-1. XEvent union and XAnyEvent structure

```
typedef union _XEvent {
    int type;               /* must not be changed; first member */
    XAnyEvent xany;
    XButtonEvent xbutton;
    XCirculateEvent xcirculate;
    XCirculateRequestEvent xcirculaterequest;
    XClientMessageEvent xclient;
    XColormapEvent xcolormap;
    XConfigureEvent xconfigure;
    XConfigureRequestEvent xconfigurerequest;
    XCreateWindowEvent xcreatewindow;
    XDestroyWindowEvent xdestroywindow;
    XCrossingEvent xcrossing;
    XExposeEvent xexpose;
    XFocusChangeEvent xfocus;
    XNoExposeEvent xnoexpose;
    XGraphicsExposeEvent xgraphicsexpose;
    XGravityEvent xgravity;
    XKeymapEvent xkeymap;
    XKeyEvent xkey;
    XMapEvent xmap;
    XUnmapEvent xunmap;
    XMappingEvent xmapping;
    XMapRequestEvent xmaprequest;
    XMotionEvent xmotion;
    XPropertyEvent xproperty;
    XReparentEvent xreparent;
    XResizeRequestEvent xresizerequest;
    XSelectionClearEvent xselectionclear;
    XSelectionEvent xselection;
    XSelectionRequestEvent xselectionrequest;
    XVisibilityEvent xvisibility;
} XEvent;

typedef struct {
    int type;
    unsigned long serial;/* # of last request processed by server */
    Bool send_event;       /* true if this came from SendEvent request */
    Display *display;      /* display the event was read from */
    Window window;         /* window on which event was requested in
                            * event mask */
} XAnyEvent;
```

The first member of the XEvent union is the type of event. When an event is received (with XNextEvent, for example), the application checks the type member in the XEvent union. Then the specific event type is known. and the specific event structure (such as xbutton) is used to access information specific to that event type.

Before the branching depending on the event type, only the XEvent union is used. After the branching, only the event structure which contains the specific information for each event type should be used in each branch. For example, if the XEvent union were called report, the report.xexpose structure should be used within the branch for Expose events.

You'll notice that each event structure also begins with a type member. This member is rarely used, since it is an identical copy of the type member in the XEvent union.

Most event structures also have a window member. The only ones that don't are selection events (SelectionNotify, SelectionRequest, and SelectionClear) and events selected by the graphics_exposures member of the GC (GraphicsExpose and NoExpose). The window member indicates the event window that selected and received the event. This is the window where the event arrives if it has propagated through the hierarchy as described in Volume One, Section 8.3.2. One event type may have two different meanings to an application, depending on which window it appears in.

Many of the event structures also have a display and/or root member. The display member identifies the connection to the server that is active. The root member indicates which screen the window that received the event is linked to in the hierarchy. Most programs only use a single screen and therefore don't need to worry about the root member. The display member can be useful since you can pass the display variable into routines by simply passing a pointer to the event structure, eliminating the need for a separate display argument.

All event structures include a serial member, that gives the number of the last protocol request processed by the server. This is useful in debugging, since an error can be detected by the server but not reported to the user (or programmer) until the next routine that gets an event. That means several routines may execute successfully after the error occurs. The last request processed will often indicate the request that contained the error.

All event structures also include a send_event flag, which if True indicates that the event was sent by XSendEvent (i.e., by another client rather than by the server).

The following pages describe each event type in detail. The events are presented in alphabetical order, each on a separate page. Each page describes the circumstances under which the event is generated, the mask used to select it, the structure itself, its members, and useful programming notes. Note that the description of the structure members does not include those members common to many structures. If you need more information on these members, please refer to this introductory section.

ButtonPress, ButtonRelease

When Generated

There are two types of pointer button events: `ButtonPress` and `ButtonRelease`. Both contain the same information.

Select With

May be selected separately, using `ButtonPressMask` and `ButtonReleaseMask`.

XEvent Structure Name

```
typedef union _XEvent {
    . . .
    XButtonEvent xbutton;
    . . .
} XEvent;
```

Event Structure

```
typedef struct {
    int type;              /* of event */
    unsigned long serial;  /* # of last request processed by server */
    Bool send_event;       /* true if this came from a SendEvent request */
    Display *display;      /* display the event was read from */
    Window window;         /* event window it is reported relative to */
    Window root;           /* root window that the event occurred under */
    Window subwindow;      /* child window */
    Time time;             /* when event occurred, in milliseconds */
    int x, y;              /* pointer coords relative to receiving window *
    int x_root, y_root;    /* coordinates relative to root */
    unsigned int state;    /* mask of all buttons and modifier keys */
    unsigned int button;   /* button that triggered event */
    Bool same_screen;      /* same screen flag */
} XButtonEvent;
typedef XButtonEvent XButtonPressedEvent;
typedef XButtonEvent XButtonReleasedEvent;
```

Event Structure Members

subwindow   If the source window is the child of the receiving window, then the `subwindow` member is set to the ID of that child.

time   The server time when the button event occurred, in milliseconds. `Time` is declared as `unsigned long`, so it wraps around when it reaches the maximum value of a 32 bit number (every 49.7 days).

x, y   If the receiving window is on the same screen as the root window specified by `root`, then x and y are the pointer coordinates relative to the receiving window's origin. Otherwise, x and y are zero.

When active button grabs and pointer grabs are in effect (see Volume One, Section 9.4), the coordinates relative to the receiving window may not be within the window (they may be negative or greater than window height or width).

x_root, y_root

The pointer coordinates relative to the root window which is an ancestor of the event window. If the pointer was on a different screen, these are zero.

state

The state of all the buttons and modifier keys just before the event, represented by a mask of the button and modifier key symbols: Button1Mask, Button2Mask, Button3Mask, Button4Mask, Button5Mask, Shift-Mask, ControlMask, LockMask, Mod1Mask, Mod2Mask, Mod3Mask, Mod4Mask, and Mod5Mask. If a modifier key is pressed and released when no other modifier keys are held, the ButtonPress will have a state member of 0 and the ButtonRelease will have a nonzero state member indicating that itself was held just before the event.

button

A value indicating which button changed state to trigger this event. One of the constants: Button1, Button2, Button3, Button4, or Button5.

same_screen

Indicates whether the pointer is currently on the same screen as this window. This is always True unless the pointer was actively grabbed before the automatic grab could take place.

Notes

Unless an active grab already exists, or a passive grab on the button combination that was pressed already exists at a higher level in the hierarchy than where the ButtonPress occured, an automatic active grab of the pointer takes place when a ButtonPress occurs. Because of the automatic grab, the matching ButtonRelease is sent to the same application that received the ButtonPress event. If OwnerGrabButtonMask has been selected, the ButtonRelease event is delivered to the window which contained the pointer when the button was released, as long as that window belongs to the same client as the window in which the ButtonPress event occurred. If the ButtonRelease occurs outside or the client's windows, or OwnerGrabButtonMask was not selected, the ButtonRelease is delivered to the window in which the ButtonPress occurred. The grab is terminated when all buttons are released. During the grab, the cursor associated with the grabbing window will track the pointer anywhere on the screen.

If the application has invoked a passive button grab on an ancestor of the window in which the ButtonPress event occurs, then that grab takes precedence over the automatic grab, and the ButtonRelease will go to that window, or it will be handled normally by that client depending on the owner_events flag in the XGrabButton call.

CirculateNotify

When Generated

`CirculateNotify` events are generated when a window is actually restacked from a call to either `XCirculateWindowUp` or `XCirculateWindowDown`. If the window manager prevents such an operation, then no `XCirculateNotify` event is generated.

Select With

This event type is selected using `StructureNotifyMask` in the `XSelectInput` call for the window to be raised, or by selecting `SubstructureNotifyMask` for the parent of the window to be raised.

XEvent Structure Name

```
typedef union _XEvent {
    . . .
    XCirculateEvent xcirculate;
    . . .
} XEvent;
```

Event Structure

```
typedef struct {
    int type;
    unsigned long serial;/* # of last request processed by server */
    Bool send_event;        /* true if this came from SendEvent request */
    Display *display;       /* display the event was read from */
    Window event;
    Window window;
    int place;              /* PlaceOnTop, PlaceOnBottom */
} XCirculateEvent;
```

Event Structure Members

event   The window receiving the event. If the event was selected by `Structure-NotifyMask`, event will be the same as `window`. If the event was selected by `SubstructureNotifyMask`, event will be the parent of `window`.

window   The window that was restacked.

place   Either `PlaceOnTop` or `PlaceOnBottom`. Indicates whether the window was raised to the top or bottom of the stack.

Event Reference

CirculateRequest

When Generated

CirculateRequest events report when another client calls XCirculateSubwindows, XCirculateSubwindowsUp or XCirculateSubwindowsDown for a specified parent window, and the stacking order is actually changed. If this event type is selected, the window is not moved in the stacking order. This gives the client that selects this event (usually the window manager) the opportunity to review the request in the light of its window management policy, before executing the circulate request itself, or deny the request.

Select With

This event type is selected for the parent window with the SubstructureRedirectMask.

XEvent Structure Name

```
typedef union _XEvent {
    . . .
    XCirculateRequestEvent xcirculaterequest;
    . . .
} XEvent;
```

Event Structure

```
typedef struct {
    int type;
    unsigned long serial;/* # of last request processed by server */
    Bool send_event;       /* true if this came from SendEvent request */
    Display *display;      /* display the event was read from */
    Window parent;
    Window window;
    int place;             /* PlaceOnTop, PlaceOnBottom */
} XCirculateRequestEvent;
```

Event Structure Members

parent   The parent of the window that was restacked. This is the window that selected the event.

window   The window being restacked.

place   PlaceOnTop or PlaceOnBottom. Indicates whether the window was to be placed on top or on the bottom of the stacking order.

ClientMessage

When Generated

`ClientMessage` events are generated only when a client calls the function `XSendEvent`. Any type of event can be sent with `XSendEvent`, but it will be distinguished from normal events by the the `send_event` member being set to `True`. If your program wants to be able to treat events sent with `XSendEvent` as different from normal events, you can read this member.

Select With

There is no event mask for `ClientMessage` events and they are not selected with `XSelectInput`. Instead, `XSendEvent` directs them to a specific window, which is given as a window ID: the `PointerWindow` or the `InputFocus`.

XEvent Structure Name

```
typedef union _XEvent {
    ...
    XClientMessageEvent xclient;
    ...
} XEvent;
```

Event Structure

```
typedef struct {
    int type;
    unsigned long serial;/* # of last request processed by server */
    Bool send_event;       /* true if this came from SendEvent request */
    Display *display;      /* display the event was read from */
    Window window;
    Atom message_type;
    int format;
    union {
        char b[20];
        short s[10];
        int l[5];
    } data;
} XClientMessageEvent;
```

Event Structure Members

message_type
> An atom that specifies how the data is to be interpreted by the receiving client. The X server places no interpretation on the type or the data, but it must be a list of 8-bit, 16-bit, or 32-bit quantities, so that the X server can correctly swap bytes as necessary. The data always consists of twenty 8-bit values, ten 16-bit values, or five 32-bit values, although each particular message might not make use of all of these values.

format
> Specifies the format of the property specified by `message_type`. This will be on of the values 8, 16, or 32.

ColormapNotify

When Generated

ColormapNotify events herald changes relating to the colormap specified in the colormap attribute for a particular window, or changes to the attribute itself.

Select With

To receive this event type, pass ColormapChangeMask to XSelectInput.

XEvent Structure Name

```
typedef union _XEvent {
    ...
    XColormapEvent xcolormap;
    ...
} XEvent;
```

Event Structure

```
typedef struct {
    int type;
    unsigned long serial;/* # of last request processed by server */
    Bool send_event;      /* true if this came from SendEvent request */
    Display *display;     /* display the event was read from */
    Window window;
    Colormap colormap;    /* Colormap or None */
    Bool new;
    int state;            /* ColormapInstalled, ColormapUninstalled */
} XColormapEvent;
```

Event Structure Members

window   The window whose associated colormap or attribute changes.

colormap   The colormap associated with the window, either a colormap ID or the constant None. It will be None only if this event was generated due to an XFree-Colormap call.

new   True when the colormap attribute has been changed, or False when the colormap is installed or uninstalled.

state   Either ColormapInstalled or ColormapUninstalled; it indicates whether the colormap is installed or uninstalled.

When Generated

`ConfigureNotify` events announce actual changes to a window's configuration (size, position, border, stacking order).

Select With

To receive this event type for a single window, specify the window ID of that window and pass `StructureNotifyMask` as the `event_mask` argument to `XSelectInput`. To receive this event for all children of a window, specify the parent window ID and pass `SubstructureNotifyMask`.

XEvent Structure Name

```
typedef union _XEvent {
    ...
    XConfigureEvent xconfigure;
    ...
} XEvent;
```

Event Structure

```
typedef struct {
    int type;
    unsigned long serial;/* # of last request processed by server */
    Bool send_event;       /* true if this came from SendEvent request */
    Display *display;      /* display the event was read from */
    Window event;
    Window window;
    int x, y;
    int width, height;
    int border_width;
    Window above;
    Bool override_redirect;
} XConfigureEvent;
```

Event Structure Members

event   The window that selected the event. The `event` and `window` members are identical if the event was selected with `StructureNotifyMask`.

window The window whose configuration was changed.

x, y   The final coordinates of the reconfigured window relative to its parent.

width, height
        The width and height in pixels of the window after reconfiguration.

border_width
        The width in pixels of the border after reconfiguration.

Event
Reference

above   If this member is None, then the window is on the bottom of the stack with respect to its siblings. Otherwise, the window is immediately on top of the specified sibling window.

override_redirect
          The override_redirect attribute of the reconfigured window. If True, it indicates that the client wants this window to be immune to interception by the window manager of configuration requests. Window managers normally should ignore this event if override_redirect is True.

ConfigureRequest

When Generated

`ConfigureRequest` events announce another client's attempt to change a window's size, position, border, and/or stacking order. The X server generates this event type when another client attempts to reconfigure the window with `XConfigureWindow` or another configuration control function. If this event type is selected, the window is not reconfigured. This gives the client that selects this event (usually the window manager) the opportunity to revise the requested configuration before executing the `XConfigureWindow` request itself, or to deny the request.

Select With

To receive this event type for any window in a group of children, specify the parent window and pass `SubstructureRedirectMask` to `XSelectInput`.

XEvent Structure Name

```
typedef union _XEvent {
    ...
    XConfigureRequestEvent xconfigurerequest;
    ...
} XEvent;
```

Event Structure

```
typedef struct {
    int type;
    unsigned long serial;/* # of last request processed by server */
    Bool send_event;      /* true if this came from SendEvent request */
    Display *display;     /* display the event was read from */
    Window parent;
    Window window;
    int x, y;
    int width, height;
    int border_width;
    Window above;
    int detail;           /* Above, Below, TopIf, BottomIf, Opposite */
    unsigned long value_mask;
} XConfigureRequestEvent;
```

Event Structure Members

parent   The window that selected the event. This is the parent of the window being configured.

window   The window that is being configured.

x, y   The requested position for the upper-left pixel of the window's border relative to the origin of the parent window.

width, height
         The requested width and height in pixels for the window.

border_width
> The requested border width for the window.

above   None, Above, Below, TopIf, BottomIf, or Opposite. Specifies the sibling window on top of which the specified window should be placed. If this member has the constant None, then the specified window should be placed on the bottom.

Notes

The geometry is derived from the XConfigureWindow request that triggered the event.

When Generated

The X server reports `CreateNotify` events to clients when windows are created.

Select With

To receive this event type on children of a window, specify the parent window ID and pass `SubstructureNotifyMask`. Note that this event type cannot selected by `Structure-NotifyMask`.

XEvent Structure Name

```
typedef union _XEvent {
    ...
    XCreateWindowEvent xcreatewindow;
    ...
} XEvent;
```

Event Structure

```
typedef struct {
    int type;
    unsigned long serial;/* # of last request processed by server */
    Bool send_event;       /* true if this came from SendEvent request */
    Display *display;      /* display the event was read from */
    Window parent;         /* parent of the window */
    Window window;         /* window ID of window created */
    int x, y;              /* window location */
    int width, height;     /* size of window */
    int border_width;      /* border width */
    Bool override_redirect;   /* creation should be overridden */
} XCreateWindowEvent;
```

Event Structure Members

parent   The ID of the created window's parent.

window   The ID of the created window.

x, y   The coordinates of the created window relative to its parent.

width, height   The width and height in pixels of the created window.

border_width   The width in pixels of the border of the created window.

override_redirect

The `override_redirect` attribute of the created window. If `True`, it indicates that the client wants this window to be immune to interception by the window manager of configuration requests. Window managers normally should ignore this event if `override_redirect` is `True`.

Notes

For descriptions of these members, see the `XCreateWindow` function and the `XSet-WindowAttributes` structure.

DestroyNotify

When Generated

DestroyNotify events announce that a window has been destroyed.

Select With

To receive this event type on children of a window, specify the parent window ID and pass SubstructureNotifyMask as part of the *event_mask* argument to XSelectInput. This event type cannot be selected with StructureNotifyMask.

XEvent Structure Name

```
typedef union _XEvent {
    . . .
    XDestroyWindowEvent xdestroywindow;
    . . .
} XEvent;
```

Event Structure

```
typedef struct {
    int type;
    unsigned long serial;/* # of last request processed by server */
    Bool send_event;       /* true if this came from SendEvent request */
    Display *display;      /* display the event was read from */
    Window event;
    Window window;
} XDestroyWindowEvent;
```

Event Structure Members

event   The window that selected the event.

window   The window that was destroyed.

When Generated

EnterNotify and LeaveNotify events occur when the pointer enters or leaves a window.

When the pointer crosses a window border, a LeaveNotify event occurs in the window being left and an EnterNotify event occurs in the window being entered. Whether or not each event is queued for any application depends on whether any application selected the right event on the window in which it occured.

In addition, EnterNotify and LeaveNotify events are delivered to windows that are *virtually crossed*. These are windows that are between the origin and destination windows in the hierarchy but not on the screen. Further explanation of virtual crossing is provided two pages following.

Select With

Each of these events can be selected separately with XEnterWindowMask and XLeaveWindowMask.

XEvent Structure Name

```
typedef union _XEvent {
    ...
    XCrossingEvent xcrossing;
    ...
} XEvent;
```

Event Structure

```
typedef struct {
    int type;              /* of event */
    unsigned long serial;  /* # of last request processed by server */
    Bool send_event;       /* true if this came from SendEvent request */
    Display *display;      /* display the event was read from */
    Window window;         /* event window it is reported relative to */
    Window root;           /* root window that the event occurred on */
    Window subwindow;      /* child window */
    Time time;             /* milliseconds */
    int x, y;              /* pointer x, y coordinates in receiving window */
    int x_root, y_root;    /* coordinates relative to root */
    int mode;              /* NotifyNormal, NotifyGrab, NotifyUngrab */
    int detail;            /* NotifyAncestor, NotifyVirtual, NotifyInferior
                            * NotifyNonLinear, NotifyNonLinearVirtual */
    Bool same_screen;      /* same screen flag */
    Bool focus;            /* Boolean focus */
    unsigned int state;    /* key or button mask */
} XCrossingEvent;
typedef XCrossingEvent XEnterWindowEvent;
typedef XCrossingEvent XLeaveWindowEvent;
```

Event
Reference

Event Structure Members

The following list describes the members of the XCrossingEvent structure.

subwindow In a LeaveNotify event, if the pointer began in a child of the receiving window then the child member is set to the window ID of the child. Otherwise, it is set to None. For an EnterNotify event, if the pointer ends up in a child of the receiving window then the child member is set to the window ID of the child. Otherwise, it is set to None.

time The server time when the crossing event occurred, in milliseconds. Time is declared as unsigned long, so it wraps around when it reaches the maximum value of a 32 bit number (every 49.7 days).

x, y The point of entry or exit of the pointer relative to the event window.

x_root, y_root
The point of entry or exit of the pointer relative to the root window.

mode Normal crossing events or those caused by pointer warps have mode Notify-Normal; events caused by a grab have mode NotifyGrab; and events caused by a released grab have mode NotifyUngrab.

detail The value of the detail member depends on the hierarchical relationship between the origin and destination windows and the direction of pointer transfer. Determining which windows receive events and with which detail members is quite complicated. This topic is described in the next section.

same_screen
Indicates whether the pointer is currently on the same screen as this window. This is always True unless the pointer was actively grabbed before the automatic grab could take place.

focus If the receiving window is the focus window or a descendant of the focus window, the focus member is True; otherwise it is False.

state The state of all the buttons and modifier keys just before the event, represented by a mask of the button and modifier key symbols: Button1Mask, Button2Mask, Button3Mask, Button4Mask, Button5Mask, Shift-Mask, ControlMask, LockMask, Mod1Mask, Mod2Mask, Mod3Mask, Mod4Mask, and Mod5Mask.

Virtual Crossing and the detail Member

Virtual crossing occurs when the pointer moves between two windows that do not have a parent-child relationship. Windows between the origin and destination windows in the hierarchy receive EnterNotify and LeaveNotify events. The detail member of each of these events depends on the hierarchical relationship of the origin and destination windows and the direction of pointer transfer.

Virtual crossing is an advanced topic that you shouldn't spend time figuring out unless you have an important reason to use it. I have never seen an application that uses this feature, and I know of no reason for its extreme complexity. With that word of warning, proceed.

Let's say the pointer has moved from one window, the origin, to another, the destination. First we'll specify what types of events each window gets, and then the detail member of each of those events.

The window of origin receives a LeaveNotify event and the destination window receives an EnterNotify event, if they have requested this type of event. If one is an inferior of the other, the detail member of the event received by the inferior is NotifyAncestor and the detail of the event received by the superior is NotifyInferior. If the crossing is between parent and child, these are the only events generated.

However, if the origin and destination windows are not parent and child, other windows are *virtually crossed* and also receive events. If neither window is an ancestor of the other, ancestors of each window up to but not including the least common ancestor receive LeaveNotify events if they are in the same branch of the hierarchy as the origin and EnterNotify events if they are in the same branch as the destination. These events can be used to track the motion of the pointer through the hierarchy.

- In the case of a crossing between a parent and a child of a child, the middle child receives a LeaveNotify with detail NotifyVirtual.

- In the case of a crossing between a child and the parent of its parent, the middle child receives an EnterNotify with detail NotifyVirtual.

- In a crossing between windows whose least common ancestor is two or more windows away, both the origin and destination windows receive events with detail NotifyNonlinear. The windows between the origin and the destination in the hierarchy, up to but not including their least common ancestor, receive events with detail NotifyNonlinearVirtual. The least common ancestor is the lowest window from which both are descendants.

- If the origin and destination windows are on separate screens, the events and details generated are the same as for two windows not parent and child, except that the root windows of the two screens are considered the least common ancestor. Both root windows also receive events.

Event Reference

Table E-2 shows the event types generated by a pointer crossing from window *A* to window *B* when window *C* is the least common ancestor of *A* and *B*.

Table E-2. Border Crossing Events and Window Relationship

LeaveNotify	EnterNotify
Origin window (*A*)	Destination window (*B*)
Windows between *A* and *B* exclusive if *A* is inferior	Windows between *A* and *B* exclusive if *B* is inferior
Windows between *A* and *C* exclusive	Windows between *B* and *C* exclusive
Root window on screen of origin if different from screen of destination	Root window on screen of destination if different from screen of origin

Table E-3 lists the `detail` members in events generated by a pointer crossing from window *A* to window *B*.

Table E-3. Event detail Member and Window Relationship

`detail` Flag	Window Delivered To
`NotifyAncestor`	Origin or destination when either is descendant
`NotifyInferior`	Origin or destination when either is ancestor
`NotifyVirtual`	Windows between *A* and *B* exclusive if either is descendant
`NotifyNonlinear`	Origin and destination when *A* and *B* are two or more windows distant from least common ancestor *C*
`NotifyNonlinearVirtual`	Windows between *A* and *C* exclusive and between *B* and *C* exclusive when *A* and *B* have least common ancestor *C*. Also on both root windows if *A* and *B* are on different screens.

For example, Figure E-1 shows the events that are generated by a movement from a window (window *A*) to a child (window *B1*) of a sibling (window *B*). This would generate three events: a LeaveNotify with detail NotifyNonlinear for the window *A*, an EnterNotify with detail NotifyNonlinearVirtual for its sibling window *B*, and an EnterNotify with detail NotifyNonlinear for the child (window *B1*).

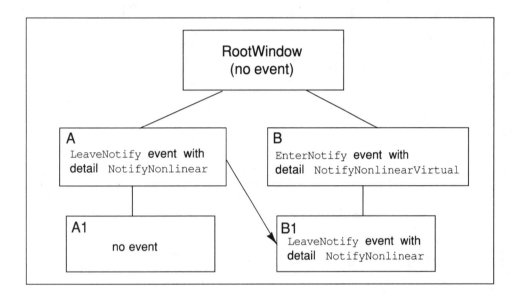

Figure E-1. Events generated by a move between windows

EnterNotify and LeaveNotify events are also generated when the pointer is grabbed, if the pointer was not already inside the grabbing window. In this case, the grabbing window receives an EnterNotify and the window containing the pointer receives a LeaveNotify event, both with mode NotifyUngrab. The pointer position in both events is the position before the grab. The result when the grab is released is exactly the same except that the two windows receive EnterNotify instead of LeaveNotify and vice versa.

Event Reference

Figure E-2 demonstrates the events and details caused by various pointer transitions, indicated by heavy arrows.

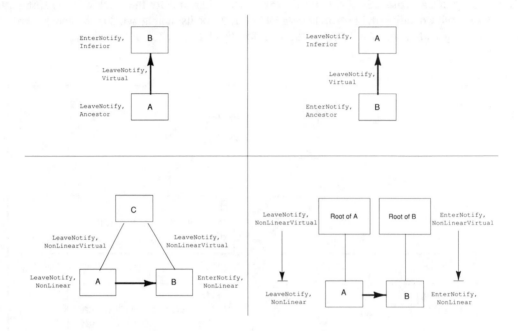

*Figure E-2. Border crossing events and detail member for pointer movement
from window A to window B, for various window relationships*

Expose

When Generated

Expose events are generated when a window becomes visible or a previously invisible part of a window becomes visible. Only InputOutput windows generate or need to respond to Expose events; InputOnly windows never generate or need to respond to them. The Expose event provides the position and size of the exposed area within the window, and a rough count of the number of remaining exposure events for the current window.

Select With

ExposureMask

XEvent Structure Name

```
typedef union _XEvent {
    ...
    XExposeEvent xexpose;
    ...
} XEvent;
```

Event Structure

```
typedef struct {
    int type;
    unsigned long serial;/* # of last request processed by server */
    Bool send_event;       /* true if this came from SendEvent request */
    Display *display;      /* display the event was read from */
    Window window;
    int x, y;
    int width, height;
    int count;             /* if nonzero, at least this many more */
} XExposeEvent;
```

Event Structure Members

x, y   The coordinates of the upper-left corner of the exposed region relative to the origin of the window.

width, height   The width and height in pixels of the exposed region.

count   The approximate number of remaining contiguous Expose events that were generated as a result of a single function call.

Notes

A single action such as a window movement or a function call can generate several exposure events on one window or on several windows. The server guarantees that all exposure events generated from a single action will be sent contiguously, so that they can all be handled before moving on to other event types. This allows an application to keep track of the rectangles specified in contiguous Expose events, set the clip_mask in a GC to the areas specified in the rectangle using XSetRegion or XSetClipRectangles, and then finally redraw the window clipped with the GC in a single operation after all the Expose events have arrived.

Event
Reference

The last event to arrive is indicated by a count of 0. In Release 2, XUnionRectWith-Region can be used to add the rectangle in Expose events to a region before calling XSet-Region.

If your application is able to redraw partial windows, you can also read each exposure event in turn and redraw each area.

FocusIn, FocusOut

When Generated

`FocusIn` and `FocusOut` events occur when the keyboard focus window changes, as a result of an `XSetInputFocus` call. They are much like `EnterNotify` and `LeaveNotify` events except that they track the focus rather than the pointer.

Select With

`FocusIn` and `FocusOut` events are selected with `FocusChangeMask`. They cannot be selected separately.

XEvent Structure Name

```
typedef union _XEvent {
    . . .
    XFocusChangeEvent xfocus;
    . . .
} XEvent;
```

Event Structure

```
typedef struct {
    int type;               /* FocusIn or FocusOut */
    unsigned long serial;/* # of last request processed by server */
    Bool send_event;        /* true if this came from SendEvent request */
    Display *display;       /* display the event was read from */
    Window window;          /* window of event */
    int mode;               /* NotifyNormal, NotifyGrab, NotifyUngrab */
    int detail;             /* NotifyAncestor, NotifyVirtual, Notify-
                             * Inferior, NotifyNonLinear, NotifyNonLinear-
                             * Virtual, NotifyPointer, NotifyPointerRoot,
                             * NotifyDetailNone */
} XFocusChangeEvent;
typedef XFocusChangeEvent XFocusInEvent;
typedef XFocusChangeEvent XFocusOutEvent;
```

Event Structure Members

mode   For events generated when the keyboard is not grabbed, mode is `Notify-Normal`; when the keyboard is grabbed, mode is `NotifyGrab`; and when a keyboard is ungrabbed, mode is `NotifyUngrab`.

detail The `detail` member identifies the relationship between the window that receives the event and the origin and destination windows. It will be described in detail after the description of which windows get what types of events.

Notes

The *keyboard focus* is a window that has been designated as the one to receive all keyboard input irrespective of the pointer position. Only the keyboard focus window and its descendants receive keyboard events. By default, the focus window is the root window. Since all

Most window managers allow the user to set a focus window, to avoid the problem where the pointer sometimes gets bumped into the wrong window and your typing doesn't go to the intended window. If the pointer is pointing at the root window, all typing is usually lost since there is no application for this input to propagate to. Some applications may set the keyboard focus so that they can get all keyboard input for a given period of time, but this practice is not encouraged.

Focus events are used when an application wants to act differently when the keyboard focus is set to another window or to itself. `FocusChangeMask` is used to select `FocusIn` and `FocusOut` events.

`FocusOut` events are delivered to the old focus window and `FocusIn` events to the window which receives the focus. Windows in between in the hierarchy are virtually crossed and receive focus change events depending on the relationship and direction of transfer between the origin and destination windows. Some or all of the windows between the window containing the pointer at the time of the focus change and that window's root can also receive focus change events. By checking the `detail` member of `FocusIn` and `FocusOut` events, an application can tell which of its windows can receive input.

The `detail` member gives clues about the relationship of the event receiving window to the origin and destination of the focus. The `detail` member of `FocusOut` and `FocusIn` events is analogous to the `detail` member of `LeaveNotify` and `EnterNotify` events, but with even more permutations to make life complicated.

Virtual Focus Crossing and the detail Member

We will now embark on specifying the types of events sent to each window and the `detail` member in each event, depending on the relative position in the hierarchy of the origin window (old focus), destination window (new focus), and the pointer window (window containing pointer at time of focus change). Don't even try to figure this out unless you have to.

Table E-4 shows the event types generated by a focus transition from window *A* to window *B* when window *C* is the least common ancestor of *A* and *B*, and *P* is the window containing the pointer. This table includes most of the events generated, but not all of them. It is quite possible for a single window to receive more than one focus change event from a single focus change.

Table E-4. FocusIn and FocusOut Events and Window Relationship

`FocusOut`	`FocusIn`
origin window (*A*)	destination window (*B*)
windows between *A* and *B* exclusive if *A* is inferior	windows between *A* and *B* exclusive if *B* is inferior
windows between *A* and *C* exclusive	windows between *B* and *C* exclusive
root window on screen of origin if different from screen of destination	root window on screen of destination if different from screen of origin
pointer window up to but not including origin window if pointer window is descendant of origin	pointer window up to but not including destination window if pointer window is descendant of destination
pointer window up to and including pointer window's root if transfer was from `PointerRoot`	pointer window up to and including pointer window's root if transfer was to `PointerRoot`

Event Reference

Table E-5 lists the detail members in events generated by a focus transition from window *A* to window *B*, with *P* being the window containing the pointer.

Table E-5. Event detail Member and Window Relationship

detail Flag	Window Delivered To
NotifyAncestor	Origin or destination when either is descendant
NotifyInferior	Origin or destination when either is ancestor
NotifyVirtual	Windows between *A* and *B* exclusive if either is descendant
NotifyNonlinear	Origin and destination when *A* and *B* are two or more windows distant from least common ancestor *C*
NotifyNonlinearVirtual	Windows between *A* and *C* exclusive and between *B* and *C* exclusive when *A* and *B* have least common ancestor *C*. Also on both root windows if *A* and *B* are on different screens
NotifyPointer	Window *P* and windows up to but not including the origin or destination windows
NotifyPointerRoot	Window *P* and all windows up to its root, and all other roots, when focus is set to or from Pointer-Root
NotifyNone	All roots, when focus is set to or from None

The following two pages show all the possible combinations of focus transitions and of origin, destination, and pointer windows and shows the types of events that are generated and their detail member. Solid lines indicate branches of the hierarchy. Dotted arrows indicate the direction of transition of the focus. At each end of this arrow are the origin and destination windows, windows *A* to *B*. Arrows ending in a bar indicate that the event type and detail described are delivered to all windows up to the bar.

In any branch, there may be windows that are not shown. Windows in a single branch between two boxes shown will get the event types and details shown beside the branch.

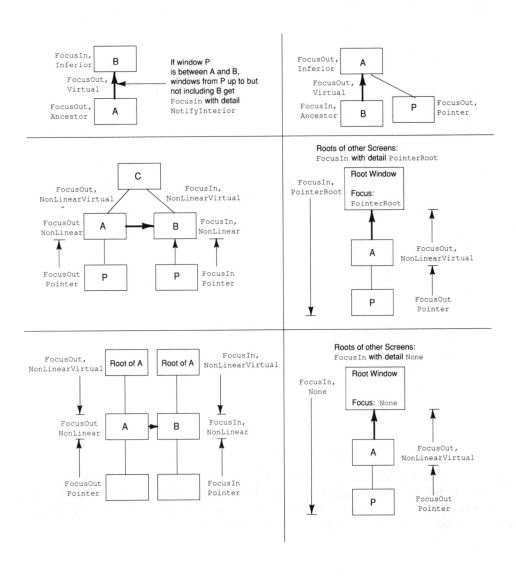

Figure E-3. FocusIn and FocusOut event schematics

Event Reference

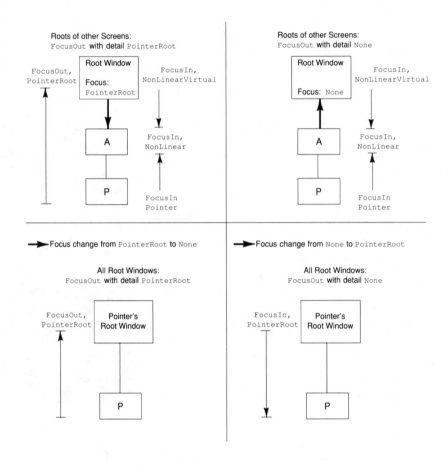

Figure E-3. FocusIn and FocusOut event schematics (cont'd)

FocusIn and FocusOut events are also generated when the keyboard is grabbed, if the focus was not already assigned to the grabbing window. In this case, all windows receive events as if the focus was set from the current focus to the grab window. When the grab is released, the events generated are just as if the focus was set back.

GraphicsExpose, NoExpose

When Generated

GraphicsExpose events indicate that the source area for a XCopyArea or XCopyPlane request was not available because it was outside the source window or obscured by a window. NoExpose events indicate that the source region was completely available.

Select With

These events are not selected with XSelectInput, but are sent if the GC in the XCopy-Area or XCopyPlane request had its graphics_exposures flag set to True. If graphics_exposures is True in the GC used for the copy, either one NoExpose event or one or more GraphicsExpose events will be generated for every XCopyArea or XCopyPlane call made.

XEvent Structure Name

```
typedef union _XEvent {
    . . .
    XNoExposeEvent xnoexpose;
    . . .
} XEvent;
```

Event Structure

```
typedef struct {
    int type;
    unsigned long serial;/* # of last request processed by server */
    Bool send_event;      /* true if this came from SendEvent request */
    Display *display;     /* display the event was read from */
    Drawable drawable;
    int x, y;
    int width, height;
    int count;            /* if nonzero, at least this many more */
    int major_code;       /* core is CopyArea or CopyPlane */
    int minor_code;       /* not defined in the core */
} XGraphicsExposeEvent;

typedef struct {
    int type;
    unsigned long serial;/* # of last request processed by server */
    Bool send_event;      /* true if this came from SendEvent request */
    Display *display;     /* display the event was read from */
    Drawable drawable;
    int major_code;       /* core is CopyArea or CopyPlane */
    int minor_code;       /* not defined in the core */
} XNoExposeEvent;
```

Event Structure Members

drawable   A window or an off-screen pixmap. This specifies the destination of the graphics request that generated the event.

Event
Reference

x, y	The coordinates of the upper-left corner of the exposed region relative to the origin of the window.
width, height	The width and height in pixels of the exposed region.
count	The approximate number of remaining contiguous GraphicsExpose events that were generated as a result of the XCopyArea or XCopy-Plane call.
major_code	The graphics request used. This may be one of the symbols CopyArea or CopyPlane, or a symbol defined by a loaded extension.
minor_code	Zero unless the request is part of an extension.

Notes

Expose events and GraphicsExpose events both indicate the region of a window that was actually exposed (x, y, width, and height). Therefore they can often be handled similarly.

GravityNotify

When Generated

GravityNotify events report when a window is moved because of a change in the size of its parent. This happens when the win_gravity attribute of the child window is something other than StaticGravity or UnmapGravity.

Select With

To receive this event type for a single window, specify the window ID of that window and use StructureNotifyMask as part of the event_mask argument to XSelectInput. To receive notification of movement due to gravity for a group of siblings, specify the parent window ID and use SubstructureNotifyMask.

XEvent Structure Name

```
typedef union _XEvent {
    ...
    XGravityEvent xgravity;
    ...
} XEvent;
```

Event Structure

```
typedef struct {
    int type;
    unsigned long serial;/* # of last request processed by server */
    Bool send_event;     /* true if this came from SendEvent request */
    Display *display;     /* display the event was read from */
    Window event;
    Window window;
    int x, y;
} XGravityEvent;
```

Event Structure Members

event   The window that selected the event.

window   The window that was moved.

x, y   The new coordinates of the window relative to its parent.

Event
Reference

KeymapNotify

When Generated

`KeymapNotify` events are reported immediately after `EnterNotify` or `FocusIn` events.

This is a way for the application to read the keyboard state as the application is "woken up," since the two triggering events usually indicate that the application is about to receive user input.

Select With

`KeymapStateMask`

XEvent Structure Name

```
typedef union _XEvent {
    . . .
    XKeymapEvent xkeymap;
    . . .
} XEvent;
```

Event Structure

```
typedef struct {
    int type;
    unsigned long serial;/* # of last request processed by server */
    Bool send_event;     /* true if this came from SendEvent request */
    Display *display;     /* display the event was read from */
    Window window;
    char key_vector[32];
} XKeymapEvent;
```

Event Structure Members

window   Reports the window which was reported in the `window` member of the preceeding `EnterNotify` or `FocusIn` event.

key_vector A bit vector or mask, each bit representing one physical key, with a total of 256 bits. For a given key, its keycode is its position in the keyboard vector. You can also get this bit vector by calling `XQueryKeymap`.

Notes

The `serial` member of `KeymapNotify` does not contain the serial number of the most recent Protocol Request processed, because this event always follows immediately after `FocusIn` or `EnterNotify` events in which the `serial` member is valid.

When Generated

KeyPress and KeyRelease events are generated for all keys, even those mapped to modifier keys such as Shift or Control.

Select With

Each type of keyboard event may be selected separately with KeyPressMask and Key-ReleaseMask.

XEvent Structure Name

```
typedef union _XEvent {
    ...
    XKeyEvent xkey;
    ...
} XEvent;
```

Event Structure

```
typedef struct {
    int type;               /* of event */
    unsigned long serial;   /* # of last request processed by server */
    Bool send_event;        /* true if this came from SendEvent request */
    Display *display;        /* display the event was read from */
    Window window;          /* event window it is reported relative to */
    Window root;            /* root window that the event occurred on */
    Window subwindow;       /* child window */
    Time time;              /* milliseconds */
    int x, y;               /* pointer coords relative to receiving window */
    int x_root, y_root;     /* coordinates relative to root */
    unsigned int state;     /* modifier key and button mask */
    unsigned int keycode;   /* server-dependent code for key */
    Bool same_screen;       /* same screen flag */
} XKeyEvent;
typedef XKeyEvent XKeyPressedEvent;
typedef XKeyEvent XKeyReleasedEvent;
```

Event Structure Members

subwindow   If the source window is the child of the receiving window, then the subwindow member is set to the ID of that child.

time   The server time when the button event occurred, in milliseconds. Time is declared as unsigned long, so it wraps around when it reaches the maximum value of a 32-bit number (every 49.7 days).

x, y   If the receiving window is on the same screen as the root window specified by root, then x and y are the pointer coordinates relative to the receiving window's origin. Otherwise, x and y are zero.

When active button grabs and pointer grabs are in effect (see Volume One, Section 9.4), the coordinates relative to the receiving window may not be within the window (they may be negative or greater than window height or width).

x_root, y_root
: The pointer coordinates relative to the root window which is an ancestor of the event window. If the pointer was on a different screen, these are zero.

state
: The state of all the buttons and modifier keys just before the event, represented by a mask of the button and modifier key symbols: `Button1Mask`, `Button2Mask`, `Button3Mask`, `Button4Mask`, `Button5Mask`, `ShiftMask`, `ControlMask`, `LockMask`, `Mod1Mask`, `Mod2Mask`, `Mod3Mask`, `Mod4Mask`, and `Mod5Mask`.

keycode
: The `keycode` member contains a server-dependent code for the key that changed state. As such it should be translated into the portable symbol called a keysym before being used. It can also be converted directly into ASCII with `XLookupString`. For a description and examples of how to translate keycodes, see Volume One, Section 9.1.1.

Notes

Remember that not all hardware is capable of generating release events, and that only the main keyboard (a-z, A-Z, 0-9), Shift, and Control keys are always found.

Keyboard events are analogous to button events, though of course there are many more keys than buttons, and the keyboard is not automatically grabbed between press and release.

All the structure members have the same meaning as described for `ButtonPress` and `ButtonRelease` events except that `button` is replaced by `keycode`.

MapNotify, UnmapNotify

When Generated

The X server generates `MapNotify` and `UnmapNotify` events when a window changes state from unmapped to mapped or vice versa.

Select With

To receive these events on a single window, use `StructureNotifyMask` in the call to `XSelectInput` for the window. To receive these events for all children of a particular parent, specify the parent window ID and use `SubstructureNotifyMask`.

XEvent Structure Name

```
typedef union _XEvent {
    ...
    XMapEvent xmap;
    XUnmapEvent xunmap;
    ...
} XEvent;
```

Event Structure

```
typedef struct {
    int type;
    unsigned long serial;/* # of last request processed by server */
    Bool send_event;        /* true if this came from SendEvent request */
    Display *display;       /* display the event was read from */
    Window event;
    Window window;
    Bool override_redirect;    /* Boolean, is override set */
} XMapEvent;

typedef struct {
    int type;
    unsigned long serial;/* # of last request processed by server */
    Bool send_event;        /* true if this came from SendEvent request */
    Display *display;       /* display the event was read from */
    Window event;
    Window window;
    Bool from_configure;
} XUnmapEvent;
```

Event Structure Members

`event`   The window that selected this event.

`window`   The window that was just mapped or unmapped.

`override_redirect` (XMapEvent only)
            `True` or `False`. The value of the `override_redirect` attribute of the window that was just mapped.

Event
Reference

from_configure (XUnmapEvent only)

     True if the event was generated as a result of a resizing of the window's parent when the window itself had a win_gravity of UnmapGravity. See the description of the win_gravity attribute in Volume One, Section 4.3.4. False otherwise.

MappingNotify

When Generated

`MappingNotify` events occur when any of the following are changed by another client: the mapping between physical keyboard keys (keycodes) and keysyms; the mapping between modifier keys and logical modifiers; or the mapping between physical and logical pointer buttons. These events are triggered by a call to `XSetModifierMapping` or `XSetPointer-Mapping` if the return status is `MappingSuccess`, or by any call to `ChangeKeyboard-Mapping`.

This event type should not be confused with the event that occurs when a window is mapped; that is a `MapNotify` event. Nor should it be confused with the `KeymapNotify` event, which reports the state of the keyboard as a mask instead of as a keycode.

Select With

The X server sends `MappingNotify` events to all clients. It is never selected, and cannot be masked with the window attributes.

XEvent Structure Name

```
typedef union _XEvent {
    ...
    XMappingEvent xmapping;
    ...
} XEvent;
```

Event Structure

```
typedef struct {
    int type;
    unsigned long serial;/* # of last request processed by server */
    Bool send_event;       /* true if this came from SendEvent request */
    Display *display;      /* display the event was read from */
    Window window;         /* unused */
    int request;           /* one of MappingModifier, MappingKeyboard,
                            * MappingPointer */
    int first_keycode;     /* first keycode */
    int count;             /* range of change with first_keycode*/
} XMappingEvent;
```

Event Structure Members

request The kind of mapping change that occurred: `MappingModifier` for a successful `XSetModifierMapping` (keyboard Shift, Lock, Control, Meta keys), `MappingKeyboard` for a successful `XChangeKeyboardMapping` (other keys), and `MappingPointer` for a successful `XSetPointerMapping` (pointer button numbers).

Event Reference

first_keycode

> If the request member is MappingKeyboard or MappingModifier, then first_keycode indicates the first in a range of keycodes with altered mappings. Otherwise it is not set.

count   If the request member is MappingKeyboard or MappingModifier, then count indicates the number of keycodes with altered mappings. Otherwise it is not set.

Notes

If the request member is MappingKeyboard, clients should call XRefreshKeyboard-Mapping.

The normal response to a request member of MappingPointer or MappingModifier is no action. This is because the clients should use the logical mapping of the buttons and modifiers to allow the user to customize the keyboard if desired. If the application requires a particular mapping regardless of the user's preferences, it should call XGetModifierMapping or XGetPointerMapping to find out about the new mapping.

MapRequest

When Generated

The X server generates `MapRequest` events when the functions `XMapRaised` and `XMap-Window` are called. If this event type is selected, the window is not mapped. This gives the client that selects this event (usually the window manager) the opportunity to revise the size or position of the window before executing the map request itself, or deny the request.

Select With

To receive this event type, you specify the window ID of the parent of the receiving window and pass `SubstructureRedirectMask` as the `event_mask` argument to `XSelect-Input`. In addition, the `override_redirect` member of the `XSetWindow-Attributes` structure for the specified window must be `False`.

XEvent Structure Name

```
typedef union _XEvent {
    . . .
    XMapRequestEvent xmaprequest;
    . . .
} XEvent;
```

Event Structure

```
typedef struct {
    int type;
    unsigned long serial;/* # of last request processed by server */
    Bool send_event;       /* true if this came from SendEvent request */
    Display *display;      /* display the event was read from */
    Window parent;
    Window window;
} XMapRequestEvent;
```

Event Structure Members

parent   The ID of the parent of the window being mapped.

window   The ID of the window being mapped.

MotionNotify

When Generated

The X server generates MotionNotify events when the user moves the pointer, or when a program warps the pointer to a new position within a single window.

Select With

This event type is selected with PointerMotionMask, PointerMotionHintMask, ButtonMotionMask, Button1MotionMask, Button2MotionMask, Button3-MotionMask, Button4MotionMask, and Button5MotionMask. These masks determine the specific conditions under which the event is generated. See Volume One, Section 8.3.3.3 for a description of selecting button events.

XEvent Structure Name

```
typedef union _XEvent {
    ...
    XMotionEvent xmotion;
    ...
} XEvent;
```

Event Structure

```
typedef struct {
    int type;               /* of event */
    unsigned long serial;   /* # of last request processed by server */
    Bool send_event;        /* true if this came from SendEvent request */
    Display *display;       /* display the event was read from */
    Window window;          /* event window it is reported relative to */
    Window root;            /* root window that the event occurred on */
    Window subwindow;       /* child window */
    Time time;              /* milliseconds */
    int x, y;               /* pointer coords relative to receiving window *
    int x_root, y_root;     /* coordinates relative to root */
    unsigned int state;     /* button and modifier key mask */
    char is_hint;           /* is this a motion hint */
    Bool same_screen;       /* same screen flag */
} XMotionEvent;
typedef XMotionEvent XPointerMovedEvent;
```

Event Structure Members

subwindow   If the source window is the child of the receiving window, then the subwindow member is set to the ID of that child.

time   The server time when the button event occurred, in milliseconds. Time is declared as unsigned long, so it wraps around when it reaches the maximum value of a 32 bit number (every 49.7 days).

x, y   If the receiving window is on the same screen as the root window specified by root, then x and y are the pointer coordinates relative to the receiving window's origin. Otherwise, x and y are zero.

When active button grabs and pointer grabs are in effect (see Volume One, Section 9.4), the coordinates relative to the receiving window may not be within the window (they may be negative or greater than window height or width).

x_root, y_root
> The pointer coordinates relative to the root window which is an ancestor of the event window. If the pointer was on a different screen, these are zero.

state
> The state of all the buttons and modifier keys just before the event, represented by a mask of the button and modifier key symbols: Button1Mask, Button2Mask, Button3Mask, Button4Mask, Button5Mask, ShiftMask, ControlMask, LockMask, Mod1Mask, Mod2Mask, Mod3Mask, Mod4Mask, and Mod5Mask.

is_hint
> Either the constant NotifyNormal or NotifyHint. NotifyHint indicates that the PointerMotionHintMask was selected. In this case, just one event is sent when the mouse moves, and the current position can be found by calling XQueryPointer, or by examining the motion history buffer with XGetMotionEvents, if a motion history buffer is available on the server. NotifyNormal indicates that the event is real, but it may not be up to date since there may be many more later motion events on the queue.

same_screen
> Indicates whether the pointer is currently on the same screen as this window. This is always True unless the pointer was actively grabbed before the automatic grab could take place.

Notes

If the processing you have to do for every motion event is fast, you can probably handle all of them without requiring motion hints. However, if you have extensive processing to do for each one, you might be better off using the hints and calling XQueryPointer or using the history buffer if it exists. XQueryPointer is a round-trip request, so it can be slow.

EnterNotify and LeaveNotify events are generated instead of MotionEvents if the pointer starts and stops in different windows.

PropertyNotify

When Generated

`PropertyNotify` events indicate that a property of a window has changed, or at least that a zero-length append has been done in order to get the X server time.

Select With

They can be selected with `PropertyChangeMask`.

XEvent Structure Name

```
typedef union _XEvent {
    . . .
    XPropertyEvent xproperty;
    . . .
} XEvent;
```

Event Structure

```
typedef struct {
    int type;
    unsigned long serial;/* # of last request processed by server */
    Bool send_event;        /* true if this came from SendEvent request */
    Display *display;       /* display the event was read from */
    Window window;
    Atom atom;
    Time time;
    int state;              /* NewValue, Deleted */
} XPropertyEvent;
```

Event Structure Members

window   The window whose property was changed, not the window that selected the event.

atom   The property that was changed.

state   Either `PropertyNewValue` or `PropertyDelete`. Whether the property was changed to a new value or deleted.

time   The `time` member specifies the server time when the property was changed.

ReparentNotify

When Generated

ReparentNotify events report information about the changing of a window's parent.

Select With

To receive this event type, specify the window ID of the old or the new parent window and pass SubstructureNotifyMask as the event_mask argument to XSelectInput, or specify the window ID and pass StructureNotifyMask.

The X server generates this event type when it reparents the specified window.

XEvent Structure Name

```
typedef union _XEvent {
    . . .
    XReparentEvent xreparent;
    . . .
} XEvent;
```

Event Structure

```
typedef struct {
    int type;
    unsigned long serial;/* # of last request processed by server */
    Bool send_event;     /* true if this came from SendEvent request */
    Display *display;     /* display the event was read from */
    Window event;
    Window window;
    Window parent;
    int x, y;
    Bool override_redirect;
} XReparentEvent;
```

Event Structure Members

window   the window whose parent window was changed.

parent   The new parent of the window.

x, y   the coordinates of the upper-left pixel of the window's border relative to the new parent window's origin.

override_redirect
          The override_redirect attribute of the reparented window. If True, it indicates that the client wants this window to be immune to meddling by the window manager. Window managers normally should not have reparented this window to begin with.

Event
Reference

When Generated

ResizeRequest events report another client's attempt to change the size of a window. The X server generates this event type when another client calls XConfigureWindow, XResizeWindow, or XMoveResizeWindow. If this event type is selected, the window is not resized. This gives the client that selects this event (usually the window manager) the opportunity to revise the new size of the window before executing the resize request itself, or to deny the request.

Select With

To receive this event type, specify a window ID and pass ResizeRedirectMask as part of the event_mask argument to XSelectInput. Only one client can select this event on a particular window. When selected, this event is triggered instead of resizing the window.

XEvent Structure Name

```
typedef union _XEvent {
    . . .
    XResizeRequestEvent xresizerequest;
    . . .
} XEvent;
```

Event Structure

```
typedef struct {
    int type;
    unsigned long serial;/* # of last request processed by server */
    Bool send_event;      /* true if this came from SendEvent request */
    Display *display;     /* display the event was read from */
    Window window;
    int width, height;
} XResizeRequestEvent;
```

Event Structure Members

window   The window whose size another client attempted to change.

width, height   The requested size of the window, not including its border.

SelectionClear

When Generated

The X server reports SelectionClear events to the current owner of a selection when a new owner is being defined.

Select With

This event is not selected. It is sent to the previous selection owner when another client calls XSetSelectionOwner for the same selection.

XEvent Structure Name

```
typedef union _XEvent {
    ...
    XSelectionClearEvent xselectionclear;
    ...
} XEvent;
```

Event Structure

```
typedef struct {
    int type;
    unsigned long serial;/* # of last request processed by server */
    Bool send_event;     /* true if this came from SendEvent request */
    Display *display;    /* display the event was read from */
    Window window;
    Atom selection;
    Time time;
} XSelectionClearEvent;
```

Event Structure Members

window
The window that is receiving the event and losing the selection.

selection
The selection atom specifying the selection that is changing ownership.

time
The last-change time recorded for the selection.

Event Reference

SelectionNotify

When Generated

SelectionNotify events are sent only by clients, not by the server. They are sent by calling XSendEvent. The owner of a selection sends this event to a requester (a client that calls XConvertSelection for a given property) when a selection has been converted and stored as a property, or when a selection conversion could not be performed (indicated with property None).

Select With

There is no event mask for SelectionNotify events and they are not selected with XSelectInput. Instead, XSendEvent directs them to a specific window, which is given as a window ID: the PointerWindow or the InputFocus.

XEvent Structure Name

```
typedef union _XEvent {
    . . .
    XSelectionEvent xselection;
    . . .
} XEvent;
```

Event Structure

```
typedef struct {
    int type;
    unsigned long serial;/* # of last request processed by server */
    Bool send_event;        /* true if this came from SendEvent request */
    Display *display;       /* display the event was read from */
    Window requester;       /* must be next after type */
    Atom selection;
    Atom target;
    Atom property;          /* Atom or None */
    Time time;
} XSelectionEvent;
```

Event Structure Members

The members of this structure have the values specified in the XConvertSelection call that triggers the selection owner to send this event, except that the property member will return either the atom specifying a property on the requestor window with the data type specified in target, or it will be None, which indicates that the data could not be converted into the target type.

When Generated

SelectionRequest events are sent to the owner of a selection when another client requests the selection by calling XConvertSelection.

Select With

There is no event mask for SelectionRequest events and they are not selected with XSelectInput.

XEvent Structure Name

```
typedef union _XEvent {
    ...
    XSelectionRequestEvent xselectionrequest;
    ...
} XEvent;
```

Event Structure

```
typedef struct {
    int type;
    unsigned long serial;/* # of last request processed by server */
    Bool send_event;      /* true if this came from SendEvent request */
    Display *display;     /* display the event was read from */
    Window owner;         /* must be next after type */
    Window requester;
    Atom selection;
    Atom target;
    Atom property;
    Time time;
} XSelectionRequestEvent;
```

Event Structure Members

The members of this structure have the values specified in the XConvertSelection call that triggers this event.

The owner should convert the selection based on the specified target type, if possible. If a property is specified, the owner should store the result as that property on the requester window, and then send a SelectionNotify event to the requester by calling XSendEvent. If the selection cannot be converted as requested, the owner should send a Selection-Notify event with property set to the constant None.

Event Reference

When Generated

VisibilityNotify events report any change in the visibility of the specified window. This event type is never generated on windows whose class is InputOnly. All of the window's subwindows are ignored when calculating the visibility of the window.

Select With

This event is selected with VisibilityChangeMask.

XEvent Structure Name

```
typedef union _XEvent {
    ...
    XVisibilityEvent xvisibility;
    ...
} XEvent;
```

Event Structure

```
typedef struct {
    int type;
    unsigned long serial;/* # of last request processed by server */
    Bool send_event;        /* true if this came from SendEvent request */
    Display *display;       /* display the event was read from */
    Window window;
    int state;              /* Visibility Unobscured,*/
                            /* Visibility Partially Obscured, or */
                            /* Visibility Obscured */
} XVisibilityEvent;
```

Event Structure Members

state   A symbol indicating the final visibility status of the window: Visibility-Unobscured, VisibilityPartiallyObscured, or Visibility-Obscured.

Notes

Table E-5 lists the transitions that generate VisibilityNotify events and the corresponding state member of the XVisibilityEvent structure.

Table E-6. The State Element of the XVisibilityEvent Structure

Visibility Status Before	Visibility Status After	State Member
Partially obscured, fully obscured, or not viewable	Viewable and completely unobscured	`Visibility-Unobscured`
Viewable and completely unobscured, or not viewable	Viewable and partially obscured	`VisibilityPartially-Obscured`
Viewable and completely unobscured, or viewable and partially obscured, or not viewable	Viewable and partially obscured	`VisibilityPartially-Obscured`

Structure Reference

This appendix describes the contents of the include files for Xlib.

Description of Contents

All include files are normally located in */usr/include/X11*. All Xlib programs require *<X11/Xlib.h>*, which includes *<X11/X.h>*. *<X11/Xlib.h>* contains most of the structure declarations, while *<X11/X.h>* contains most of the defined constants. Virtually all programs will also require *<X11/Xutil.h>*, which include structure types and declarations applicable to window manager hints, colors, visuals, regions, standard geometry strings, and images.

Here is a summary of the contents of the include files:

<X11/Xlib.h>	structure declarations for core Xlib functions.
<X11/X.h>	constant definitions for Xlib functions.
<X11/Xutil.h>	additional structure types and constant definitions for miscellaneous Xlib functions.
<X11/Xatom.h>	the predefined atoms for properties, types, and font characteristics.
<X11/cursorfont.h>	the constants used to select a cursor shape from the standard cursor font.
<X11/keysym.h>	predefined key symbols corresponding to keycodes. It includes *<X11/keysymdef.h>*.
<X11/Xresource.h>	resource manager structure definitions and function declarations.

Resource Types

The following types are defined in *<X11/X.h>*:

```
unsigned long XID
XID Colormap
XID Cursor
XID Drawable
XID Font
XID GContext
XID KeySym
XID Pixmap
XID Window
unsigned long Atom
unsigned char KeyCode
unsigned long Mask
unsigned long Time
unsigned long VisualID
```

Structure Definitions

This section lists all Xlib structure definitions in `Xlib.h` and `Xutil.h`, in alphabetical order, except the event structures which are listed separately in the next section.

Note that the first few structure types do not begin with X. These structures are intended to be opaque, so that Xlib's authors are free to change them in later releases. You are discouraged from accessing their members directly. However, only the **GC** structure is dangerous to access, because of the way GCs are implemented.

Before each structure is a description of what the structure is used for and a list of the Xlib routines that use the structure.

Depth

Depth defines a valid depth and list of associated visuals. A list of these structures is contained in the `Screen` structure, which is itself a member of the `Display` structure. Not used directly in any Xlib function. This structure should not be accessed directly, but instead through `XGetVisualInfo` and `XMatchVisualInfo`.

```
typedef struct {
    int depth;                  /* this depth (Z) of the depth */
    int nvisuals;               /* number of Visual types at this depth */
    Visual *visuals;            /* list of visuals possible at this depth */
} Depth;
```

Display

Display describes the connection to the X server. A pointer to a structure of this type is returned by XOpenDisplay, and is subsequently the first argument to nearly every Xlib routine. Macros are provided to access most members of this structure.

```
/*
 * Display datatype maintaining display specific data.
 */
typedef struct _XDisplay {
    XExtData *ext_data;            /* hook for extension to hang data */
    struct _XDisplay *next;        /* next open Display on list */
    int fd;                        /* network socket */
    int lock;                      /* is someone in critical section? */
    int proto_major_version;       /* major version of server's X protocol */
    int proto_minor_version;       /* minor version of servers X protocol */
    char *vendor;                  /* vendor of the server hardware */
    long resource_base;            /* resource ID base */
    long resource_mask;            /* resource ID mask bits */
    long resource_id;              /* allocator current ID */
    int resource_shift;            /* allocator shift to correct bits */
    XID (*resource_alloc)();       /* allocator function */
    int byte_order;                /* screen byte order, LSBFirst, MSBFirst */
    int bitmap_unit;               /* padding and data requirements */
    int bitmap_pad;                /* padding requirements on bitmaps */
    int bitmap_bit_order;          /* LeastSignificant or MostSignificant */
    int nformats;                  /* number of pixmap formats in list */
    ScreenFormat *pixmap_format;   /* pixmap format list */
    int vnumber;                   /* Xlib's X protocol version number */
    int release;                   /* release of the server */
    struct _XSQEvent *head, *tail; /* input event queue */
    int qlen;                      /* length of input event queue */
    int last_request_read;         /* sequence number of last event read */
    int request;                   /* sequence number of last request */
    char *last_req;                /* beginning of last request, or dummy */
    char *buffer;                  /* output buffer starting address */
    char *bufptr;                  /* output buffer index pointer */
    char *bufmax;                  /* output buffer maximum+1 address */
    unsigned max_request_size;     /* maximum number 32 bit words in request*/
    struct _XrmHashBucketRec *db;
    int (*synchandler)();          /* synchronization handler */
    char *display_name;            /* "host:display" string used on this connect*/
    int default_screen;            /* default screen for operations */
    int nscreens;                  /* number of screens on this server*/
    Screen *screens;               /* pointer to list of screens */
    int motion_buffer;             /* size of motion buffer */
    Window current;                /* for use internally for Keymap notify */
    int min_keycode;               /* minimum defined keycode */
    int max_keycode;               /* maximum defined keycode */
    KeySym *keysyms;               /* this server's keysyms */
    XModifierKeymap *modifiermap;  /* this server's modifier keymap */
    int keysyms_per_keycode;       /* number of rows */
    char *xdefaults;               /* contents of defaults from server */
    char *scratch_buffer;          /* place to hang scratch buffer */
    unsigned long scratch_length;  /* length of scratch buffer */
    int ext_number;                /* extension number on this display */
```

```
    _XExtension *ext_procs;        /* extensions initialized on this display */
    /*
     * the following can be fixed size, as the protocol defines how
     * much address space is available.
     * While this could be done using the extension vector, there
     * may be MANY events processed, so a search through the extension
     * list to find the right procedure for each event might be
     * expensive if many extensions are being used.  */

    Bool (*event_vec[128])();      /* vector for wire to event */
    Status (*wire_vec[128])();     /* vector for event to wire */
} Display;
```

GC

GC describes a graphics context. A pointer to a structure of this type is returned by
XCreateGC and subsequently used in all routines that draw or modify the GC. The
members of this structure must not be accessed directly.

```
typedef struct _XGC {
    XExtData *ext_data;       /* hook for extension to hang data */
    GContext gid;             /* protocol ID for graphics context */
    Bool rects;               /* Boolean: TRUE if clipmask is list of rectangles */
    Bool dashes;              /* Boolean: TRUE if dash-list is really a list */
    unsigned long dirty;      /* cache dirty bits */
    XGCValues values;         /* shadow structure of values */
} *GC;
```

Screen

Screen describes the characteristics of a screen. A pointer to a list of these structures is a
member of the Display structure. A pointer to a structure of this type is returned by
XGetWindowAttributes. Macros are provided to access most members of this structure.

```
typedef struct {
    XExtData *ext_data;             /* hook for extension to hang data */
    struct _XDisplay *display;      /* back pointer to display structure */
    Window root;                    /* root window ID */
    int width, height;              /* width and height of screen */
    int mwidth, mheight;            /* width and height of  in millimeters */
    int ndepths;                    /* number of depths possible */
    Depth *depths;                  /* list of allowable depths on the screen */
    int root_depth;                 /* bits per pixel */
    Visual *root_visual;            /* root visual */
    GC default_gc;                  /* GC for the root root visual */
    Colormap cmap;                  /* default colormap */
    unsigned long white_pixel;
    unsigned long black_pixel;      /* white and black pixel values */
```

```
    int max_maps, min_maps;        /* max and min colormaps */
    int backing_store;             /* Never, WhenMapped, Always */
    Bool save_unders;
    long root_input_mask;          /* initial root input mask */
} Screen;
```

ScreenFormat

ScreenFormat is a member of the Display structure. This structure is used internally for image operations. It is not used as an argument to or returned by any Xlib function. Macros are provided to access the members of this structure.

```
typedef struct {
    XExtData *ext_data;            /* hook for extension to hang data */
    int depth;                     /* depth of this image format */
    int bits_per_pixel;            /* bits/pixel at this depth */
    int scan_line_pad;             /* scan line must be padded to this multiple */
} ScreenFormat;
```

Visual

Visual describes a way of using color resources on a particular screen. A pointer to a visual structure is an argument to XCreateColormap, XCreateImage, and XCreate-Window. The valid visual structures for a screen can be determined with XGetVisual-Info or XMatchVisualInfo, or with the DefaultVisual(screen) macro. The visual used to create a window is returned by XGetWindowAttributes.

```
typedef struct {
    XExtData *ext_data;            /* hook for extension to hang data */
    VisualID visualid;             /* visual ID of this visual */
    int class;                     /* class of screen (PseudoColor, etc.) */
    unsigned long red_mask;        /* TrueColor, DirectColor only */
    unsigned long green_mask;      /* TrueColor, DirectColor only */
    unsigned long blue_mask;       /* TrueColor, DirectColor only */
    int bits_per_rgb;              /* log base 2 of distinct color values */
    int map_entries;               /* number of colormap entries */
} Visual;
```

XArc

XArc specifies the bounding box for an arc and two angles indicating the extent of the arc within the box. A list of these structures is used in XDrawArcs and XFillArcs.

```
typedef struct {
    short x, y;
    unsigned short width, height;
    short angle1, angle2;
} XArc;
```

XChar2b

XChar2b specifies a character in a two-byte font. A list of structures of this type is an argument to XDrawImageString16, XDrawString16, XDrawText16, XQuery-TextExtents16, XTextExtents16, and XTextWidth16. The only two-byte font currently available is Kanji (Japanese).

```
typedef struct {                       /* normal 16 bit characters are two bytes */
    unsigned char byte1;
    unsigned char byte2;
} XChar2b;
```

XCharStruct

XCharStruct describes the metrics of a single character in a font, or the overall charac-teristics of a font. This structure is the type of several of members of XFontStruct, and is used to return the overall characteristics of a string in XQueryTextExtents* and XTextExtents*.

```
typedef struct {
    short lbearing;             /* origin to left edge of raster */
    short rbearing;             /* origin to right edge of raster */
    short width;                /* advance to next char's origin */
    short ascent;               /* baseline to top edge of raster */
    short descent;              /* baseline to bottom edge of raster */
    unsigned short attributes;  /* per char flags (not predefined) */
} XCharStruct;
```

XClassHint

XClassHint is used to set or get the XA_WM_CLASS_HINT property for an application's top-level window, as arguments to XSetClassHint or XGetClassHint.

```
typedef struct {
    char *res_name;
    char *res_class;
} XClassHint;
```

XColor

XColor describes a single colorcell. This structure is used to specify and return the pixel value and RGB values for a colorcell. The flags indicate which of the RGB values should be changed when used in XStoreColors, XAllocNamedColor or XAllocColor. Also used in XCreateGlyphCursor, XCreatePixmapCursor, XLookupColor, XParseColor, XQueryColor, XQueryColors, and XRecolorCursor.

```
typedef struct {
    unsigned long pixel;
    unsigned short red, green, blue;
    char flags;                    /* DoRed, DoGreen, DoBlue */
    char pad;
} XColor;
```

XComposeStatus

XComposeStatus describes the current state of a multikey character sequence. Used in calling XLookupString. This processing is not implemented in the Release 2 sample servers.

```
typedef struct _XComposeStatus {
    char *compose_ptr;            /* state table pointer */
    int chars_matched;           /* match state */
} XComposeStatus;
```

XExtCodes

XExtCodes is a structure used by the extension mechanism. This structure is returned by XInitExtension which is not a standard Xlib routine but should be called within the extension code. Its contents are not normally accessible to the application.

```
typedef struct {                     /* public to extension, cannot be changed */
    int extension;                   /* extension number */
    int major_opcode;                /* major opcode assigned by server */
    int first_event;                 /* first event number for the extension */
    int first_error;                 /* first error number for the extension */
} XExtCodes;
```

XExtData

XExtData provides a way for extensions to attach private data to the existing structure types GC, Visual, Screen, Display, and XFontStruct. This structure is not used in normal Xlib programming.

```
typedef struct _XExtData {
    int number;                      /* number returned by XRegisterExtension */
    struct _XExtData *next;          /* next item on list of data for structure */
    int (*free_private)();           /* called to free private storage */
    char *private_data;              /* data private to this extension */
} XExtData;
```

XFontProp

XFontProp is used in XFontStruct. This structure allows the application to find out the names of additional font properties beyond the predefined set, so that they too can be accessed with XGetFontProperty. This structure is not used as an argument or return value for any core Xlib function.

```
typedef struct {
    Atom name;
    unsigned long card32;
} XFontProp;
```

XFontStruct

XFontStruct specifies metric information for an entire font. This structure is filled with the XLoadQueryFont and XQueryFont routines. ListFontsWithInfo also fills it but with metric information for the entire font only, not for each character. A pointer to this structure is used in the routines XFreeFont, XFreeFontInfo, XGetFontProp, XTextExtents*, and XTextWidth*.

```
typedef struct {
    XExtData *ext_data;              /* hook for extension to hang data */
    Font fid;                        /* font ID for this font */
    unsigned direction;              /* direction the font is painted */
    unsigned min_char_or_byte2;      /* first character */
    unsigned max_char_or_byte2;      /* last character */
    unsigned min_byte1;              /* first row that exists */
    unsigned max_byte1;              /* last row that exists */
    Bool all_chars_exist;            /* flag if all characters have nonzero size*/
    unsigned default_char;           /* char to print for undefined character */
    int n_properties;                /* how many properties there are */
    XFontProp *properties;           /* pointer to array of additional properties*/
    XCharStruct min_bounds;          /* minimum bounds over all existing char*/
    XCharStruct max_bounds;          /* minimum bounds over all existing char*/
    XCharStruct *per_char;           /* first_char to last_char information */
    int ascent;                      /* logical extent above baseline for spacing */
    int descent;                     /* logical descent below baseline for spacing */
} XFontStruct;
```

XGCValues

XGCValues is used to set or change members of the GC by the routines XCreateGC and XChangeGC.

```
typedef struct {
    int function;                /* logical operation */
    unsigned long plane_mask;    /* plane mask */
    unsigned long foreground;    /* foreground pixel */
    unsigned long background;    /* background pixel */
    int line_width;              /* line width */
    int line_style;              /* LineSolid, LineOnOffDash, LineDoubleDash */
    int cap_style;               /* CapNotLast, CapButt, CapRound, CapProjecting */
    int join_style;              /* JoinMiter, JoinRound, JoinBevel */
    int fill_style;              /* FillSolid, FillTiled, FillStippled */
    int fill_rule;               /* EvenOddRule, WindingRule */
    int arc_mode;                /* ArcPieSlice, ArcChord */
    Pixmap tile;                 /* tile pixmap for tiling operations */
    Pixmap stipple;              /* stipple 1 plane pixmap for stippling */
    int ts_x_origin;             /* offset for tile or stipple operations */
    int ts_y_origin;
    Font font;                   /* default text font for text operations */
    int subwindow_mode;          /* ClipByChildren, IncludeInferiors */
    Bool graphics_exposures;     /* Boolean, should exposures be generated */
    int clip_x_origin;           /* origin for clipping */
```

```
        int clip_y_origin;
        Pixmap clip_mask;               /* bitmap clipping; other calls for rects */
        int dash_offset;                /* patterned/dashed line information */
        char dashes;
} XGCValues;
```

XHostAddress

XHostAddress specifies the address of a host machine that is to be added or removed
from the host access list for a server. Used in XAddHost, XAddHosts, XListHosts,
XRemoveHost, and XRemoveHosts.

```
typedef struct {
        int family;                     /* for example FAMILY_INTERNET */
        int length;                     /* length of address, in bytes */
        char *address;                  /* pointer to where to find the bytes */
} XHostAddress;
```

XIconSize

XIconSize is used to set or read the XA_WM_ICON_SIZE property. This is normally set
by the window manager with XSetIconSizes and read by each application with XGet-
IconSizes.

```
typedef struct {
        int min_width, min_height;
        int max_width, max_height;
        int width_inc, height_inc;
} XIconSize;
```

XImage

XImage describes an area of the screen. As you can tell from the funcs member, this
structure is used in XCreateImage, XDestroyImage, XGetPixel, XPutPixel,
XSubImage, and XAddPixel. It is also used in XGetImage, XGetSubImage and
XPutImage.

```
typedef struct _XImage {
        int width, height;              /* size of image */
        int xoffset;                    /* number of pixels offset in X direction */
        int format;                     /* XYBitmap, XYPixmap, ZPixmap */
        char *data;                     /* pointer to image data */
        int byte_order;                 /* data byte order, LSBFirst, MSBFirst */
        int bitmap_unit;                /* quant. of scan line 8, 16, 32 */
        int bitmap_bit_order;           /* LSBFirst, MSBFirst */
```

```
    int bitmap_pad;                 /* 8, 16, 32 either XY or ZPixmap */
    int depth;                      /* depth of image */
    int bytes_per_line;             /* accelerator to next line */
    int bits_per_pixel;             /* bits per pixel (ZPixmap) */
    unsigned long red_mask;         /* bits in z arrangement */
    unsigned long green_mask;
    unsigned long blue_mask;
    char *obdata;                   /* hook for the object routines to hang on */
    struct funcs {                  /* image manipulation routines */
    struct _XImage *(*create_image)();
    int (*destroy_image)();
    unsigned long (*get_pixel)();
    int (*put_pixel)();
    struct _XImage *(*sub_image)();
    int (*add_pixel)();
    } f;
} XImage;
```

XKeyboardControl

XKeyboardControl is used to set user preferences with XChangeKeyboard-Control.

```
typedef struct {
    int key_click_percent;
    int bell_percent;
    int bell_pitch;
    int bell_duration;
    int led;
    int led_mode;
    int key;
    int auto_repeat_mode;    /* AutoRepeatModeOn, AutoRepeatModeOff,
                              * AutoRepeatModeDefault */
} XKeyboardControl;
```

XKeyboardState

XKeyboardState is used to return the current settings of user preferences with XGet-KeyboardControl.

```
typedef struct {
    int key_click_percent;
    int bell_percent;
    unsigned int bell_pitch, bell_duration;
    unsigned long led_mask;
    int global_auto_repeat;
    char auto_repeats[32];
} XKeyboardState;
```

XModifierKeymap

XModifierKeymap specifies which physical keys are mapped to modifier functions. This structure is returned by XGetModifierMapping, and is an argument to XDelete-ModifiermapEntry, XFreeModifiermap, InsertModifiermapEntry, XNew-Modifiermap, and XSetModifierMapping.

```
typedef struct {
    int max_keypermod;              /* server's max # of keys per modifier */
    KeyCode *modifiermap;           /* an 8 by max_keypermod array of modifiers */
} XModifierKeymap;
```

XPoint

XPoint specifies the coordinates of a point. Used in XDrawPoints, XDrawLines, XFillPolygon, and XPolygonRegion.

```
typedef struct {
    short x, y;
} XPoint;
```

XRectangle

XRectangle specifies a rectangle. Used in XClipBox, XDrawRectangles, XFill-Rectangles, XSetClipRectangles, and XUnionRectWithRegion.

```
typedef struct {
    short x, y;
    unsigned short width, height;
} XRectangle;
```

XSegment

XSegment specifies two points. Used in XDrawSegments.

```
typedef struct {
    short x1, y1, x2, y2;
} XSegment;
```

XSetWindowAttributes

XSetWindowAttributes contains all the attributes that can be set without window manager intervention. Used in XChangeWindowAttributes and XCreateWindow.

```
typedef struct {
    Pixmap background_pixmap;         /* background or None or ParentRelative */
    unsigned long background_pixel;/* background pixel */
    Pixmap border_pixmap;             /* border of the window */
    unsigned long border_pixel;       /* border pixel value */
    int bit_gravity;                  /* one of bit gravity values */
    int win_gravity;                  /* one of the window gravity values */
    int backing_store;                /* NotUseful, WhenMapped, Always */
    unsigned long backing_planes;     /* planes to be preserved if possible */
    unsigned long backing_pixel;      /* value to use in restoring planes */
    Bool save_under;                  /* should bits under be saved? (popups) */
    long event_mask;                  /* set of events that should be saved */
    long do_not_propagate_mask;       /* set of events that should not */
                                      * propagate */

    Bool override_redirect;           /* Boolean value for override-redirect */
    Colormap colormap;                /* colormap to be associated with window */
    Cursor cursor;                    /* cursor to be displayed (or None) */
} XSetWindowAttributes;
```

XSizeHints

XSizeHints describes a range of preferred sizes and aspect ratios. Used to set the XA_WM_NORMAL_HINTS and XA_WM_ZOOM_HINTS properties for the window manager with XSetNormalHints, XSetZoomHints, XSetStandardProperties or XSet-SizeHints. Also used in reading these properties with XGetSizeHints, XGet-NormalHints, or XGetZoomHints.

```
typedef struct {
    long flags;                       /* marks defined fields in structure */
    int x, y;
    int width, height;
    int min_width, min_height;
    int max_width, max_height;
    int width_inc, height_inc;
    struct {
        int x;                        /* numerator */
        int y;                        /* denominator */
    } min_aspect, max_aspect;
} XSizeHints;
```

XStandardColormap

XStandardColormap describes a standard colormap, giving its ID and its color characteristics. This is the format of the standard colormap properties set on the root window, which can be changed with XSetStandardProperties and changed with XGetStandardProperties.

```
typedef struct {
    Colormap colormap;
    unsigned long red_max;
    unsigned long red_mult;
    unsigned long green_max;
    unsigned long green_mult;
    unsigned long blue_max;
    unsigned long blue_mult;
    unsigned long base_pixel;
} XStandardColormap;
```

XTextItem

XTextItem describes a string, the font to print it in, and the horizontal offset from the previous string drawn or from the location specified by the drawing command. Used in XDrawText.

```
typedef struct {
    char *chars;              /* pointer to string */
    int nchars;              /* number of characters */
    int delta;               /* delta between strings */
    Font font;               /* font to print it in, None don't change */
} XTextItem;
```

XTextItem16

XTextItem16 describes a string in a two-byte font, the font to print it in, and the horizontal offset from the previous string drawn or from the location specified by the drawing command. Used in XDrawText16.

```
typedef struct {
    XChar2b *chars;          /* two-byte characters */
    int nchars;              /* number of characters */
    int delta;               /* delta between strings */
    Font font;               /* font to print it in, None don't change */
} XTextItem16;
```

XTimeCoord

XTimeCoord specifies a time and position pair, for use in tracking the pointer with XGet-MotionEvents. This routine is not supported on all systems.

```
typedef struct {
    Time time;
    unsigned short x, y;
} XTimeCoord;
```

XVisualInfo

XVisualInfo is used in XGetVisualInfo and XMatchVisualInfo to specify the desired visual type. The visual member of XVisualInfo is used for the *visual* argument of XCreateWindow or XCreateColormap.

```
typedef struct {
    Visual *visual;
    VisualID visualid;
    int screen;
    unsigned int depth;
    int class;
    unsigned long red_mask;
    unsigned long green_mask;
    unsigned long blue_mask;
    int colormap_size;
    int bits_per_rgb;
} XVisualInfo;
```

XWMHints

XWMHints describes various application preferences for communication to the window manager via the XA_WM_HINTS property. Used in XSetWMHints and XGetWMHints.

```
typedef struct {
    long flags;                  /* marks defined fields in structure */
    Bool input;                  /* does application need window manager for
                                  * keyboard input */
    int initial_state;           /* see below */
    Pixmap icon_pixmap;          /* pixmap to be used as icon */
    Window icon_window;          /* window to be used as icon */
    int icon_x, icon_y;          /* initial position of icon */
    Pixmap icon_mask;            /* icon mask bitmap */
    /* this structure may be extended in the future */
} XWMHints;
```

XWindowAttributes

XWindowAttributes describes the complete set of window attributes, including those that can't be set without window manager interaction. This structure is returned by XGet-WindowAttributes. It is *not* used by XChangeWindowAttributes or XCreate-Window.

```
typedef struct {
    int x, y;                          /* location of window */
    int width, height;                 /* width and height of window */
    int border_width;                  /* border width of window */
    int depth;                         /* depth of window */
    Visual *visual;                    /* the associated visual structure */
    Window root;                       /* root of screen containing window */
    int class;                         /* InputOutput, InputOnly*/
    int bit_gravity;                   /* one of bit gravity values */
    int win_gravity;                   /* one of the window gravity values */
    int backing_store;                 /* NotUseful, WhenMapped, Always */
    unsigned long backing_planes;      /* planes to be preserved if possible */
    unsigned long backing_pixel;       /* value to be used when restoring planes */
    Bool save_under;                   /* Boolean, should bits under be saved */
    Colormap colormap;                 /* colormap to be associated with window */
    Bool map_installed;                /* Boolean, is colormap currently installed*/
    int map_state;                     /* IsUnmapped, IsUnviewable, IsViewable */
    long all_event_masks;              /* events all people have interest in*/
    long your_event_mask;              /* my event mask */
    long do_not_propagate_mask;        /* set of events that should not propagate */
    Bool override_redirect;            /* Boolean value for override-redirect */
    Screen *screen;
} XWindowAttributes;
```

XWindowChanges

XWindowChanges describes a configuration for a window. Used in XConfigure-Window, which can change the screen layout and therefore can be intercepted by the window manager. This sets some of the remaining members of XWindowAttributes that cannot be set with XChangeWindowAttributes or XCreateWindow.

```
typedef struct {
    int x, y;
    int width, height;
    int border_width;
    Window sibling;
    int stack_mode;
} XWindowChanges;
```

G
Symbol Reference

This appendix presents an alphabetical listing of the symbols used in X. The routines in parentheses following the descriptions indicate the routines associated with those symbols.

A

Above	stacking method (XConfigureWindow)
AllHints	XA_WM_HINTS property, all members set (XGetWMHints, XSetWMHints)
AllTemporary	resource ID passed to XKillClient
AllValues	mask used by XParseGeometry, returns those set by user
AllocAll	allocate entire map writable (XCreateColormap)
AllocNone	create map with no entries (XCreateColormap)
AllowExposures	screen saver (XSetScreenSaver, XGetScreenSaver)
AlreadyGrabbed	XGrabPointer, XGrabKeyboard return Status
Always	backing_store attribute (XCreateWindow, XChangeWindowAttributes)
AnyButton	button name for XGrabButton, or for ButtonPress or ButtonRelease detail
AnyKey	keycode for XGrabKey
AnyModifier	modifier key mask for XGrabButton, XGrabKey, results of XQueryPointer, event state
AnyPropertyType	atom for XGetProperty
ArcChord	arc_mode in GC, join endpoints of arc (XFillArcs)
ArcPieSlice	arc_mode in GC, join endpoints to center of arc (XFillArcs)
AsyncBoth	XAllowEvents mode
AsyncKeyboard	XAllowEvents mode
AsyncPointer	XAllowEvents mode
AutoRepeatModeDefault	keyboard preferences (XChangeKeyboardControl, XGetKeyboardControl)
AutoRepeatModeOff	keyboard preferences (XChangeKeyboardControl, XGetKeyboardControl)
AutoRepeatModeOn	keyboard preferences (XChangeKeyboardControl, XGetKeyboardControl)

B

BadAccess	used by extensions only, depending on context
BadAlloc	used by extensions only, insufficient resources
BadAtom	used by extensions only, parameter not an Atom
BadColor	used by extensions only, no such colormap
BadCursor	used by extensions only, parameter not a Cursor
BadDrawable	used by extensions only, parameter not a Pixmap or Window
BadFont	used by extensions only, parameter not a Font
BadGC	used by extensions only, parameter not a GC
BadIDChoice	used by extensions only, choice not in range or already used
BadImplementation	used by extensions only, server is defective
BadLength	used by extensions only, request length incorrect
BadMatch	used by extensions only, parameter mismatch
BadName	used by extensions only, font or color name doesn't exist
BadPixmap	used by extensions only, parameter not a Pixmap
BadRequest	used by extensions only, bad request code
BadValue	used by extensions only, integer parameter out of range
BadWindow	used by extensions only, parameter not a Window
Below	stacking method, XConfigureWindow
BitmapFileInvalid	returned status for XReadBitmapFile, XWriteBitmapFile
BitmapNoMemory	returned status for XReadBitmapFile, XWriteBitmapFile
BitmapOpenFailed	returned status for XReadBitmapFile, XWriteBitmapFile
BitmapSucces	returned status for XReadBitmapFile, XWriteBitmapFile
BottomIf	stacking method (XConfigureWindow)
Button1	button name in event detail (XGrabButton)
Button1Mask	button mask (XQueryPointer)
Button1MotionMask	event mask
Button2	button name in event detail (XGrabButton)
Button2Mask	button mask (XQueryPointer)
Button2MotionMask	event mask
Button3	button name in event detail (XGrabButton)
Button3Mask	button mask (XQueryPointer)
Button3MotionMask	event mask
Button4	button name in event detail (XGrabButton)
Button4Mask	button mask (XQueryPointer)
Button4MotionMask	event mask
Button5	button name in event detail (XGrabButton)
Button5Mask	button mask (XQueryPointer)
Button5MotionMask	event mask

`ButtonMotionMask`	event mask
`ButtonPress`	event type
`ButtonPressMask`	event mask
`ButtonRelease`	event type
`ButtonReleaseMask`	event mask

C

`CapButt`	line `cap_style` of GC (`XSetLineAttributes`)
`CapNotLast`	line `cap_style` of GC (`XSetLineAttributes`)
`CapProjecting`	line `cap_style` of GC (`XSetLineAttributes`)
`CapRound`	line `cap_style` of GC (`XSetLineAttributes`)
`CenterGravity`	`bit_gravity` and `win_gravity` attribute constant
`CirculateNotify`	event type
`CirculateRequest`	event type
`ClientMessage`	event type
`ClipByChildren`	`subwindow_mode` of GC, don't draw through children (`XSetSubwindowMode`)
`ColormapChangeMask`	event mask
`ColormapInstalled`	`ColormapNotify` event state
`ColormapNotify`	event type
`ColormapUninstalled`	`ColormapNotify` event state
`Complex`	polygon shapes, paths may intersect (`XFillPolygon`)
`ConfigureNotify`	event type
`ConfigureRequest`	event type
`ControlMapIndex`	modifier names for `XSetModifierMapping`, `XGetModifierMapping`
`ControlMask`	modifier key mask for `XGrabButton`, `XGrabKey`, results of `XQueryPointer`, event state
`Convex`	polygon shapes, wholly convex (`XFillPolygon`)
`CoordModeOrigin`	interpret points relative to origin (`XDrawLines`, `XDrawPoints`)
`CoordModePrevious`	interpret points relative to previous point (`XDrawLines`, `XDrawPoints`)
`CopyFromParent`	border pixmap, visual ID, window class (`XCreateWindow`, `XChangeWindowAttributes`)
`CreateNotify`	event type
`CurrentTime`	most time arguments
`CursorShape`	largest displayable size (`XQueryBestSize`, `XQueryBestCursor`)
`CWBackPixel`	window attribute mask (`XCreateWindow`, `XChangeWindowAttributes`)

CWBackPixmap	window attribute mask (XCreateWindow, XChangeWindowAttributes)
CWBackingPixel	window attribute mask (XCreateWindow, XChangeWindowAttributes)
CWBackingPlanes	window attribute mask (XCreateWindow, XChangeWindowAttributes)
CWBackingStore	window attribute mask (XCreateWindow, XChangeWindowAttributes)
CWBitGravity	window attribute mask (XCreateWindow, XChangeWindowAttributes)
CWBorderPixel	window attribute mask (XCreateWindow, XChangeWindowAttributes)
CWBorderPixmap	window attribute mask (XCreateWindow, XChangeWindowAttributes)
CWBorderWidth	XConfigureWindow mask
CWColormap	window attribute mask (XCreateWindow, XChangeWindowAttributes)
CWCursor	window attribute mask (XCreateWindow, XChangeWindowAttributes)
CWDontPropagate	window attribute mask (XCreateWindow, XChangeWindowAttributes)
CWEventMask	window attribute mask (XCreateWindow, XChangeWindowAttributes)
CWHeight	XConfigureWindow mask
CWOverrideRedirect	window attribute mask (XCreateWindow, XChangeWindowAttributes)
CWSaveUnder	window attribute mask (XCreateWindow, XChangeWindowAttributes)
CWSibling	XConfigureWindow mask
CWStackMode	XConfigureWindow mask
CWWidth	XConfigureWindow mask
CWWinGravity	window attribute mask (XCreateWindow, XChangeWindowAttributes)
CWX	XConfigureWindow mask
CWY	XConfigureWindow mask

DEF

DefaultBlanking	screen saver (XSetSreenSaver, XGetScreenSaver)
DefaultExposures	screen saver (XSetSreenSaver, XGetScreenSaver)
DestroyAll	mode in XSetCloseDownMode
DestroyNotify	event type
DirectColor	visual class, read/write (XGetVisualInfo, XMatchVisualInfo)

DisableAccess	host access (XSetAccessControl)
DisableScreenInterval	internal to Xlib
DisableScreenSaver	internal to Xlib
DoBlue	mask for flags member of XColor structure (XStoreNamedColor, XStoreColors)
DoGreen	mask for flags member of XColor structure (XStoreNamedColor, XStoreColors)
DoRed	mask for flags member of XColor structure (XStoreNamedColor, XStoreColors)
DontAllowExposures	screen saver (XSetSreenSaver, XGetScreenSaver)
DontCareState	window state, don't know or care (value for member of XWMHints)
DontPreferBlanking	screen saver (XSetSreenSaver, XGetScreenSaver)
EastGravity	bit_gravity and win_gravity attribute constant
EnableAccess	host access (XSetAccessControl)
EnterNotify	event type
EnterWindowMask	event mask
EvenOddRule	fill_rule of GC, for polygons (XSetFillRule, XPolygonRegion)
Expose	event type
ExposureMask	event mask
FamilyChaos	host address families for XAddHost
FamilyDECnet	host address families for XAddHost
FamilyInternet	host address families for XAddHost
FillOpaqueStippled	fill_style of GC (XSetFillStyle)
FillSolid	fill_style of GC (XSetFillStyle)
FillStippled	fill_style of GC (XSetFillStyle)
FillTiled	fill_style of GC (XSetFillStyle)
FirstExtensionError	use if writing extension
FocusChangeMask	event mask
FocusIn	event type
FocusOut	event type
FontChange	internal to Xlib
FontLeftToRight	draw direction (XQueryFont)
FontRightToLeft	draw direction (XQueryFont)
ForgetGravity	bit_gravity attribute constant

G

GCArcMode	GC setting mask (XCreateGC, XCopyGC, XChangeGC)
GCBackground	GC setting mask (XCreateGC, XCopyGC, XChangeGC)

GCCapStyle	GC setting mask (XCreateGC, XCopyGC, XChangeGC)
GCClipMask	GC setting mask (XCreateGC, XCopyGC, XChangeGC)
GCClipXOrigin	GC setting mask (XCreateGC, XCopyGC, XChangeGC)
GCClipYOrigin	GC setting mask (XCreateGC, XCopyGC, XChangeGC)
GCDashList	GC setting mask (XCreateGC, XCopyGC, XChangeGC)
GCDashOffset	GC setting mask (XCreateGC, XCopyGC, XChangeGC)
GCFillRule	GC setting mask (XCreateGC, XCopyGC, XChangeGC)
GCFillStyle	GC setting mask (XCreateGC, XCopyGC, XChangeGC)
GCFont	GC setting mask (XCreateGC, XCopyGC, XChangeGC)
GCForeground	GC setting mask (XCreateGC, XCopyGC, XChangeGC)
GCFunction	GC setting mask (XCreateGC, XCopyGC, XChangeGC)
GCGraphicsExposures	GC setting mask (XCreateGC, XCopyGC, XChangeGC)
GCJoinStyle	GC setting mask (XCreateGC, XCopyGC, XChangeGC)
GCLastBit	higher than last GC mask value
GCLineStyle	GC setting mask (XCreateGC, XCopyGC, XChangeGC)
GCLineWidth	GC setting mask (XCreateGC, XCopyGC, XChangeGC)
GCPlaneMask	GC setting mask (XCreateGC, XCopyGC, XChangeGC)
GCStipple	GC setting mask (XCreateGC, XCopyGC, XChangeGC)
GCSubwindowMode	GC setting mask (XCreateGC, XCopyGC, XChangeGC)
GCTile	GC setting mask (XCreateGC, XCopyGC, XChangeGC)
GCTileStipXOrigin	GC setting mask (XCreateGC, XCopyGC, XChangeGC)
GCTileStipYOrigin	GC setting mask (XCreateGC, XCopyGC, XChangeGC)
GrabFrozen	XGrabPointer, XGrabKeyboard return Status
GrabInvalidTime	XGrabPointer, XGrabKeyboard return Status
GrabModeAsync	XGrabPointer, XGrabButton, XGrabKeyboard, XGrabKey mode
GrabModeSync	XGrabPointer, XGrabButton, XGrabKeyboard, XGrabKey mode
GrabNotViewable	XGrabPointer, XGrabKeyboard return Status
GrabSuccess	XGrabPointer, XGrabKeyboard return Status
GraphicsExpose	event type
GravityNotify	event type
GrayScale	visual class, read/write (XGetVisualInfo, XMatchVisualInfo)
GXand	logical function of GC, src AND dst (XSetFunction, XCreateGC, XChangeGC, XCopyGC)
GXandInverted	logical function of GC, NOT src AND dst (XSetFunction, XCreateGC, XChangeGC, XCopyGC)
GXandReverse	logical function of GC, src AND NOT dst (XSetFunction, XCreateGC, XChangeGC, XCopyGC)

GXclear	logical function of GC, don't draw (XSetFunction, XCreateGC, XChangeGC, XCopyGC)
GXcopy	logical function of GC, src (XSetFunction, XCreateGC, XChangeGC, XCopyGC)
GXcopyInverted	logical function of GC, NOT src (XSetFunction, XCreateGC, XChangeGC, XCopyGC)
GXequiv	logical function of GC, NOT src XOR dst (XSetFunction, XCreateGC, XChangeGC, XCopyGC)
GXinvert	logical function of GC, NOT dst (XSetFunction, XCreateGC, XChangeGC, XCopyGC)
GXnand	logical function of GC, NOT src OR NOT dst (XSetFunction, XCreateGC, XChangeGC, XCopyGC)
GXnoop	logical function of GC, dst (XSetFunction, XCreateGC, XChangeGC, XCopyGC)
GXnor	logical function of GC, NOT src AND NOT dst (XSetFunction, XCreateGC, XChangeGC, XCopyGC)
GXor	logical function of GC, src OR dst (XSetFunction, XCreateGC, XChangeGC, XCopyGC)
GXorInverted	logical function of GC, NOT src OR dst (XSetFunction, XCreateGC, XChangeGC, XCopyGC)
GXorReverse	logical function of GC, src OR NOT dst (XSetFunction, XCreateGC, XChangeGC, XCopyGC)
GXset	logical function of GC, set pixel (XSetFunction, XCreateGC, XChangeGC, XCopyGC)
GXxor	logical function of GC, src XOR dst (XSetFunction, XCreateGC, XChangeGC, XCopyGC)

HIJ

HeightValue	mask used by XParseGeometry, returns those set by user
HostDelete	used internally to distinguish XAddHost and XRemoveHost
HostInsert	used internally to distinguish XAddHost and XRemoveHost
IconMaskHint	XA_WM_HINTS property, icon pixmap mask mask (XGetWMHints, XSetWMHints)
IconPixmapHint	XA_WM_HINTS property, icon pixmap mask (XGetWMHints, XSetWMHints)
IconPositionHint	XA_WM_HINTS property, position mask (XGetWMHints, XSetWMHints)
IconWindowHint	XA_WM_HINTS property, input window mask (XGetWMHints, XSetWMHints)
IconicState	window state, application wants to be an icon (value for member of XWMHints)
InactiveState	window state, application believes it is seldom used (value for member of XWMHints)
IncludeInferiors	subwindow_mode of GC, draw through children (XSetSubwindowMode)

InputFocus	window in XSendEvent
InputHint	XA_WM_HINTS property, input member mask (XGetWMHints, XSetWMHints)
InputOnly	window class (XCreateWindow)
InputOutput	window class (XCreateWindow)
IsCursorKey	keysym class macro
IsFunctionKey	keysym class macro
IsKeypadKey	keysym class macro
IsMiscFunctionKey	keysym class macro
IsModifierKey	keysym class macro
IsPFKey	keysym class macro
IsUnmapped	map_state member of XWindowAttributes (XGetWindowAttributes)
IsUnviewable	map_state member of XWindowAttributes (XGetWindowAttributes)
IsViewable	map_state member of XWindowAttributes (XGetWindowAttributes)
JoinBevel	line join_style of GC (XSetLineAttributes)
JoinMiter	line join_style of GC (XSetLineAttributes)
JoinRound	line join_style of GC (XSetLineAttributes)

KL

KBAutoRepeatMode	mask for setting keyboard preferences (XChangeKeyboardControl, XGetKeyboardControl)
KBBellDuration	mask for setting keyboard preferences (XChangeKeyboardControl, XGetKeyboardControl)
KBBellPercent	mask for setting keyboard preferences (XChangeKeyboardControl, XGetKeyboardControl)
KBBellPitch	mask for setting keyboard preferences (XChangeKeyboardControl, XGetKeyboardControl)
KBKey	mask for setting keyboard preferences (XChangeKeyboardControl, XGetKeyboardControl)
KBKeyClickPercent	mask for setting keyboard preferences (XChangeKeyboardControl, XGetKeyboardControl)
KBLed	mask for setting keyboard preferences (XChangeKeyboardControl, XGetKeyboardControl)
KBLedMode	mask for setting keyboard preferences (XChangeKeyboardControl, XGetKeyboardControl)
KeyPress	event type
KeyPressMask	event mask
KeyRelease	event type
KeyReleaseMask	event mask

KeymapNotify	event type
KeymapStateMask	event mask
LASTEvent	bigger than any event type value
LastExtensionError	use if writing extension
LeaveNotify	event type
LeaveWindowMask	event mask
LedModeOff	keyboard preferences (XChangeKeyboardControl, XGetKeyboardControl)
LedModeOn	keyboard preferences (XChangeKeyboardControl, XGetKeyboardControl)
LineDoubleDash	line_style of GC (XSetLineAttributes)
LineOnOffDash	line_style of GC (XSetLineAttributes)
LineSolid	line_style of GC (XSetLineAttributes)
LockMapIndex	modifier names for XSetModifierMapping, XGetModifierMapping
LockMask	modifier key mask for XGrabButton, XGrabKey, results of XQueryPointer, event state
LowerHighest	circulation direction, XCirculateSubwindows
LSBFirst	byte order, used in image structure (XCreateImage, ImageByteOrder)

M

MapNotify	event type
MapRequest	event type
MappingBusy	pointer or modifier mapping Status (XSetModifierMapping, XSetPointerMapping)
MappingFailed	pointer or modifier mapping Status (XSetModifierMapping, XSetPointerMapping)
MappingKeyboard	MappingNotify event
MappingModifier	MappingNotify event
MappingNotify	event type
MappingPointer	MappingNotify event
MappingSuccess	pointer or modifier mapping Status (XSetModifierMapping, XSetPointerMapping)
Mod1MapIndex	modifier names for XSetModifierMapping, XGetModifierMapping
Mod1Mask	modifier key mask for XGrabButton, XGrabKey, results of XQueryPointer, event state
Mod2MapIndex	modifier names for XSetModifierMapping, XGetModifierMapping
Mod2Mask	modifier key mask for XGrabButton, XGrabKey, results of XQueryPointer, event state

Symbols

Mod3MapIndex	modifier names for XSetModifierMapping, XGetModifierMapping
Mod3Mask	modifier key mask for XGrabButton, XGrabKey, results of XQueryPointer, event state
Mod4MapIndex	modifier names for XSetModifierMapping, XGetModifierMapping
Mod4Mask	modifier key mask for XGrabButton, XGrabKey, results of XQueryPointer, event state
Mod5MapIndex	modifier names for XSetModifierMapping, XGetModifierMapping
Mod5Mask	modifier key mask for XGrabButton, XGrabKey, results of XQueryPointer, event state
MotionNotify	event type
MSBFirst	byte order, used in image structure (XCreateImage, ImageByteOrder)

N

NoEventMask	event mask
NoExpose	event type
NoSymbol	keysym for no symbol
NoValue	mask used by XParseGeometry, returns those set by user
Nonconvex	polygon shapes, no paths intersect, but not convex (XFillPolygon)
None	universal null resource or null atom
NormalState	window state, not iconified or zoomed (value for member of XWMHints)
NorthEastGravity	bit_gravity and win_gravity attribute constant
NorthGravity	bit_gravity and win_gravity attribute constant
NorthWestGravity	bit_gravity and win_gravity attribute constant
NotUseful	backing_store attribute (XCreateWindow, XChangeWindowAttributes)
NotifyAncestor	FocusIn, FocusOut, EnterNotify, LeaveNotify detail
NotifyDetailNone	FocusIn, FocusOut, EnterNotify, LeaveNotify detail
NotifyGrab	FocusIn, FocusOut, EnterNotify, LeaveNotify mode
NotifyHint	MotionNotify event hint
NotifyInferior	FocusIn, FocusOut, EnterNotify, LeaveNotify detail
NotifyNonlinear	FocusIn, FocusOut, EnterNotify, LeaveNotify detail
NotifyNonlinear-Virtual	FocusIn, FocusOut, EnterNotify, LeaveNotify detail
NotifyNormal	FocusIn, FocusOut, EnterNotify, LeaveNotify mode
NotifyPointer	FocusIn, FocusOut, EnterNotify, LeaveNotify detail
NotifyPointerRoot	FocusIn, FocusOut, EnterNotify, LeaveNotify detail

NotifyUngrab	FocusIn, FocusOut, EnterNotify, LeaveNotify mode
NotifyVirtual	FocusIn, FocusOut, EnterNotify, LeaveNotify detail
NotifyWhileGrabbed	FocusIn, FocusOut, EnterNotify, LeaveNotify mode

OP

Opposite	stacking method (XConfigureWindow)
OwnerGrabButtonMask	event mask
PAllHints	size hints, all program specified hints mask (XGetNormalHints, XSetNormalHints)
ParentRelative	pixmap origin (XCreateWindow, XChangeWindowAttributes)
PAspect	size hints, program specified min and max aspect ratio mask (XGetNormalHints, XSetNormalHints)
PlaceOnBottom	circulation direction in CirculateNotify event
PlaceOnTop	circulation direction in CirculateNotify event
PMaxSize	size hints, maximum desired window size mask (XGetNormalHints, XSetNormalHints)
PMinSize	size hints, minimum desired window size mask (XGetNormalHints, XSetNormalHints)
PointerMotionHintMask	event mask
PointerMotionMask	event mask
PointerRoot	window in XSetInputFocus
PPosition	size hints, program specified position mask (XGetNormalHints, XSetNormalHints)
PreferBlanking	screen saver (XSetSreenSaver, XGetScreenSaver)
PResizeInc	size hints, program specified resize increments mask (XGetNormalHints, XSetNormalHints)
PropModeAppend	property mode (XChangeProperty)
PropModePrepend	property mode (XChangeProperty)
PropModeReplace	property mode (XChangeProperty)
PropertyChangeMask	event mask
PropertyDelete	PropertyNotify event state
PropertyNewValue	PropertyNotify event state
PropertyNotify	event type
PseudoColor	visual class, read/write (XGetVisualInfo, XMatchVisualInfo)
PSize	size hints, program specified size mask (XGetNormalHints, XSetNormalHints)

R

| RaiseLowest | circulation direction (XCirculateSubwindows) |
| RectangleIn | rectangle is inside region (XRectInRegion) |

RectangleOut	rectangle is outside region (XRectInRegion)
RectanglePart	rectangle is part inside region (XRectInRegion)
ReparentNotify	event type
ReplayKeyboard	XAllowEvents mode
ReplayPointer	XAllowEvents mode
ResizeRedirectMask	event mask
ResizeRequest	event type
RetainPermanent	mode in XSetCloseDownMode
RetainTemporary	mode in XSetCloseDownMode
RevertToNone	backup keyboard focus window (XSetInputFocus, XGetInputFocus)
RevertToParent	backup keyboard focus window (XSetInputFocus, XGetInputFocus)
RevertToPointerRoot	backup keyboard focus window (XSetInputFocus, XGetInputFocus)

S

ScreenSaverActive	turn screen saver on (XForceScreenSaver)
ScreenSaverReset	turn screen saver off (XForceScreenSaver)
SelectionClear	event type
SelectionNotify	event type
SelectionRequest	event type
SetModeDelete	change_mode argument of XChangeSaveSet
SetModeInsert	change_mode argument of XChangeSaveSet
ShiftMapIndex	modifier names for XSetModifierMapping, XGetModifierMapping
ShiftMask	modifier key mask for XGrabButton, XGrabKey, results of XQueryPointer, event state
SouthEastGravity	bit_gravity and win_gravity attribute constant
SouthGravity	bit_gravity and win_gravity attribute constant
SouthWestGravity	bit_gravity and win_gravity attribute constant
StateHint	XA_WM_HINTS property, window state mask (XGetWMHints, XSetWMHints)
StaticColor	visual class, read-only (XGetVisualInfo, XMatchVisualInfo)
StaticGravity	bit_gravity and win_gravity attribute constant
StaticGray	visual class, read-only (XGetVisualInfo, XMatchVisualInfo)
StippleShape	size tiled fastest (XQueryBestSize, XQueryBestStipple)
StructureNotifyMask	event mask
SubstructureNotifyMask	event mask

SubstructureRedirect-Mask	event mask
Success	return code, everything's okay
SyncBoth	XAllowEvents mode
SyncKeyboard	XAllowEvents mode
SyncPointer	XAllowEvents mode

TU

TileShape	size tiled fastest (XQueryBestSize, XQueryBestTile)
TopIf	stacking method (XConfigureWindow)
TrueColor	visual class, read-only (XGetVisualInfo, XMatchVisualInfo)
UnmapGravity	win_gravity constant
UnmapNotify	event type
Unsorted	order of clip rectangles (XSetClipRectangles)
USPosition	size hints, user specified position mask (XGetNormalHints, XSetNormalHints)
USSize	size hints, user specified size mask (XGetNormalHints, XSetNormalHints)

VW

VisibilityChangeMask	event mask
VisibilityFully-Obscured	VisibilityNotify event state
VisibilityNotify	event type
VisibilityPartially-Obscured	VisibilityNotify event state
VisibilityUnobscured	VisibilityNotify event state
VisualAllMask	mask for determining desired visual structure (XGetVisualInfo, MatchVisualInfo)
VisualBitsPerRGBMask	mask for determining desired visual structure (XGetVisualInfo, MatchVisualInfo)
VisualBlueMaskMask	mask for determining desired visual structure (XGetVisualInfo, MatchVisualInfo)
VisualClassMask	mask for determining desired visual structure (XGetVisualInfo, MatchVisualInfo)
VisualColormapSize-Mask	mask for determining desired visual structure (XGetVisualInfo, MatchVisualInfo)
VisualDepthMask	mask for determining desired visual structure (XGetVisualInfo, MatchVisualInfo)
VisualGreenMaskMask	mask for determining desired visual structure (XGetVisualInfo, MatchVisualInfo)
VisualIDMask	mask for determining desired visual structure (XGetVisualInfo, MatchVisualInfo)

Symbols

VisualNoMask	mask for determining desired visual structure (XGetVisualInfo, MatchVisualInfo)
VisualRedMaskMask	mask for determining desired visual structure (XGetVisualInfo, MatchVisualInfo)
VisualScreenMask	mask for determining desired visual structure (XGetVisualInfo, MatchVisualInfo)
WestGravity	bit_gravity and win_gravity attribute constant
WhenMapped	backing_store attribute (XCreateWindow, XChangeWindowAttributes)
WidthValue	mask used by XParseGeometry, returns those set by user
WindingRule	fill_rule of GC, for polygons (XSetFillRule, XPolygonRegion)
WindowGroupHint	XA_WM_HINTS property, group property mask (XGetWMHints, XSetWMHints)

X

XA_ARC	predefined type atom
XA_ATOM	predefined type atom
XA_BITMAP	predefined type atom
XA_CAP_HEIGHT	predefined font atom
XA_CARDINAL	predefined type atom
XA_COLORMAP	predefined type atom
XA_COPYRIGHT	predefined font atom
XA_CURSOR	predefined type atom
XA_CUT_BUFFER0	predefined cut buffer atom
XA_CUT_BUFFER1	predefined cut buffer atom
XA_CUT_BUFFER2	predefined cut buffer atom
XA_CUT_BUFFER3	predefined cut buffer atom
XA_CUT_BUFFER4	predefined cut buffer atom
XA_CUT_BUFFER5	predefined cut buffer atom
XA_CUT_BUFFER6	predefined cut buffer atom
XA_CUT_BUFFER7	predefined cut buffer atom
XA_DRAWABLE	predefined type atom
XA_END_SPACE	predefined font atom
XA_FAMILY_NAME	predefined font atom
XA_FONT	predefined type atom
XA_FONT_NAME	predefined font atom
XA_FULL_NAME	predefined font atom
XA_INTEGER	predefined type atom
XA_ITALIC_ANGLE	predefined font atom
XA_LAST_PREDEFINED	predefined font atom

XA_MAX_SPACE	predefined font atom
XA_MIN_SPACE	predefined font atom
XA_NORM_SPACE	predefined font atom
XA_NOTICE	predefined font atom
XA_PIXMAP	predefined type atom
XA_POINT	predefined type atom
XA_POINT_SIZE	predefined font atom
XA_PRIMARY	predefined selection atom
XA_QUAD_WIDTH	predefined font atom
XA_RECTANGLE	predefined type atom
XA_RESOLUTION	predefined font atom
XA_RESOURCE_MANAGER	predefined resource manager atom
XA_RGB_BEST_MAP	predefined colormap atom
XA_RGB_BLUE_MAP	predefined colormap atom
XA_RGB_COLOR_MAP	predefined type atom
XA_RGB_DEFAULT_MAP	predefined colormap atom
XA_RGB_GRAY_MAP	predefined colormap atom
XA_RGB_GREEN_MAP	predefined colormap atom
XA_RGB_RED_MAP	predefined colormap atom
XA_SECONDARY	predefined selection atom
XA_STRIKEOUT_ASCENT	predefined font atom
XA_STRIKEOUT_DESCENT	predefined font atom
XA_STRING	predefined type atom
XA_SUBSCRIPT_X	predefined font atom
XA_SUBSCRIPT_Y	predefined font atom
XA_SUPERSCRIPT_X	predefined font atom
XA_SUPERSCRIPT_Y	predefined font atom
XA_UNDERLINE_POSITION	predefined font atom
XA_UNDERLINE_THICKNESS	predefined font atom
XA_VISUALID	predefined type atom
XA_WEIGHT	predefined font atom
XA_WINDOW	predefined type atom
XA_WM_CLASS	predefined font atom
XA_WM_CLIENT_MACHINE	predefined string atom
XA_WM_COMMAND	predefined window manager hints atom
XA_WM_HINTS	predefined window manager hints atom
XA_WM_ICON_NAME	predefined window manager hints atom
XA_WM_ICON_SIZE	predefined window manager hints atom
XA_WM_NAME	predefined window manager hints atom

Symbols

XA_WM_NORMAL_HINTS	predefined window manager hints atom
XA_WM_SIZE_HINTS	predefined type atom
XA_WM_TRANSIENT_FOR	predefined font atom
XA_WM_ZOOM_HINTS	predefined window manager hints atom
XA_X_HEIGHT	predefined font atom
XCNOENT	association table lookup return codes, No entry in table
XCNOMEM	association table lookup return codes, Out of memory
XCSUCCESS	association table lookup return codes, No error
XK_*	keysyms, see Appendix H, *Keysyms*
XNegative	mask used by XParseGeometry, if position is outside
X_PROTOCOL	current protocol version
X_PROTOCOL_REVISION	current minor revision
XValue	mask used by XParseGeometry, returns those set by user
XYBitmap	depth 1 (XPutImage, XGetImage)
XYPixmap	depth == drawable depth (XPutImage, XGetImage)

YZ

YNegative	mask used by XParseGeometry, if position is outside
YSorted	order of clip rectangles (XSetClipRectangles)
YValue	mask used by XParseGeometry, returns those set by user
YXBanded	order of clip rectangles (XSetClipRectangles)
YXSorted	order of clip rectangles (XSetClipRectangles)
ZoomState	window state, application wants to be zoomed (value for member of XWMHints)
ZPixmap	depth == drawable depth (XPutImage, XGetImage)

H
Keysyms

This appendix provides a list of keysyms and a brief description of each keysym. Keysyms, as you may remember, are the portable representation of the symbols on the caps of keys.

The normal way to process a keyboard event is to use XLookupKeysym to determine the keysym or, if the application allows remapping of keys to strings, it may use XLookup-String to get the ASCII string mapped to the key or keys pressed. This allows the application to treat keys in a simple and portable manner, and places the responsibility of tailoring the mapping between keys and keysyms on the server vendor.*

Many keysyms do not have obvious counterparts on the keyboard, but may be generated with certain key combinations. You will need a table for each particular model of hardware you intend the program to work on, to tell you what key combination results in each keysym that is not present on the caps of the keyboard. For real portability, you will want to use only the keysyms that are supported on all vendors equipment you intend the program to be displayed on.

The keysyms are defined in two standard include files: *<X11/keysym.h>* and *<X11/keysymdef.h>*. There are several families of keysyms defined in *<X11/keysymdef.h>*; LATIN1, LATIN2, LATIN3, LATIN4, KATAKANA, ARABIC, CYRILLIC, GREEK, TECHNICAL, SPECIAL, PUBLISHING, APL, HEBREW, and MISCELLANY. The *<X11/keysym.h>* file specifies which families are enabled. Only the LATIN1, LATIN2, LATIN3, LATIN4, GREEK, and MISCELLANY families are enabled in the standard *<X11/keysym.h>* file, probably because some compilers have an upper limit on the number of defined symbols that are allowed.

The developers of X at MIT say that to the best of their knowledge the Latin, Kana, Arabic, Cyrillic, Greek, Technical, APL, and Hebrew keysym sets are from the appropriate ISO (International Standards Organization) and/or ECMA international standards. There are no Technical, Special nor Publishing international standards, so these sets are based on Digital Equipment Corporation standards.

---

* While keycode information is not necessary for normal application programming, it may be necessary for writing certain programs that change the keycode to keysym mapping. You will need to obtain a list of keycodes and their normal mappings from the system manufacturer. Any program that uses this mapping is not fully portable.

Keysyms are four byte long values. In the standard keysyms, the least significant 8 bits indicate a particular character within a set. and the next 8 bits indicate a particular keysym set. The order of the sets is important since not all the sets are complete. Each character set contains gaps where codes have been removed that were duplicates with codes in previous (that is, with lesser keysym set) character sets.

The 94 and 96 character code sets have been moved to occupy the right hand quadrant (decimal 129 - 256), so the ASCII subset has a unique encoding across the least significant byte which corresponds to the ASCII character code. However, this cannot be guaranteed in the keysym sets of future releases and does not apply to all of the MISCELLANY set.

As far as possible, keysym codes are the same as the character code. In the LATIN1 to LATIN4 sets, all duplicate glyphs occupy the same position. However, duplicates between GREEK and TECHNICAL do not occupy the same code position. Thus, applications wishing to use the TECHNICAL character set must transform the keysym using an array.

The MISCELLANY set is a miscellaneous collection of commonly occurring keys on keyboards. Within this set, the keypad symbols are generally duplicates of symbols found on keys on the alphanumeric part of the keyboard but are distinguished here because they often have distinguishable keycodes associated with them.

There is a difference between European and US usage of the names Pilcrow, Paragraph, and Section, as shown in Table H-1.

Table H-1. European vs. US usage of Pilcrow, Paragraph, and Section symbol names

US name	European name	Keysym in LATIN1	Symbol
Section sign	Paragraph sign	`XK_section`	§
Paragraph sign	Pilcrow sign	`XK_paragraph`	¶

X has adopted the names used by both the ISO and ECMA standards. Thus, `XK_paragraph` is what Europeans call the pilcrow sign, and `XK_section` is what they would call the paragraph sign. This favors the US usage.

Keysyms and Description

Tables H-2 through H-7 list the six commonly available sets of keysyms (MISCELLANY, LATIN1 through LATIN4, and GREEK) and describe each keysym briefly. When necessary and possible, these tables show a representative character or characters that might appear on the cap of the key or on the screen when the key or keys corresponding to the keysym were typed.

Keysym	Description
XK_BackSpace	Backspace, Back Space, Back Char
XK_Tab	Tab
XK_Linefeed	Linefeed, LF
XK_Clear	Clear
XK_Return	Return, Enter
XK_Pause	Pause, Hold, Scroll Lock
XK_Escape	Escape
XK_Delete	Delete, Rubout
XK_Multi_key	Multi-key character preface
XK_Kanji	Kanji, Kanji convert
XK_Home	Home
XK_Left	Left, move left, left arrow
XK_Up	Up, move up, up arrow
XK_Right	Right, move right, right arrow
XK_Down	Down, move down, down arrow
XK_Prior	Prior, previous
XK_Next	Next
XK_End	End, EOL
XK_Begin	Begin, BOL
XK_Select	Select, mark
XK_Print	Print
XK_Execute	Execute, run, do
XK_Insert	Insert, insert here
XK_Undo	Undo, oops
XK_Redo	Redo, again
XK_Menu	Menu
XK_Find	Find, search
XK_Cancel	Cancel, stop, abort, exit
XK_Help	Help, question mark
XK_Break	Break
XK_Mode_switch	Mode switch, script switch, character set switch
XK_script_switch	Alias for mode switch, script switch, character set switch
XK_Num_Lock	Num Lock
XK_KP_Space	Keypad Space
XK_KP_Tab	Keypad Tab
XK_KP_Enter	Keypad Enter
XK_KP_F1	Keypad F1, PF1, a
XK_KP_F2	Keypad F2, PF2, b
XK_KP_F3	Keypad F3, PF3, c
XK_KP_F4	Keypad F4, PF4, d
XK_KP_Equal	Keypad equals sign
XK_KP_Multiply	Keypad multiplication sign, asterisk
XK_KP_Add	Keypad plus sign

Keysyms

Keysym	Description
XK_KP_Separator	Keypad separator, comma
XK_KP_Subtract	Keypad minus sign, hyphen
XK_KP_Decimal	Keypad decimal point, full stop
XK_KP_Divide	Keypad division sign, solidus
XK_KP_0	Keypad digit zero
XK_KP_1	Keypad digit one
XK_KP_2	Keypad digit two
XK_KP_3	Keypad digit three
XK_KP_4	Keypad digit four
XK_KP_5	Keypad digit five
XK_KP_6	Keypad digit six
XK_KP_7	Keypad digit seven
XK_KP_8	Keypad digit eight
XK_KP_9	Keypad digit nine
XK_F1	F1 function key
XK_F2	F2 function key
XK_F3	F3 function key
XK_F4	F4 function key
XK_F5	F5 function key
XK_F6	F6 function key
XK_F7	F7 function key
XK_F8	F8 function key
XK_F9	F9 function key
XK_F10	F10 function key
XK_F11	F11 function key
XK_L1	L1 function key
XK_F12	F12 function key
XK_L2	L2 function key
XK_F13	F13 function key
XK_L3	L3 function key
XK_F14	F14 function key
XK_L4	L4 function key
XK_F15	F15 function key
XK_L5	L5 function key
XK_F16	F16 function key
XK_L6	L6 function key
XK_F17	F17 function key
XK_L7	L7 function key
XK_F18	F18 function key
XK_L8	L8 function key
XK_F19	F19 function key
XK_L9	L9 function key
XK_F20	F20 function key
XK_L10	L10 function key
XK_F21	F21 function key

Keysym	Description
XK_R1	R1 function key
XK_F22	F22 function key
XK_R2	R2 function key
XK_F23	F23 function key
XK_R3	R3 function key
XK_F24	F24 function key
XK_R4	R4 function key
XK_F25	F25 function key
XK_R5	R5 function key
XK_F26	F26 function key
XK_R6	R6 function key
XK_F27	F27 function key
XK_R7	R7 function key
XK_F28	F28 function key
XK_R8	R8 function key
XK_F29	F29 function key
XK_R9	R9 function key
XK_F30	F30 function key
XK_R10	R10 function key
XK_F31	F31 function key
XK_R11	R11 function key
XK_F32	F32 function key
XK_R12	R12 function key
XK_R13	F33 function key
XK_F33	R13 function key
XK_F34	F34 function key
XK_R14	R14 function key
XK_F35	F35 function key
XK_R15	R15 function key
XK_Shift_L	Left Shift
XK_Shift_R	Right Shift
XK_Control_L	Left Control
XK_Control_R	Right Control
XK_Caps_Lock	Caps Lock
XK_Shift_Lock	Shift Lock
XK_Meta_L	Left Meta
XK_Meta_R	Right Meta
XK_Alt_L	Left Alt
XK_Alt_R	Right Alt
XK_Super_L	Left Super
XK_Super_R	Right Super
XK_Hyper_L	Left Hyper
XK_Hyper_R	Right Hyper

Table H-3. LATIN1

Keysym	Description	Character
XK_space	Space	
XK_exclam	Exclamation point	!
XK_quotedbl	Quotation mark	,,
XK_numbersign	Number sign	#
XK_dollar	Dollar sign	$
XK_percent	Percent sign	%
XK_ampersand	Ampersand	&
XK_quoteright	Apostrophe	,
XK_parenleft	Left parenthesis	(
XK_parenright	Right parenthesis	)
XK_asterisk	Asterisk	*
XK_plus	Plus sign	+
XK_comma	Comma	,
XK_minus	Hyphen, minus sign	−
XK_period	Full stop	.
XK_slash	Solidus	/
XK_0	Digit zero	0
XK_1	Digit one	1
XK_2	Digit two	2
XK_3	Digit three	3
XK_4	Digit four	4
XK_5	Digit five	5
XK_6	Digit six	6
XK_7	Digit seven	7
XK_8	Digit eight	8
XK_9	Digit nine	9
XK_colon	Colon	:
XK_semicolon	Semicolon	;
XK_less	Less than sign	<
XK_equal	Equals sign	=
XK_greater	Greater than sign	>
XK_question	Question mark	?
XK_at	Commercial at	@
XK_A	Latin capital A	A
XK_B	Latin capital B	B
XK_C	Latin capital C	C
XK_D	Latin capital D	D
XK_E	Latin capital E	E

Table H-3. LATIN1 (continued)

Keysym	Description	Character
XK_F	Latin capital F	F
XK_G	Latin capital G	G
XK_H	Latin capital H	H
XK_I	Latin capital I	I
XK_J	Latin capital J	J
XK_K	Latin capital K	K
XK_L	Latin capital L	L
XK_M	Latin capital M	M
XK_N	Latin capital N	N
XK_O	Latin capital O	O
XK_P	Latin capital P	P
XK_Q	Latin capital Q	Q
XK_R	Latin capital R	R
XK_S	Latin capital S	S
XK_T	Latin capital T	T
XK_U	Latin capital U	U
XK_V	Latin capital V	V
XK_W	Latin capital W	W
XK_X	Latin capital X	X
XK_Y	Latin capital Y	Y
XK_Z	Latin capital Z	Z
XK_bracketleft	Left square bracket	[
XK_backslash	Reverse solidus	\
XK_bracketright	Right square bracket	]
XK_asciicircum	Circumflex accent	^
XK_underscore	Low line	_
XK_quoteleft	Grave accent	`
XK_a	Latin small a	a
XK_b	Latin small b	b
XK_c	Latin small c	c
XK_d	Latin small d	d
XK_e	Latin small e	e
XK_f	Latin small f	f
XK_g	Latin small g	g
XK_h	Latin small h	h
XK_i	Latin small i	i
XK_j	Latin small j	j

Keysyms

Table H-3. LATIN1 (continued)

Keysym	Description	Character
XK_k	Latin small k	k
XK_l	Latin small l	l
XK_m	Latin small m	m
XK_n	Latin small n	n
XK_o	Latin small o	o
XK_p	Latin small p	p
XK_q	Latin small q	q
XK_r	Latin small r	r
XK_s	Latin small s	s
XK_t	Latin small t	t
XK_u	Latin small u	u
XK_v	Latin small v	v
XK_w	Latin small w	w
XK_x	Latin small x	x
XK_y	Latin small y	y
XK_z	Latin small z	z
XK_braceleft	Left brace	{
XK_bar	Vertical line	|
XK_braceright	Right brace	}
XK_asciitilde	Tilde	~
XK_nobreakspace	No-break space	
XK_exclamdown	Inverted exclamation mark	¡
XK_cent	Cent sign	¢
XK_sterling	Pound sign	£
XK_currency	Currency sign	¤
XK_yen	Yen sign	¥
XK_brokenbar	Broken vertical bar	¦
XK_section	Paragraph sign, section sign	§
XK_diaeresis	Diaeresis	¨
XK_copyright	Copyright sign	©
XK_ordfeminine	Feminine ordinal indicator	ª
XK_guillemotleft	Left angle quotation mark	«
XK_notsign	Not sign	¬
XK_hyphen	Short horizontal hyphen	-
XK_registered	Registered trade mark sign	®
XK_macron	Macron	¯
XK_degree	Degree sign, ring above	°

Keysym	Description	Character
XK_plusminus	Plus-minus sign	±
XK_twosuperior	Superscript two	²
XK_threesuperior	Superscript three	³
XK_acute	Acute accent	´
XK_mu	Micro sign	μ
XK_paragraph	Pilcrow sign	¶
XK_periodcentered	Middle dot	·
XK_cedilla	Cedilla	¸
XK_onesuperior	Superscript one	¹
XK_masculine	Masculine ordinal indicator	º
XK_guillemotright	Right angle quotation mark	»
XK_onequarter	Vulgar fraction one quarter	¼
XK_onehalf	Vulgar fraction one half	½
XK_threequarters	Vulgar fraction three quarters	¾
XK_questiondown	Inverted question mark	¿
XK_Agrave	Latin capital A with grave accent	À
XK_Aacute	Latin capital A with acute accent	Á
XK_Acircumflex	Latin capital A with circumflex accent	Â
XK_Atilde	Latin capital A with tilde	Ã
XK_Adiaeresis	Latin capital A with diaeresis	Ä
XK_Aring	Latin capital A with ring above	Å
XK_AE	Latin capital diphthong AE	Æ
XK_Ccedilla	Latin capital C with cedilla	Ç
XK_Egrave	Latin capital E with grave accent	È
XK_Eacute	Latin capital E with acute accent	É
XK_Ecircumflex	Latin capital E with circumflex accent	Ê
XK_Ediaeresis	Latin capital E with diaeresis	Ë
XK_Igrave	Latin capital I with grave accent	Ì
XK_Iacute	Latin capital I with acute accent	Í
XK_Icircumflex	Latin capital I with circumflex accent	Î
XK_Idiaeresis	Latin capital I with diaeresis	Ï
XK_Eth	Icelandic capital ETH	
XK_Ntilde	Latin capital N with tilde	Ñ
XK_Ograve	Latin capital O with grave accent	Ò
XK_Oacute	Latin capital O with acute accent	Ó
XK_Ocircumflex	Latin capital O with circumflex accent	Ô
XK_Otilde	Latin capital O with tilde	Õ

Keysym	Description	Character
XK_Odiaeresis	Latin capital O with diaeresis	Ö
XK_multiply	Multiplication sign	×
XK_Ooblique	Latin capital O with oblique stroke	Ø
XK_Ugrave	Latin capital U with grave accent	Ù
XK_Uacute	Latin capital U with acute accent	Ú
XK_Ucircumflex	Latin capital U with circumflex accent	Û
XK_Udiaeresis	Latin capital U with diaeresis	Ü
XK_Yacute	Latin capital Y with acute accent	Ý
XK_Thorn	Icelandic capital THORN	
XK_ssharp	German small sharp s	
XK_agrave	Latin small a with grave accent	à
XK_aacute	Latin small a with acute accent	á
XK_acircumflex	Latin small a with circumflex accent	â
XK_atilde	Latin small a with tilde	ã
XK_adiaeresis	Latin small a with diaeresis	ä
XK_aring	Latin small a with ring above	å
XK_ae	Latin small diphthong ae	æ
XK_ccedilla	Latin small c with cedilla	ç
XK_egrave	Latin small e with grave accent	è
XK_eacute	Latin small e with acute accent	é
XK_ecircumflex	Latin small e with circumflex accent	ê
XK_ediaeresis	Latin small e with diaeresis	ë
XK_igrave	Latin small i with grave accent	ì
XK_iacute	Latin small i with acute accent	í
XK_icircumflex	Latin small i with circumflex accent	î
XK_idiaeresis	Latin small i with diaeresis	ï
XK_eth	Icelandic small eth	
XK_ntilde	Latin small n with tilde	ñ
XK_ograve	Latin small o with grave accent	ò
XK_oacute	Latin small o with acute accent	ó
XK_ocircumflex	Latin small o with circumflex accent	ô
XK_otilde	Latin small o with tilde	õ
XK_odiaeresis	Latin small o with diaeresis	ö
XK_division	Division sign	÷
XK_oslash	Latin small o with oblique stroke	ø
XK_ugrave	Latin small u with grave accent	ù
XK_uacute	Latin small u with acute accent	ú

Table H-3. LATIN1 (continued)

Keysym	Description	Character
XK_ucircumflex	Latin small u with circumflex accent	û
XK_udiaeresis	Latin small u with diaeresis	ü
XK_yacute	Latin small y with acute accent	ý
XK_thorn	Icelandic small thorn	
XK_ydiaeresis	Latin small y with diaeresis	ÿ

Keysyms

Table H-4. LATIN2

Keysym	Description	Character
XK_Aogonek	Latin capital A with ogonek	Ą
XK_breve	Breve	˘
XK_Lstroke	Latin capital L with stroke	Ł
XK_Lcaron	Latin capital L with caron	Ľ
XK_Sacute	Latin capital S with acute accent	Ś
XK_Scaron	Latin capital S with caron	Š
XK_Scedilla	Latin capital S with cedilla	Ş
XK_Tcaron	Latin capital T with caron	Ť
XK_Zacute	Latin capital Z with acute accent	Ź
XK_Zcaron	Latin capital Z with caron	Ž
XK_Zabovedot	Latin capital Z with dot above	Ż
XK_aogonek	Latin small a with ogonek	ą
XK_ogonek	Ogonek	˛
XK_lstroke	Latin small l with stroke	ł
XK_lcaron	Latin small l with caron	ľ
XK_sacute	Latin small s with acute accent	ś
XK_caron	Caron	ˇ
XK_scaron	Latin small s with caron	š
XK_scedilla	Latin small s with cedilla	ş
XK_tcaron	Latin small t with caron	ť
XK_zacute	Latin small z with acute accent	ź
XK_doubleacute	Double acute accent	˝
XK_zcaron	Latin small z with caron	ž
XK_zabovedot	Latin small z with dot above	ż
XK_Racute	Latin capital R with acute accent	Ŕ
XK_Abreve	Latin capital A with breve	Ă
XK_Cacute	Latin capital C with acute accent	Ć
XK_Ccaron	Latin capital C with caron	Č
XK_Eogonek	Latin capital E with ogonek	Ę
XK_Ecaron	Latin capital E with caron	Ě
XK_Dcaron	Latin capital D with caron	Ď
XK_Nacute	Latin capital N with acute accent	Ń
XK_Ncaron	Latin capital N with caron	Ň
XK_Odoubleacute	Latin capital O with double acute accent	Ő
XK_Rcaron	Latin capital R with caron	Ř
XK_Uring	Latin capital U with ring above	Ů
XK_Udoubleacute	Latin capital U with double acute accent	Ű
XK_Tcedilla	Latin capital T with cedilla	Ţ

Keysym	Description	Character
XK_racute	Latin small r with acute accent	ŕ
XK_abreve	Latin small a with breve	ă
XK_cacute	Latin small c with acute accent	ć
XK_ccaron	Latin small c with caron	č
XK_eogonek	Latin small e with ogonek	ę
XK_ecaron	Latin small e with caron	ě
XK_dcaron	Latin small d with caron	ď
XK_nacute	Latin small n with acute accent	ń
XK_ncaron	Latin small n with caron	ň
XK_odoubleacute	Latin small o with double acute accent	ő
XK_rcaron	Latin small r with caron	ř
XK_uring	Latin small u with ring above	ů
XK_udoubleacute	Latin small u with double acute accent	ű
XK_tcedilla	Latin small t with cedilla	ţ
XK_abovedot	Dot above	·

Keysyms

Keysym	Description	Character
XK_Hstroke	Latin capital H with stroke	
XK_Hcircumflex	Latin capital H with circumflex accent	Ĥ
XK_Iabovedot	Latin capital I with dot above	İ
XK_Gbreve	Latin capital G with breve	Ğ
XK_Jcircumflex	Latin capital J with circumflex accent	Ĵ
XK_hstroke	Latin small h with stroke	
XK_hcircumflex	Latin small h with circumflex accent	ĥ
XK_idotless	Small dotless i	ı
XK_gbreve	Latin small g with breve	ğ
XK_jcircumflex	Latin small j with circumflex accent	ĵ
XK_Cabovedot	Latin capital C with dot above	Ċ
XK_Ccircumflex	Latin capital C with circumflex accent	Ĉ
XK_Gabovedot	Latin capital G with dot above	Ġ
XK_Gcircumflex	Latin capital G with circumflex accent	Ĝ
XK_Ubreve	Latin capital U with breve	Ŭ
XK_Scircumflex	Latin capital S with circumflex accent	Ŝ
XK_cabovedot	Latin small c with dot above	ċ
XK_ccircumflex	Latin small c with circumflex accent	ĉ
XK_gabovedot	Latin small g with dot above	ġ
XK_gcircumflex	Latin small g with circumflex accent	ĝ
XK_ubreve	Latin small u with breve	ŭ
XK_scircumflex	Latin small s with circumflex accent	ŝ

Keysym	Description	Character
XK_kappa	Latin small kappa	
XK_Rcedilla	Latin capital R with cedilla	Ŗ
XK_Itilde	Latin capital I with tilde	Ĩ
XK_Lcedilla	Latin capital L with cedilla	Ļ
XK_Emacron	Latin capital E with macron	Ē
XK_Gcedilla	Latin capital G with cedilla	Ģ
XK_Tslash	Latin capital T with oblique stroke	
XK_rcedilla	Latin small r with cedilla	ŗ
XK_itilde	Latin small i with tilde	ĩ
XK_lcedilla	Latin small l with cedilla	ļ
XK_emacron	Latin small e with macron	ē
XK_gacute	Latin small g with acute accent	ģ
XK_tslash	Latin small t with oblique stroke	
XK_ENG	Lappish capital ENG	
XK_eng	Lappish small eng	
XK_Amacron	Latin capital A with macron	Ā
XK_Iogonek	Latin capital I with ogonek	Į
XK_Eabovedot	Latin capital E with dot above	Ė
XK_Imacron	Latin capital I with macron	Ī
XK_Ncedilla	Latin capital N with cedilla	ņ
XK_Omacron	Latin capital O with macron	Ō
XK_Kcedilla	Latin capital K with cedilla	Ķ
XK_Uogonek	Latin capital U with ogonek	Ų
XK_Utilde	Latin capital U with tilde	Ũ
XK_Umacron	Latin capital U with macron	Ū
XK_amacron	Latin small a with macron	ā
XK_iogonek	Latin small i with ogonek	į
XK_eabovedot	Latin small e with dot above	ė
XK_imacron	Latin small i with macron	ī
XK_ncedilla	Latin small n with cedilla	ņ
XK_omacron	Latin small o with macron	ō
XK_kcedilla	Latin small k with cedilla	ķ
XK_uogonek	Latin small u with ogonek	ų
XK_utilde	Latin small u with tilde	ũ
XK_umacron	Latin small u with macron	ū

Keysyms

Keysym	Description	Character
XK_Greek_ALPHAaccent	Greek capital alpha with accent	
XK_Greek_EPSILONaccent	Greek capital epsilon with accent	
XK_Greek_ETAaccent	Greek capital eta with accent	
XK_Greek_IOTAaccent	Greek capital iota with accent	
XK_Greek_IOTAdiaeresis	Greek capital iota with diaeresis	
XK_Greek_IOTAaccentdiaeresis	Greek capital iota with accent+dieresis	
XK_Greek_OMICRONaccent	Greek capital omicron with accent	
XK_Greek_UPSILONaccent	Greek capital upsilon with accent	
XK_Greek_UPSILONdieresis	Greek capital upsilon with dieresis	
XK_Greek_UPSILONaccentdieresis	Greek capital upsilon with accent+dieresis	
XK_Greek_OMEGAaccent	Greek capital omega with accent	
XK_Greek_alphaaccent	Greek small alpha with accent	
XK_Greek_epsilonaccent	Greek small epsilon with accent	
XK_Greek_etaaccent	Greek small eta with accent	
XK_Greek_iotaaccent	Greek small iota with accent	
XK_Greek_iotadieresis	Greek small iota with dieresis	
XK_Greek_iotaaccentdieresis	Greek small iota with accent+dieresis	
XK_Greek_omicronaccent	Greek small omicron with accent	
XK_Greek_upsilonaccent	Greek small upsilon with accent	
XK_Greek_upsilondieresis	Greek small upsilon with dieresis	
XK_Greek_upsilonaccentdieresis	Greek small upsilon with accent+dieresis	
XK_Greek_omegaaccent	Greek small omega with accent	
XK_Greek_ALPHA	Greek capital alpha	A
XK_Greek_BETA	Greek capital beta	B
XK_Greek_GAMMA	Greek capital gamma	Γ
XK_Greek_DELTA	Greek capital delta	Δ
XK_Greek_EPSILON	Greek capital epsilon	E
XK_Greek_ZETA	Greek capital zeta	Z
XK_Greek_ETA	Greek capital eta	H
XK_Greek_THETA	Greek capital theta	Θ
XK_Greek_IOTA	Greek capital iota	I
XK_Greek_KAPPA	Greek capital kappa	K
XK_Greek_LAMBDA	Greek capital lambda	Λ
XK_Greek_MU	Greek capital mu	M
XK_Greek_NU	Greek capital nu	N
XK_Greek_XI	Greek capital xi	Ξ
XK_Greek_OMICRON	Greek capital omicron	O
XK_Greek_PI	Greek capital pi	Π

Keysym	Description	Character
XK_Greek_RHO	Greek capital rho	Ρ
XK_Greek_SIGMA	Greek capital sigma	Σ
XK_Greek_TAU	Greek capital tau	Τ
XK_Greek_UPSILON	Greek capital upsilon	Υ
XK_Greek_PHI	Greek capital phi	Φ
XK_Greek_CHI	Greek capital chi	Χ
XK_Greek_PSI	Greek capital psi	Ψ
XK_Greek_OMEGA	Greek capital omega	Ω
XK_Greek_alpha	Greek small alpha	α
XK_Greek_beta	Greek small beta	β
XK_Greek_gamma	Greek small gamma	γ
XK_Greek_delta	Greek small delta	δ
XK_Greek_epsilon	Greek small epsilon	ε
XK_Greek_zeta	Greek small zeta	ζ
XK_Greek_eta	Greek small eta	η
XK_Greek_theta	Greek small theta	θ
XK_Greek_iota	Greek small iota	ι
XK_Greek_kappa	Greek small kappa	κ
XK_Greek_lambda	Greek small lambda	λ
XK_Greek_mu	Greek small mu	μ
XK_Greek_nu	Greek small nu	ν
XK_Greek_xi	Greek small xi	ξ
XK_Greek_omicron	Greek small omicron	ο
XK_Greek_pi	Greek small pi	π
XK_Greek_rho	Greek small rho	ρ
XK_Greek_sigma	Greek small sigma	σ
XK_Greek_finalsmallsigma	Greek small final small sigma	ς
XK_Greek_tau	Greek small tau	τ
XK_Greek_upsilon	Greek small upsilon	υ
XK_Greek_phi	Greek small phi	φ
XK_Greek_chi	Greek small chi	χ
XK_Greek_psi	Greek small psi	ψ
XK_Greek_omega	Greek small omega	ω
XK_Greek_switch	Switch to Greek set	

Keysyms

I

The Cursor Font

A standard font consisting of a number of cursor shapes is available. This font is loaded automatically when XCreateFontCursor, the routine used to create a standard cursor, is called. To specify a cursor shape from the standard font, use one of the symbols defined in the file <X11/cursorfont.h>, by including it in your source code. The symbols for the available cursors and an illustration of their shapes is provided here. The procedure for creating a cursor is described in Volume One, Section 6.6.

You may notice that the symbol values skip the odd numbers; there are really two font characters for each shape but we are only showing you one. Each odd-numbered character (not shown) is a mask that selects which pixels in the screen around the cursor are modified.

The standard cursor shapes are shown in Figure I-1. The mask shapes have been removed. Each row in Figure I-1 contains twelve cursor shapes (except the last one). Table I-1 shows the symbol definitions from <X11/cursorfont.h> grouped by rows corresponding to the rows in Figure I-1.

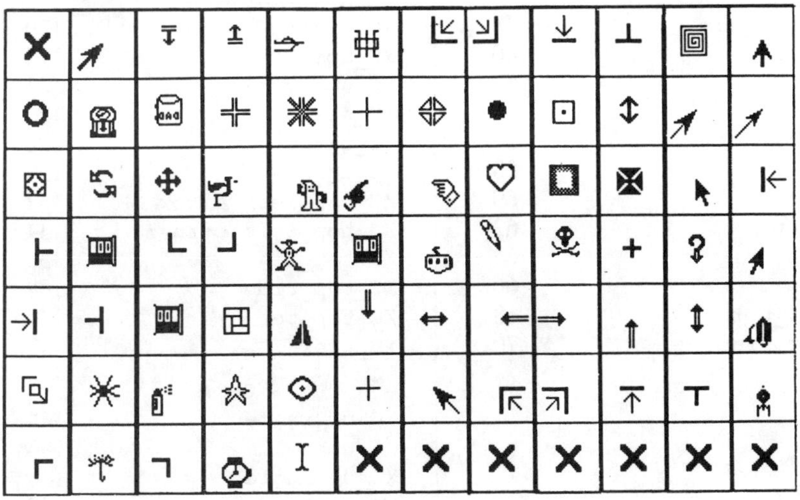

Figure I-1. The Standard Cursors

Table I-1. Standard Cursor Symbols

Symbol	Value	Symbol	Value
Row 1		**Row 4**	
XC_X_cursor	0	XC_left_tee	72
XC_arrow	2	XC_left_button	74
XC_based_arrow_down	4	XC_ll_angle	76
XC_based_arrow_up	6	XC_lr_angle	78
XC_boat	8	XC_man	80
XC_bogosity	10	XC_middlebutton	82
XC_bottom_left_corner	12	XC_mouse	84
XC_bottom_right_corner	14	XC_pencil	86
XC_bottom_side	16	XC_pirate	88
XC_bottom_tee	18	XC_plus	90
XC_box_spiral	20	XC_question_arrow	92
XC_center_ptr	22	XC_right_ptr	94
Row 2		**Row 5**	
XC_circle	24	XC_right_side	96
XC_clock	26	XC_right_tee	98
XC_coffee_mug	28	XC_rightbutton	100
XC_cross	30	XC_rtl_logo	102
XC_cross_reverse	32	XC_sailboat	104
XC_crosshair	34	XC_sb_down_arrow	106
XC_diamond_cross	36	XC_sb_h_double_arrow	108
XC_dot	38	XC_sb_left_arrow	110
XC_dotbox	40	XC_sb_right_arrow	112
XC_double_arrow	42	XC_sb_up_arrow	114
XC_draft_large	44	XC_sb_v_double_arrow	116
XC_draft_small	46	XC_shuttle	118
Row 3		**Row 6**	
XC_draped_box	48	XC_sizing	120
XC_exchange	50	XC_spider	122
XC_fleur	52	XC_spraycan	124
XC_gobbler	54	XC_star	126
XC_gumby	56	XC_target	128
XC_hand1	58	XC_tcross	130
XC_hand2	60	XC_top_left_arrow	132
XC_heart	62	XC_top_left_corner	134
XC_icon	64	XC_top_right_corner	136
XC_iron_cross	66	XC_top_side	138
XC_left_ptr	68	XC_top_tee	140
XC_left_side	70	XC_trek	142
		Row 7	
		XC_ul_angle	144
		XC_umbrella	146
		XC_ur_angle	148
		XC_watch	150
		XC_xterm	152
		XC_num_glyphs	154

J

Fonts

This appendix should tell you everything you need to know about the fonts in the X distribution. Not every font may be supported by particular server vendors, and some vendors may supplement the set. Also, a more descriptive naming scheme has been proposed, but it has not been accepted as part of the X standard at this writing.

Table J-1 lists the fonts provided in the standard X distribution. Fixed-width and variable-width fonts are listed in separated columns. Table J-2 describes the maximum metrics for characters in the font. This should help you choose a font and decide how much space to allow for strings using the font. Finally, all or most of the characters in each font are shown actual size, as they would appear on a 900 × 1180 pixel, 10" × 13.5" screen (Sun). On a screen with different pixel density, these fonts would appear a different size.

Table J-1. Fonts in the Standard Distribution

Fixed-width Fonts			Variable-width Fonts			
6x10	fgb1-25	oldera	apl-s25	hbr-s40	vg-25	vr-30
6x12	fgb1-30	rot-s16	arrow3	krivo	vg-31	vr-31
6x13	fgi-20	sans12	chp-s25	met25	vg-40	vr-40
8x13	fgi1-25	sansb12	chs-s50	mit	vgb-25	vrb-25
8x13bold	fgs-22	sansi12	cursor	plunk	vgb-31	vrb-30
9x15	fixed	serif10	cyr-s25	runlen	vgbc-25	vrb-31
crturz	fqxb-25	serif12	cyr-s30	stan	vgh-25	vrb-35
dancer	fr-25	serifb10	cyr-s38	sub	vgi-20	vrb-37
fg-13	fr-33	serifb12	ent	subsub	vgi-25	vri-25
fg-16	fr1-25	serifi10	fcor-20	sup	vgi-31	vri-30
fg-18	fr2-25	serifi12	fgb-13	supsup	vgl-40	vri-31
fg-20	fr3-25	stempl	fgb-25	sym-s25	vgvb-31	vri-40
fg-22	frb-32	swd-s30	fri-33	sym-s53	vmic-25	vsg-114
fg-25	ipa-s25	vtbold	fri1-25	variable	vply-36	vsgn-57
fg-30	lat-s30	vtsingle	ger-s35	vbee-36	vr-20	vshd-40
fg-40	micro	xif-s25	grk-s25	vctl-25	vr-25	vxms-37
fg1-25			grk-s30	vg-13	vr-27	vxms-43
			hbr-s25	vg-20		

Fonts

Table J-2 describes the maximum metrics for each font. These are the values of the `max_bounds` member of `XFontStruct` (which is an `XCharStruct` structure with the members shown in the table). Note that it is unlikely that any single character will be the biggest in all the measurements simultaneously; these describe the largest `lbearing` of any character in the font, the largest `rbearing` for any character in the font, and so on. For a description of each of the character measurements, see Volume One, Section 6.2.3.

Table J-2. Maximum Font Metrics

Font Name	lbearing	rbearing	ascent	descent	width
6x10	0	6	8	2	6
6x12	0	6	8	4	6
6x13	0	6	10	3	6
8x13	0	8	10	3	8
8x13bold	0	8	10	3	8
9x15	0	9	12	3	9
a14	0	7	12	2	7
apl-s25	0	27	20	5	27
arrow3	0	59	8	18	59
chp-s25	0	34	23	2	34
chs-s50	0	50	40	10	50
crturz	0	100	0	155	100
cursor	1	16	15	16	17
cyr-s25	0	28	24	5	28
cyr-s30	0	37	30	8	37
cyr-s38	0	37	30	8	37
dancer	0	47	36	10	47
ent	0	640	0	170	640
fcor-20	0	16	16	4	16
fg-13	0	9	11	2	9
fg-16	0	10	11	5	10
fg-18	0	12	13	5	12
fg-20	0	12	15	5	12
fg-22	0	13	17	5	13
fg-25	0	16	20	5	16
fg-30	0	19	25	5	19
fg-40	0	25	33	7	25
fg1-25	0	14	20	5	14
fgb-13	0	10	11	2	10
fgb-25	0	17	20	5	17
fgb1-25	0	16	20	5	16
fgb1-30	0	16	20	10	16
fgi-20	0	12	15	5	12
fgi1-25	0	16	20	5	16
fgs-22	0	13	17	5	13
fixed	0	6	10	3	6

Font Name	lbearing	rbearing	ascent	descent	width
fqxb-25	0	22	20	5	22
fr-25	0	17	20	5	17
fr-33	0	23	23	10	23
fr1-25	0	16	20	5	16
fr2-25	0	16	20	5	16
fr3-25	0	16	20	5	16
frb-32	0	19	24	8	19
fri-33	0	26	24	9	26
fri1-25	0	17	20	5	17
ger-s35	0	32	30	5	32
grk-s25	0	27	20	5	27
grk-s30	0	35	26	5	35
hbr-s25	0	20	32	13	20
hbr-s40	0	29	50	14	29
ipa-s25	0	16	20	5	16
kana14	0	7	12	2	7
krivo	0	49	50	50	49
lat-s30	0	16	25	5	16
met25	0	7	21	9	7
micro	0	4	5	0	4
mit	0	161	143	2	161
oldera	0	15	9	6	15
plunk	0	26	21	9	26
r14	0	7	12	2	7
rot-s16	0	25	16	0	25
runlen	0	96	3	0	96
sans12	0	11	11	3	11
sansb12	0	11	11	3	11
sansi12	0	11	11	3	11
serif10	0	8	10	3	8
serif12	0	11	11	3	11
serifb10	0	8	10	3	8
serifb12	0	11	11	3	11
serifi10	0	8	10	3	8
serifi12	0	11	11	3	11
stan	0	225	108	108	225
stempl	0	28	28	0	28
sub	0	20	9	12	20
subsub	0	13	0	14	13
sup	0	20	28	−7	20
supsup	0	13	36	−22	13
swd-s30	0	16	25	5	16
sym-s25	0	24	20	5	24
sym-s53	0	34	35	18	34

Fonts

Font Name	lbearing	rbearing	ascent	descent	width
variable	16	16	11	3	16
vbee-36	0	38	29	7	38
vctl-25	0	25	19	6	25
vg-13	0	13	11	2	13
vg-20	0	20	16	4	20
vg-25	0	23	20	5	23
vg-31	0	31	24	7	31
vg-40	0	37	32	8	37
vgb-25	0	23	20	5	23
vgb-31	0	32	24	7	32
vgbc-25	0	22	20	5	22
vgh-25	0	23	20	5	23
vgi-20	0	20	16	4	20
vgi-25	0	23	20	5	23
vgi-31	0	31	24	7	31
vgl-40	0	37	32	8	37
vgvb-31	0	32	24	7	32
vmic-25	0	28	20	5	28
vply-36	0	16	27	9	16
vr-20	0	24	15	5	24
vr-25	0	25	21	4	25
vr-27	0	28	20	7	28
vr-30	0	31	22	8	31
vr-31	0	28	25	6	28
vr-40	0	38	30	10	38
vrb-25	0	25	20	5	25
vrb-30	0	30	22	8	30
vrb-31	0	30	25	6	30
vrb-35	0	35	26	9	35
vrb-37	0	51	27	10	51
vri-25	0	27	20	5	27
vri-30	0	30	22	8	30
vri-31	0	28	25	6	28
vri-40	0	43	33	7	43
vsg-114	0	189	100	12	189
vsgn-57	0	95	50	7	95
vshd-40	0	38	32	8	38
vtbold	0	8	10	3	8
vtsingle	0	9	12	3	9
vxms-37	0	44	28	9	44
vxms-43	0	56	35	8	56
xif-s25	0	16	20	5	16

The remaining pages of this appendix show the characters in each font, actual size, as they would appear on a 900 × 1180 pixel, 10" × 13.5" screen (Sun). On a screen with different pixel density, these fonts would appear a proportionally different size.

For most fonts, the entire character set is shown. For very large fonts, we have sometimes shown just a few characters to save space. Also, fonts that begin with many blank characters are shown with most leading blanks removed. Therefore, you can't always get the character number of each cell in the font by counting from the first cell we have shown. Use *xfd* to quickly determine the code for a particular cell.

Fonts

6x10

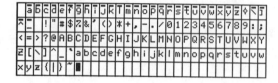

6x12

6x13

8x13

8x13bold

9x15

a14

Fonts

apl-s25

	;	:	[		!	φ	φ	I						
▯	⊕	⋏	⋎	Ⴀ	⍋	⍒	⊖	⌿	⍀	⋉⋊	⍢	▼	⊟
⊟	⊡	$	Φ		(	)	]	$	=	×	≥	∨	∧
≠	÷	,	+	.	/	0	1	2	3	4	5	6	7
8	9	≤	<	¯	⋅⋅	>	\	←	∝	⊥	∩	⌊	∈
_	∇	Δ	⍳	∘	'	□	∣	⊤	○	*	?	ρ	⌈
~	↓	∪		⊃	↑	⊂	{		}		⁻	→	A
B	C	D	E	F	G	H	I	J	K	L	M	N	O
P	Q	R	S	T	U	V	W	X	Y	Z	∀	ⱻ	↔

arrow3

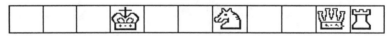

chp-s25

chs-s50

cyr-s25

				ю	ы	я		Ш	А	Б		Д
Е	Ф	Г	Х	И		К	Л	М	Н	О	П	
Р	С	Т	У	В			Й	З				Ж
Ц	ъ	а	б		д	е	ф	г	х	и		к

cyr-s30

Ф	Г	Х	И		К	Л	М	Н		О
П		Р	С	Т	У	В			Й	
З				Ж	Ц	ъ	а		б	
д	е	ф	г	х	и		к	л		М
н	о	п		р	с	т	У	в		
	й	з								

cyr-s38

dancer

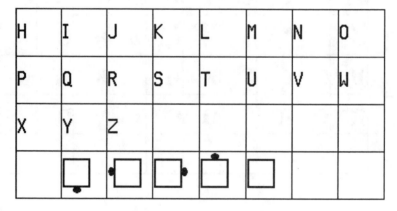

ent

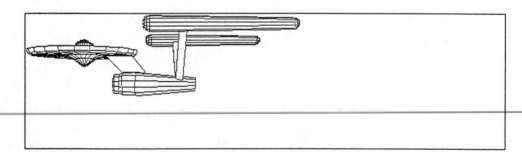

fr2-25

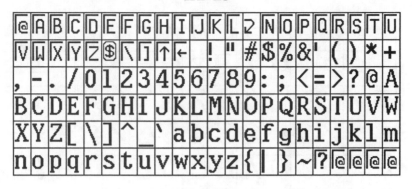

fr3-25

frb-32

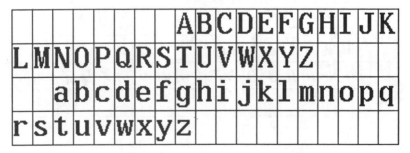

fri-33

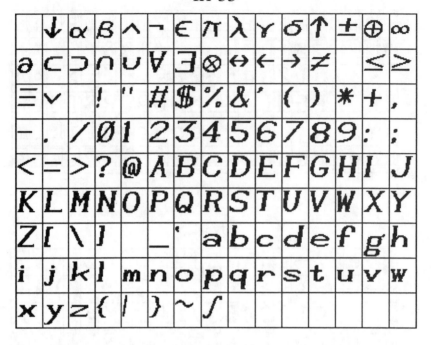

fri1-25

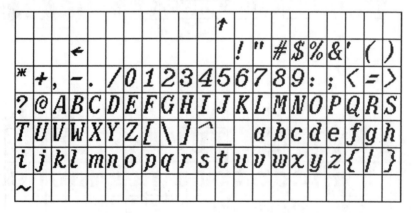

fr1-25

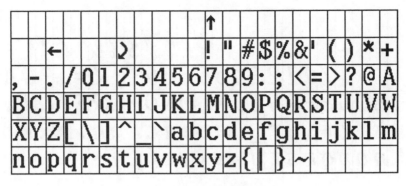

fr-33

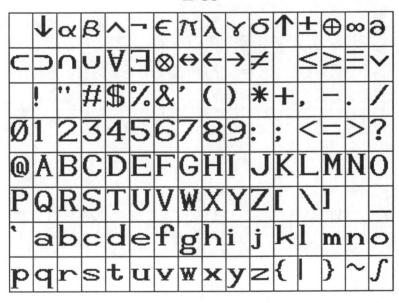

fgi1-25

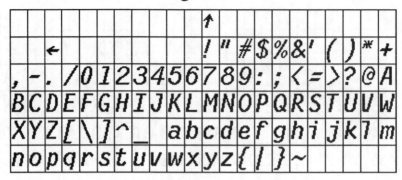

fgs-22

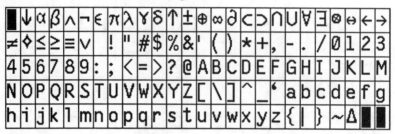

fixed

fqxb-25

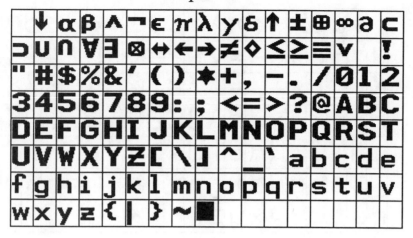

fr-25

fg-30

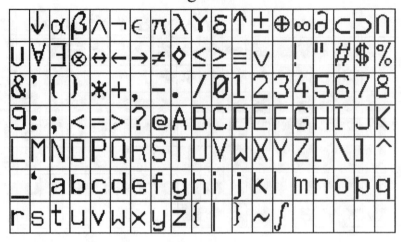

fg-40

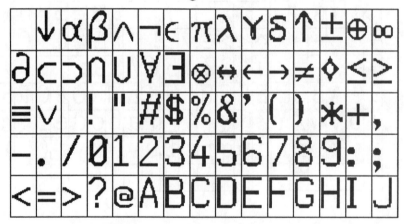

fg1-25

Xlib Reference Manual

fgb-13

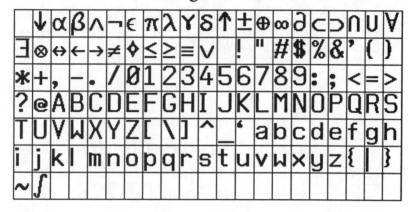

fgb-25

fgb1-25

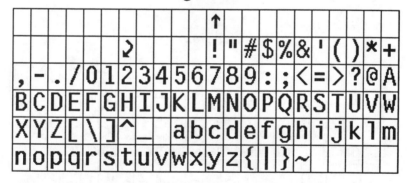

Fonts

fgb1-30

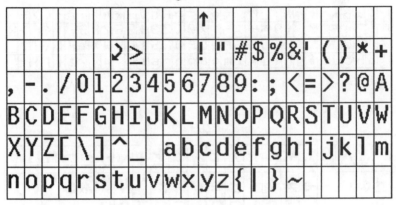

fgi-20

fg-25

fcor-20

fg-13

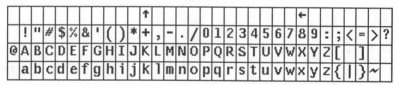

fg-16

fg-18

Fonts

fg-20

```
↓αβ∧¬∈πλ   ↑  ℤω∂⊂⊃∪∀∃⊗↔←→≠◇
≤≥≡∨ ! " #$%&' ( ) *+, −. /01234567
89: ; <=>? @ABCDEFGHIJKLMNOPQRS
TUVWXYZ[ \]^_` abcdefghijklmno
pqrstuvwxyz{ | } ~
```

fg-22

```
                 ↑              ⊗  ←
         ≡     ! " #$%&' ( ) *+, −. /0123
456789: ; <=>? @ABCDEFGHIJKLM
NOPQRSTUVWXYZ[ \]^_` abcdefg
hijklmnopqrstuvwxyz{ | } ~Δ
```

ger-s35

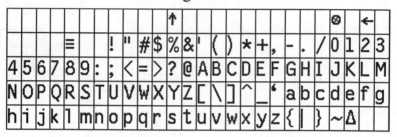

grk-s25

								Α	Β	Χ	Δ	Ε
Φ	Γ	Η	Ι	φ	Κ	Λ	Μ	Ν	Ο	Π	Θ	Ρ	Σ
Τ	Υ	ε	Ω	Ξ	Ψ	Ζ							α
β	χ	δ	ε	φ	γ	η	ι	ϑ	κ	λ	μ	ν	o
π	θ	ρ	σ	τ	υ	s	ω	ξ	ψ	ζ			

grk-s30

Β	Χ	Δ	Ε	Φ	Γ	Η	Ι	φ	Κ	Λ
Μ	Ν	Ο	Π	Θ	Ρ	Σ	Τ	Υ		Ω
Ξ	Ψ	Ζ						α	β	
χ	δ	ε	φ	γ	η	ι	ϑ	κ	λ	μ
ν	o	π	θ	ρ	σ	τ	υ	s	ω	ξ
ψ	ζ									

hbr-s25

hbr-s40

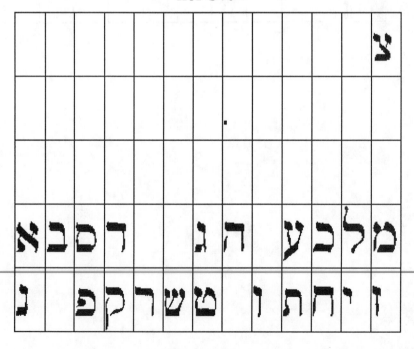

ipa-s25

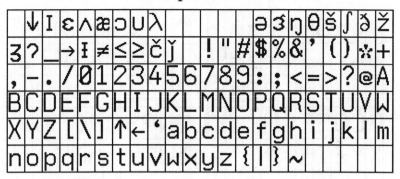

kana14

																																														|○|「|」|、|・|ヲ|ァ|ィ|ゥ
ェ	ォ	ャ	ュ	ョ	ッ	ー	ア	イ	ウ	エ	オ	カ	キ	ク	ケ	コ	サ	シ	ス	セ	ソ	タ	チ	ツ	テ	ト	ナ	ニ	ヌ	ネ	ノ	ハ	ヒ	フ	ヘ	ホ	マ	ミ	ム	メ	モ
ヤ	ユ	ヨ	ラ	リ	ル	レ	ロ	ワ	ン	゛	゜

krivo

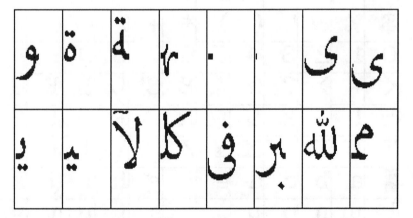

Fonts

lat-s30

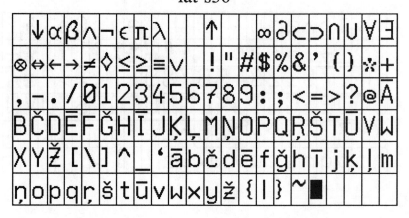

met25

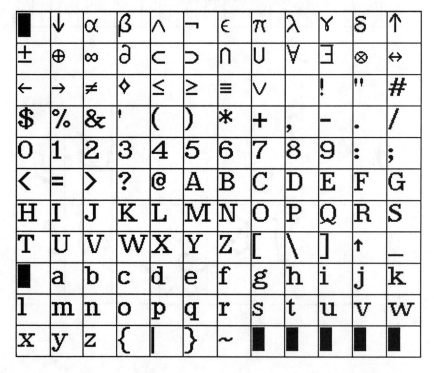

micro

mit

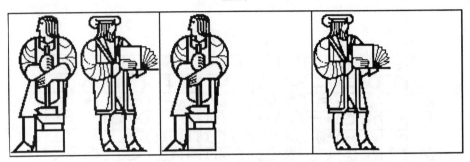

oldera

plunk

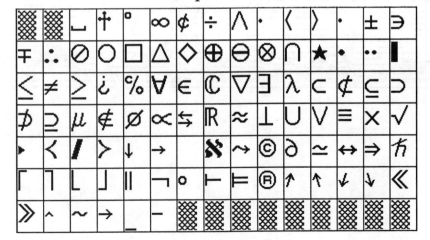

r14

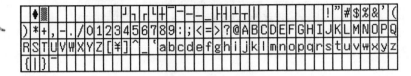

rot-s16

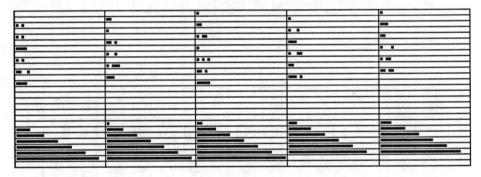

runlen

sans12

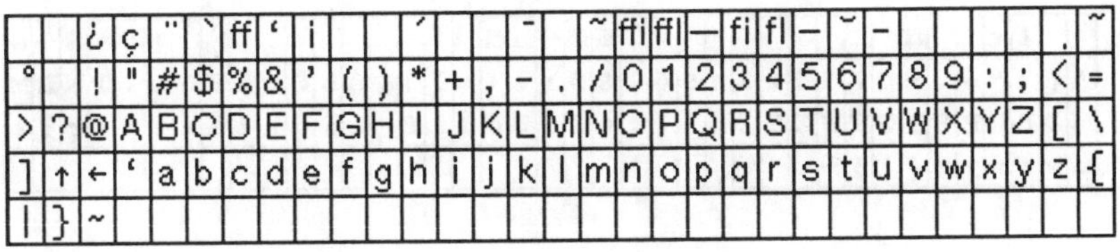

sansb12

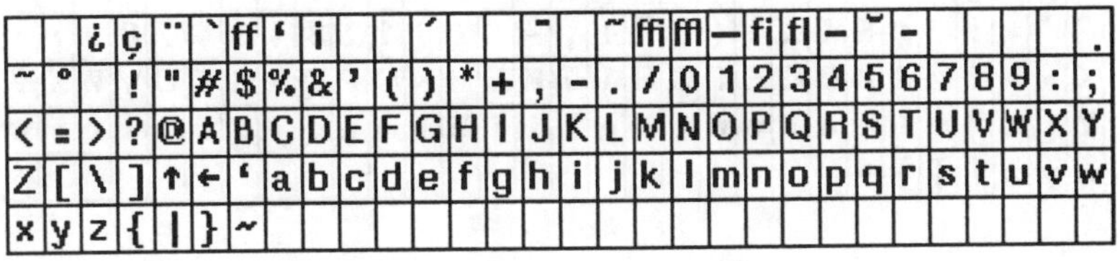

sansi12

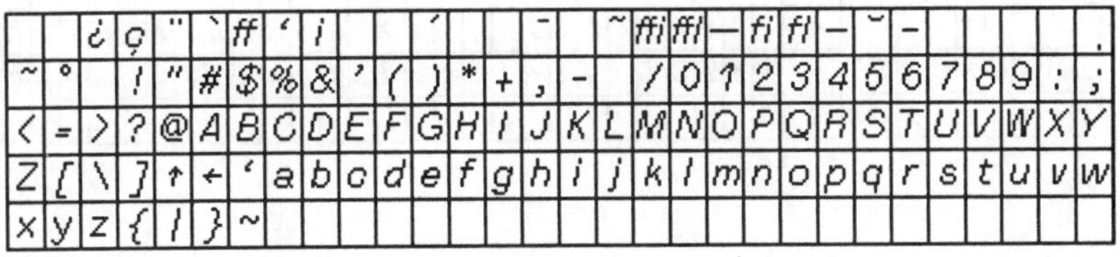

serif10

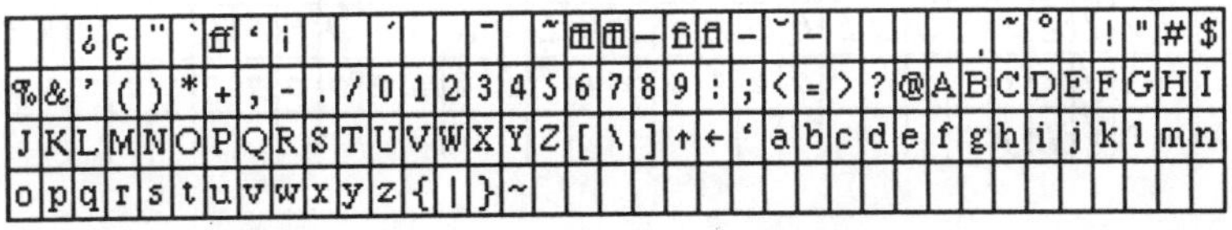

serif12

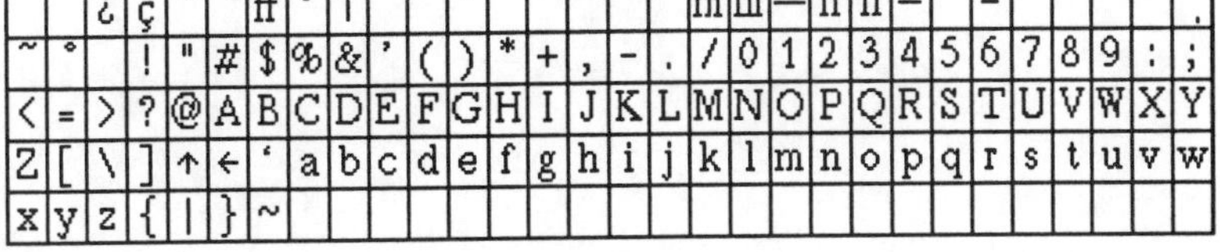

serifb10

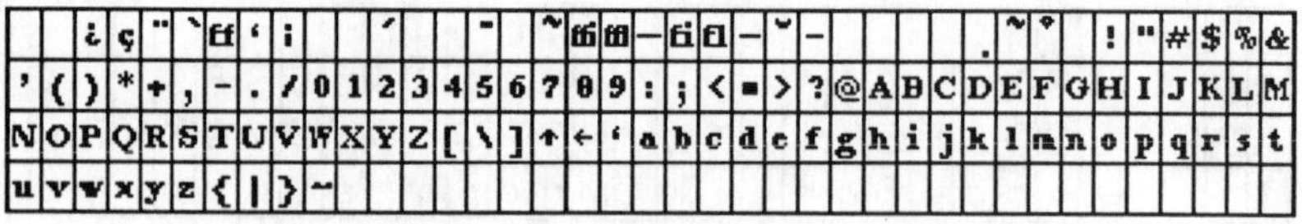

serifb12

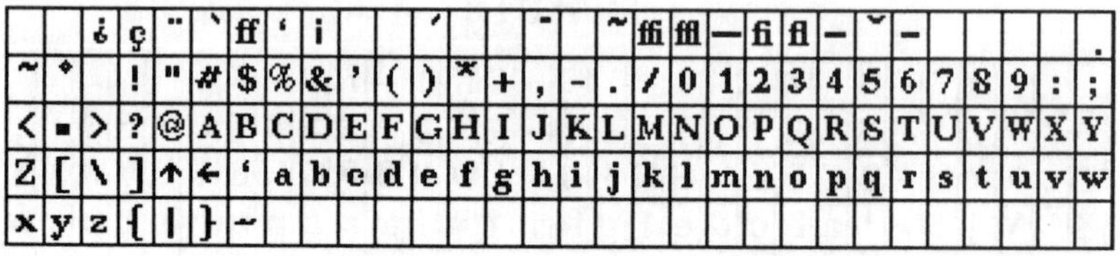

serifi10

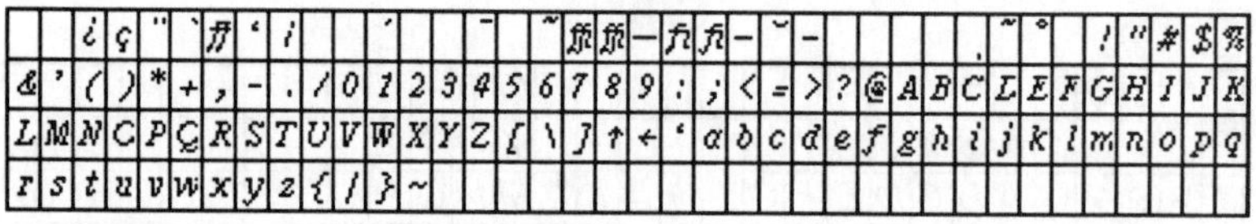

serifi12

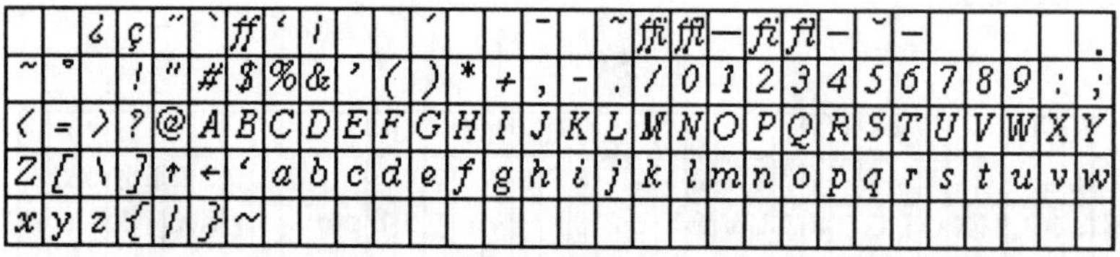

stan

stempl

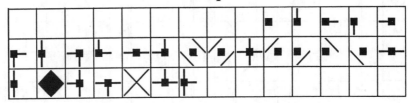

sub

	↓	∝	ß	∧	¬	∈	π	λ			↑				∞	∂	⊏	⊐
∩	∪	∀	∃	⊗	↔	←	→	≠	~	≤	≥	≡	∨		!	"	#
$	%	&	'	(	)	*	+	,	-	.	/	0	1	2	3	4	5
6	7	8	9	:	;	<	=	>	?	@	A	B	C	D	E	F	G
H	I	J	K	L	M	N	O	P	Q	R	S	T	U	V	W	X	Y
Z	[	\	]		_	'	a	b	c	d	e	f	g	h	i	j	k
l	m	n	o	p	q	r	s	t	u	v	w	x	y	z	{			}
~																	

subsub

	↓	∝	ß	∧	¬	∈	π	λ			↑			∞	∂	⊂	⊃	∩	∪	∀	∃	⊗	↔	←	→
≠	∾	≤	≥	≡	∨		!	"	#	$	%	&	'	(	)	*	+	,	-	.	/	0	1	2	3
4	5	6	7	8	9	:	;	<	=	>	?	@	A	B	C	D	E	F	G	H	I	J	K	L	M
N	O	P	Q	R	S	T	U	V	W	X	Y	Z	[	\	]		_	'	a	b	c	d	e	f	g
h	i	j	k	l	m	n	o	p	q	r	s	t	u	v	w	x	y	z	{	|	}	∾			

sup

supsup

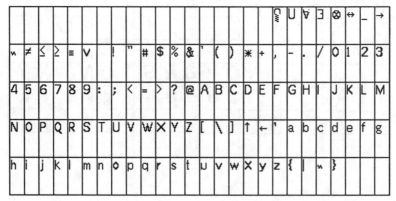

swd-s30

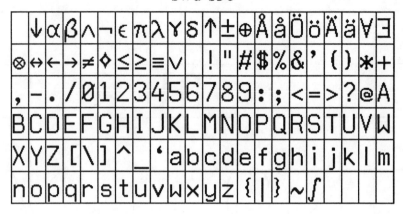

sym-s25

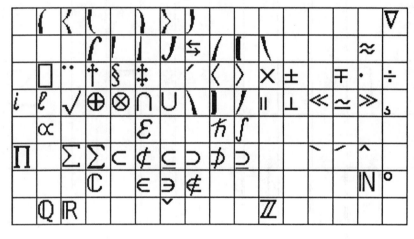

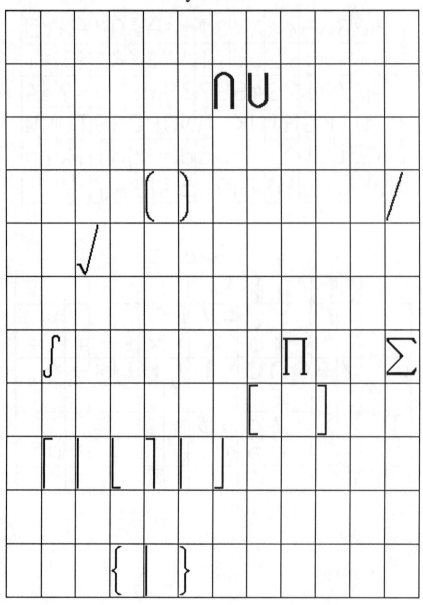

variable

	ˇ	¿	ç	¨	`	ff	'	i			'		-		~	ffi	ffl	—	fi	fl
-	˘		-				.		~	°		!	"	#	$	%	&	'	(	)	*	+
,	-		.	/	0	1	2	3	4	5	6	7	8	9	:	;	<	=	>	?	@	A
B	C	D	E	F	G	H	I	J	K	L	M	N	O	P	Q	R	S	T	U	V	W
X	Y	Z	[	\	]	↑	←	'	a	b	c	d	e	f	g	h	i	j	k	l	m
n	o	p	q	r	s	t	u	v	w	x	y	z	{			}	~				

vbee-36

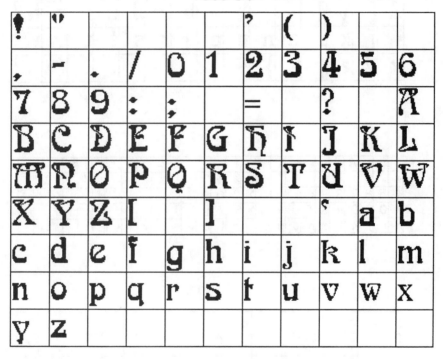

vctl-25

vg-13

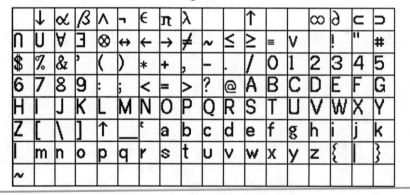

vg-20

vg-25

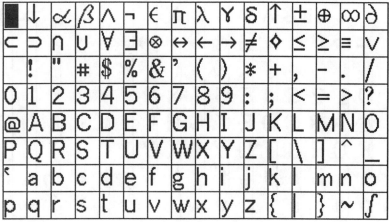

vg-31

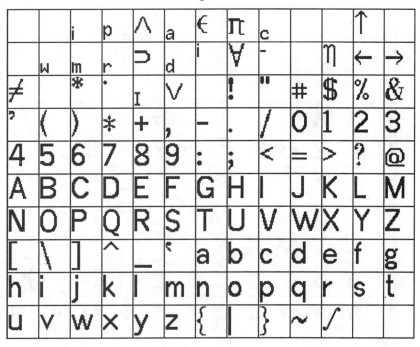

vgb-25

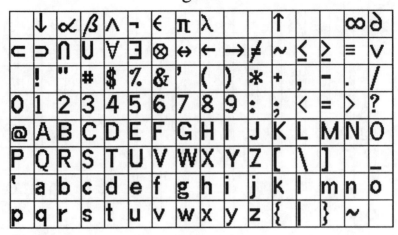

vgb-31

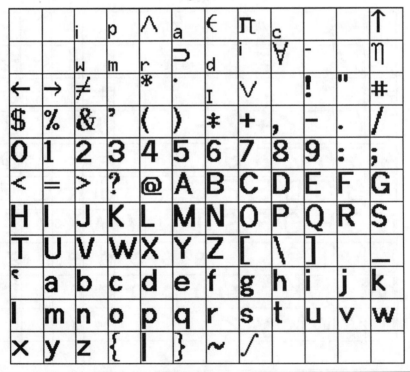

vgbc-25

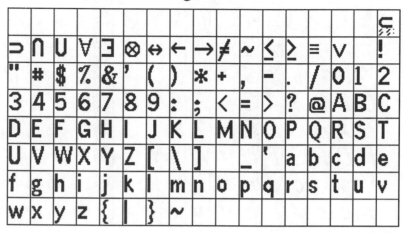

vgh-25

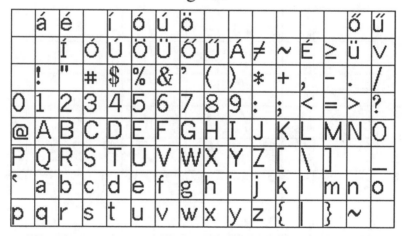

vgi-20

vgi-25

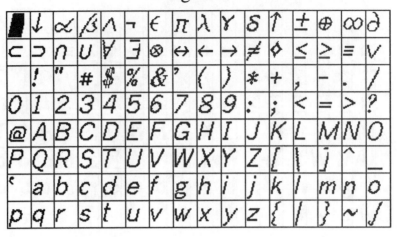

vgi-31

	↓	∝	β	∧	¬	∈	π	λ		
↑			∞	∂	⊂	⊃	∩	∪	∀	∃
⊗	↔	←	→	≠	◇	≤	≥	≡	∨	
!	"	#	$	%	&	'	(	)	*	+
,	-	.	/	Ø	1	2	3	4	5	6
7	8	9	:	;	<	=	>	?	@	A
B	C	D	E	F	G	H	I	J	K	L
M	N	O	P	Q	R	S	T	U	V	W
X	Y	Z	[	\	]		_	`	a	b
c	d	e	f	g	h	i	j	k	l	m
n	o	p	q	r	s	t	u	v	w	x
y	z	{	|	}	~					

Fonts

vgvb-31

vmic-25

vply-36

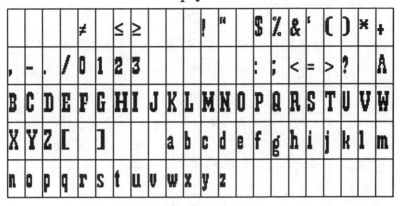

vr-20

	a	b	c	d	e	f	g	h	i	j	k	l	m	n
o	p	q	r	s	t	u	v	w	x	y	z			
			!	"	#	$	%		'	(	)	*	+	,
-	.		/	0	1	2	3	4	5	6	7	8	9	:	;
<	=	>	?		A	B	C	D	E	F	G	H	I	J
K	L	M	N	O	P	Q	R	S	T	U	V	W	X	Y
Z	[	\	]		_	`	a	b	c	d	e	f	g	h
i	j	k	l	m	n	o	p	q	r	s	t	u	v	w
x	y	z		|		~								

vr-25

vr-27

vr-30

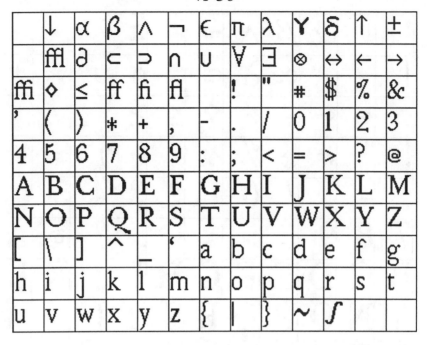

vr-31

	↓	∝	ß	∧	¬	∈	π	λ		
↑		∞	∂	⊂	⊃	∩	∪	∀	∃	
⊗	↔	←	→	≠	◊	≤	≥	≡	∨	
!	"	#	$	%	&	'	(	)	*	+
,	-	.	/	0	1	2	3	4	5	6
7	8	9	:	;	<	=	>	?	@	A
B	C	D	E	F	G	H	I	J	K	L
M	N	O	P	Q	R	S	T	U	V	W
X	Y	Z	[	\	]		_	`	a	b
c	d	e	f	g	h	i	j	k	l	m
n	o	p	q	r	s	t	u	v	w	x
y	z	{	|	}	~					

vrb-25

vrb-30

	↓	∝	β	∧	¬	∈	π	λ		↑	
	∞	∂	⊂	⊃	⊇	∩	∪	∀	∃	⊗	↔	←	→
≠	◇	≤	≥	≡	∨		!	"	#	$	%	&
'	(	)	*	+	,	-	.	/	0	1	2	3
4	5	6	7	8	9	:	;	<	=	>	?	@
A	B	C	D	E	F	G	H	I	J	K	L	M
N	O	P	Q	R	S	T	U	V	W	X	Y	Z
[	\	]		_	`	a	b	c	d	e	f	g
h	i	j	k	l	m	n	o	p	q	r	s	t
u	v	w	x	y	z	{	|	}	~			

	↓	∝	ß	∧	¬	∈	π	λ		
↑			∞	∂	⊂	⊃	∩	∪	∀	∃
⊗	↔	←	→	≠	~	≤	≥	≡	∨	
!	"	#	$	%	&c	'	(	)	*	+
,	-	.	/	0	1	2	3	4	5	6
7	8	9	:	;	<	=	>	?	@	A
B	C	D	E	F	G	H	I	J	K	L
M	N	O	P	Q	R	S	T	U	V	W
X	Y	Z	[	\	]		_	`	a	b
c	d	e	f	g	h	i	j	k	l	m
n	o	p	q	r	s	t	u	v	w	x
y	z	{	|	}	~					

					ffl		
		ffi			ff	fi	fl
	"	#	$	%	×	?	
(	)		+	,	-	.	/
0	1	2	3	4	5	6	7
8	9	:	;	<	=	>	?
	A	B	C	D	E	F	G
H	I	J	K	L	M	N	O
P	Q	R	S	T	U	V	W
X	Y	Z	[	\	]		_
`	a	b	c	d	e	f	g
h	i	j	k	l	m	n	o
p	q	r	s	t	u	v	w
x	y	z	{	|	}	~	∫

vri-25

vri-30

	↓	α	β	∧	¬	∈	π	λ		↑	
∞	∂	⊂	⊃	∩	∪	∀	∃	⊗	↔	←	→	≠	◊
≤	≥	≡	∨		!	"	#	$	%	&	'	(	)
*	+	,	–	.	/	0	1	2	3	4	5	6	7
8	9	:	;	<	=	>	?	@	A	B	C	D	E
F	G	H	I	J	K	L	M	N	O	P	Q	R	S
T	U	V	W	X	Y	Z	[	\	;		_	`	a
b	c	d	e	f	g	h	i	j	k	l	m	n	o
p	q	r	s	t	u	v	w	x	y	z	{	|	}
~													

	↓	∝	β	∧	¬	∈	π	λ
	↑	ff			∞	∂	⊂	⊃
∩	∪	∀	∃	⊗	↔	←	→	≠
~	≤	≥	≡	∨		!	"	#
$	%	&	'	(	)	*	+	,
-	.	/	0	1	2	3	4	5
6	7	8	9	:	;	<	=	>
?	@	A	B	C	D	E	F	G
H	I	J	K	L	M	N	O	P
Q	R	S	T	U	V	W	X	Y
Z	[	\	]		_	`	a	b
c	d	e	f	g	h	i	j	k
l	m	n	o	p	q	r	s	t
u	v	w	x	y	z	{			}
~								

vsg-114

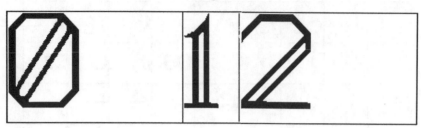

vsgn-57

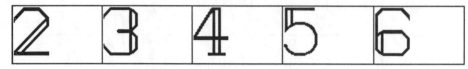

vshd-40

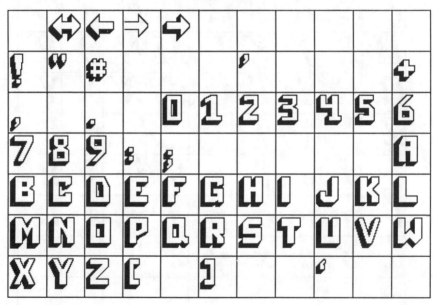

vtbold

vtsingle

vxms-37

Fonts

				(	)
					0
1	2	3	4	5	6	7
8	9					
?		A	B	C	D	E
F	G	H	I	J	K	L
M	N	O	P	Q	R	S
T	U	V	W	X	Y	Z
						a
b	c	d	e	f	g	h
i	j	k	l	m	n	o
p	q	r	s	t	u	v
w	x	y	z			

xif-s25

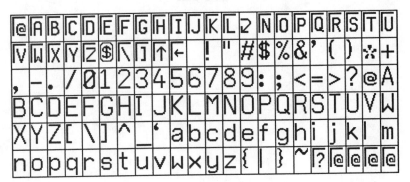

Fonts

K
Xlib Release 3 Update

This appendix is an update to Volume Two, *Xlib Reference Manual*. It describes the changes to Xlib, and to application writing standards in general, that took place in Release 3. Next, there is a description of corrections to the book based on Release 3 protocol clarifications. Some of these apply to Release 2 as well.

New Routines

Five new routines have been added to Xlib in Release 3. They are all very simple, and in fact four of them could actually have been simple macros. Here are their definitions:

Example K-1. Code for routines added to Xlib in Release 3 Update

```
long XMaxRequestSize(dpy)
    Display *dpy;
{
    return dpy->max_request_size;
}

char *XResourceManagerString(dpy)
    Display *dpy;
{
    return dpy->xdefaults;
}

unsigned long XDisplayMotionBufferSize(dpy)
    Display *dpy;
{
    return dpy->motion_buffer;
}

XDisplayKeycodes(dpy, min_keycode_return, max_keycode_return)
    Display *dpy;
    int *min_keycode_return, *max_keycode_return;
{
    *min_keycode_return = dpy->min_keycode;
    *max_keycode_return = dpy->max_keycode;
}
```

```
VisualID XVisualIDFromVisual(visual)
    Visual *visual;
{
    return visual->visualid;
}
```

All of these routines were added to allow applications access to members of structures that are intended to be opaque, namely `Display` and `Visual`. Applications should reference only the pointers to these structures. When applications are coded without direct reference to members of the opaque structures, this allows the X Consortium or an Xlib implementor on a particular system to change the contents of the `Display` and `Visual` structures if necessary.

`XMaxRequestSize` tells you the maximum request size on the server, in units of four bytes. This would be used when reading and writing properties, since the maximum property data length that can be stored in a single property is one unit (four bytes) less than the value returned by `XMaxRequestSize`.

The `XResourceManagerString` routine accesses the RESOURCE_MANAGER property resource database string that is stored in the server with *xrdb*, and returned to the client in the `Display` structure by `XOpenDisplay`. This is used by applications that use the resource manager routines to merge appropriate program and user defaults. All serious applications will do this.

`XDisplayMotionBufferSize` tells you whether the server has a motion history buffer, and if it does, how large it is in units of events. Most current servers do not have a motion history buffer, and in that case this function will return 0.

`XDisplayKeycodes` lets you determine the range of valid keycodes on a particular server. This should not be needed in most applications that use the standard keyboard interface through keysyms. It is only needed if you intend to change the mapping between keycodes and keysyms (server-wide) or perhaps to process key events using keycodes in a non-text application such as for music.

`XVisualIDFromVisual` is provided for completeness. It should not be necessary in most applications, and certainly not in those that use `XGetVisualInfo` or `XMatch-VisualInfo` to determine color characteristics, since these routines return the `XVisual-Info` structure which contains the `VisualID`.

Command Line Options

The convention until Release 3 has been that any command line argument containing : was a display specification and any argument beginning with = was a geometry specification. These no longer hold, and none of the core clients now operate this way. Applications should require an explicit *-display* or *-geometry* option. The = in the geometry specification is now optional.

Fonts

There is no standard that specifies the fonts a server must provide. However, this should not be a portability problem for properly written applications, because fonts should be resources that can be specified by the user or system administrator. You'll probably want to "build in" default font names, either in an *app-defaults* file or in your code, but your code ought to be robust enough to fall back on the default font in the GC if all else fails.

We bring this up because the font environment provided in the MIT distribution has changed substantially since Release 2. In Release 3, a unified family of fonts has been donated by Adobe, Inc. and BitStream, Inc. These include fonts of various sizes in the Courier, Times Roman, Helvetica, New Century Schoolbook, and Bitstream Charter families in regular weight, bold, and italic, and symbol fonts in various sizes from Adobe/DEC are also provided. Furthermore, font aliasing has been added so that font names in code and resource files can be long enough to fully describe a font, but the actual files containing the fonts may be 14 characters or less for compatibility with System V. An organized font-naming scheme has also been instituted.

The new font names look like this:*

```
-adobe-courier-bold-o-normal--10-100-75-75-m-60-iso8859-1
```

Because the font names that applications and users must specify are now so long, wildcards are now permitted as arguments to the Xlib routines `XLoadFont`, `XQueryFont`, and `XLoadQueryFont`. They were already permitted for the routines `XListFonts` and `XListFontsWithInfo`.

To specify a font, you specify only the fields that are important to you. For example, if you wanted to use a 12 point Roman Courier font for an xterm, you could use the either of the following names:

```
-adobe-courier-medium-r-normal--12-120-75-75-m-70-iso8859-1
*-courier-*-r-*-120-*
```

Note that you should match the point size field which is measured in tenths of a point (the 120 in this example) rather than the pixel size field (the 12). This allows your defaults to

---

*Most of this description of the new font-naming scheme was provided by Jim Fulton of the X Consortium.

work properly on tubes of different resolution. For example, to specify a 24 point, normal italic Charter,

```
*-charter-medium-i-*-240-*
```

will match either:

```
-bitstream-charter-medium-i-normal--25-240-75-75-p-136-iso8859-1
-bitstream-charter-medium-i-normal--33-240-100-100-p-179-iso8859-1
```

depending on whether the 75 dpi or 100 dpi font directory comes first in your font path. This example also demonstrates why the pixel size should not be used when wildcarding. On a 75 dpi monitor, a 24 point font will be 25 pixels tall; on a 100 dpi monitor, it will be 33 pixels tall.

If your application depends on the Release 2 fonts, they can be used with a Release 3 server by placing the Release 2 fonts in a directory and allowing users to add it to their font path (see the *mkfontdir* man page). If you have particular fonts that you want to use, and you have them in source (BDF) form, then most server vendors should supply a font compiler with their server, allowing you to import fonts.

Internal and Invisible Changes to Xlib

Xlib has been modified internally so that it will compile and run on Cray machines. This does not change the programming interface. Untested support for Mips computers has also been contributed.

Other internal changes include improvements to Graphics Context cache flushing. The region code was improved, including fix for overflow on complex regions.

Small Interface Changes

The routines XChangeProperty and XGetWindowProperty now take care of converting arrays of chars, shorts, and longs to and from the formats required by the protocol (8-bit, 16-bit, and 32-bit signed integers respectively). XGetWindowProperty now always mallocs space for its return data even if the data has zero elements.

XLookupString now has list of key bindings per display, can cope with modifier mapping changes, handles upper and lower case of all Latin-1 keysyms, doesn't convert non-Latin-1 keysyms, understands Control 2-8 and /, and uses the preferred protocol definition for CapsLock.

XrmPutFileDatabase will write file with proper special char quoting.

Server Fixes

Some problems that existed in sample server code affected application programming under Release 2. You may wish to inspect programs for workarounds for these problems. We cannot list and explain all the bugs that were found and fixed; see the CHANGES file in the appropriate directory of the X distribution. However, the following changes to the device-independent (dix) part of the server were among the most likely to affect client programming:

- The `AllocColorPlanes` request has been fixed to allow allocation of all planes at once.

- Delayed/Buffered writes for client events implemented. Delayed writes are simply a performance improvement; the server now queues all events generated by a single request for greater network efficiency. Buffered writes fix a bug that appeared when reading long properties from the server. Client connections would be severed when the client refused or was slow in reading a long message from the server.

- `SelectionClear` events are now sent to the selection owner (set by `XSet-SelectionOwner`, not the window creator.

- Font routines and color name lookup routines now fold upper case in names to lower case. Case is no longer significant in the color database, and items in the database differing only in case have been removed.

- Save under support has been added to the device-independent portion of the server. This code supplies save unders to any server which has backing store but not save unders implemented in the device-dependent portion.

- Mixing window gravity and bit gravity has been fixed.

- Many other specious requests also generate Value errors now.

The Xmu library

A new miscellaneous utilities library has been placed on the X distribution tape. This library is not part of the Xlib standard. It contains routines which only use public interfaces so that it may be layered on top of any proprietary implementation of Xlib or Xt.

It is intended to support clients in the MIT distribution; vendors may choose not to distribute this library if they wish. Therefore, applications developers who depend on this library should be prepared to treat it as part of their software base when porting.

The following routines apply to Xlib (there are a few not described here that are for use with the X Toolkit):

- Routines to cache atoms, avoiding multiple server round-trips. `XmuMakeAtom` creates and initializes an opaque `AtomRec`. `XmuInternAtom` fetches an atom from cache or server. `XmuInternStrings` fetches multiple atoms as strings. `XmuGetAtomName` returns name of an atom. `XmuNameOfAtom` returns name from an `AtomPtr`.

- `XmuCreatePixmapFromBitmap` routine converts a bitmap to a pixmap. The routine uses `XCopyPlane`).

- `XmuConvertStandardSelection` converts a known selection into the appropriate target type.

- `XmuPrintDefaultErrorMessage` prints a nice error that looks like the usual message. Returns 1 if the caller should consider exiting, else 0.

- `XmuDrawRoundedRectangle` draws a rounded rectangle. x, y, w, h are the dimensions of the rectangle, *ew* and *eh* are the sizes of a bounding boxes that each corner is drawn inside of.

- `XmuReadBitmapDataFromFile` reads X10 or X11 format bitmap files and return data.

Release 3 Protocol Clarifications

The following changes are not errors, per se. They reflect clarifications of the protocol specification made in Release 3. These changes, where noted, were also true in Release 2.

Page 36
The return type from `XAddPixel` is deleted. `XAddPixel` has its *value* argument changed from `int` to `long`.

Page 53
`XChangeActivePointerGrab` is capable of generating a `BadValue` error.

Page 70
`XCheckMaskEvent` has its *mask* argument changed from `unsigned long` to `long`.

Page 73
`XCheckWindowEvent` has its *mask* argument changed from `int` to `long`.

Page 77
On the `XClearArea` page, the first sentence of the third paragraph should end: "…the rectangle is tiled with a `plane_mask` of all 1's, a function of `GXcopy`, and a `subwindow_mode` or `ClipByChildren`." This should be true in Release 2.

Page 90
`XCopyGC` now generates a `BadValue` error when bits outside the set of valid GC mask bits are set.

Page 92
The *plane* argument of `XCopyPlane` must be a plane that exists in the source drawable, or a `BadValue` error is generated.

Page 213
On the second page of XGetImage, the first sentence should say that the source window must be *viewable*, not just mapped (all its ancestors also must be mapped). The page should also mention that the pointer cursor is not included in the image. This is also true in Release 2.

Page 219
The XTimeCoord structure has its x and y members changed from type unsigned short to short.

Page 248
The XGrabButton page should mention that the call overrides all previous passive grabs by the same client on the same key/button combinations on the same window. This is also true in Release 2.

Page 255
For XGrabPointer, the constant GrabNotViewable is returned for the reasons given at the bottom of the page, but also if the confine_to window is completely outside the root window. This was true in Release 2.

Page 284
The string that XLookupString returns in the *buffer* argument is in Latin-1 encoding, not necessarily in ASCII. (Latin-1 uses codes 128 to 255 to specify foreign characters, while ASCII uses only up to 127. ASCII is a subset of Latin-1.)

Page 291
The *event_mask* argument of XMaskEvent changes from unsigned long to long.

Page 349
The XReparentWindow page should say that the reparenting leaves unchanged the absolute coordinates (relative to the root window) of the upper-left outer corner of the window. This was true in Release 2.

Page 391
The *event_mask* argument of XSelectInput changes from type unsigned long to type long.

Page 393
The *event_mask* argument of XSendEvent changes from type unsigned long to type long. Also, XSendEvent can now generate a BadValue error if the event type sent is not valid in the core or an extension.

Page 410
The error_code, request_code, and minor_code members of XErrorEvent have been changed from type char to type unsigned char.

Page 429
In the paragraph about server restrictions on the XSetModifierMapping page, it should mention that one restriction may be that it might not be possible to disable auto-repeat on certain keys. This is also true in Release 2.

Page 481, 482

XUngrabButton and XUngrabKey may generate a BadValue error if the *button* or *keycode* argument is invalid.

Page 484

The XUngrabPointer pointer should mention that a grab is released automatically if the confine_to window is moved completely outside the root window. This is also true in Release 2.

Page 547

The XClientMessageEvent structure contains a union of three data types. The l[5] member has been changed from type int to type long.

Page 605

The XTimeCoord structure has its x and y members changed from type unsigned short to short.

Page 643

As described above, the fonts provided in Release 3 are no longer those shown in the book.

Window Attributes at a Glance

Member	Values / Default	Mask	Convenience Function
`Pixmap background_pixmap;`	pixmap (depth of window), ParentRelative / **None**	CWBackPixmap	XSetWindowBackgroundPixmap
`unsigned long background_pixel;`	pixel value / **undefined**	CWBackPixel	XSetWindowBackground
`Pixmap border_pixmap;`	pixmap (depth of window), None / **CopyFromParent**	CWBorderPixmap	XSetWindowBorderPixmap
`unsigned long border_pixel;`	pixel value / **undefined**	CWBorderPixel	XSetWindowBorder
`int bit_gravity;`	StaticGravity, NorthWestGravity, NorthGravity, NorthEastGravity, WestGravity, CenterGravity, SouthWestGravity, SouthGravity, EastGravity, SouthEastGravity / **ForgetGravity**	CWBitGravity	none
`int win_gravity;`	same as above, UnmapGravity / **NorthWestGravity**	CWWinGravity	none
`int backing_store;`	WhenMapped, Always / **NotUseful**	CWBackingStore	none
`unsigned long backing_planes;`	bit mask / **AllPlanes**	CWBackingPlanes	none
`unsigned long backing_pixel;`	pixel value / **0**	CWBackingPixel	none
`Bool save_under;`	True / **False**	CWOverrideRedirect	none
`long event_mask;`	OR of event mask symbols * / **0**	CWSaveUnder	XSelectInput
`long do_not_propagate_mask;`	OR of event mask symbols * / **0**	CWEventMask	none
`Bool override_redirect;`	True / **False**,	CWDontPropagate	none
`Colormap colormap;`	colormap ID, None / **CopyFromParent**	CWColormap	XSetWindowColormap
`Cursor cursor;`	cursor ID / **None** (copy from parent)	CWCursor	XDefineCursor, XUndefineCursor

All attributes can be set with XCreateWindow or XChangeWindowAttributes.

* The `event_mask` **symbols are:**
NoEventMask, KeyPressMask, KeyReleaseMask, ButtonPressMask, ButtonReleaseMask, EnterWindowMask, LeaveWindowMask, PointerMotionMask, PointerMotionHintMask, Button1MotionMask, Button2MotionMask, Button3MotionMask, Button4MotionMask, Button5MotionMask, ButtonMotionMask, KeymapStateMask, ExposureMask, VisibilityChangeMask, StructureNotifyMask, ResizeRedirectMask, SubstructureNotifyMask, SubstructureRedirectMask, FocusChangeMask, PropertyChangeMask, ColormapChangeMask, OwnerGrabButtonMask.

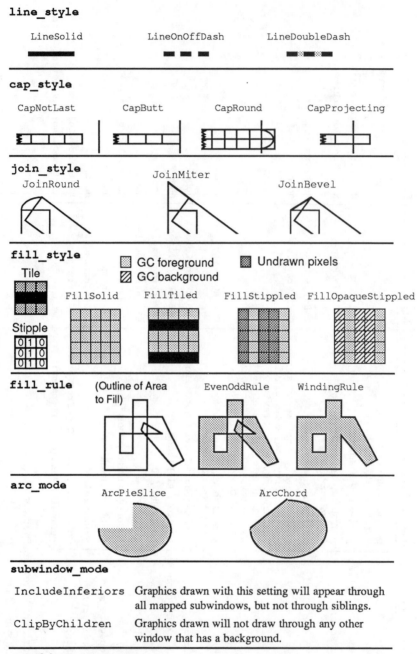

line_style

LineSolid   LineOnOffDash   LineDoubleDash

cap_style

CapNotLast   CapButt   CapRound   CapProjecting

join_style

JoinRound   JoinMiter   JoinBevel

fill_style

GC foreground   Undrawn pixels
GC background

Tile

Stipple

FillSolid   FillTiled   FillStippled   FillOpaqueStippled

fill_rule

(Outline of Area to Fill)   EvenOddRule   WindingRule

arc_mode

ArcPieSlice   ArcChord

subwindow_mode

IncludeInferiors   Graphics drawn with this setting will appear through all mapped subwindows, but not through siblings.

ClipByChildren   Graphics drawn will not draw through any other window that has a background.

graphics_exposures

True   Generate GraphicsExpose or NoExpose events when XCopyArea or XCopyPlane is called with this GC.

False   Don't generate GraphicsExpose or NoExpose events.

The GC at a Glance

Member	Values / Default	Mask	Convenience Function
int function;	GXclear, GXand, GXandReverse, GXandInverted, GXnoop, GXxor, GXor, GXnor, GXequiv, GXinvert, GXorReverse, GXset, GXcopyInverted, GXorInverted, GXnand / **GXcopy**	GCFunction	XSetFunction
unsigned long plane_mask;	bit for each plane / all 1's	GCPlaneMask	XSetPlaneMask
unsigned long foreground;	pixel value / 0	GCForeground	XSetForeground
unsigned long background;	pixel value / 1	GCBackground	XSetBackground
int line_width;	in pixels / 0	GCLineWidth	XSetLineAttributes
int line_style;	LineOnOffDash, LineDoubleDash / **LineSolid**	GCLineStyle	XSetLineAttributes
int cap_style;	CapNotLast, CapRound, CapProjecting / **CapButt**	GCCapStyle	XSetLineAttributes
int join_style;	JoinRound, JoinBevel / **JoinMiter**	GCJoinStyle	XSetFillStyle
int fill_style;	FillTiled, FillStippled, FillOpaqueStippled / **FillSolid**	GCFillStyle	XSetFillStyle
int fill_rule;	WindingRule / **EvenOddRule**	GCFillRule	XSetFillRule
int arc_mode;	ArcChord / **ArcPieSlice**	GCArcMode	XSetArcMode
Pixmap tile;	depth of destination / filled with **foreground**	GCTile	XSetTile
Pixmap stipple;	depth 1 / all 1's	GCStipple	XSetStipple
int ts_x_origin;	from drawable origin / 0	GCTileStipXOrigin	XSetTSOrigin
int ts_y_origin;	from drawable origin / 0	GCTileStipYOrigin	XSetTSOrigin
Font font;	ID, not necessarily loaded / **server-dependent**	GCFont	XSetFont
int subwindow_mode;	IncludeInferiors / **ClipByChildren**	GCSubwindowMode	XSetSubwindowMode
Bool graphics_exposures;	False / **True**	GCGraphicsExposures	XSetGraphicsExposures
int clip_x_origin;	from drawable origin / 0	GCClipXOrigin	XSetClipOrigin
int clip_y_origin;	from drawable origin / 0	GCClipYOrigin	XSetClipOrigin
Pixmap clip_mask;	depth 1 / **None**	GCClipMask	XSetClipMask, XSetClipRectangles, XSetRegion
int dash_offset;	in pixels / 0	GCDashOffset	XSetDashes
char dashes;	lengths of dashes / **4**	GCDashList	XSetDashes

About the Editor

Adrian Nye is a senior technical writer at O'Reilly and Associates. In addition to the X Window System programming manuals, he has written user's manuals for data acquisition products, and customized UNIX documentation for Sun Microsystems and Prime. Adrian has also worked as a programmer writing educational software in C, and as a mechanical engineer designing offshore oil-spill cleanup equipment. He has long-term interests in using his technical writing skills to promote recycling and other environmentally-sound technologies. He graduated from the Massachusetts Institute of Technology in 1984 with a B.S. in Mechanical Engineering.

☐ Please send me the information
I have asked for on the reverse
side of this card.

Name _____

Company _____

Address _____

City _____

State, ZIP _____

(Fill out or tape
business card here)

Nutshell Handbooks

 O'Reilly & Associates, Inc.
632 Petaluma Avenue
Sebastopol CA 95472

☐ Please send me the information
I have asked for on the reverse
side of this card.

Name _____

Company _____

Address _____

City _____

State, ZIP _____

(Fill out or tape
business card here)

Nutshell Handbooks

 O'Reilly & Associates, Inc.
632 Petaluma Avenue
Sebastopol CA 95472

O'Reilly & Associates, Inc.
Creators and Publishers of Nutshell Handbooks

Nutshell Handbooks

Learning the UNIX Operating System
DOS Meets UNIX
Learning the vi Editor
UNIX in a Nutshell, System V
UNIX in a Nutshell, Berkeley

Handbooks on Communications:

!%@:: A Directory of Electronic
    Mail Addressing and Networks
Using UUCP and Usenet
Managing UUCP and Usenet

Handbooks on Programming:

Using C on the UNIX System
Checking C Programs with lint
Understanding and Using COFF
Programming with curses
termcap and terminfo
Managing Projects with make

The X Window System series

Vol. 0 *X Protocol Reference Manual*
Vol. 1 *Xlib Programming Manual*
Vol. 2 *Xlib Reference Manual*
Vol. 3 *X Window System User's Guide*
Vol. 4 *X Toolkit Intrinsics*
        Programming Manual
Vol. 5 *X Toolkit Intrinsics Reference*
        Manual

For HyperCard on Macintosh:

UNIX in a Nutshell for HyperCard
(includes 1.8MB of HyperCard
stackware, *User's Guide,* and a copy of
Learning the UNIX Operating System)

Other UNIX books:

UNIX Text Processing

Send me more information on:

☐ Retail sales
☐ Licensing
☐ Review copies for instructors
☐ Magazine press kits for new books
☐ Education policy
☐ Bookstore locations
☐ Overseas distributors
☐ Additional copy of Nutshell News
☐ Upcoming books on the subject:

_____

_____

☐ Writing a Nutshell Handbook

O'Reilly & Associates, Inc.
Creators and Publishers of Nutshell Handbooks

Nutshell Handbooks

Learning the UNIX Operating System
DOS Meets UNIX
Learning the vi Editor
UNIX in a Nutshell, System V
UNIX in a Nutshell, Berkeley

Handbooks on Communications:

!%@:: A Directory of Electronic
    Mail Addressing and Networks
Using UUCP and Usenet
Managing UUCP and Usenet

Handbooks on Programming:

Using C on the UNIX System
Checking C Programs with lint
Understanding and Using COFF
Programming with curses
termcap and terminfo
Managing Projects with make

The X Window System series

Vol. 0 *X Protocol Reference Manual*
Vol. 1 *Xlib Programming Manual*
Vol. 2 *Xlib Reference Manual*
Vol. 3 *X Window System User's Guide*
Vol. 4 *X Toolkit Intrinsics*
        Programming Manual
Vol. 5 *X Toolkit Intrinsics Reference*
        Manual

For HyperCard on Macintosh:

UNIX in a Nutshell for HyperCard
(includes 1.8MB of HyperCard
stackware, *User's Guide,* and a copy of
Learning the UNIX Operating System)

Other UNIX books:

UNIX Text Processing

Send me more information on:

☐ Retail sales
☐ Licensing
☐ Review copies for instructors
☐ Magazine press kits for new books
☐ Education policy
☐ Bookstore locations
☐ Overseas distributors
☐ Additional copy of Nutshell News
☐ Upcoming books on the subject:

_____

_____

☐ Writing a Nutshell Handbook